Understanding and Managing Behaviors of Children with Psychological Disorders

Understanding and Managing Behaviors of Children with Psychological Disorders

A Reference for Classroom Teachers

JERED B. KOLBERT AND LAURA M. CROTHERS

BLOOMSBURY

NEW YORK · LONDON · NEW DELHI · SYDNEY

BH

Bloomsbury Academic

An imprint of Bloomsbury Publishing Plc

175 Fifth Avenue
New York
NY 10010
USA

50 Bedford Square
London
WC1B 3DP
UK

www.bloomsbury.com

First published 2013

Library of Congress Cataloging-in-Publication Data
Understanding and managing behaviors of children with psychological disorders : a reference for classroom teachers / edited by Jered B. Kolbert and Laura M. Crothers.
p. cm.
Includes bibliographical references and index.
ISBN 978-1-4411-5836-9 (pbk. : alk. paper) 1. Children with mental disabilities–Education. 2. Children with mental disabilities–Behavior modification. 3. Classroom management. I. Kolbert, Jered B. II. Crothers, Laura M.
LC4601.U53 2012
371.92–dc23
2012020236

ISBN: PB: 978-1-4411-5836-9

Typeset by Fakenham Prepress Solutions, Fakenham, Norfolk NR21 8NN
Printed and bound in the United States of America

12/9/13

Dedicated to

Kennedy Isabel, Karlena Swanhild Kolbert and Meredith Julia Lipinski

CONTENTS

LIST OF FIGURES

LIST OF TABLES & APPENDICES

ACKNOWLEDGMENTS

The editors wish to thank Chas Albright, Jane Lang'at and Dan Wells for their review of chapters, and finally, David Barker and his editorial team for all of their support throughout the writing of this book.

ABOUT THE EDITORS

Laura M. Crothers, DEd, NCSP, is a Professor in the School Psychology Program at Duquesne University, Pittsburgh, Pennsylvania. She received her D.Ed. in School Psychology in 2001, her Ed.S. in School Psychology in 1997, and her M.Ed. in Educational Psychology in 1995 from Indiana University of Pennsylvania, Indiana, Pennsylvania. She received her B.A. in Psychology from Grove City College, Grove City, Pennsylvania, in 1994. Dr Crothers has been named a national expert in childhood bullying by the National Association of School Psychologists, and serves on several journal editorial boards. Dr Crothers is the author of over thirty peer-reviewed manuscripts and monographs, three books, several book chapters, and has conducted presentations regionally, nationally, and internationally. Dr Crothers has contributed to the source literature by studying bullying in children, adolescents, and adults.

Jered B. Kolbert, PhD, LPC, is an Associate Professor in the Department of Counseling, Psychology, and Special Education at Duquesne University. Dr Kolbert is a certified school counselor and Licensed Professional Counselor (LPC) in Pennsylvania, and he is a National Certified Counselor (NCC). Dr Kolbert teaches graduate level courses in counseling, including family counseling, counseling and developmental theories, research, school counseling fieldwork courses, and a professional orientation course for school counselors. He has also taught at The College of William and Mary in Virginia, Virginia Commonwealth University, and Slippery Rock University of Pennsylvania. Dr Kolbert obtained his doctorate in counseling from The College of William and Mary, Williamsburg, Virginia. He has worked as a school counselor, marriage and family counselor, and substance abuse counselor. Dr Kolbert has authored publications in nationally refereed journals on a variety of topics, including bullying, relational aggression, gender identity, and moral development.

CONTRIBUTORS

Charles M. Albright, MEd, is a third year doctoral student in the school psychology program at Duquesne University in Pittsburgh Pennsylvania. He holds a Masters of Education in child psychology from Duquesne University and a Bachelors of Arts in psychology from Ohio Northern University.

Beth Barbarasch, BA, is a doctoral student in the School Psychology Program at Rutgers University.

Melissa A. Bray, PhD, is a professor and licensed psychologist at the University of Connecticut. Her main research interests are in intervention science especially for health-related areas such as asthma, stuttering, and classroom disruptive behaviors.

Sierra L. Brown, MSEd, is a graduate student at Duquesne University's School Psychology PhD program. Ms Brown earned her undergraduate degree in psychology from the University of Pittsburgh and after graduation, worked as a research assistant at the University of Pittsburgh Medical Center. Her research interests include examining factors and racial differences related to high school dropout rates and school readiness of preschool children.

Kathleen M. Chard, PhD, is the Director of the PTSD and Anxiety Disorders Division at the Cincinnati VA Medical Center and Associate Professor of Clinical Psychiatry at the University of Cincinnati. As the VA CPT Implementation Director, Dr Chard oversees the dissemination of Cognitive Processing Therapy to VA clinicians across the United States. She is the author of the CPT for Sexual Abuse treatment manual and is co-author of the Cognitive Processing Therapy: Military Version manual. Dr Chard has trained clinicians throughout the Veterans Administration, Department of Defense and public sector on using CPT with veterans and active duty personnel in individual and group formats. She is an active researcher and she has conducted several funded studies on the treatment and etiology of PTSD. Currently Dr Chard is exploring the efficacy of CPT with veterans with PTSD and comorbid traumatic brain injury.

Amanda B. Clinton, PhD, is an Assistant Professor of Psychology in the Department of Social Sciences at the University of Puerto Rico, Mayagüez (UPRM). Dr Clinton is a licensed psychologist, a credentialed school psychologist, and a certified infant-toddler specialist. She has taught courses at the undergraduate and graduate level in biopsychology, child-adolescent development, cognition and learning, abnormal psychology, and cross-cultural psychology at the UPRM and in the California State University system. She has worked as a neuropsychologist, a clinical psychologist, and a school psychologist. Dr Clinton further developed prevention curricula for use in several Latin American countries and contributed to test adaptation for Spanish-speaking populations. Dr Clinton's publications include articles in English and Spanish related to violence/drug abuse prevention, cultural adaptation, bilingualism, and effective educational methods for reaching under-represented minority students.

Christopher M. Dudek, BA, is the project manager for a multi-state federally funded grant from the US Department of Education—Institute of Educational Sciences and a graduate student in the Counseling Psychology Program at Rutgers University.

Gregory A. Fabiano, PhD, is an associate professor of Counseling, School, and Educational Psychology in the Graduate School of Education at the University at Buffalo. His interests are in the area of evidence-based assessments and treatments for children with AD/HD. He is author or co-author of over forty peer-reviewed publications and book chapters. Dr Fabiano's work has been funded by the Administration for Children and Families, Centers for Disease Control and Prevention, National Institutes of Health, and the Department of Education. In 2007 Dr Fabiano was nominated by the Department of Education and invited to the White House to receive the Presidential Early Career Award for Scientists and Engineers, the nation's highest honor for early career investigators.

Eric J. Fenclau Jr., MSEd, is a third year doctoral student studying School Psychology at Duquesne University in Pittsburgh, PA. He holds a MSEd in Child Psychology from Duquesne University, and a B.A. in Psychology from Le Moyne College, in Syracuse, NY.

Julaine E. Field, PhD, LPC, NCC, is an Associate Professor and the Associate Dean of the College of Education at the University of Colorado—Colorado Springs. Dr Field is a Licensed Professional Counselor (LPC) in Colorado and she is a National Certified Counselor (NCC). Dr Field teaches graduate level courses in individual counseling, group counseling, sexuality in counseling, crisis counseling, marriage and family and school counseling fieldwork courses. She has also taught at Slippery Rock University of Pennsylvania and North Carolina State University. Dr Field obtained her doctorate in counseling and supervision from North Carolina State University, Raleigh, NC. Dr Field has practiced as a school counselor, mental health counselor, college counselor and in private practice. She has also provided crisis and trauma counseling to victims of sexual abuse, sexual assault and domestic violence in North Carolina, Pennsylvania and Colorado. Dr Field has presented at the international, national and state levels and has authored publications related to counselor advocacy, relational aggression, gender identity and crisis intervention.

Rich Gilman, PhD, is the Coordinator of the Psychology and Special Education programs at Cincinnati Children's Hospital Medical Center, and Associated Professor in the Department of General Pediatrics at the University of Cincinnati Medical School. His research interests are in risk/resiliency factors in children and families. His scholarship has been recognized by the American Psychological Association. He is a Fellow of APA Division 16 (school psychology).

Amanda Graham, MSEd, earned her undergraduate degree in psychology from the University of Cincinnati. She then served as a research assistant and study coordinator at Cincinnati Children's Hospital Medical Center. Recently, Ms Graham earned her MSEd. in Child Psychology from Duquesne University where she is currently a graduate student in the School Psychology Program. Her research interests include developing evidenced-based treatments for skill deficits in children with AD/HD, and the treatment of pediatric disorders in schools.

Lauren J. Holleb, PhD, is a postdoctoral fellow in the Division of Developmental and Behavioral Pediatrics at Cincinnati Children's Hospital Medical Center. Dr Holleb received her PhD in Developmental-Clinical Psychology from the University of Maine. Her primary research interests focus on the psychosocial functioning of socially withdrawn and socially anxious children and adolescents with specific interests in peer relationships and social cognitive influences on these relationships.

Tammy L. Hughes, PhD, is the Martin A. Hehir Endowed Chair for Scholarly Excellence, and Professor and Chair of the Department of Counseling, Psychology and Special Education at Duquesne University. Active at the national level she currently serves on the American Psychological Association's (APA) Board of Educational Affairs (BEA) She is the Past-President of the Division of School Psychology (16) of

APA, Past-President of Trainers of School Psychologists (TSP), and served on the 2009 APA Presidential Task Force on the *Future of Psychology Practice*. Dr Hughes is an Associate-Editor for *Psychology in the Schools* and serves on the editorial boards of the *Journal of School Violence* and *International Journal of Offender Therapy and Comparative Criminology*. Her writing is in the area of childhood aggression including: differentiating emotional disturbance and social maladjustment, identifying the treatment needs of youth with autism in detention facilities (specifically those who are incarcerated for sexual offenses) and understanding the relationship between emotional dysregulation and conduct problems in children. Her clinical experience includes assessment, counseling and consultation services in alternative education and juvenile justice settings focusing on parent-school-interagency treatment planning and integrity monitoring.

Shane R. Jimerson, PhD, is a Professor at the University of California, Santa Barbara. His scholarly publications and presentations have provided insights regarding: school violence and school safety, school crisis prevention and intervention, developmental pathways of school success and failure, the efficacy of early prevention and intervention programs, school psychology internationally, and developmental psychopathology. Among numerous publications, he is the lead-editor of *The Handbook of Bullying in Schools: An International Perspective* (2010, Routledge), he is also the lead-editor of *The Handbook of School Violence and School Safety: International Research and Practice 2nd Edition* (2012, Lawrence Erlbaum, Inc), a co-editor of *Best Practices in School Crisis Prevention and Intervention 2nd Edition* (2012, National Association of School Psychologists), the lead-editor of *The Handbook of International School Psychology* (2007, SAGE Publishing), and the lead editor of *The Handbook of Response to Intervention: The Science and Practice of Assessment and Intervention* (2007, Springer Science). He is also co-author of *School Crisis Prevention and Intervention: The PREPaRE Model* (2009, National Association of School Psychologists), a co-author of a five-book grief support group curriculum series *The Mourning Child Grief Support Group Curriculum* (2001, Taylor and Francis), co-author of *Identifying, Assessing, and Treating Autism at School* (2006, Springer Science), co-author of *Identifying, Assessing, and Treating Conduct Disorder at School* (2008, Springer Science), co-author of *Identifying, Assessing, and Treating PTSD at School* (2008, Springer Science), co-author of *Identifying, Assessing, and Treating AD/HD at School* (2009, Springer Science), and co-author of the *Promoting Positive Peer Relationships (P3R): Bullying Prevention Program* (2008, Stories of Us). Dr Jimerson is the Editor of *School Psychology Quarterly*.

Thomas J. Kehle, PhD, is Professor and Director of School Psychology at the University of Connecticut. He is a fellow of the American Psychological Association, the Association for Psychological Science, and the American Association of Applied and Preventive Psychology. He is also a member of the Council for the National Register for Health Service Providers in Psychology, and a licensed psychologist in the state of Connecticut. Dr Kehle's primary research interests include individual differences, self-modeling, selective mutism, and psychological wellness.

Jinhee Kim, PhD, is an Assistant Professor in the Department of Instruction and Leadership in Education at Duquesne University. Dr Kim teaches undergraduate and graduate level courses in early childhood education program. She was a preschool and kindergarten teacher and taught young children from diverse backgrounds. Dr Kim's recent scholarly works are published in *Journal of Research in Childhood Education* and *Early Childhood Education Journal.*

Jamie King, PhD, is a postdoctoral fellow presently practicing in Greensburg, Pennsylvania. She is a graduate of Duquesne University where she earned her PhD in School Psychology and MSEd. in Child Psychology. She also holds a M.A. in Counseling Psychology with a specialization in Marriage and Family Therapy from Seton Hill University. Her undergraduate training was completed at Clarion University of Pennsylvania where she earned a B.A. in Psychology. Dr King presently works with both adolescents and adult populations and services the community by providing individual therapy, couples/family therapy, drug and alcohol treatment, and psychological assessment. She spent the majority of her clinical pre-doctoral training working in community mental health where she worked with patients from diverse clinical backgrounds and she has experience treating various psychiatric conditions including but not limited to: depression, anxiety, addiction, mood disorders, and eating disorders. She also has an extensive background in marital and family counseling. Dr King has authored publications in nationally refereed journals and has also delivered lectures and conducted presentations nationally and internationally on various topics including eating disorders, bullying/victimization, and methods for accessing mental health services in schools.

Stacie A. Leffard, PhD, is a Clinical Neuropsychologist at The Children's Institute of Pittsburgh where she provides inpatient and outpatient neuropsychological and rehabilitation services to children with developmental and acquired neurological impairment. She is a Licensed Psychologist and Certified School Psychologist in Pennsylvania. She is also an Adjunct Professor in the Department of Psychology at Saint Vincent College. Dr Leffard obtained her doctorate in School Psychology from Duquesne

University and completed a post-doctoral fellowship in pediatric rehabilitation/neuropsychology at The University of Michigan, Department of Physical Medicine & Rehabilitation. She has authored peer-reviewed publications on topics including working memory, processing speed, AD/HD symptoms, and cerebral palsy.

Huijun Li, PhD, is the Director of Multicultural Research at the Commonwealth Research Center, Instructor of Psychology, Division of Public Psychiatry, Beth Israel Deaconess Medical Center, Harvard Medical School. She is also a Nationally Certified School Psychologist. Dr Li was born in China and came to the US in 1996 to pursue a PhD degree in School Psychology at the University of Arizona. She has experiences working with children, adolescents, and young adults from different racial/ethnic backgrounds who experience emotional, behavioral and academic challenges. Her current research focuses on psychosocial and cultural factors that affect pathways to care, patient help-seeking behaviors, and mental illness interpretation models. Dr Li also conducts multicultural competency trainings at the Harvard Medical School community.

Elizabeth McCallum, PhD, is an Associate Professor in the school psychology program at Duquesne University, an APA accredited and NASP approved program. Additionally, Dr McCallum is a Pennsylvania state certified school psychologist. Dr McCallum conducts research in the area of academic and behavioral interventions for school-aged students. She has published scholarly articles in journals such as *School Psychology Review, Psychology in the Schools,* and the *Journal of Evidence-Based Practices for Schools.*

Lindsay McGuirk, MSEd, is a fourth year PhD student in the School Psychology program at Duquesne University. She has experience working with children in both the public school setting, as well as in an approved private school setting for children with various disabilities and diagnoses. Lindsay's research interests include working with children with moderate to severe disabilities and remediating the behaviors associated with those disabilities and diagnoses. Her dissertation topic is examining the workings of transition teams of children with disabilities and the perception of transition from school to employment of those children. Lindsay has served as a Teacher's Assistant for various graduate-level courses, including research methods and statistics classes. She is currently a board member for both Duquesne's local chapter, as well as at the national level of Student Affiliates of School Psychology (SASP). She is also a member of the American Psychological Association (APA-Division 16) and the National Association of School Psychologists (NASP). Lindsay has presented at local, as well as national conferences on various topics, including childhood AD/HD, autism, and executive functioning in elementary students.

Jeffrey A. Miller, PhD, ABPP, is the Associate Dean for Graduate Studies and Research and a Professor of School Psychology in the School of Education at Duquesne University. He is a Board Certified School Psychologist by the American Board of Professional Psychology, licensed psychologist, and certified school psychologist. He is a Fellow and Past-President of the American Academy of School Psychology. Dr Miller also serves on the Board of the American Board of School Psychology, is Vice-President of the Council of Specialties in Professional Psychology, and is the current chair of the School Psychology Specialty Council. He has published over thirty books, book chapters, and refereed journal articles. His most recent book is entitled Specialty Competencies in School Psychology published by Oxford University Press. Dr Miller is on the editorial boards of the *Journal of Psychoeducational Assessment* and the *Journal of Applied School Psychology*. Dr Miller is recipient of the 2010 Eugene P. Beard Award for Leadership in Ethics and is a Fellow of the American Psychological Association. His research focuses on the translation of neuropsychological knowledge to improve teaching and learning and professional issues in school psychology.

Elizabeth A. Pask, MSEd, is a graduate student in the School Psychology program at Duquesne University. She earned her undergraduate degree in psychology at Canisius College in Buffalo, New York. Ms Pask works as a Graduate Assistant for Duquesne University's School of Education and is involved in research examining children and adolescents with pervasive developmental disabilities and factors related to their involvement in the juvenile justice system.

Melissa Pearrow, PhD, is an Associate Professor and the Program Director of the School Psychology program at the University of Massachusetts Boston. She has more than twenty years of experience in public education as a school psychologist and special educator, with field-placement trainings in urban schools as well as inpatient, outpatient, and community mental health settings. Her research focuses on school-based mental health services and empowerment of youth in urban communities. With the other authors of this chapter, she has co-authored *Identifying, Assessing, and Treating AD/HD at School* (2010, Springer Science). She is also the former President of the Massachusetts School Psychologists Association and is currently the Regional Representative to the National Association of School Psychologists Ethics Committee.

Linda A. Reddy, PhD, is an Associate Professor of Psychology at Rutgers University, where she serves as Director of the Child AD/HD and AD/

HD-Related Disorders Clinic. Dr Reddy has published five books and over sixty manuscripts/book chapters in the areas of assessment and interventions for children with AD/HD, test development and validation, and school-based interventions. She has received over two million dollars in research funding and is currently the PI of an Institute of Educational Sciences NCER teacher measurement grant.

Ara J. Schmitt, PhD, an Associate Professor and Director of the School Psychology in the School of Education at Duquesne University, is a certified school psychologist and a licensed psychologist. Dr Schmitt's research interests include the neuropsychological assessment and intervention of learning problems and neurologic disorders, manifestations of chronic illness within schools, and professional issues in school psychology and special education. Among other scholarly works, he is an author of many peer-reviewed journal articles and a well-regarded Guilford School Practitioner Series book titled, *Patterns of Learning Disorders: Working Systematically from Assessment to Intervention*. Dr Schmitt is on the editorial board of several peer reviewed publications including the *Journal of School Psychology*, *Journal of Applied School Psychology*, *Journal of Psychoeducational Assessment*, *The School Psychologist*, and the Woodcock-Munoz Foundation Press. He recently served as a guest editor for the *Journal of Evidence Based Practices for Schools* regarding the use of assistive technology in educational interventions.

Michael Tansy, PhD, ABPP, is a psychologist in private practice evaluating and serving children, adolescents and adults with psychological and addictive disease. Currently he is the president of the American Board of School Psychology (ABSP), serves on the board of trustees of the American Board of Professional Psychology (ABPP) and is a past-president of the American Academy School Psychology (AASP). Dr Tansy has practiced in mental health and school settings for over thirty years, administering inpatient and outpatient treatment programs, directing school-psychological services within public school settings, and consulting with school districts across the US

Angelique R. Teeters, MA, is an O'Grady Resident in Psychology at Cincinnati Children's Hospital Medical Center and will receive her PsyD from Xavier University in May, 2012. She has spent the past five years working on several research grants, including a study examining program retention in home visitation and another examining the efficacy of an adaptation of cognitive behavioral therapy for treatment of depression in first-time mothers participating in a home visitation program. Ms Teeters has conducted research examining the effects of childhood maltreatment history of maternal sensitivity to infant facial expressions of emotion.

Her research interests include infant mental health, the effects of maternal maltreatment history on parenting behaviors, and maternal depression. Ms Teeters is an adjunct faculty member in the Psychology Department at the College of Mt. St. Joseph in Cincinnati, Ohio.

Lea A. Theodore, PhD, is an associate professor in the School Psychology Program at The College of William and Mary. She is currently Vice President of Professional Affairs for Division 16 of the American Psychological Association and an associate editor for *School Psychology Quarterly*. Her research interests include interventions for behavior, health, and communication disorders.

Sandra Ward, PhD, is a professor in the School Psychology program at the College of William and Mary. She has published more than thirty papers in professional journals and actively presents at both state and national conferences. Her primary interest areas include assessment and diagnosis, consultation, and supervision. Dr Ward has been a Primary Investigator for grants in the area of substance abuse totaling more than $1,000,000. Dr Ward is a board member of the Virginia Academy of School Psychologists and is the editor of the organization's newsletter, *School Psychology in Virginia*.

Kara Giron Wisniewski, PhD, is currently director of psychological services at the Brewer School Department, Brewer, Maine. She is responsible for coordinating and providing school psychological services for both general and special education students.

CHAPTER ONE

Introduction to Understanding and Managing Behaviors of Children with Psychological Disorders: A Reference for Classroom Teachers

Jered B. Kolbert and
Laura M. Crothers
Duquesne University

Abstract

In this chapter, authors will outline a framework for the text, and identify the theoretical frameworks for understanding common childhood mental health disorders and behavioral problems. The theoretical frameworks are discussed in terms of how they contribute to the Response to Intervention (RtI) and Schoolwide Positive Behavioral Intervention and Supports (SWPBS) models.

Introduction

Among the different options for books in which their authors review various theories and techniques for classroom behavior management, there are no texts that offer a set of behavior management strategies specific to various psychopathology issues manifested in children and adolescents. In this work, authors offer a relatively concise description of various mental health and behavioral disorders, and then outline a classroom management approach designed specifically to address the needs and challenges presented by children and adolescents, hereafter referred to as children, with each disorder. Interventions are provided for use with a variety of ages (from early childhood to adolescence).

As classrooms become more inclusive, teachers are responsible for accommodating students with a variety of mental health and behavioral disorders in general education settings. It is our hope that this book will be a useful reference for educators who wish to either prevent or diminish problem behaviors exhibited by children in the classroom. Although there often is a lack of consensus in the extant literature base about how best to treat various symptoms of childhood mental health and behavioral disorders, the variety of treatment strategies presented in this book will allow teachers to select the level of intervention that best suits the needs of the child and the classroom environment.

Identifying evidence-based treatment strategies appropriate for childhood emotional and behavioral disorders seems of particular importance when considering that the 1% to 5% of students with the most severe emotional and behavioral problems consume more than 50% of teachers' and administrators' time (Cheney, Flower, & Templeton, 2009; US Department of Education, 2000). Such problems disadvantage both students and teachers. Although student misbehavior has historically been a concern of teachers, the issue of lack of discipline has reached heightened proportions, being seen as one of the most problematic of school systems in the United States (Bear, 1998). In particular, externalizing behavior problems exhibited by children, including antisocial conduct, impulsivity, aggression, defiance, and overactivity can be disruptive and stressful for both students and educators (Hinshaw, 1992). Moreover, serious problem behaviors are associated with a variety of negative outcomes for students, including removal of children from regular classrooms, jobs, and homes, high dropout rates, and adult criminal behavior (Cheney et al., 2008; Reichle, 1990; Wagner et al., 2006).

In this text, in addition to the introductory (Chapter 1) and concluding (Chapter 16) chapters, educators will be presented with chapters regarding various mental health diagnoses and behavior problems, including children with: 1) Attention-Deficit/Hyperactivity Disorder, 2) Anxiety Disorders, 3) Autism Spectrum Disorders, 4) Bullying Problems, 5) Childhood Schizophrenia, 6) Chronic Illnesses, 7) Eating Disorders, 8) Mood Disorders, 9) Oppositional Defiant and Conduct Disorders, 10) Post-traumatic Stress Disorder, 11) Behavior Problems during the Preschool Years, 12) Social and Relational Aggression Problems, 13) Substance Abuse Problems, and 14) Traumatic Brain Injury. After reviewing the associated features with a particular disorder, the authors will then provide a set of classroom management techniques, for students at-risk or already identified as having emotional or behavioral problems, designed to target the adverse behaviors associated with various childhood diagnoses. In essence, the framework for intervention selection, implementation, and evaluation that will be presented in each chapter is consistent with a three-tiered model of intervention, which will be discussed later in this chapter.

The Biomedical Model in Conceptualizing Mental Illness and Behavioral Problems in Children

The medical model is currently the prevailing framework for conceptualizing mental illness in youth (Foltz, 2006), emphasizing the role of brain pathology and chemical imbalances in the etiology of mental illness. Practitioners of the medical model devote extensive time to diagnosing mental disorders, classifying symptoms, and developing and applying treatments that eliminate detrimental behaviors. Arguably, the prevalence of the medical model is closely associated with the increased use of psychotropic mediations amongst youth in the past two decades.

While the research literature supports the strong contribution of bio-chemical processes in the etiology of some mental disorders, such as schizophrenia and psychotic disorders, it does not provide definitive support for many other mental disorders (e.g. Eaves, Silberg, & Erkanli, 2003; Eley et al., 2003). For example, Cosgrove et al. (2011) found that among adolescents, both genetic and environmental influences contribute to the etiology of major depressive disorder, generalized anxiety disorder, separation anxiety disorder, attention-deficit/hyperactivity disorder, oppositional defiant disorder, and conduct disorder. Most experts believe that biological, genetic, or organic components interact with environmental experiences to result in a child being identified with an emotional or behavioral disorder (EBD; Fergusson & Woodward, 2002; Youngblade & Nackashi, 2003). Moreover, unlike other illnesses, EBD cannot be linked to a specific gene or chromosomal anomaly.

The Systems-Ecological Model in Conceptualizing Mental Illness and Behavioral Problems in Children

The systems-ecological framework represents an alternative framework for understanding childrens' dysfunctional behavior and is reflective of the belief that emotional and behavioral disorders are the result of a complex interaction of environmental and biochemical influences. We are using the term "systems-ecological" to refer to two similar theories: general systems theory (von Bertalanffy, 1968) and social ecology theory (Bronfenbrenner, 1979). The main assumption of the systems-ecological framework is that behavior is the result of the interaction between the child and the environment. General systems theory represents a paradigm shift in that it rejects the traditional linear causal perspective of western science and the medical model, which conceptualizes behavior as being the result of a single cause or chain of causes. The medical model tends to presume that the etiology for problem behavior exists within the individual child. In contrast, general systems theory posits a circular causal perspective in which a child's behavior instead is believed to be a function of numerous interacting variables that reciprocally influence each other.

Parents, teachers, and peers are seen as potentially impacting a child's behavior, and in turn, being impacted by the child in question. No one person or environmental context is regarded as causative; persons and contexts are seen as potential contributors to problematic behavior, and consequently are eligible for intervention. Bronfenbrenner's (1979) theory of social ecology shares some of the basic principles of systems theory, including the importance of reciprocal interaction, but is broader in scope than systems theory. Whereas systems theory tends to focus upon the interactions within a system, particularly the family system, Bronfenbrenner claimed that the multiple embedded systems in which the child exists, which includes the peer, family, school, community and cultural environments, may be equally as important in influencing behavior. Children do not develop in isolation but instead are influenced by various contexts (e.g. society, peers, family, etc), which interact.

Systems-ecological theory may be utilized less often than the medical model in part due to the limitations of current research methods to examine interacting relationships. Proponents of the systems-ecological perspective argue that the medical model perspective may dominate our understanding of emotional and behavioral disorders among children not because of its superiority but because of its simplicity; a linear perspective that is more amenable to the methods of research currently available. Despite these challenges, some studies have directly evaluated systems-ecological models for childhood issues, providing empirical support for the model's application to school violence (Khoury-Kassabri, Benbenishty, Astor, & Zeira, 2004) and bullying (Espelage & Swearer, 2010). Henggeler's (1996) review of the research literature revealed that "serious antisocial behavior is multi-determined by the reciprocal interplay of characteristics of the individual youth and the key social systems in which youths are embedded (i.e. family, peer, social, neighborhood, and community)" (pp. 6–7).

Epigenetics is an emerging field that incorporates the fundamental assumptions of both the medical model and the systems-ecological by studying the interaction between genes and the environment (Brendtro & Mitchell, 2010). Twardosz and Lutzker (2010) concluded from a review of the literature that abuse and neglect during childhood affects both the structure and functioning of the brain and imparts lifelong consequences for mental health. Maltreatment appears to result in a heightened responsiveness to stress that enables the child to survive and reproduce in an unsafe environment but is associated with an increased risk for mental illness, including anxiety, depression, and other mood disorders. Thankfully, there is evidence to suggest that the brain is modified by experience throughout life, which is often referred to as "brain plasticity." For example, Tarullo and Gunnar (2006) found that training foster parents to be more sensitive resulted in reduced hormones associated with stress and behavioral problems compared to the children of foster parents who did not receive such training.

The Behavioral Model in Conceptualizing Mental Illness and Behavioral Problems in Children

Behavior theory is another common model for understanding mental illness. Behavior theory consists of several theoretical foundations, the most prominent including classical conditioning, operant conditioning, and social learning theory (Wilson, 2008). The fundamental assumption of operant conditioning is that behavior is a product of its consequences. Children are taught new behaviors through the use of reinforcement and unwanted behaviors are decreased or eliminated through the use of punishment and extinction, in which adults and peers learn to ignore a child's inappropriate behaviors. Classical conditioning is a type of associative learning in which in the case of maladaptive behavior, a neutral stimulus becomes paired with a frightening event so that the neutral stimulus elicits anxiety. Classical conditioning is frequently used as a framework for understanding anxiety and obsessive compulsive disorders in children. In social cognitive theory, which was developed by Albert Bandura (1997), the impact of environmental events is mediated by cognitive processes concerning how an individual perceives and interprets the events, with cognitions and behaviors reciprocally influencing each other. According to Bandura (1997), "The experiences generated by behavior also partly determine what individuals think, expect, and can do, which in turn affect their subsequent behavior" (p. 345). Learning or reinforcement is more likely to occur when children are aware of the rules concerning the consequences of their behaviors (Wilson, 2008). Eliminating children's maladaptive behaviors often requires helping children to modify the cognitions associated with the unwanted behavior, and teaching the cognitions required for the expected behaviors.

Behavioral theory is similar to the systems-ecological model in that there is an emphasis on the role of the environment and interactions with others affecting learning. However, behavioral theory's focus on identifying the antecedents and consequences of behaviors and its assumption that the causes for behavior are identifiable may be regarded as a linear perspective and similar to the medical model. In contrast, the systems-ecological model assumes that contextual variables mutually interact in reverberating cycles in a manner that precludes identification of causality. Furthermore, whereas behavior theory tends to focus on dyadic relationships, systemic-ecological models emphasize the patterns of interaction between a child and parent and/or teacher.

One of the primary conceptual foundations from which the Response to Intervention (RtI) model was developed is the behavioral consultation model (BC) model (Kratochwill & Bergan, 1990). The BC model utilizes principles of behavioral theory to define student performance problems using methods of objective measurement, identify contributing factors, implement interventions to target those factors, and measure the success of interventions. Indeed, schools have applied the RtI model not only to academic problems, but also to behavior and mental health issues. Given RtI's behavioral theory underpinnings, it is understandable that many school districts have incorporated other behavioral models as part of the RtI model in order to address students' maladaptive behavior or mental health difficulties (Buffum, Mattos, & Weber, 2009).

Schoolwide Positive Behavioral Interventions and Supports (SWPBIS) is a universal, prevention program that is based in behavioral theory (Bradshaw, Mitchell, & Leaf, 2010), and has been adopted by many schools that use the RTI model. SWPBIS, encouraged by the US Department of Education (Knoff, 2000) and several state departments of education, uses a three-tiered model to address disruptive behavior by developing and maintaining primary (schoolwide/universal), secondary (targeted/selective), and tertiary (individual/indicated) interventions (Bradshaw et al., 2010). Whereas traditionally school-based behavioral interventions primarily focused upon the individual student, SWPBIS and other types of "proactive classroom management" programs seek to alter the school environment through the universal application of principles of behavioral theory (Gettinger & Kohler, 2005). Research indicates that the implementation of SWPBIS has resulted in reduced student suspensions (Barrett, Bradshaw, & Lewis-Palmer, 2008; Bradshaw et al., 2010), office discipline referrals (Bradshaw et al., 2010; Horner et al., 2009; Muscott, Mann, & LeBrun, 2008a), and increased student perceptions of safety at school (Horner et al., 2009). Additionally, some studies have found that the implementation of SWPBIS is associated with academic improvement (e.g. Horner et al., 2009), whereas other have not (e.g. Bradshaw et al., 2010).

Teachers play a more active role in addressing the behavioral issues of students who are identified with emotional and behavioral disorders in SWPBIS and other tiered behavioral intervention programs. The discrepancy model, which has been the traditional model for identifying students with a specific learning disability or behavioral or emotional disorder, has been criticized as a "wait to fail" approach because students' performance had to be very low in order to evaluate to determine eligibility for special education services under the Individuals with Disabilities Education Act (IDEA).

At the primary level in SWPBIS, teachers seek to prevent behavioral problems by using positive instructional and classroom management practices. Teachers collaborate in identifying three to five positively-stated school-wide expectations (Simonsen, Sugai, & Negron, 2008). Typical expectations include, "Be Safe, Be Respectful, and Be Responsible." These expectations for the various school settings (e.g. classroom, cafeteria, hallway, and bathroom) are taught to the students through scripted lessons in the beginning of the school year. Teachers collaboratively develop a continuum of strategies to reinforce appropriate behaviors, including use of verbal praise, token economies, among others, and punishment of unacceptable behaviors. For a first offense, students are typically reminded of the expected behavior, and for a second offense, students are re-taught the behavior, the assumption being that the student has not acquired the expected behavior. In this model, supervision of classroom and non-classroom settings is increased. Data are collected to evaluate both the efficacy of the intervention, which often includes decreases in the percentage of office discipline referrals and increased frequency in students' achievement of the lesson objectives, and staff's consistency of implementation, which is referred to as treatment fidelity.

Horner (2007) found that approximately 11%, 26%, and 29% of elementary, middle, and high school students, respectively, will require secondary and/or tertiary interventions in order to demonstrate improvements in behavior. The secondary tier is for an identified group of students who did not respond to the primary intervention but whose behaviors do not pose a risk of harm to themselves or others (Simonsen et al., 2008).

Teachers continue to play a primary role in secondary interventions, as strategies often involve increasing the supports provided in the primary tier. For example, secondary tier interventions typically include providing more frequent behavioral prompts and praise, social skills training, self-monitoring strategies, peer tutoring, and check in and check out (CICO; Fairbanks, Simonsen, & Sugai, 2008).

CICO, also known as the Behavior Education Program (BEP; Hawken & Horner, 2003), is a common secondary tier intervention that involves having students check in with an adult in the beginning of the day and receive a point sheet that they carry throughout the day and use to obtain feedback from teachers regarding their progress in meeting behavioral expectations. A token economy is used with the CICO technique whereby students receive tokens (e.g. points, bucks) for achieving their individualized, pre-established point percentage goals for that day. Students may accumulate tokens and exchange them for backup reinforcers (e.g. tangible items, privileges). For interested readers, Myers and Briere (2010) provide a list of excellent practical suggestions for implementing a CICO system. Moreover, research suggests that the CICO system is particularly effective for attention-seeking students and may be less helpful for students who appeared to be motivated to avoid work (Hawken & Hess, 2006; Hawken & Horner, 2003).

Tertiary tier interventions are highly specialized and tailored to address the specific needs of individual students whose behaviors may pose a risk to themselves or others (Fairbanks et al., 2008). Most tertiary tier interventions involve the development of a behavior support plan following a functional behavioral assessment (FBA), which is a process that attempts to identify the potential functions of the student's behavior by formally observing and analyzing the antecedents, or "setting events", and consequences of the behavior in question. Behavior support plans often involve providing teacher attention through praise and/or points, self-monitoring, teaching social skills, dividing and teaching the various components of a behavior, alternating between instruction and preferred activities, such as breaks with adults and peers, and wraparound services.

Wraparound services involve the creation of a team, which works to develop constructive relationships and support networks among the student, his or her family, and school personnel, including teachers (Eber, Breen, Rose, Unizycki, & London, 2008). The wraparound process is the most comprehensive intervention in the SWPBS RtI continuum, and is applied to 1% to 2% of students, many of whom are diagnosed with serious emotional/behavioral disorders and for whom school personnel believe there are "setting events" or environmental contributions that occur outside of school. Wraparound is related to the System of Care movement that emphasizes fully involving families and youth in the planning and selecting of interventions, the coordination of services of multiple providers, and use of a culturally relevant process (Stroul, 2002). Such a process involves the identification of a team facilitator who is trained in the family-centered and strength-based philosophy, who can facilitate constructive relationships between the important adults in the student's life, manage the adults' frustration related to failed interventions, identify the student's needs and the child's and adults' strengths to achieve those needs that are contained in the student's and adults' stories, and organize data to guide the multiple levels of interventions (Eber et al., 2008). The team facilitator uses a strength-based philosophy to manage the frustration of parents, teachers, and other school personnel by encouraging the team to focus upon the student's needs as opposed to problems or deficits, which often appear overwhelming.

Wraparound services often entail many of the interventions used in secondary tier interventions, including CICO, adult and peer mentoring, etc., but the process differs in that there is more intensive emphasis upon tailoring the interventions to meet the unique needs and strengths of the child. These strengths and needs are identified through a collaborative approach between the school and family, which relies upon the encouragement of family members to be a part of the behavioral support plan in order to address those setting events occurring outside of school. Although systems-ecological theory is not explicitly identified as a foundational theory for wraparound services, there appears to be a similar focus in the heavy emphasis on repairing the relationships between the student and important adults, and between the important adults in the child's life. Although a full review of wraparound services is beyond the scope of this chapter, Eber et al. (2008) provide a descriptive case study that is helpful in further understanding this service delivery model.

SWPBIS emphasizes the importance of family-school collaboration in a comprehensive manner in order to prevent students' behavioral issues, and as a component of secondary and tertiary tier interventions (Muscott, Szczesiul, Berk, Staub, Hoover, & Perry-Chisolm, 2008a). SWPBS draws upon Epstein's (2001) framework for promoting family engagement. In this framework, Epstein advocates for a partnership model in which parents' strengths and participation are more fully valued and communication is reciprocal as opposed to the more traditional family-school relationships, in which communication is more unilateral. In traditional family-school relationships, families often receive information from the school through newsletters and parent handbooks without a formal, systematic process for parents to communicate with the school.

In explanation, Epstein's model includes six types of involvement: 1) helping parents provide supportive home environments, 2) communicating (establishing reciprocal exchanges regarding school programs and children's progress), 3) volunteering (increased use of parents in the classroom), 4) learning at home (educating parents on how they can assist with homework), 5) decision-making (including parents of various backgrounds on school committees), and 6) collaborating with the community (integrating resources and services). Studies have revealed that increased family involvement has resulted in increased academic achievement as well as reduced student behavior problems (Epstein, 2005; Muscott, Mann, & LeBrun, 2008) and school violence (Boulter, 2004). Moreover, Hoagwood et al.'s (2007) review of the literature of school-based mental health interventions targeting academic and mental health interventions revealed that programs that positively impacted both academic and mental health functioning were more likely to include parents and teachers than programs that did not result in such favorable outcomes.

The Role of Classroom Teachers

As mentioned throughout the chapter, classroom teachers play a pivotal role in preventing and managing students' behavior problems, particularly in SWPBIS and Tiers I and II of RtI models. In a review of the research literature, those educators who demonstrate effective behavior management skills have been found to exhibit an authoritative disciplinary style that integrates the use of three types of strategies, "classroom management and positive climate strategies for preventing behavior problems, operant learning strategies for the short-term management and control of behavior problems, and decision-making and social problem-solving strategies for achieving the long-term goal of self-discipline" (Bear, 1998, p. 23). Other theories that may be helpful in helping teachers to conceptualize their roles as behavior managers include Max Weber's investigations regarding authority (particularly legal/rational, and charismatic; 1947).

As teachers are often the primary responders in addressing students' behavior problems, they may wish to consider classroom management as an aspect of school climate, instruction, and curriculum rather than one of control (Levin & Nolan, 2004). One of the methods which teachers can use to improve their classroom management is school-based consultation, either with an educational specialist, such as a school psychologist or a school counselor, or with another teacher. Consultation in schools can be described as a service delivery model in which an educator, serving as a consultant, uses problem-solving strategies (in order to alter an existing set of circumstances to become a desired set of circumstances) to address the needs of a consultee and a client (Crothers, Hughes, & Morine, 2008). Consultants and consultees work collaboratively to share their knowledge bases to help solve academic, behavioral, and social/emotional problems in children. Thus, consultation is an indirect vehicle through which school-based educational and mental health professionals can pool resources together to positively impact upon children's development and functioning in several domains.

Although there are a number of different theoretical models for consultation (see Crothers et al., 2008), Vargo (1998) provides a practical model of the communication, consultation, and provision of services that can be used with children who are at risk for or demonstrating the symptoms of a variety of emotional and behavioral disorders. This model can be used teacher-to-teacher, whereas other approaches, such as mental health consultation, typically require that a consultant be a mental health specialist, such as a school psychologist or school counselor.

Vargo (1998) describes the initiation of consultation as the first step, such as a special educator speaking with each of the classroom teachers who are working with a child. The goal of such conversations is to facilitate open communication between the teachers, clarify roles, and identify challenges with a particular student or group of students. After this has been accomplished, ongoing communication can be developed by weekly conversations between the consulting teacher and the consultee teachers regarding their specific plans for working with the target student(s) for the coming week. Using a journal for the weekly information gleaned from these conversations may be helpful for ongoing reference.

During these conversations, the consulting educator can ask about: 1) what topics are planned to be reviewed for the week; 2) given the student's difficulty in a particular area, what type of instruction or assistance is needed to be provided by the consultant; 3) what are the expectations and evaluation criteria for the activities for the week; 4) to what extent was the student's performance typical; 5) how does the consultee plan instruction for the student; 6) what options for intervention can be identified through brainstorming; 7) which of these options are likely to have desired results; 8) which of the options the consultee is willing to try; 8) what are the objectives of the interventions that have been chosen; 9) what are the evaluation criteria for the outcomes; 10) how and when will progress be monitored; 11) what roles and responsibilities will each person have for implementing the intervention; 12) who will adapt the curriculum and instruction; 13) how will the content be presented; 14) who will evaluate which group of students; 15) who will communicate with parents and administrators regarding progress made; and when will the next meeting occur (and who should attend; Vargo, 1998).

Vargo (1998) also recommends that the consulting teacher provide positive feedback frequently, being as specific as possible, both through verbal and written means. When the consultant conducts an observation of a student, he or she should offer verbal feedback to the classroom teacher immediately after the observation, making sure to describe something that worked well or was positive. Furthermore, the observation notes from the consultant should be provided to the consultee teacher, outlining the goals of the observation and what information was noted. Ideally, the consultant should schedule time within classrooms in 45-minute intervals, in order to have enough time to spend with each teacher. Finally, consulting teachers should be aware of teachers' potential resistance to having another person in the classroom. Consultants should be mindful to demonstrate respect, warmth, and flexibility, as well as to acknowledge different points of view, which will encourage optimal collaboration in the problem-solving process.

Conclusion

The medical model has made considerable advances in identifying the biochemical contributions to children's mental illness and behavior problems. However, research based on the systems-ecological and behavioral theories also indicates that the environment contributes, often in a reciprocal manner, to the development and continuance of students' mental illness and behavioral problems. The increased prominence of the RtI and SWPBIS models, which are based on behavioral theory, imply that educators are expected to play an active role in assisting students with mental illness and behavior problems, and provide teachers with a framework for differentiation. Both systems-ecological and behavior theory suggest that the educator must be able to reflect upon the larger patterns that influence a child's behavior and consider modifying those patterns of interaction that are to some degree influenced by the teacher. These patterns of interaction include the structure of the classroom, peer interactions, the teacher-child relationship, and the relationship between the teacher and parents.

References

Bandura, A. (1977). *Social learning theory*. Englewood Cliffs, NJ: Prentice-Hall.

Barrett, S. B., Bradshaw, C. P., & Lewis-Palmer, T. (2008). Maryland statewide PBIS initiative: Systems, evaluation, and next steps. *Journal of Positive Behavior Interventions, 10*, 105–14. doi:10.1177/1098300707312541

Bear, G. G. (1998). School discipline in the United States: Prevention, correction, and long-term social development. *School Psychology Review, 27*, 14–32.

Bertalanffy, L. von. (1968). *General systems theory: Foundation, development, applications*. New York: Braziller.

Boulter, L. (2004). Family-school connection and school violence prevention. *The Negro Educational Review, 55*, 27–40.

Bradshaw, C. P., Mitchell, M. M., & Leaf, P. J. (2010). Examining the effects of schoolwide positive behavioral interventions and supports on student outcomes: Results from a randomized controlled effectiveness trial in elementary schools. *Journal of Positive Behavioral Interventions, 12*, 133–48. doi:10.1177/1098300709334798

Brendtro, L. K., & Mitchell, M. L. (2010). The profound power of groups. *Reclaiming children and youth, 19*, 5–10.

Bronfenbrenner, U. (1979). *The ecology of human development: Experiments by nature and design.* Cambridge, MA: Harvard University Press.

Buffum, A., Mattos, M., & Weber, C. (2009). *Pyramid response to intervention: RTI, professional learning communities, and how to respond when kids don't learn.* Bloomington, IN: Solution Tree Press.

Carter, J., & Sugai, G. (1989). Survey on prereferral practices: Responses from state departments of education. *Exceptional Children, 55*, 298–302.

Cheney, D., Flower, A., & Templeton, T. (2008). Applying response to intervention metrics in the social domain for students at risk of developing emotional or behavioral disorders. *The Journal of Special Education, 42*, 108–26. doi:10.1177/0022466907313349

Cosgrove, V. E., Rhee, S. H., Gelhorn, H. L., et al., (2011). Structure and etiology of co-occurring internalizing and externalizing disorders in adolescents. *Journal of Abnormal Child Psychology, 39*, 109–23. doi:10.1007/s10802-010-9444-8

Cousin, P. T., Diaz, E., Flores, B., & Hernandez, J. (1995). Looking forward: Using a sociocultural perspective to reform the study of learning disabilities. *Journal of Learning Disabilities, 28*, 656–63.

Crothers, L. M., Hughes, T. L., & Morine, K. A. (2008). *Theory and cases in school-based consultation: A resource for school psychologists, school counselors, special educators, and other mental health professionals.* NY: Routledge.

Drame, E. R., & Xu, Y. (2008). Examining sociocultural factors in response to intervention models. *Childhood Education, 85*, 26–32.

Eaves, L., Silberg, J., & Erkanli, A. (2003). Resolving multiple epigenetic pathways to adolescent depression. *The Journal of Child Psychology and Psychiatry and Allied Disciplines, 44*, 1006–14. doi:10.1111/1469-7610.00185

Eber, L., Breen, K., Rose, J., Unizycki, R., M., & London, T. H. (2008). Wraparound as a tertiary level intervention for students with emotional/behavioral needs. *Teaching Exceptional Children, 40*, 16–22.

Eley, T. C., Bolton, D., O'Connor, T. et al., (2003). A twin study of anxiety-related behaviors in pre-school children. *Journal of Child Psychology and Psychiatry and Allied Disciplines, 44*, 945–60. doi:10.1111/1469-7610.00179

Epstein, J. L. (2001). *School, family, and community partnerships: Preparing educators and improving schools.* Boulder, CO: Westview Press.

—(2005). Results of the Partnership Schools-CSR model for student achievement over three years. *Elementary School Journal, 106*, 151–70. doi:10.1086/499196

Espelage, D. L., & Swearer, S. M. (2010). A social-ecological model for bullying prevention and intervention: Understanding the impact of adults in the social ecology of youngsters. In S. R., Jimerson, S. M., Swearer, S. M., & D. L. Espelage (eds). *Handbook of bullying in schools: An international perspective* (pp. 61–72). New York: Routledge.

Fairbanks, S., Simonsen, B., & Sugai, B. (2008). Classwide secondary and tertiary tier practices and systems. *Teaching Exceptional Children, 40*, 44–52.

Fergusson, D. M., & Woodward, L. J. (2002). Mental health, educational and social role outcomes of depressed adolescents. *Archives of General Psychiatry, 59*, 225–31.

Foltz, R. (2006). Balancing the imbalance: Integrating a strength-based approach with a medical model. *Reclaiming Children and Youth, 15*, 92–4.

Gettinger, M., & Kohler, K. M. (2005). Process-outcome approaches to classroom management. In M. Everston & C. S. Weinstein (eds), *Handbook of classroom management: Research, practice, and contemporary issues* (pp. 73–96). Mahwah, NJ: Erlbaum.

Gresham, F. M. (2004). Current status and future directions of school-based behavioral interventions. *School Psychology Review, 33*, 326–43.

Hawken, L. S., & Hess, R. S. (2006). School psychologists as leaders in the implementation of a targeted intervention: The Behavioral Education Program. *School Psychology Quarterly, 21*, 91–111. doi:10.1521/scpq.2006.21.1.91

Hawken, L., & Horner, R. (2003). Evaluation of a targeted group intervention within a schoolwide system of behavior support. *Journal of Behavioral Education, 12*, 225–40. doi:10.1023/A:1025512411930

Henggeler, S. W. et al. (1996). *Multisystemic treatment of antisocial behavior in children and adolescents*. New York: The Guilford Press.

Hinshaw, S. P. (1992). Externalizing behavior problems and academic underachievement in childhood and adolescence: Causal relationships and underlying mechanisms. *Psychological Bulletin, 111*, 127–55.

Hoagwood, K. E., Olin, S. S., Kerker, B. D., Kratochwill, T. R., Crowe, M., & Saka, M. (2007). Empirically based school interventions targeted at academic and mental health functioning. *Journal of Emotional and Behavior Disorders, 15*, 66–92. doi:10.1177/10634266070150020301

Horner, R. H. (2007). *Discipline prevention data*. Eugene, OR: OSEP Center on Positive Behavioral Interventions and Supports, University of Oregon.

Horner, R. H., Sugai, G., Smolkowski, K., et al. (2009). A randomized, wait-list controlled effectiveness trial assessing School-wide Positive Behavior Support in elementary schools. *Journal of Positive Behavior Interventions, 11*, 133–44. doi:10.1177/1098300709332067

Khoury-Kassabri, M., Benbenishty, R., Astor, R. A., & Zeira, A. (2004). The contributions of community, family, and school variables to student victimization. *American Journal of Community Psychology, 34*, 187–204. doi:10.1007/s10464-004-7414-4

Knoff, H. M. (2000). Organizational development and strategic planning for the millennium: A blueprint toward effective school discipline, safety, and crisis prevention. *Psychology in the Schools, 37*, 17–32.

Kratochwill, T. R., & Bergan, J. R. (1990). *Behavioral consultation: An individual guide*. New York: Plenum Press.

Levin, J., & Nolan, J. F. (2004). *Principles of classroom management: A professional decision-making model*. New York: Pearson.

Malecki, C. K., & Demaray, M. K. (2007). Social behavior assessment and response to intervention. In S. R. Jimerson, M. K., Burns, & A. M.

VanDerHeyden (eds), *Handbook of response to intervention: The science and practice of assessment and intervention* (pp. 161–71). New York: Springer.

Muscott, H., Mann, E., LeBrun, M. R. (2008). Positive behavioral interventions and supports in New Hampshire: Effects of large-scale implementation of schoolwide positive behavior support on student discipline and academic achievement. *Journal of Positive Behavior Interventions, 10,* 190–205. Muscott, H. S., Szczesiul, S., & Berk, B., doi:10.1177/1098300708316258

Myers, D. M., & Briere, D. E. (2010). Lessons learned from implementing a check-in/check-out behavioral program in an urban middle school. *Beyond Behavior, 19,* 21–7.

Reichle, J. (1990). *National working conference on positive approaches to the management of excess behavior: Final report and recommendations.* Minneapolis, MN: Institute on Community Integration.

Simonsen, B., Sugai, G., & Negron, M. (2008). Schoolwide positive behavior supports: Primary systems and practices. *Teaching Exceptional Children, 40,* 32–40.

Staub, K., Hoover, J., & Perry-Chisolm, P. (2008). Creating home-school partnerships by engaging families in Schoolwide Positive Behavior Supports. *Teaching Exceptional Children, 40,* 6–14.

Stroul, B. A. (2002). *Issue-brief-system of care: A framework for system reform in children's mental health.* Washington, DC: Georgetown University Child Development Center, National Technical Assistance Center for Children's Mental Health.

Tarullo, A. R., & Gunnar, R. (2006). Child maltreatment and the developing HPA axis. *Hormones and Behavior, 50,* 632–9.

Tilly, W. D. (2002). Best practices in school psychology as a problem solving enterprise. In A. Thomas & J. Grimes (eds), *Best practices in school psychology IV* (pp. 21–36). Bethesda, MD: The National Association of School Psychologists Publications.

Upah, K. R. F. (2008). Best practices in designing, implementing, and evaluating quality interventions. In A. Thomas & J. Grimes (eds), *Best practices in school psychology V* (pp. 209–24). Bethesda, MD: The National Association of School Psychologists Publications.

US Department of Education (2000). *Annual report to Congress on the implementation of the Individuals With Disabilities Act.* Washington, DC: Office of Special Education and Rehabilitative Services.

Vargo, S. (1998). Consulting teacher-to-teacher. *Teaching Exceptional Children, 30,* 54–5.

Wagner, M., Friend, M., Bursuck, W. D. (2006). Educating students with emotional disturbances: A national perspective on school programs and services. *Journal of Emotional and Behavioral Disorders, 14,* 12–30. doi:10.11 77/10634266060140010201

Walker, H. M., & Shinn, M. R. (2002). Structuring school-based interventions to achieve integrated primary, secondary, and tertiary prevention goals for safe and effective schools. In M. R. Shinn, H. M. Walker, & G. Stoner (eds), *Interventions for academic and behavior problems II: Preventative and remedial approaches* (pp. 1–25). Bethesda, MD: The National Association of School Psychologists Publications.

Wilson, G. T. (2008). Behavior therapy. In R. J. Corsini & D. Wedding (eds). *Current psychotherapies* (8ᵗʰ ed.). Belmont, CA: Brooks/Cole.

Youngblade, L. M., & Nackashi, J. (2003). Evaluation of children's spontaneous reports of social difficulties: "I don't have any friends." *Pediatric Case Reviews, 3,* 157–67.

CHAPTER TWO

Understanding and Managing Behaviors of Children Diagnosed with Attention-Deficit/Hyperactivity Disorder (AD/HD)

Linda A. Reddy
Rutgers University

Gregory Fabiano
University of Buffalo

Beth Barbarasch and Christopher Dudek
Rutgers University

Abstract

AD/HD is a neurocognitive disorder which represents a multifaceted and heterogeneous mix of cognitive, behavioral, and social behaviors. These symptoms often challenge the teaching and learning process for teachers and students. This chapter offers school personnel an overview of this population, common comorbid disorders and conditions, as well as overlapping symptom dimensions associated with AD/HD. To help school personnel guide their classroom practices and student focused interventions, readers are provided a detailed description of new teacher and student progress monitoring tools which are illustrated in a case example.

Introduction

Effective classroom management is an important component for delivering quality instruction and promoting student learning. The educational and behavioral needs of children at risk for and with Attention-Deficit/Hyperactivity Disorder (AD/HD) pose unique challenges for educators and school personnel in schools. AD/HD is a complex neurocognitive disorder which represents a heterogeneous mix of symptom dimensions that can impair students' academic, social, and behavioral functioning in school and home (e.g. DuPaul & Stoner, 2004; Fabiano et al., 2006; Reddy & DeThomas, 2006). Symptoms are often exacerbated by the presence of co-occurring symptomotology or comorbid disorders (Barkley, 2006). AD/HD is now widely conceptualized as being a chronic disorder, and children with AD/HD continue to experience clinically significant impairment from symptoms throughout adolescence and adulthood (Kent et al., 2011; Kessler et al., 2005).

To this end, this chapter offers school personnel an overview of AD/HD, common comorbid disorders and conditions, as well as overlapping symptom dimensions associated with this population. Additionally, progress monitoring tools that inform intervention planning are described and illustrated in a case example.

What is AD/HD?

AD/HD is a neurocognitive disorder found in approximately 5% of all school aged children, representing, on average at least one student in every classroom (Polanczyk, Silva de Lima, Horta, Biederman, & Rohde, 2007). Although generally misunderstood as a behavior disorder, AD/HD comprises an array of neurocognitive deficits that manifest as impairments in attention, hyperactivity, impulsivity, planning, organization, and evaluation skills across settings (Douglas, 2005; Reddy & Hale, 2007). Many scholars have asserted that core deficits in executive function underlie the neurocognitive and behavioral difficulties in the AD/HD population (e.g. Barkley, Fischer, Edelbrock, & Smallish, 1990; Castellanos & Tannock, 2002; Douglas, 2005). Executive functioning is often described as the cognitive abilities necessary for implementing goal directed behavior and adapting goal directed behavior to social and environmental demands and changes (DeShazo, Lyman, & Klinger, 2002). Students with executive functioning deficits exhibit difficulties in planning, self-monitoring, and social problem solving skills (Reddy, Hale, & Weissman, in press; Hale et al., 2009). Youngsters with executive functioning deficits may exhibit difficulties in working memory and experience low frustration tolerance and vigilance in the face of difficult tasks (Hale et al., 2009). Regardless of the exact underlying cause of these problems, the neurocognitive deficits and manifested behavior difficulties result in impairments in academic, social, and behavioral functioning.

According to the Diagnostic and Statistical Manual Fourth Edition—Text Revision (DSM-IV-TR), the essential features of AD/HD are persistent patterns (i.e. high rates of frequency and severity) of inattention and/or hyperactivity-impulsivity than are typically observed in individuals at a comparable level of development (American Psychological Association [APA], 2000).[1] The symptoms of AD/HD must be persistent across settings (home and school) and linked to impairment in social and/or academic functioning (e.g. APA, 2000; Junond, DuPaul, Jitendra, Volpe, & Cleary, 2006). The symptoms of AD/HD are usually classified into three categories: Inattention, Hyperactivity, or Impulsivity. These categories are used to generally differentiate between three AD/HD unique and distinct subtypes: AD/HD-Inattention, AD/HD-Hyperactivity/Impulsivity or AD/HD-Combined. In general, children with AD/HD-Inattentive type often appear distracted and withdrawn, while children with AD/HD-hyperactive/inattentive or combined type typically display higher levels of motor activity as they are frequently moving or talking. These students often act impulsively as they may talk out of turn, or seem to act without thinking. For a more detailed discussion of AD/HD subtypes, see Reddy and Hale (2007).

Comorbidity and Common Symptom Dimensions

Students with AD/HD represent a heterogeneous population, which often includes high rates of comorbid disorders, conditions and overlapping symptom dimensions with other childhood disorders that complicate the assessment and intervention process (MTA Cooperative Group, 1999). Due to these factors, children may be misdiagnosed with AD/HD when they have other related childhood disorders (e.g. learning disabilities, language-based disorders, disruptive behavior disorders, anxiety, and depression) and conditions (e.g. medical, family, environmental).

The comorbidity rate for this population varies across disorder, gender, and age. For example, research has found 25% to 70% of youth with AD/HD have specific learning disabilities (Kellner, Houghton, & Douglas, 2003; Reddy et al., in press). Approximately 25 to 40% of youth with AD/HD Inattentive or Combined Type are diagnosed with reading disabilities (Reddy & Hale, 2007; Willcutt & Pennington, 2000). Children with both AD/HD and reading disabilities often exhibit difficulties following verbal and/or written directions and may appear confused because of difficulties with basic oral comprehension skills (Muir-Broaddus, Rosenstein, Medina, & Soderberg, 2002; Tannock & Brown, 2000). It is important to note that children with reading disabilities are more likely to have comorbid symptoms of inattention, rather than hyperactivity or impulsivity (Willcutt, Pennington, Olson, & DeFries, 2007). Areas of distinction between reading disabilities and AD/HD may include phonological awareness, verbal memory, and automatic-processing skills (O'Connor & Jenkins, 1999; Tannock & Brown, 2000).

Although reading disabilities are common in AD/HD, writing may be the greatest challenge for these children, with approximately 65% experiencing written expression disorder (Kellner, Houghton, & Douglas, 2003; Mayes, Calhoun, & Crowell, 2000). Evidence suggests children with AD/HD have poorer handwriting, spelling, vocabulary, lexical-semantic knowledge, grammar, and syntax than typical children. They also tend to produce short, disorganized writing samples with many errors (e.g., Mayes et al., 2000; Re, Pedron, & Cornoldi, 2007). Because executive functions are required to plan, organize, monitor, evaluate, and revise written expression, deficits in these areas that underlie AD/HD may contribute to a learning disability in written language (Hale & Fiorello, 2004).

Language-based disorders (commonly referred to as auditory processing disorder) are common among youth with AD/HD. For example, prevalence rates of auditory processing disorder among school-aged children range from 5% to 10%, while 45% to 75% of these children have comorbid AD/HD (Riccio, Hynd, Cohen, Hall, & Molt, 1994; Tannock & Brown, 2000). Common symptoms associated with AD/HD and auditory processing disorder include inattentiveness, distractability, listening problems, and difficulty following oral instructions (Chermak, Tucker, & Seikel, 2002; Katz & Tillery, 2004). Their shared characteristics have led some to conclude that auditory processing disorder is largely an attention problem (Moore, Ferguson, Edmonson-Jones, Ratib, & Riley, 2010). Children with AD/HD also share common symptoms with autism spectrum disorders such as clinical levels of inattention (Goldstein & Schwebach, 2004; Holtmann, Bolte, & Poustka, 2005) and executive functioning deficits;

most notably response inhibition or the ability to think and plan before responding (Happe, Booth, Charlton, & Hughes, 2006). Additionally, research has suggested that AD/HD-related symptoms parallel those of sensory processing disorder, specifically difficulty processing sensory input (e.g. visual, auditory, tactical, smell, textures, taste) in the classroom (Yochman, Shula, & Ornoy, 2004).

Other disruptive behavior disorders such as oppositional defiant disorder and/or conduct disorder have been found to coexist in approximately 30% to 60% of AD/HD Hyperactive/Impulsive or Combined types samples (Kadesjö, Hägglöf, Kadesjö, & Gillberg, 2003). AD/HD youth with aggressive behavior patterns tend to have more family and peer interpersonal conflicts than AD/HD youth without aggressive behavior patterns (Johnston & Mash, 2001). Youngsters with AD/HD and oppositional defiant disorder display higher rates of teacher conflict, school refusal, anxiety, and depression than those with AD/HD or oppositional defiant disorder alone (Harada, Yamazaki, & Saitoh, 2002).

It is not surprising that children with AD/HD have high rates of comorbid anxiety and/or depression that resemble the symptoms of AD/HD. Anxiety is one of the most common mental problems in youth that can be found in approximately 25% to 50% of children with AD/HD (e.g. Bowen, Chavira, Bailey, Stein, & Stein, 2008; Reynolds & Lane, 2009). Some research has suggested that children exhibiting AD/HD and anxiety may present with lowered rates of school failure, attention problems, and social impairments (Bowen et al., 2008).

Depression disorders have become increasingly identified in school-aged children with estimates ranging from 11% to 15% (APA, 2000; Kessler, Avenevoli, & Merikangas, 2001). Comorbidity rates among children with AD/HD are comparatively low, with comorbidity rates among adolescents with AD/HD ranging from 20% to 30% (Kessler et al., 2001) with 14% meeting criteria of major depressive disorder (Cole, Ball, Martin, Scourfield, & McGuffin, 2009; Kessler et al., 2005) and 28% meeting criteria of dysthymic disorder (Kessler et al., 2005). Overlapping depressive symptoms similar to AD/HD symptoms can include irritability, low self-esteem, and poor concentration. However, other depressive symptoms such as fatigue, feelings of hopelessness, diminished interest in activities or recurrent thoughts of death or dying are distinct to major depressive disorder (APA, 2000).

AD/HD-related symptoms of inattentiveness, hyperactivity, and impulsivity often resemble other medical conditions, and familial and environmental factors (Cushman & Johnson, 2001; Reddy & DeThomas, 2006). For example, research has established that clinical levels of inattention can manifest from at least 38 different sources (Goodman & Poillion, 1992), such as family genetic history, low birth weight, prenatal exposure to alcohol, smoking, drugs, lead poisoning, asthma, and/or allergies. Inattention or impulsivity also has been linked to the complexity of social or academic task demands, use of home and/or classroom behavioral techniques, anxiety, frustration, family discourse (low cohesion and high parental disagreement), as well as poor peer and adult relationships (Reddy & DeThomas, 2006; Samudra & Cantwell, 1999). Parental approaches such as the quality of mothers' caregiving has been shown to predict distractibility in 3 year olds and hyperactivity in 6 to 8 year olds (Carlson, Jacobvitz, & Sroufe, 1995). Mothers' use of inappropriate control strategies with children (e.g. harsh comments without explanation and physical restraints), as well as a lack of affection and approval of their children are associated with AD/HD symptoms (Johnston, Murray, Hinshaw, Pelham, & Hoza, 2002).

In sum, numerous childhood disorders and biological and environmental factors can resemble AD/HD-related symptoms. High rates of comorbid childhood disorders also exacerbate children's AD/HD-related symptom frequency and severity, further impacting their academic, social and behavior functioning in the classroom. Thus, it is clear that most educators will find that no two children with AD/HD in their classroom are alike. For this reason, practitioners often find it helpful to focus on targeted behaviors related to areas of functional impairment, and that interventions need careful progress monitoring across these important domains (e.g. academic achievement and productivity, social relationships with adults/peers) to ensure improvement in all areas of functioning.

What does AD/HD look like in the classroom?

Academically, students with AD/HD bring their own set of unique difficulties to the classroom. For example, many children with AD/HD struggle with following multiple step instructions (i.e. more than three steps), checking and correcting their written work, and organizing and planning for short- and long-term assignments. Their work is often messy and performed quickly and carelessly. Children with AD/HD often struggle to sustain attention, remain academically engaged in tasks (Junond et al., 2006; Rapport, Chung, Shore, & Isaacs, 2001), and thus miss key concepts or important information needed to understand a lesson. Academic engagement is typically referred to as a set of specific classroom behaviors such as writing, participating in tasks, reading aloud or silently, and asking and answering questions. Children with AD/HD tend to be the most engaged during active lessons when they have frequent opportunities to respond aloud or use tools such as computers or white boards (Junond et al., 2006). Students with AD/HD may also have difficulty sustaining attention and often have trouble persevering through tasks (e.g. they may only complete a portion of the work that other students complete, or have a low frustration tolerance). Students' difficulty persevering through tasks should not be due to problems with task demands or instructions, but with a struggle to organize thoughts or materials, and sustain efforts (attention) through successful completion of tasks (Reddy & Hale, 2007).

Children with AD/HD often display their hyperactivity through fidgeting or squirming in their seats, not remaining seated when expected to do so, and appearing "on the go" or as if "driven by a motor". Impulsive children often struggle in delaying verbal or motoric responses, have difficulty waiting their turn and frequently interrupting or intruding on others. In the classroom, hyperactive and impulsive students also experience difficulty in remaining engaged on tasks. It is important to note that hyperactivity or impulsivity can lead to engagement of potentially dangerous activities or accidents. In fact, youth with AD/HD are more prone to emergency room visits and hospitalizations than those with other childhood disorders such as LD, speech and language impairments and Aspergers Syndrome (Bruce, Kirkland, Waschbusch, 2007; Lahey et al., 1998).

Research has suggested that boys exhibit more disruptive behavior than girls (Abikoff et al., 2002; Gaub & Carlson, 1997). Typically, boys with AD/HD display higher rates of off task behavior, noncompliance, and aggression. Girls with AD/HD tend to show less externalizing behavior, they are observed to be equally off task, and seek out the teacher's attention more frequently than their typical peers (Abikoff et al., 2002). Additionally, girls with AD/HD have been shown to have higher cognitive impairment than boys. Because of these gender differences, scholars assert girls are at risk for being under-identified, referred, diagnosed, and treated for AD/HD than boys (Gaub & Carlson, 1997).

Socially, students with AD/HD may exhibit a range of difficulties when relating to peers, most notably engaging in appropriate social interactions. Children with AD/HD tend to have interpersonal difficulties with negotiating the "give-and-take" of social situations and engage in more aggressive and noisier play (Whalen & Henker, 1998). As a result, these youngsters are invited less frequently to participate in games and activities (Pelham & Milich, 1984). Children with inattentive type tend to approach social situations passively and exhibit a general lack of social knowledge (Maedgen & Carlson, 2000). Due to these social difficulties, children with AD/HD are often perceived negatively by their peers and are rejected at much higher rates than their typical peers (Pelham & Milich, 1984).

Use of Teacher and Student Progress Monitoring for Intervention Plans

We offer an overview of two approaches for assessing teacher and student functioning within elementary school classrooms:[2] *Classroom Strategies Scale for Elementary School* and the *Daily Report Card* for AD/HD students as a progress monitoring tool. For students at risk for and with AD/HD, progress monitoring methods can serve as clinically useful approaches to identify intervention plans and monitor the implementation of intervention plans for the classroom and student levels. Incorporating assessment-intervention approaches that track both teacher and student behavior are particularly helpful for students at risk for and with AD/HD (Reddy et al., 2009b). A case example is provided to illustrate the application of these approaches for promoting educators' classroom practices and student identified behavioral needs.

Using the Classroom Strategies Scale for Elementary School to Inform Teacher Practices

The Classroom Strategies Scale (CSS) for Elementary School is a multi-source, multi-method approach for identifying and monitoring K–5 grade general education teachers' usage of empirically-supported instructional and behavioral management strategies. The CSS was developed based on evidence-based general classroom practices (e.g. Gable, Hester, Rock, & Hughes, 2009; Hattie, 1992; Heward, 2003; Leflot, van Lier, Onghena, & Colpin, 2010; Marzano, 1998; Sugai & Horner, 2007; Sutherland, Wehby, & Yoder, 2002; Stichter et al., 2009) and principles from the response-to-intervention framework (Fletcher, Lyon, Fuchs, & Barnes, 2007). Research on teachers' use of positive instructional and classroom behavior management strategies has been found related to academic and behavior success for school-aged children (e.g. Epstein, Atkins, Cullinan, Kutash, & Weaver, 2008; Leflot, van Lier, Onghena, & Colpin, 2010; Marzano, 1998; Reddy et al., 2009a; Sugai & Horner, 2002). For example, Leflot and colleagues (2010) found that teacher behavior management (e.g. reduced use of negative remarks, increased rate of praise statements) predicted improved students' on-task behavior and talking out behavior, which in turn mediated the impact of a universal classroom prevention intervention on the development of disruptive behaviors (hyperactive and oppositional behavior). Thus, assessment approaches focused on informing teachers' classroom practices are critical for educating and managing students at risk for and with AD/HD (Epstein et al., 2008; Reddy et al., 2009a, 2009b).

The CSS was designed to generate scores that inform individual K–5 general education teachers' classroom practices (primary goal) which then subsequently improve student academic and behavioral outcomes (distal goal). The CSS is a multi-stage assessment composed of two brief user-friendly forms: (1) Principal/School Personnel Form and (2) Teacher Form.

The CSS *Principal/School Personnel Form* (Pilot 3) is composed of three stages of assessment:

1 Stage 1 (Classroom Observations) consists of two 30-minute classroom observations, which are conducted by the principal/school personnel, who tallies the frequency of eight teacher behaviors: (1) Concept Summaries, (2) Academic Response Opportunities, (3) Clear 1 to 2 Step Directives, (4) Vague Directives, (5) Praise Statements for Academic Performance, (6) Praise Statements for Appropriate Behavior, (7) Corrective Feedback for Academic Performance, and (8) Corrective Feedback for Appropriate Behavior. The eight teacher behaviors (strategies) are further described and illustrated in the case example.

2 Stage 2 (Strategy Rating Scales) consists of a Positive Instructional Scale (PIS) including 28 items and Behavioral Management Scale (BMS) including 26 items. After each classroom observation, principal/school personnel rate on a 7-point Likert scale ("1" Not used to "7" Always Used) how often teachers used specific positive instructional and behavioral management strategies (*Frequency Rating Scale)* and then how often the teachers should have used each strategy (*Ideal Frequency Rating Scale)* in the specific observed lesson. Change scores are based on subtracting the frequency ratings from the ideal frequency ratings. Stage 2 Strategy Rating Scales are completed after each classroom observation.

3 Stage 3 (Classroom Checklist) consists of 14 items that assess the presence of: specific learning materials and resources and procedures/methods for classroom structure, organization, assignments, and behavioral management/reward systems. The Stage 2 Classroom Checklist is completed after two 30-minute classroom observations (Stage 1) and Strategy Rating Scales (Stage 2).

The CSS *Teacher Form* includes two stages of assessment (i.e., Stage 1: Strategy Rating Scales and Stage 2: Classroom Checklist) that parallel the Principal/School Personnel Form. After the principal or school personnel conducts each of the CSS Classroom Observations, the teacher then completes the Stage 1 Strategy Rating Scales by rating on the 7-point Likert scale how often he/she used each strategy (*Frequency Rating Scale)* and how often he/she should have used each strategy (*Ideal Frequency Rating Scale)* in the specific 30-minute lesson observed. The Stage 2 Classroom Checklist is completed by the teacher after he/she completes the Strategy Rating Scales twice.

The CSS (Pilot 3) is being extensively validated through field testing and collaborative consumer and expert input. The Pilot 2 version of CSS

Principal/School Personnel Form has strong face, content, and construct validity based on school personnel (consumer) input and decades of evidence-based instructional and behavioral management research. The Stage 2 PIS and BMS Total scales, Composite scales, and Subscales are theoretically and factor analytically derived (confirmatory factor analysis) within and across classroom observations. The CSS has strong internal consistency (Cronbach alphas of 0.93 and 0.92) across Stages 1 through 3. Good inter-rater reliability was found for the Stage 1 (Classroom Observation) Total Behaviors ($r=0.94$; percent agreement 92%), Stage 2 (Strategy Rating Scales) PIS and BMS Total scales ($r=0.80$, $r =0.72$; percent agreement 92% and 88%), and Stage 3 Classroom Checklist ($r =0.86$; percent agreement 91%). Good test-retest reliability (approximately 2 to 3 weeks, unadjusted) was found for the Stage 1 Total Behaviors ($r =0.70$; percent agreement 81%), Stage 2 PIS and BMS Total scales ($r=0.86$, $r=0.80$, percent agreement 93% and 85%), and Stage 3 Classroom Checklist ($r = 0.77$; percent agreement was 81%). The CSS has been found to have good concurrent and divergent validity with the Classroom Assessment Scoring System (Pianta, La Paro, & Hamre, 2008; Reddy, Fabiano, & Dudek, under review). Differential item functioning analyses have revealed that the Stage 2 Strategy Rating Scales and items are free of item bias for important teacher demographic variables (e.g. educational degree, tenure status, years of teaching experience). Preliminary validity studies have found the CSS scores sensitive to change following brief teacher consultation for improving classroom practices (Reddy et al., under review).

Evidence for CSS Stage 1 Teacher Strategies

The CSS Principal/School Personnel Stage 1 (Classroom Observation) includes the assessment of eight teacher behaviors (strategies) that are important for effectively educating students with and without disabilities in the classroom. A brief description of the Stage 1 eight teacher strategies is provided. The use of CSS Stage 1 teacher behaviors is further discussed in the illustrative case example. The CSS Stage 2 Strategy Rating Scales and Stage 3 Classroom Checklist are not described in the case example due to space limitations.

Concept summaries are defined as the teacher summarizing or highlighting key concepts or facts (steps) taught during the lesson. Lesson content or concept summarization statements are typically brief, clear, and should be provided throughout the lesson, not just at the beginning or end. This strategy has been found to improve students' organization and recall of material taught as well as to increase their overall understanding of lesson content (e.g. Brophy & Alleman, 1991; Brophy 1999; Hines, Cruickshank, & Kennedy, 1985; Rosenshine & Stevens, 1986). Techniques that reinforce key concepts and facts (concept summaries) are particularly important for students with executive functioning and/or auditory processing disorders as these students often require lesson content to be repeated and emphasized for successful integration and skill application (Hale et al., 2009; Tannock & Brown, 2000). A general guideline for educators is to provide brief concept summaries every two to three minutes during learning activities. Examples may include "we learned today that a hypothesis is a scientist's best guess about how an experiment will turn out", "Yesterday we learned that A, E, I, O, and U are vowels", and "DeShawn, to find a cube's volume we multiply the length times the width times the height".

Academic response opportunities are a powerful strategy for teachers to systematically elicit and encourage students to share their ideas and understanding of lesson content in class. Academic response opportunities can be verbal or nonverbal responses (e.g. explain answers, repeat key points, brainstorm ideas, and show answers on the board). They may include when teachers ask the entire class a question, call on a student with his or her hand raised, and/or asking students to show their answers on their individual white boards. Research on "opportunities to respond" (OTR) among students with behavior disorders underscores the utility of teachers creating opportunities for their students to response to questions and learning activities during instructional time (e.g., Partin, Robertson, Maggin, Oliver, & Wehby, 2010; Sutherland, Alder, & Gunter, 2003; Stichter et al., 2009). Research has found that increasing opportunities to respond and praising students for effort and/or correct responses can lead to higher levels of both on task behavior, prosocial behavior, and correct student answers (Sutherland et al., 2002). Additionally, the Council for Exceptional Children (1987) has recommended that educators should elicit 4 to 6 responses per minute when teaching new learning material and 9 to 12 responses per minute when reviewing previously taught learning material (practice or drill work).

For decades, national organizations and scholars have recognized the impact of academic feedback on the quality of instruction and student learning (e.g., Council for Exceptional Children (1987); Institute of Educational Sciences What Works Clearing House; Bender, 2008; Gable et al., 2009; Tomlinson et al., 2003). For the CSS Stage 1 assessment, academic feedback consists of two strategies: *praise for academic performance (or effort)* and *corrective feedback for incorrect academic performance.* Praise for academic performance is verbal or nonverbal statements or gestures provided by teachers to individual or groups of students immediately following academic responses. Likewise, corrective feedback for academic performance is verbal or nonverbal statements or gestures provided by teachers to individual or groups of students immediately following incorrect academic responses.

Praise statements should be frequent, immediate, enthusiastic, and describe the specific behaviors of the student's success. Praise statements that are implemented consistently will orient students towards a better appreciation of students' own task-related behavior (Brophy, 1981; Gable et al., 2009). Examples of effective praise for academic performance may include "Good Job dividing 10 and 2 to get 5" or "I like how hard you worked to come up with a compound word". Similarly, feedback for students' incorrect academic responses should be immediate and explain what is specifically incorrect about their answers (Hattie & Timperely, 2007). Simply telling children their answer is right or wrong is not enough. Students need to be told what specifically is correct or incorrect about their answers. This is especially true of children with AD/HD as their difficulties with attention to detail, planning, and organization may make it challenging for them to check and then correct their work. An example of well-phrased corrective feedback would be, "Your answer is incorrect because you forgot to carry over the one when you added the tens column".

Praise and corrective feedback for academic performance serve as natural consequences for academic response opportunities. Following academic response opportunities, teachers should specifically praise students for their correct answers or efforts to answer questions if answers are incorrect. However, teachers should also provide corrective feedback that specifically explains why responses were incorrect. For all students, but especially students with AD/HD, academic response opportunities and academic feedback (praise and correct feedback) are critically important for encouraging, monitoring, and reinforcing task persistence and completion. There is a long-standing history of studies supporting these feedback approaches for children with AD/HD in classroom settings (e.g., O'Leary, Kaufman, Kass, & Drabman, 1970; Pfiffner & O'Leary, 1987).

The CSS Stage 1 assessment also includes four behavior management strategies (i.e. clear one to two step directives, vague directives, praise statements for appropriate behavior, corrective feedback for inappropriate behavior) that have substantial empirical support (e.g. Forehand & McMahon, 1981; Gable et al., 2009; IES What Works Clearinghouse; Kalis, Vannest, & Rich, 2007; Kern & Clemens, 2007; Walker, Colvin, & Ramsey, 1995). Effective delivery of instructions (directives) is a key strategy for promoting appropriate behavior (Kern & Clemens, 2007). *Clear one to two step directives* are brief verbal instructions that direct specific student behavior. Directives are clear, declarative statements (not questions or favors) that specifically describe the desired behavior in no more than two steps. Directives are most effective when phrased as "do" commands (i.e., telling children what they should do rather then what they should not). For example, 'Sarah please line up at the door", "Take out your math book and turn to page 10", and "Class, put your homework folders on the back desk". Other key features of effective directives include: first gaining the student's attention before issuing the directive, issuing the directives one at a time in a firm (but not angry) voice, and waiting for student compliance (e.g. Forehand & McMahon, 1981; Kern & Clemens, 2007).

It is advised after giving directives teachers should wait (pause) approximately five seconds to assess for compliance and remain within close proximity to the student(s) (Matherson, 2005; Reddy, Hale, & Weissman, in press). Specific praise should be given immediately after directives are followed. Directives not followed should be briefly repeated and monitored for compliance. The contingent delivery of one to two step directives, compliance monitoring (wait time), and praise and/or corrective feedback is particularly helpful to students with disabilities (Forehand & McMahon, 1981). Research has found that clear brief directives increase compliance and improve adult and child interactions among children with AD/HD (Forehand & McMahon, 1981; Peed, Roberts, & Forehand, 1977; Pisterman et al., 1989).

In contrast, *vague directives* are verbal directives that are unclear, issued as questions, and include unnecessary verbalizations (more than two steps). Examples of vague directives may include "Everyone needs to be behaving", "You are not listening", and "Open your math books, turn to page 7, start problem 6, and then complete your ditto and put it here". Vague directives often do not explicitly communicate the behavior expectation required and thus are difficult to successfully follow.

Effective classroom management has been linked to contingent use of praise statements and corrective feedback for behavior for decades (e.g. Brophy, 1981; Kern & Clemens, 2007; O'Leary et al., 1970; Gable et al., 2009). For the CSS Stage 1 assessment, behavior feedback consists of two strategies: *praise for appropriate behavior* and *corrective feedback for inappropriate behavior.* Praise for appropriate behavior is verbal or nonverbal statements or gestures provided by teachers to individuals or groups of students immediately following appropriate behavior. As with praise for academic performance, key features of effective praise statements for behavior are high frequency, immediacy, and specifically labeling the appropriate behavior. Examples may include "I like the way John is following directions", "Table 2 is working hard and sharing materials", and "Good job going back to your seat quietly".

Research has shown that levels of on task behavior significantly increase when students were given specific praise about their behavior compared to simply positive praise (i.e. Good job; Chalk & Bizo, 2004; Brophy, 1982). This is especially true for children with AD/HD, where praise is used to shape behavior to meet expectations (Chalk & Bizo, 2004). Using specific positive praise reinforces students for positive behavior, tells students specifically what they are doing well, and reinforces others to follow appropriate behaviors.

On the CSS Stage 1, corrective feedback for inappropriate behavior is verbal or nonverbal statements or gestures provided by teachers to redirect inappropriate behavior. Like praise, corrective feedback should be specifically labeled and given immediately after inappropriate behavior is observed (Bangert-Downs, Kulik, Kulik, & Morgan, 1991). Corrective feedback also should point out what appropriate behavior should be displayed by students and tailored to the individual student's developmental/cognitive level to enhance follow through (Hattie & Timperley, 2007). Examples of effective corrective feedback statements include: "Get back to your seat Robert. While we work on the ditto we need to remain seated" or "please be quiet in the hallway, John". In general, teachers should aim to give approximately *one* corrective feedback statement for *every three* praise statements in the classroom (White, 1975; Stitcher et al., 2009).

Case Example

Teacher and Classroom Characteristics

Sarah is a 62-year-old, Caucasian, certified general education teacher with a Master's degree in reading. She has 31 years of experience as a teacher in elementary school education and has worked at the school for 15 years. She currently teaches a first grade classroom with twenty-four students and has two students classified with specific learning disabilities (reading) and one student (Emily) with a 504 plan who has been independently diagnosed with AD/HD Combined Type by a pediatric neuropsychologist and licensed psychologist when she was 6.5 years old. The teacher describes Emily as a highly bright student who often engages in impulsive behaviors which disrupt the classroom. Emily frequently calls out in class, acts without thinking, and struggles to follow directions the first time they are given. The student often fidgets in her chair or gets up and walks around the room. While the teacher tries to ignore many of Emily's behaviors, she frequently finds herself reprimanding Emily, especially when her behavior appears to trigger other students to act out. The teacher seldom praises Emily or the other students for appropriate behavior.

The teacher requested behavioral consultation with the school psychologist to help improve her classroom practices and behavioral management of Emily. The initial phase of consultation was focused on "fine tuning" classroom strategies (CSS) and the subsequent phase of consultation (Daily Report Card) focused on Emily's specific behaviors. The CSS Principal/ School Personnel Form was used as a progress monitoring tool for informing changes in teacher classroom practices.

Teacher Consultation, CSS scores, and Visual Performance Feedback

Consultation was conducted by a supervised doctoral student in school psychology. The consultant and teacher met for 30-minutes once a week for four weeks. After sessions 1, 2, and 3, the consultant visited the teacher's classroom and completed the CSS Principal/School Personnel Form during math and literacy. To facilitate the consultation process, the consultant's CSS Stage 1 scores of the eight teacher strategies were graphically displayed to offer the teacher weekly visual performance feedback (VPF) on her progress towards her strategy goals (see Figures 2.1 and 2.2).

During each consultation session, the consultant reviewed the CSS scores through visual performance feedback with the teacher and provided her with a copy. After each session, the consultant faxed and e-mailed the teacher a memo outlining what was discussed during the meeting. The consultant was available via e-mail and cell phone to provide support to the teacher outside of consultation sessions.

Prior to the start of the consultation, an independent observer trained on the CSS completed the CSS Principal/School Personnel Form during two 30-minute lessons identified by the teacher (i.e. math and literacy). Two baseline assessments were completed, each approximately four weeks apart. After the fourth consultation session, the same independent observer completed the CSS during the same lessons (serving as a post-test). Due to

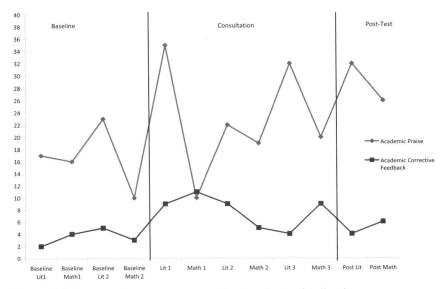

Figure 2.1 Instructional strategy goals: Academic feedback

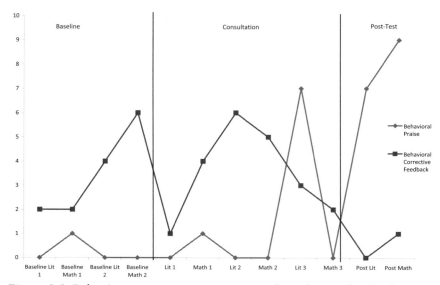

Figure 2.2 Behavior management strategy goals: Behavior feedback

space limitation, the CSS scores and VPF for the teacher's targeted goals only are presented.

Session 1

During session 1, the consultant and teacher discussed her general approaches to teaching and classroom management and her specific use of strategies. Collaboratively, the teacher and consultant reviewed and discussed the eight teacher strategies on the CSS Principal/School Personnel Form. Initial plans for strategy goals were discussed. The teacher originally chose to work on corrective feedback for both academic performance and behavior, hoping to improve delivery effectiveness by increasing specificity of the incorrect answers or inappropriate behavior. However, after further discussion, the consultant and teacher agreed to also work on increasing her use of praise statements for both academic performance and behavior. The teacher acknowledged that her use of praise for appropriate behavior and perhaps academic performance could be improved, especially for Emily. Thus, the identified strategy goals were: (1) praise statements for academic performance (or effort), (2) corrective feedback for academic performance, (3) praise statements for appropriate behavior, and (4) correct feedback for inappropriate behavior. The meeting concluded with the consultant arranging times to observe the classroom for two lessons (i.e. math and literacy).

Session 2

During session 2, the initial four strategy goals were confirmed. The consultant complimented the teacher on her two lessons that were observed. The consultant and teacher first briefly reviewed the graphed consultant CSS Stage 1 scores (VPF), which reflected the frequency with which she used the eight CSS strategies. The VPF was obtained before session 2 during math and literacy. Discussion then focused on the four identified strategy goals with a particular emphasis on the two instructional goals. The objective of session 2 was to establish a practical plan to build upon the teacher's current approaches, as well as define and operationalize the two target instructional strategies for improved implementation. For praise and corrective feedback for academic performance, it was observed that the teacher provided her students with academic feedback (praise or corrective feedback) about half the time she provided academic response opportunities. It was noted that use of academic response opportunities was an area of strength for her.

The consultant suggested that the teacher increase her rate of praise and corrective feedback for academic performance (or effort) to approximate the number of times academic response opportunities were given. The teacher agreed with this goal. The consultant provided some tips on how to make corrective feedback a positive learning experience for students as opposed to a negative affirmation of poor performance. In order to create such an opportunity, it was suggested that the teacher specifically explain what was incorrect about the students' responses. Although concept summaries were not an identified goal, it was noted that she used concept summaries at a low rate during the lessons observed. For example, the teacher was observed utilizing concept summaries only at the beginning of the lesson. Thus, it was suggested that the teacher try to summarize concepts, facts, and instructional steps throughout the lesson to enhance student organization and recall of lesson content. The meeting was concluded with setting up times to observe the classroom.

Session 3

During the beginning of the meeting, the consultant and teacher briefly reviewed the graphed consultant CSS Stage 1 scores (VPF), which reflected the frequency in which she used the CSS eight strategies. The VPF was obtained before session 3 during math and literacy. The four identified strategy goals were reviewed with a particular emphasis on the two behavioral management goals. The teacher was praised for her efforts to improve her use of the two instructional goals. Similar to session 2, the goal for this session was to establish a plan to build upon the teacher's current approaches, as well as define and operationalize the two target behavioral management strategies for improved implementation. While it was noted that the teacher used behavioral corrective feedback, her feedback was somewhat vague and did not specify (label) the inappropriate behavior. The consultant and teacher worked on ways to deliver more behaviorally specific corrective feedback and direct students to the appropriate behavior. Of significant note, the teacher used almost no behavioral praise as a strategy to manage behavior during the lessons observed.

Further discussion revealed that the teacher struggled to separate academic and behavioral praise, as she saw behavioral praise as praising students for what they "should be doing". The consultant and the teacher discussed the differences between each type of praise and the benefits of each, especially for students with special needs like Emily. It was discussed that praising students for behaving appropriately increases their likelihood of engaging in more prosocial behavior, subsequently decreasing student inappropriate behavior and the rate of corrective feedback. A strategy to help remind teachers to use behavioral praise was suggested (i.e. 10 pennies in a pocket, moving one penny from the left to right pocket after giving specific praise). The teacher agreed to incorporate more praise strategies. While clear one to two step directives were not one of the teacher's goals, it was noted that she often made requests in the form questions (i.e. favors; "Can you please clean up for me?") rather than directives (declarative statements). The teacher thanked the consultant for pointing out this observation. Again, the meeting concluded with setting up times to observe the classroom.

Session 4

The final consultant CSS scores (VPF) was completed before session 4 during math and literacy. Once again the teacher and the consultant reviewed her progress on the CSS eight teacher strategies with a focus on the four identified goals. The teacher was commended for her hard work on improving and refining her use of the four strategies. The consultant noted that her strong efforts to use labeled praise statements during literacy and greater specificity in behavioral corrective feedback. Likewise, improvements in the teacher's use of praise statements and corrective feedback for academic performance were discussed.

While the teacher's use of academic response opportunities remained constant, the overall quality of her academic response opportunities improved as she asked students questions that fostered detailed answers and explanations on how they arrived at answers. Increases in the use of concept summaries were also observed. The teacher noted her increased use of praise appeared to improve the overall classroom climate and consequently, she found herself using behavioral corrective feedback less often. She reported reprimanding Emily less and felt as though her relationship with Emily was beginning to improve. Also, the teacher indicated she felt her use of all eight strategies had improved and she started to find her students more engaged and on task during her lessons. Overall, she reported the consultation as a positive experience.

Visual analysis of the CSS Stage 1 scores revealed positive improvements on the level (quantity) of the teacher's use of praise and corrective feedback, for both academic performance and behavior. The goal of providing feedback (praise or corrective) for each academic response opportunities proved to be an effective strategy to improve the teacher's use of specific labeled praise and corrective feedback for correct and incorrect academic performance (See Figure 2.1). As consultation progressed, the teacher's praise was more enthusiastic and specific to the particulars of students' accomplishment. The teacher also became more effective at specifying why an answer was incorrect when giving corrective feedback. As shown on Figure 2.2, the teacher demonstrated significant improvements in her use of behavioral praise statements and corrective feedback at post-test. It was found that the teacher decreased her use of behavioral corrective feedback as a function of increasing praise. Also, the quality of behavioral corrective feedback improved on the specificity of what students were doing inappropriately and what appropriate behaviors should be performed.

Single-case design effect sizes[3] were computed to assess the practical significance of the teacher's change in classroom practices between baseline(s) to post-test as assessed by a trained independent observer (Busk & Serlin, 1992). For a general guideline, effect sizes of 0.20 to 0.49 are considered small, 0.50 to 0.79 are medium, and 0.80 and above large (Cohen, 1988). For academic and behavioral feedback (i.e. praise and corrective feedback), the effect sizes between baselines one and two were less than 0.20, reflecting that the teacher consistently used the four strategies across time (4 weeks) and academic area (math and literacy). For academic feedback, the teacher produced large positive effect sizes from baseline to post-test for her increased use of praise statements and correct feedback for academic performance or effort (praise ES=2.53; corrective feedback ES=1.06), respectfully. Similarly, the teacher produced large effect sizes from baseline to post-test for her increased use of praise statements for appropriate behavior (praise ES=22.0) and reduced use of corrective feedback for inappropriate behavior (ES=4.24).

Applying the Daily Report Card to Inform Student Behavior

As outlined, improving educators' use of evidence-based instructional and behavior management strategies within the general education classroom is an essential first step (intervention) for nondisabled and disabled students.

However, for some children with AD/HD, tailored individualized interventions are required to further improve academic and/or behavioral functioning in the general education setting (e.g., Epstein et al., 2008). Consistent with the emphasis on progress monitoring in this chapter, the use of a Daily Report Card (DRC) as an intervention and progress monitoring tool will be briefly reviewed and applied to the case of Emily.

A cornerstone effective treatment for AD/HD is the DRC, also known as a school home note or daily behavior report card (DuPaul & Eckert, 1997; DuPaul & Stoner, 2004; Kelley, 1990; Pelham & Fabiano, 2008; Pelham, Wheeler, & Chronis, 1998). The DRC is an operationalized list of a student's target behaviors (e.g., interrupting, noncompliance, academic productivity, behavior in unstructured areas such as hallways, cafeteria), and includes specific criteria for meeting each behavioral goal (e.g., interrupts three or fewer times during math instruction). Teachers provide immediate feedback to the child regarding target behaviors on the DRC as well as liberal praise for working toward and meeting goals. Often, the DRC is sent home with the child each day, and parents provide home-based privileges (e.g., use of bicycle, computer time) contingent on meeting DRC goals.

The targets listed on a DRC have also been conceptualized as a means of progress monitoring as well (e.g., Evans & Youngstrom, 2006; Fabiano, Vujnovic, Naylor, Pariseau, & Robins, 2009; Pelham, Fabiano, & Massetti, 2005; Riley-Tillman, Chafouleas, & Briesch, 2007). DRC outcomes have been found to be sensitive to pharmacological (e.g., Pelham et al., 2001; Pelham et al., 2002) and behavioral treatment effects (e.g., Pelham et al., 2005). Thus, DRCs may be used as a data-driven monitoring device for schools to use to evaluate the progress of students in classrooms. Indeed, information collected DRCs would provide idiographic feedback on socially valid target behaviors that are tailored to each child.

Teacher Consultation to Establish a DRC

Following the CSS-focused consultation to establish effective general education instructional and behavioral management strategies, a consultant could continue with three or more additional consultation visits to establish a DRC for Emily, if her behavior is not improved to an acceptable degree. Below we outline the content of the additional consultation visits, and discuss how student progress monitoring data might guide efforts to tailor an effective intervention.

Session 5

During this meeting, the consultant and teacher would discuss Emily's recent classroom functioning and construct a list of targeted behaviors.

Typically, consultants would only focus on three to five behaviors at a time and each would be clearly operationally defined (e.g. "work must be completed within the time provided at 80% accuracy" rather than "Seatwork is handed in"). The consultant and teacher would also decide how often to evaluate each target behavior (e.g. mid-day and end of the day; after each subject, etc.). Finally, each target would have an initial criterion established so teachers would know when the child met the target versus when the child did not (i.e. interrupts the lesson five or fewer times). Between the first and second meeting, the teacher was asked to implement the intervention. Figure 2.3 lists a sample DRC for Emily.

EMILY'S DAILY REPORT CARD

Emily's Goals	Reading		Writing		Math		Social Studies	
Completes all work within the time given at 80% accuracy or better.	Yes	No	Yes	No	Yes	No	Yes	No
Needs no more than 2 reminders to follow a direction.	Yes	No	Yes	No	Yes	No	Yes	No
Needs no more than 3 reminders to stay in her seat	Yes	No	Yes	No	Yes	No	Yes	No
Has no more than 5 interruptions during lessons.	Yes	No	Yes	No	Yes	No	Yes	No

Comments:
_____
_____
_____
_____
_____

Emily's Good Behavior Privileges
12–16 Yes's Choose 3: 30 minutes of TV, 30 minutes of computer, dessert, extra bedtime story, prize box
8–11 Yes's Choose 2: 20 minutes of TV, 20 minutes of computer, dessert, extra bedtime story
4–7 Yes's Choose 1: Extra bedtime story, dessert

Figure 2.3 Sample daily report card for Emily

At the same time, the consultant meets with the child's parent(s) to establish home-based rewards contingent on the child's daily DRC performance. Parents are typically asked to establish a menu of rewards and to place the rewards in a hierarchy (i.e. the longest duration of computer time is provided for obtaining the majority of DRC goals, whereas a shorter duration is awarded for obtaining a modest number of DRC goals). Parents are typically encouraged to use activities or privileges the child currently receives non-contingently (e.g. television, snacks) as rewards now only provided contingent on meeting DRC goals.

Session 6

During this meeting, target behaviors are refined based on teacher data and student outcomes. For example, by using the data collected by the teacher, criteria for each target behavior may be modified (e.g. a child who averaged five verbally intrusive behaviors per class would have a target behavior changed to "Has four or fewer interruptions during class"). Often another follow-up consultant visit is conducted to fine-tune and trouble-shoot the DRC and inform the teacher of the home rewards established by the parents.

Following this visit, on an ongoing basis, the percentage of goals met each day can serve as an ongoing indicator of progress monitoring. For instance, a graphical representation of percent of targets met could be generated and used during consultant-teacher follow-up meetings as a means for data driven decision-making related to target modification, addition, or deletion (Fabiano et al., 2010). The DRC has adequate psychometric properties as a measure of ongoing progress monitoring (Cheney, Flower, & Templeton, 2008; Fabiano et al., 2009; Pelham, et al., 2005).

Future Directions and Implications

This chapter reviews the potential impact of AD/HD symptoms on classrooms and procedures for enhancing the general education environment to promote successful learning and behavior regulation for students at risk for and with AD/HD. New progress monitoring approaches for teacher practices (behavior) and student behavior were described and illustrated through case study. These approaches are promising for educational practice and offer evidence to guide directions in the field of school-based interventions for students with AD/HD.

First, the approaches focus on impaired areas of functioning (e.g. corrective feedback to remediate academic and behavioral concerns; specific DRC targets) rather than specific symptoms of AD/HD. The field should continue to move toward emphasizing improvement in functioning, rather than the reduction of psychiatric symptoms as the impaired areas of functioning are the social valid targets of intervention. Second, the approaches afford school personnel practical repeated assessments rather than time-limited assessments. With AD/HD widely conceptualized as a chronic disorder, educators must move away from time-limited or short-term interventions to those that are implemented in an ongoing fashion for as long as is needed—sometimes entire school years or longer. Finally, this chapter emphasizes the utilization of progress monitoring tools that generate specific behavioral feedback (scores) for informing decision-making to develop effective intervention plans for both educators and students in schools. Future work should continue to investigate effective consultative and assessment-intervention strategies to enhance outcomes for educators and their students with AD/HD in schools.

Notes

1 The DSM-V will be released in 2013 and will likely include some changes in diagnostic criteria for AD/HD.

2 The Classroom Strategies Scale for Elementary School (PI Reddy; R305A080337) and study of a Daily Report Card for children with AD/HD in special education (PI Fabiano; R324J06024) were funded by the US Department of Education, Institute of Educational Sciences.

3 Busk and Serlin's (1992) single-subject ES was used to assess change in teacher behavior from baseline to post-tests. The ESs were calculated by subtracting the mean of the treatment phase from the mean of the baseline phase and dividing the sum by the standard deviation of the baseline. The number of data points per phase was used in these computations rather than the number of participants. This method is sometimes referred to as the *No Assumptions* approach because there are no assumptions made about the normality of the distribution or the equality of variances.

References

Abikoff, H. B., Jensen, P.L., Arnold, E. L. L., et al., (2002). Observed classroom behavior of children with AD/HD: Relationship to gender and comorbidity. *Journal of Abnormal Child Psychology, 30*, 349–59. doi:10.1023/A:1015713807297

American Psychiatric Association. (2000). *Diagnostic and statistical manual of mental disorders* (4th ed.-text revision). Washington, DC: Author.

Bangert-Downs, R. L., Kulik, C. C., Kulik, J. A., & Morgan, M. (1991). The instructional effect of feedback in test-like events. *Review of Educational Research, 61*, 213–38. doi:10.3102/00346543061002213

Barkley, R. A. (2006). Attention-deficit/hyperactivity disorder. In D. A. Wolfe & E. J. Mash (eds), *Behavioral and emotional disorders in adolescents: Nature, assessment and treatment* (pp. 91–152). New York, NY: The Guilford Press.

Barkley, R. A., Fischer, M., Edelbrock, C. S., & Smallish, L. (1990). The adolescent outcome of hyperactive children diagnosed by research criteria: I. An 8-year prospective follow-up study. *Journal of the American Academy of Child and Adolescent Psychiatry, 29,* 233–55. doi:10.1111/j.1469-7610.1991.tb00304.x

Bender, G. (2008). Exploring conceptual models for community engagement at higher education institutions in South Africa. *Perspectives in Education, 26,* 81–95. Accessed from http://supportservices.ufs.ac.za/dl/userfiles/Documents/00000/530_eng.pdf

Bowen, R., Chavira, D., Bailey, K., Stein, M., & Stein, M. (2008). Nature of anxiety comorbid with attention deficit hyperactivity disorder in children from a pediatric primary care setting. *Psychiatry Research, 157,* 201–9. doi:10.1016/j.psychres.2004.12.015

Brophy, J. (1981). Teacher praise: A functional analysis. *Review of Educational Research, 51,* 5–32. doi:10.3102/00346543051001005

—(1982). Classroom management and organization. *The Elementary School Journal, 83,* 264–85. doi:10.1086/461318

—(1999). Toward a model of the value aspects of motivation in education: Developing an appreciation for particular learning domains and activities. *Educational Psychologist, 34,* 75–85. doi:10.1207/s15326985ep3402_1

Brophy, J., & Alleman, J. (1991). Activities as instructional tools: A framework for analysis and evaluation. *Educational Researcher, 20,* 9–23. doi:10.3102/0013189X020004009

Bruce, B., Kirkland, S., & Waschbusch, D. (2007). The relationship between childhood behaviour disorders and unintentional injury event. *Pediatrics and Child Health, 12,* 749–54.

Busk, P., & Serlin, R. (1992). Meta-analysis for single-participant research. In T. R. Kratochwill & J. R. Levin (eds), *Single-case research design and analysis: New directions for psychology and education* (pp. 187–212). Mahwah, NJ: Erlbaum.

Carlson, E. A., Jacobvitz, D., & Sroufe, L. A. (1995). A developmental investigation of inattentiveness and hyperactivity. *Child Development, 66,* 37–54. doi:10.1111/j.1467-8624.1995.tb00854.x

Castellanos, X., & Tannock, R. (2002). Neuroscience of attention-deficit/hyperactivity disorder: The search for endophenotypes. *Nature Reviews Neuroscience, 3,* 617–28. doi:10.1038/nrn896

Chalk, K., & Bizo, L. (2004). Specific praise improves on-task behavior and numeracy enjoyment: A study of year four pupils engaged in the numeracy hour. *Educational Psychology in Practice, 20,* 335–52. doi:10.1080/0266736042000314277

Cheney, D., Flower, A., & Templeton, T. (2008). Applying response to intervention metrics in the social domain for students at risk of developing emotional or behavioral disorders. *The Journal of Special Education, 42,* 108–26. doi:10.1177/0022466907313349

Chermak, G. D., Tucker, E., & Seikel, J. A. (2002). Behavioral characteristics of auditory processing disorder and attention-deficit hyperactivity disorder: Predominately inattentive type. *Journal of the American Academy of Audiology, 13*, 332–8.

Cohen, J. (1988). *Statistical power analysis for the behavioral sciences* (2nd ed.). Hillside, New Jersey: Erlbaum.

Cole, J., Ball, H. A., Martin, N. C., Scourfield, J., & McGuffin, P. (2009). Genetic overlap between measures of hyperactivity/inattention and mood in children and adolescents. *Journal of the American Academy of Child and Adolescent Psychiatry, 48*, 1094–101. doi:10.1097/CHI.0b013e3181b7666e

Council for Exceptional Children (1987). *Academy for effective instruction: Working with mildly handicapped students.* Reston, VA: Author.

Cushman, T. P., & Johnson, T. B. (2001). Understanding 'inattention' in children and adolescents. *Ethical Human Sciences & Services, 3*, 107–25.

DeShazo, T., Lyman, R, D., & Klinger, L.G. (2002). Academic underachievement and attention-deficit/hyperactivity disorder: The negative impact of symptom severity on school performance. *Journal of School Psychology, 40*, 259–83. doi:10.1016/S0022-4405(02)00100-0

DuPaul, G. J., & Eckert, T. L. (1997).The effects of school-based interventions for attention deficit/hyperactivity disorder: A meta-analysis. *School Psychology Review, 26*, 5–27.

DuPaul, G. J., & Stoner, G. (2004). *AD/HD in the schools: Assessment and intervention strategies* (2nd ed.). New York, NY: The Guilford Press.

Epstein, M., Atkins, M., Cullinan, D., Kutash, K., & Weaver, R. (2008). *Reducing behavior problems in the elementary school classroom: A practice guide (NCEE #2008–12).* Washington, D.C.: National Center for Educational Evaluation and Regional Assistance.

Evans, S. W., & Youngstrom, E. (2006). Evidence-based assessment of attention-deficit/hyperactivity disorder: Measuring outcomes. *Journal of the American Academy of Child and Adolescent Psychiatry, 45*, 1132–7. doi:10.1097/01. chi.0000228355.23606.14

Fabiano, G. A., Pelham, W. E., Coles, E. L., Gnagy, et al., (2009). A meta-analysis for behavior treatments for attention-deficit/hyperactivity disorder. *Clinical Psychology Review, 29*, 129–40. doi:10.1016/j.cpr.2008.11.001

Fabiano, G. A., Pelham, W. E., Waschbusch, D. A., et al., (2006). A practical measure of impairment: Psychometric properties of the Impairment Rating Scale in samples of children with attention-deficit/hyperactivity disorder and two school-based samples. *Journal of Clinical Child and Adolescent Psychology, 35*, 369–85. doi:10.1207/s15374424jccp3503_3

Fabiano, G. A., Vujnovic, R., Naylor, J., Pariseau, M., & Robins, M. L. (2009). An investigation of the technical adequacy of a daily behavior report card (DBRC) for monitoring progress of students with attention-deficit/hyperactivity disorder in special education placements. *Assessment for Effective Intervention, 34*, 231–41. doi:10.1177/1534508409333344

Fabiano, G. A., Vujnovic, R. K., Pelham, W. E., et al., (2010). Enhancing the effectiveness of special education programming for children with attention deficit hyperactivity disorder using a daily report card. *School Psychology Review, 39*, 219–39.

Fletcher, J. M., Lyon, G. R., Fuchs, L. S., & Barnes, M. A. (2007). *Learning disabilities: From assessment to intervention.* New York, NY: The Guilford Press.

Forehand, R., & McMahon, R. J. (1981). *Helping the noncompliant child: A clinician's guide to parent training.* New York, NY: The Guilford Press.

Gable, R., Hester, P., Rock, M., & Hughes, K. (2009). Back to basics: Rules, praise, ignoring, and reprimands revisited. *Intervention in School & Clinic, 44,* 195–205. doi:10.1177/1053451208328831

Gaub, M., & Carlson, C. L. (1997). Gender differences in AD/HD: A meta-analysis and critical review. *Journal of the American Academy of Child and Adolescent Psychiatry, 36,* 1036–45. doi:10.1097/00004583-199708000-00011

Goldstein, S., & Schwebach, A. J. (2004). The comorbidity of pervasive developmental disorder and attention deficit hyperactivity disorder: Results from a retrospective chart review. *Journal of Autism and Developmental Disorders, 34,* 329–39. doi:10.1023/B:JADD.0000029554.46570.68

Goodman, G., & Poillion, M. J. (1992). ADD: Acronym for any dysfunction or difficulty. *Journal of Special Education, 26,* 37–56. doi:10.1177/002246699202600103

Hale, J. B., & Fiorello, C. A. (2004). *School neuropsychology: A practitioner's handbook.* New York, NY: The Guilford Press.

Hale, J. B., Reddy, L. A., Decker, S. L., et al., (2009). Development and validation of an attention-deficit/hyperactivity disorder (AD/HD) executive function and behavior rating screening battery. *Journal of Clinical and Experimental Neuropsychology, 31,* 897–912. doi:10.1080/13803390802687423

Happe, F., Booth, R., Charlton, R., & Huges, C. (2006). Executive function deficits in autism spectrum disorders and attention-deficit/hyperactivity disorder: Examining profiles across domains and ages. *Brain and Cognition, 61,* 25–39. doi:10.1016/j.bandc.2006.03.004

Harada, Y., Yamazaki, T., & Saitoh, K. (2002). Psychosocial problems in attention-deficit hyperactivity oppositional defiant disorder. *Psychiatry and Clinical Neurosciences, 56,* 365–9. doi:10.1046/j.1440-1819.2002.01024.x

Hattie, J. (1992). Measuring the effects of schooling. *Australian Journal of Education, 36,* 5–13.

Hattie, J., & Timperley, H. (2007). The power of feedback. *Review of Educational Research, 77,* 81–112. doi:10.3102/003465430298487

Heward, W. L. (2003). Ten faulty notions about teaching and learning that hinder the effectiveness of special education. *The Journal of Special Education, 36,* 186–205. doi:10.1177/00224669030360040

Hines, C., Cruickshank, D. R., & Kennedy, J. J. (1985). Teacher clarity and its relationship to student achievement and satisfaction. *American Educational Research Journal, 22,* 87–99. doi:10.3102/00028312022001087

Holtmann, M., Bölte, S., & Poustka, F. (2005). Letters to the editor: AD/HD, Asperger syndrome, and high functioning autism. *Journal of the American Academy of Child and Adolescent Psychiatry, 44,* 1101. doi:10.1097/01. chi.0000177322.57931.2a

Institute of Educational Sciences What Works Clearinghouse (2011, December 14). Accessed from http://ies.ed.gov/ncee/wwc/

Johnston, C., & Mash, E. J. (2001). Families of children with AD/HD: Review and recommendations for future research. *Clinical Child and Family Psychology Review, 4*, 183–207. doi:10.1023/A:1017592030434

Johnston, C., Murray, C., Hinshaw, S. P., Pelham, W. E., & Hoza, B. (2002). Responsiveness in interactions of mothers and sons with AD/HD: Relations to maternal and child characteristics. *Journal of Abnormal Child Psychology, 30*, 77–88. doi:10.1023/A:1014235200174

Junod, R., DuPaul, G. J., Jitendra, A. K., Volpe, R. J., & Cleary, K. S. (2006). Classroom Observations of students with and without AD/HD: Differences across types of engagement. *Journal of School Psychology, 44*, 87–104. doi:10.1007/s10802-006-9046-7

Kadesjö, C., Hägglöf, B., Kadesjö, B., & Gillberg, C. (2003) Attention-deficit-hyperactivity disorder with and without oppositional defiant disorder in 3- to 7-year-old children. *Developmental Medicine & Child Neurology, 45*, 693–9. doi:10.1111/j.1469-8749.2003.tb00872.x

Kalis, T. M., Vannest, K. J., & Parker, R. (2007). Praise counts: Using self-monitoring to increase effective teaching practices. *Preventing School Failure: Alternative Education for Children and Youth, 51*, 20–7. doi:10.3200/PSFL.51.3.20-27

Katz, J., & Tillery, K. (2004). Central auditory processing. In L. Verhoeven & H. van Balkom (eds), *Classification of developmental language disorders: Theoretical issues and clinical implications* (pp. 191–208). Mahwah, NJ: Lawrence Erlbaum Associates.

Kelley, M. L. (1990). *School-home notes: Promoting children's classroom success.* New York, NY: The Guildford Press.

Kellner, R., Houghton, S., & Douglas, G. (2003). Peer-related personal experiences of children with attention-deficit/hyperactivity with and without comorbid learning disabilities. *International Journal of Disability, Development and Education, 50*, 119–36. doi:10.1080/1034912032000089639

Kent, K. M., Pelham, W. E., Molina, B. S. G., et al., (2011). The academic experience of male high school students with AD/HD. *Journal of Abnormal Child Psychology, 39*, 451–62. doi:10.1007/s10802-010-9472-4

Kern, L., & Clemens, N. H. (2007). Antecedent strategies to promote appropriate classroom behavior. *Psychology in the schools, 44*, 65–75. doi:10.1002/pits.20206

Kessler, R. C., Adler, L. A., Barkley, R., et al., (2005). Patterns and predictors of Attention-Deficit/Hyperactivity Disorder persistence into adulthood: Results from the national comorbidity survey replication. *Biological Psychiatry, 57*, 1442–51. doi:10.1016/j.biopsych.2005.04.001

Kessler, R. C., Avenevoli, S., & Merikangas, K. R. (2001). Mood disorders in children and adolescents: An epidemiologic perspective. *Biological Psychiatry, 49*, 1002–14. doi:10.1016/S0006-3223(01)01129-5

Lahey, B. B., Pelham, W. E., Stein, M. A., et al.,(1998). Validity of DSM-IV attention-deficit/hyperactivity disorder for younger children. *Journal of the American Academy of Child and Adolescent Psychiatry, 37*, 695–702. doi:10.1097/00004583-199807000-00008

Leflot, G., van Lier, P. A. C., Onghena, P., & Colpin, H. (2010). The role of teacher behavior management in the development of disruptive behaviors: An intervention study with the Good Behavior Game. *Journal of Abnormal Child Psychology, 38*, 869–82. doi:10.1007/s10802-010-9411-4

Maedgen, J. W., & Carlson, C. L. (2000). Social functioning and emotional regulation in the attention deficit hyperactivity disorder subtypes. *Journal of Clinical Child Psychology, 29*, 30–42. doi:10.1207/S15374424jccp2901_4

Marzano, R. J. (1998). Rethinking tests and performance tasks. *School Administrator, 55*, 10–12.

Matherson, A. S. (2005). Training teachers to give effective commands: Effects on student compliance and academic behaviors. *School Psychology Review, 34*, 202–19.

Mayes, S. D., Calhoun, S. L., & Crowell, E. W. (2000). Learning disabilities and AD/HD: Overlapping spectrum disorders. *Journal of Learning Disabilities, 30*, 417–24. doi:10.1177/002221940003300502

Moore D. R., Ferguson M. A., Edmondson-Jones A. M., Ratib S., & Riley A. (2010). Nature of auditory processing disorder in children. *Pediatrics, 126*, 382–90. doi:10.1542/peds.2009-2826

MTA Cooperative Group. (1999). 14-month randomized clinical trial of treatment strategies for attention deficit hyperactivity disorder. *Archives of General Psychiatry, 56*, 1073–86.

Muir-Broaddus, J. E., Rosenstein, L. D., Medina, D. E., & Soderberg, C. (2002). Neuropsychological test performance of children with AD/HD relative to test norms and parent behavioral ratings. *Archives of Clinical Neuropsychology, 17*, 671–89. doi:10.1093/arclin/17.7.671

O'Connor, R. E., & Jenkins, J. R. (1999). Prediction of reading disabilities in kindergarten and first grade. *Scientific Studies of Reading, 3*, 159–97. doi:10.1207/s1532799xssr0302_4

O'Leary, K. D., Kaufman, K. F., Kass, R. E., & Drabman, R. S. (1970). The effects of loud and soft reprimands on the behavior of disruptive students. *Exceptional Children, 37*, 145–55.

Partin, T. M., Robertson, R. E., Maggin, D. M., Oliver, R. M., & Wehby, J. H. (2010). Using teacher praise and opportunities to respond to promote appropriate studentbehavior. *Preventing School Failure, 54*, 172–8. doi:10.1080/10459880903493179

Peed, S., Roberts, M., & Forehand, R. (1977). Evaluation of the effectiveness of a standardized parent training program in altering the interaction of mothers and their noncompliant children. *Behavior Modification, 1*, 323–50. doi:10.1177/014544557713003

Pelham, W. E., & Fabiano, G. A. (2008). Evidence-based psychosocial treatment for AD/HD: An update. *Journal of Clinical Child and Adolescent Psychology, 37*, 184–214. doi:10.1080/15374410701818681

Pelham, W. E., Fabiano, G. A., & Massetti, G. M. (2005). Evidence-based assessment for attention-deficit/hyperactivity disorder in children and adolescents. *Journal of Clinical Child and Adolescent Psychology, 34*, 449–76. doi:10.1207/s15374424jccp3403_5

Pelham, W. E., Gnagy, E. M., Burrows-Maclean, L., et al., (2001). Once-a-day Concerta methylphenidate versus three-times-daily methylphenidate in laboratory and natural settings. *Pediatrics, 107*, e105–19. doi:10.1542/peds.107.6.e105

Pelham, W. E., Hoza, B., Pillow, D. R., Gnagy, E. M., et al., (2002). Effects of methylphenidate and expectancy on children with AD/HD: Behavior, academic performance, and attributions in a summer treatment program and regular classrooms. *Journal of Consulting and Clinical Psychology, 70,* 320–35. doi:10.1542/peds.107.6.e105

Pelham, W. E., & Milich, R. (1984). Peer relations of children with hyperactivity/ attention deficit disorder. *Journal of Learning Disabilities, 17,* 560–7. doi:10.1177/002221948401700911

Pelham, W. E., Wheeler, T., & Chronis, A. (1998). Empirically supported psychosocial treatments for attention deficit hyperactivity disorder. *Journal of Clinical Child Psychology, 27,* 190–205. doi:10.1207/ s15374424jccp2702_6

Pfiffner, L. J., & O'Leary, S. G. (1987). The efficacy of all-positive management as a function of the prior use of negative consequences. *Journal of Applied Behavior Analysis, 20,* 265–71. doi:10.1901/jaba.1987.20-265

Pianta, R., La Paro, K., & Hamre, B. K. (2005). *Classroom Assessment Scoring System (CLASS).* Unpublished measure, University of Virginia, Charlottesville, VA.

Pisterman, S., McGrath, P., Firestone, P., et al., (1989). Outcome of parent mediated treatment of preschoolers with attention deficit disorder with hyperactivity. *Journal of Consulting and Clinical Psychology, 57,* 628–35. doi:10.1037//0022-006X.57.5.628

Polanczyk, G., Silva de Lima, M., Horta, B. L., Biederman, J., & Rohde, L. A. (2007). The worldwide prevalence of AD/HD: A systematic review and metaregression analysis. *American Journal of Psychiatry, 164,* 942–8. doi:10.1176/appi.ajp.164.6.942

Rapport, M. D., Chung, K. M., Shore, G., & Isaacs, P. (2001). A conceptual model of child psychopathology: Implications for understanding attention deficit hyperactivity disorder and treatment efficacy. *Journal of Clinical Child Psychology, 30,* 48–58. doi:10.1207/S15374424JCCP3001_6

Re, A. M., Pedron, M., & Cornoldi, C. (2007) Expressive writing difficulties in children described as exhibiting AD/HD symptoms. *Journal of Learning Disabilities, 40,* 244–55. doi:10.1177/00222194070400030501

Reddy, L., & De Thomas, C. (2006). Assessment of Attention-Deficit/ Hyperactivity Disorder with children. In S. R. Smith and L. Handler (eds), *The clinical assessment of children and adolescents: A practitioner's guide,* pp. 367–87. Lawrence, NJ: Erlbaum Associates Inc.

Reddy, L. A., De Thomas, C. A., Newman, E., & Chun, V. (2009a). Effectiveness of school-based prevention and intervention programs for children and adolescents with emotional disturbance: A meta analysis. *Journal of School Psychology, 47,* 77–99. doi:10.1016/j.jsp.2008.11.001

—(2009b). School-based prevention and intervention programs for children with emotional disturbance: A review of treatement components and methodology. *Psychology in the Schools, 46,* 132–53. doi:10.1002/pits.20359

Reddy, L. A., Fabiano, G., & Dudek, C. (2011). *Concurrent validity of the Classroom Strategies Scale for Principal/School Personnel Form.* Manuscript submitted for publication.

Reddy, L. A., & Hale, J. (2007). Inattentiveness. In A. R. Eisen (ed.), *Treating childhood behavioral and emotional problems: A step-by-step evidence-based approach* (pp. 156–211). New York, NY: The Guilford Press.

Reddy, L. A., Hale, J. B., & Weissman, A. (in press). Integration of neuropsychological assessment and clinical intervention for youth with AD/HD. In L. A. Reddy, A. Weissman., & J. B. Hale (eds), *Neuropsychological assessment and intervention for emotional and behavior disordered youth: An integrated step-by-step evidence-based approach*. Washington, DC: American Psychological Association Press.

Reynolds, S., & Lane, S. J. (2009). Sensory overresponsivity and anxiety in children with AD/HD. *American Journal of Occupational Therapy, 63,* 433–40. doi:10.5014/ajot.63.4.433

Riccio, C. A., Hynd, G. W., Cohen, M. J., Hall, J., & Molt, L. (1994). Comorbidity of central auditory processing disorder and attention-deficit hyperactivity disorder. *Journal of the American Academy of Child and Adolescent Psychiatry, 33,* 849–57. doi:10.1097/00004583-199407000-00011

Riley-Tillman, T. C., Chafouleas, S. M., & Briesch, A. M. (2007). A school practitioner's guide to using daily behavior report cards to monitor student behavior. *Psychology in the Schools, 44,* 77–89. doi:10.1002/pits.20207

Rosenshine, B., & Stevens, R. (1986). Teaching functions. In M. C. Wittrock (ed.), *Handbook of research on teaching* (3rd ed.). New York, NY: Macmillan.

Samudra, K., & Cantwell, D. P. (1999). Risk factors for attention-deficit/hyperactivity disorder. In H. C. Quay & A. E. Hogan (eds), *Handbook of disruptive behavior disorders* (pp. 199–220). New York, NY: Kluwer Academic/Plenum Publishers.

Stichter, J. P, Lewis, T. J., Whittaker, T. A., et al., (2009). Assessing teacher use of opportunities to respond and effective classroom management strategies: Comparisons among high- and low-risk elementary schools. *Journal of Positive Behavior Interventions, 11,* 68–81. doi:10.1177/1098300708326597

Sugai, G., & Horner, R. (2002). The evolution of discipline practices: School-wide positive behavior supports. *Child & Family Behavior Therapy, 24,* 23–50. doi:10.1300/J019v24n01_03

—(2006). A promising approach for expanding and sustaining the implementation of school-wide positive behavior support. *School Psychology Review, 35,* 245–59.

Sutherland, K. S., Alder, N., & Gunter, P. L. (2003). The effect of varying rates of opportunities to respond to academic requests on the classroom behavior of students with EBD. *Journal of Emotional and Behavioral Disorders, 11,* 239–48. doi:10.1177/10634266030110040501

Sutherland, K. S., Wehby, J. H., & Yoder, P. J. (2002). Examination of the relationship between teacher praise and opportunities for students with EBD to respond to academic requests. *Journal of Emotional and Behavioral Disorders, 10,* 5–13. doi:10.1177/106342660201000102

Tannock, R., & Brown, T. E. (2000). Attention-deficit disorders with learning disorders in children and adolescents. In T. E. Brown (ed.), *Attention-deficit disorders and comorbidities in children, adolescents and adults* (pp. 231–95). Washington, D.C.: American Psychiatric Publishing.

Tomlinson, C., Brighton, C., Hertberg, H., et al., (2003). Differentiating instruction in response to student readiness interest, and learning profile in academically diverse classrooms: A review of the literature. *Journal of the Education of the Gifted, 27,* 119–45. doi:10.4219/jeg-2003-219

Walker, H. M., Colvin, G., & Ramsey, E. (1995). *Antisocial behavior in school: Strategies and best practices.* Pacific Grove, CA: Brooks/Cole Publishing Company.

Whalen, C. K., & Henker, B. (1998). Attention-deficit/hyperactivity disorders. In T. H. Ollendick & M. Hersen (eds), *Handbook of child psychopathology* (pp. 181–211). New York, NY: Plenum Press.

White, M. A. (1975). Natural rates of teacher approval and disapproval in the classroom, *Journal of Applied Behavior Analysis, 8,* 367–72. doi:10.1901/jaba.1975.8–367

Willcutt, E. G., & Pennington, B. F. (2000). Comorbidity of reading disability and attention-deficit/hyperactivity disorder: Differences by gender and subtype. *Journal of Learning Disabilities, 33,* 179–91. doi:10.1177/002221940003300206

Willcutt, E. G., Pennington, B. F., Olson, R. K., & DeFries, J. C. (2007). Understanding comorbidity: A twin study of reading disability and attention-deficit/hyperactivity disorder. *American Journal Medical Genetics Part B: Neuropsychiatric Genetics, 144B,* 709–14. doi:10.1002/ajmg.b.30310

Yochman, A., Parush, S., & Ornoy, A. (2004). Responses to preschool children with and without AD/HD to sensory events in daily life. *The American Journal of Occupational Therapy, 58,* 294–302. doi:10.5014/ajot.58.3.294

CHAPTER THREE

Understanding and Managing Behaviors of Children Diagnosed with Anxiety Disorders (AD)

Elizabeth McCallum and
Elizabeth A. Pask
Duquesne University

Abstract

Anxiety disorders are among the most prevalent mental health problems facing children and adolescents today. Because of the accessibility, efficiency, and naturalistic practice opportunities associated with school-based interventions, schools may be the ideal setting for the prevention and treatment of childhood anxiety. While empirical research validating school-based interventions for anxiety disorders is promising, the field is still in its infancy. To date, Cognitive Behavioral Therapy (CBT) is the most well-documented treatment for anxiety problems in children, although most studies have been conducted in mental health clinic settings. Teachers and school personnel should work collaboratively with mental health professionals, and be equipped with an understanding of the symptoms and implications of common childhood anxiety disorders. They should have a knowledge base of empirically validated interventions as resources. Informal strategies and techniques for use in the classroom may also be advantageous for students with anxiety disorders. However, future research is needed for further evaluating the effectiveness of school-based formal CBT programs and informal classroom strategies in reducing anxiety symptoms in children.

Overview

The term anxiety refers to the brain's response to perceived danger. This emotional response is present from birth and falls on a continuum from mild to severe. Usually, anxiety is not pathological and can be adaptive as it encourages organisms to attempt to avoid dangerous situations. Anxiety only becomes maladaptive when it interferes with an individual's ability to function in everyday life activities (e.g. school, work, social performance). While adults with heightened anxiety usually have the capacity and self-awareness to report feelings of distress due to the excessive anxiety, differentiating between typical and atypical anxiety in children can be difficult due to the normal manifestation of some fears and anxieties during childhood (Beesdo, Knappe, & Pine, 2009). Furthermore, children may be less able or willing than adults to communicate anxiety-related cognitions, emotions, and impairments to parents, teachers, and/or mental health professionals. Teachers, who interact with students on a regular basis, may be in an ideal position to aid students with anxiety problems. Therefore, teachers must be aware of the signs and symptoms of pathological anxiety in children and adolescents. They also should be equipped with knowledge of empirically-validated interventions and instructional techniques for the prevention and treatment of anxiety disorders.

Until the latter half of the twentieth century, the study of anxiety disorders among children and adolescents was largely ignored. Prior to the publication of the Diagnostic and Statistical Manual of Mental Disorders, Third Edition (American Psychiatric Association [APA], 1980), most researchers suggested that fears and anxieties of childhood were simply part of the normal course of child development. They reported that because childhood fears were common, declined with age, and that the focus of these fears tended to change over time, they should not be considered cause for making clinical diagnoses (Albano, Chorpita, & Barlow, 2003). More recently, research on pathological anxiety in children and adolescents has increased somewhat, although it continues to lag behind the corresponding adult research on anxiety disorders. This relative lack of research is problematic for a variety of reasons. First of all, anxiety disorders are among the most prevalent of all psychiatric disorders affecting children and adolescents and are one of the most common reasons for childhood and adolescent mental health referrals (Achenbach, Howell, McConaughy, & Stanger, 1995; Cartwright-Hatton, McNicol, & Doubleday, 2006; Costello, Mustillo, Erkanli, Keeler, & Angold, 2003). Furthermore, researchers suggest that fewer than 20% of children in need of mental health services for any emotional or behavioral problems actually receive the proper treatment (Collins, Westra, Dozois, & Burns, 2004; Kendall, 1994).

Further complicating matters is the fact that, unlike many of the other mental health disorders of childhood (Attention Deficit Hyperactivity Disorder [AD/HD], Conduct Disorder, etc.), anxiety disorders are *internalizing* disorders which often are not associated with outwardly disruptive behaviors. Due to their tendency to be quiet and compliant, students' difficulties are frequently underestimated and overlooked by teachers and parents, who often assume that the presumable "shyness" of their students will be outgrown (Masia-Warner, Fisher, Ludwig, Rialon, & Ryan, 2011). As such, parents and teachers must be particularly attuned to the signs and symptoms of anxiety disorders in children and adolescents. Because children spend a substantial amount of time in schools, teachers and other school personnel are in a prime role to aid students suffering from high levels of anxiety. However, research suggests that oftentimes, teachers may perceive students' anxiety and other emotional problems as beyond the scope of their expertise, and therefore, they may be hesitant or unwilling to intervene (Huberty, 2009). In order to help these children, educators should have a toolkit of classroom strategies and be knowledgeable about more intensive evidence-based interventions for reducing anxiety.

Anxiety Disorders of Childhood and Adolescence

Anxiety disorders of childhood and adolescence are defined by a persistent pattern of excessive worry accompanied by marked distress or impairment in school, social, or family functioning (Essau, Conradt, & Petermann, 2000; Ezpeleta, Keeler, Erkanli, Costello, & Angold, 2001). Prevalence estimates of anxiety disorders vary. Most researchers suggest that between 10% and 21% of children suffer from anxiety disorders (e.g. Garber, Keiley, & Martin, 2002; Gurley, Cohen, Pine, & Brook, 1996; Shaffer et al., 1996), although some have reported the prevalence rate to be as high as 41% (Carwright-Hatton et al., 2006). These prevalence rates place these disorders among the most commonly reported psychiatric disorders of childhood and adolescence (Costello et al., 2003).

There are data to suggest that childhood anxiety disorders are chronic, and often persist into adulthood if left untreated (Angelosante, Colognori, Goldstein, & Warner, 2011; Hirshfeld, Micco, Simoes, & Henin, 2008; Kendall, Safford, Flannery-Schroeder, & Webb, 2004). Furthermore, childhood anxiety disorders have been identified as risk factors for depression, suicidal ideation and suicide attempts, substance abuse, and psychiatric hospitalizations (Cole, Peeke, Martin, Truglio, & Seroczynski, 1998; Kendall et al., 2004). Because of the high prevalence of anxiety disorders in childhood and their comorbidity with other psychiatric problems, there exists a need for evidence-based treatment approaches and strategies for preventing and combating anxiety in children and adolescents, particularly when the disorders interfere with school and social functioning.

The Diagnostic and Statistical Manual of Mental Disorders, Fourth Edition, Text -Revision (DSM-IV-TR; APA, 2000) identifies a number of anxiety disorders that can manifest during childhood. The most common of these are Generalized Anxiety Disorder (GAD), Specific and Social Phobias, Obsessive-Compulsive Disorder (OCD), Posttraumatic Stress Disorder (PTSD), and Separation Anxiety Disorder. Each of these disorders and the associated symptoms most likely to be present in school settings are discussed next.

Generalized Anxiety Disorder

GAD is associated with excessive anxiety and worry about particular activities or events that persists for at least 6 months (DSM-IV-TR). In children and adolescents with GAD, the worries often revolve around school performance, including academics, athletics, and other school-related extra-curricular activities. Students with GAD may present as perfectionists, often redoing tasks because of dissatisfaction with what they perceive as poor performance. In school, these students tend to seek continuous approval from teachers and require excessive reassurance about the quality of their work. GAD is also often associated with other disorders such as AD/HD, depression, or other anxiety disorders (Albano et al., 2003). GAD alone, or in conjunction with one or more of these other psychological disorders, is problematic for students because they may exacerbate negative school experiences such as reluctance to attend school, difficulty concentrating, or not participating in peer activities. Adults who seek treatment for GAD most often report that the onset of symptoms occurred during childhood.

Specific phobias

Specific phobias are identified by marked and persistent fears of specific objects or situations with exposure to the phobic object provoking immediate and intense anxiety. Common types of specific phobias of childhood include fears of animals, heights, darkness, loud noises, and injections. Young children often do not recognize the phobias as problematic and do not report distress due to the phobia. For this reason, childhood phobias should only be diagnosed if they significantly impair the child's daily activities. School phobia is a relatively common specific phobia in children and adolescents. School phobia is diagnosed when the fear response is attributable to a specific school-related situation (e.g. class pet, fire drills, bus rides). However, if the emotional response is triggered by the fear of humiliation or embarrassment that is anticipated to take place in school, social phobia is more likely the appropriate diagnosis. In children, specific phobias (including school phobias) may be expressed by crying, throwing tantrums, freezing, or clinging to caregivers in response to the feared object or situation. Adolescents and adults may actively attempt to avoid the feared situation or object. Children may express psychosomatic complaints, claiming that they feel ill, or engage in disruptive behaviors to avoid the feared school object. Truancy and poor attendance become issues for those with school phobia, which may then lead to a number of problems for the students such as falling behind academically, poor academic achievement, trouble meeting social demands, or school or legal conflicts. Family distress from the struggle to help the child manage anxiety, other psychological disorders and other phobias, like social phobia, may also develop (Paige, 1996).

Social Phobias

Social phobia (sometimes called Social Anxiety Disorder) is defined by a marked and persistent fear of social situations in which an individual may become embarrassed or humiliated, with exposure to social situations provoking an immediate anxiety response. For instance, students may fear situations like reading aloud in class, musical or athletic performances, writing on the blackboard, speaking to adults, attending dances, or joining peer conversations. Typically, adolescents and adults recognize these fears as being excessive and irrational, although often children do not. Children may cry, throw tantrums, freeze, or cling to caregivers when faced with the feared situation. Adults with Social Phobia tend to avoid social situations when possible. However, when the feared situation is school or a school-related activity, children and adolescents often do not have the option of avoidance. Symptoms associated with childhood and adolescent Social Phobias are poor social performance, impaired academic performance, school refusal, and avoidance of age-appropriate social activities. Additionally, children may become selectively mute in school in an effort to avoid looking incompetent or making mistakes (Black & Uhde, 1992). In other words, despite having the physical capabilities, children may withhold speech in uncomfortable social situations in an effort to avoid humiliation or mistakes they think they will make. If left untreated, social phobia may persist into adulthood, and result in severe distress for the individual and family.

Obsessive-Compulsive Disorder

OCD involves recurrent obsessions (abnormal thoughts, images, or impulses) or compulsions (repetitive acts) that are time-consuming or impair an individual's daily functioning. While adults usually recognize the obsessions or compulsions as excessive, often children do not. Typically, it is the parents who seek help for their child's symptoms. Children with OCD tend to exhibit frequent washing, checking, or ordering rituals that cause parental concern. Both children and adults with OCD tend to exhibit their obsessive and/or compulsive behaviors more frequently at home rather than in public, making it particularly difficult for teachers to identify symptoms of the disorder in their students. However, gradually deteriorating academic performance and impaired concentration have been associated with OCD in children and adolescents. Additionally, with increasing severity, OCD ordering and arranging rituals may become more difficult to hide from teachers and classmates. In school, obsessive thinking may mimic AD/HD because students may be distracted by their obsessions or attempts to delay or hide their rituals. Likewise, OCD can also look like school avoidance or phobia because students may want to avoid places that increase their obsessions or compulsions or spend time trying to perform rituals privately. Teachers should understand that students with OCD may appear agitated as well, and if left untreated, may be vulnerable to victimization, bullying, and academic difficulties (Paige, 2007).

Posttraumatic Stress Disorder

PTSD is characterized by intense fear, helplessness, horror, or agitation following exposure to an extreme traumatic stressor. Commonly, individuals with PTSD re-experience the traumatic event through recurrent and intrusive recollections, flashbacks, or nightmares during which the event is replayed. These individuals attempt to avoid any stimuli associated with the traumatic event, including thoughts, feelings, and conversations about the event. For young children with PTSD, as time elapses following the trauma, specific dreams of the traumatic event may give way to generalized nightmares of monsters or other feared objects. Additionally, young children may exhibit the reliving of the traumatic event through repetitive play rather than literally feeling that they are reliving the experience, as adults often will through flashbacks. Symptoms of childhood and adolescent PTSD that may be evidenced in school include talking excessively about the traumatic event, loss of interest in previously enjoyed activities, and difficulty concentrating. Also exhibited by school aged children with PTSD are increased aggressiveness, trouble sleeping, and higher risk of substance abuse and suicide in teenagers, as well as disruptiveness in class, beliefs of not living into adulthood, or theories of omens predicting future trauma (Brock & Cowan, 2004). These significant symptoms have obvious implications for difficulties in school, making awareness by school personnel imperative for the sake of the students' well-being.

Separation Anxiety Disorder

Separation Anxiety Disorder (SAD) is characterized by excessive anxiety about becoming physically separated from one's attachment figures (parents or caregivers) or home. Separation Anxiety Disorder begins in childhood and can cause impairment in social and academic functioning. Children with SAD often express fears that they will never be reunited with their parents. They are often resistant to attending school or social functions without their parents. Upon being left at school, young children with SAD may cry, throw tantrums, or cling to their parent. As children get older, they express more specific fears of dangers befalling them or their loved ones. In middle childhood, children with SAD begin to anticipate the separation and exhibit related anxiety even prior to becoming separated from the attachment figure. Older children and adolescents with SAD may exhibit mild to severe avoidance behaviors, including refusing to attend school (Albano et al., 2003). Similar to social anxiety and school phobia, the symptoms of separation anxiety may lead to a frustratingly difficult school experience which makes treatment as well as parental and teacher support crucial to alleviate separation anxiety.

Anxiety Disorders and School

Childhood anxiety disorders have been identified as a form of emotional disturbance eligible for services under federal special education law. Specifically, the Individuals with Disabilities Education Improvement Act of 2004 (IDEIA) requires that schools provide accommodations to children with anxiety and other psychiatric disorders that are interfering with their ability to engage in and/or benefit from educational and other school-related activities.

Theoretical and applied researchers have suggested a model linking high anxiety and impaired cognitive functioning to explain the association between excessive anxiety and decreased academic performance. Specifically, this theoretical model suggests that heightened anxiety may evoke a state of physiological arousal and an accompanying narrowed focus on the object of perceived threat. This heightened arousal toward the feared object inhibits one's concentration on stimuli that are not perceived as threatening at the time (Wood, 2006). It follows that if students experiencing high levels of anxiety perceive academic tasks as nonthreatening, their concentration on these tasks may be impaired. Alternatively, students whose anxiety responses are triggered by academic tasks may focus too narrowly on the tasks, leading to excessive anxiety over completing the activities correctly. This, in turn, may lead to extreme dissatisfaction with school performance and additional anxieties over potential future failures. Finally, high levels of stress may interfere with students' recall of previously mastered content material (Ma, 1999).

In addition to academic achievement, anxiety can have adverse effects on students' social performance. Anxious children and adolescents may be overly cautious and avoidant of social situations. They may also be less socially competent than typical children, perhaps due to a preoccupation with perceived threats and an inability to focus on the present social task (Barrett & Heubeck, 2000; Langley, Bergman, McCracken, & Piacentini, 2004; Wood, 2006). Additionally, avoidance of social situations limits the opportunities for children and adolescents with anxiety disorders to practice social skills with peers in real-world settings. Despite the negative effects of anxiety on children and adolescents, there is emerging evidence to suggest that interventions aimed at reducing childhood anxiety can improve academic and social performance (Wood, 2006).

Evidence-Based Interventions for Anxiety Disorders

Cognitive behavioral therapy (CBT) is the most well-established, evidence-based treatment for anxiety disorders (Wood, Chiu, Hwang, Jacobs, & Ifekwunigwe, 2008). CBT is an empirically supported treatment technique that involves changing maladaptive thought patterns and their underlying beliefs. CBT has been identified as a developmentally appropriate treatment for anxiety disorders in children as young as five years old, although treatment for children under the age of seven usually involves significant parent participation (Rapee, Kennedy, Ingram, Edwards, & Sweeney, 2005; Wood, Piacentini, Southam-Gerow, Chu, & Sigman, 2006). Researchers have suggested that CBT is successful at alleviating anxiety symptoms for as many as 80% of children involved in treatment programs (Barnett, Dadds, & Rapee, 1996; Kendall et al., 2003; Wood et al., 2006). What is more, CBT has also been shown to lead to an improvement in school performance over time due to the reduction in anxiety. As previously mentioned, theory suggests that excessive anxiety prevents concentration on academic tasks. It has been shown that CBT, and the ensuing reduction in anxiety, predicts improvements in perceptions of children's school performance. In other words, perhaps reduced anxiety due to CBT leads to increased capability to attend to academic tasks at school, such as lessons, tests, and materials. For those children anxious about school in particular, reduction of anxiety levels may lead to a greater engagement and improved performance in the school environment (Wood et al., 2006). Although most CBT studies for treating children with anxiety disorders have been conducted in mental health clinic settings, recently some have taken place within schools.

More so than community mental health centers, researchers have suggested that schools may be in a better position to provide intervention and treatment to students with mental health disorders for a variety of reasons. School-based services are cost-effective and have virtually unlimited access to children (Anglin, 2003). Additionally, the reduced reliance on parental transportation to and from clinics may increase the treatment compliance and attendance of children with mental health disorders (Armbruster & Lichtman, 1999). In fact, research suggests that as many as 80% of students who receive mental health services receive them in schools (Burns et al., 1995). Furthermore, interventions that take place in schools may have heightened external validity because they allow for practice of skills in real-world settings.

Particularly with respect to the treatment of anxiety disorders, schools may be the ideal settings for intervention because, for children and adolescents with anxiety disorders, the unwanted emotional response is often triggered by school-related phenomena (e.g.. answering questions in class, eating in the cafeteria, initiating conversation with unfamiliar peers/personnel, etc.). Therefore, interventionists in schools have access to naturally anxiety-provoking situations in which to have students practice the skills they are learning in therapy (Angelosante et al., 2011). Moreover, students may be reluctant to seek services due to the stigma and labels that may be attached, which may be particularly worrisome to students with social anxiety. Receiving intervention in a familiar school setting where several other students also receive an array of services may reduce the worry and stigma, making treatment more acceptable and providing further evidence for school settings being an optimal place for delivering mental health services (Masia-Warner et al., 2011).

Despite the potential benefits of school based interventions for treating children with anxiety disorders, research support in this area is relatively limited. Very few studies have been conducted evaluating the effectiveness of school-based interventions for reducing anxiety in children and adolescents. The research that has been conducted fits a three tier model that includes: (1) universal prevention of anxiety disorders for all students, (2) selective intervention for students at-risk for developing anxiety disorders, and (3) direct intervention for students with clinically significant levels of anxiety (Angelosante et al., 2011).

The majority of the evidence based interventions for preventing and/or treating anxiety disorders in children and adults involve cognitive behavioral therapeutic techniques including psychoeducation about stress and anxiety, behavioral management techniques, cognitive restructuring, and problem-solving strategies (Dadds & Roth, 2008; Kendall, Aschenbrand, & Hudson, 2003). To date, relatively few studies have been conducted that apply prevention methods to reduce the incidence of anxiety in children and adolescents (Ginsburg, 2009), and even fewer have been conducted within school settings. A review of the literature reveals some programs that have been used successfully within schools to prevent anxiety in children and adolescents. Knowledge of these and similar programs may help teachers and school personnel identify formal anxiety prevention and intervention programs as well as embedded techniques that may be applicable to their settings.

Tier I: School-Based Universal Prevention Programs

In a typical high school of 1000 students, researchers have suggested that as many as 200 may be suffering from anxiety disorders (Doll, 1996). Research further suggests that most students suffering from anxiety do not receive adequate treatment (Doll, 1996; Hirshfeld et al., 1997). Given the high prevalence rates of anxiety disorders in children and adolescents and the fact that many more students may suffer from anxiety that has not yet reached clinical levels, interventions aimed at preventing these disorders have merit. Because of the common trajectory of anxiety disorders preceding other serious mental health problems (e.g.. depression, suicidal ideation, substance abuse, etc.), prevention programs have the additional benefit of potentially preventing these associated psychological problems. Finally, schools may be the most appropriate place for intervention programs aimed at the prevention of mental health disorders due to their relatively unlimited access to children and adolescents. The following are some school-based interventions that have been documented as effective prevention programs targeting anxiety in children and adolescents.

Penn Resiliency Program for Children and Adolescents

The Penn Resiliency Program for Children and Adolescents (PRP-CA) is a cognitive behavioral depression and anxiety prevention program that, when combined with a parent intervention component, has been demonstrated to lead to lower levels of clinical anxiety in middle-school students than a control condition (Gillham et al., 2006). The PRP-CA is a school-based, manualized treatment prevention program aimed at increasing the resilience and emotional well-being of children and adolescents, and thereby preventing the onset of depression and anxiety disorders. The program can be conducted class-wide and led by trained teachers using the manualized procedures. This study tested a new version of the PRP-CA program, which consisted of teaching both adolescents and their parents such skills as challenging pessimistic cognitions and thinking optimistically about adversity. Twenty sixth- and seventh-grade students and their parents completed the intervention, which consisted of eight weekly 90-minute group counseling sessions focused on such topics as teaching students the concept of "thinking styles" and the consequences they have on emotions and behaviors so they are able to evaluate the accuracy of their own thoughts. The program also teaches restructuring negative thoughts about the future and encourages students to dispute negative beliefs in the moment, as they occur. There is also a social-problem solving techniques component that practices assertiveness, decision making, creative brainstorming, and problem solving with the students through role plays, skits, and hypothetical questions. Results suggested that, when compared to the control group, students who participated in the intervention had significantly fewer symptoms of both depression and anxiety over a one-year follow up period.

FRIENDS

The FRIENDS program is a school based CBT program aimed at preventing anxiety in school-aged children (Barrett & Turner, 2001). *FRIENDS* was developed based on the *Coping Cat* manualized CBT treatment program (Kendall, 1994). *FRIENDS* is an acronym designed to help students remember the learned skills. The acronym includes: feeling worried (F), relax and feel good (R), inner thoughts (I), explore plans of action (E), nice work, reward yourself (N), don't forget to practice (D), and stay cool (S). The *FRIENDS* program involves ten weekly group therapy sessions and two additional booster sessions one and three months post intervention. The program involves the teaching of skills such as emotion recognition, how to regulate emotions, relaxation techniques, cognitive restructuring, and social problem-solving. The program also provides controlled exposure to real life social settings that may provoke anxiety in which participants can practice using the *FRIENDS* technique in vivo.

A number of studies have been conducted evaluating the effectiveness of the *FRIENDS* prevention program. Two studies comparing *FRIENDS* with control, non-intervention conditions have reported promising results for preventing anxiety in 10–13 year old students (Barrett & Turner, 2001; Lowry-Webster, Barrett, & Dadds, 2001). Both studies reported a reduction in self-reported anxiety symptoms following treatment. Additionally, research suggests that, particularly for younger students, the beneficial effects of the *FRIENDS* program may be maintained over time (Barrett,

Farrell, Ollendick, & Dadds, 2006; Lock & Barrett, 2003; Lowry-Webster et al., 2001).

Tier II: School-Based Prevention Programs for At-Risk Students

Oftentimes, limited resources prevent schools from initiating universal prevention programs for all students. Programs aimed at preventing mental health problems for at-risk students are particularly useful when financial and personnel resources are scarce and therefore, universal programs are not possible. The following are two empirically validated anxiety prevention programs developed for students with risk factors for developing anxiety disorders.

FRIENDS plus Parent-Training

This program is an adaptation of the previously described *FRIENDS* program that incorporates weekly group parent training sessions (Bernstein, Layne, Egan, & Tennison, 2005). The parent component was added to address how children's anxiety can impact family interactions. It is also important to include parents in intervention because children's coping and explanatory styles are often learned from those of their caregivers. Parents are taught how their current family interactions may be maintaining high anxiety levels in children. Additionally, parents learn behavioral techniques that they can use to encourage their children to cope with their fears. Finally, parents are taught stress management techniques for coping with their own anxieties. Bernstein and colleagues (2005) found the *FRIENDS* plus Parent-Training program to be as effective as the *FRIENDS* program alone at reducing anxiety of school-aged children with some features of SAD, GAD, or Social Phobias. Both programs were found to be more effective than a no-treatment control condition.

Cool Kids

Cool Kids is an eight-session, small group CBT counseling program led by a trained mental health care provider (Mifsud & Rapee, 2005). *Cool Kids* has separate child and adolescent manuals, with varying amounts of parental involvement. Topics of early sessions include education about what anxiety is, identifying and restructuring anxious thoughts, and identifying associated emotions and regulating these maladaptive emotions. Later sessions consist of social problem-solving, dealing with bullying, and increasing assertiveness. Additionally, a large component of the *Cool*

Kids program is working with families to develop ranked live exposure hierarchies for children to approach homework. Participants engage in each step up the hierarchies and are rewarded for successful attempts. Children in the program are asked to try at least one step a week as homework and to report back their experiences to the group. *Cool Kids* was evaluated in a low socioeconomic area with 8–11 year-old students. Program participants showed significant improvements in anxiety symptoms immediately after treatment and at a four-month follow up.

Tier III: School-Based Treatment Programs

Sometimes, school-based interventions are warranted for students with clinical levels of anxiety. When students present with diagnosable anxiety disorders, more intensive treatment programs may be necessary. As with prevention programs, the most empirically sound programs for these students seem to involve various forms of CBT. The following are two such evidence-based programs for treating anxiety disorders within school settings.

Skills for Academic and Social Success

Skills for Academic and Social Success (SASS) is a CBT oriented, small group therapy treatment program designed to be implemented with adolescents with social anxiety disorders in schools (Masia et al., 1999). Facilitated by one or two group leaders, SASS consists of twelve group sessions, two individual sessions, two parent meetings, two teacher meetings, and four school social events. Group sessions include such topics as realistic thinking, social skills training, relapse prevention, and closely monitored exposure sessions for social practice opportunities. Individual counseling sessions focus on setting goals for treatment and problem-solving predicted treatment obstacles. The four social events are designed to provide real-life practice of learned skills and to promote generalization of group-practiced skills. Parent and teacher meetings are held to bolster the understanding of signs, symptoms, and difficulties associated with social anxiety. Parents may also learn appropriate strategies and techniques to aid in their children's treatment, and teachers are additionally involved through helping to identify student areas of difficulty and providing feedback throughout intervention. Research findings report that SASS is effective in reducing and/or eliminating symptoms of social anxiety in adolescents as well as enhancing the recognition of social anxiety in adolescents through education of parents and school personnel (Masia, Klein, Storch, & Corda, 2001; Masia-Warner et al., 2005; Masia-Warner et al., 2007; Masia-Warner et al., 2011).

Baltimore Child Anxiety Treatment Study in the Schools

The Baltimore Child Anxiety Treatment Study in the Schools (BCATSS) was developed as an individually-administered treatment program for inner city students with anxiety disorders. BCATSS is a manualized CBT program consisting of twelve sessions led by a school psychologist. A unique feature of the BCATSS program is that the content is given in modules that can be sequenced to tailor to the individual needs of the student. The modular set up is also conducive to receiving treatment in the inconsistency of school schedules (e.g.. holidays, semester change, breaks, etc.) Topics of sessions include psychoeducation about anxiety, relaxation techniques, exposure to anxiety provoking situations, cognitive restructuring, problem-solving, and relapse prevention. In a pilot study, BCATSS was implemented with students with diagnoses of GAD, specific phobia, or social phobia. Following treatment, three of the four participants no longer met the diagnostic criteria for an anxiety disorder (Ginsburg & Drake, 2002).

Implications for Practitioners

Universal prevention techniques may be the best method of intervention due to the costliness of mental health services. Additionally, because of the association between anxiety disorders and other mental health problems (depression, substance abuse, etc.), preventing anxiety disorders may also prevent the development of these often subsequent conditions. While the majority of the empirically-validated, school based interventions for anxiety disorders have been CBT programs offered by specialized therapists (Angelosante et al., 2011), there are also steps teachers can take in preventing and helping students cope with anxiety.

At the universal prevention level (Tier I), teachers can emphasize the importance of effort over ability in student work products. Students with anxiety are often concerned with achieving perfection with regard to their academic assignments. It may be beneficial for teachers to sometimes draw attention to assignments that have required a great deal of effort, even if they are not perfectly accurate. One way teachers may do this is by posting sample assignments on display boards in the classroom (as long as doing so does not create heightened anxiety levels).

For students with social anxiety problems, teachers may use peer-mediated learning techniques in which they deliberately pair students with anxiety with outgoing, friendly students, and require the pairs to complete an activity for which there is a high likelihood of success. This technique combines opportunities for anxious students to practice social skills in a relatively safe environment with modeling of appropriate social behaviors by the socially competent peer.

Teachers may also be able to adapt some of the CBT intervention skills for classroom implementation. For instance, teachers can lead group relaxation techniques, and encourage students to self-monitor their own anxiety behaviors (Huberty, 2009). Similarly, teachers may adapt appropriate gradual exposure strategies such as those suggested in the previously mentioned SASS intervention. For instance, if a student fears answering questions in class, first a teacher could provide the student with an answer to a question prior to class, followed by providing a question, but no answer, and so on until eventually the student is able to practice answering questions more spontaneously (Masia-Warner et al., 2011).

Developing a plan of action with the family of the student can also be beneficial in supporting anxious students. Perhaps a safe place in the school can be identified for the student to go in order to take a time-out to ease anxiety when it escalates. A cue worked out between teacher and student can be used so that the student may quietly leave the classroom and go to the safe spot. Involving parents could also substantially ease anxiety for students, particularly those with separation anxiety or social anxiety. Caregivers could leave a comforting note or trinket in the student's lunch box or locker that can provide reassurance. Short phone calls home for a minute or two during periods of severe anxiety could also be a plausible possibility for comfort.

Support and encouragement of participation in activities by adults, like teachers, principals or other authority figures, can be beneficial as well as gratifying for students with anxiety. Contingencies, rewards, and praise should be given for effort and successes and assistance should be provided when necessary and appropriate. For particular anxieties in which the child is avoiding school and absence is a problem, the child should be helped to return to school as quickly as possible. It may be an option for the school to work out a shorter school day or late arrival at first and gradually move toward regular school days as necessary in order to give the child and family time to work through anxiety issues whether they are from separation, phobia, or socially based issues.

Teachers should work collaboratively with school psychologists or other mental health personnel in identifying appropriate therapeutic techniques and implementing them properly. Additionally, all implemented interventions should be monitored closely for effectiveness and acceptability. Formative evaluation is necessary to determine when interventions need to be adapted and summative evaluation is necessary to determine whether interventions were effective in reducing anxiety symptoms in students. While older children and adolescents may be able to self-report reductions in anxiety, direct observations or parent feedback may be necessary to determine the effectiveness of interventions for young children.

Anxiety disorders are among the most prevalent mental health problems facing children and adolescents today. Because of the accessibility, efficiency, and naturalistic practice opportunities associated with school-based interventions, schools may be the ideal setting for the prevention and treatment of childhood anxiety. While empirical research validating school-based intervention for anxiety disorders is promising, the field is still in its infancy. To date, CBT is the most well-documented treatment for anxiety problems in children, although most studies have been conducted in mental health clinic settings. Future research is needed for further evaluating the effectiveness of school-based formal CBT programs and informal classroom strategies in reducing anxiety symptoms in children.

References

Achenbach, T. M., Howell, C. T., McConaughy, S. H., & Stanger, C. (1995). Six-year predictors of problems in a national sample of children and youth: Cross-informant syndromes. *Journal of the American Academy of Child and Adolescent Psychiatry, 34,* 336–47. doi:10.1097/00004583-199503000-00020

Albano, A., Chorpita, B. F., & Barlow, D. H. (2003). Childhood anxiety disorders. In E. J. Mash, R. A. Barkley (eds), *Child psychopathology (2nd ed.,* pp. 279–329). New York, NY: The Guilford Press.

American Psychiatric Association. (1980). *Diagnostic and statistical manual of mental disorders* (3rd ed., rev.). Washington, DC.

—(2000). *Diagnostic and statistical manual of mental disorders* (4th ed., text rev.). Washington, DC.

Angelosante, A., Colognori, D., Goldstein, C. R., & Warner, C. (2011). School-based interventions for anxiety in youth. In D. McKay, E. A. Storch, D. McKay, & E. A. Storch (eds), *Handbook of child and adolescent anxiety disorders* (pp. 419–34). New York, NY: Springer Science + Business Media.

Anglin, T. M. (2003). Mental health in schools: Programs of the federal government. In M. D. Weist, S. W. Evans, & N. A. Lever (eds), *Handbook of school mental health: Advancing practice and research* (pp. 89–106). New York, NY: Kluwer Academic/Plenum.

Armbruster, P., & Lichtman, J. (1999). Are school based mental health services effective? Evidence from 36 inner city schools. *Community Mental Health Journal, 35,* 493–504. doi:10.1023/A:1018755100381

Barrett, P. M., Dadds, M. R., & Rapee, R. M. (1996). Family treatment of childhood anxiety: A controlled trial. *Journal of Consulting and Clinical Psychology, 64,* 333–42. doi:10.1037/0022-006X.64.2.333

Barrett, P. M., Farrell, L. J., Ollendick, T. H., & Dadds, M. (2006). Long-term outcomes of an Australian universal prevention trial of anxiety and depression symptoms in children and youth: An evaluation of the *FRIENDS* program. *Journal of Clinical Child and Adolescent Psychology, 35,* 403–11. doi:10.1207/s15374424jccp3503_5

Barrett, S., & Heubeck, B. G. (2000). Relationships between school hassles and uplifts and anxiety and conduct problems in grades 3 and 4.

Journal of Applied Developmental Psychology, 21, 537–54. doi:10.1016/ S0193-3973(00)00053-8

Barrett, P., & Turner, C. (2001). Prevention of anxiety symptoms in primary school children: Preliminary results from a universal school-based trial. *British Journal of Clinical Psychology, 40,* 399–410. doi:10.1348/014466501163887

Beesdo, K., Knappe, S., & Pine, D. S. (2009). Anxiety and anxiety disorders in children and adolescents: Developmental issues and implications for DSM-V. *Psychiatric Clinics of North America, 32,* 483–524. doi:10.1016/j. psc.2009.06.002

Bernstein, G. A., Layne, A. E., Egan, E. A., & Tennison, D. M. (2005). School-based interventions for anxious children. *Journal of the American Academy of Child & Adolescent Psychiatry, 44,* 1118–27. doi:10.1097/01. chi.0000177323.40005.a1

Black, B., & Uhde, T. W. (1992). Case study: Elective mutism as a variant of social phobia. *Journal of the American Academy of Child & Adolescent Psychiatry, 31,* 1090–4. doi:10.1097/00004583-199211000-00015

Brock, S. E., & Cowan, K. (2004). Coping after a crisis. *Principal Leadership,* 9–13. Accessed from http:// www. nasponline.org/resources/principals/ PTSD%20NASSP%20January%2004.pdf.

Burns, B. J., Costello, E. J., Angold, A., Tweed, D. L., Stangl, D. K., Farmer, E. M., & Erklani, A. (1995). Children's mental health service use across service sectors. *Health Affairs, 14,* 147–59. doi:10.1377/hlthaff.14.3.147

Cartwright-Hatton, S., McNicol, K., & Doubleday, E. (2006). Anxiety in a neglected population: Prevalence of anxiety disorders in pre-adolescent children. *Clinical Psychology Review, 26,* 817–33. doi:10.1016/j. cpr.2005.12.002

Cole, D. A., Peeke, L. G., Martin, J. M., Truglio, R., & Seroczynski, A. D. (1998). A longitudinal look at the relation between depression and anxiety in children and adolescents. *Journal of Consulting and Clinical Psychology, 66,* 451–60. doi:10.1037/0022-006X.66.3.451

Collins, K. A., Westra, H. A., Dozois, D. A., & Burns, D. D. (2004). Gaps in accessing treatment for anxiety and depression: Challenges for the delivery of care. *Clinical Psychology Review, 24,* 583–616. doi:10.1016/j. cpr.2004.06.001

Costello, E., Mustillo, S., Erkanli, A., Keeler, G., & Angold, A. (2003). Prevalence and development of psychiatric disorders in childhood and adolescence. *Archives of General Psychiatry, 60,* 837–44. doi:10.1001/archpsyc.60.8.837

Dadds, M. R., & Roth, J. H. (2008). Prevention of anxiety disorders: Results of a universal trial with young children. *Journal of Child and Family Studies, 17,* 320–35. doi:10.1007/s10826-007-9144-3

Doll, B. (1996). Prevalence of psychiatric disorders in children and youth: An agenda for advocacy by school psychology. *School Psychology Quarterly, 11,* 20–46. doi:10.1037/h0088919

Essau, C. A., Conradt, J., & Petermann, F. (2000). Frequency, comorbidity, and psychosocial impairment of depressive disorders in adolescents. *Journal of Adolescent Research, 15,* 470–81. doi:10.1177/0743558400154003

Ezpeleta, L., Keeler, G., Erkanli, A., Costello, E., & Angold, A. (2001). Epidemiology of psychiatric disability in childhood and adolescence. *Journal of Child Psychology and Psychiatry, 42,* 901–14. doi:10.1111/1469-7610.00786

Garber, J., Keiley, M. K., & Martin, N. C. (2002). Developmental trajectories of adolescents' depressive symptoms: Predictors of change. *Journal of Consulting and Clinical Psychology, 70,* 79–95. doi:10.1037/0022-006X.70.1.79

Gillham, J. E., Reivich, K. J., Freres, D. R., Lascher, et al., (2006). School-based prevention of depression and anxiety symptoms in early adolescence: A pilot of a parent intervention component. *School Psychology Quarterly, 21,* 323–48. doi:10.1521/scpq.2006.21.3.323

Ginsburg, G. S. (2009). The child anxiety prevention study: Intervention model and primary outcomes. *Journal of Consulting and Clinical Psychology, 77,* 580–7. doi:10.1037/a0014486

Ginsburg, G. S., & Drake, K. L. (2002). School-based treatment for anxious African-American adolescents: A controlled pilot study. *Journal of the American Academy of Child & Adolescent Psychiatry, 41,* 768–775. doi:10.1097/00004583-200207000-00007

Gurley, D., Cohen, P., Pine, D. S., & Brook, J. (1996). Discriminating depression and anxiety in youth: A role for diagnostic criteria. *Journal of Affective Disorders, 39,* 191–200. doi:10.1016/0165-0327(96)00020-1

Hirshfeld, D. R., Keller, M., Panico, S., Arons, B., Barlow, D., & Davidoff, F., et al. (1997). The National Depressive and Manic Depressive Association consensus statement on the undertreatment of depression. *Journal of the American Medical Association, 277,* 333–40. doi:10.1001/jama.1997.03540280071036

Hirshfeld, D. R., Micco, J. A., Simoes, N. A., & Henin, A. (2008). High risk studies and developmental antecedents of anxiety disorders. *American Journal of Medical Genetics, Part C (Seminar in Medical Genetics), 148,* 99–117.

Huberty, T. J. (2009). Interventions for internalizing disorders. In A. Akin-Little, S. G. Little, M. A. Bray, & T. J. Kehle (eds), *Behavioral interventions in schools: Evidence-based positive strategies* (pp. 281–96). Washington, DC: American Psychological Association.

Kendall, P. C. (1994). Treating anxiety disorders in children: Results of a randomized clinical trial. *Journal of Consulting and Clinical Psychology, 62,* 100–10. doi:10.1037/0022-006X.62.1.100

Kendall, P. C., Aschenbrand, S. G., & Hudson, J. L. (2003). Child-focused treatment of anxiety. In A. E. Kazdin, J. R. Weisz, A. E. Kazdin, & J. R. Weisz (eds), *Evidence-based psychotherapies for children and adolescents* (pp. 81–100). New York, NY: The Guilford Press.

Kendall, P. C., Safford, S., Flannery-Schroeder, E., & Webb, A. (2004). Child anxiety treatment: Outcomes in adolescence and impact on substance use and depression at 7.4-year follow-up. *Journal of Consulting and Clinical Psychology, 72,* 276–87. doi:10.1037/0022-006X.72.2.276

Langley, A. K., Bergman, R., McCracken, J., & Piacentini, J. C. (2004). Impairment in childhood anxiety disorders: Preliminary examination of the Child Anxiety Impact Scale-Parent Version. *Journal of Child and Adolescent Psychopharmacology, 14,* 105–14. doi:10.1089/104454604773840544

Lock, S., & Barrett, P. M. (2003). A longitudinal study of developmental differences in universal preventive intervention for child anxiety. *Behavior Change, 20,* 183–99. doi:10.1375/bech.20.4.183.29383

Lowry-Webster, H. M., Barrett, P. M., & Dadds, M. R. (2001). A universal prevention trial of anxiety and depressive symptomatology in childhood: Preliminary data from an Australian study. *Behavior Change, 18,* 36–50. doi:10.1375/bech.18.1.36

Ma, X. (1999). A meta-analysis of the relationship between anxiety toward mathematics and achievement in mathematics. *Journal for Research in Mathematics Education, 30,* 520–40. doi:10.2307/749772

Masia, C., Beidel, D. C., Fisher, P. H., Albano, A. M., Rapee, R. M., & Turner, S. M., et al. (1999). *Skills for academic and social success.* New York: University School of Medicine.

Masia, C. L., Klein, R. G., Storch, E. A., & Corda, B. (2001). School-based behavioral treatment for social anxiety disorder in adolescents: Results of a pilot study. *Journal of the American Academy of Child & Adolescent Psychiatry, 40,* 780–6. doi:10.1097/00004583-200107000-00012

Masia-Warner, C., Fisher, P. H., Ludwig, K. A., Rialon, R., & Ryan, J. L. (2011). Adapting treatment of social anxiety disorder for delivery in schools: A school-based intervention for adolescents. In C. A. Alfano & D. C. Beidel (eds), *Social anxiety in adolescents and young adults: Translating developmental science into practice* (pp. 281–96). Washington, DC: American Psychological Association.

Masia-Warner, C., Fisher, P. H., Shrout, P. E., Rathor, S., & Klein, R. G. (2007). Treating adolescents with social anxiety disorder in school: An attention control trial. *Journal of Child Psychology and Psychiatry, 48,* 676–86. doi:10.1111/j.1469-7610.2007.01737.x

Masia-Warner, C., Klein, R. G., Dent, H. C., Fisher, P. H., Alvir, J., Albano, A., & Guardino, M. (2005). School-based intervention for adolescents with social anxiety disorder: Results of a controlled study. *Journal of Abnormal Child Psychology: An official publication of the International Society for Research in Child and Adolescent Psychopathology, 33,* 707–22.

Mifsud, C., & Rapee, R. M. (2005). Early intervention for childhood anxiety in a school setting: Outcomes for an economically disadvantaged population. *Journal of the American Academy of Child & Adolescent Psychiatry, 44,* 996–1004. doi:10.1097/01.chi.0000173294.13441.87

Paige, L. M. (1996). School refusal/avoidance phobia: A handout for parents. *National Association of School Psychologists.* Accessed from http://www.amphi.com/~psych/refusal.html.

Paige, L. Z. (2007). Obsessive-compulsive disorder. *Principal Leadership,* 12–15. Accessed from www.naspcenter.org/principals.

Rapee, R. M., Kennedy, S., Ingram, M., Edwards, S., & Sweeney, L. (2005). Prevention and early intervention of anxiety disorders in inhibited preschool children. *Journal of Consulting and Clinical Psychology, 73,* 488–97. doi:10.1037/0022-006X.73.3.488

Shaffer, D., Fisher, P., Dulcan, M. K., Davies, M., Piacentini, J., Schwab-Stone, M. E., Lahey, B. B. ... Regier, D. A. (1996). The NIMH Diagnostic Interview Schedule for Children Version 2.3 (DISC-2.3): Description, acceptability, prevalence rates, and performance in the MECA study. *Journal of the*

American Academy of Child & Adolescent Psychiarity, 35, 865–77. doi:10.1097/00004583-199607000-00012

Wood, J. J. (2006). Effect of anxiety reduction on children's school performance and social adjustment. *Developmental Psychology, 42,* 345–9. doi:10.1037/0012-1649.42.2.345

Wood, J. J., Chiu, A. W., Hwang, W., Jacobs, J., & Ifekwunigwe, M. (2008). Adapting cognitive-behavioral therapy for Mexican American students with anxiety disorders: Recommendations for school psychologists. *School Psychology Quarterly, 23,* 515–32. doi:10.1037/1045-3830.23.4.515

Wood, J. J., Piacentini, J. C., Southam-Gerow, M., Chu, B. C., & Sigman, M. (2006). Family cognitive behavioral therapy for child anxiety disorders. *Journal of the American Academy of Child & Adolescent Psychiatry, 45,* 314–21. doi:10.1097/01.chi.0000196425.88341.b0

CHAPTER FOUR

Understanding and Managing Behaviors of Children Diagnosed with Autism Spectrum Disorders (ASD)

Charles M. Albright, Laura M. Crothers, and Jered B. Kolbert
Duquesne University

Abstract

Autistic spectrum disorders are characterized by deficits in social interaction and communication skills, as well as restricted, repetitive, and stereotyped behavior patterns, and include symptoms that affect almost all areas of child development (APA, 2000; Stahmer & Aarons, 2009). Recent studies have suggested that between 1 in 88 of children can be diagnosed with one of the variants of ASD (Baio & Autism and Developmental Disabilities Monitoring Network Surveillance Year 2008 Principal Investigators, 2012), representing an increase in the incidence of the disorder within the last two decades. In this chapter, the authors will discuss the history of the diagnosis and epidemiology of autistic spectrum disorders, as well as their etiology and diagnostic criteria. The full spectrum of autism is described, as well as the symptoms that may be observed in the school setting. Empirically-based intervention strategies appropriate to the school setting are examined with a particular focus on multi-tiered interventions that allow for monitoring of a child's response to these interventions.

Overview

Autistic spectrum disorders (ASD) are a group of lifelong neurodevelopmental disorders that are characterized by deficits in social interaction and communication skills, as well as restricted, repetitive, and stereotyped behavior patterns, and include symptoms that affect almost all areas of child development (APA, 2000; Stahmer & Aarons, 2009). Also known as pervasive developmental disorders (PDD), symptoms associated with ASD widely vary from relatively mild impairments to severe symptoms that profoundly interfere with functioning. In *The Diagnostic and Statistical Manual of Mental Disorders, Fourth Edition, Text Revision* (DSM-IV-TR), published by the American Psychiatry Association, the umbrella term of pervasive developmental disorder includes autistic disorder, Asperger syndrome, and pervasive developmental disorder, not otherwise specified (Mouridsen, Rich, & Isager, 2009).

In this chapter, information is provided to educators regarding the necessary information for identifying and treating symptoms associated with ASD in children at school. The authors will discuss the history of the diagnosis and epidemiology of autistic spectrum disorders, as well as their etiology and diagnostic criteria. The full spectrum of autism is described, as well as the symptoms that may be observed in the school setting. Empirically-based intervention strategies appropriate to the school setting are examined with a particular focus on multi-tiered interventions that allow for monitoring of a child's response to these interventions.

Brief Historical Perspective

The first meaningful identification of individuals with autism occurred almost 70 years ago (1943), in Kanner's writings, "Autistic Disturbances of Affective Contact," in which he introduced the label, "early infantile autism," published in *The Nervous Child*. Prior to that time, symptoms now associated with ASD were described in a legal case in Scotland in 1747 (Frith, 2003; Houston & Frith, 2000) and then in the work, *Observations* on *Madness and Melancholy,* published by Haslam in 1809 (Wolff, 2004). Additionally, in the early 1900s, Swiss psychiatrist Bleuler used the term, "autism" to characterize people who demonstrated profound disturbances in their ability to socially connect with others (Dycher, Wilder, Sudweeks, Obiakor, & Algozzine, 2004). Despite these references in the psychological literature, early accounts of the history of child psychiatry did not include childhood autism (Crutcher, 1943; Harmes, 1960; Lowrey, 1944; Wolff, 2004).

After Kanner's descriptions of "early infantile autism," in the 1960s, Rutter's comparative studies validated the symptoms and features of autism (Rutter, 1968; Rutter & Lockyer, 1967), and in 1981, Wing identified Asperger's syndrome (Wing, 1981; Wolff, 2004). Since that time, many researchers have substantially contributed studies of the epidemiology, etiology, and clinical management of children with autistic features (Wolff, 2004), the findings of which will be explored in this chapter.

DSM-IV-TR vs. DSM-VAs

Previously mentioned, the DSM-IV-TR includes the three disorders of autistic disorder, Asperger syndrome, and pervasive developmental disorder, not otherwise specified.

The term, Asperger syndrome (AS), is often used synonymously with the label, high-functioning autism (HFA). In AS/HFA, there are no developmental delays in the first 36 months of life, and only two of the three domains of autistic behavior are evidenced, including impairment in social interaction, and stereotyped, repetitive patterns of behavior (Matilla et al., 2011). However, impairments in communication are also considered to be a significant feature in individuals with HFA. PDD-NOS is typified by lack of criteria for autism because of either late onset, atypical or sub-threshold symptomatology, or all of these.

In the draft DSM-V criteria, the whole spectrum of PDDs are to be replaced with one disorder, "autism spectrum disorder." In a Finnish study regarding the prevalence rates of ASDs and Autism according to the DSM-IV-TR in a group of over 5,000 8-year-old children, 8.4% in 1,000 met the criteria for ASD, with 65% of these classified as high functioning (e.g. FSIQ $\geq$ 70), 2.5% in 1,000 met the criteria for AS, while 4.1% in 1,000 met the criteria for autism, with 61% of these children also classified as high functioning. In the same group of children, using the DSM-V draft criteria, 46% of the children with ASDs (36% of children with ASDs FSIQ $\geq$ 70; 100% of children with ASDs FSIQ $\leq$ 70), 0% of the children with AS, and 73% of the high-functioning children with autism (100% of the children with autism FSIQ $\leq$ 70) could be identified (Mattila et al., 2011). Mattila and colleagues (2011) found the DSM-V draft criteria to be less sensitive regarding the identification of children with ASD; in particular, those with AS and some high-functioning children with autism.

Moreover, Mattila et al. (2011) suggest modifications to five details of the DSM-V draft criteria (e.g., one example includes changing the requirement of deficits in social communication and interactions in nonverbal communication, peer relationships, and social reciprocity to at least two out of these three being met; Mattila et al., 2011). Supporting this finding, Wing, Gould, and Gillberg (2011) argue that the DSM-V committee has overlooked a number of important issues in their conceptualization of ASD, including the issue of social imagination, diagnosis in infancy and adulthood, and the potential for girls and women with autism to continue to be unrecognized or misdiagnosed using the criteria of ASD in the new manual. These authors consequently recommend that a number of changes be made to increase the reliability and validity of the new criteria in clinical practice and research (Wing et al., 2011).

Epidemiology of ASD

Estimates of the prevalence of ASD vary from 10 to 18.4 per 1000 persons (Baird et al., 2006; Baio et al., 2012) to 1 and 88, considering the full spectrum of ASD behaviors (Baio et al., 2012). Males are more likely to be diagnosed with ASD; in a review of 34 epidemiological surveys, 30 studies reported male to female ratios of children with ASD from 1.27 to 16.0:1, with a mean ratio of 4:1 (Baio et al., 2012; Mouridsen et al., 2009). Less is known about the female presentation of ASD during early childhood than male presentation. Although one study found that boys and girls demonstrated a similar pattern of developmental profiles, autism symptoms, and comorbid behavior problems, subtle differences exist; girls with ASD evidenced greater communication deficits than boys, sleep problems, and anxious or depressed affect than boys, while boys demonstrated more restrictive, repetitive, and stereotyped behavior than girls (Hartley & Sikora, 2009).

The reason that males are more likely to suffer from autism is not well understood. However, in a number of articles, Baron-Cohen (2002), Baron-Cohen, Knickmeyer, and Belmonde (2005), Knickmeyer, Baron-Cohen, Raggat, and Taylor (2005), and Knickmeyer, Baron-Cohen, Raggat, Taylor, and Hackett (2006) have posed a theory combining the "extreme male brain" school of thought with the androgen conceptualization of autism. In this approach, the behaviors of ASD are viewed as an exaggeration of typical male personality traits, with the notion that exposure to high levels of prenatal testosterone may be a risk factor in developing ASD (Mouridsen et al., 2009). Evidence to support this claim was provided in a Danish study, in which in a sample of 513 siblings of 326 children with ASD, there was a higher birth rate of males (58.5%) in comparison to the Danish live-births of males during the same period (51.4%), suggesting a higher level of maternal testosterone in the mothers of children with ASD and their siblings (Mouridsen et al., 2009).

Another theory, proposed by Skuse (2000, 2009) to account for a higher rate of autism in males is based on males having a single X chromosome, which is thought to render males more vulnerable to genetic abnormalities. The X chromosome contains more genes that are expressed in the brain than the other chromosomes (Nguyen & Disteche, 2006). Skuse (2000, 2009) advances the notion that there is an imprinted social cognitive locus on the short arm of the paternally derived X chromosome, responsible for the female superiority in socio-cognitive abilities as well as a greater propensity of males toward developmental disorders, including ASD (Mouridsen, 2009; Skuse, 2000, 2009). However, the majority of linkage or association studies have not found "regions of interest" on the X chromosome, X-linked mutations are only occasionally seen in ASC, and large copy number variation (CNV) scans have yielded no significant findings on the X chromosome (Baron-Cohen et al., 2011). Baron-Cohen and colleagues (2011) hypothesize that these theories, as well as the Y chromosome theory (the male limited expression of genes on the Y chromosome) and the reduced autosomal penetrance theory (dominant de novo mutations on the autosomes, which have reduced penetrance in females), are likely not mutually exclusive and may collectively explain the male prevalence of ASD.

Autism is believed to occur equitably across demographic groups. Indeed, the Autism Society of America notes, "Autism ... knows no racial, ethnic, or social boundaries. Family income, lifestyle, and educational levels do not affect the chance of autism's occurrence" (2000, p. 3). In 2001, Fombonne, Simmons, Ford, Meltzer, and Goodman conducted an epidemiological study, finding no significant differences for ethnicity in the prevalence rates of autism in the United Kingdom. However, researchers have also argued that much of the published research on the diagnosis of ASD has been conducted with populations that are primarily Anglo and has failed to identify students with autism according to culture (Dycher et al., 2004). Consequently, additional research is likely needed to adequately consider multicultural issues in the diagnosis and treatment of ASD.

Necessity of Early Intervention

Although early intervention has been suggested as producing the best long-term outcomes for children with a variety of mental health and behavioral disorders, such service provision to children with ASD has proven to be particularly important. There is an ever-increasing evidence base for the beneficial effects of comprehensive interventions for children with ASD. Specifically, Early Intensive Behavioral Intervention (EIBI) has been found to be an effective intervention in comparison to either no intervention controls or eclectic/autism-specific special education interventions (Eikeseth, 2009; Eldevik, Hastings, Hughes, Jahr, Eikeseth, & Cross, 2009; Rogers & Vismara, 2008). A meta-analysis conducted by Eldevik et al. in 2009 investigated change in full scale intelligence and adaptive behavior in response to EIBI, and found a large effect size in full scale intelligence and a moderate effect size in adaptive behavior. These authors conclude that EIBI should be the intervention of choice for children with autism.

EIBI programs, of which the Lovaas treatment approach is an example, include the following components: 1) individualized, comprehensive intervention that includes all skill domains; 2) numerous behavioral analytic approaches used to build new repertoires as well as reduce interfering behavior; 3) at least one individual with advanced training in ABA and experience with young children with autism directs the intervention; 4) normal developmental sequences guide the selection of short-term objectives and intervention goals; 5) parents serve as active co-therapists for their child; 6) intervention begins one-to-one, with gradual transitions to small- or large-group formats when possible; 7) intervention usually begins in the home and is transferred to other environments, with gradual, systematic transitions to preschool, kindergarten, and elementary school classrooms when children have developed the skills to learn in those environments; 8) programming is intensive, spans the year, and includes 20 to 30 hours of structured sessions each week in addition to informal instruction and practice throughout most of the other waking hours of the child; 9) typically is 2 or more years in duration; and 10) begins in the preschool years, at ages 3 or 4 (Eldevik et al., 2009; Green, Brennan, & Fein, 2002, p. 70).

Moreover, the increase in identification in ASD in addition to treatment investigations documenting that substantial gains are more likely when effective interventions are provided at a very early age has led to the promotion of early intervention in ASD (Lovaas, 1987; McGee, Daly, & Jacobs, 1994; Stahmer & Aarons, 2009; Strain & Cordisco, 1994). Research conducted by Stahmer and Aarons (2009) has found that early intervention providers reported significantly more favorable attitudes in adopting evidence based practices (EBP) in working with children with ASD than did mental health providers. Furthermore, the early intervention providers perceived less of a disparity between their current practices and EBPs than did the mental health providers, suggesting that the implementation of new interventions complement the values of the innovation-users in those providing early intervention services.

Etiology

Genetic Factors

A single etiology for Autism Spectrum Disorders has proven to be elusive. It is likely that the pervasive nature of the disorder makes understanding a single cause to be unrealistic at this time. What is known is that there is a clear genetic susceptibility that influences the development of an ASD. This is evidenced by the prevalence of ASD in siblings of children with an ASD that is 15 to 30 times the rate of the general population (Szatmari, 1999). Further evidence for this genetic link is that when one monozygotic twin has an ASD, there is as much as a 91 percent chance that the other also will have the disorder (Losh, Trembath, & Piven, 2008). ASD in distant family members (i.e. cousins) is considerably less likely than those of immediate siblings (Szatmari et al., 1995). The genetic influence on ASD is also evidenced by its association with a number of genetic disorders, including: Fragile X syndrome, Rett's syndrome, Tuberous Sclerosis Complex, Down's syndrome, Angelman's disorder, CHARGE, and Phenylketonuria (Moss & Howlin, 2009). Although there are subtle differences between ASD and these disorders, the similarities in presentation suggest that the causes of ASD share some similarities to these disorders.

The heritability of ASD suggests that there is a genetic component to the expression of the disorder. What is unclear, however, is what the exact genetic link is. There have been many studies that have tried to identify genes that cause ASD (Grafodatskaya, Chung, Szatmari, & Weksberg, 2010). While many genes have been implicated, no single gene has been found to cause ASD. It is most likely that the genetic impact on the disorder results from a number of genes, each of which play an independent role in causing the spectrum of disorders (Klinger, Dawson, & Renner, 2003).

The convoluted and incomplete explanation of the causes of ASD in the genetic research has led researchers to discuss epigenetic explanations for the development of ASD disorders. Epigenetic factors are environmental variables that can impact the way that genes are expressed in a particular genome. These factors affect the genome by suppressing gene expression without altering the genetic sequence (Crews, 2011). Prenatal exposure to the drug Valproate is one example of an environmental exposure that can increase the likelihood of an ASD. Some studies also suggest that there are a number of early gestational and neonatal factors that can potentially influence the development of ASD (Grafodatskaya et al., 2010). While these findings do not represent a causal source of ASD, they do add to a growing body of literature suggesting that ASD is a complex disorder with both genetic and environmental causes. There has been open speculation in the popular media that the Measles, Mumps, and Rubella combination

(MMR) vaccination causes autism, and the increase in the diagnosis of ASD is related to the increase in children being immunized. This has resulted in an understandable concern expressed by many parents. Currently, however, there is no evidence in the literature to support an association between the MMR vaccination and ASD (Klinger et al., 2003).

While there is a clear genetic influence in the causes of ASD, finding the etiology of the disorder is difficult. In an attempt to capture a fuller understanding of the heritability of ASD, researchers are beginning to consider a broader autism phenotype (Klinger et al., 2003). The term, phenotype, refers to how genes are expressed as observable traits. The way the term is used regarding the broader autism phenotype considers the inheritance of traits that are associated with ASD. For example, family members of children with ASD who do not have the disorder occasionally demonstrate some social perception difficulties (Bauminger & Yirmiya, 2001). Such observations have led some researchers to move from considering a singular autism diagnosis to instead examining individual symptoms as a spectrum of behavioral phenotypes in the general population. Chen and Yoon (2011) found that individuals in the general population who scored lower on a scale of autistic symptoms also showed a greater tendency to look at actors on a video whose gaze was directed toward the participant. In contrast, participants who scored higher in autistic symptoms did not gaze at individuals who were gazing at them. This helps to suggest that features of ASD are seen in the general population at varying levels; when deficits are seen in a number of skill areas, an individual will likely meet the diagnostic criteria for ASD.

Diagnostic Criteria

Autism spectrum disorders are, according to the Diagnostic and Statistics Manual 4th Edition-Text Revision (DSM-IV-TR), included in a broader categorization of disorders known as pervasive developmental disorders (APA, 2000). These disorders include the three types of ASD: autistic disorder, Asperger's Syndrome, and pervasive developmental disorder-not otherwise specified, as well as Rett's syndromes and childhood disintegrative disorder. Assessment of autistic symptomatology is obtained through an interview with a child's parents, teachers, and the child, as well as direct observation of the child's behavior. The DSM-IV-TR identifies three core areas that define ASD: deficits in social interaction, deficits in communication, and restricted and repetitive movement. These deficits vary slightly between the individual disorders, but in each disorder, impediments will be seen in all three areas.

Social Interaction Deficit

Deficits in social interaction are considered by some to be the core deficit of ASD (Landa, Holman, O'Neill, & Stuart, 2011). Social impairment in ASD varies widely across individuals; however, in order to meet the DSM-IV-TR criteria for an autistic disorder, an individual must demonstrate two of the four areas of deficit. The first area of deficit is impairment in the use of multiple nonverbal behaviors, such as eye-to-eye gaze, facial expression, body postures, and gestures to regulate social interaction (APA, 2000). Thus, children with ASD will not only use fewer nonverbal behaviors to communicate with others, but they will also have difficulty accurately interpreting the nonverbal behaviors of others. The second area of impairment is the failure to develop peer relationships at an appropriate developmental level. Children with ASD will struggle to initiate and maintain close interpersonal relationship with same-age peers. It is not uncommon for a child with ASD to be more comfortable interacting with adults or much younger children than same-age children. The third area of impairment is a lack of spontaneous seeking to share enjoyment, interests, or achievements with other people, and the last area of deficit is a lack of social or emotional reciprocity. Children with ASD will be less likely than typically developing children to share objects, as well as thoughts and feelings with other people. They will also have a tendency to not be interested in the back and forth exchange of typical human interaction. It has been hypothesized that this inability to have reciprocal interactions is a symptom of deficits in theory of mind, essentially difficulty predicting the thoughts and motivations of others (Baron-Cohen, Leslie, & Frith, 1985). Moreover, these social interaction deficits are stable and present in some combination in every child with an ASD (APA, 2000).

Communication Deficit

The second core area of deficit outlined in the DSM-IV-TR for the diagnosis of autistic disorder is in the area of communication. In order for the diagnosis of autism to be appropriate, impairment must be found in at least one of four areas. The first area is the delay or lack of spoken language, without an attempt to compensate with another form of communication. The second area of impairment requires that children with autism having adequate language skills but have a marked impairment in the ability to initiate or sustain a conversation with others. The third criterion is stereotyped and repetitive use of language or using language in idiosyncratic ways. Some children with autism may use the same stereotyped phrases over and over again without regard to the appropriateness of the situation. Children may also simply echo the phrases of others, as opposed to engaging in spontaneous conversation (APA, 2000).

The last criterion in the communication domain is that children with autism will show a lack of spontaneous play skills. Children with autism will not engage in appropriate play with toys at all, and when they do, they will enact stereotyped play activities, as opposed to engaging in spontaneous play. Overall, children with autism have an inability to effectively relate their thoughts and feelings to other individuals, whether it is verbally, or through play activities (APA, 2000).

Restricted Repetitive and Stereotyped Behavior

The third area of deficit that should be considered in the diagnosis of autistic disorder is restricted and repetitive and stereotyped behavior. The DSM-IV-TR requires that a child with autism demonstrate at least one of these behaviors: an encompassing preoccupation with one or more stereotyped and restricted patterns of interest that is abnormal in frequency or focus, apparently inflexible adherence to specific, nonfunctional routines or rituals, stereotyped and repetitive motor mannerisms, or persistent preoccupation with parts of objects. While many children demonstrate some repetitive behaviors and preoccupations as part of normal development, children with autism engage in these behaviors in excess, both in the insistence on adherence to these behaviors, as well as the level of reaction when interests or routines are interrupted. While a typically developing child would be able to stop talking about an interest in trains and instead talk about his day at school, a child with autism may insist on continuing to speak about trains and become actively upset when conversation moves away from this topic (APA, 2000).

Other Criteria

In addition to impairment in these areas of functioning, a child with autism must also demonstrate these impairments before the age of three years old. The impairments must also not be able to be better understood by a diagnosis of Rett's disorder or childhood disintegrative disorder (APA, 2000).

Asperger's Disorder and PDD-NOS

Two variations of autism spectrum disorders are presented in the DSM-IV-TR, completing the continuum of disorders: Asperger's disorder and pervasive developmental disorder-not otherwise specified. Both of these disorders are based on the criteria for autistic disorder. Asperger's disorder is characterized by the same impairments in social awareness as well as restricted and repetitive behaviors. Children with Asperger's disorder, however, do not demonstrate any delays in language skills or in cognitive development. PDD-NOS is characterized as a diagnostic category for children who demonstrate significant social and communicative deficits as well as restricted and repetitive behaviors, but do not meet the criteria for autistic disorder. Though these diagnostic categories are still currently in use, they are becoming antiquated as autistic symptoms are increasingly considered as a continuum of symptoms as opposed to discrete diagnostic categories (APA, 2000).

Comorbid Disorders

There are a number of disorders that commonly co-occur with autism spectrum disorders. When understanding the individual needs of a child with ASD, it is important to identify what other cognitive, social-emotional, and behavioral difficulties may be co-occurring with ASD symptoms. The first disorder that is frequently comorbid with ASD is intellectual disability (ID). While children with ASD demonstrate wide variability in intellectual functioning, a significant number of children will have IQ scores in the impaired range. Approximately 40 percent of children will demonstrate a comorbid intellectual disability that extends past the social impairment of ASD symptoms (Baird et al., 2001). Comorbid intellectual disability will typically lead to children having more difficulty learning in the classroom and requiring more individualized and intensive teaching strategies.

Another disorder that is highly correlated with ASD is Attention-Deficit/Hyperactivity Disorder (AD/HD). The current DSM-IV-TR does not allow for AD/HD to be diagnosed with ASD; however, there is significant overlap in the presentations between the two disorders (Reiersen, 2011). It is likely that teachers who work with a child with ASD will also notice symptoms of inattention and possibly hyperactivity.

In addition to intellectual disabilities, there are a number of psycho-pathologies that can commonly occur with ASD. One such psychopathology is mood disorders. Ghaziuddin, Tsai, and Ghaziuddin (1992) found that depression is comorbid with ASD in 2 percent of those that they studied. This number increases to 30 percent of children with Asperger's disorder (Ghaziuddin, Weidmer-Mikhail, & Ghaziuddin, 1998). The likelihood of mood problems increases for higher functioning children, as these children have more insight into their difficulties and a greater understanding of their differences from other children (Klinger et al., 2003).

Another psychopathology that is comorbid with ASD is anxiety disorders, which are seen in approximately 7 to 84% of children with ASD (Lainhart, 1999). Generalized anxiety disorder, agoraphobia, separation anxiety, and simple phobia are most commonly associated with ASD (Klinger et al., 2003). Obsessive-compulsive disorder (OCD) is another anxiety disorder that is commonly associated with ASD; however, it is debated how often OC symptoms are truly comorbid and how often they can be categorized under the core symptoms of ASD (Matson & Nebel-Schwalm, 2007).

While there are a number of disorders that co-occur with autism spectrum disorders, there are also a number of behavioral difficulties that a teacher working with a child with an ASD will encounter. Children with ASD often present with oppositional, aggressive, and self-injurious behavior in addition to the inattentive and hyperactive behavior that was previously mentioned. These behavioral difficulties can stem from a child's rigidities in his or her thought patterns and/or an inability to express one's own needs at a given time. In the case of self-injurious behavior, difficulties can also serve a self-stimulatory function. Regardless of the form of behavior, strategies will need to be implemented in order to maximize the ability of a child with ASD to learn in the classroom.

Symptomatology in a School Setting

A considerable range in symptom severity for children with ASD may be evident for each of the three primary categories of deficits, communication impairment, social interaction impairment, and repetitive and restrictive behaviors, which are referred to as the 'triad of impairments' (Wing, 2002).

There is considerable variation in the communication abilities between children with ASD, and the individual child with ASD may also exhibit widely discrepant capabilities. Some children diagnosed with ASD may have extremely advanced vocabularies and oral expression abilities, but may show inconsistencies in their communication abilities, including discrepancies between receptive and expressive language capabilities. Receptive language is the comprehension of language, and involves attending to speech, comprehending the message, and the speed of processing the message, with many ASD students struggling with comprehending simple directions. Expressive language refers to the production of speech and communicating a message. Higher functioning ASD students tend to have higher receptive than expressive language abilities (APA, 2000). Children with ASD may have an advanced vocabulary, but may not able to use it to communicate their needs, or they may not understand the meaning of the words they frequently use.

Approximately one-half of autistic children fail to develop any form of functional language (Tager-Flusberg, 2000) and some may exhibit impairments in all aspects of language, including the lexical, semantic, syntactic, phonological, and pragmatic components (Tager-Flusberg, 1999). Obviously, many of the language impairments exhibited by children with

ASD have direct relevance to academic learning and the school context. Moreover, all autistic children demonstrate Pragmatic Language Disorders (PLD; Young, Diehl, Morris, Hyman, & Bennetto, 2005).

Specific language deficits that are associated with PLD include a poor command of indirect speech acts such as questions (Aarons & Gittens, 1999), difficulties with presuppositions (Young et al., 2005), person pronouns reversal (using "I" instead of "you"), and the inaccurate use of prepositions (as in "in", "under"; Aarons & Gittens, 1999). Children with autism are at increased risk for phonological impairments, as their speech often lacks intonation and tends towards monotony (Baron-Cohen, 1995). Grammatical difficulties of children with autism may include the inappropriate use of verbs and adjectives (Van Lancker, Cornelius, & Needleman, 1991), and the morphological marking of finite verbs, such as failure to use past tense morpheme "ed" or "s" indicating the third person of the singular (Tager-Flusberg, 2004).

Children with ASD often exhibit social skills deficits, which interferes with their ability to develop and maintain relationships. Such social skills deficits may become even more apparent in school rather than the home setting, as autistic children interact with children of the same age. Children with ASD may have difficulty engaging in reciprocal social exchanges, fail to initiate conversations that may be of interest to other children, or engage in long monologues that are of interest to them but not their peers (Ashcroft, Argiro, & Keohane, 2010). They may engage with peers in a developmentally inappropriate manner, selecting games, toys, and activities that are not attractive to children their age. Children with ASD often find large group and cooperative activities such as circle time or play groups to be overwhelming, and they typically prefer to spend time alone. Young children with ASD may lack reciprocal and imaginative play, and may fail to understand the rules for such games as tag. They do not generally engage in make-believe or pretend play. For example, in a toy kitchen, they may organize the food rather than pretending to cook or eat the food. Children with ASD may avoid sports and find physically challenging activities difficult because their motor skills may be mildly impaired.

The restricted repetitive and stereotyped patterns of behavior demonstrated by autistic children may be evident in their response to changes in routine and in learning. Some children with ASD become extremely anxious in response to changes in routines (Ashcroft et al., 2010). Such children often notice minor variations in schedules, settings, people, and instructional materials. Even changes from less to more preferred activities may be distressing. The child with ASD may exhibit ritualistic behaviors associated with routines that are similar to compulsive behaviors seen in OCD. An example of a ritualistic behavior related to routines includes having specific ways of entering a school building, regardless of the distance from the intended location, or touching a series of objects, including one's hair, chair, and shirt before eating. Other examples of ritualistic behaviors may include excessively organizing toys by color and other geometric shapes, or smelling the clothes of strangers. Children diagnosed with ASD may overly focus on irrelevant details to a degree that may interfere with comprehension and are not relevant to understanding the concept or situation. Furthermore, children with ASD may have difficulty translating learning to new situations. These children may overgeneralize, which involves performing the behavior when it is not appropriate. For example, upon being taught to raise their hands to ask a question, children with ASD may continue to raise their hands to speak any time, even outside of school. Or, they may undergeneralize, failing to use the behavior or concept when it would be appropriate. There are several theories regarding the function of restricted repetitive and stereotyped behavior patterns of autistic children, but a prevailing theory is that these behaviors help children to manage their difficulties in processing sensory information (Ayers, 1979).

Autistic children are at a greater risk for other academically at-risk behaviors. Minshew, Goldstein, Taylor, and Siegel (1994) found that compared to controls, individuals with autism exhibited lower scores on reading comprehension tasks but not on mechanical reading, spelling, and computational tasks. Once again, children with ASD may exhibit unevenness in their academic profiles. Some children with ASD may demonstrate characteristics associated with a nonverbal learning disability (Rourke, 1995), such as difficulties with tactile perception, psychomotor coordination, mathematical reasoning, visual-spatial organization, and nonverbal problem solving. However, they tend to have advanced rote verbal skills and strong verbal memory and auditory linguistic capabilities.

Multimodal Interventions

When a teacher works with a child with an ASD in the school setting, there are a number of considerations that need to be made. While the three tiered, Response to Intervention (RtI) model of assessment does not apply to the diagnosing of ASD, it can be useful to consider it as a broad framework for levels of intervention that can be used with children with ASD. In this section, the authors will begin by outlining a few general considerations that will be useful for teachers preparing to work with a child with ASD. The authors will then outline types of intervention that will likely be necessary at the primary, secondary, and tertiary levels of intervention for children with ASD. These intervention overviews will take into account all three areas of core deficit in ASD, as well as peripheral considerations that may be applicable at each level.

General Intervention Considerations

When working with a child with an ASD, there are a few strategies that should be considered across levels of functioning. These strategies include behavior modification techniques that will help individuals, first to understand, and then to modify the behaviors of children with ASD. Four strategies that will be useful in working with any child on the autism spectrum are: functional behavior assessment, task analysis, differential reinforcement, and antecedent-based interventions.

Functional behavior assessment

As stated previously, children with ASD present with wide variations of behavior within their core areas of deficit. For this reason, functional behavior assessment (FBA) is necessary to understand these idiosyncratic behavior presentations. FBA is a method of assessing the variables that influence behavior problems, and then to use these identified variables to develop interventions (Carr & Durand, 1985). While the FBA may not be conducted directly by the teacher, one should be completed either by a school psychologist, or a special education support staff, to help clarify and understand the functions of the child's behavior. Common functions that maintain behaviors are receiving attention, obtaining a need, and avoiding an aversive stimulus.

The process of functional assessment helps to identify antecedents and consequences that maintain a child's behavioral repertoire (Rogers & Vismara, 2008). Antecedents are stimuli that occur before a behavior occurs; for example, a teacher telling a student that he or she needs to finish his or her classwork before going to recess. Consequences of behavior are the immediate results of a child's behavior; for example, a teacher providing a child with kind words after successfully completing an assignment. If a teacher can understand the functional relationship that antecedents and consequences have with behaviors, then more targeted intervention techniques can be developed to successfully affect the child's behavioral repertoires. While FBA is often utilized to understand how to intervene when children are demonstrating negative behaviors, assessments can also be used to learn how to increase positive behaviors, as well as learn about the child's preferences (Harris & Glasberg, 2007). These preference analyses can be used to find methods of reinforcement that will increase preferred behaviors. Overall, FBA is the first step in systematically understanding a child with ASD's behavioral needs in the classroom.

Task analysis

Task analysis, like FBA, is an effective process to help understand the individual behavioral needs of a child with an ASD. Task analysis is the process of systematically segmenting a skill that a child with ASD cannot perform into each of its component parts. For example, a seemingly singular task of a child getting ready for a math test actually involves a number of steps (Matson, Taras, Seven, Love, & Fridley, 1990). Analyzing the components of a skill can help a teacher understand where the breakdown in the development of a skill is occurring (Browder, Trela, & Jimenez, 2007). The child may have to put his books away in his desk, remove a pencil from his desk, stand up from his chair and retrieve his calculator from his cubby, walk to the pencil sharpener and sharpen his pencil and then return to his seat. When these individual tasks are monitored, it may be identified that a child perseverates on sharpening his pencil, focusing on the stimulation of the vibration of the pencil sharpener while sharpening his pencil. So while ostensibly the child cannot remain on task when getting ready for his test, task analysis shows that the child's self stimulatory behavior is slowing the child as he prepares for a new task. Utilizing task analysis when working with children with ASD can help to create effective, individualized interventions that are parsimonious and therefore take up less of the teacher's instruction time. Task analysis can be implemented for any skill that needs to be developed, whether it is in the academic, social, or behavioral domains of a child's functioning.

Differential reinforcement

As behaviors that need to be increased or decreased are identified using FBA and task analysis, systems of behavior change will need to be implemented. A basic, yet powerful behavior modification system is differential reinforcement. Simply put, differential reinforcement is the process of manipulating the consequences of behavior in order to affect the occurrence of a behavior. The goal of differential reinforcement is to reinforce behaviors that a teacher wants a child to increase, while ignoring, or extinguishing, behaviors in which the teacher does not want the child to engage. Reinforcement is considered to be anything that increases the likelihood that a behavior will occur. Behaviors that are not reinforced will reduce and eventually cease to occur, via a process called extinction. FBA and task analysis are critical in the implementation of a differential reinforcement schedule, as without identified functions of behavior, mechanisms of reinforcement and extinction cannot be identified and affected. While this intervention strategy seems simple, it has been identified as effective in intervention programs that address issues as varied as reducing destructive behavior and increasing self-monitoring skills (Adelinis, Piazza, & Han-Leong, 2001; Newman, Tuntigian, Ryan, & Reinecke, 1997).

When executing differential reinforcement techniques, it is important to always consider the function of the behavior being modified. Some children with ASD may use undesirable behaviors to obtain needs because they lack the requisite skills to meet these needs appropriately. In these cases, it is not considered to be best practice (or fair to the child) to extinguish this problem behavior without teaching a replacement behavior to provide a means to obtain the need that the child possesses.

Antecedent interventions

Another strategy that has been found to be successful in working with children with ASD is antecedent interventions. Antecedent interventions, much like differential reinforcement, use information taken from FBA and task analysis to create interventions to help increase or decrease target behaviors. Antecedents, however, affect behavior by manipulating the antecedents to behavior as opposed to the consequences. An example that could necessitate an antecedent intervention is a child who has sensitivities to loud noises and crowded areas, and tantrums when the bell rings at the end of the day and he has to walk to his locker in the crowded school hallway. An antecedent intervention in this situation would be to allow the child to gather his books prior to the bell ringing, therefore avoiding the antecedent to the behavior problem. Another simple and effective antecedent intervention would be moving a child who has difficulty focusing on class instruction to the front of the classroom. Antecedent interventions are proactive and seek to allow the child to function in an environment that is optimal for his or her learning needs. When working with children with ASD, antecedent interventions can be especially helpful in decreasing repetitive behaviors in children with ASD (Sigafoos, Green, Payne, O'Reilly, & Lancioni, 2009).

Tiers of Intervention

Now that a few general principles of assessment and intervention of children with ASD have been discussed, techniques can be investigated at three levels of intervention. We will discuss working with higher functioning children with ASD at a first tier level. We will then review considerations for working with children at the Tier II level, who will need a greater frequency and/or magnitude of strategies to be successful in class. Finally, third tier levels of intervention will be discussed for the needs of children who require intensive intervention. It is important to note that while certain interventions have been classified at different levels in the three tier model, this is not to suggest that such interventions will only be effective at that level. Many interventions can be applied to a variety of children at different points of the ASD spectrum and still be considered effective. Also, all of the interventions that are mentioned are considered to be evidence-based practices by the National Professional Development Center on Autism Spectrum Disorders (2011).

Tier I

While autism spectrum disorders are pervasive in nature, it will not be necessary for every child to require intensive intervention in the classroom. Children with high functioning autism (e.g. Asperger's disorder) will likely have good technical language skills and adequate-to-strong academic skills. A child with ASD at a Tier I level will be well suited for a general education classroom with some considerations. It will not be necessary to focus more on the child's disability than is warranted by his or her skill sets. That being said, there will be some areas in which a high functioning ASD child will need help from the school support system to optimize his or her performance in school. These areas will be especially evident when the child's restricted, concrete thinking and resistance to changes in routine can interfere with the dynamic environment of a classroom.

The main need for children with ASD at the Tier I level will be for social support. Although the child will likely be prepared for the class academically, there are many subtle social interactions from day-to-day that could prove overwhelming for a child with ASD. In such instances, the teacher can help the child understand the social environment with which the child will interact. The teacher can do this by using the information he or she knows about the child to try to predict the situations in which the child may have difficulty interacting with others. In these situations, the teacher can explain the situation to the student and what he or she should expect. For example, if the child is required to participate in a group project, it will be helpful for the student to understand what is involved in doing a group project; that he or she will need to ask other students to be a part of the group, that they will have to pick a time to meet together and work on the project, that they will have to agree on how to segment the work in the project, and then schedule a time to get together to finish the project.

Although this step-by-step explanation may seem tedious and obvious for most children, it will be necessary to help the child with ASD to understand how to be successful in his or her environment. In some situations, it will also be useful to model social behaviors for a child with ASD. For example if a child is going to have to ask students to be in a work group with him or her, the teacher may first demonstrate for the child how to approach another student and ask him or her to be in a group. Providing video models for appropriate social behaviors has also been found to improve the child's social interaction skills (Nikopoulos & Keenan, 2004).

In the area of communication, children with ASD at the Tier I level will likely need little or no intervention as far as the technical aspects of language; however, the tendency for problems with pragmatic language, or the social aspects of language do exist (Volen & Phillips, 2010). Children with ASD will have problems understanding nuance in language and thus often misunderstand their peers and teachers. An example of this is children with ASD often misunderstanding idioms, such as, "you are on fire." Children with ASD may believe that the speaker is literally referring to someone catching on fire. Teachers will need to help facilitate understanding for children by interacting with the child using clear, concrete instruction. It will also be useful to let the child know that the teacher can help him or her to understand what other students are trying to say. Other than this, the child at the Tier I level of ASD should be capable of communicating at an adequate level for a general classroom setting.

In the area of behavior, children at the Tier I level will demonstrate only mild behavioral difficulties. Common issues at a Tier I level would be a child speaking too loudly, or standing too close to others as well as some repetitive movements like hand flapping and other socially inappropriate behaviors. For behaviors at this level of intensity, teaching self management skills have been found to be successful (Koegel & Koegel, 1990). Teaching these skills involve helping the child to identify appropriate and inappropriate behaviors in a given situation. The teacher can also work with the child to develop his or her own reinforcement for behaving appropriately. An example of a self monitoring intervention would be teaching a child with ASD who tends to hand flap to identify that a classroom is not an appropriate time for hand flapping and to subsequently have the child monitor how many times per class period he hand flaps, reinforcing himself on every day that he does not engage in the behavior. This allows the child to practice appropriate behavior without needing external support to do it.

At a Tier I level of intervention a child will be reasonably capable to participate in a general education classroom. If the child's individual needs can be considered and accounted for, it is likely that he or she will be successful in his or her academic pursuits. The enriched social environment of a general education setting can improve the social skills of children with ASD, allowing them to become more prepared for future social exchanges encountered in life.

Tier II

Children with ASD who require a second tier level of intervention will need more support than a general education classroom can provide. Children with social difficulties at the Tier II level will require more attention from the teacher. The child will likely have difficulty remaining engaged in classroom instruction and participating in class. Children with more significant skill deficits will also have notable difficulties interacting with other students. Moreover, these skill weaknesses will require more of the teacher's time to keep the child engaged and actively participating in class.

One tool that a teacher can use to facilitate both is prompting (Bryan & Gast, 2000; Taylor & Harris, 1995). Prompts are subtle instructions that can be used to keep a child on task as well as cue him or her to use a skill that he or she may not use spontaneously. For a child with an ASD, a prompt also helps him or her to organize and make sense of situations in which they do not know how to act appropriately. Prompts can be given verbally (e.g. What do we need to do now? It is time to get your books out and place them on your desk) or nonverbally (tapping a child's worksheet as a nonverbal prompt to continue working). Prompts can also be used to help elicit a child's social skills (e.g. What do you say? Maybe your friend would like to try your toy). Children with ASD will require many of these prompts, as they tend to have difficulty taking information that has been learned in one setting and applying it to other settings (Klinger & Dawson, 2001). When using prompts, a teacher should always start with one that is least intrusive (what do you need now?) and only moving to more intensive (physically prompting the child to pick up his or her book) when subsequent prompts are not successful.

Children with ASD who have social deficits that require services in the second tier of intervention will also need to have systematic instruction in social interaction skills. This will require that children at this level take part in a social skills group apart from the classroom. Social skills groups can be an effective strategy to teach and model new skills, as well as to allow children to practice these skills under supervision (Licciardello, Harchik, & Luiselli, 2008) In such groups, children will learn the routines of social interaction as well as how to adjust to new social situations. It is likely that these children will need this level of support throughout most of their academic career.

Another means to facilitate improved social skills in children with ASD is through peer-mediated instruction. In peer mediated instruction, a teacher instructs typically developing students in working through instruction materials with a child with ASD (Laushey & Heflin, 2000). This approach allows for opportunities for the child with ASD to have social interactions in the classroom, in a controlled, yet natural setting.

Children with communication deficits that require services in the second tier of intervention will require more intensive communication intervention. While these children will have some functional language skills, their communication deficits will significantly impact their ability to function in the classroom. Having communication difficulties does not necessarily mean that the child will be incapable of completing work in the classroom, but his or her communication skills will provide a barrier to effectively interacting in the classroom environment. One strategy for improving communication skills in children with this level of impairment is by using functional communication training (FCT; Casey & Merical, 2006). FCT is a process by which a problem behavior can be analyzed, through FBA, to understand what the child is communicating with the behavior and then teach a more appropriate verbal response to achieve the same goal. For example, a child who is prone to tantrum when he or she wants to go to the reading station and read a favorite book, could instead be taught to ask, "can I go to the station?" The goal is to use communicative behavior to guide what functional verbal skills the child will learn.

Another effective communicative intervention for children with second tier levels of communication impairment is visual supports. Children with ASD often have more advanced nonverbal abilities than verbal abilities, so using visual stimuli can often be more effective than verbal stimuli (Klinger et al., 2003). These stimuli can range in purpose from giving instructions to setting schedules, among other functions (Massey & Wheeler, 2000). An example of this would be using a visual schedule in the classroom so that children can see what activity is next. The schedule would have pictures of the activities that will occur (for example, a picture of the gym for gym class) in the order that they occur during the day. Instead of telling the student that it is time to go to gym class, the teacher can simply point to the picture of the gym. Visual supports can be especially helpful for children who can have difficulty with transitions from one activity to another and have few communication skills to prepare for the next activity.

Children who demonstrate rigid and repetitive behaviors requiring a Tier II level of intervention will demonstrate behavioral difficulties that will cause significant impediments in the classroom. A number of strategies can be implemented to help reduce these difficulties, including redirection and token economies. Redirection is a strategy that is especially useful in reducing restricted and repetitive behaviors that children with ASD may demonstrate (Duker & Schaapveld, 1996; Hagopian, Bruzek, Bowman, & Jennet, 2007). This intervention involves interrupting a behavior by introducing another stimulus in order to interrupt the problem behavior. This is especially useful in working with repetitive behaviors, as they are not maintained by external contingencies, but internal stimulation. An example of this would be a teacher who taps on a child's desk and says, "quiet hands," when the child is engaging in hand flapping. Another intervention option, token economy, tends to be effective for children whose behavior is mediated by external contingencies (Matson & Boisjoli, 2009). Token economies work by creating a goal of reducing a particular behavior or demonstrating a positive behavior. When the child meets a particular goal, he or she receives a token. These tokens can be saved and eventually redeemed for reinforcement. An example of this would be a child who shouts out during class. The intervention could be that for every class period the child does not shout out, he or she receives a star. When the child receives five stars, then he or she can trade them in for 15 minutes of extra recess time. Both token economies as well as redirection are effective in reducing moderate problem behaviors demonstrated by children with ASD.

Tier III

Children who have impairments at the Tier III level demonstrate significant impairments that will require intensive intervention. It is likely that children with impairments at this level will not benefit from a general education setting and require placement in a special education classroom because of the severity of their symptomatology. Given this level of impairment, a number of intervention techniques will need to be implemented together in order to help improve the child's social and communicative skills, and reduce restricted and repetitive behaviors.

Children with ASD symptoms in the Tier III level will require intensive intervention in order to master basic social skills. Task analysis will have to be conducted on even the simplest social interactions, such as starting a conversation, and reinforcement will be necessary for any social response. With this level of impairment, teaching instruction will need to be individualized and systematic. Discrete trials training is an instructional method that provides one-on-one instruction in a manner that is broken down into step-by-step instructions (Smith, Groen, & Wynn, 2000). This method allows a teacher to give instructions explicitly and provide immediate feedback for responses, both of which are necessary for learning at such basic levels. Discrete trial training is also beneficial in that individual instruction allows the trials to be tailored to the behavioral and cognitive needs of the individual child. Unfortunately, this intense level of instruction involves a lot of a teacher's time and resources as each new skill needs to be practiced and mastered before a new skill can be presented.

Children with communication deficits at a Tier III level will have little to no functional communication skills. For children with this level of impairment, it will be necessary to teach compensatory communication skills. One such resource for developing an alternative communication is the picture exchange communication system (PECS). PECS involves training a child with ASD to communicate with other individuals, not by verbally communicating, but by using pictures to represent objects the child is requesting (Kravits, Kamps, & Kemmerer, 2002). For example, a child who has his choice of objects to play with will respond to the prompt, "What do you want to play with?" by giving the teacher the picture of a truck. These systems, when used effectively, can provide the child with a repertoire of functional communication skills that he or she can use in the classroom.

Children with restricted and repetitive behavior issues at a Tier III level demonstrate extreme levels of restricted and repetitive behaviors. At this level, behavior problems will be intense enough to have a significant impact on children's ability to benefit from instruction of any kind. In the case of self-injurious behavior, there can also be danger for the child. If behaviors are this extreme, an individual behavior intervention plan should be made for the child. This plan will likely combine elements of differential reinforcement, extinction, redirection, and reinforcement, depending on the situation. Whatever the plan, it will be of the utmost importance to ensure that the child is safe and that he or she can benefit from instruction in the classroom.

Progress-Monitoring of Interventions

Progress monitoring of interventions for use with children with ASD is an essential component of successful treatment programs. Because the plasticity of these disorders tends to diminish as children age, it is essential that interventions are focused most intensively after a diagnosis of ASD has been made (Fenske, Zalenski, Krantz, & McClannahan, 1985). There is a marked relationship between age at intervention and treatment outcomes, with younger children (e.g. in one study, a mean age of 42 months) tending to benefit more significantly from high quality treatment than older children (e.g. mean age of 54 months; Harris & Handelman, 2000).

Progress-Monitoring of Social Skills Intervention

Because social skills deficits are a pervasive and enduring feature of ASD, social skills training should be a critical feature of programming for students with these disorders. Moreover, evaluation of social skills and social competence is a key component of social skills training programs. The goal of such assessments is to identify skill deficits that will comprise the target of the intervention, and then to monitor the outcomes of the training. Social skills assessment methods can be delineated into three categories, each measuring different levels of social functioning. Type I measures feature rating scales and interviews designed to assess the social competence of a child or perceptions of his or her social performance. Such measures require the judgments of parents or teachers, and thus are the most socially valid of the three types of assessments discussed. Type II measures include a direct assessment of a child's social skills or social behaviors, and are thus most valuable to progress-monitoring of the success of an intervention. Type II assessments tend to be sensitive to small changes in behavior due to their direct linkage to treatment objectives. Finally, Type III measures refer to role-playing scenarios or asking questions of the child with ASD related to social cognition. Although these approaches have clinical utility, they are among the least valid assessment measures (Bellini & Peters, 2008; Gresham, Sugai, & Horner, 2001).

Progress-Monitoring of Communication Interventions

Outcomes research has identified that language abnormalities contribute to an overall negative prognosis over an individual's lifespan (Lord & Venter, 1992), and that improvements in language may affect the positive developmental trajectory of children with ASD (Szatmari, 2000). However, the three most common ASD screeners in the literature base, the Autism Spectrum Rating Scale (ASRS), the Gilliam Autism Rating Scale—Second Edition (GARS–2), and the Child Autism Rating Scale—Second Edition (CARS–2) were not designed to monitor the success or failure of various communication skills interventions (Naglieri & Chambers, 2009; Livanis & Mouzakitis, 2010).

However, the educator can prioritize intervention efforts depending upon the symptom presentation of the child with ASD, and link categories from these assessment instruments with the interventions designed to target a child's specific skill deficits. For example, while the CARS–2 measures 15 categories, in monitoring the progress of interventions designed to increase communication skills, the categories of relating to people, verbal communication, and nonverbal communication will likely be more helpful in measuring skills changes than, for example, the category of body use (Livanis & Mouzakitis, 2010). Moreover, Livanis and Mouzakitis (2010) suggest that educators identify keystone items on autism screeners that correspond to ASD children's communication deficits and may be used as a measure of progress in response to intervention.

Progress-Monitoring of Restricted and Repetitive Behaviors

A group of behaviors that frequently co-varies with ASD are self-injury, aggression, noncompliance, and stereotype. Unfortunately, such behaviors tend to be physically dangerous, and also may impede learning and access to normal activities. The assessments for such behaviors first include diagnostic instruments that provide a detailed analysis in order to establish targets for interventions and to evaluate treatment outcomes, such as the Behavior Problems Inventory (Rojahn, Matson, Lott, Esbensen, &

Smalls, 2001), the PDD Behavior Inventory (Cohen, 2003), and the Overt Aggression Scale (Hellings et al., 2005; Matson & Nebel-Schwalm, 2007).

Another form of progress-monitoring of restricted and repetitive behaviors is the applied behavior analysis (ABA) approach to assessment. Typical ABA methods include operational definitions, observation intervals, and functional assessment to evaluate challenging behaviors. In using operational definitions, educators note the actual description of the behavior treated as a measure of change. Observational intervals refer to such techniques as videotaping students in short time samples, with educators coding target behaviors. Partial interval recording (PIR; e.g. blocking off 10 minute segments into 10 second intervals, and marking whether the behavior occurred or did not occur) and momentary time sampling (MTR; e.g. 60 1-second intervals randomly sampled from a total of 600 seconds in 10-, 20-, or 30-second blocks) are both used as evaluating outcomes for challenging behaviors (Matson & Nebel-Schwalm, 2007). Finally, functional behavior assessments (FBA), as discussed earlier in the chapter, can be used dynamically to assess behavior change and to make alterations in treatment programs. The idea of FBA is to systematically assess which behaviors are maintaining a challenging behavior in the environment, so such responses can be targeted for change (Matson & Nebel-Schwalm, 2007).

Conclusion

Given the complexity of needs with children with ASD, which may include speech/language, motor, sensory, behavioral, social, and academic problems, and the considerable range in severity of behaviors, it is probably not surprising that teachers tend to report a lack of self-efficacy in meeting the needs of such children (Spears, Tollefson, & Simpson, 2001). Obviously, this is problematic, given the increasing number of children with ASD in public schools (Accardo, Magnusen, & Capute, 2000) and the trend toward their inclusion in mainstream settings (US Department of Education, 2000). Consequently, it seems important that teachers are encouraged to learn more about ASD. In illustration of this point, Lecavalier, Leone, and Wiltz (2006) found that there was a negative relationship between teachers' report of familiarity with ASD and stress in regards to teaching children with ASD.

Furthermore, teachers are encouraged to utilize the frameworks and resources which have been designed to support them in meeting the varied needs of children with ASD. RtI and the Autism Spectrum Disorder Inclusion Collaboration Model (Simpson, de Boerr-Ott, & Smith-Myles, 2003) emphasize the need for teachers to closely collaborate with the various school- and community-based professionals that are typically assisting the child with ASD in order to provide the comprehensive program such children need. Professionals from other disciplines are not only important for the direct services they provide to the child with ASD, but also as a part of the team that develops, implements, evaluates, and modifies the educational program of the child with ASD to encourage the best outcomes possible for children with this diagnosis.

References

Aarons, M., & Gittens, T. (1999). *The handbook of autism*. London: Routledge.

Accardo, P., Magnusen, D., & Capute, A. (2000). *Autism: Clinical and research issues*. Baltimore, MD: York Press.

Adelinis, J., Piazza, C., & Goh, H. L. (2001). Treatment of multiply controlled destructive behavior with food reinforcement. *Journal of Applied Behavior Analysis, 34*, 97–100. doi:10.1901/jaba.2001.34-97

American Psychiatric Association (2000). *Diagnostic and statistical manual of mental disorders* (4th ed., text revision). Washington, DC: Author.

Ashcroft, W., Argiro, S., & Keohane, J. (2010). *Success strategies for teaching kids with autism*. Waco, TX: Prufrock Press.

Autism Society of America. (2000). What is autism? *Advocate: The newsletter of the American Autism Society of America, 33*, 3.

Ayers, A. J. (1979). *Sensory integration and the child*. Los Angeles, CA: Western Psychological Services.

Baio, J. and Autism and Developmental Disabilities Monitoring Network Surveillance Year 2008 Principle Investigators. (2012). Prevalence of Austism Spectrum Disorders – Autism and developmental disablties monitoring network, 14 sites, United States, 2008. *Surveillance Summaries, 61*, 1–19.

Baird, G., Charman, T., Cox, A., Baron-Cohen, S., Swettenham, J., et al., (2001). Screening and surveillance for autism and pervasive developmental disorders. *Archives of the Disabled Child, 84*, 468–75. doi:10.1136/adc.84.6.468

Baird, G., Simonoff, E., Pickles, A., Chandler, S., Loucas, T., Meldrum, D., & Charman, T. (2006). Prevalence of disorders of the autism spectrum in a population cohort of children in South Thames: The special needs and autism project (SNAP). *Lancet, 368*, 210–15. doi:10.1016/S0140-6736(06)69041-7

Baron-Cohen, S. (1995). The eye direction detector (EDD) and the shared attention mechanism (SAM): Two cases for evolutionary psychology. In C. Moore & P. J. Dunham (eds), *Joint attention* (pp. 41–60). Hillsdale, NJ: Lawrence Erlbaum Associates, Inc.

—(2002). The extreme male brain theory of autism. *Trends in Cognitive Science, 6*, 248–54. doi:10.1016/S1364-6613(02)01904-6

Baron-Cohen, S., Knickmeyer, R. C., & Belmonde, M. K. (2005). Sex differences in the brain: Implications for explaining autism. *Science, 310*, 819–23. doi:10.1126/science.1115455

Baron-Cohen, S., Leslie, A. M., & Frith, U. (1985). Does the autistic child have a 'theory of mind'?. *Cognition, 21*, 37–46. doi:10.1016/0010-0277(85)90022-8

Baron-Cohen, S., Lombardo, M. V., Auyeung, B., Ashwin, E., Chakrabarti, B., & Knickmeyer, R. (2011). Why are autism spectrum conditions more prevalent in males? *Plos Biology, 9*, 1–10. doi:10.1371/journal.pbio.1001081

Bauminger, N., & Yirmiya, N. (2001). The functioning and well-being of siblings of children with autism: Behavioral-genetic and familial contributions. In J. A. Burack, T. Charman, N. Yirmiya, & P. R. Zelazo, (eds), *The development of autism: Perspectives from theory and research* (pp. 61–80). Mahwah, NJ: Lawrence Erlbaum Associates Publishers.

Bellini, S., & Peters, J. K. (2008). Social skills training for youth with autism spectrum disorders. *Child and Adolescent Psychiatric Clinics of North America, 17*, 857–73. doi:10.1016/j.chc.2008.06.008

Browder, D., Trela, K., & Jimenez, B. (2007). Training teachers to follow a task analysis to engage middle school students with moderate and severe developmental disabilities in grade appropriate literacy. *Focus on Autism and Other Developmental Disabilities, 22*, 206–19. doi:10.1177/10883576070220040301

Bryan, L. C., & Gast, D. L. (2000). Teaching on-task and on-schedule behaviors to high-functioning children with autism via picture activity schedules. *Journal of Autism and Developmental Disorders, 30*, 553–67. doi:10.1023/A:1005687310346

Carr, E. G., & Durand, V. M. (1985). Reducing behavior problems through functional communication training. *Journal of Applied Behavioral Analysis, 18*, 111–126. doi:10.1901/jaba.1985.18-111

Casey, S., & Merical, C. (2006). The use of functional communication training without additional treatment procedures in an inclusive school setting. *Behavioral Disorders, 32*, 46–54. Accessed from http://www.ccbd.net/sites/default/files/BD%2032-01-46.pdf

Chen, F. S., & Yoon, J. M. D. (2011). Brief report: Broader autism phenotype predicts spontaneous reciprocity of direct gaze. *Journal of Autism and Developmental Disorders, 41*, 1131–4. doi:10.1007/s10803-010-1136-2

Cohen, I. L. (2003). Criterion-related validity of the PDD Behavior Inventory. *Journal of Autism and Developmental Disorders, 33*, 31–45. doi:10.1023/A:1022278420716

Crews, D. (2011). Epigenetic modifications of brain and behavior: Theory and practice. *Hormones and Behavior, 59*, 393–8. doi:10.1016/j.yhbeh.2010.07.001

Crutcher, R. (1943). Child psychiatry: A history of its development. *Psychiatry, 6*, 191–201.

Duker, P. C., & Schaapveld, M. (1996). Increasing on-task behaviour through interruption-prompting. *Journal of Intellectual Disability Research, 40*, 291–7. doi:10.1046/j.1365-2788.1996.775775.x

Dyches, T. T., Wilder, L. K., Sudweeks, R. R., Obiakor, F. E., & Algozzine, B. (2004). Multicultural issues in autism. *Journal of Autism and Developmental Disorders, 34*, 211–22. doi:10.1023/B:JADD.0000022611.80478.73

Eikeseth, S. (2009). Outcome of comprehensive psycho-educational interventions for young children with autism. *Research in Developmental Disabilities, 30*, 158–78. doi:10.1016/j.ridd.2008.02.003

Eldevik, S., Hastings, R. P., Hughes, J. C., Eikeseth, S., & Cross, S. (2009). Meta-analysis of early intensive behavioral intervention for children with autism. *Journal of Clinical Child and Adolescent Psychology, 38,* 439–50. doi:10.1080/15374410902851739

Fenske, E. C., Zalenski, S., Krantz, P. J., & McClannahan, L. E. (1985). Age at intervention and treatment outcome for autistic children in a comprehensive intervention program. *Analysis and Intervention in Developmental Disabilities, 5,* 49–58. doi:10.1016/S0270-4684(85)80005-7

Fombonne, E. (2003). The prevalence of autism. *Journal of the American Medical Association, 289,* 87–9. doi:10.1001/jama.289.1.87

Fombonne, E., Simmons, H., Ford, T., Meltzer, H., & Goodman, R. (2001). Prevalence of pervasive developmental disorders in the British nationwide survey of child mental health. *Journal of the American Academy of Child and Adolescent Psychiatry, 40,* 820–7. doi:10.1097/00004583-200107000-00017

Frith, U. (2003). *Autism: Explaining the enigma* (2nd ed.). Oxford, UK: Blackwell.

Ghaziuddin, M., Tsai, L., & Ghaziuddin, N. (1992). Comorbidity of autistic disorder in children and adolescents. *European Child and Adolescent Psychiatry, 1,* 209–13. doi:10.1007/BF02094180

Ghaziuddin, M., Weidmer-Mikhail, E., & Ghaziuddin, N. (1998). Comorbidity of Asperger syndrome: A preliminary report. *Journal of Intellectual Disability Research, 42,* 279–83. doi:10.1111/j.1365-2788.1998.tb01647.x

Grafodatskaya, D., Chung, B., Szatmari, P., & Weksberg, R. (2010). Autism spectrum disorders and epigenetics. *Journal of The American Academy Of Child & Adolescent Psychiatry, 49,* 794–809. doi:10.1016/j.jaac.2010.05.005

Green, G., Brennan, L. C., & Fein, D. (2002). Intensive behavioral treatment for a toddler at high risk for autism. *Behavior Modification, 26,* 69–102. doi:10.1177/0145445502026001005

Gresham, F. M., Sugai, G., & Horner, R. H. (2001). Interpreting outcomes of social skills training for students with high-incidence disabilities. *Teaching Exceptional Children, 67,* 331–44.

Hagopian, L. P., Bruzek, J. L., Bowman, L. G., & Jennett, H. K. (2007). Assessment and treatment of problem behavior occasioned by interruption of free-operant behavior. *Journal of Applied Behavior Analysis, 40,* 89–103. doi:10.1901/jaba.2007.63–05

Harms, E. (1960). At the cradle of child psychiatry: Hermann Emminghaus' "Psychiatrische Störungen des Kindesalters (1887)". *American Journal of Orthopsychiatry, 30,* 186–90. doi:10.1111/j.1939-0025.1960.tb03025.x

Harris, S. L., & Glasberg, B. A. (2007). Functional behavioral assessment in practice: Concepts and applications. In J. Jacobson, J. Mulick, & J. Rojahn (eds), *Handbook of intellectual and developmental disabilities* (pp. 317–32). New York, NY: Springer Science + Business Media.

Harris, S. L., & Handelman, J. S. (2000). Age and IQ at intake as predictors of placement for young children with autism: A four- to six-year follow up. *Journal of Autism and Developmental Disorders, 30,* 137–42. doi:10.1023/A:1005459606120

Hartley, S. L., & Sikora, D. M. (2009). Sex differences in autism spectrum disorder: An examination of developmental functioning, autistic symptoms, and coexisting behavior problems in toddlers. *Journal of Autism and Developmental Disorders, 39,* 1715–22. doi:10.1007/s10803-009-0810-8

Haslam, J. (1809). Cases of insane children. In *Observations on madness and melancholy* (2nd ed., Chapter 4). London: J. Callow.

Hellings, J. A., Nickel, M. A., Weckbaugh, R. N., McCarter, K., Mosier, M., & Schroeder, S. R. (2005). The Overt Aggression Scale for rating aggression in outpatient youth with autistic disorder: Preliminary findings. *The Journal of Neuropsychiatry and Clinical Neuroscience, 17,* 29–35. Accessed from http://neuro.psychiatryonline.org/data/Journals/NP/3931/29.pdf

Houston, R., & Frith, U. (2000). *Autism in history: The case of Hugh Blair of Borgue.* Oxford, UK: Blackwell.

Kanner, L. (1943). Autistic disturbances of affective contact. *The Nervous Child, 2,* 217–50. Accessed from http://www.autismtruths.org/pdf/Autistic%20 Disturbances%20of%20Affective%20Contact%20-%20Leo%20Kanner.pdf

Klinger, L. G., & Dawson, G. (2001). Prototype formation in autism. *Development and Psychopathology, 29,* 479–92.

Klinger, L., Dawson, G., & Renner, P. (2003). Autistic disorder. In E. J. Mash & R. A. Barkley (eds), *Child psychopathology* (2nd ed., pp. 409–54). New York, NY: The Guilford Press.

Knickmeyer, R. C., Baron-Cohen, S., Raggatt, P., & Taylor, K. (2005). Foetal testosterone, social relationships, and restricted interests in children. *Journal of Child Psychology and Psychiatry, 46,* 198–210. doi:10.1111/j.1469 7610.2004.00349.x

Knickmeyer, R. C., Baron-Cohen, S., Raggatt, P., & Taylor, K., & Hackett, G. (2006). Fetal testosterone and empathy. *Hormones and Behavior, 49,* 282–92. doi:10.1016/j.yhbeh.2005.08.010

Koegel, R. L., & Koegel, L. K. (1990). Extended reductions in stereotypic behavior of students with autism through a self-management treatment package. *Journal of Applied Behavior Analysis, 23,* 119–27. doi:10.1901/jaba.1990.23-119

Kravits, R. R., Kamps, D. M., & Kemmerer, K. (2002). Brief report: Increasing communication skills for an elementary-aged learner with autism using the picture exchange communication system. *Journal of Autism and Developmental Disorders, 32,* 225–30. doi:10.1023/A:1015457931788

Lainhart, J. E. (1999). Psychiatric problems in individuals with autism, their parents and siblings. *International Review of Psychiatry, 11,* 278–98. doi:10.1080/09540269974177

Landa, R. J., Holman, K. C., O'Neill, A. H., & Stuart, E. A. (2011). Intervention targeting development of socially synchronous engagement in toddlers with autism spectrum disorder: A randomized controlled trial. *Journal of Child Psychology and Psychiatry, 52,* 13–21. doi:10.1111/j.1469-7610.2010.02288.x

Laushey, K. M., & Heflin, L. J. (2000). Enhancing social skills of kindergarten children with autism through the training of multiple peers as tutors. *Journal of Autism and Developmental Disabilities, 30,* 183–93. doi:10.1023/A:1005558101038

Lecavalier, L., Leone, S., & Wiltz, J. (2006). The impact of behavior problems on caregiver stress in young people with autism spectrum disorders. *Journal of Intellectual Disability Research, 50,* 172–83. doi:10.1111/j.1365-2788.2005.00732.x

Licciardello, C. C., Harchik, A. E., & Luiselli, J. K. (2008). Social skills intervention for children with autism during interactive play at a public elementary school. *Education and Treatment of Children, 31,* 28–37. doi:10.1353/etc.0.0010

Livanis, A., & Mouzakitis, A. (2010). The treatment validity of autism screening instruments. *Assessment for Effective Intervention, 35,* 206–17. doi:10.1177/1534508410481041

Lord, C., & Venter, A. (1992). Outcome and follow-up studies of high functioning autistic individuals. In E. Schopler & G. B. Mesibov (eds), *High functioning individuals with autism* (pp. 187–200). New York, NY: Plenum.

Losh, M., Trembath, D., & Piven, J. (2008). Current developments in the genetics of autism: From phenome to genome. *Journal of Neuropathology and Experimental Neurology, 67,* 829–37. doi:10.1097/NEN.0b013e318184482d

Lovaas, O. I. (1987). Behavioral treatment and normal educational and intellectual functioning in young autistic children. *Journal of Consulting and Clinical Psychology, 55,* 3–9. doi:10.1037/0022-006X.55.1.3

Lowrey, L. G. (1944). Psychiatry for children: A brief history of developments. *American Journal of Psychiatry, 101,* 375–88.

Massey, G., & Wheeler, J. (2000). Acquisition and generalization of activity schedules and their effects on task engagement in a young child with autism in an inclusive pre-school classroom. *Education and Training in Mental Retardation and Developmental Disabilities, 35,* 326–35.

Matson, J. L., & Boisjoli, J. A. (2009). The token economy for children with intellectual disability and/or autism: A review. *Research in Developmental Disabilities: A Multidisciplinary Journal, 30,* 240–8. doi:10.1016/j.ridd.2008.04.001

Matson, J. L., & Nebel-Schwalm, M. (2007a). Assessing challenging behaviors in children with autism spectrum disorders: A review. *Research in Developmental Disabilities, 28,* 567–79. doi:10.1016/j.ridd.2006.08.001

—(2007b). Comorbid psychopathology with autism spectrum disorder in children: An overview. *Research in Developmental Disabilities: A Multidisciplinary Journal, 28,* 341–52. doi:10.1016/j.ridd.2005.12.004

Matson, J. L., Taras, M., Seven, J., Love, S., & Fridley, D. (1990). Teaching self-help skills to autistic and mentally retarded children. *Research in Developmental Disabilities, 11,* 361–78. doi:10.1016/0891-4222(90)90023-2

Mattila, M., Kielinen, M., Linna, S., Jussila, K., Ebeling, H., Bloigu, R., Joseph, R., & Moilanen, I. (2011). Autism spectrum disorders according to DSM-IV-TR and comparison with DSM–5 draft criteria: An epidemiological study. *Journal of the American Academy of Child and Adolescent Psychiatry, 50,* 583–92. doi:10.1016/j.jaac.2011.04.001

McGee, G. G., Daly, T., & Jacobs, H. A. (1994). The Walden Preschool. In S. L. Harris, & J. S. Handleman (eds), *Preschool education programs for children with autism* (pp. 127–62). Austin, TX: Pro-Ed.

Minshew, N. J., Goldstein, G., Taylor, H. G., & Siegel, D. J. (1994). Academic achievement in high functioning autistic individuals. *Journal of Clinical and Experimental Psychology, 16,* 261–70. doi:10.1080/0168839408402637

Moss, J. J., & Howlin, P. P. (2009). Autism spectrum disorders in genetic syndromes: Implications for diagnosis, intervention and understanding the wider autism spectrum disorder population. *Journal of Intellectual Disability Research, 53,* 852–73. doi:10.1111/j.1365-2788.2009.01197.x

Mouridsen, S. E., Rich, B., & Isager, T. (2009). Sibling sex ratio of individuals diagnosed with autism spectrum disorder as children. *Developmental Medicine and Child Neurology, 52,* 289–92. doi:10.1111/j.1469-8749.2009.03368.x

Naglieri, J. A., & Chambers, K. M. (2009). Psychometric issues and current scales for assessing autism spectrum disorders. In S. Goldstein, J. A. Naglieri, & Sally Ozonoff (eds), *Assessment of autism spectrum disorders* (pp. 55–90). New York, NY: The Guilford Press.

National Professional Development Center on Autism Spectrum Disorders. (2011). *Evidence-based practice briefs.* Accessed from http://autismpdc.fpg.unc.edu/content/briefs

Newman, B., Tuntigian, L., Ryan, C. S., & Reinecke, D. R. (1997). Self-management of a DRO procedure by three students with autism. *Behavioral Interventions, 12,* 149–56. doi:10.1002/(SICI)1099-078X (199707)12:3<149::AID-BRT173>3.0.CO;2-M

Nguyen, D. K., & Disteche, C. M. (2006). High expression of the mammalian X chromosome in brain. *Brain Research, 1126,* 46–9. doi:10.1016/j.brainres.2006.08.053

Nikopoulos, C. K., & Keenan, M. (2004). Effects of video modeling on social initiations by children with autism. *Journal of Applied Behavior Analysis, 37,* 93–6. doi:10.1901/jaba.2004.37-93

Reiersen, A. M. (2011). Links between autism spectrum disorder and AD/HD symptom trajectories: Important findings and unanswered questions. *Journal of the American Academy of Child and Adolescent Psychiatry, 50,* 857–9. doi:10.1016/j.jaac.2011.06.012

Rice, C., & Autism and Developmental Disabilities Monitoring Network Surveillance of the Year 2000 Principal Investigators. (2007). Prevalence of autism and autism spectrum disorder: Autism and developmental disabilities monitoring network, six sites, United States, 2000. *Morbidity and Mortality Weekly Report, 56,* 1–11.

Rogers, S. J., & Vismara, L. A. (2008). Evidence-based comprehensive treatments for early autism. *Journal of Clinical Child and Adolescent Psychology, 37,* 8–38. doi:10.1080/15374410701817808

Rojahn, J., Matson, J. L., Lott, J. L., Esbensen, A. J., & Smalls, Y. (2001). The Behavior Problems Inventory: An instrument for the assessment of self-injury, stereotyped behavior, and aggression/destruction in individuals with developmental disabilities. *Journal of Autism and Developmental Disorders, 31,* 577–88. doi:10.1023/A:1013299028321

Rourke, B. P. (ed.). (1995). *Syndrome of nonverbal learning disabilities: Neurodevelopmental manifestations.* New York, NY: The Guilford Press.

Rutter, M. (1968). Concepts of autism: A review of research. *Journal of Child Psychology and Psychiatry, 9,* 1–25. doi:10.1111/j.1469-7610.1968.tb02204.x

Rutter, M., & Lockyer, L. (1967). A five to fifteen year follow-up study of infantile psychosis. I: Description of sample. *British Journal of Psychiatry, 113,* 1169–82. doi:10.1192/bjp.113.504.1169

Sigafoos, J., Green, V. A., Payne, D., O'Reilly, M. F., & Lancioni, G. E. (2009). A classroom-based antecedent intervention reduces obsessive-repetitive behavior in an adolescent with autism. *Clinical Case Studies, 8*, 3–13. doi:10.1177/1534650108327475

Simpson, R. L., de Boerr-Ott, S. R., & Smith-Myles, B. (2003). Inclusion of learners with autism spectrum disorders in general education settings. *Topics in Language Disorders, 23*, 116–33. doi:10.1097/00011363-200304000-00005

Skuse, D. H. (2000). Imprinting, the X-chromosome, and the male brain: Explaining sex difference in the liability to autism. *Pediatric Research, 47*, 33–7. doi:10.1203/00006450-200001000-00006

—(2009). Is autism really a coherent syndrome in boys, or girls? *British Journal of Psychology, 100*, 33–7. doi:10.1348/000712608X369459

Smith, T., Groen, A., & Wynn, J. W. (2000). Randomized trial of intensive early intervention for children with pervasive developmental disorder. *American Journal on Mental Retardation, 105*, 269–85. doi:10.1352/0895-8017(2000)105<0269:RTOIEI>2.0.CO;2

Spears, R., Tollefson, N., & Simpson, R. (2001). Usefulness of different types of assessment data in diagnosing and planning for a student with high-functioning autism. *Behavioral Disorders, 26*, 227–42.

Stahmer, A. C., & Aarons, G. A. (2009). Attitudes toward adoption of evidence-based practices: A comparison of autism early intervention providers and children's mental health providers. *Psychological Services, 6*, 223–34. doi:10.1037/a0010738

Strain, P., & Cordisco, L. (1994). LEAP Preschool. In S. L. Harris, & J. S. Handleman (eds), *Preschool education programs for children with autism* (pp. 225–44). Austin, TX: Pro-Ed.

Sztamari, P. (1999). Heterogeneity and the genetics of autism. *Journal of Psychiatry and Neuroscience, 24*, 159–65.

Szatmari, P. (2000). Perspectives on the classification of Asperger syndrome. In A. Klin, F. R. Volkmar, & S. S. Sparrow (eds), *Asperger syndrome* (pp. 403–17). New York, NY: The Guilford Press.

Szatmari, P., Jones, M., Fisman, S., Tuff, L., Bartolucci, G., Mahoney, W., & Bryson, S. (1995). Parents and collateral relatives of children with pervasive developmental disorders: A family history study. *American Journal of Medical Genetics, 60*, 282–9. doi:10.1002/ajmg.1320600405

Tager-Flusberg, H. (1999). A psychological approach to understanding the social and language impairments in autism. *International Review of Psychiatry, 11*, 325–34. doi:10.1080/09540269974203

—(2000). Language development in children with autism. In L. Menn & N. Bernstein Ratner (eds), *Methods for studying language production* (pp. 312–32). Mahwah, NJ: Lawrence Erlbaum.

—(2004). Do autism and specific language impairment represent overlapping language disorders? In M. L. Rice & S. F. Warren (eds), *Developmental language disorders: From phenotypes to etiologies* (pp. 31–52). London: Lawrence Erlbaum Associates.

Taylor, B. A., & Harris, S. L. (1995). Teaching children with autism to seek information: Acquisition of novel information and generalization of responding. *Journal of Applied Behavior Analysis, 28*, 3–14. doi:10.1901/jaba.1995.28-3

US Department of Education (2000). *Twenty-second annual report to congress on the implementation of the individuals with disabilities act*. Washington, DC: Author.

Van Lancker, D., Cornelius, C., & Needleman, R. (1991). Comprehension of verbal terms for emotions in normal, autistic, and schizophrenic children. *Developmental Neuropsychology, 7*, 1–18. doi:10.1080/87565649109540474

Volen, J., & Phillips, L. (2010). Measuring pragmatic language in speakers with autism spectrum disorders: Comparing the children's communication checklist–2 and the test of pragmatic language. *American Journal of Speech-Language Pathology, 19*, 204–12. doi:10.1044/1058-0360(2010/09-0011)

Wing, L. (1981). Asperger's syndrome: A clinical account. *Psychological Medicine, 11*, 115–29. doi:10.1017/S0033291700053332

—(2002). *The autistic spectrum: A guide for parents and professionals*. London, UK: Robinson.

Wing, L., Gould, J., & Gillberg, C. (2011). Autism spectrum disorders in the DSM-V: Better or worse than the DSM-IV? *Research in Developmental Disabilities, 32*, 768–73. doi:10.1016/j.ridd.2010.11.003

Wolff, S. (2004). The history of autism. *European Child and Adolescent Psychiatry, 13*, 201–9. doi:10/1007/s00787-004-0363-5

Young, E. C., Diehl, J. J., Morris, D., Hyman, S. L., & Bennetto, L. (2005). The use of two language tests to identify pragmatic language problems with children with autism spectrum disorders. *Language, Speech and Hearing Services in Schools, 36*, 62–72. doi:10.1044/0161-1461(2005/006)

CHAPTER FIVE

Understanding and Managing Behaviors of Children Involved in Bully/Victim Conflicts

Laura M. Crothers, Eric J. Fenclau, Jr., Charles M. Albright, and Jered B. Kolbert
Duquesne University

Abstract

Bullying is one of the most common forms of school violence, with a recent population study of elementary, middle school, and high school students revealing that 41% of students were frequently involved in bullying, 23% were victims of bullying, 8% were bullies, and 9% were bully/victims (Bradshaw, Sawyer, & O'Brennan, 2007). Because of the relative frequency of bullying behaviors evidenced by students while at school (e.g. 9–32% are bullied once a week or more often; Berger, 2007), teachers are most often the adults required to respond to incidents of bullying. In this chapter, bullying is conceptualized as a behavior management issue, with recommendations for interventions appropriate for Tiers I, II, and III according to a Response to Intervention (RtI) model.

Overview

Childhood bullying has been recognized as a pervasive problem in schools that has negative effects upon both perpetrators and victims (e.g. Bradshaw, O'Brennan, & Sawyer, 2007; Brunstein-Klomek, Marrocco, Kleinman, Schoneld, & Gould, 2007). It is one of the most common forms of school violence, with a recent population study of elementary, middle school, and high school students revealing that 41% of students were frequently involved in bullying, 23% were victims of bullying, 8% were bullies, and 9% were bully/victims (Bradshaw, Sawyer, & O'Brennan, 2007). Among primary school children, 3–27% reported bullying peers, while 9–32% indicated that they are bullied at least once a week (Berger, 2007).

There is evidence suggesting that teachers may contribute to or tolerate the problem. Students often report that teachers do not intervene when a student is being bullied in school and that teachers are not aware of bullying, even though students frequently indicate that bullying occurs in the classroom while the teacher is present (Olweus, 1991). Olweus (1993a) found that when teachers are aware of bullying incidents, they often do relatively little to put a stop to the behavior, and make only limited contact with students involved in the bullying to discuss the problem. Unfortunately, such inaction can be particularly dangerous since children who engage in bullying may interpret the resulting adult non-intervention as tacit approval of their behavior. Since childhood bullying is a common behavioral problem evidenced by students in schools, in this chapter, educators will be presented with information regarding the conceptual foundations, definitions, relevant symptomatology, and a three-tier prevention/intervention system for teachers to use in the classroom to address this form of school violence.

A variety of comprehensive theoretical frameworks have been used to explain the etiology and characteristics associated with bullying and victimization, with the more prominent including the ecological systems model, social learning theory, and dominance theory. According to Bronfenbrenner's (1979) ecological systems model, children's behavior is the product of the reciprocal interaction between multiple factors existing on different contextual levels, and includes individual traits, family dynamics, interpersonal relationships, school climates, and community characteristics. In other words, the probability that a child is likely to engage in bullying or be the victim of bullying depends upon the interaction between these various variables, and thus it is unlikely that there is a single and clearly identifiable cause. A recent meta-analytic study of predictors of bullying behavior indicated that both individual and contextual factors were strong predictors of bullying perpetration (Cook, Williams, Guerra, Kim, & Sadek, 2010). Furthermore, it is probable that such individual and contextual factors mutually influence each other. For example, defiance of adult authority, an individual trait which predicted perpetration, may influence a contextual variable associated with perpetration, such as poor parental monitoring, and vice versa.

Bandura's (1977) social learning theory focuses upon the reciprocal interaction between an individual's cognitions, his or her behaviors, and the environment. In this model, it is posited that children acquire bullying behaviors through operant and vicarious conditioning mechanisms. The behaviors of perpetrators of bullying are positively reinforced through the attainment of goals, such as social status, and are negatively reinforced through the removal of threats to their power (Batsche & Knoff, 1994). Youth who support the primary perpetrator, who are sometimes referred to as the bully's henchmen, receive vicarious reinforcement in observing the benefits accrued by the perpetrator. Youth may also initially acquire bullying behaviors through witnessing violence between adults and/or peers, including through the media, and by observing or experiencing the use of physical or inconsistent punishment. Through such observation, children learn that aggression is an effective strategy to obtain goals and they learn the rationale and motivations for using violence. Patterson, Reid, and Dishion (1992) propose that some families reinforce aggression in their children by attending to, laughing about, or approving aggressive behavior and ignoring pro-social behavior.

Dominance theorists assert that a primary motivation of perpetrators of bullying is to obtain social status in order to establish a high position within the social hierarchy of their peers (Pellegrini & Long, 2003). Social status provides greater access to resources, such as toys for younger children, or access to relationships, either social or romantic, for adolescents. Physical bullying demonstrates the perpetrator's physical dominance, verbal bullying likely indicates the perpetrator's superior intellect and/or verbal acumen, and in relational bullying, which consists of threats to end a relationship, spreading rumors, or humiliating in public, the aim of the perpetrator is either to obtain power within the relationship or to attack the social status of the intended target. Of note, Pellegrini and Long (2003) found that perpetrators of bullying are often more likely to be perceived as leaders by their peers and more attractive to the opposite sex.

Definitions of Bullying

Bullying is a form of instrumental aggression, meaning that it is proactive and frequently not a response to aggressive behavior demonstrated by a victim (Espelage & Swearer, 2003). A power differential exists between perpetrator and victim, such that the victim is typically unable to defend himself or herself from the bully's aggression (Espelage & Swearer, 2003). Bullying behavior tends to be repeated over time, although in some cases, a single incident can also be seen as an instance of this type of aggression (Olweus, 1993a).

Three types of peer victimization have been described in the literature: physical bullying, verbal bullying, and relational bullying. Physical bullying is a purposeful attempt to injure or make someone uncomfortable through the use of physical contact (e.g. hitting, pushing, hair-pulling; Olweus, 1993a). Verbal bullying, also called direct verbal aggression, consists of behaviors such as name-calling, shouting, abusing, and accusing (Björkqvist, Lagerspetz, & Kaukianinen, 1992). Finally, relational bullying includes harming peers through purposeful manipulation (e.g. gossiping, ignoring, and rumor-spreading) or causing damage to relationships or friendships (Crick & Grotpeter, 1996).

What characteristics are associated with victims of bullying?

It is important for teachers to be aware of the signs of victimization and psychosocial characteristics associated with victimization for several reasons. Victims often do not inform teachers about bullying incidents (Fekkes, Pijpers, & Verloove-Vanhorick, 2005), and one study found that only 4% of 8th grade students reported that they would tell a teacher about an incident of teasing (Shapiro, Baumeister, & Kessler, 1991). Furthermore, bullying occurs most often in areas of the school where there is a lack of adult supervision (Fekkes et al., 2005). For these reasons, teachers need to identify potential indications of victimization and pursue talking with a possible victim to gather more information and enhance their observation of bullying behavior.

Teachers may look for signs of the effects upon victims and perpetrators mentioned earlier, such as decreased self-esteem for victims, etc. There is evidence to suggest that for some of the common effects of victimization, the relationship is bi-directional. For example, a longitudinal study found that among early adolescents, victimization resulted in increased levels of depressive symptoms and that students with elevated levels of depressive symptoms were more likely to be victimized (Sweeting, Young, West, & Ger, 2006). In other words, some of the effects of victimization may exist prior to victimization, and may increase victims' vulnerability to peer aggression. Moreover, the subsequent victimization may exacerbate these vulnerabilities.

A recent meta-analytic study revealed which variables are most consistently associated with victimization within the research literature since 1970 (Cook et al., 2010). Victims were more likely than their non-bullying peers to exhibit internalizing symptoms, use externalizing behaviors, lack social skills and be isolated and rejected by peers, have a negative family environment, and have negative cognitions about themselves. The findings of Cook and colleagues (2010) regarding the self-concept of victims is consistent with Carney and Merrell's (2001) assertion that victims "... see themselves as stupid, ugly, and worthless, and (usually) wrongly blame themselves for the attacks" (p. 368).

Victims have varying emotional responses to victimization. Borg (1998) found that among 9- to 14-year-old victims, 38% reported feeling vengeful, 37% felt angry, 37% indicated feeling sorry for themselves, 25% reported indifference, and 24% felt helpless. Additionally, there is evidence suggesting that victims often lack a sense of hope. Hunter and Boyle (2002) discovered that 45% of 9–11 year-olds who had been bullied for a short time reported feeling a lack of control regarding the situation.

Most victims of bullying are generally submissive or passive, but a significant minority of victims has been called "provocative victims" or "bully-victims" because of their apparent tendency to provoke the ire of peers in response to their frequent demonstrations of aggression (Salmivalli & Niemenen, 2002). McAdams and Schmidt (2007) identify bully-victims as "reactive aggressors", suggesting that such youth desire close interpersonal relationships but are insecure, anxious, and highly emotional. These researchers posit that reactive aggressors tend to inaccurately appraise other students as threatening and thus respond impulsively to these misperceived threats. In contrast, proactive aggressors are more deliberate in targeting those whom they perceive to be vulnerable, deriving a sense of status or power. Cook et al.'s (2010) meta-analysis indicated that in comparison to their non-bullying and non-victimized peers, bully-victims tend to exhibit both internalizing and externalizing symptoms, have negative beliefs about themselves and others, lack social competence, have lower academic achievement, and are rejected and negatively influenced by peers.

What are the effects upon victims?

Numerous studies have suggested that being bullied by peers can have negative, pervasive effects upon psychological functioning (Nansel et al., 2004). The results of bullying behavior upon victims include anxiety, depression, low self-esteem, physical and psychosomatic complaints, posttraumatic stress disorder, and suicidal ideation (Crosby, Oehler, &

Capaccioli, 2010; Kaltiala-Heino, Rimpela, Marttunen, Rimpela, & Rantenan, 1999; McKenney, Pepler, Craig, & Connolly, 2002; Williams, Chambers, Logan, & Robinson, 1996). Victims tend to have poor relationships with their peers, which increases their vulnerability to future attacks (Dill, Vernberg, Fonagy, Twemlow, & Gamm, 2004). Additionally, those who are aggressively victimized are less likely to feel connected to others at school (O'Brennan, Bradshaw, & Sayer, 2009; Wilson, 2004). In fact, children victimized by peers through bullying are more likely than those who are not abused by peers to bring weapons to school (Carney & Merrell, 2001).

Unfortunately, these risks are not limited only to victims' short-term functioning. Olweus (1993b) found that when childhood victims of bullying became young adults (e.g. age 23 years), such individuals were more vulnerable to depression and low self-esteem than those who were not victimized by peers. Since the effects of being bullied can potentially last for a lifetime, it seems all the more important that educators are assertive in intervening in instances of peer victimization.

What characteristics are associated with perpetrators of bullying?

In addition to its focus on victimization, the meta-analysis completed by Cook and colleagues (2010) documented the variables that are most consistently associated with perpetration of bullying. The findings of this analysis indicated that perpetrators of bullying are more likely than non-bullying peers to exhibit externalizing behaviors, including defiant, aggressive, disruptive, and non-compliant responses, as well as internalizing symptoms, such as withdrawal, depressive, anxious, and avoidant responses. Perpetrators were more likely than their non-bullying peers to display social competence but to experience academic challenges, which supports O'Moore and Kirkman's (2001) suggestion that such children have high self-esteem in regard to their social and emotional functioning, but lack self-esteem related to their school functioning. Perpetrators were more likely than their non-bullying peers to have negative attitudes towards others, including a lack of empathy for others (Cook et al., 2010). They were also more likely than their non-bullying peers to experience trouble resolving social conflicts. Perpetrators were more likely than their non-bullying peers to experience poor parental monitoring and high levels of family conflict.

What are the consequences for perpetrators?

Children who engage in instrumental aggression, such as perpetrators of bullying, are also more likely to demonstrate beliefs supporting aggressive retaliation to others (Bradshaw et al., 2008), exhibit higher levels of aggressive-impulsive behavior than non-aggressive peers (O'Brennan et al., 2009), and, like victims, are less likely to feel a sense of connection to others at their school (Wilson, 2004). There are also established negative effects for perpetrators of bullying, including an increased risk of mental health disorders, such as attention deficit/hyperactivity disorder, depression, oppositional defiant disorder, and conduct disorder (Kumpulainen, Rasanen, & Puura, 2001), as well as a greater likelihood of engaging in criminal behavior, domestic violence, and substance abuse as adults (Farrington, 1993).

Children who bully are more likely than non-aggressive peers to have poor academic achievement, drop out of school, and struggle with career performance in adulthood (Carney & Merrell, 2001). Finally, researchers have found that childhood bullies are often severely punitive with their own children, who are subsequently more likely to be aggressive with peers (Eron, Huesmann, Dubow, Romanoff, & Yarmel, 1987; Smokowski & Kopasz, 2005).

Using a Response to Intervention Framework to Intervene with Bullies and Victims

In a Response to Intervention (RtI) model (three-tiered intervention structure), the levels of intervention may be classified as primary, secondary, and tertiary prevention. Primary interventions target whole schools and are often efforts to build protective factors to prevent behavior problems from initially occurring. Secondary interventions are designed for students who are already at-risk for emotional or social behavior problems. Such efforts are often delivered to small groups of students. Finally, tertiary intervention is focused upon addressing the needs of children already demonstrating emotional and social behavior problems. These interventions are typically much more intensive and individualized in focus (Malecki & Demaray, 2007; Walker & Shinn, 2002). Although three-tiered intervention systems are often suggested for use in remedying children's academic problems, problematic behavior evidenced by students can also be targeted through a system of primary, secondary, and tertiary prevention. Accordingly, bully and victim behaviors in students may be addressed through a tiered intervention system used in the classroom, an approach that will be discussed throughout the remainder of this chapter.

Tier I Prevention and Intervention

Student Code of Conduct

Although the establishment of a whole-school anti-bullying policy is critically important to a successful Tier I intervention in childhood peer victimization, a classroom climate also must be created that is inhospitable to bullying. Thus, one of the first strategies in addressing bullying is to establish rules prohibiting it. Teaching clear anti-bullying rules to students appears to be important in molding their explicit attitudes toward bullying behavior (Van Goethem, Scholte, & Wiers, 2010). Students need to be provided with information that instructs them in the way in which they should handle bullying behavior, both as bystanders and as victims (Batsche, 1997; Boulton & Underwood, 1992). However, it may be helpful to recognize that educators and children sometimes differ in their definitions regarding bullying. In an investigation of whether the themes that emerged from children's definitions of bullying were compatible with theoretical and methodological descriptions of bullying, researchers noted that students' explanations rarely included the three prominent definitional criteria of bullying: intentionality, repetition, and power imbalance. Instead, younger children were more focused upon physical and verbal aggression and general harassment, while middle school students, particularly females, were more apt to describe relational aggression in their depiction of bullying (Vaillancourt et al., 2008). These researchers (Vaillancourt et al., 2008) also reported that students given a definition of bullying reported less victimization than students who were not provided with a definition; findings that were also noted by Kert, Codding, Tyron, and Shiyko (2010). Thus, it may be important to standardize a definition of bullying in order to verify that educators and students are referring to the same behaviors.

In addition to explicitly prohibiting bullying behavior, educators may also need to consider children's implicit attitudes about peer victimization, meaning their impulsive, spontaneous, uncontrolled emotional reactions and evaluations (Van Goethem et al., 2010). Not surprisingly, Van Goethem and colleagues (2010) found that in a sample of primary school children, explicit bullying attitudes predicted bullying behavior. However, a significant interaction between implicit and explicit bullying attitudes revealed that in children with relatively positive explicit attitudes about peer victimization, implicit attitudes regarding bullying also predicted bullying behavior. Essentially, for children who had relatively positive explicit attitudes toward bullying, which are deliberate, reflective, controlled, and consciously self-reported evaluations (e.g. one should not bully others; Gawronski & Bodenhausen, 2006), having negative implicit attitudes toward bullying (e.g. an uncontrolled emotional reaction that bullying is acceptable) was an important predictor of bullying behavior.

Another point of consideration is that some children may not have good models upon which to base their conceptualization of a healthy friendship. Unfortunately, not all children smoothly develop the skills required to cultivate social relationships, and a child's overall happiness can be seriously hampered by the desire to make friends and being unable to do so. Consequently, students may also need to be presented with positive examples of peer relationships, which can be accomplished informally, by being exposed to children modeling good social skills and relationships with others. However, teachers can also engage in more formal friendship development building skills for students (see activities such as the Role, Meaning and Value of Friendships in Field, Kolbert, Crothers, & Hughes, 2009), which will be discussed later in this chapter.

Classroom Climate

In addition to anti-bullying policies in the school, as well as in each classroom, educators may also consider the climate of the classroom as a Tier I anti-bullying intervention. Research has identified that there is a robust relationship between childhood bullying and a negative school climate (Guerra, Williams, & Sadek, 2011; Kasen, Berenson, Cohen, & Johnson, 2004). Not surprisingly, this linkage appears to extend to the classroom. Smith, Ananiadou, and Cowie (2003) reported on a Norwegian study that found that the quality of teacher-student relationships and the social structure of the classroom both predicted victimization rates through childhood bullying (Roland & Galloway, 2002).

In their research, Guerra et al. (2011) defined a positive school climate as encompassing trust between students and teachers, respectful interactions among and between students, and rules that were fair. These researchers further suggested that this can be achieved by providing resources for positive youth development and establishing an environment in which children are encouraged to be fair to peers and are also empowered to identify and report bullying behavior to adults (Guerra et al., 2011). In the classroom, teachers can model respectful interactions with others and encourage students to collaborate with each other in developing the code of conduct for the group. Moreover, it is important for educators to create a classroom environment in which pro-social skills are valued and children's friendships and inclusion in social groups are encouraged.

Tier II Intervention

Tier II interventions focus more specifically on group populations that exhibit at-risk behavior, and typically consist of approximately 5–10% of the general population (Anderson & Borgmeier, 2010). Moreover, this level of intervention targets specific at-risk behaviors of interest and tends to be implemented in a targeted small group, or in a classroom wide format (Anderson & Borgmeier, 2010). The purpose of this targeted intervention format is to identify students who are at risk and to provide sufficient and appropriate systematic instruction so that such students change their negative behaviors.

Nickerson et al. (2006) suggest that Tier II interventions should include the following: parental education specific to bullying awareness, problem-solving skills training, social integration activities, counseling, and school to home communication regarding specific incidents of unwanted behavior. Through these intervention strategies, pro-social replacement behaviors are instilled, maintenance of such behaviors increases, and generalization strategies help educators to identify and diminish the possible function(s) of the problem behavior.

Selecting Students for Intervention

When identifying students who are "at-risk" for bully or victim behaviors and are in need of a Tier II intervention, teachers should identify students based on discipline, teacher, and parent referrals as well as direct assessment procedures (e.g. observations, checklists, interviews). After selecting students for this level of intervention, the multidisciplinary team should discuss each student's reason for referral and set goals that are obtainable and measurable. After discussing these goals with the referral team, the classroom teacher should arrange to meet and develop a contract with each student and the overall group (Lassman, Jolivette, & Wehby, 1999).

For potential or emerging bullies, a behavioral contract may include such targeted behaviors as identifying and eliminating expressions of instrumental aggression and replacing these aggressive impulses with pro-social behaviors, such as initiating a friendly interaction. Behavioral goals for likely victims of bullying may consist of demonstrations of assertiveness or friend-seeking efforts. Including the at-risk students in this process helps increase "buy-in" and internal motivation to succeed within the group dynamic. After the intervention process has started, teachers should check in with these children periodically to ensure that they are still on track in reaching their preset goals (Lassman et al., 1999).

Selecting a Tier II Intervention

Second Step

Second Step is a school-based curriculum for pre-school through junior high school students and focuses on promoting social skills and altering attitudes that lead to violence through the development of empathy, impulse control, and anger management (Committee for Children, 2004). This program facilitates teachers' interventions of classroom disruptions and students' behavior issues, while teaching children how to recognize and understand their feelings, how to make positive and effective choices and keep anger from escalating into violence or bullying. Furthermore, the Second Step curriculum focuses on three competencies: empathy, impulse control and problem solving, and anger management (Committee for Children, 2004). The program is easy to teach, flows sequentially, and requires minimal teacher preparation time. Moreover, academic lessons can be integrated into the Second Step activities—helping teachers build on what they are already teaching in class to their students.

Steps to Respect

Steps to Respect is an anti-bullying program that targets children in the upper elementary school years. Hanish and Guerra (2004) report that because bullying behavior seems to increase at the end of elementary school, and acceptance of aggression also grows and begins to stabilize, this age range is an ideal target for intervention techniques (Huesmann & Guerra, 1997). Therefore, the program represents an important time in which to intervene and change bullying related skills, beliefs, and behaviors (Frey et al., 2009). Specifically, this program is designed to decrease school bullying problems by: "(a) increasing adult monitoring and intervention in bullying events, (b) improving systemic supports for socially responsible behavior, (c) change student normative beliefs that support bullying, and (d) addressing student social-emotional skills that counter bullying and support social competence" (Frey et al., 2009, p. 467). Steps to Respect is a multilevel curriculum that can be used as a Tier I, II, or III intervention and contains classroom and individual intervention materials based on need.

The classroom lessons of Steps to Respect use cognitive-behavioral techniques to encourage socially responsible norms (Huesman & Guerra, 1997). Lessons and instructional material are designed for use for third through sixth graders and consists of a 10-week period of bi-weekly basic lessons, followed by 8–10 literature-based lessons (Frey et al., 2009). The program aims to counter expectations that students can bully with impunity, and to remove the stigma from "tattling." Further, the Steps to Respect classroom curricula affords the facilitator with many pathways to influence social behavior by building bullying prevention and fundamental social-emotional skills (Frey et al., 2009). Moreover, the program works to teach the following social-emotional skills: perspective taking, emotional management, conflict resolution, and other skills that provide a buffer to bullying (Espelage & Swearer, 2003).

Behavior Education Programs (BEPs)

Behavior Education Programs (BEPs) also may be an intervention that helps educators to expose and intervene with a student's at-risk behaviors. With a child who is prone to demonstrate bullying behaviors, such a program would typically begin with a daily morning check-in with the classroom teacher, with the student obtaining his or her daily BEP form. The child then would be instructed to review his or her daily goals (e.g. being a good friend by avoiding aggressive interactions) and asked to reflect on the expected behavior(s). At the end of each class period, the student submits the form to his or her teacher, who assigns tallies to all successfully completed behaviors. At the end of the day, the student "checks-out," has his or her points tallied and is able to select a reward or prize based on the accrued points. The student must then take the BEP form home, have it signed by a parent or guardian, and then return the copy the following morning. This last step may be particularly useful with students who are at-risk for bullying other children, as there is research suggesting that parents of bullies may minimize or deny their child's aggressive behaviors (Crothers & Kolbert, 2008).

Social Skills Groups

Programs that teach coping strategies and academic, social, and life skills have been shown to substantially improve children's behavior (Macarthur & Ferretti, 2001). In school settings, social skills groups are typically focused upon identifying critical skills that students fail to exhibit naturally; either the result of a skill deficit or a production problem due to external environmental issues. Through social skills instruction, the goal is to have teachers develop social skill lessons that instruct, demonstrate, and allow children to practice the missing skill. While concrete, structured examples of how and when to use the learned social skills are necessary, it is also critical to ensure that the students can generalize the strategies for future use. Furthermore, social skills training holds great importance for limiting future victimization, as researchers have found that a child's poor social skills are a major risk factor for victimization (Boulton, Trueman, Chau, Whitehand, & Amataya, 1999; Hodges, Boivin, Vitaro, & Bukowski, 1999).

Tier III Intervention

No matter the preventative efforts utilized, it is likely impossible to prevent all cases of bullying in the classroom. Consequently, a Tier III level of bullying intervention is necessary when there are clear or reoccurring cases of bullying in a classroom or school. When intervening, there are short- and long-term steps that can be utilized not only to protect and empower victims, but also to work with perpetrators to reduce their bullying behaviors.

Selecting Students for Intervention

The first course of action when a student has been bullied by peers is to speak with the victim to understand the nature of the problem. It is likely that the student will be concerned that talking to a teacher will make the problem worse. Thus, it is important that the teacher builds rapport with the student by letting him or her know that everything he or she decides to discuss will be held in confidence. Additionally, it may be helpful for the teacher to confide in the child by explaining that classroom bullying has occurred before, and that the teacher has been successful in remedying the problem. This will provide the child with hope and will also assist the child in trusting the teacher. Furthermore, as the child divulges information to the teacher, his or her feelings should be validated, and the teacher should let the student know that he or she did not cause the bullying to occur.

Once the relevant information is gathered, the teacher should reaffirm that the child made the right decision in divulging the bullying to the educator and explain the next steps in the process. The teacher should talk to other students and gather information to order to assist him or her in accurately understanding the bullying behavior. Then, steps can be taken to correct the problem, including negative consequences for the bully as well as protecting the victim from future peer harassment.

Selecting a Tier III Intervention

Although there is empirical support for individual interventions for rejected youth (Nickerson, Brock, Chang, O'Malley, 2006), there is currently little empirical investigation of individual interventions for victims and perpetrators of bullying, and neither are there empirically supported methods for identifying students for Tier III interventions. Obviously, continuation or escalation of victimization and/or perpetration following the application of Tier II interventions would indicate eligibility. Indications that victims need continued individual interventions would be extremely low self-esteem, continued or increased signs of depressive symptoms, negative views of self—including possibly accepting that the perpetrator's taunts are an accurate portrayal of them, and increased social isolation. Perpetrators who maintain a defensive position and fail to develop any behaviors of empathy for their victims or remorse, insight regarding the impact of their behaviors upon victims or their motivations, or a willingness to change would be likely candidates for continued individual interventions.

Working with Victims of Bullying

One of the reasons that bullying occurs at school is because of the power imbalances between children that are exploited in order to inflict harm upon the weaker individual (Olweus, 1993a). Thus, when working with the victims of bullying, it is important to create supports both external to and within the child in order to promote a sense of control and safety in one's environment as well as to build resiliency skills. Social skills difficulties are one of the central weaknesses that leave children open to bullying (Fox & Boulton, 2005). Students who do not have the skills necessary to seek and maintain friendships tend to be isolated in the school culture and are vulnerable to being bullied. Consequently, it is often necessary to target victims of bullying for participation in a social skills group to help them to build the skills necessary to be successful in the social climate of the school.

Teachers can also help to facilitate social interactions for the bullied student. This may be difficult to do initially, as the student's history with classmates will make integration into the school culture difficult. Therefore, it likely will be helpful to encourage the victim to engage with other children in structured social activities, such as class projects in which the teacher can help support the bullied student as well as facilitate positive interactions with other children. Because of the child's past history of negative interactions with peers, he or she will probably need guidance in identifying when and how to approach another child for a social interaction. The classroom teacher can encourage the student to engage in some of the risk taking behaviors that are necessary to start a friendship. This likely will be especially difficult for the student, as past attempts to engage socially with other children may not have been successful. However, changing this pattern in the child's life may be the most effective way to stop him or her from continuing to be bullied.

While developing social skills and friendships, it will also be necessary for the child to build resilience. Children who are the victims of bullying tend to internalize their negative interactions with peers as well as have low self-esteem. It is likely that the bullied student will have negative thoughts about himself or herself. It is therefore important for the teacher to talk to the student about these misperceptions, helping him or her to restructure his or her thoughts in more positive and accurate ways. The teacher can also help the victim learn to identify his or her strengths and positive qualities to which some other students may be attracted.

The objective of promoting the victim's social skills is to reduce the victim's social isolation by developing at least a few friends, which hopefully reduces the victim's vulnerability as a target to the perpetrator, and provides the victim with an outlet for expressing his or her frustrations. Unfortunately, it may be very difficult for the victim to develop friends, as there is evidence that students who are socially isolated in the early grades of elementary school typically remain so throughout childhood (Booth-LaForce & Oxford, 2008). Thus, teachers can encourage victims to reinforce themselves for attempting to connect with others and learn to focus less on the immediate results and more upon the effort of making friends. Since victims may lack social perspective-taking skills, teachers can ask victims to consider who is likely to respond to their friendship overtures.

Another skill that victims often lack is assertiveness. Victimized students should be encouraged to believe that they have the power to affect their environment as well as to have their needs met. Again, this will be difficult, as the student likely has not had a history of positive consequences achieved through assertiveness. It will be important for the teacher to provide the student with continuous positive regard when he or she is asserting his or her thoughts and feelings. Additionally, as the child gains confidence in these skills, he or she can be encouraged to begin to handle conflicts assertively. Such encouragement may come in the form of bibliotherapy, in which children demonstrate appropriate assertiveness, as well as in role-playing conflictual peer interactions, in which the student can practice assertive problem solving behavior. As the child learns these skills, it is essential that the teacher continues to offer positive feedback and identifies instances of success. Such techniques will help to improve the student's self-efficacy and develop the confidence to use these techniques in actual peer interactions.

Working with Perpetrators

When working with perpetrators, it is important for teachers to use a straightforward delivery of the facts of the aggression demonstrated toward peers and the resulting consequences. Teachers should begin calmly by identifying the reason for the conversation and the evidence of the bullying behavior. This will result in the notification of the seriousness of the infraction without judgment or vilification for bad behavior. The teacher should communicate to the student the consequences for the bullying behavior, as well as the fact that other school personnel will be apprised of the episode(s) so that the bully's actions can be monitored. Thus, the bully will be made aware that steps have been taken that will make it more difficult for him or her to continue his or her bullying of other students. Perpetrators often deny any wrongdoing and will dispute the facts regarding the incident, and in such cases teaches are encouraged to focus on the victim's feelings.

After the student has been informed of the rule infractions and the resulting consequences, it is then important for the teacher to talk to the student about his or her behavior from a non-punitive perspective. This will potentially allow the educator to build rapport with the child and begin to develop insight into the bully's perspective. Students who bully tend to have poorer psychological health than other students (Önder & Yurtal, 2008). However, it is important to note the misconception that bullies are aggressive because of feelings of inadequacy; on the contrary, bullies tend to feel justified in their behavior and are often popular with classmates (Olweus, 1993a). With this in mind, it will be important to work with the student who bullies his or her classmates to understand the mutual benefits of being supportive with peers. For example, some perpetrators have a higher need for dominance than non-bullying peers (Graham & Juvonen, 1998; Olweus, 1993a), and may perceive bullying as an effective means for increasing status. In such a situation, teachers can help the perpetrator identify the possible long-term consequences of continuing to use dominance-oriented strategies, as studies suggest that while perpetrators tend to be popular in elementary and middle/junior high school, the popularity of perpetrators declines upon entry into the high school level (Olweus, 1993a). Teachers can assist perpetrators in identifying the socially acceptable ways the perpetrator currently uses to obtain status, and also help explore additional ways to obtain status.

Unfortunately, perpetrators of bullying often tend not to evidence empathy for their victims (Olweus, 1993a). It is important for teachers to understand this, as it will likely be ineffective to tell the student how hurtful the other child found his or her behavior. Instead, empathy and perspective taking should be built slowly through modeling, role playing, and restructuring the way that the student perceives interactions with other individuals. Because it is likely that the cognitions and emotions associated with the bullying behavior developed over time, so also will the development of pro-social skills take time to manifest. However, through patience and compassion, progress will likely occur.

Progress Monitoring of Interventions

When implementing an RtI model in a school system, it is essential that the interventions chosen are based upon evidence of their effectiveness.

However, it is important to recognize that while such interventions may have a body of literature supporting their efficacy for a significant number of students, there is no guarantee that an intervention will be effective for specific students or classes. In order to implement interventions that are truly evidence based, implementers need to utilize data to make decisions regarding intervention through the use of progress monitoring tools (Gresham, 2010).

Progress monitoring involves using objective benchmarks to quantify children's behaviors, as well as their beliefs, attitudes and values in order to track their changes over time. Progress monitoring can measure short- and long-term changes, as well as the changes of individuals, classrooms, and even schools (Shapiro, 2004). In order to gauge student progress over time, student behavior needs to be measured prior to the implementation of the intervention. These measurements should be repeated; either after the intervention is concluded, or as the intervention is being implemented. Repeating these measures will allow teachers to evaluate how the intervention has affected students' behaviors over time and to conclude whether the intervention was successful, whether it should continue to be implemented, or whether it should be discontinued.

It is also recommended that progress monitoring involves more than one form of evaluation (Rathvon, 2008). For example, using objective rating forms as well as direct observation will allow more diverse and numerous data points. The more robust the collected data, the more confidence that the teacher will have in the decisions that are made. Moreover, no single monitoring tool will ever provide all of the information necessary to properly evaluate a bullying intervention plan (Algozinne, 2010).

Determining appropriate progress monitoring measures will depend greatly on the type of intervention that is being implemented. Consequently, the teacher should first consider whether he or she is working with perpetrators or victims of bullying, and what type of thoughts, attitudes, and/ or behaviors the intervention is targeting. If the teacher is working on an intervention with an individual student, the progress monitoring tools can be specifically tailored to the child's needs. However, if the program being implemented is a classroom-based strategy, progress monitoring measures will likely be dependent upon objective behavioral rating scales. Though less individualized, these scales have been found to be sensitive to intervention changes over time (Volpe & Gadow, 2010). Regardless, the key to successfully choosing a progress monitoring procedure is clearly defining what type of change the intervention is seeking to effect and choosing a progress monitoring tool that will accurately measure that change.

Direct Behavior Observation

School-based behavioral observation is a direct observation and rating of a child's behaviors in the classroom based upon a set of pre-established behavioral categories. Behavioral observation is useful because it provides concrete examples of the disruptive or maladaptive social behavior, and for the purposes of progress monitoring, should be conducted to observe bullying behaviors in a structured manner. To that end, the observer should have predetermined, operationally-defined behaviors in mind, and record the frequency, duration, and intensity of each behavioral occurrence. This method provides the examiner with "real-life" examples of the student's disruptive behavior. After a baseline has been established, the examiner can select a desired time interval, and compare the frequency, duration, and intensity information between sessions. Such a technique permits the examiner to track progress over time.

Daily Behavior Report Cards (DBRCs) & Electronic Daily Report Card (e-DBRC)

Because an individual's behaviors or response to interventions typically cannot reliably be predicted, frequent progress monitoring for any intervention is essential. Although direct observation is considered by many to be the gold standard of behavior monitoring, this process requires substantial time, resources and potentially inhibits the observed behaviors in the applied setting (Chafouleas, Riley-Tillman, & McDougal, 2002). Daily Behavior Report Cards (DBRCs) are an alternative to the aforementioned technique, and can be used as a performance, behavior-based recording system used to collect teachers' ratings of predetermined behaviors (Chafouleas et al., 2002). Traditionally, DBRCs have been used to record disruptive behaviors in the classroom; they can also serve as a measure of behavior progress monitoring (McDougal, Nastasi, & Chafouleas, 2005). The DBRCs should include no more than three behaviors, each rated on a Likert scale. The student's teacher is responsible for completing the DBRC each day, including during the baseline and intervention phases (McDougal et al., 2005). Obtaining this information is important for establishing a student's rate of improvement, identifying students who are not responding to the present intervention, and informing decision making about continuing or altering an intervention (Gresham et al., 2010).

Another form of daily report cards is *The Electronic Daily Report Card (e-DBRC)*, which is a criterion-referenced behavioral progress monitoring system (Burke & Vannest, 2008). This system affords educators a comprehensive approach utilizing a web-based program that summarizes behavioral rating data into a concise behavioral report card (Burke & Vannest, 2008).

The program records and reports upon a student's behaviors across time and presents the student's progress in a graph format. Reports also include a presentation of the student's daily target behaviors. Chafouleas et al. (2005) found this method to be efficacious and efficient when monitoring, reporting upon, and intervening with a student's problem behaviors.

Behavioral Scales for Progress Monitoring

Behavioral rating scales are questionnaires that measure behaviors, thoughts, and feelings (Riccio & Rodriguez, 2007), and can be completed by students, teachers, or parents. In the case of bullying intervention, behavioral scales can be used to measure teachers' perceptions of students' behavior as well as students' attitudes and perceptions of conflict management and victimization.

The *Conflict Resolution Scale* (CRS) is a measure that helps to evaluate how a child or adolescent handles conflict. The two parts of the scale helps the examiner to gain a comprehensive view of how the student engages in conflict resolution behaviors. In the first part of the scale, the student is asked to choose the frequency with which certain behaviors or events occur, such as problems with friends and getting in trouble in school. This portion of the scale consists of twenty-five items, with each item including a 5-point Likert scale (e.g. 1 = Never; 5 = Once a Day or More). In the second part of the scale, the student is asked to answer how easy or hard it is for him or her to participate in the behavior, such as asking other children to play or standing up to his or her friends. This portion of the scale consists of twenty-two items, with each item also including a 5-point Likert scale (e.g. 1 = Never; 5 = Once a Day or More; Smith, Daunic, Miller, & Robinson, 2002).

The *Young Adult Social Behavior Scale* (YASB; Crothers, Schreiber, Field, & Kolbert, 2009) is a measure that examines both pro-social and aggressive social behaviors in adolescence and young adulthood. Specifically, the fourteen-item scale assesses such behaviors as spreading rumors, handling arguments with friends, and keeping secrets. The examinee is asked to choose the frequency with which he or she engages in specific behaviors through a 5-point Likert scale (e.g. 1 = Always; 5 = Never). Confirmatory factor analyses supports that the YASB measures three internally consistent constructs: relationally aggressive behaviors, socially aggressive behaviors, and interpersonally mature behaviors. This measure has been used both epidemiologically (e.g. Clinton et al., under review), and as a pretest-posttest measure (e.g. Comstock et al., in press) to assess the indirect types of bullying most often seen in females and adolescents.

The *Social Skills Improvement System (SSIS) Rating Scales* is a norm-based system used to gauge and monitor students' social behaviors.

This system is comprised of four main components, including the Social Skills Scale, Behavior Problems Scale, Autism Spectrum Scale and Academic Competence Scale. In addition, the SSIS has three validity scales that allow examiners to collect information on the veracity and certitude of the responses of each individual rater. Collaboratively, each component provides a greater understanding of the student's current level of functioning in the many domains typically associated with disruptive behavioral problems. The SSIS has alternative forms that can be administered to the student, his or teachers, and his or her parents. This method affords great depth and breadth into the student's adaptive or maladaptive social behaviors. Moreover, these scales can be administered every four weeks to progress monitor a student's response to interventions (Gresham & Steven, 2008).

Discussion and Recommendations

Recent meta-analytic investigations of school-based bullying prevention programs have indicated that such programs may have no impact (Merrell, Gueldner, Ross, & Isava, 2008) or only a small positive impact (Ferguson, San Miguel, Kilburn, & Sanchez, 2007) upon students' bullying behavior. Despite such findings, teachers have a moral obligation to address bullying given the considerable short-term and long-term consequences for both victims and perpetrators, as well as a legal obligation in many states since school personnel are required to address incidents of peer victimization.

The ineffectiveness of bullying prevention programs is frustrating. However, the issue of bullying may be regarded as a public health issue requiring a multi-faceted approach involving sustained efforts within both the schools and the community in order to change the common perception that bullying is normative. Thus, the path of progress for bullying prevention may be similar to other public health crises, such as tobacco use prevention, which failed to achieve demonstrable effects until decades had passed. One of the consistent components of bullying prevention programs is the focus on comprehensive, multi-systemic approaches targeting the school climate, classroom, and individual students, and there has been an increased call to use the ecological systems model to understand and address bullying (e.g. Espelage & Swearer, 2010). Accordingly, the Response to Intervention (RtI) model's emphasis on comprehensive approaches and data-based decision-making offers considerable potential for addressing and intervening with bullying behavior.

Although bullying prevention programs have not received considerable empirical support, there is evidence that teachers make a difference in reducing bullying behavior. Teachers who use effective management techniques in their classroom had a lower prevalence of student bullying

(Roland & Galloway, 2002). Bowllan (2011) found that after one year of implementing Olweus's Bullying Prevention Program, teachers reported that they were better able to identify bullying and talk to perpetrators and victims. Consequently, there is data to suggest that teachers' behaviors do matter in the prevention and intervention of childhood bullying. It is therefore critically important to both the short- and long-term functioning of victims and perpetrators that educators consider themselves to be the first responders to bullying in the classroom.

References

Anderson, C. M., & Borgmeier, C. (2010). Tier II interventions within the framework of school-wide positive behavior support: Essential features for design, implementation, and maintenance. *Behavior Analysis in Practice, 3,* 33–45.

Bandura, A. (1977). *Social learning theory.* Englewood Cliffs, NJ: Prentice-Hall.

Batsche, G. M. (1997). Bullying. In G. G. Bear, K. M. Minke, & A. Thomas, (eds). *Children's needs II: Development, problems, and alternatives* (pp. 171–9). Bethesda, MD: National Association of School Psychologists.

Batsche, G. M., & Knoff, H. (1994). Bullies and their victims: Understanding a pervasive problem in the schools. *School Psychology Review, 23,* 165–74.

Björkqvist, K., Lagerspetz, K., & Kaukiainen, A. (1992). Do girls manipulate and boys fight? Developmental trends in regard to direct and indirect aggression. *Aggressive Behavior, 18,* 117–27.

Booth-LaForce, C., & Oxford, M. L. (2008). Trajectories of social withdrawal from grades 1 to 6: Prediction from early parenting, attachment, and temperament. *Developmental Psychology, 44,* 1298–313.

Bowllan, N. M. (2011). Implementation and evaluation of a comprehensive, school-wide bullying prevention program in an urban/suburban middle school. *Journal of School Health, 81,* 167–73. doi:10.1111/j.1746-1561.2010.00576.x

Borg, M. G. (1998). The emotional reactions of school bullies and their victims. *Educational Psychology, 18,* 433–4.

Boulton, M. J., & Smith, P. K. (1994). Bully/victim problems in middle school children: stability, self-perceived competence, peer-perceptions and peer acceptance. *British Journal of Developmental Psychology, 12,* 315–29. doi:10.1111/j.2044-835X.1994.tb00637.x

Boulton, M. J., Trueman, M., Chau, C., Whitehand, C., & Amataya, K. (1999). Concurrent and longitudinal links between friendship and peer victimization: Implications for befriending interventions. *Journal of Adolescence, 22,* 461–6. doi:10.1006/jado.1999.0240

Bradshaw, C. P., Sawyer, A. L., & O'Brennan, L. M. (2007). Bullying and peer victimization at school: Perceptual differences between students and school staff. *School Psychology Review, 36,* 361–82.

Bronfenbrenner, U. (1979). *The ecology of human development: Experiments by nature and design.* Cambridge, MA: Harvard University Press.

Brunstein-Klomek, A., Marrocco, F., Kleinman, M., Schonfeld, I. S., & Gould, M. S. (2007). Bullying, depression, and suicidality in adolescents. *Journal of the American Academy of Child and Adolescent Psychiatry, 46,* 40–9. doi:10.1097/01.chi.0000242237.84925.18

Carney, A. G., & Merrell, K. W. (2001). Bullying in schools: Perspectives on understanding and preventing an international problem. *School Psychology International, 22,* 364–82.

Carter, J., & Sugai, G. (1989). Survey on prereferral practices: Responses from state departments of education. Exceptional Children, 55, 298–302.

Cenkseven Önder, F., & Yurtal, F. (2008). An investigation of the family characteristics of bullies, victims, and positively behaving adolescents. *Kuram ve Uygulamada Eğitim Bilimleri, 8,* 821–32.

Clinton, A., Crothers, L. M., Kolbert, J. B., Hughes, T. L., Schreiber, J. B., Schmitt, A. J., Lipinski, J., Vázquez, G. R., & Field, J. E. (under review). A cross-cultural investigation of relational and social aggression in Puerto Rican and American female college students. *Journal of Agression, Maltreatment, and Trauma.*

Committee for Children. (2004). *Knowledge assessment for Second Step: A violence prevention curriculum.* Seattle, WA: author.

Comstock, L. A., Crothers, L. M., Schreiber, J. B., Schmitt, A. J., Field, J. E., Hughes, T. L., Kolbert, J. B., & Lipinski, J. (in press). Relational, social, and overt aggression among diverse female adolescents. *Journal of Child and Adolescent Trauma.*

Cook, C. R., Williams, K. R., Guerra, N. G., Kim, T. E., & Sadek, S. (2010). Predictors of Bullying and victimization in childhood in adolescence: A meta-analytic investigation. *School Psychology Quarterly, 25,* 65–83.

Cousin, P. T., Diaz, E., Flores, B., & Hernandez, J. (1996). Looking forward: Using a sociocultural perspective to reframe the study of learning disabilities. In M. Poplin & P. Cousin (eds), Alternative views of learning disabilities (pp. 656–63). Austin, TX: Pro-Ed.

Crick, N. R., & Grotpeter, J. K. (1996). Children's treatment by peers: Victims of relational and overt aggression. *Development and Psychopathology, 8,* 367–80.

Crosby, J. W., Oehler, J., & Capaccioli, K. (2010). The relationship between peer victimization and post-traumatic stress symptomatology in a rural sample. *Psychology in the Schools, 47,* 297–310.

Crothers, L. M., & Kolbert, J. B. (2008). Tackling a problematic behavior management issue: Teachers' intervention in childhood bullying problems. *Intervention in School and Clinic, 43,* 132–9.

Dill, E. J., Vernberg, E. M., Fonagy, P., Twemlow, S. W., & Gamm, B. K. (2004). Negative affect in victimized children: The roles of social withdrawal, peer rejection, and attitudes toward bullying. *Journal of Abnormal Psychology, 32,* 159–73.

Drame, E. R., & Xu, Y. (2008). Examining sociocultural factors in response to intervention models. *Childhood Education, 85,* 26–32.

Eron, L. D., Huesmann, R. L., Dubow, E., Romanoff, R., & Yarmel, P. W. (1987). Childhood aggression and its correlates over 22 years. In D. Crowell, I. M. Evans, & C. R. O'Donnell (eds), *Childhood aggression and violence* (pp. 249–62). New York: Plenum.

Espelage, D. L., & Swearer, S. M. (2003). Research on school bullying and victimization: What have we learned and where do we go from here? *School Psychology Review, 32,* 365–83.

Espelage, D. L., & Swearer, S. M. (2010). A social-ecological model for bullying prevention and intervention: Understanding the impact of adults in the social ecology of youngsters. In S. R., Jimerson, S. M., Swearer, S. M., & D. L. Espelage (eds). *Handbook of bullying in schools: An international perspective* (pp. 61–72). New York: Routledge.

Farrington, D. P. (1993). Understanding and preventing bullying. In M. Tonry (ed.), *Crime and justice: A review of research* (pp. 381–458). Chicago: University of Chicago Press.

Fekkes, M. F., Pijpers, I. M., & Verloove-Vanhorick, S. P. (2005). Bullying: Who does what, when and where? Involvement of children, teachers, and parents in bullying behavior. *Health Education Research, 20,* 81–91.

Ferguson, C. J., Miguel, C. S., Kilburn, Jr., J. C., & Sanchez (2007). The effectiveness of school-based anti-bullying programs: A meta-analytic review. *Criminal Justice Review, 32,* 401–14.

Field, J. E., Kolbert, J. B., Crothers, L. M., & Hughes, T. L. (2009). *Understanding girl bullying and what to do about it: Strategies to help heal the divide.* Thousand Oaks, CA: Corwin.

Fox, C. L., & Boulton, M. J. (2005). The social skills problems of victims of bullying: Self, peer and teacher perceptions. *British Journal of Educational Psychology, 75,* 313–28. doi:10.1348/000709905X25517

Frey, K. S., Hirschstein, M. K., Edstrom, L. V., & Snell, J. L. (2009). Observed reductions in school bullying, nonbullying aggression, and destructive bystander behavior: A longitudinal evaluation. *Journal of Educational Psychology, 101,* 466–81. doi:10.1037/a0013839

Gawronski, B., & Bodenhausen, G. V. (2006). Associative and propositional in evaluation: An integrative review of implicit and explicit attitude change. *Psychological Bulletin, 132,* 692–731.

Graham, S., & Juvonen, J. (1998). A social cognitive perspective on peer aggression and victimization. *Annals of Child Development, 12,* 21–66.

Gresham, F. M. (2004). Current status and future directions of school-based behavioral interventions. *School Psychology Review, 33,* 326–43.

Griffin, R., & Gross, A. (2004). Childhood bullying: Current empirical findings and future directions for research. *Aggression and Violent Behavior, 9,* 379–400.

Guerra, N. G., Williams, K. R., & Sadek, S. (2011). Understanding bullying and victimization during childhood and adolescence: A mixed methods study. *Child Development, 82,* 295–310.

Hanish, L. D., & Guerra, N. G. (2004). Aggressive victims, passive victims, and bullies: Developmental continuity or developmental change? *Merrill-Palmer Quarterly, 50,* 17–38.

Hodges, E. V. E., Boivin, M., Vitaro, F., Bukowski, W. M. (1999). The power of friendship: Protection against an escalating cycle of peer victimization. *Developmental Psychology, 35,* 94–101.

Huesmann, L. R., & Guerra, N. G. (1997). Children's normative beliefs about aggression and aggressive behavior. *Journal of Personality and Social Psychology, 72,* 408–19.

Hunter, S. C., & Boyle, J. M. E. (2002). Perceptions of control in the victims of school bullying: The importance of early intervention. *Educational Research, 44*, 323–36.

Kaltiala-Heino, R., Rimpela, M., Marttunen, M., Rimpela, A., & Rantenan, P. (1999). Bullying, depression, and suicidal ideation in Finnish adolescents: School survey. *British Medical Journal, 319*, 348–51.

Kasen, S., Berenson, K., Cohen, P., &, & Johnson, J. G. ((2004).). The effects of school climate on changes in aggressive and other behaviors related to bullying. In D. L. Espelage & S. M. Swearer (eds), *Bullying in American schools* (pp. 187–210). Mahwah, NJ: Lawrence Erlbaum.

Kert, A. S., Codding, R. S., Tyron, G. S., & Shiyko, M. (2010). Impact of the word "bully" on the reported rate of bullying behavior. *Psychology in the Schools, 47*, 193–204.

Kumpulainen, K., Rasanen, E., & Puura, K. (2001). Psychiatric disorders and the use of mental health services among children involved in bullying. *Aggressive Behavior, 27*, 102–10.

Lassman, K. A., Jolivette, K., & Wehby, J. H. (1999). "My Teacher Said I Did Good Work Today!": Using collaborative behavioral contracting. *Teaching Exceptional Children, 31*, 12–18.

Malecki, C. K., & Demaray, M. K. (2007). Social behavior assessment and response to intervention. In S. R. Jimerson, M. K., Burns, & A. M. VanDerHeyden (eds), *Handbook of response to intervention: The science and practice of assessment and intervention* (pp. 161–71). New York: Springer.

McAdams, C. R., & Schmidt, C. D. (2007). How to help a bully: Recommendations for counseling the proactive aggressor. *Professional School Counseling, 11*, 121–8.

McKenney, K. S., Pepler, D. J., Craig, W. M., & Connolly, J. A. (2002). Psychosocial consequences of peer victimization in elementary and high school—An examination of posttraumatic stress disorder symptomatology. In K. A. Kendall-Tackett & S. M. Giacomoni (eds), *Child victimization: Maltreatment, bullying and dating violence, prevention and intervention* (pp. 151–7). Kingston, NJ: Civic Research Institute.

Merrell, K. W., Gueldner, B. A., Ross, S. W., & Isava, D. M. (2008). How effective are school bullying intervention programs? A meta-analysis of intervention research. *School Psychology Quarterly, 23*, 26–42.

Nansel, T. R., Craig, W., Overpeck, M. D., Saluja, G., Ruan, W. J., & the Health Behaviour in School-aged Children Bullying Analyses Working Group. (2004). Cross-national consistency in the relationship between bullying behaviors and psychosocial adjustment. *Journal of the American Medical Association, 158*, 730–6.

Nickerson, A. B., Brock, S. E., Chang, Y., & O'Malley, M. D. (2006). Responding to children victimized by their peers. *Journal of School Violence, 5*, 19–32. doi:10.1300/J202v05n03_03

O'Brennan, L. M., Bradshaw, C. P., & Sawyer, A. L. (2009). Examining developmental differences in the social-emotional problems among frequent bullies, victims, and bully/victims. *Psychology in the Schools, 46*, 100–15.

Olweus, D. (1978). *Aggression in the schools: Bullies and whipping boys.* Washington, DC: Hemisphere Press.

—(1993a). *Bullying at school: What we know and what we can do.* Cambridge, MA: Blackwell Publishers Ltd.

—(1993b). Victimization by peers: Antecedents and long-term outcomes. In K. H. Rubin & J. B. Asendorf (eds), *Social withdrawal, inhibition, and shyness in childhood* (pp. 315–42). Hillsdale, NJ: Erlbaum.

O'Moore, A. M., & Kirkman, C. (2001). Self-esteem and its relationship to bullying behavior. *Aggressive Behavior, 27,* 283–96.

Patterson, G. R., Reid, J. B., & Dishion, T. J. (1992). *Antisocial boys.* Eugene, Oregon: Castalia.

Pellegrini, A. D., & Long, J. D. (2003). A sexual selection theory longitudinal analysis of sexual segregation and integration in early adolescence. *Journal of Experimental Child Psychology, 85,* 257–78. doi:10.1016/S0022-0965(03)00060-2

Roland, E., & Galloway, D. (2002). Classroom influences on bullying. *Educational Research, 44,* 299–312.

Salmivalli, C., & Nieminen, E. (2002). Proactive and reactive aggression among school bullies, victims, and bully-victims. *Aggressive Behavior, 28,* 30–44.

Shapiro, J. P., Baumeister, R. F., & Kessler, J. W. (1991). A three component model of children's teasing: Aggression, humor and ambiguity. *Journal of Social and Clinical Psychology, 10,* 459–72. doi:10.1521/jscp.1991.10.4.459

Smith, P. K., Ananiadou, K., & Cowie, H. (2003). Interventions to reduce school bullying. *Canadian Journal of Psychiatry, 48,* 591–9.

Sweeting, H., Young, R., West, P., & Der, G. (2006). Peer victimization and depression in early-mid-adolescence: A longitudinal study. *British Journal of Educational Psychology, 76,* 577–94. doi:10.1348/000709905X49890

Tilly, W. D. III (2002). *Best practices in school psychology as a problem solving enterprise.* In A. Thomas & J. Grimes (eds), Best practices in school psychology IV (pp. 21–36). Bethesda, MD: The National Association of School Psychologists.

Upah, K. R. F. (2008). Best practices in designing, implementing, and evaluating quality interventions. In A. Thomas & J. Grimes (eds), *Best practices in school psychology V* (pp. 209–24). Bethesda, MD: The National Association of School Psychologists Publications.

Vaillancourt, T., McDougall, P., Hymel, S., Krygsman, A., Miller, J., Stiver, K., & Davis, C. (2008). Bullying: Are researchers and children/youth talking about the same thing? *International Journal of Behavioral Development, 32,* 486–95. doi:10.1177/0165025408095553

Van Goethem, A. A. J., Scholte, R. H. J., & Wiers, R. W. (2010). Explict- and implicit bullying attitudes in relation to bullying behavior. *Journal of Abnormal Child Psychology, 38,* 829–42. doi:10.1007/s10802-010-9405-2

Walker, H. M., & Shinn, M. R. (2002). Structuring school-based interventions to achieve integrated primary, secondary, and tertiary prevention goals for safe and effective schools. In M. R. Shinn, H. M. Walker, & G. Stoner (eds), *Interventions for academic and behavior problems II: Preventative and remedial approaches* (pp. 1–25). Bethesda, MD: The National Association of School Psychologists Publications.

Ward, L., Mallett, R., Heslop, P., & Simons, K. (2003). Transition planning: how well does it work for young people with learning disabilities and their families? *British Journal of Special Education, 30,* 132–7. doi:10.1111/1467-8527.00298

Williams, K., Chambers, M., Logan, S., & Robinson, D. (1996). Association of common health symptoms with bullying in primary school children. *British Medical Journal, 313,* 17–19.

Wilson, D. (2004). The interface of school climate and school connectedness and relationships with aggression and victimization. *Journal of School Health, 74,* 293–9. doi:10.1111/j.1746-1561.2004.tb08286.x

Understanding and Managing Behaviors of Children Diagnosed with Childhood Schizophrenia

Melissa Pearrow

University of Massachusetts

Huijun Li

Beth Israel Deaconess Medical Center and Harvard Medical School

Shane R. Jimerson

University of California, Santa Barbara

Abstract

Early Onset Schizophrenia (EOS), identified prior to the age of 18, is among the most pervasive and debilitating of all childhood psychopathologies. In the school context, schizophrenia is associated with impairments in cognitive abilities, language skills, motor skills, social skills, and creative thought, among other domains. This chapter reviews the etiology and diagnostic criteria of schizophrenia, as well as the phases of illness and the symptoms that may be observed in the school setting. The application of empirically-based psychosocial strategies to the school setting are examined with a particular focus on multi-tiered interventions that can monitor the child's development and progress in school.

Overview

The identification of schizophrenia in children first occurred in the early twentieth century (Kraepelin, 1919). Those who are diagnosed as having schizophrenia between ages 13 and 18 are usually referred to as having Early Onset Schizophrenia (EOS), and those at or before age 12 as having Very Early Onset Schizophrenia (VEOS) or Childhood—Onset Schizophrenia (COS). In this chapter, we will use the term EOS to refer to diagnosis of schizophrenia before age 18. The symptoms of children and adolescents diagnosed with schizophrenia seem to be consistent with those of adults (Asarnow, Thompson, & McGrath, 2004). The diagnostic classification of EOS is characterized by an individual experiencing delusions, hallucinations, disorganized or incoherent speech, grossly disorganized or catatonic behavior or negative symptoms such as lack of emotion (American Psychiatric Association [APA], 2000). It has been estimated that about 1 in 10,000 children will develop some form of schizophrenic disorder, with childhood-onset schizophrenia (COS) occurring at a rate of roughly 1 in 40,000 children (Asarnow & Asarnow, 2003; Remschmidt, 2002). Mueser and McGurk (2004) report a lifetime prevalence of schizophrenia to be 1 in 100 and it is estimated that 2.5 million people in the United States are living with the disorder. In approximately one-third of the cases, individuals begin experiencing psychotic symptoms in adolescence (Kodish & McClellan, 2008), and most frequently, the age of onset of schizophrenia is between 16 and 35 years old (Asarnow et al., 2004).

Over the course of development, EOS is often more severe than adult onset schizophrenia (Asarnow et al., 2004; Kumra & Shulz, 2008). When schizophrenia develops during childhood or adolescence, the symptoms impact the individual as well as his or her family, peers, teachers, and other school professionals. The importance of understanding EOS is that its effects are among the most pervasive and debilitating of all childhood psychopathologies. Of notable significance in the educational context, schizophrenia is associated with impairments in cognitive abilities, language skills, motor skills, social skills, and creative thought, among other domains (Andreasen, 2000; Nicolson et al., 2000; Remschmidt, 2002). Problem behaviors common among students with EOS include social withdrawal, isolation, disruptive behavior disorders, problems paying attention, impaired memory and reasoning, inappropriate or flattened expression of emotion, achievement difficulties, speech and language problems, and developmental delays (McClellan et al., 2001).

Early identification and intervention are important components that influence developmental trajectories of students with EOS. Identifying risk factors and recognizing early signs are important steps in supporting students with EOS. The premorbid abnormalities and early onset of psychotic symptoms found in children with schizophrenia often lead to a severe disruption in the child's global development. Skill deficits in numerous domains often exist due to the child's inability to develop or acquire new skills during the early stages of the disorder, which heightens the importance of early identification.

While EOS is relatively rare, it is imperative that educators, school psychologists, and other mental health professionals working in the schools are well informed about it so that they are fully prepared to meet the needs of these students. A basic understanding of EOS is crucial to increase the likelihood of success in all domains of a child's life. This chapter provides educators and child mental health professionals with the essential information they need to be better prepared to identify and address the needs of students with EOS. The chapter begins with conceptual foundations underlying the etiology of EOS and clearly defines the diagnostic criteria for EOS. Next, it highlights the symptomatology that is most likely seen in school settings and discusses a three-tier prevention/intervention strategy for school professionals and teachers to use in the classroom setting, including progress-monitoring strategies. Finally, recommendations conclude the chapter.

Conceptual Foundations Underlying Influences on EOS

The precise etiological process of schizophrenia remains elusive. The confluence of contemporary scholarship suggests that multiple factors contribute to the development of schizophrenia, including: (a) genes that cause structural brain deviations which make some individuals vulnerable to schizophrenia and (b) environmental factors such as negative pre- and post-natal impacts and social stresses such as trauma and stigma. Furthermore, considering a transactional-ecological developmental perspective (e.g. Sameroff, 2009), there may be an interaction or interplay between genetic vulnerability, neurobiological, and environmental factors that put a child or adolescent at risk of developing schizophrenia. The *transactional-ecological developmental model* is a framework for understanding the dynamic processes by which children and contexts shape each other (Sameroff, 2009). Specifically, this model posits that all human development is an adaption that is shaped at three primary levels: the (a) *genotype* (i.e. genetic and biochemical makeup), (b) *phenotype* (i.e. phenomenological experience and current developmental expressions), and (c) *environtype* (i.e. multilevel nested environments; Sameroff, 2000). These three levels interface via transactions—or multilevel interactions throughout time—continuously taking place among them.

Table 6.1 Etiological Factors of Schizophrenia

Risk Genes
Neuregulin, Dysbindin, D-amino acid oxidase, Catechol-O-methyltransferase, Proline dehydrogenase, Reelin, serotonin type 2a receptor, dopamine D3 receptor

---

Early Insults: Pre, peri, and postnatal risks
Viral Infections: herpes simplex, influenza, rubella
Toxins: Lead, alpha-aminolevulinic acid
Obstetric: Mother hypertension, loss of husband while being pregnant, malnutrition
Delivery complications

Other Environmental Factors
Vitamin D deficiency, winter birth, high latitude, inner city residence, drug use, natural disasters

---

Trauma
Stigma; emotional, physical, sexual, and psychological abuse; neglect; bullying, loss of a beloved one

---

Brain Abnormality
Reduction in whole brain and hippocampal volume, low volume of total cortical gray matter, high volumes of white matter, ventricular, and basal ganglia; larger superior temporal gyri relative to brain size; lack of normal right-greater-than left hippocampal asymmetry; larger ventricles, smaller temporal lobes, reduced metabolism in frontal lobe, significant reduction of mid sagittal thalamus

---

Researchers generally agree on a multifaceted etiological model of schizophrenia, including genetic, neurobiological, neuroanatomical mechanisms, and environmental factors, since a single cause is unlikely to explain its origin (Table 6.1 includes a multifaceted model). It is hypothesized that "schizophrenia is probably neither a single disease entity and nor is it a circumscribed syndrome—it is likely to be a conglomeration of phenotypically similar disease entities and syndromes" (Tandon, Nasrallah, & Keshavan, 2009, p. 1). Future studies are needed to clarify and specify the nature of the complex interplay among the different factors and their unique contribution to the development of schizophrenia in general and EOS in particular.

Diagnostic Criteria and Developmental Course for Early Onset Schizophrenia

The diagnostic criteria for Schizophrenia and Other Psychotic Disorders are delineated in the *Diagnostic and Statistical Manual of Mental Disorders* (Text Rev, 4th ed.; DSM IV-TR; APA, 2000). Some of the criteria of schizophrenia, according to the *DSM IV-TR*, include the following: delusions (i.e. having beliefs not based on reality), hallucinations (i.e. seeing or hearing things that do not exist), disorganized speech, grossly disorganized or catatonic behavior, and negative symptoms (i.e. affective flattening). A diagnosis is appropriate when two of the preceding symptoms are present during a one-month period, and those symptoms persist for at least six months. When the onset is prior to the age of 18 years, the condition is considered to be Early Onset Schizophrenia.

Developmentally, some individuals who have EOS may have a seemingly normal childhood or adolescence and others begin to manifest deficits in different domains at an early age, thus making the diagnostic assessment of EOS challenging as many symptoms of EOS also appear in other psychiatric disorders such as Attention Deficit Hyperactivity Disorder (AD/HD), autism, depression, or anxiety. Some warning signs or at-risk behaviors of EOS can last several months or a few years as nonspecific psychological, behavioral, emotional, and social disturbances of varying intensity, and sometimes they can be difficult to distinguish from characteristics related to normal child or adolescent development (Woods, Miller, & McGlashan, 2001; Yung et al., 2006). The DSM IV-TR (APA, 2000) includes the following five subtypes of schizophrenia:

1 *Paranoid-type* schizophrenia is characterized by delusions and auditory hallucinations.

2 *Disorganized-type* schizophrenia is characterized by speech and behavior that are disorganized or difficult to understand, and flattening or inappropriate emotions.

3   *Catatonic-type* schizophrenia is characterized by disturbances of movement (e.g. grossly disorganized or immobility).

4   *Undifferentiated-type* schizophrenia is characterized by some symptoms seen in the other subtypes of schizophrenia, but not enough of any one of them to define it as another particular type of schizophrenia.

5   *Residual-type schizophrenia* is characterized by a past history of at least one episode of schizophrenia, but the person currently has no positive symptoms (delusions, hallucinations, disorganized speech or behavior).

The clinical course of EOS is characterized by three phases, based on the symptom presentation and treatment response—*prodromal, acute,* and *residual* phases (Kodish & McClellan, 2008). The *prodromal phase* "begins with the first changes in behavior and lasts up until the onset of psychosis" (Cornblatt, Lencz, & Kane, 2001, p. 32). Prodromal symptoms are the first nonspecific indicators of active psychosis, and the most frequently reported initial signs include restlessness and vague feelings of uneasiness, depression, anxiety, sleep disturbance, stress vulnerability, social withdrawal, poor hygiene, and difficulty with thinking or concentrating (Hafner & Maurer, 2006; Kodish & McClellan, 2008; Yung & McGorry, 1996). In adult studies, the prodromal phase is organized into two stages: *prepsychotic prodromal stage*, which is the period from the first sign of illness until the first psychotic symptom, and the *psychotic prephase stage*, which is the period between the first positive symptom and the first psychiatric admission (Hafner & Maurer, 2006). The *acute phase* is marked by a sharp decline in functioning and an increase in hallucinations, delusions, and disorganized speech/behavior. The symptoms present during this phase can appear suddenly and typically last between one and six months, depending on the interventions. The *residual phase* is manifested through the lower intensity and frequency of positive symptoms (frequently due to medical intervention) though there continues to be impairment due to negative symptoms (social withdrawal, avolition, and depression, etc.). This phase can be evident for months at a time but may also be demonstrated throughout the course of the individual's life (Kodish & McClellan, 2008).

Symptomatology observed in school settings

Schizophrenia is among the least understood psychiatric disorders among school personnel, yet also among the most disabling mental disorders. Schizophrenia is a type of "Emotional Disturbance" (ED) based on the latest definitions of disabilities of the Individuals with Disabilities Education Improvement Act-IDEIA (2004). The onset of EOS is an insidious process usually with a prodromal phase preceding the symptoms, yet with about 25% of cases assuming an acute onset. However, it should be noted that there are different illness development trajectories based on the aforementioned complicated interaction between genetic, biological, and environmental factors. The following is a case that illustrates the symptom development.

Case study

John had an unremarkable childhood apart from being somewhat shy. According to his parents, he was "too good" a child. At age 15, he began withdrawing from family members and friends. This solitary teenager spent hours in his room. He was not paying attention in classes. At age 17, he was seen by a doctor for "anxiety attack" and the doctor noted in John a strange "flatness of affect." John was prescribed an antidepressant. John graduated from high school and he went on to college where he drifted aimlessly for two years, then dropped out. John attempted suicide at age 20 and became further withdrawn. John told his psychiatrist about his obsession with an actress. He wrote: "My mind is on the breaking point the whole time." At age 21, he wrote to the "girlfriend" he was thinking of kidnapping her, hijacking a plane, and asking to be installed in the White House. This letter was not mailed. A few hours later after he wrote the letter, he was attempting to assassinate President Reagan to impress his "girlfriend." This John is John Hinckley, who was later found not guilty due to insanity and is still held in a psychiatric hospital, diagnosed as having schizophrenia.

John's case, along with many other research findings, demonstrates a prodromal/clinical high risk phase which occurs before the onset of psychotic symptoms—a functional decline marked by social withdrawal, deterioration in school performance, decreased ability to perform daily activities, changes in affect and mood, hostility and aggression, and disorganized and/or unusual behavior. Symptoms demonstrated by children and youth with EOS are consistent with adult populations and can take two major forms—positive symptoms and negative symptoms. Positive signs and symptoms refer to hallucinations and delusions. Auditory hallucinations were found to be the most frequent positive symptoms especially in young patients with schizophrenia (childhood onset schizophrenia). In comparison to adult schizophrenic patients, the hallucination themes for children with EOS are vaguer and the conversing and commenting voices may be less frequent. Visual and tactile hallucinations are even less common in children and adolescents (Masi, Mucci, & Pari, 2006). Delusion themes are usually related to childhood themes, such as monsters under the bed or monsters controlling one's voices, persecutory, somatic complaints, reference (the character on TV or in music talks to me), grandiose ("I can stop the global warming if I focus my mind"), or religious (claiming to have special supernatural power, e.g. Russell, 1994). Individuals with disorganized speech in the form of formal thought disorder present incoherent/incomprehensible speech, poverty of content (e.g. speech that lacks meaning), or illogical thinking (APA, 2000).

Negative symptoms include flattened affect, alogia (e.g. poverty of speech) and avolition (e.g. lack of desire, drive, or motivation, APA, 2000). One key distinction among others between true negative symptoms and depressive symptoms is that depressive symptoms "typically experience an intensely painful affect, whereas those with schizophrenia have a diminution or emptiness of affect" (APA, 2000, p. 301). Besides positive and negative symptoms, behavioral problems and dysphoria are often observed among school-age children and adolescents (Masi et al., 2006). Among the four main symptom categories (positive, negative, behavioral, and dysphoria), negative symptoms have been found to be highly predictive of the diagnosis of schizophrenia in children and adolescents, while the other three categories also occur in other disorders (Masi et al., 2006).

One notable symptom that educators and school mental health professionals should watch for in students who are experiencing schizophrenia symptoms is marked deterioration of social and role functioning, such as progressive social withdrawal and decline of school grades, poor self-care, and neurocognitive decline (such as attention, memory, and information processing speed). In addition, these students may have been receiving special education services before being diagnosed as having schizophrenia due to language delays, motor abnormalities, emotional disturbances, learning disabilities, and attention related difficulties (Nicolson, Lenane, Singaracharlu, & Rapoport, 2000). In fact, cognitive dysfunction has been regarded as a hallmark feature of schizophrenia (the prototypical primary psychotic disorder) from the time of its earliest conceptualizations by Kraepelin (1919) and Bleuler (1950).

A meta-analysis of follow-back studies of childhood IQ in adults with schizophrenia (based on premorbid assessments conducted in mid-childhood to adolescence) documented reliable medium size deficits in premorbid IQ (Cohen $d = -0.54$; Woodberry et al., 2008), well before the onset of any diagnosable symptoms of the illness and likely reflecting an important early neurodevelopmental abnormality. A meta-analysis on the relationship of age of onset and cognition in schizophrenia indicates that individuals with EOS have larger cognitive deficits than those with first-episode schizophrenia (within the first five years of being diagnosed as having schizophrenia) in the areas of arithmetic, executive function, full-scale IQ, psychomotor speed of processing, and verbal memory (Rajji, Ismail,

& Mulsant, 2009). Prevalence rates of schizophrenia among individuals with learning disabilities are estimated at 3%, which is three times the rate within the general population, which makes diagnosis a challenge as a result of both comprehension and expression of communication problems (Doody, Johnstone, Sanderson, Owens, & Muir, 1998; Reid, 1989; Turner, 1989). Additionally, in a multi-site study, more than a quarter of students with EOS had repeated a grade (Frazier et al., 2007).

Therefore, the symptoms of schizophrenia in school-age children and adolescents are manifested in the areas of social, emotional, behavioral, and academic functioning. They can be related to truncated educational achievement, poor overall life outcome, and financial burden to the schools, families, and society in general. The President's New Freedom Commission (2003) called for a transformation in the delivery of mental health services in the United States. The role of school mental health services was highlighted in the commission's report. School mental health professionals are uniquely positioned to play a central role in improving early identification, early referral, and access to specialized mental health services, and in enhancing capacity for mental health promotion and prevention programming (Nastasi, Varjas, Bernstein, & Pluymert, 1997).

Designing and Monitoring Multi-tiered Interventions for the School Setting

Effective interventions for EOS must be global and all-encompassing, just as the symptoms of EOS fully encompass a young person's life (Sikich, 2005). With the impoverished social networks and need for social contact associated with the symptoms of EOS, supportive strategies demonstrated by all school personnel can help bring the student back into the social world (Davidson, Stayner, & Haglund, 1998). In the school setting, children and adolescents with EOS may be especially responsive to the nonspecific elements of a supportive therapeutic relationship, particularly if the professionals are accessible to them in their daily life. Appropriately targeting interventions for students with EOS involves consideration of the developmental stage of the child, the specific phase of the disorder, and the coordination of treatment with various professionals on the child's team— including doctors, family members, and educators.

In recent years, there has been considerable advancement in the interventions for individuals with schizophrenia, especially in the area of pharmacology. It is important to note that individuals with schizophrenia receiving both pharmacological and psycho-educational interventions demonstrated significantly improved functioning in areas related to their schizophrenic symptoms, psychosocial functioning, and quality of life compared to those receiving only pharmacological interventions (Linden, Pyrkosch, & Hundemer, 2008). A thorough review of the intervention literature conducted by the full name (NIMH)-sponsored Schizophrenia Patient Outcomes Research Team (PORT) identified twenty state-of-the-art interventions for adult populations (Lehman et al., 2004). Of the twenty recommended interventions, six of them were psychosocial strategies that positively affected relapse rates, symptoms, and/or social impairments, while the remaining fourteen focused on pharmacological interventions (which are beyond the scope of this chapter). Moreover, treatments that are effective with adults may be effective in children when adapted to address their development needs, as EOS has been found to be continuous with adult-onset schizophrenia (American Academy of Child and Adolescent Psychiatry, 2001). Thus, we will briefly describe the six psychosocial interventions identified by the Schizophrenia PORT, present modifications that address the developmental needs of children and adolescents, and build on the review of childhood-focused treatments as discussed in Asarnow et al. (2004). Each of these interventions will be examined within the three-tiered model of prevention and intervention; however, unlike other disorders, the implementation and targeting of these interventions may vary considerably based on the severity of symptoms, phase of illness, and need for intensive supports. As such, we will discuss how each intervention can be integrated into the supports of the classroom and school setting. These interventions are examined more extensively by Li, Pearrow, and Jimerson (2010).

Cognitive-Behavioral Therapy

Cognitive Behavioral Therapy (CBT) focuses on the identification of target symptoms, strategies to cope with these symptoms, interpretations of reality, affect regulation, and recognition of sources and signs of stress (Asarnow et al., 2004; Lehman et al., 2004). CBT "attempts to reduce certain symptoms and enhance functioning by entering into a dialogue that provides rational alternative perspectives to the patient's experiences, with the goal of helping him or her to better understand and cope with issues and experiences that are especially problematic for the individual" (Shean, 2009, p. 312). It also encourages individuals to re-appraise delusional beliefs in order to reduce distress and more effectively manage stressful environments. CBT treatment appears to be the most effective in the early course of the disorder and is most appropriate for older children and adolescents with higher cognitive functioning and capacities. Outcomes are most noteworthy for those demonstrating persistent, or residual, symptoms, and these interventions do not provide the same outcomes for those who are in the acute phase of illness (Dickerson, 2000; Dilk & Bond, 1996).

Through active collaboration, the school mental health professionals can work intensively (Tier III) with the student as they create a shared understanding of the illness and manifestations of the disorder as demonstrated in the school environment. These individualized meetings can offer supportive feedback about perceptions and gently confront illogical thoughts and speech. In addition, the school mental health professionals can provide encouragement to focus on the reality of the external world, and support the development of coping strategies for the stressful aspects of the school day. These skills would primarily be the focus of more intensive sessions; yet within the classroom, teachers can support the development of these skills by maintaining communication regarding the student's functioning, both academically and socially, and allow increased access to support services during periods of stress. Moreover, the classroom setting provides opportunities for students with EOS to learn from and engage with normal developing peers and practice strategies that enhance their coping skills.

Skills Training

Skills deficits in numerous domains often exist due to the child's inability to develop or acquire new skills during the early stages of the disorder. The focus of skills training targets specify deficit areas and the learning of age-appropriate skills needed to function in the social environment. Areas typically emphasized include communication skills, social skills, and basic self-care and daily living skills (AACAP, 2001; Asarnow et al., 2004; Gunther & Lyon, 2004). Sikich (2005) also recommends that social skills training should focus on nonverbal behavior such as eye contact, posture, facial expression, tone, and volume of speech. The most effective skills training groups include behaviorally based instruction that includes modeling, corrective feedback, and the use of contingent social reinforcements and reward systems (Dulmus & Smith, 2000).

Schools are ideal settings for the practice and generalization of new social and organizational skills. The acquisition of new skills may occur in a small group setting (Tier II) with targeted strategies to support generalization to other settings (Tier I), including the classroom, lunch room, and transition times. These strategies may be integrated into a study skills period that assists with organization with agenda books and/or calendars, skill development and daily check-ins on hygiene and reality orientation, and social skills lessons that focus on making and keeping friends and create a supportive peer group. Classroom teachers enhance student success by breaking down large assignments, allowing students to complete assignments in a small group, modifying assignments, and encouraging students to use organization and social supports.

Token Economy Interventions

Token economy systems, based on social learning theory, are comprehensive behavioral programs that provide positive reinforcements, in the form of tokens or points, for displaying targeted behaviors and have proven to be effective when applied to the school setting targeting academic and social skill development (Matson & Boisjoli, 2009). With a token economy program, tokens are used to increase motivation by providing reinforcement for the performance of specified target behaviors, and may be later exchanged for individually selected reinforcers (Shean, 2009). The Schizophrenia PORT recognized that a token economy system demonstrated efficacy as it establishes clear expectations and consequences for behaviors, particularly when implemented in a controlled setting (Lehman et al., 2004). Token economy systems have demonstrated improvements on behavior such as interpersonal skills, cooperation and self-care, and reduced inappropriate behavior such as rocking; however, they do not decrease bizarre cognitions or emotional behaviors such as crying or screaming (Paul & Lentz, 1977).

The use of a token economy system can be fully implemented into any general classroom or school setting (Tier I) when there is consistency among staff and reinforcements are positive, immediate, and specific (Dickerson, Tenhula, & Green-Paden, 2005). There is a specific need, however, to allow for the intensity and severity of the disorder, as a student in the acute phase (e.g. actively psychotic) may not be fully responsive to behavioral interventions. Token economy systems explicitly clarify expectations of academic and social behaviors and build reinforcers for the student when targeted goals are met. Goals may include issues such as self-care, smooth transitions, assignment completion, participation in class discussions, or collaborative engagement with peer. The design of contingency plans and reinforcement schedules would occur as a Tier III strategy though full implementation would include an entire school day throughout the school setting.

Supported Employment and Education

The Schizophrenia PORT recommended supported employment that focused on individualized job development, ongoing job support, and the integration of vocational and mental health services (Lehman et al., 2004). The "job" of young people is school. These supports will vary based on the needs of student and the phase of the illness. For example, one author worked with a 15-year-old boy who demonstrated high average to superior skills on achievement tests and was very successful academically, when he was stable. However, during acute phases, he clearly demonstrated the need for organizational, social, and ancillary support services. Although the *Individuals with Disabilities Education Improvement Act* (IDEIA, 2004) clearly stipulates eligibility for special education services under "emotional disturbance" for "students who are schizophrenic," youth with high premorbid functioning may still function adequately academically, especially with appropriate pharmacological and psychosocial treatment. For example, in a multi-site national study of children and adolescents with EOS, 51% continued to be educated in the regular education setting and roughly one-third were educated in resource rooms or self-contained special education classrooms (Frazier et al., 2007).

For a student who has obtained an EOS diagnosis, there is a range of academic and behavioral supports, accommodations, and modifications that may be made available. Accommodations may support behaviors such as assignment completion and attendance, where flexibility is critical, or being allowed to attend the same class twice during the day to make certain that the material is mastered. Supports can include allowing the student to use gum or have water, as dryness of mouth can be a medication side effect, partnering the student with a peer, or being allowed to leave class early to ease the transition between classes. Other modifications include being allowed to take exams in a quiet room or eat lunch in a smaller setting. There are a range of strategies to offer the three-tiers of support for students with EOS as they manage the school environment, and additional information and examples of these interventions can be found in Li et al. (2010).

Assertive Community Treatment and Wrap-Around Services

The efficacy of Assertive Community Treatment has been demonstrated with randomized trials (Burns & Santos, 1995). This treatment model provides comprehensive services to address the needs of adults with severe mental illnesses that have not been well met with traditional approaches. In many ways, there are similarities to the System of Care movement that develops comprehensive, coordinated, and community-based services and supports for children and adolescents with serious and profound mental illness (Kendziora, Bruns, Osher, Pacchiano, & Mejia, 2001). The "wrap–around" support for individual youth using this System of Care model maintains a strength-based approach that takes advantage of community-based and natural resources. Wraparound services are primarily initiated through mental health or child welfare systems; nonetheless, they can result in improved outcomes in school performance (Eber, Sugai, Smith, & Scott, 2002). In a five site study of youth engaging in Wraparound services, significant improvements were demonstrated in several areas of school functioning, including grades and access to support services (Taub & Pearrow, 2007).

School mental health professionals are appropriate liaisons to these teams given the range and depth of needs of students with EOS. By providing the team with information about the academic and social performance in the school environment, school mental health professionals can help identify early indicators of difficulty (e.g. limited frustration tolerance or increased anxiety) as well as stay abreast of changes in medical and community-based treatments. Classroom teachers can support these interventions by maintaining ongoing communication with other school providers regarding changes in academic or social behaviors, concerns of performance in the classroom, or reactions to changes in medications.

Family Interventions

Even for adults with schizophrenia, family interventions greatly impact functional outcomes. According to a meta-analytic study, family therapy significantly prevented psychotic relapses and readmissions to psychiatric hospitals, reduced family burden, and improved treatment adherence (Pillings et al., 2002). Family involvement and intervention become particularly critical when treating children with EOS as they most likely reside with their family and are dependent upon them for support and access to treatment (Asarnow et al., 2004). Family interventions have demonstrated improved family problem-solving and enhanced psychosocial functioning, which may be critical since parents of children with EOS experience greater levels of social isolation, introversion, suspiciousness, and hostility (Hogarty, 2002; Nicholson et al., 2000). Elements of effective family intervention programs have been identified by Goldstein and Miklowitz (1995) to include engaging the family with a "no-fault atmosphere," educating them about the etiology, prognosis, and treatment for schizophrenia, and strategies for coping with the disorder. They also focus on strategies to improve communication, problem-solving, and crisis intervention.

School mental health professionals can assist families by creating a welcoming environment and connecting those in need with community providers and resources. Classroom teachers can support family interventions by connecting and collaborating with them as they learn new strategies to understand and support their children with EOS. Schools can also examine their success at engaging families by monitoring attendance at family programs and gathering feedback from families about their support services and responses to needs.

School-based Prevention Programs

Thus far, the interventions outlined have been those identified by the Schizophrenia PORT. Given the unique setting of schools, which can proactively address student needs, they are also positioned to reduce the risk of stigma by maximizing resources and providing services to large groups of children (Macklem, 2011). School-wide intervention programs, conceptualized through a public health orientation, involve peers, teachers, families, community members, and have been shown to produce positive outcomes even for the most vulnerable youth (Power, Mautone, & Ginsburg-Block, 2010). The impact of stigma and discrimination can have profound implications for youth in development as they struggle with mental illness, and schools can address these issues and educate youth with the facts about mental illness. *The Science of Mental Illness* curriculum was sponsored by the National Institutes of Health (NIH) Office of Science Education and the NIMH to introduce middle schools students to *the biological basis of mental illness*. The modules address symptoms, causes, and treatments for areas such as AD/HD, depression, and schizophrenia. An evaluation of this program indicated significant improvement in knowledge and attitudes regarding mental illness, and this program was most effective in improving attitudes for those who initially indicated more negative attitudes (Watson et al., 2004). Thus, schools have a unique opportunity to educate all students about mental illness with the hope of reducing stigma and discrimination for those with mental illness.

Progress Monitoring of Interventions

Given the dearth of interventions that have been studied using randomized control testing for students with EOS, creative strategies are needed by school professionals. Thus, interventions that are flexible and responsive to the unique needs of each student will need to be designed, implemented, and monitored for effectiveness. Functional behavioral assessments and behavior intervention plans, with ongoing progress monitoring, can serve as the basis for creating successful school experiences for students with EOS, and when conducted in a variety of school settings (e.g. classroom, lunchroom, and hallways) can identify academic areas and social situations where the student demonstrates competencies and struggles (Kodish & McClellan, 2008; Li et al., 2010; O'Neill et al., 1997). These observations can determine functional abilities and serve as the foundation for educational planning. For example, a student with EOS may perform adequately in a lecture-based course, such as a math class with restricted opportunities for social interactions and clear, straightforward answers. This same student may present with more difficulties in a class such as health, where there are frequent class discussions that focus on areas of personal difficulty (e.g. hygiene and social relationships).

Moreover, given the dynamic nature of the illness, it is important to obtain multiple data points, especially when the EOS is emerging or in various phases (Wozniak, White, & Schulz, 2005). Before a full psychotic episode, which looms throughout the prodromal phase, the student may or may not be targeted for interventions. In the acute phase of the illness, however, immediate interventions may be needed which may allow for only limited baseline data collection in the school setting as a more restrictive environment may be temporarily needed. As the student becomes more stable and enters into the recovery phase, then a return to normal daily activities – such as school – may commence. In this phase, the task would primarily focus on monitoring the student's transition into the environment and his or her capacity to manage the stress associated with the school environment. Once in the maintenance, or residual, phase, then interventions and strategies would support the student in the least restrictive environment meeting the academic and social demands of the school setting.

Information gathered from academic and social observations serve as the foundation for the functional analysis of behavioral difficulties. Given the broad range of symptoms demonstrated through the manifestation of this disorder, targeted interventions can be designed that address the unique needs of the student. As an example, it may be evident that a student with EOS has consistently been skipping class following lunch. Observations indicate that stress around social interaction and engagement is highly problematic for this student, and that this period of time has only minimal supervision and support. A simple strategy of allowing the student to eat lunch in a quiet location with a small, supportive peer group may resolve this problem. Using a single case design, hypotheses can be tested and interventions can target specific problem behaviors, and moreover, the effectiveness of interventions can be monitored. Whichever interventions or strategies are implemented to support the student as he or she masters the tasks of school, data on their effectiveness with each student needs ongoing monitoring and adjusting to respond to his or her unique needs.

Discussion and Recommendations

School professionals play an important role in early identification of children with EOS, as well as providing support and modifications in the school context that will help to facilitate the development of children with EOS. In addition, school professionals can assist by directing families toward effective interventions. Given the range of misperceptions of causes and treatments, it is important that these professionals maintain accurate and scientifically-based information to support families as they navigate the complex medical, mental health, and education systems.

The optimal treatment for EOS is multi-modal. Each of the previously reviewed treatment approaches has benefits for a young person with EOS, and it is important to incorporate the various strategies to address the different symptoms and functional impairments faced by the child and family. The first line of treatment is usually pharmacological because of the debilitating effects of psychotic symptoms. Although there is research to show that neuroleptics and anti-psychotics are less effective with children than with adults, there is also evidence to show that these drugs are effective in reducing psychotic symptoms for some children with EOS. To date, however, recovery from negative symptoms remains elusive (Erhart et al., 2006).

As discussed in this chapter, cognitive-behavioral therapy is the method of psychotherapy that has been shown to be the most effective in treating adults with schizophrenia. This type of intervention involves a close working relationship between the patient and therapist and active participation of the youth. Unfortunately, this therapy is restricted to older children and adolescents with higher cognitive functioning and capacities because of the cognitive capabilities required to benefit from the therapy. A younger child would most likely not be able to understand and focus on the thoughts, emotions and behaviors associated with symptoms of the disorder, nor the triggers, consequences, and responses to symptoms. Therefore, when the child with EOS is cognitively advanced enough, CBT is highly recommended to help him or her devise strategies to best cope with their symptoms, improve his or her capacity to test reality, monitor behavior, and alter dysfunctional beliefs and attributions.

Because EOS leads to a disruption of global functioning, psycho-educational treatment with skills training focusing on communication skills, social skills, and daily life skills are essential components of treatment (AACAP, 2001; Asarnow et al., 2004; Gonthier & Lyon, 2004; Lehman et al., 2004). Skills training should be sensitive to the developmental level of the child and targeted to the identified areas of impairment for the child with EOS, such as learning Conversational skills, basic self-care skills, and money management skills.

Incorporating the family into the treatment process is very beneficial for the youth with EOS because the family learns how to better interact with the child or adolescent, anticipate and deal with psychotic and negative symptoms, and provide emotional and psychological support for the child. Therefore, a multi-modal treatment package must include a family treatment component if it is to be effective in reducing symptomatology. Family therapy should be targeted at reducing the environmental stressors brought on by the disorder so as to reduce the likelihood of relapse (Clark & Lewis, 1998). Strategies involved in family therapy may include family behavioral management strategies (including lecture, role playing, modeling, rehearsal, and homework) aimed at understanding the nature of the disorder, developing coping strategies, and strengthening problem solving skills and basic communication skills.

Systemic interventions, through interagency collaboration such as wraparound services, with coordinated services can implement cohesive plans to support youth with schizophrenia to stay in the home and community (Kendziora et al., 2001). However, depending upon the severity of the disorder, placement of the child outside of the family home, especially during the acute phase of the disorder, may be necessary. In all cases, the least restrictive setting ensuring optimal treatment effectiveness should be considered. See Li and colleagues (2010) for a thorough discussion of the etiology, epidemiology, assessment, and treatment of EOS, with particular focus on school-based professionals.

Interventions that target academic and social development in the school setting can help mitigate stress during various phases of the illness. School personnel, particularly classroom teachers, can provide a range of supported educational practices, academic accommodations, and optimal treatment by using token economy systems. Not only can schools support the individual with EOS in this setting, they also have the opportunity to educate the peer group to reduce stigma and discrimination.

References

American Academy of Child and Adolescent Psychiatry (2001). Practice parameter for the assessment and treatment of children and adolescents with schizophrenia, *Journal of the American Academy of Child and Adolescent Psychiatry, 40,* 5s–23s.

American Psychiatric Association (2000). *Diagnostic and statistical manual of mental disorders (DSM-IV-TR)*. Washington, D.C.: American Psychiatric Association.

Andreasen, N. C. (2000). Schizophrenia: The fundamental questions. *Brain Research Reviews, 31,* 106–12. doi:10.1016/S0165-0173(99)00027-2

Asarnow, J. R., & Asarnow, R. F. (2003). Childhood-onset schizophrenia. In E. J. Mash & R. A. Barkley (eds), *Developmental psychopathology* (2nd ed., pp. 455–85). New York: The Guilford Press.

Asarnow, J. R., Thompson, M. C., & McGrath, E. P. (2004). Annotation: Childhood-onset schizophrenia: Clinical and treatment issues. *Journal of Child Psychology and Psychiatry, 45,* 180–94. doi:10.1111/j.1469-7610.2004.00213.x

Bleuler, E. (1950). *Dementia praecox or the group of schizophrenias*. Oxford, England: International Universities Press.

Burns, B. J., & Santos, A. B. (1995). Assertive community treatment: An update of randomized trials. *Psychiatric Services, 46,* 669–75.

Clark, A. F., & Lewis, S. W. (1998). Practitioner review: Treatment of schizophrenia in childhood and adolescence, *Journal of Child Psychology and Psychiatry, 39,* 1071–81. doi:10.1111/1469-7610.00412

Cornblatt, B., Lencz, T., & Kane, J. M. (2001). Treatment of schizophrenia prodrome: Is it presently ethical? *Schizophrenia Research, 51,* 31–8. doi:10.1016/S0920-9964(01)00236-5

Davidson, L., Stayner, D., & Haglund, K. E. (1998). Phenomological perspectives on the social functioning of people with schizophrenia. In K. T. Mueser & N. Tarrier (eds), *Handbook of social functioning in schizophrenia* (pp. 97–120). Needham Heights, MA: Allyn and Bacon.

Dickerson, F. B. (2000). Cognitive behavioral psychotherapy for schizophrenia: A review of recent empirical studies. *Schizophrenia Research, 16*, 71–90. doi:10.1016/S0920-9964(99)00153-X

Dickerson, F. B., Tenhula, W. N., & Green-Paden, L. D. (2005). The token economy for schizophrenia: Review of the literature and recommendations for future research. *Schizophrenia Research, 75*, 405–16. doi:10.1016/j.schres.2004.08.026

Dilk, M. N., & Bond, G. R. (1996). Meta-analytic evaluation of skills training research for individuals with severe mental illness: Review of recent studies. *Journal of Consulting and Clinical Psychology, 64*, 1337–46. doi:10.1037/0022-006X.64.6.1337

Doody, G. A., Johnstone, E. C., Sanderson, T. L., Owens D. G., & Muir W. J. (1998). 'Pfropfschizophrenie' revisited: Schizophrenia in people with mild learning disability. *British Journal of Psychiatry, 173*, 145–53. doi:10.1192/bjp.173.2.145

Dulmus, C. N., & Smyth, N. J. (2000). Early-onset schizophrenia: A literature review of empirically based interventions. *Child and Adolescent Social Work Journal, 17*, 55–69. doi:10.1023/A:1007567609909

Eber, L., Sugai, G., Smith, C. R., & Scott, T. M. (2002). Wraparound and positive behavioral interventions and supports in the schools. *Journal of Emotional and Behavioral Disorders, 10*, 171–80. doi:10.1177/10634266020100030501

Erhart, S. M., Marder, S. R., & Carpenter, W. T. (2006). Treatment of schizophrenia negative symptoms: Future prospects. *Schizophrenia Bulletin, 32*, 234–7. doi:10.1093/schbul/sbj055

Frazier, F. A., McClellan, J., Findling, R. L., Vitiello, B., Anderson, R., Zablotsky, B., .. Sikich, L. (2007). Treatment of early-onset schizophrenia spectrum disorders (TEOSS): Demographic and clinical characteristics. *Journal of American Academy of Child and Adolescent Psychiatry, 46*, 979–88. doi:10.1097/chi.0b013e31807083fd

Gonthier, M., & Lyon, M. A. (2004). Childhood-onset schizophrenia: An overview. *Psychology in the Schools, 41*, 803–11. doi:10.1002/pits.20013

Hafner, H., & Maurer, K. (2006). Early detection of schizophrenia: Current evidence and future perspectives. *World Psychiatry, 5*, 130–8.

Hogarty, G. E. (2002). Personal therapy: A practical psychotherapy for stabilization of schizophrenia. In S. G. Hoffman & M. C. Tompson (eds), *Treating chronic and severe mental disorders: a handbook of empirically-supported interventions* (pp. 53–68). New York: The Guilford Press.

Goldstein, M. J. & Miklowitz, D. J. (1995). The effectiveness of psychoeducational family therapy in the treatment of schizophrenic disorders. *Journal of Marital and Family Therapy, 21*, 361–76. doi:10.1111/j.1752-0606.1995.tb00171.x

Kendziora, K., Bruns, E., Osher, D., Pacchiano, D., & Mejia, B. (2001). *Systems of care: Promising practices in children's mental health, 2001 Series, Volume 1.* Washington, D.C.: Center for Effective Collaboration and Practice, American Institutes for Research.

Kodish, I., & McClellan, J. (2008). Early-onset schizophrenia. In M. Hersen & D.

Reitman (eds), *Handbook of psychological assessment, case conceptualization, and treatment, Vol. 2: Children and adolescents* (pp. 405–43). Hoboken, NJ: John Wiley & Sons Inc.

Kraepelin, E. (1919). *Dementia praecox and paraphrenia* (Barclay RM, translator). (8th ed.) Edinburg: S. Livingston.

Kumra, S., & Schulz, S. C. (2008). Editorial: Research progress in Early-Onset Schizophrenia. *Schizophrenia Bulletin, 34*, 15–17. doi:10.1093/schbul/sbm123

Lehman, A. F., Kreyenbuhl, J., Buchanan, R. W., Dickerson, F. B., Dixon, L. B., Goldberg, R., ... Steinwachs, D. M. (2004). The Schizophrenia Patient Outcomes Research Team (PORT): Updated treatment recommendations 2003. *Schizophrenia Bulletin, 30*, 193–217.

Li, H., Pearrow, M., & Jimerson, S. (2010). *Identifying, assessing, and treating early onset schizophrenia in the schools.* New York: Springer.

Linden, M., Pyrkosch, L., & Hundemer, H. (2008). Frequency and effects of psychosocial interventions additional to olanzapine treatment in routine care of schizophrenic patients. *Social Psychiatry and Psychiatric Epidemiology, 43*, 373–9. doi:10.1007/s00127-008-0318-0

Macklem, G. (2011). *Evidence-based school mental health services: Affect education, emotion regulation training, and cognitive behavioral therapy.* New York: Springer.

Masi, G., Mucci, M., & Pari, C. (2006). Children with schizophrenia; Clinical picture and pharmacological treatment. *Central Nerves System Drugs, 20*, 841–66

Matson, J. L., & Boisjoli, J. A. (2009). The token economy for children with intellectual disability and/or autism: A review. *Research in Developmental Disabilities, 30*, 240–8. doi:10.1016/j.ridd.2008.04.001

McClellan, J., & Werry, J. (2001). Practice parameters for the assessment and treatment of children and adolescents with schizophrenia. *Journal of the American Academy of Child and Adolescent Psychiatry, 40*, 4S–23S. doi:10.1097/00004583-200107001-00002

Mueser, K. T., & McGurk, S. R. (2004). Schizophrenia. *The Lancet, 363*, 2063–72. doi:10.1016/S0140-6736(04)16458-1

Nastasi, B. K., Varjas, V., Bernstein, R., & Pluymert, K. (1997). *Exemplary mental health programs: School psychologists as mental health service providers.* Bethesda, MD: NASP.

Nicholson, R., Lenane, M., Hamburger, S. D., Fernandez, T., Bedwell, J., & Rapoport, J. L. (2000). Lessons from childhood-onset schizophrenia. *Brain Research Reviews, 31*, 147–56. doi:10.1016/S0165-0173(99)00032-6

Nicholson, R., Lenane, M., Singaracharlu, S., & Rapoport, J. L. (2000). Premorbid speech and language impairments in childhood-onset schizophrenia : Association with risk factors. *American Journal of Psychiatry, 157*, 794-800. doi:10.1176/appi.ajp.157.5.794

O'Neill, R. E., Horner, R. H., Albin, R. W., Sprague, J. R., Storey, K., & Newton, J. S. (1997). *Functional assessment and program development for problem behavior: A practical handbook* (2nd ed.). Pacific Grove, CA: Brooks/Cole.

Paul, G. L., & Lentz, R. J. (1977). *Psychosocial treatment of chronic mental patients: Milieu versus social learning programs.* Cambridge, Massachusetts: Harvard University Press.

Pilling, S., Bebbington, P. Kuipers, E., Garety, P., Geddes, J., Orbach, G., ... Morgan, C. (2002). Psychological treatments in schizophrenia: II. Meta-analyses of randomized controlled trials of social skills training and cognitive remediation. *Psychological Medicine, 32,* 783–91. doi:10.1017/S0033291702005640

Power, T. J., Mautone, J. A., & Ginsburg-Block, M. (2010). Training school psychologists for prevention and intervention in a three-tiered model. In M.R. Shinn & H.M. Walker (eds), *Interventions for achievement and behavior problems in a three-tiered model including RTI* (pp. 151–73). Bethesda, MD: NASP Publications.

President's New Freedom Commission on Mental Health. (2003). *Remarks by President Bush in announcing the New Freedom Commission on Mental Health.* Accessed on June 1st, 2008 from http://govinfo.library.unt.edu/mentalhealthcommission/address.html

Rajji, T. K., Ismail, Z., & Mulsant, B. H. (2009). Age at onset and cognition in schizophrenia: Meta-analysis. *The British Journal of Psychiatry, 195,* 286–93. doi:10.1192/bjp.bp.108.060723

Reid, A. (1989). Schizophrenia in mental retardation: Clinical features. *Research in Developmental Disabilities, 10,* 241–9. doi:10.1016/0891-4222(89)90013-9

Remschmidt, H. (2002). Early-onset schizophrenia as a progressive-deteriorating developmental disorder: Evidence from child psychiatry. *Journal of Neural Transmission, 109,* 101–17. doi:10.1007/s702-002-8240-3

Russell, T. T. (1994). The clinical presentation of childhood onset schizophrenia. *Schizophrenia Bulletin, 20,* 631–46.

Sameroff, A. J. (2000). Dialectical processes in developmental psychopathology. In A. J. Sameroff, M. Lewis, & S. M. Miller (eds), *Handbook of developmental psychopathology* (2nd ed., pp. 23–40). New York, NY: Kluwer Academic/Plenum.

—(ed.). (2009). *The transactional model of development: How children and contexts shape each other.* Washington, D.C.: American Psychological Association.

Shean, G. D. (2009). Evidence-based psychosocial practices and recovery from schizophrenia. *Psychiatry, 72,* 307–20. doi:10.1521/psyc.2009.72.4.307

Sikich, L. (2005). Individual psychotherapy and school interventions for psychotic youth. In R. L. Findling & S. C. Schulz (eds), *Juvenile-onset schizophrenia: assessment, neurobiology, and treatment* (pp. 257–87). Baltimore, MD: John Hopkins Press.

Tandon, R., Nasrallah, H. A., & Keshavan, M. S. (2009). Schizophrenia, "just the facts" 4. Clinical features and conceptualization. *Schizophrenia Research, 110,* 1–23. doi:10.1016/j.schres.2009.03.005

Taub, J., & Pearrow, M. (2007). School functioning for children enrolled in community based wraparound services. In C. Newman, C. J. Liberton, K. Kutash & R. Friedman, (eds), *The 19th Annual Research Conference Proceedings: a system of care for children's mental health: expanding the research base* (pp. 323–6). Tampa: University of South Florida, Louis de la Parte Florida Mental Health Institute, Research and Training Center for Children's Mental Health.

Turner, T. H. (1989). Schizophrenia and mental handicap: A historical review with implications for further research. *Psychological medicine, 19*, 301–14. doi:10.1017/S0033291700012344

Watson, A. C., Otey, E., Westbrook, A. L., Gardner, A. L., Lamb, T. A., Corrigan, P. W., & Fenton, W. S. (2004). Changing middle schoolers' attitudes about mental illness through education. *Schizophrenia Bulletin, 30*, 563–72.

Woodberry, K. A., Giuliano, A. J., & Seidman, L. J. (2008). Premorbid IQ in schizophrenia: A meta-analytic review. *American Journal of Psychiatry*, AiA 1–9.

Woods, S. W., Miller, T. J., & McGlashan, T. H. (2001b). The prodromal patient: Both symptomatic and at risk. *CNS Spectrums, 6*, 223–32.

Wozniak, J. R., White, T., & Schulz, S. C. (2005). Neuropsychological factors in early-onset schizophrenia. In R. L. Findling & S. C. Schulz (eds), *Juvenile-onset schizophrenia: assessment, neurobiology, and treatment.* (pp. 125–7). Baltimore, MD: The John Hopkins University Press.

Yung, A. R., & McGorry, P. D. (1996). The initial prodrome in psychosis: Descriptive and qualitative aspects. *Australian and New Zealand Journal of Psychiatry, 30*, 587–99. doi:10.3109/00048679609062654

Yung, A. R., Phillips, L., Simons, J., Ward, J., Thompson, K., French, P., … McGorry, P. (2006). *Comprehensive assessment of at risk mental states* (CAARMS). Melbourne, Australia: PACE Clinic, Department of Psychiatry, University of Melbourne.

CHAPTER SEVEN

Understanding and Managing Behaviors of Children Diagnosed with Chronic Illnesses

Ara J. Schmitt and
Amanda J. Graham
Duquesne University

Abstract

Classroom teachers perform an invaluable role in the education of children with chronic illnesses. The child's teacher may be the only professional on the medical and school teams to bring detailed knowledge regarding the child's previous educational performance, grade-level psychoeducational expectations, the upcoming curriculum and related challenges, and the current classroom climate including the child's peer relationships. This chapter presents issues to which children with chronic illness must adjust and illustrates the broad continuum of intervention strategies, ranging from positive classroom support to formal re-entry programs, which involve classroom teachers. Pediatric leukemia will be used as an illustrative example of a chronic illness for which teachers will likely be involved in the classroom intervention and progress monitoring of functioning.

Overview

Previous chapters of this book have addressed the classroom implications of distinct psychological disorders, such as depression and Attention-Deficit/Hyperactivity Disorder (AD/HD). The current chapter complements the others in that the psychoeducational implications of *chronic medical conditions* will be reviewed, with pediatric leukemia used as an illustrative disease. The term, chronic illness, refers to a medical condition that lasts from three months to a lifetime (American Academy of Pediatrics, 2011) and may manifest in some degree of limitation to a child's cognitive, academic, and social functioning (Sexson & Madan-Swain, 1993). With up to 18% of school-aged children suffering from a chronic illness (Glaser, Ouimet, & Shaw, 2010), this statistic suggests that in a classroom of twenty-five students, approximately four to five students may have a persistent health condition that manifests in functional limitations. In order to meet the needs of students with chronic illnesses, teachers must possess disease-specific knowledge and skills. Regrettably, teachers often report a lack of disease-specific and child-specific information necessary to provide appropriate instruction (Clay, 2004; Sexson & Maden-Swain, 1993). Given that asthma, diabetes, and cancer are among the most commonly encountered pediatric conditions in the schools (Clay, 2004), teachers should at least have a working knowledge of these conditions. However, many teachers do not report having awareness of these diseases.

Nabors, Little, Akin-Little, and Iobst (2008) recently conducted a study investigating teachers' knowledge of distinct chronic illnesses and confidence in their own ability to meet the needs of students with specific medical conditions. Consistent with previous research, only 34.2% of teachers reported being well informed regarding asthma, 24.4% felt well informed regarding diabetes, and 17.5% indicated being well informed regarding pediatric cancer. Likewise, when asked about their confidence in meeting the academic needs of students with the same medical conditions, only 51.4% of teachers felt very confident in the ability to meet the academic needs of students with asthma, 42.5% felt very confident in meeting the academic needs of students with diabetes, and 32.8% of teachers felt very confident in meeting the academic needs of students with cancer. A similar pattern of results were found when teachers were asked about confidence in meeting the students' social needs. These data are not surprising given that as recently as 2004, 59% of teachers reported no academic training regarding chronic illness in childhood and 64%

reported no such training in their schools positions (Clay, Cortina, Harper, Cocco, & Drotar, 2004).

One aim of this chapter is to provide teachers with practical information regarding chronic illness in childhood, and disease-specific information regarding cancer, as teachers report having a very limited working knowledge of this medical condition. This disease was also selected as it may be used to demonstrate the continuum of intensity of services in the schools that may be required for students with chronic illnesses. As Cunningham and Wodrich (2006) found that providing teachers disease-specific information increased the educators' ability to generate disease-specific accommodations, by focusing on pediatric leukemia, another goal is to help educators address the needs of children with this disease. Finally, we desire to motivate teachers to examine their professional philosophy of educating students with chronic illnesses. In a recent survey of 454 educators, only 43.4% reported feeling at least moderately responsible for meeting the educational needs of students with chronic medical conditions (Clay et al., 2004). Although there are many reasons for this finding, lack of awareness of federal mandates that require educators to take an active role in the education of children with chronic conditions and lack of awareness of the classroom manifestations of chronic illnesses are likely among them.

Mandates to Consider Services for Students with Chronic Illnesses

As data show that educators do not necessarily consider themselves to be responsible for meeting the educational needs of children with chronic illnesses, a general overview seems warranted regarding federal legislation that each require schools to: 1) convene a multidisciplinary team of professionals, including medical professionals, and the student's parents, 2) consider if a student with a chronic illness is eligible for special services, and 3) create a formal plan to meet the educational needs of the sick student as identified by a team of professionals. The primary pieces of legislation include the Individuals with Disabilities Education Act (IDEA; Federal Register, 2006) and Section 504 of the Rehabilitation Act of 1973. These federal regulations require schools to provide a free and appropriate public education (FAPE) to qualifying students with disabilities. As noted by Schmitt, Wodrich, and Lazar (2010), the mere presence of a chronic illness does not automatically qualify a student for special services. Instead, a team of professionals knowledgeable about the student must find that certain eligibility criteria have been met and such services are *necessary* to receive FAPE.

With respect to the IDEA, the eligibility category that directly allows students with chronic illnesses to receive special education services is other health impairment (OHI). The codification of IDEA within the Federal Register (2006) provides a definition of OHI that teams must reference when determining eligibility:

§300.8 (9) Other health impairment means having limited strength, vitality, or alertness, including a heightened alertness to environmental stimuli, that results in limited alertness with respect to the educational environment, that— (i) Is due to chronic or acute health problems such as asthma, attention deficit disorder or attention deficit hyperactivity disorder, diabetes, epilepsy, a heart condition, hemophilia, lead poisoning, leukemia, nephritis, rheumatic fever, sickle cell anemia, and Tourette syndrome; and (ii) Adversely affects a child's educational performance.

For those students found to be eligible for special education services, an individual education program (IEP) is then constructed. Among other components, federal regulations mandate that the IEP must outline student-specific goal and objectives, related services (e.g. speech-language therapy, physical therapy, and occupational therapy) to be provided to the child, and accommodations and modifications necessary for the student to receive FAPE. Important to note is that the definition of related services included in the code makes direct reference to "school health services and school nurse services" as examples of services that may be required for a student with a chronic illness to benefit from the special education outlined in the IEP.

The other piece of legislation that directs schools to consider the educational needs of children with chronic illnesses is Section 504 of the Rehabilitation Act of 1973. This type of planning is often used for students who do not require a significantly modified curriculum and intensive services, but still have needs that warrant agreed upon interventions. This law also requires schools to create a multidisciplinary team of professionals, including medical professionals and the student's parents, to evaluate for suspected disabilities and apply "aides, benefits, and services" that "afford handicapped persons equal opportunity to obtain the same result, to gain the same benefit, or to reach the same level of achievement, in the most integrated setting appropriate to the person's needs" (34 C.F.R. § 104.4 (2)). In order to qualify for a Section 504 Plan, the student must have physical or mental impairment that substantially limits a major life activity, including learning. Germane to this chapter, chronic medical conditions are specifically mentioned in the definition of physical or mental impairment:

34 C.F.R. § 104.3(j)(2)(i) *Physical or mental impairment means* (A) any physiological disorder or condition, cosmetic disfigurement, or anatomical loss affecting one or more of the following body systems:

neurological; musculoskeletal; special sense organs; respiratory, including speech organs; cardiovascular; reproductive, digestive, genito-urinary; hemic and lymphatic; skin; and endocrine; or (B) any mental or psychological disorder, such as mental retardation, organic brain syndrome, emotional or mental illness, and specific learning disabilities.

In brief, federal regulations clearly mandate that schools provide formal services to students with chronic illnesses, provided that a sufficient level of functional impairment is present and services are required to receive a reasonable education. Legislation also requires the direct participation of classroom teachers when determining eligibility for specialized services and when developing an IEP or Section 504 Plan. Given these facts and teachers' self-reported lack of knowledge of the classroom manifestations of chronic illnesses, the following sections include a review of issues related to adapting to a chronic illness at school, as well as classroom interventions tied to each.

Adaptation to a Chronic Illness at School

Within the chronic illness literature, the term adaptation has been broadly characterized as general adjustment to a medical condition or overall adjustment to an outcome related to the disease (Clay, 2004). Adapting to a chronic illness is a process that occurs across time and involves multiple intrapersonal (within the individual) and interpersonal (between individuals) features. In order to better understand this process, researchers have created models to explain the manner by which children with chronic illnesses adjust to their condition. Clay (2004) proposed a "coping experience" model that incorporates child characteristics, stressor parameters, cognitive processes, and coping strategies that lead to adaptation, arguably inside and outside of the classroom (see Figure 7.1).

Boekaerts and Roder (1999), in their review of the extant chronic illness literature, proposed that Perrez and Reicherts' (1992) characteristics of a stressful situation also apply to adapting to a chronic medical condition. These characteristics have been infused under the heading of stress parameters within the model displayed in Figure 7.1. A thorough discussion of each element is beyond the scope of this chapter; however, awareness of the components of this revised model is important for classroom teachers who are very much involved in helping a student adapt to their chronic illness in the educational setting. In order to make the features of this model more salient, we suggest that the readers of this chapter recall a medical condition from his or her own health history and work through the model to gain insight into the process of adaptation.

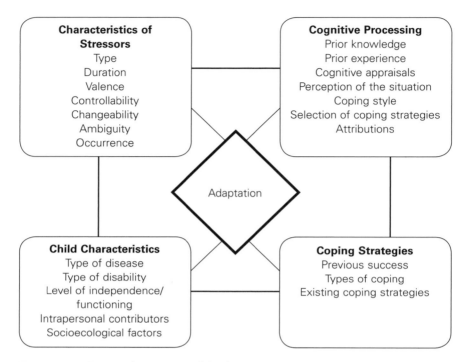

Figure 7.1 Comprehensive model of coping with a chronic illness. Adapted from Clay (2004) and Perrez and Reicherts (1992).

The pediatric chronic illness literature references a number of disease-related issues to which a child with any chronic illness must adapt. It is not our intent to suggest that classroom teachers are primarily responsible for, or necessarily intricately involved in, facilitating a student's adjustment in each of the following five areas. Without question, a team approach that includes the child's parents, medical staff, school nurses, school psychologists, school counselors and social workers, related service therapists (e.g. speech, physical therapy, occupational therapy, etc.), and teachers is necessary to meet the psychoeducational needs of a student with a chronic illness (Harris, 2009; Shaw & McCabe, 2008). However, among these professionals, classroom teachers have the most contact with the student across the school day and may be able to, at a minimum, play a supportive role in helping a child adapt to a chronic illness at school. Specific roles for teachers regarding each of the following appear later in this chapter.

The first disease-related issue requiring adjustment is knowledge of the *diagnosis itself*. Consistent with the developmental maturity of the student, the child or adolescent will likely have an emotional reaction to the literal diagnosis (i.e. the diagnosis of asthma, diabetes, leukemia, etc.). That emotional reaction is largely related to the stressor parameters listed in Figure 7.1. For example, the perceived seriousness (e.g. lethality), duration, controllability, changeability, ambiguity, and likelihood of reoccurrence may all play a role. Second, a child must adapt to the *response of others* after learning of their condition or observing the effects of the disease and its treatment. The response of classmates is an oft-cited concern of children with chronic illnesses. Likewise, children must adapt to *symptoms of the disease* and *effects of the disease's treatment,* such as pain, cognitive decline, loss of physical functioning, and changes in appearance, among others. These negative effects will vary by medical condition and course of treatment, and also differ in terms of severity. Disease-specific information will be required for the classroom teacher to understand the student's adaptation in these areas. Finally, children with chronic illness must adapt to the experience of *medical procedures.* Understandably, children often dread the prospect of procedures like injections, body imaging/scans, surgeries, dialysis, and chemotherapy. Medical procedures may require the use of restraints, take a long period of time to complete, and cause varying degrees of pain, among other potentially negative aspects.

For the purposes of this chapter, a specific chronic illness was selected to illustrate the five domains of adaptations outlined above. Given the findings of Clay et al. (2004) and Nabors et al. (2008) that teachers lack information regarding pediatric cancer, perhaps more than other high incidence chronic illnesses, we chose acute lymphoblastic leukemia (ALL) because it is the most common cancer of childhood. Next, we will review ALL from a medical perspective, highlight symptoms and disease-related issues commonly seen in the classroom, and finally provide psychoeducational intervention and progress monitoring suggestions that also apply across medical conditions.

Acute Lymphoblastic Leukemia (ALL)

The term cancer refers to a group of related diseases that are characterized by uncontrollable cell growth that results in the spread of abnormal cells (American Cancer Society, 2003). Cancer can occur in any part of the body and be exhibited in several forms. The most common form seen in children is acute lymphoblastic leukemia (ALL), which comprises 40 percent of all diagnosed pediatric cases (Armstrong, Blumberg, & Toledano, 1999). The second most common form of childhood cancer manifests as various types of brain tumors. The prevalence rates of pediatric cancer, characterized as occurring between birth and 19 years of age, are rising due to improved treatments and increasing survival rates (American Cancer Society, 2007). Current prevalence rates for pediatric cancer are estimated at approximately 270,000 children (American Cancer Society, 2007). A child returning to school after cancer treatment, or attending school while in treatment, presents complex academic, social and medical needs (Power, DuPaul, Shapiro, & Kazak, 2003). Disease-specific information and collaboration among professionals are integral to meeting the demands placed on children with chronic illnesses at school.

As just referenced, the most common form of cancer seen in children is ALL. This cancer of the blood is particularly dangerous as the disease affects the child's white blood cells, which are critical to fighting infections within the body. Children with ALL are therefore highly susceptible to serious infections that put the child at substantial risk for death (Armstrong et al., 1999). In addition to an impact on white blood cells, ALL can have negative effects on blood platelets and red blood cells resulting in difficult to control bleeding, bruising, and severe anemia (Armstrong et al., 1999). Important to recognize is that the effects of ALL can manifest across the child's entire body system as blood is required for the functioning of all major organs and the central nervous system.

Common treatments

The treatment of ALL typically involves chemotherapy, radiation, or both. Most commonly, ALL treatment includes two to three years of intense intrathecal chemotherapy, which is injected directly into the spinal fluid that surrounds the brain and spinal cord (American Cancer Society, 2007). This treatment is often used alone; however, neuro-axis (whole brain) radiation may be needed if the cancer has spread across the central nervous system. The immediate treatment effects can be vast, but common side effects from systemic chemotherapy include hair loss, weight gain or loss, fatigue, constipation, low blood counts, and temporary difficulties with fine motor skills (Copeland et al., 1988; Margolin & Poplack, 1997). Radiation therapy is known to have even more serious negative effects on a child's cognitive performance (Armstrong et al., 1999; Silber et al., 1992). The combination of younger age (under the age of 6) and higher dose of radiation seems to increase the risk that the child will experience severe cognitive impairment (Mulhern et al., 2009). In addition to immediate treatment effects, these treatments are also associated with long term psychoeducational deficits that will be reviewed later in this chapter.

Manifestations of ALL by Domain of Adaptation

Adjustment to the diagnosis

Much like adults when faced with a serious illness, a child with ALL must adapt to learning of his or her own diagnosis. Many children react with confusion, sadness, fear, and anger, along with the continuum of emotional reactions to learning of their possibly terminal medical condition (DeGood, Crawford, & Jongsma, 1999). However, for most children, these reactions are considered adjustment in nature as children with ALL are generally not given to major psychopathology after learning of their condition, or even throughout the treatment process (Noll et al., 1997). In fact and perhaps counter to intuition, children with ALL are only at a slightly elevated risk of significant psychosocial stress (Barlow & Ellard, 2006). One risk factor for psychosocial stress, however, is decline in physical health that negatively impacts daily classroom functioning (DeGood et al., 1999). Although most children with ALL will not meet diagnostic criteria for depression or an anxiety disorder, the child will likely require some degree of support in the classroom. This may be particularly true of elementary-aged children who experience slightly higher levels of anxiety-related behavior than middle-school or high school students (Bessell, 2001).

Adjustment to the response of peers

A major area of adjustment that can be troublesome for chronically ill children is dealing with the reactions of peers. The child with ALL may have a fear of telling a peer about his or her condition and experiencing subsequent rejection. This may manifest in the child avoiding conversations with peers on anything other than superficial topics in an attempt to avoid discussing the cancer and related difficulties (DeGood et al., 1999). Clearly, this social approach can significantly impact a child's ability to make and retain friends.

However, once peers are aware of the illness, the child can be at risk for exclusion in activities or *covert* relational aggression. Research shows that peers typically do not overtly physically and verbally bully a child with cancer (Noll, Bukowski, Davies, Koontz, & Kulkarni, 1993; Noll et al., 1999). However, the child with cancer may still be at risk of subtle forms of relational aggression such as being excluded from activities, or being the topic of gossip among other students. One example of this is the exclusion of a child with a chronic illness from a sporting activity. Participation in sports is a crucial developmental activity that contributes to the child's well-being and self-esteem (Vitulano, 2003). Whether due to lack of skill, or for safety reasons, children with chronic illness often report this type of exclusion to be particularly distressing. Teacher-encouraged, noncompetitive group activities may help alleviate the child's feelings of being left out. In brief, it is important for teachers to monitor for the presence of discreet forms of relational aggression in the event that the child with a chronic illness does not report it.

Peers' reactions to a classmate with a chronic illness may also directly involve the classroom teacher. This may be particularly true when the chronically ill child has been out of school for an extended period of time, or when the child returns to school. At these times, it is normal for peers to have questions regarding their classmate's illness (Sexson & Madan-Swain, 1993). These questions may be directly posed to the student, but often, questions are asked of the classroom teacher. As will be reviewed later, in order to respond effectively, the classroom teacher will need disease-specific information and to know the wishes of the student and family regarding the level of detail to share with the other children. Table 7.1 includes a list of questions commonly asked by peers about a child with a chronic illness.

Table 7.1 Common Questions Regarding a Classmate with a Chronic Illness

What is wrong with Steven?
Is Steven ever going to get better?
Is Steven going to die?
When will Steven come back to school?
Will Steven look different after he comes back?
Will Steven get sick at school?
Can I catch what Steven has?
Can I still be friends and/or play with Steven?
What should I do if the other kids make fun of Steven?
Can we ask Steven about what's wrong with him?
Can I do anything to help Steven feel better?

Adjustment to the illness and its symptoms

Childhood cancer as a disease process manifests in a wide-range of symptoms that can be categorized into three areas. These include physical effects, including excessive fatigue (McCabe & Shaw, 2010; Zins et al., 1998). First, a child with ALL must learn to adjust to the direct physical manifestations of the disease. For example, weight fluctuation, hair loss, motor difficulties, and jaundice are all commonly experienced symptoms of ALL. The physical effects are also the subject of classmates' questions that could be posed to the child with ALL or the classroom teacher. Furthermore, a child with ALL may also experience fatigue to the extent that classroom performance is negatively impacted. Classroom fatigue hinders the learning of new material due to difficulty with sustained attention and concentration and keeping pace with the class. Because of this, arranging for rest breaks may be necessary. This could take the form of quiet time spent at the child's desk, lying down in the nurse's office, or even partial days of attendance.

Adjustment to medical procedures

Children with ALL may experience adjustment difficulties from the medical procedures associated with treatment. Take, for example, chemotherapy. Chemotherapy requires a long period of time to administer and involves the use of needles, possibly the placement of subcutaneous mediports, and a burning sensation at the injection site (American Cancer Society, 2011). All the while, the child must remain reasonably still as the chemotherapy is applied directly to the spinal column (intrathecal chemotherapy). It is easy to understand that a child with ALL may become anxious and afraid of needles, or even of the medication itself due to pain and discomfort associated with the actual treatment process (Kazak et al., 1997). Children must also adjust to radiation therapy procedures. The goal of radiation therapy is to kill the cancer cells by administering a high dosage of radiation at a particular location (American Cancer Society, 2011). The actual therapy process requires the child to be immobilized with some degree of restraint for a long period of time while enclosed in medical machinery that makes loud noises. This process can be upsetting for many children. Other types of cancers require other invasive procedures, such as bone marrow aspirations and lumbar punctures (Cruce & Stinnett, 2006). On the whole, treatments for pediatric ALL and other chronic illnesses often require painful procedures. Children may develop skin rashes, have insomnia, become nauseous, or even vomit in the anticipation of these treatments as a result (Kazak et al., 1997). Furthermore, if the medical procedures are perceived as traumatic, the child may develop long lasting aversions to hospitals, doctors, and needles or other medical-related equipment (Cruce & Stinnett, 2006). Classroom teachers may witness anxious or irritable behavior as the child anticipates an upcoming medical procedure.

Adjustment to the effect of treatments

Treatments associated with ALL are also related to a variety of short-term and long-term effects. As Herrmann, Thurber, Miles, and Gilbert

(2011) allude to, side effects of treatment and long term psychoeducational outcomes will differ for each child. Well established, however, is that early age of diagnosis and multimodal treatment (chemotherapy and radiation) put children at greatest risk for negative outcomes (Silber et al., 1992). Physical effects of treatments include hair loss, abnormal growth and maturation, death of bone tissue, heart problems, Hepatitis C, weakness, fatigue, obesity or weight loss, constipation, and dental problems (Copeland et al., 1988; Gorin & McAuliffe, 2009; Margolin & Poplack, 1997). The psychoeducational effects of chemotherapy and/or radiation therapy may not be fully appreciated for several years after treatment (Brown, Sawyer, Antoniou, Toogood, & Rice, 1999). Overall IQ, attention and concentration, working memory, planning and organization, visual motor integration, processing speed, fine motor speed, and reading, spelling, and math skills are commonly reported (Armstrong et al., 1999; Harris, 2009). There is some evidence that girls may experience greater negative effects of treatment than boys (Schlieper, Esseltine, & Tarshis, 1989). Clearly, all of aforementioned potential outcomes have implications for the child's functioning in the classroom.

It goes without saying that school attendance is significantly impacted by a chronic illness and its treatment. This is particularly true of pediatric cancer (Vance & Eiser, 2004). Moore, Kaffenberger, Goldberg, Oh, and Hudspeth (2009) recently found that in their sample of children with cancer, 83, 58, and 32 days were missed across the first, second, and third years after diagnosis, respectively. Negative effects of the illness, side effects of treatments, side effects of medical tests (e.g. spinal taps and bone marrow tests), and other medical complications are often cited as reasons for school absences (Sullivan, Fulmer, & Zigmond, 2001).

In addition to chemotherapy and radiation, medication management is often necessary to control the child's pain. Pain medications also carry side effects that may impact the child's classroom performance. The side effects from these medications vary widely based on the type, frequency, and duration of use (Cruce & Stinnett, 2006). Examples of common medication side effects that can affect a child's classroom experience include irritability, difficulty sustaining attention, nausea, fatigue, gastrointestinal problems, pain, and anemia (McCabe & Shaw, 2010; Vance & Eiser, 2004). Often more disruptive to a child than medication side effects is uncontrolled pain (DeGood et al., 1999).

Intervention Considerations for Children with Chronic Illnesses, including ALL

Thus far we have reviewed legislation that requires educators to provide school-based services to qualified children with a medical condition and five domains of adaptation to a chronic illness that could have implications for the child's functioning within the classroom, as well as a teacher's classroom management. Clearly, the teacher's role in the psychoeducational management of a chronic illness can vary by the nature of the medical condition, the age/grade of the child and peers, classroom size, the subject being taught (particularly for middle and high school teachers), and the availability of district resources, among other factors. Despite these and other factors, a continuum of classroom interventions can be implemented to address the manifestations of a particular chronic illness. In order to illustrate the continuum of interventions that can be implemented, we again turn to a discussion of ALL.

Brief teacher education

Teachers consistently report that a lack of disease-specific knowledge hinders the ability to adapt instruction for a student with a chronic illness (e.g. Clay et al., 2004; Nabors et al., 2008). In their study regarding the inclusion of students with chronic illnesses, Mukherjee, Lightfoot, and Sloper (2000) found that teachers are often eager to gain health-related information from families to not only learn how to modify the classroom, but also learn of the family's reaction to the disease. That being said, teachers in the same study also reported the desire to get advice regarding the classroom implications of the illness directly from medical professionals without having to go through the child's parents. A number of reasons were cited for this including not wanting to burden the parents, fear of inaccurate information coming from anyone other than medical staff, and wanting to maintain parent confidence by not revealing lack of knowledge. Teachers should examine their own knowledge of a specific condition and then consider if consultation with a school-based health professional (e.g. school nurse) or the child's medical staff would be helpful (Sexson & Madan-Swain, 1993). Specific information to obtain through such a consultation might include the disease's nature, symptoms, treatment, and the treatment's side effects; the teacher's role in the child's medical treatment, the natural course of the disease, the perceived implications for the classroom, and in the case of ALL, mortality information. Of course, a number of online medial resources are available, in addition to print resources (e.g. American Academy of Pediatrics, 2010); however, it is best to get such information from those who have specific knowledge of the child and how the disease is manifesting for that child in particular. By seeking disease-specific information, teachers can make more informed decisions regarding classroom modifications, as well as how to respond to the questions of peers, and even the child him or herself.

Brief peer education

Another intervention of low intensity is to conduct peer education with the chronically ill student's classmates. Many children with a chronic illness, including ALL, want help in explaining their condition to classmates (Clay, 2004; Mukherjee et al., 2000). The children in the study conducted by Mukherjee et al. specifically cited the desire for peers to know what to expect from them, how to respond to an emergency, limitations of physical contact, and simply understand what they are going through. Not all children wish for classmates to be informed of the medical condition (Clay, 2004; Mukherjee et al., 2000). Therefore, it is imperative that the school ask the child and the child's family what information can be shared with peers. Having this conversation is necessary for the classroom teacher to respond appropriately to the questions of classmates. Table 7.1 includes a list of questions commonly asked by peers of a classmate with a chronic illness. Not all of these questions are easily answered without prior knowledge (e.g. "Can I catch what Johnny has?") and some of the questions (e.g. "Is Johnny going to die?") require carefully planned, thoughtful responses. Again, consultation with the child's family and medical staff can be very helpful in anticipating the questions of peers, and having a prepared response that is truthful and respects the privacy of the chronically ill child. Furthermore, by providing peers with health-related information to address misperceptions and fears, the child's social standing may be protected.

Ongoing emotional support by teachers

Children with chronic illnesses often report that they would like to be able to talk to their classroom teacher about their illness (Mukherjee et al., 2000). Specifically, the child may be interested in discussing worries related to their disease, as well as any learning and social difficulties. Recall, a child with chronic illness may experience anxiety in the face of a diagnosis, like ALL, with a possible terminal outcome (DeGood et al, 1999). This may be particularly true of middle-school or high school aged children with a chronic illness (Bessell, 2001). If extreme emotional distress is present, a referral to a school mental health professional, such as a school counselor or school psychologist, is warranted. However, in most cases, ongoing emotional support can be provided by classroom teachers to show an interest in the child and his or her treatment, make time to talk with the student, and help the student maintain a positive outlook regarding the future. Warm words of encouragement are welcomed by all children, including those with a medical condition.

Ongoing academic support by teachers

As referenced earlier, a student with a chronic illness may require consistent classroom support during treatment and across the long term management of the disease. In many instances, the student can be reasonably supported by providing relatively straightforward classroom accommodations and modifications. For the purpose of this chapter, we characterize accommodations as removing "construct-irrelevant variance caused by physical, cognitive, or sensory barriers to accessing material" (Ketterlin-Geller, Yovanoff, & Tindal, 2007, p. 331) so that the student with a chronic illness gains equal access the classroom's curriculum and the student is able to better demonstrate his or her learning. In order to thoughtfully select accommodations, rather than applying a cookie cutter approach, some knowledge of the manifestations of the chronic illness is necessary. As referenced below, problem-solving teaming will be essential in this regard. Additionally, Clay (2004) and Phelps (2006) are excellent resources to consult for a review of the psychoeducational implications of chronic illnesses commonly seen in the classroom.

To illustrate the application of accommodations, recall the major neuropsychological deficits associated with ALL and its treatment: general reasoning, attention and concentration, working memory, planning and organization, visual motor integration, processing speed, fine motor speed, and reading, spelling, and math skills (Armstrong et al., 1999; Harris, 2009). To the extent that each of these deficits is present, the problem-solving team should identify accommodations and modifications that "bypass" the nature of the deficit. For example, if the student is either by observation or formal evaluation shown to have decreased processing speed, the student in all likelihood would have difficulty keeping pace with classmates and would lag behind on classroom tasks such as note taking and test taking. Extended time would be a reasonable accommodation in this instance. However, due to classroom scheduling or remarkably slow processing speed, additional time may not reasonably accommodate the student. In such cases, reduced expectations for the time period or assistance with note taking (e.g. copy of peer's notes, audio recording) may be necessary. With respect to general reasoning, peer tutoring, additional teacher scaffolding of concepts, and advanced graphic organizers may be useful. Regarding attention and organization, a discreet teacher signal to get back on task, a behavior plan that rewards work completion, or home-school notes are suggested. Visual motor integration and fine motor problems can result in inability to keep up with classroom tasks that involve handwriting. As such, keyboarding, dictation software, or as previously mentioned, providing the student with notes would help bypass these problems. With respect to academic deficits, accommodations such as text-to-speech assistive technology, books on tape, use of a spell checker, and use of a calculator may allow the child to better access the curriculum and demonstrate learning.

At a minimum, educators should establish a firm line of communication with the student's parents and medical team through the use of home-school notes. Home-school notes are known to not only be an effective means of communication, but also known to act as an intervention to improve academic and behavioral functioning in the classroom (Cox, 2005). As advocated throughout this chapter, Phelps (2006) and Power et al. (2003) advocate for home-school collaboration to help focus the team on achieving the best possible outcomes for the student. Knowing that behavior report cards may be used to monitor and effectively treat a variety of behavior problems (Vannest, Davis, Davis, Mason, & Burke, 2010), we suggest educators use behavior report cards as a model home-school notes for children with chronic illnesses. Figure 7.2 presents a model for home-school note for students with a chronic illness.

Daily Home-School Note

Student's Name:_____

Date:_____

Teacher/Class:_____

Behaviors to Observe	Present today?	Behavior Intensity (if desired)		
1 _____	Yes/No	Mild	Moderate	Severe
2 _____	Yes/No	Mild	Moderate	Severe
3 _____	Yes/No	Mild	Moderate	Severe
4 _____	Yes/No	Mild	Moderate	Severe
5 _____	Yes/No	Mild	Moderate	Severe

Behaviors unusual for the student:

Additional comments or concerns:

Figure 7.2 Example daily home-school note for a student with a chronic illness

The principal components of a note include behaviors to monitor; scaling to reflect the frequency, intensity, or duration of the behavior; space to communicate unusual behavior or complaints of the student; and space for additional comments or concerns regarding the student and his or her functioning at school.

The specific behaviors to be monitored must be determined through a team approach. For example, medical staff may ask the school to monitor for behavior that reflects upon the success of the treatment or severity of the disease process. Parents may desire to learn of their child's diet, level of fatigue, and treatment compliance. Monitoring treatment compliance may be particularly important for students with diseases that require medical attention during the school day, like diabetes. Finally, teachers may be especially interested in monitoring the student's work completion and communicating this with the home in order to promote productivity. Aside from monitoring specific behaviors, this home-school note may also be used as a means for teachers to communicate unusual behavior or somatic complaints of the child. Keeping such records can be invaluable to medical staff who may desire to look for patterns of behavior to determine how well a child is tolerating a treatment, gauge the effectiveness of the treatment, or track the disease process.

Although accommodations and modifications can be provided on an informal basis, we suggest that these services be provided through a Section 504 Plan. After a review of case law regarding type 1 diabetes mellitus (T1DM), Schmitt et al. (2010) warned educators that courts have found schools culpable when a string of informal accommodations did not trigger the construction of a formal Section 504 Plan. In effect, it is the responsibility of well-intentioned educators to recognize that providing a multitude of informal accommodations and modifications signals that a student has a disability that warrants Section 504 protections.

Clay (2004) has provided educators with a sample Section 504 Plan that can be used for a student with a chronic illness. The core elements of a Section 504 Plan are: 1) the accommodation/modification to be provided, 2) the implementors of the plan and, 3) the date on which the plan will be reviewed. The American Academy of Pediatrics (2010) calls upon schools to also create an "emergency plan" to be implemented in case a serious medical event should occur while in the classroom or at a school function. Again, Schmitt et al. (2010) found many instances in the T1DM case law where the lack of an emergency plan, or an ineffectively implemented emergency plan, was a source of conflict. Thoughtfully ensuring the participation of the student's parents, medical staff, teachers, school nurse, building administration, and school psychologist in Section 504 Plan writing will help ensure that all of the student's medical and educational needs have been addressed.

Intensive school re-entry

If a child has missed school for an extended period of time due to a chronic illness, formal school re-entry planning is often required. This re-entry planning should involve comprehensive hospital-to-school strategies that are tailored to the needs of the student (Harris, 2009; Shaw & McCabe, 2008). Herrmann et al. (2011) advocate that successful school re-entry necessitates school-medical team collaboration during hospitalization, in-service training for school personnel, short- and long-term support services as necessary, and continuing care by rehabilitation professionals. After a thorough search of the literature, Prevatt, Heffer, and Lowe (2000) reviewed fourteen school re-entry programs and found the nature of the programs fell into one of three categories: school staff informational workshops, peer education, and what the authors termed comprehensive.

There are few studies that have collected large scale data on the positive effects of comprehensive school re-entry programs. As examples, Katz, Rubinstein, Hubert, and Blew (1988) and Katz, Varni, Rubenstein, Blew, and Hubert (1992) studied the effects of a comprehensive school re-entry program for children with cancer. This complex program included elements such as consultation among the child, parents, medical staff, and teachers regarding the return to school; interim educational planning until the child could return to school; identification of a hospital-based professional to act as a liaison between the medical team and school personnel; direct counseling surrounding issues related to school re-entry (e.g. classmate questions and possible teasing); planning for foreseeable school problems; consultation with school staff regarding psychoeducational needs, and assistance in identifying special education services; informational workshops for school staff; informational classroom presentations; and follow-up with all stakeholders regarding educational services. This program resulted in children displaying fewer signs of anxiety, depression, and general behavior problems, and also enjoying greater social adjustment at school.

The classroom teacher plays a vital professional role in the re-entry of a child with a chronic illness. Although it is the case that the teacher may have much to learn from other professionals regarding the nature of the child's medical condition and current level of functioning, arguably, it is impossible for the team to adequately establish the child's need without learning of the current classroom curriculum and behavioral expectations. Consider the child who has been continuously absent from school for several months, but who has received homebound services. Homebound services (i.e. one or two hours per week) would inform parents and medical professionals of the current curriculum and corresponding needs. However, the classroom teacher must be available to explain the *upcoming* content and pacing of the curriculum, as well as what challenges may lie ahead for the student within the immediate curriculum. This knowledge may not only be helpful for learning purposes, but also for reasons of safety. This is particularly true of physical education classes, as well as classes that require the use of potentially dangerous equipment (e.g. chemistry, shop classes, home studies). The classroom teacher is likely the only professional that can speak to the complexity of the upcoming curriculum, as well as what safety concerns may be around the corner.

Furthermore, in the child's absence, classroom behavioral expectations may have changed. In the course of only a few months, teacher modeled math exercises may have shifted towards independent drill using worksheets and this may be difficult for a child with slow processing speed and attention span (e.g. difficult for a child with ALL treated with chemotherapy and radiation). Likewise, the students may now be expected to manage their own organization system, or even independently transition between classes while carrying their own materials. Gauging the perceived intensity of the challenges can help determine if no formal services are necessary, if Section 504 accommodations will reasonably meet the child's needs, or if a significantly modified curriculum with other related services (e.g. physical therapy, occupational therapy, speech language therapy) is necessary through special education (IDEA).

Psychoeducational Progress Monitoring for Students with ALL

In addition to intervening in the classroom, teachers play an invaluable role in the monitoring of the psychoeducational status of students with chronic illnesses. Particularly in diseases and/or treatments that impact the central nervous system, immediate psychoeducational deficits may not be present (see Yeates, Ris, Taylor, & Pennington, 2010 for a review of the neuropsychological manifestations of various neurological disorders). Generally speaking, crystallized skills, or over-learned and well-established cognitive and academic skills (Sattler, 2001), remain intact in children with ALL in the period closely following treatment. For example, immediately after a student with ALL begins to attend regularly, the basic reading, math calculation, and spelling skills of the student may not stand out compared to peers as being deficient. This may give the false impression that the student has escaped the disease and treatment process unscathed. However, impairment in the ability to *learn new skills* may be present (Brown et al., 1998). In a longitudinal study of the intellectual and academic functioning of children with ALL who received chemotherapy compared to healthy peers, results indicated that three to four years may pass before academic discrepancies begin to appear (Brown et al., 1999). This pattern of performance across time is common in children with chronic illnesses involving the neurological system.

For children with a chronic illness or treatment protocol known to manifest in cognitive and academic deficits over time, a neuropsychological evaluation is often conducted by pediatric neuropsychologists prior to the termination of treatment. Particularly if the student received inpatient treatment for an extended period of time, or if the student received homebound services, a recent neuropsychological evaluation will prove helpful with respect to identifying student needs and determining eligibility for formal services (i.e. IDEA and Section 504). Herrmann et al. (2011) identified eight domains of neuropsychological functioning with implications for the psychoeducational intervention of students with ALL. These include general intelligence, language, memory, sustained attention, sensory/perception, academic achievement, behavior/personality, and affective/psychosocial. These are domains of functioning that are commonly assessed as a part of neuropsychological evaluations. As such, information regarding these skills may be present for students returning to school after intensive treatment. Educators should ask medical staff and parents if any psychological testing was conducted as part of the treatment process in order to facilitate planning. Follow-up evaluations by school psychologists are also recommended every six months to a year for students with ALL (Herrmann et al., 2011). We advocate for the follow-up testing of any student for which cognitive decline is expected.

The purposes of follow-up evaluations are to monitor the psychoeducational impact of the illness and determine what interventions may be necessary. As part of the teaming process, a teacher may hear that a student's standard scores have dropped since the previous evaluation. A bit of clarification for all educators is warranted here. As referenced earlier and explained by Schmitt (2011), *standardized* test scores from instruments commonly administered by neuropsychologists and school psychologists may drop over time for students with conditions with neurological involvement. A decline in scores typically does not suggest the student has lost previously learned skills, as one may infer from lower *standard scores* (a measure of performance compared to peers). Instead, examining the *raw score* performance of the student will likely reveal that learning, although slower than classmates, did occur since the last evaluation. To illustrate, the mathematics standard score performance of a student may have dropped from 95 to 84 across three school years. This suggests that a gap in achievement is forming between the student and his or her peers. However, the corresponding raw score performance may reveal a literal increase in raw score performance from 32 raw score points to 36 raw score points. Previously learned skills were not lost and new learning did actually occur. If a teacher needs assistance interpreting test scores from any psychological report, the school psychologist will be very helpful in this regard.

Thus far we have discussed evaluations completed by psychologists and other specialists; however, teachers can play a very active role in monitoring the psychoeducational status of students with a chronic illness. Aside from providing parents with frequent updates using home-school notes and reporting observations of behavior, Herrmann et al. (2011) suggested that curriculum based measurement (CBM) techniques could be used as a tool to monitor the status of a child after treatment for cancer. The same would be true of any chronic illness. Curriculum based measurement probes are designed to be fast, reliable, and easily repeated measures of a discreet academic skill, such as oral reading fluency, reading comprehension, math calculation, and math reasoning (Shinn, 1989). For example, an oral reading fluency probe requires a student to read to a teacher for only one minute and then the student's performance is recorded in terms of words read correct per minute. Use of CBM techniques to screen for students in need of additional intervention is increasing in popularity with the advent of response to intervention (RTI). Within the context of RTI as an academic problem-solving process for all students, universal screening data are collected three times per year to identify those who are struggling. This data is plotted on a graph to: 1) visually analyze a student's performance compared to others and by connecting the three data points; and 2) determine the student's growth rate (learning slope) across the school year. A sizeable decline in performance compared to peers may be an indication that the disease process or treatment is manifesting in academic declines. A change in learning slope between years may also suggest the same. If educators notice this pattern, additional problem-solving and consultation with the student's medical team is suggested.

Conclusions

Classroom teachers perform an invaluable role in the education of children with chronic illnesses. Foremost, teachers must actively participate in the group process that determines if a child with a chronic illness is eligible for federally mandated special services in the schools. The classroom teacher may be the only professional on the medical and school teams to bring detailed knowledge of the student's previous educational performance, typical psychoeducational expectations of the child at the present time, the current and upcoming curriculum and related challenges, and the current classroom climate including peer relationships. Understanding of the different issues to which children with chronic illness must adjust, likely assists teachers to better respond to the child's needs, classmates' needs, and implement educational accommodations and modifications. By involving themselves in applying a broad continuum of interventions (e.g. from positive classroom support to involvement in formal re-entry programs) and actively engaging in progress monitoring strategies, teachers can help to facilitate the most positive outcomes possible for a child with a chronic illness.

References

American Academy of Pediatrics (2010). *Managing chronic health needs in child care and schools: A quick reference guide.* Elk Grove Village, IL: Author.

—(2011). Accessed from http://www.healthychildren.org/english/health- issues/ conditions/chronic/Pages/ default.aspx

American Cancer Society (2011). Accessed from http://www.cancer.org/Treatment/ TreatmentsandSideEffects/TreatmentTypes/index

American Cancer Society (2007). *Cancer facts & figures.* Oklahoma City, OK: Author.

—(2003). *Cancer facts & figures.* Oklahoma City, OK: Author.

Armstrong, F. D., Blumberg, M. J., & Toledano, S. R. (1999). Neurobehavioral issues in childhood cancer. *School Psychology Review, 28,* 194–203. Accessed from http://nasponline.org/publications/spr/abstract.aspx?ID=1474

Barlow, J. H., & Ellard, D. R. (2006). The psychosocial well-being of children with chronic disease, their parents and siblings: An overview of the research evidence base. *Child Care, Health, and Development, 32,* 19–31. doi:10.1111/j.1365-2214.2006.00591.x

Bessell, A. (2001). Children surviving cancer: Psychosocial adjustment, quality of life, and school experiences. *Exceptional Children, 67,* 345–59. Accessed from http://sbac.edu/~werned/DATA/RESEARCH/journals/Excep%20Children/ children%20and%20cancer.pdf

Boekaerts, M., & Roder, I. (1999). Stress, coping, and adjustment in children with a chronic disease: A review of the literature. *Disability and Rehabilitation, 21,* 311–37. doi:10.1080/096382899297576

Brown, R. T., Madan-Swain, A., Walco, G. A., et. al., (1998). Cognitive and academic late effects among children previously treated for acute lymphoblastic leukemia receiving chemotherapy as CNS prophylaxis. *Journal of Pediatric Psychology, 23,* 333–40. doi:10.1093/jpepsy/23.5.333

Brown, R. T., Sawyer, M. G., Antoniou, G., Toogood, I., & Rice, M. (1999). Longitudinal follow-up of the intellectual and academic functioning of children receiving central nervous system prophylactic chemotherapy for leukemia: A four-year final report. *Developmental and Behavioral Pediatrics, 20,* 373–7. Accessed from http://hdl.handle.net/2440/7477

Clay, D. L. (2004). *Helping schoolchildren with chronic health conditions: A practical guide.* New York, NY: The Guilford Press.

Clay, D. L., Cortina, S., Harper, D. C., Cocco, K. M., & Drotar, D. (2004). School teachers' experiences with childhood chronic illness. *Children's Health Care, 33,* 227–39. doi:10.1207/s15326888chc3303_5

Copeland, D. R., Dowell, R. E., Fletcher, J. M., Sullivan, M. P., Jaffe, N., Cangir, A., … Judd, B. W. (1988). Neuropsychological test performance of pediatric cancer patients at diagnosis and one year later. *Journal of Pediatric Psychology, 13,* 183–96. doi:10.1093/jpepsy/13.2.183

Cox, D. D. (2005). Evidence-based interventions using home-school collaboration. *School Psychology Quarterly, 20,* 473–97. doi:10.1521/ scpq.2005.20.4.473

Cruce, M. K., & Stinnett, T. A. (2006). Children with cancer. In L. Phelps (ed.).

Chronic health-related disorders in children: Collaborative medical and psychoeducational interventions (pp. 41–55). Washington, DC: American Psychological Association.

Cunningham, M. M., & Wodrich, D. L. (2006). The effect of sharing health information on teachers' production of classroom accommodations. *Psychology in the Schools, 43,* 553–64. doi: 10.1002/pits.20166

DeGood, D. E., Crawford, A.L., & Jongsma, A. E. (1999). *The behavioral medicine treatment planner.* New York, NY: Wiley.

Federal Register: Assistance to States for the Education of Children with Disabilities; Final Rule, 71 Fed. Reg. 156 (Aug. 14, 2006) (codified at 34 C.F.R. pt. 300).

Glaser, S., Ouimet, T., & Shaw, S. R. (2010). Collaboration between educators and medical professionals. In P. C. McCabe and S. R. Shaw (eds), *Pediatric disorders: Current topics and interventions for educators* (pp. 8–21). Washington, DC: National Association of School Psychologists.

Gorin, S. & McAuliffe, P. (2009). Implications of childhood cancer survivors in the classroom and the school. *Health Education, 109,* 25–48. doi:10.1108/09654280910923363

Harris, M. S. (2009). School reintegration for children and adolescents with cancer: The role of school psychologists. *Psychology in the Schools, 46,* 579–92. doi:10.1002/pits.20399

Herrmann, D. S., Thurber, J.R., Miles, K., & Gilbert, G. (2011). Childhood leukemia survivors and their return to school: A literature review, case study, and recommendations. *Journal of Applied School Psychology, 27,* 252–75. doi:10.1080/15377903.2011.590777

Kazak, A. E., Barakat, L. P., Meeske, K., et al., (1997). Posttraumatic stress, family functioning, and social support in survivors of childhood leukemia and their mothers and fathers. *Journal of Consulting and Clinical Psychology, 65,* 120–9. doi:10.1037/0022-006X.65.1.120

Katz, E. R., Rubinstein, C. L., Hubert, N. C., & Blew, A. (1988). School and social reintegration of children with cancer. *Journal of Psychosocial Oncology, 6,* 123–40. doi:10.1300/J077v06n03_09

Katz, E. R., Varni, J., W., Rubenstein, C. L., Blew, A., & Hubert, N. (1992). Teachers, parent, and child evaluative ratings of school reintegration intervention for children with a newly diagnosed cancer. *Children's Health Care, 21,* 69–75. doi:10.1207/s15326888chc2102_1

Ketterlin-Geller, L. R., Yovanoff, P., & Tindal, G. (2007). Developing a new paradigm for conducting research on accommodations in mathematics testing. *Exceptional Children, 73,* 331–47. Accessed from http://cec.metapress.com/content/ur76527844050286/

Margolin, J. F., & Poplack, D. G. (1997). Acute lymphoblastic leukemia. In P.A. Pizzo & D.G. Poplack (eds), *Principles and practice of pediatric oncology* (3rd ed., pp. 409–62). Philadelphia, PA: Lippincott-Raven.

McCabe, P. C. & Shaw, S. R. (2010). *Pediatric disorders: Current topics and interventions for educators.* Bethesda, MD: National Association of School Psychologists Publications.

Moore, J., Kaffenberger, C., Goldberg, P., Oh, K., & Hudspeth, R. (2009). School reentry for children with cancer: Perceptions of nurses, school personnel, and parents. *Journal of Pediatric Oncology Nursing, 26,* 86–99. doi:10.1177/1043454208328765

Mukherjee, S., Lightfoot, J., & Sloper, P. (2000). The inclusion of pupils with a chronic health condition in mainstream school: What does it mean for teachers? *Educational Research, 42,* 59–72. doi:10.1080/001318800363917

Mulhern, R. K., Kepner, J. L., Thomas, P. R., Armstrong, F. D., Friedman, H. S., & Kun, L. E. (1998). Neuropsychologic functioning of survivors of childhood medulloblastoma randomized to receive conventional or reduced dose craniospinal irradiation: A pediatric oncology group study. *Journal of Clinical Oncology, 16,* 1723–28. Accessed from http://www.jcojournal.org/content/16/5/1723.short

Nabors, L. A., Little, S. G., Akin-Little, A., & Iobst, E.A. (2008). Teacher knowledge of and confidence in meeting the needs of children with chronic medical conditions: Pediatric psychology's contribution to education. *Psychology in the Schools, 45,* 217–26. doi:10.1002/pits.20292

Noll, R. B., Bukowski, W. M., Davies, W. H., Koontz, K., & Kulkarni, R. (1993). Adjustment in the peer system of children with cancer: A two-year follow-up study. *Journal of Pediatric Psychology, 18,* 351–64. doi:10.1093/jpepsy/18.3.351

Noll, R. B., MachLean, W. E., Whitt, J. K., et al., (1997). Behavioral adjustment and social functioning of long-term survivors of childhood leukemia: Parent and teacher reports. *Journal of Pediatric Psychology, 22,* 827–41. doi:10.1093/jpepsy/22.6.827

Noll, R. B., Martstein, M. A., Vannatta, K., Correll, J., Bukowski, W. M., & Davies, W. H. (1999). Social, emotional, and behavioral functioning of children with cancer. *Pediatrics, 103,* 71–9. Accessed from http://pediatrics.aappublications.org/content/103/1/71.short

Perez, M., & Reicherts, M. (1992). *Stress, coping, and health: A situation-behavior approach, theory, methods, applications.* Seattle: WA: Hogrefe & Huber.

Phelps, L. (ed.). (2006). *Chronic health-related disorders in children: Collaborative medical and psychoeducational interventions.* Washington DC: American Psychological Association.

Power, T. J., DuPaul, G. J., Shapiro, E.S., & Kazak, A.E. (2003). *Promoting children's health: Integrating school, family and community.* New York, NY: The Guilford Press.

Prevatt, F. F., Heffer, R. W., & Lowe, P. A. (2000). A review of school reintegration programs for children with cancer. *Journal of School Psychology, 38,* 447–67. doi:10.1016/S0022-4405(00)00046-7

Sattler, J. M. (2001). *Assessment of children: Cognitive applications* (4th ed.). San Diego, CA: Jerome M. Sattler Publishing, Inc.

Schlieper, A. E., Esseltine, D. W., & Tarshis, E. (1989). Cognitive function in long survivors of childhood acute lymphoblastic leukemia. *Pediatric Hematology Oncology, 6,* 1–9. doi:10.3109/08880018909014573

Schmitt, A. J. (2011). Commentary on "Childhood leukemia survivors and their return to school: A literature review, case study, and recommendations". *Journal of Applied School Psychology, 27,* 276–83. doi:10.1080/15377903.2011.590771

Schmitt, A. J., Wodrich, D. L., & Lazar, S. (2010). Type I diabetes mellitus case decisions: Health-related service considerations for school psychologists. *Psychology in the Schools, 47*, 803–16. doi:10.1002/pits.20505

Section 504 Amendment to the Rehabilitation Act of 1973 (enacted under the Workforce Investment Act of 1998, Pub. L. 105–220, 112 Stat. 936 [1998]).

Sexson, S. B., & Madan-Swain, A. (1993). School reentry for the child with chronic illness. *Journal of Learning Disabilities, 26*, 115–37. doi:10.1177/002221949302600204

Shaw, S. R., & McCabe, P. C. (2008). Hospital-to-school transition for children with chronic illness: Meeting the new challenges of an evolving health care system. *Psychology in the Schools, 45*, 74–87. doi:10.1002/pits.20280

Shinn, M. R. (1989). *Curriculum-based measurement: assessing special children.* New York, NY: The Guilford Press.

Silber, J. H., Radcliffe, J., Peckham, V., et al., (1992). Whole-brain irradiation and decline in intelligence: The influence of dose and age on IQ score. *Journal of Clinical Oncology, 10*, 1390–6. Accessed from http://jco.ascopubs.org/content/10/9/1390.short#cited-by

Sullivan, N. A., Fulmer, D. L., & Zigmond, N. (2001). School: The normalizing factor for children with childhood leukemia. Perspectives of young survivors and their parents. *Preventing School Failure, 46*, 4–13. doi:10.1080/10459880109603338

Vance, Y. H., & Eiser, C. (2004). Caring for a child with cancer: A systematic review. *Pediatric Blood and Cancer, 42*, 249–53. doi:10.1002/pbc.10440

Vannest, K. J., Davis, J. L., Davis, C. R., Mason, B. A., & Burke, M. D. (2010). Effective intervention for behavior with a daily behavior report card: A meta-analysis. *School Psychology Review, 39*, 654–72. Accessed from http://www.nasponline.org/publications/spr/39-4/spr394vannest.pdf

Vitulano, L. A. (2003). Psychosocial issues for children and adolescents with chronic illness: Self-esteem, school functioning and sports participation. *Child and Adolescent Psychiatry, 12*, 585–92. doi:10.1016/S1056-4993(03)00027-0

Yeates, K. O., Ris, M. D., Taylor, H. G., & Pennington, B. F. (2010). *Pediatric neuropsychology: Research, theory, and practice* (2nd ed.). New York, NY: The Guilford Press.

Zins, J. E., Elias, M. J., Weissberg, R. P., et al., (1998). Enhancing learning through social and emotional education. *Think: The Journal of Creative and Critical Thinking, 9*, 18–20.

CHAPTER EIGHT

Understanding and Managing Behaviors of Children Diagnosed with Eating Disorders

Jamie M. King, Tammy L. Hughes, Laura M. Crothers, and Jered B. Kolbert

Duquesne University

Abstract

Childhood and adolescence represents formative years in which there are many developmental experiences (e.g. puberty, identity formation, dating) that if not successfully navigated, may put a youngster at greater risk for developing a range of eating problems, disturbances, and for some, full-blown disorders. Indeed, early eating problems (either overeating or undereating) can put a child at risk for disturbed eating patterns across the lifespan (Neumark-Sztainer, 2003). Researchers note that weight related problems, unhealthy dieting, and body dissatisfaction are common to both eating disorders and obesity (Neumark-Sztainer et al., 2002).

Formal eating disorders (e.g. Anorexia Nervosa and Bulimia Nervosa) are medical conditions characterized by unhealthy attempts at controlling weight. Obesity, in contrast, is a medical condition in which there is an excess of body fat and weight (eMedicineHealth, 2009) that is often the result of unhealthy overeating. Although there is a clear contrast, problematic eating patterns, such as binge eating, are associated with both eating disorders and obesity (Yanovski, 2002). It is important to note that obesity is not typically referred to as an eating disorder; rather, as we have written in this chapter, it is often referenced as an eating disturbance.

While the majority of children will not develop a clinical eating disorder, many youth do display subsyndromal eating problems that may require medical and psychiatric attention. Therefore, early intervention and prevention are important in improving outcomes for students with eating problems. As many children spend a large portion of their time at school, educators can play an important role in early identification and intervention. Furthermore, the educational milieu is an ideal setting to promote healthy living behaviors designed to decrease the incidence of childhood eating disorders and disturbances in today's youth.

As such, this chapter will address issues concerned with the behavior and classroom management of children and adolescents with various forms of eating problems. Specifically, the following areas will be discussed: how eating disorders develop, eating disorder definitions and diagnoses, signs and symptoms of eating disorders and various other eating problems, a three-tiered plan for prevention and intervention, and steps for monitoring prevention programming.

Overview

Eating disorders that occur between the ages of 7 and 13 are termed childhood-onset eating disorders (Bryant-Waugh & Lask, 2002). Although the research on eating disorders that occur before the age of 14 is limited, the available research indicates that those who are diagnosed with childhood-onset eating disorders tend to manifest severe symptoms, accompanied by a less than acceptable treatment prognosis (Bryant-Waugh & Lask, 2002). Additionally, researchers have shown that children with eating disorders are at greater risk of having eating disorders in their adult years (Johnson, Cohen, Kasen, & Brook, 2002). Similarly, child-onset obesity is associated with adult symptoms and poorer physical and mental health outcomes (Centers for Disease Control and Prevention,

2009). Unfortunately child-onset obesity is reported to be increasing at an alarming rate, with the number of obese youth doubling every three years (National Center for Health Statistics, 2002).

Although there are some individuals who exhibit symptoms of childhood-onset eating disorders (e.g. Anorexia Nervosa or Bulimia Nervosa), there are many more with childhood eating disturbances. Eating disturbances refer to variant forms of eating problems that either are different in symptom presentation from clinical eating disorders or lack all of the requisite symptoms of a clinical eating disorder. In addition to obesity, other common forms of childhood eating disturbances are as follows: food avoidance emotional disorders, selective eating, and pervasive refusal syndrome (Bryant-Waugh & Lask, 2002).

Anorexia nervosa is the most common full-syndrome eating disorder in young children, whereas the required criteria for full-syndrome bulimia are rarely met prior to age 14 (Bryant-Waugh & Lask, 2002). In older youth, it is more common to observe disordered eating such as dieting, bingeing and overeating cycles, and purging episodes that do not alone meet the full criteria for an individual to be diagnosed with a clinical eating disorder.

The best estimates have shown that between 0.3% to 4.2% of adolescents and young adults will go on to develop a clinically diagnosed eating disorder (Hoek & Van Hoeken, 2003; Keski-Rahkonen et al., 2007; Keski-Rahkonen et al., 2009). These estimates do not include those who experience eating disturbances that reflect eating problems that do not meet the diagnostic threshold of a formal eating disorder. Reports indicate prevalence rates for disordered eating behaviors are as high as 16% and 30% for males and females, respectively (Scott & Sobczak, 2002). Furthermore, researchers have estimated that 25% of all children in the US are overweight or at high risk of becoming overweight (Ogden, Flegal, Carroll, & Johnson, 2002; Rich et al., 2005); however, it is noteworthy to mention that there is likely some unaccounted overlap in the prevalence rates for disordered eating and overweight groups.

The majority of individuals diagnosed with clinical eating disorders are female (*DSM-IV-TR*, 2000). Although it seems to be much less common, eating disorders do occur in males as well. Current estimates indicate that for every ten to fifteen females diagnosed with anorexia or bulimia, there will be one male diagnosed with an eating disorder (Woodside et al., 2001). Overweight and obesity rates are reported to be the highest among African American females and Mexican Americans males (Rand Health, 2004). Furthermore, the number of overweight African American and Hispanic children are increasing at a faster rate than the number of overweight Caucasian children (Strauss & Pollack, 2001).

Morbidity (incidence of ill health in a population) associated with eating disorders is alarmingly high. The Fourth Edition, Text Revision of the Diagnostic and Statistical Manual for Mental Disorders (DSM-IV-TR, American Psychiatric Association [APA], 2000) estimates mortality rates (number of deaths in a population) to be over 10% for Anorexia Nervosa, which is often considered the most dangerous eating disorder. Crude estimates of mortality rates for other types of eating disorders are reported to be as high as 5.2% (Crow et al., 2009). When examining mortality rates for individuals who are 20 years of age and younger, research has estimated that approximately seven out of every 1,000 people will die from an eating disorder (Crow et al., 2009). Although the mortality rate is not reported to be as high as those found in children with eating disorders, in both short and long-term comparisons, overweight and obese children disproportionately report suffering from chronic cardiovascular, metabolic, pulmonary, gastrointestinal, skeletal, neurological, and psychosocial problems (Daniels, 2006).

Given the serious risk associated with eating disorders and obesity, early detection and intervention are important to obtain the best prognosis (Duker & Slade, 1988). School systems can play a vital role in the prevention and early intervention of eating problems in children. School personnel (e.g. teachers, guidance counselors, coaches, school nurses) are in a unique position to observe and recognize the warning signs and symptoms of eating behaviors. As such, school personnel can provide viable support in averting problems before they begin or identifying problems while they are in the early stages, which is associated with better outcomes for youth (Bardick et al., 2004). The following sections will provide a general overview of eating problems specific to child and adolescent years. Specifically, the following topics will be covered: risk factors for childhood eating problems, the signs and symptoms that educators may observe in schools, a three-tiered prevention and intervention plan to address disordered eating behaviors in the school setting, and methods for monitoring the effectiveness of intervention plans.

Conceptual foundations

Body image disturbances are associated with all types of disturbed eating patterns, including disordered eating (e.g. obesity) and eating disorders (e.g. anorexia and bulimia) (Neumark-Sztainer et al., 2002). Body image (one's perception of the aesthetics or attractiveness of his or her person/body) is central to self-concept (how one feels about himself or herself), which has important implications for multiple areas of psychological functioning and quality of life (Cash, Theriault, & Annis, 2004). Body image is a multidimensional construct that includes various cognitive, emotional and behavioral components. For example:

Cognitive Dimension	Emotional Dimension	Behavioral Dimension
Perception	Affect related to physical self	Excessive exercise
Attitude	Fear of Fatness	Diet Restrictiveness
Thoughts about appearance	Body Distortions	Purging
Body distortions	Body Dissatisfaction	Clothing Choices
Body dissatisfaction		Activity Choices
Investment (time spent thinking about body image)		
Evaluation (self-schemas & the internalized appearance ideals)		
Preference for thinness		

Distortions can have a cognitive (e.g. I look fat, I'll never lose weight), emotional (e.g. I feel fat, I hate my body) or behavioral component (e.g. I eat, select clothes, or attend public outings based on body exposure). Body perceptions are defined as the ability to accurately and correctly perceive one's body size. When there are perceptual disturbances, these may lead to body image dissatisfaction, disparagement, or distortions. When there are attitudinal disturbances, the accuracy of body size estimation are intact; however, there are cognitive or emotional interferences (Vocks, Lgenbauer, Ruddel, & Troje, 2007) that lead to the presence of extreme body image dissatisfaction/disparagement, or concern about body shape, body size, or body weight (e.g. my stomach is flabby; Bergstrom & Neighbors, 2006). Disturbances associated with common developmental tasks include various aspects of poor parental attachment at a young age (Unoka, Tölgyes, Czobor, & Simon, 2010), timing of puberty that is either too early or too late, peer teasing (Lunner et al., 2000; Moore, Dohm, Pike, Wilfley, & Fairburn, 2002), or onset of dating and sexual experiences that may lead to a heightened awareness of the body and associated discomfort. Sociocultural influences that promote disturbed perceptions about the body include the media, peer, social comparisons, and cultural ideals about body size and shape (Stice, 2002).

The quicker the body size change, the greater the overestimation of size. Indeed, some researchers have considered brain-based cortical deficits where there may be problems with visuospatial abilities, which lead to distorted perceptions of the body where individuals of smaller sizes are more prone to overestimate body size (Thompson & Spana, 1991). Other researchers explain difficulties in the context of the sociocultural ideal where beauty and femininity are primarily displayed through thinness (Hallewell & Harvey, 2006).

It is clear that each of these factors can and do contribute to body dissatisfaction in both males and females. However, the combination of any of these factors is likely to differ across individuals. Similarly, individuals are vulnerable to different influences, in which one factor may prove to be more salient to one person as compared to another.

Definitions: Anorexia Nervosa, Bulimia Nervosa and Obesity

Anorexia Nervosa, Bulimia Nervosa and Eating Disorders Not Otherwise Specified (ED-NOS) comprise the three categories of eating disorders in the Fourth Edition, Text Revision of the Diagnostic and Statistical Manual for Mental Disorders (DSM-IV-TR, American Psychiatric Association; [APA], 2000). The essential characteristics of Anorexia Nervosa include an intentional failure to maintain a minimally normal body weight based on age and height, excessive concern about gaining weight, and a distorted perspective of one's body shape or size. Postmenarcheal females must experience amenorrhea, which is the absence of a least three consecutive menstrual cycles to qualify for the disorder. Not only are individuals underweight, but also they show an extreme discomfort and disturbance related to the way in which one's body weight or shape is experienced and show an undue influence of body weight or shape on self-evaluation. This group is characterized by denial of the seriousness of their low body weight.

Until recently, many clinicians did not believe that children, particularly girls, could manifest "true anorexia" (Bryant-Waugh & Lask, 2002). Specifically, since children often have not yet reached menarche, they do not experience a disruption in menstruation cycles. For children, weight loss is better determined by a failure to make weight gains and is experienced by parents as food avoidance, preoccupation with weight and calories, dread of fatness, over-exercising, self-induced vomiting, laxative abuse, obsessive-compulsive features, anxiety, depression, and expressions of perfectionism (Bryant-Waugh & Lask, 2002). Early Anorexia may first present as symptoms of nausea, abdominal pain, feeling full and being unable to swallow. There is rarely a physical cause identified for these symptoms, other than poor nutrition and there is generally not a history of psychiatric problems, feeding problems, or childhood obesity in this group. Medical complications that are reported include: delayed growth, polycystic ovaries, impaired fertility, osteoporosis including reduced bone density, delay in bone age, and reduced blood flow to the limbic system which is detectable in brain scans (Bryant-Waugh & Lask, 2002). For children with anorexia, an estimated one-half to two-thirds make a full recovery, with the remainder experiencing continued persistent difficulty (Bryant-Waugh & Lask, 2002).

Bulimia Nervosa is characterized by binge eating and maladaptive compensatory strategies to prevent weight gain. Individuals with Bulimia Nervosa place excessive emphasis on their body shape and weight for self-evaluation. A binge involves eating within a two-hour period a considerably larger amount of food than most people would eat in similar circumstances. The binge eating includes a sense of lack of control. Individuals with Bulimia Nervosa can be further classified by the types of compensatory strategies he or she uses following an episode of binge eating. The Purging Type compensatory strategy involves the use of the induction of vomiting or use of laxatives, diuretics, or enemas. In the Nonpurging Type compensatory strategy, the individual has used other inappropriate methods, such as excessive exercise or fasting. To meet full criteria for the diagnosis, the binge eating and maladaptive compensatory strategies must occur twice a week for three months on average (APA, 2000). There are very few cases of bulimia before the age of 14 (Byant-Waugh & Lask, 2002). Most of the "early onset" cases documented have occurred at the beginning of adolescence and thus little to nothing is known about the clinical features, medical indicators/complications, or prognosis associated with childhood bulimia.

Childhood obesity is a medical condition in which weight significantly exceeds what is normal for age and height (Centers for Disease Control and Prevention; CDC, 2008) and is essentially an excess of body fat (eMedicine Health, 2009). Body mass index (BMI), expressed as weight/height^2 (kg/m^2), typically is used to identify and categorize children who are overweight or at risk of becoming overweight. The cutoff criteria are based on the 2000 CDC BMI-for age growth charts. According to current recommendations of medical experts, children or adolescents with a BMI at or above the 95th percentile of the sex-specific BMI growth charts are classified as overweight (CDC, 2002).

Symptomatology Most Likely Seen in School Settings

Schools are often the ideal setting for early identification of eating problems because personnel are in direct contact with the majority of the child and adolescent population, including those who are potentially at risk for the development of disordered eating patterns (Neumark-Sztainer, 1996). Schools deliver lunch to approximately 26 million children each day. For 11.3 million families, schools are also providing breakfast (School Breakfast Score Card, 2011). Although policy changes in 1996 required schools to increase nutritional requirements in federally mandated school lunch programs (Sallis et al., 1999; "The Role," 2004), there has also been a sudden increase in opportunities for children to select unregulated high calorie foods through vending machines, school stores, and concession stands (US Department of Agriculture, 1994, 2001; "The Role," 2004).

Although the importance of access to a well balanced meal is accepted throughout the educational system, it is clear that some teachers may perceive eating disturbances in children as a medical or lifestyle problem that does not fall under the purview of the school personnel. Further yet, some educators are not clear on the link between eating patterns and school performance. A recent nutrition and health survey conducted with Taiwanese elementary school students showed that poor school performance was associated with unhealthy eating patterns (Fu, Cheng, Tu, & Pan, 2007). Similarly, low nutrition associated with restrictive eating (US Department of Health and Human Services, 2005) as well as an imbalance of nutrition associated with overeating and obesity are all related to poor academic and social performance at school (Taras & Potts-Datema, 2005).

Teachers may not appreciate the opportunity they have to observe eating patterns in children. Indeed, they may hold the misperception that such disorders may be seen as a medical problem, and therefore, they better fall within the domain of responsibilities of school health personnel. Interestingly, one study conducted in the U.K. found that teachers knew of more students with eating disorders than school nurses. The authors speculated that because teachers have many more direct contact hours with students compared with school nurses, teachers may be more aware of children with diagnosed eating disorders (Rees & Clark-Stone, 2006).

Symptoms of eating disorders and obesity can negatively impact a child's behaviors, cognition, emotion, and social interactions. The core symptomatology germane to eating disorders often reflects a two-fold issue: a maladaptive relationship with one's body and a maladaptive relationship with food. In fact, Cook-Cottone (2009) reported that the two strongest predictors of eating-disordered behavior are body dissatisfaction (maladaptive relationship with one's body) and dieting (restraint behaviors, indicating a maladaptive relationship with food; Cook-Cottone & Phelps, 2006; Mintz, Borchers, Bledman, & Franko, 2009; Presnell, Bearman, & Stice, 2004; Stice & Whitenton, 2002). Similarly, body dissatisfaction and unhealthy dieting are significant risks with children who are overweight or obese (Neumark-Sztainer et al., 2002).

The first aspect of eating disorder symptomatology generally is exhibited through body dissatisfaction and poor body esteem. Peterson and colleagues (2007) further elaborate on specific aspects of body dissatisfaction.

Specifically, they report that it is common for individuals with eating disorders to have an unhealthy pursuit of muscularity (McCreary & Sasse, 2000; Ricciardelli & McCabe, 2004) and an extreme motivation toward being thin (Wertheim, Martin, Prior, Sanson, & Smart, 2002).

Further, conversations that center on body dissatisfaction and diet fads/trends tend to be frequent in today's society for both children and adults. The ubiquitous nature of these conversations may lead teachers to conclude that these discussions are affiliated with a normative age group or developmental task; some may privately feel that overweight children should be dissatisfied with their bodies while other teachers may feel free to join in discussions around dieting and body image issues. However, given that these symptoms can be associated with serious disturbances of eating, teachers and schools are advised to take note, consider the risk of these behaviors and act according to the accumulation of concern for a specific youth.

The second classical symptom of an eating disorder occurs when dysfunctional patterns with eating are exhibited. These issues can occur at two ends of the spectrum. That is, some individuals may chronically diet and avoid food, contending that food is a negative factor that leads to weight gain rather than a source of nutrition. Chronic dieters are those who intend to eat less than desired (Gorman & Allison, 1995) and constantly struggle to maintain control over eating behaviors (Herman & Polivy, 1975). On the other hand, those at the opposing end of the continuum may abuse food and intake calories for reasons other than physical hunger. Food abuse may result in overeating beyond the point of satiety without regard to the body's hunger cues.

When considering the risk factors for eating disorders, the three factors that are most commonly found in the literature include adolescents' relationships with their mothers, their susceptibility to the direct comments from and behaviors of peers, and their reaction to the messages from the media (Peterson, Paulson, & Williams, 2007). Relatedly, Arluk and colleagues (2003) and Kimbro et al. (2007) conducted studies that revealed that *maternal obesity* is the strongest independent predictor of childhood obesity; however, other research (Salsberry & Reagan, 2005) has suggested that *maternal pre-pregnancy obesity* influences early childhood obesity. Still, other correlates of risk for all types of disordered eating include negative emotionality, mood problems, internalizing tendencies (e.g. depression, anxiety), lower self-esteem, substance use, and suicidal ideation/attempts (Ackard, Fulkerson, & Neumark-Sztainer, 2011; Chamay-Weber, Narring, & Michaud, 2005; Leon, Fulkerson, Perry, & Dube, 1994).

Although not all of these factors may be readily observable by teachers, negative mood, low self-esteem, unhealthy weight reduction patterns, and body dissatisfaction are symptoms in children that may be evidenced at school. Additionally, educators can be aware of weight-related teasing and bullying; teachers need to be prepared to prevent and/or respond to such behaviors (Cook-Cottone, 2009). Although the identification of the risk factors of eating disorders in children is only one component of a comprehensive intervention approach, teachers can play an important role in providing the first step.

Eating Disorder Prevention and Intervention

In the treatment of eating disturbances and disorders, prevention is the preferred and more effective method of intervention. Given the poor prognosis often associated with eating disorders, prevention and early intervention are vital components to improving outcomes for those who are at risk. Although school personnel are not equipped to provide professional treatment for children with eating disorders, educators can play an invaluable role in the prevention of these serious psychiatric conditions.

The term "preventative medicine" is used to describe interventions that are implemented in an attempt to prevent or reduce the effects of the disease or illness. There are various levels of prevention, including primary, secondary, and tertiary methods. Primary prevention strategies are concerned with taking measures to avoid the onset of a disease; thereby intervening before the problem begins. Secondary prevention methods aim to identify a disease in its initial stages in an effort to intervene early and reduce the negative effects of the disease. Finally, tertiary prevention focuses on recovery from a disease and relapse prevention.

Three-Tiered Prevention Plan

Tier I prevention strategies are focused on measures that school districts can take to prevent eating disorders and disordered eating behaviors in all students, including those who may be at high risk. Tier II prevention strategies are for children and adolescents who have been identified as a child with an eating disorder. Interventions will focus on methods for early identification and facilitating early intervention to improve the prognosis for affected students. Finally, Tier III strategies are for assisting children and adolescents who have been identified as a child with an eating disorder and are in the recovery stage of illness. Recommended strategies focus on the transition back to school for students who required hospitalization because of an eating disorder. Also, common modifications/accommodations to student educational plans that may be warranted during the recovery phase of treatment will be discussed.

Tier I: Primary prevention

Primary prevention methods are designed to decrease the likelihood of a specific undesirable event or outcome. This level of prevention in the educational context will target a variety of disordered eating behaviors, which may place a student at risk for unhealthy outcomes, including childhood obesity or an eating disorder. The emphasis at Tier I, therefore, is on promoting a healthy school environment that will foster a healthy attitude towards eating and exercise in students, positive body esteem, and well-balanced self-image. Specific recommendations are reviewed in the sections below.

Who is at risk?

The beginning point in developing a primary prevention plan is to determine who may be at risk. Experts on eating disturbances and disorders agree that there are multiple pathways through which an individual may develop problematic eating patterns, however; there are risk factors that tend to be common to childhood and adolescence which may be used as markers to identify students who may be considered high risk (refer to Table 8.1 for a quick reference of the common risk factors seen in the school setting).

Perhaps the most well-established risk factors are related to gender (e.g. 90% of those diagnosed with an eating disorder are female; *DSM-IV-TR*, 2000) and age (e.g. mid-adolescence, around age 14, and late adolescence, around age 18; *DSM-IV-TR, 2000*). Age related risks are also associated with the onset of body changes (Walsh & Cameron, 2005).

Other studies have shown that negative comments about body weight and shape can lead to disruptions in a child's self-image and subsequently result in disruptions of normative eating patterns. As a result, children who are teased or bullied in school may be at a greater risk for developing eating disorder symptoms (Lunner et al., 2000; Moore, Dohm, Pike, Wilfley, & Fairburn, 2002). Also, some reports have indicated that involvement in various extracurricular activities where there is more focus place on body weight and shape (e.g. cheerleading, dancing, gymnastics) may also heighten the risk of a student developing eating disorder symptoms (Smolak, Murnen, & Ruble, 2000).

When considering risk factors, it is also important to understand the influence of peers and social networks. Studies have shown that beliefs about body weight are greatly influenced by the attitudes and values held within peer networks (Paxton, Schutz, Wertheim, & Muir, 1999). To be specific, one study showed that adolescents who believed that being thin would increase interpersonal success were more likely to diet and demonstrate concerns about body, weight, and shape (Gerner & Wilson, 2005). Also, researchers have shown that students who have friends that

Table 8.1 Common Risk Factors and Warning Signs of Obesity and
Eating Disorders in Children

	Obesity	Eating Disorders
Physical/ Behavioral	Insufficient physical activity, higher birth weight, dietary restraint, binge eating, using radical weight control tactics (e.g. purging, using laxatives), high birth weight, maternal pregnancy obesity, child obesity within the first five years of life, insufficient sleep, unhealthy diet and eating habits (e.g. skipping breakfast, high caloric diet)	Dieting/restrictive eating patterns, significant weight loss, binge eating, purging, excessive exercising or obsession with exercise, avoidance of eating situations, easily fatigued, weight fluctuations, dieting, frequent trips to the bathroom
Psychological	Depression, negative affect, limited coping skills to deal with emotions	Depression, anxiety, mood swings, irritability, poor self-esteem, body dissatisfaction or disturbance, feelings of inadequacy, anger, loneliness, problems expressing and identifying emotions, perfectionism, problems with concentration, all or nothing thinking, problems retaining information, indecisiveness
Social	Low socioeconomic status, parental obesity, social withdrawal, poor health behaviors in family	Social isolation, change in social patterns, history of sexual abuse, cultural pressures to conform to the thin-ideal, social messages that emphasize self-worth based on physical appearance, interpersonal problems, history of being teased or bullied, family problems

are preoccupied with weight loss and dieting tend to have higher concerns about their own body image (Paxton et al., 1999).

Students who are vulnerable to developing an eating disorder also tend to display qualities which may be easily observed, yet are often overlooked in the classroom milieu. Patterns of perfectionism and overachieving across various domains of life are often commonly observed in those who suffer from Anorexia Nervosa. As these traits are generally seen as socially acceptable and even admirable, these characteristics also tend to be symptoms commonly associated with eating disorders. As a result, well-meaning adults can unknowingly reinforce symptoms in students who may be at risk or suffering from an undiagnosed eating disorder.

What can schools do to help?

Once at risk youth are identified, the question becomes, "What, if anything, can schools do to help these youngsters?" While the task of developing a prevention plan may seem daunting and overwhelming to educators, it is definitely feasible and with some planning can be easily incorporated into the general education setting.

Staff development

An integral component to any successful eating disorder prevention program in the school setting is teacher and staff education. Karl Menninger (n.d.) once said, "What the teacher is, is more important than what he teaches," reminding us that what the student learns from the teacher extends far beyond the basic content provided in the classroom. Stated differently, teachers and educational professionals are first and foremost role models who hold great influence in the lives of their students. Leading experts in the area of eating disorders have suggested that messages promulgated in modern-day culture and society exert external pressure on youth to conform to the cultural thin-ideal (Stice, 2002). Youngsters are exposed to many different messages that attempt to define their worth and value, diminishing the measure of who they are to the numbers of their weight or the size of their clothing.

Teachers are in a unique position to counteract the potentially harmful effects of such cultural messages. It would be unwise and naïve, however, to conclude that educators have been exempt from the influence and the impact of these same messages that negatively affect our youth. Therefore, it is important for school staff to develop knowledge and insight into their own personal values, beliefs, and practices regarding weight, dieting, and body image (Graber, Archibald, & Brooks-Gunn, 1999).

The recommendation for professional development trainings and workshops is foundational to any successful prevention plan for several reasons. First, teachers must be aware of their own biases and the impact that their perceptions have on those they teach (Piran, 2004). For instance, an educator who was teased as a child for being overweight may have a prejudice against children who are naturally more slender or thin. On the other hand, someone who highly esteems healthy eating and daily activity may be more critical or look down on a student who is overweight. Researchers have shown that when teachers are unaware of their own biases, they may unknowingly display prejudices against some children while showing favoritism to others (Berg, 1996). Thus, while our own past experiences will inform our current perceptions, effective educators will be aware of and monitor the effect that those biases have on students in their classroom.

Secondly, staff development trainings can be used to promote increased sensitivity and compassion towards students. Specifically, when staff members are asked to examine their own beliefs, attitudes, and past experiences related to their own issues with weight, eating, or body esteem, they may find they can connect with students more effectively. It is very likely that at some point or another, teachers will have struggled with issues that their students may be facing in the present moment (e.g. bullying, weight problems, body dissatisfaction, not feeling accepted by peers). Reconnecting with their own experiences may help them to better relate with their students and identify more effective methods for promoting and modeling positive self-image and body esteem in their classrooms (Piran, 2004).

Finally, many educators may not be familiar with the interaction between content and the process of teaching health wellness (Piran, 2004). Evaluations of eating disorder prevention programs have emphasized that program effectiveness is not merely determined by the curriculum taught but also by the way the curriculum is modeled by the teacher (Bassler, 2001; Piran, 2004). Since, as mentioned, educators are not exempt from the influence of media messages, it is important for districts to provide in-service opportunities that offer focused discussion groups and experiential exercises that invite teachers to explore the ways their own thoughts and behaviors have been shaped by the culture (O'Dea & Maloney, 2000; Piran, 2004). Topics to examine include: teachers' attitudes toward physical exercise, teachers' attitudes towards their own bodies, teachers' biases towards various body shapes and sizes, information on age-appropriate nutrition, ways to promote positive attitudes toward physical activity in staff and students, ways to promote positive body esteem in staff and students, warning signs of eating disorders, and general education about symptoms and causes of eating disorders (Piran, 2004). Teachers can then incorporate their experiences, and those they learn from others, to best deliver health messages.

There are many persisting myths about eating disturbances and disorders. Furthermore, the field describing eating problems and medical advances are always developing and, as such, general information as well as state of the art findings should be included in staff in-services. Trainer qualifications should be current; in schools, trainers are often school psychologists, school guidance counselors, psychiatrists, nutritionists or other eating disorder specialists. Most critically, it is important for teachers and school personnel to understand that eating disorders are not just about food and weight. They are complex psychiatric conditions that can be related to less obvious issues (e.g. feelings of inadequacy, feelings of rejection, ongoing peer bullying and teasing, family problems, and identity problems).

Also, educators must realize that children with eating disorders come in all different shapes and sizes. For instance, a student with anorexia may look painfully emaciated and underweight; however, an individual with bulimia may be equally as ill while maintaining an average weight. Individuals who binge will most likely be overweight; however, there are some conditions where a person will binge and then vomit his or her food, fast, or exercise to maintain a normal weight. In essence, the symptoms (e.g. purging, bingeing, restricting) drive weight changes. However, a student's weight can fluctuate as the eating disorder progresses and for this reason, weight measurements cannot be the sole determinant for deciding if a student is at risk or is suffering from an eating disorder. Rather, weight changes may occur along a continuum from emaciation to obesity depending on the kind of disordered eating behavior a student is experiencing.

Finally, it is important for staff to recognize that eating disorders look different in children and adolescents. That is, children are most likely to show subsyndromal (not as extreme behaviors yet their impact is still significantly impairing) or atypical (deviations from the typical patterns of problem eating) in nature. That is, younger children and teens may present with symptoms of disordered eating (e.g. dieting, overeating, purging, inappropriately using diuretics, etc.) that do not meet the full criteria or in some cases or may not resemble the typical symptom profile associated with clinical eating disorders. School staff need to be prepared to develop prevention plans that will address a variety of symptoms.

Safe and healthy school environments

As Abraham Maslow taught us, safety is one of the chief fundamental needs we have as human beings. Safety extends beyond the assurance of our physical welfare but also includes our sense that we are safe emotionally and psychologically too. Therefore, another crucial element in eating disorder prevention programming is creating a safe and healthy school environment. In order to accomplish this goal, it may require some examination and possible revisions to current school policies and practices.

One issue for school districts to consider is the common practice of weighing students and obtaining body fat measurements. Also, increased concerns about the epidemic of childhood obesity have led to recent legislation in some states that would require schools to track and report student's BMI to parents. While we know that early identification and intervention are important in the prevention of eating disorders and childhood obesity, some have argued that these screening practices may be ineffective (Cogan, Smith, & Maine, 2008; Keca & Cook-Cottonne, 2005) and actually stigmatizing.

There have been many concerns presented by medical experts about the appropriateness of using BMI as a screening tool for students who are overweight or obese. The American Association for Pediatrics (AAP, 2004) recognizes BMI as a valid measurement of weight status stating that it is a "surrogate" measure of adiposity or body fat. There are, however, limitations to its effectiveness, particularly in its use with children. That is, there are a variety of developmental changes that children and adolescents experience that may lead to changes in their body mass and composition. As children grow, for instance, they may experience disproportionate spurts of growth in height and weight until they fully mature, which may impact the BMI measurement (Cogan et al., 2008). Also, BMI does not take into account variables such as body frame and muscularity which may lead to elevated BMI ratings for students that are a healthy weight (Cogan et al., 2008).

Although the BMI measurement may be imperfect, it does not necessarily mean that it is contraindicated to use for screening purposes. In fact, the AAP (2004) recommends that BMI be calculated periodically as a routine practice for children. What is unclear is whether the school setting is the most appropriate place to offer this form of preventative care. Some suggest that it is not and indeed may adversely affect the psychological or social well-being of children. Specifically, one concern is that focusing on body measurements may lead to several issues for students (e.g. bullying, negative social stigma with peers and teachers, increased self-consciousness, dietary restraint, eating disorder symptoms). Additionally, another issue is what parents will do with the information that they are provided with through BMI report cards. Moreover, schools are not treatment facilities and teacher are not trained medical professionals; therefore, schools that have adopted this practice must be able to provide information and referral sources to parents through which they can seek out professional counsel when needed (Cogan et al., 2008).

In addition to the revision of school policies about weighing and measuring students, a second topic that is important in increasing students' sense of safety in their school environment is related to the issues of bullying. While peer teasing and bullying unfortunately tend to be common, it is nonetheless unhealthy for children. Teasing that is focused on students' bodies and weight has been identified as a factor that increases the risk of developing eating disturbances and disorders (Moore et al., 2002). As a result, it is imperative that schools develop and enforce policies to reduce bullying, teasing, and prejudice (O'Dea & Maloney, 2000).

Similar to bullying issues among students, another aspect of a safe school environment concerns the student-teacher relationship. Specifically, it is important that teachers and coaches do not exert undue pressure to be thin or lose weight. With certain classes (e.g. physical education) and activities (e.g. wrestling, cheerleading), there may be more focus drawn to the physical aspects of the student. It is imperative that athletic instructors and coaches understand and respect the position they hold and the influence they have in the lives of students.

The National Eating Disorder Association (NEDA, 2005) recommends that coaches do not focus heavily on the weight of the student athletes they train and that derogatory comments about weight and body size of students should not be tolerated for any reason. Rather than focusing on weight or body fat, NEDA (2005) recommends that coaches redirect students to focus on aspects of physical training and conditioning that will help to improve their athletic performance (e.g. strength training). Always, coaches need to remember that the health of the athlete should never be compromised for the sake of athletic performance or winning a game (NEDA, 2005). Instead coaches can play an important role in preventing problematic eating, eating disturbances (e.g. unhealthy weight gain or loss) or eating disorders by promoting positive self-image and body esteem in student athletes.

Finally, in an effort to create an environment that supports health and wellness in students, a recent report by Rossen and Rossen (2011) provides several recommendations. First, the authors recommend that schools provide a wide array of healthy food options that students can choose from and limit the times available when less nutritious foods are displayed or available for purchase. Additionally, in school cafeterias or vending machines, the report suggests using a color-coded system to identify and distinguish foods which yield greater nutritional value from those which provide less nutritional benefit. For instance, foods could be colored coded similar to a traffic light (green, yellow, and red) to signify the nutritional value, indicating that students would ideally consume more green foods while occasionally treating themselves to yellow and red foods.

The authors also suggested that schools make provisions for students to participate in healthy living behaviors throughout the school day. For instance, establishing a policy that allows students to carry bottled water into classrooms may help students develop a healthy habit and ensure that they are receiving the proper amount of hydration throughout the day. Another example may be for students to have the option to spend free class periods in a recreational room or monitored outdoor track where they can walk or participate in various sports or activities for leisure. While this may be an inappropriate choice for some students diagnosed with an eating disorder, from a primary prevention perspective, an open-activity time may help students to form healthy habits and attitudes around exercise and physical activity.

Student education

The final component to an effective primary prevention plan is to educate students directly. With the strong current of cultural messages that seek to shape beliefs about beauty, attractiveness, and success, student education is a crucial element in the war on eating disorders. The rationale for educating students is not merely to impart knowledge. Rather, the purpose is to teach students to think critically about the messages that they hear and to provide alternate messages that will promote health and wellness.

There are a variety of different curricula available; however, there are basic elements that a curriculum should include to be considered for use in the classroom. Most experts agree that prevention curriculum should not spend a significant amount of time educating students about the symptoms of eating disorders because youth tend to be impressionable and may inadvertently learn dysfunctional behaviors (Russell & Ryder, 2001). Instead, the focus of lessons should be centered on teaching healthy living attitudes and behaviors. Specifically, the curriculum should include education in the following domains: *developing a healthy body and self-image* (e.g. promoting positive body esteem, helping students to develop a well-rounded self-image that is based on more than just physical appearance, encouraging the acceptance of bodies of all shapes and sizes), *establishing healthy and well-balanced eating habits* (e.g. teaching students about nutrition, moving students away from thinking food is "good or bad," helping students to develop insight into personal food preferences and eating patterns), and *forming healthy attitudes about exercise and activity* (e.g. redefining students' perceptions on exercise, brainstorming with students to identify enjoyable forms of activity, learning to exercise to have fun and enjoy a healthy body rather than exercising to lose weight). These curricular elements are essential for all children, including those with problems of under and overeating (Doak, Visscher, Renders, & Seidell, 2006).

Tier II: Secondary prevention

Despite the best prevention efforts, there will be some children and teens who proceed beyond the point of being an "at risk student" to developing a full-syndrome eating disorder or who meet the criteria for obesity (e.g. Body Mass Index of at or above the 95th percentile of the sex-specific growth charts; CDC, 2002). Under such conditions, the goals are early identification and intervention to prevent the eating problems from becoming more serious and more difficult to treat (Bardick et al., 2004). In Tier II interventions, educators are going to be primarily functioning as facilitators and it is important that the roles are clearly defined. That is, school personnel are not responsible for the treatment of an eating disorder but may be able to serve in helping a student with an eating disorder in a number of ways.

Preparedness is a key to success in secondary prevention. Specifically, it would be wise for school districts to have a protocol for handling situations where a student may be experiencing a psychiatric condition that is significant enough that it may warrant intervention and professional assistance. The NEDA (2008a) recommends that schools provide their staff with checklists of signs and symptoms associated with eating disorders/eating disturbances that can be helpful in describing the symptoms to monitor as well as descriptions regarding behavioral changes that teachers can look for in the student's condition. They also advise that schools have specific procedures for referring students who are suspected of having an eating disorder and or weight problem. Specific suggestions include the development of a Student Assistance Program (SAP), which can serve as a team that addresses non-academic related concerns about students. It has also been suggested that there be designated individuals within the school district who can serve as the school-based resource personnel (SBRP) who will field concerns about students who may have an undiagnosed eating disorder or a developing weight concern (Smolak, Harris, Levine & Shisslak, 2001). The designated SBRP may be someone who has a particular interest in the area of eating disorders (e.g. school nurse, guidance counselor, school psychologist, SAP team member) and is willing to devote time and energy to work as a liaison on behalf of the district to arrange meetings with students and their parents to discuss concerns and making appropriate referrals to specialists for treatment when it is warranted.

When symptoms of an eating disorder are observed by educational professionals, it is important that the issue be addressed with the student and his or her parents/guardians. Conversations should focus on the welfare of the student and a representative from the school should openly and honestly express the concerns of the district, describing the observed behaviors and symptoms in the student. Referral information should be provided to parents and they should be encouraged to seek a professional evaluation (Bardick et al., 2004). During this conversation, it is not uncommon for students to deny having a problem and school personnel must recognize that this is part of the illness. Denial of symptoms is often triggered by fears of gaining weight, embarrassment about the symptoms, or even can reflect impaired reasoning and judgment which can be a secondary issue to starvation (often common with anorexia; Vitousek et al., 1998).

SBRP can also play an invaluable role in working with families in districts that have implemented BMI screening programs. An executive summary by the Center for Disease Control (Nihiser et al., 2007) states that schools need to provide parents with understandable and respectful explanations of their child's health, BMI status and when appropriate, parents should be offered referral information for follow-up care.

Additionally, while it is less common, students may approach a teacher or coach whom they trust to obtain assistance with their eating or weight concerns. In such situations, staff must be mindful not to become overly involved in trying to treat the eating disorder but can instead connect the student with the formal school procedure (e.g. SBRP) or take the steps to contact the family and make needed referrals when appropriate.

Tier III: Tertiary prevention

The last tier is focused on preventing relapse and facilitating the process of recovery for students who have been identified as a child or adolescent with an eating disorder or severe weight problem. Although treatment for eating disorders is multifaceted and specialized, there tend to be three common phases of treatment and they are as follows: a) restoration of a healthy weight and normal eating behaviors, b) significant changes in thinking and behavioral patterns, and c) relapse prevention (Bardick et al., 2004). Similarly, treatments for obesity will target the specific problems a student is experiencing, such as Type II diabetes (Fagot-Campagna, Saadinem, Flegal, & Beckles, 2000), orthopedic problems, asthma, sleep apnea and high blood pressure (Daniels, 2006).

Eating disorders do not always require hospitalization to provide quality treatment; however, in some cases it is necessary. Other times, students may receive intensive outpatient treatment that enables them to continue attending school. Under either circumstance, the student will most likely require adjustments and modifications made to his or her educational plan and when a student has been hospitalized, he or she will require assistance from school personnel in the process of re-entry into the general academic setting.

The NEDA (2008b) provides a list of recommendations for schools in the process of helping a student who has been diagnosed with an eating disorder. In the process of recovery and transition back to the classroom, it is suggested that schools set up a meeting with the student and his or her family prior to the student's return to school. When a student has been out of school for an extended period of time, it is reasonable to assume that the child or teen may experience some social stress and feel disconnected from his or her peers. Therefore, the NEDA (2008b) suggests that schools offer the student a "buddy" with whom he or she can sit with at lunch or walk to classes with to ease the student back into the routine of daily academic life.

Also, adjustments may need to be made to the student's educational program. The National Association for School Psychologists (NASP; Cook-Cottonne & Scime, 2006) has suggested that schools may need to develop a modified educational plan with a reduced workload, extended deadlines for assignments, and alternative assignments/class schedules when needed (e.g. students with eating disorders may not be able to participate in physical education classes upon re-entry). Schools may need to be flexible with the student and make accommodations to his or her schedule to allow the student to attend needed doctor's appointments. Also, in assisting the student's transition back into the general education milieu, students may need supportive counseling, meal monitoring, and medical monitoring. The tertiary stage of prevention will involve frequent meetings and conversations with family, psychiatric specialists, and school personnel in addition to ongoing monitoring of the student's condition in an effort to prevent relapse.

Discuss progress monitoring of interventions

Regardless of the level of prevention (Tier I, II, or III), it is important for students and teachers to be mindful of the progress a student is making. That is, how well are students engaged and responding to curriculum or specialized interventions around appropriate eating and physical activities. Once an area of concern is identified (e.g. child is restricting food intake or child is not participating in physical activity), the intervention selected (e.g. student will weigh total food intake during lunch, student will monitor blood sugar level after lunch with school nurse) and progress is defined (e.g. student will eat 80% of selected food, or 80% of foods eaten during lunch will have the desired effects on blood sugar levels), then the interval for review should be designated. Behaviors that require smaller changes (e.g. participating in whole school curriculum from 80% to 100% of the time) can be reviewed less often, behaviors that have been intractable or are very far from acceptable (e.g. blood sugar levels are not stable more than 20% of the week at baseline) need to be tracked often so that modifications can be made in a timely fashion.

Tracking a child's progress is accomplished easily by using a graph. First, a baseline needs to be established. For instance, in a day or week, how often is the student engaged in the behavior that we seek to modify? To be more specific, how often is the student skipping meals or hiding or hoarding sweets? On the graph it is useful to record a measureable data point, such as number of days or number of lunches, (on the X-axis) and percent of activity (on the Y-axis) allowing the teacher, child and parent to review daily or weekly progress. It is recommended that the child chart (if s/he is old enough they can make their own graphs) and review his or her progress toward the (positive) behavior that is established. When it is clear that there is no (further) improvement in a given area, then the intervention should be reviewed, modified or changed completely.

Case Study

Gabby Mae is a 16-year old student in the 10th grade in her high school. Her parents have always described her as the "perfect child," stating that she is very compliant and rarely gives them any problems. She excels in her academic work and also is involved in student council and various extracurricular activities, including both track and cheerleading. Gabby is a pleasant student who gets along well with her teachers and coaches. She is also well-accepted by her peers. After joining cheerleading however, Gabby began experiencing increased self-consciousness related to her weight. Other girls on the cheerleading squad would compare their "facts and figures" which referred to various body measurements (e.g. waist circumference, weight,% body fat, etc.). While Gabby's weight was well within the average range as she compared herself with the other girls on the squad, she began to believe she was not thin enough. At first, she became self-conscious about her thighs where she naturally carried more weight because of her body shape. Gabby started a daily exercise regime intended to address her "problem area" but did not feel that she was experiencing adequate results. Next, she modified her eating plan to significantly reduce her caloric intake and increased her frequency of exercising to twice a day. Gabby's coach, Mrs. Bloom, who also is the health and physical education teacher, had just finished an in-service on the warning signs for eating disorders. She began to notice that Gabby was displaying some symptoms of an eating disorder. Specifically, she noticed that there was a considerable and noticeable drop in Gabby's weight that occurred in a short period of time. She also had overheard Gabby talking with some of the other girls and about how "fat" she looked and that she "still had a lot of weight to lose." One of the cheerleaders approached Mrs. Bloom to tell her that she was fairly sure Gabby was purging her food after lunch. At this point, Mrs. Bloom pulled Gabby aside after practice to discuss her concerns. Gabby denied the purging behaviors and stated that she was just on a diet to get in shape and lose a little weight. It was clear to Mrs. Bloom that Gabby seemed to minimize her observable problem and dismiss Mrs. Bloom's concerns. Therefore, Mrs. Bloom consulted the school guidance counselor, Miss Grace. The following plan was developed.

First, Miss Grace called Gabby's parents to preview the concerns. Next, Miss Grace and Mrs. Bloom set a meeting with Mr. and Mrs. Mae where they formalized concerns and then asked Gabby to join the meeting. Since there was no change in Gabby's school functioning (e.g. grades remained high and her relationships remained appropriate) there was little "educational" concern; however, given the developing pattern, the symptoms were significant enough to be considered for review. The parents agreed and the school provided them with contact information for follow-up evaluation by a local psychologist who specializes in the treatment of eating disorders. A follow-up meeting with the school was set up to review the results of the evaluation and any recommendations that could be helpful at school.

The initial evaluation resulted in an inpatient hospital stay when it was clear that Gabby had lost over 25% of her total body weight; a fact that she hid from her parents with long t-shirts and other loose fitting clothes. Gabby stayed in the unit for approximately one month where she participated in intensive therapy and her treatment team worked on the restoration of healthy eating patterns and a healthier weight status. After being discharged, Gabby received follow-up individual therapy two times a week to continue her progress. Prior to returning to school, Mr. and Mrs. Mae set up a meeting with the school counselor and the school psychologist. They set up a modified schedule to help her successfully transition back to the general education setting. Gabby's treatment team approved her to resume full-day classes; however, the team recommended that she refrain from participating in vigorous physical activity in class or extracurricular activities.

To help facilitate an easier social transition, the school district allowed Gabby to choose two "buddies" who were friends with whom she could walk to and from classes during the school day and with whom she ate lunch. Also, Gabby's gym schedule was modified. She was permitted to participate in low intensity activities (those that did not make her short of breath). Gabby was allowed extended time and provided with extra assistance to help her catch up with coursework missed during the hospital stay. Also, Gabby identified two staff (e.g. guidance counselor and coach) with whom she felt comfortable talking at school. She met with her guidance counselor once a week during a study hall period for supportive counseling and to address any problems during her transition back to school.

Her psychiatrist provided the parents and the school with a list of relapse indicators (e.g. frequently weighing herself, obsessing about calories, lying to family members and others about her food intake, recurring purging behaviors, exercising more than once a day, frequently measuring the circumference of body parts) and the school participated in monitoring Gabby's physical condition (e.g.% of food consumed at lunch, noting patterns of more or less consumption when eating with "buddies") and facilitating a more positive outcome for recovery (e.g. weekly thought and feeling "thermometers" to determine% of dissatisfaction with her body weight and shape and feelings of "fatness"). Gabby charted her own thoughts and feelings, was able to identify periods of worry and self-initiated support from her counselor and her coach. Note that her counselor and coach kept notes on their meetings checking for relapse symptoms. Regular meetings were held at school to discuss Gabby's progress in recovery (first monthly and then quarterly) to determine the continued need for modifications to her educational experience.

Discussion and Final Recommendations

The issue of identification and treatment of eating problems, eating distur-bances and eating disorders in children and adolescents at school is not one that is well established. That is, although school provides an excellent opportunity for prevention programming (e.g. teaching about nutrition and body health) in the same way that other types of curricula are delivered, teachers and parents are not always comfortable with the topic. Indeed, some teachers and parents consider the issue a medical one that school systems may not be fully prepared to address.

What is clear is that schools play a critical role in the education and socialization of children and to leave this portion of health education out of the school day has not been without consequences. Already, nutritional care is provided via breakfast and lunch programs and as the overeating and obesity rates in children skyrocket, it is expected that addressing the needs of the public is likely to find its way more formally into the school setting. We anticipate that the responsibility of educators to participate in the health behaviors of children will increase. Further, at the other end of the spectrum, for children with eating disorders, their needs are compre-hensive and the risk can be life threatening. As a result, the treatment of this smaller group of children will likely require specialized intervention plans (often associated with special education placement and protections) to ensure their safety at school. With good planning and increased attention to the issues of children with eating problems we are confident that educators are in an ideal position to help children develop positive behaviors and attitudes surrounding issues of eating, exercise, and body image that will lead to healthy outcomes.

References

Ackard, D. M., Fulkerson, J. A., & Neumark-Sztainer, D. (2011). Psychological and behavioral risk profiles as they relate to eating disorder diagnoses and symptomatology among a school-based sample of youth. *International Journal of Eating Disorders, 44,* 440–6. doi:10.1002/eat.20846

American Academy of Pediatrics (2003). Policy Statement: Prevention of Pediatric Overweight and Obesity: Committee on Nutrition. *Pediatrics, 112,* 424–30.

American Psychiatric Association (2000). *Diagnostic and statistical manual of mental disorders* (4th ed.). Washington, DC: Author.

—(2001). *Diagnostic and statistical manual of mental disorders* (4th ed., text revision). Washington, DC: Author.

Arluk, S. L., Branch, J. D., Swain, D. P., & Dowling, E. A. (2003). Childhood obesity's relationship to time spent in sedentary behavior. *Military Medicine*, *168*, 583–6.

Bardick, A., Bernes, K., McCulloch, A., Witko, K., Spriddle, J., Roest, A. (2004). Eating disorder intervention, prevention, and treatment: Recommendations for school counselors. *Professional School Counseling, 8*, 168–74.

Bassler, E. (2001). Challenging future nutritionists to promote normal eating. *Healthy Weight Journal, 15*, 25–46.

Berg, F. (1996). Pupil's nutrition and the school's legal position. *Croner's Head Teachers' Briefing, 134*, 6–7.

Bergstrom, R. L. & Neighbors, C. (2006). Body image disturbance and the social norms approach: An integrative review of the literature. *Journal of Social and Clinical Psychology, 25*, 975–1000. doi:10.1521/jscp.2006.25.9.975.

Bryant-Waugh, R. & Lask, B. (2002). Childhood-onset eating disorders. In C. G. Fairburn & K. D. Brownell (eds), *Eating disorders and obesity: A comprehensive handbook* (pp. 210–14). New York, NY: The Guilford Press.

Cash, T. F., Theriault, J., & Annis, N. M. (2004). Body image in an interpersonal context: Adult attachment, fear of intimacy, and social anxiety. *23*, 89–103. *Journal of Social and Clinical Psychology*. doi:10.1521/jscp.23.1.89.26987.

Centers for Disease Control and Prevention (2002). *Prevalence of overweight among children and adolescents: United States, 1999–2002*. Http://www.cdc. gov/nchs/products/pubs/pubd/hestats/overwght99.htm.

—(2008). *About BMI for children and teens*. Http://www.cdc.gov/nccdphp/dnpa/ healthyweight/assessing/bmi/childrens_BMI/about_childrens_BMI.htm.

—(2009). Overweight and Obesity. Consequences. Http://www.cdc.gov/ NCCDPHP/DNPA/obesity/childhood/consequences.htm.

Chamay-Weber, C., Narring, F., & Michaud, P. (2005). Partial eating disorders among adolescents: A review. *Journal of Adolescent Health, 37*, 417–27. doi:10.1016/j.jadohealth.2004.09.014.

Cogan, J., Smith, J., & Maine, M. (2008). The risks of a quick fix: A case against mandatory body mass index reporting laws. *Eating Disorders, 16*, 2–13.

Cook-Cottone, C. (2009). Eating disorders in childhood: Prevention and treatment supports. *Childhood Education, 85*, 300–5.

Cook-Cottone, C. P., & Phelps. L. (2006). Adolescent eating disorders. In G. G. Bear & K. M. Minke (eds), *Children's needs III* (pp. 977–88). Bethesda, MD: National Association of School Psychologists.

Cook-Cottone, C. & Scime, M. (2006). The prevention and treatment of eating disorders: An overview for school psychologists. *NASP Communique, 43*, 223–30. doi:10.1002/pits.20139.

Crow, S. J., Peterson, C. B., Swanson, S. A., Raymond, N. C., Specker, S., Eckert, E. D., & Mitchell, J. E. (2009). Increased mortality in Bulimia Nervosa and other eating disorders. *The American Journal of Psychiatry, 166*, 1342–6. doi:10.1176/appi.ajp.2009.09020247.

Daniels, S. R. (2006). The consequences of childhood overweight and obesity. *The Future of Children, 16*, 47–67. doi:10.1353/foc.2006.0004.

Doak, C. M., Visscher, T. L. S., Renders, C. M., & Seidell, J. C. (2006). The prevention of overweight and obesity in children and adolescents: A review of interventions and programmes. *Obesity Review, 7*, 111–36. doi:10.1111/j.1467-789X.2006.00234.x.

Duker, M. & Slade, R. (1988). *Anorexia nervosa and bulimia: How to help.* Buckingham: Open University Press.

Dykens, E. M., & Gerrard, M. (1986). Psychological profiles of purging bulimics, repeat dieters, and controls. *Journal of Consulting and Clinical Psychology, 54,* 283–8. doi:10.1037/0022-006X.54.3.283.

eMedicineHealth. *Obesity in children.* Http://www.emedicinehealth.com/obesity_in_children/article_em.htm.

Fagot-Campagna, A., Saadinem, J. B., Flegal, K. M., & Beckles, G. L. (2000). Emergence of type2 diabetes mellitus in children: Epidemiologic evidence. *Journal of Pediatric Endocrinology and Metabolism, 13,* 1395–1405.

Fu, M., Cheng, L., Tu, S., & Pan, W. (2007). Association between unhealthful eating patterns and unfavorable overall school performance in children. *Journal of the American Dietetic Association, 107,* 1935–42. doi:10.1016/j.jada.2007.08.010.

Gerner, B., & Wilson, P. (2005). The relationship between friendship factors and adolescent girls' body image concern, body dissatisfaction, and restrained eating. *International Journal of Eating Disorders, 37,* 313–20. doi:10.1002/eat.20094.

Gorman, B. S., & Allison, D. B. (1995). Measures of Restrained Eating. In D. B. Allison (ed.), *Handbook of assessment methods for eating behaviors and weight-related problems* (pp. 149–84). Thousand Oaks, CA: Sage Publications.

Graber, J., Archibald, A., & Brooks-Gunn, J. (1999). The role of parents in the emergence, maintenance, and prevention of eating problems and disorders. In N. Piran, M. Levine, & C. Steiner-Adair (eds), *Preventing eating disorders* (pp. 44–62). Philadelphia: Taylor & Francis.

Hallewell, E. & Harvey, M. (2006). Examination of a sociocultural model of disordered eating among male and female adolescents. *British Journal of Health Psychology, 11,* 235–48. doi:10.1348/135910705X39214.

Herman, C. P. & Polivy, J. (1975). Anxiety, restraint, and eating behavior. *Journal of Abnormal Psychology, 84,* 666–72. doi:10.1037/0021-843X.84.6.666.

Hoek, H. & Van Hoken, D. (2003). Review of the prevalence and incidence of eating disorders. *International Journal of Eating Disorders, 34,* 383–96. doi:10.1002/eat.10222.

Johnson, J., Cohen, P., Kasen, S., & Brook, J. (2002). Childhood adversities associated with risk for eating disorders or weight problems during adolescence or early adulthood. *The American Journal of Psychiatry, 159,* 394–400.

Karl Menninger (n.d.). 1-famous-quotes.com. Http://www.1-famous-quotes.com/quote/1377361

Keca, J. & Cook-Cottone, C. (2005). *Eating Disorders: Prevention is worth every ounce.* Accessed from www.nasponline.org/resources/principals/Eating%20Disorders%20WEB.pdf.

Keski-Rahkonen, A., Hoek, H.W., Linna, M.S., et al. (2009). Incidence and outcomes of Bulimia Nervosa: A nationwide population-based study. *Psychological Medicine, 39,* 823–31. doi:10.1017/S0033291708003942.

Keski-Rahkonen, A., Hoek, H. W., Susser, E. S., Linna, et al. (2007). Epidemiology and course of anorexia nervosa in the community. *The American Journal of Psychiatry, 164,* 1259–65. doi:10.1176/appi.ajp.2007.06081388.

Kimbro, R. T., Brooks-Gunn, J., & McLanahan, S. (2007). Racial and ethnic differentials in overweight and obesity among 3-year-old children. *American Journal of Public Health, 97*, 298–305. doi:10.2105/AJPH.2005.080812.

Leon, G. R., Fulkerson, J. A., Perry, C. L., & Dube, A. (1994). Family influences, school behaviors, and risk for the later development of an eating disorder. *Journal of Youth and Adolescence, 23*, 499–515. doi:10.1007/BF01537733.

Lunner, K., Werthem, E. H., Thompson, J. K., Paxton, S. J., McDonald, F., & Halvaarson, K. S. (2000). A cross-cultural examination of weight-related teasing, body image, and eating disturbance in Swedish and Australian samples. *International Journal of Eating Disorders, 28*, 430–5. doi:10.1002/1098-108X(200012)28:4<430::AID-EAT11>3.0.CO;2-Y.

McCreary, D. R., & Sasse, D. K. (2000). An exploration of the drive for muscularity in adolescent boys and girls. *Journal of American College Health, 48*, 297–304. doi:10.1080/07448480009596271.

Mintz, L., Borchers, E., Bledman, R., & Franko, D. (2008). Preventing eating and weight-related disorders: Towards an integrated best practices approach. In R. Brown & S. Lent (eds), *Handbook of counseling psychology* (4th ed., pp. 570–87). Hoboken, NJ: Wiley.

National Center for Health Statistics (2002). *Prevalence and trends of overweight among adults: United States, 1999–2000.* Http://epsl.asu.edu/ceru/ Documents / NCHS_obesity.pdf.

National Eating Disorder Association (2005). *Tips for coaches: Preventing eating disorders in athletes.* From http://www.nationaleatingdisorders.org/nedaDir/ files/documents/handouts/TipCoach.pdf.

—(2008a). *School strategies for assisting students with eating disorder.* Http:// www.nationaleatingdisorders.org/uploads/file/toolkits/NEDA-TKE-A06-SchoolStrategies.pdf.

—(2008b). *Guidance for schools on education plan for a student in treatment.* Http://www.nationaleatingdisorders.org/uploads/file/toolkits/NEDA-TKE-A11-EducationPlan.pdf.

Neumark-Sztainer, D. (1996). School-based program for preventing eating disturbances. *Journal of School Health, 66*, 64–71. doi:10.1111/j.1746-1561.1996.tb07912.x.

—(2003). Obesity and eating disorder prevention: An integrated approach. *Adolescent Medicine, 14*, 159–73.

Neumark-Sztainer, D., Story, M., Hannan, P.J., Perry, C. L., & Irving, M. (2002). Weight-related concerns and behaviors among overweight and nonoverweight adolescents: Implications for preventing weight-related disorders. *Archives of Pediatrics and Adolescent Medicine, 156*, 171–8.

Nihiser, A. J., Lee, S. M., Wechsler, H., McKenna, M., Odom, E., Reinold, C., Thompson, D., & Grummer-Strawn, L. (2007). Body mass index measurement in schools. *Journal of School Health, 77*, 651–71. doi:10.1111/j.1746-1561.2007.00249.x.

O'Dea, J. & Maloney, D. (2000). Preventing eating and body image problems in children and adolescents using the health promoting schools framework. *Journal of School Health, 70*, 18–21. doi:10.1111/j.1746-1561.2000.tb06441.x.

Ogden, C. L., Flegal, K. M., Carroll, M. D., & Johnson, C. L. (2002). Prevalence and trends in overweight among US children and adolescents, 1999–2000.

Journal of the American Medical Association, 288, 1728–32. doi:10.1001/jama.288.14.1728.

Paxton, S. J., Schutz, H. K., Wertheim, E. S., & Muir, S. L. (1999). Friendship clique and peer influences on body image concerns, dietary restraint, extreme weight loss behaviors, and binge eating in adolescent girls. *Journal of Abnormal Psychology, 108,* 255–66. doi:10.1037/0021-843X.108.2.255.

Peterson, K. A., Paulson, S. E., & Williams, K. K. (2007). Relations of eating disorder symptomology with perceptions of pressures from mother, peers, and media in adolescent girls and boys. *Sex Roles, 57,* 629–39. doi:10.1007/s11199-007-9296-z.

Phelps, L., Andrea, R., Rizzo, F. J., Johnson, L., & Main, C. M. (1993). Prevalence of self-induced vomiting and laxative/medication abuse among female adolescents: A longitudinal study. *International Journal of Eating Disorder, 14,* 375–78. doi:10.1002/1098-108X(199311)14:3<375::AID-EAT2260140316>3.0.CO;2-8.

Piran, N. (2004). Prevention series: Teachers on "being" (rather than "doing") prevention. *Eating Disorders, 12,* 1–9. doi:10.1016/S1740-1445(03)00006-8.

Presnell, K., Bearman, S. K., & Stice, E. (2004). *Risk factors for body dissatisfaction in adolescent boys and girls: A prospective study.* Wiley Interscience www.interscience.wiley.com. doi:10.1002/eat.20045.

Rand Health (2004). *Obesity and disability.* Santa Monica, CA. Http://www.rand.org/pubs/research_briefs/RB9043-1/index1.html.

Rees, L., & Clark-Stone, S. (2006). Can collaboration between education and health professionals improve the identification and referral of young people with eating disorders in schools? A pilot study. *Journal of Adolescence, 29,* 137–51. doi:10.1016/j.adolescence.2005.08.017.

Ricciardelli, L. A., & McCabe, M. P. (2004). A biopsychosocial model of disordered eating and the pursuit of muscularity in adolescent boys. *Psychological Bulletin, 130,* 179–205. doi:10.1037/0033-2909.130.2.179.

Rossen, L. & Rossen, E. (2011). Addressing obesity in secondary schools. *Principal Leadership.* Http://www.nasponline.org/resources/principals/Obesity_Mar_2011_nassp.PDF.

Russell, S. & Ryder, S. (2001). BRIDGE (Building the relationships between body image and disordered eating graph and explanation): A tool for parents and professionals. *Eating Disorders: The Journal of Treatment and Prevention, 9,* 1–14.

Sallis, J. F., McKenzie, T. L., Kolody, B., Lewis, M., Marshall, S., & Rosengard, P. (1999). Effects of health-related physical education on academic achievement: Project SPARK. *Research Quarterly for Exercise and Sport, 70,* 127–34.

Salsberry, P. J., & Reagan, P. B. (2005). Dynamics of early childhood overweight. *Pediatrics, 116,* 1329–38. doi:10.1542/peds.2004-2583.

Scott, E. & Sobczak, C. (2002). *Body aloud!* Berkeley, CA: The Body Positive. Http://www.bodypositive.com.

School breakfast score card (2011). *Food research and action center.* Http://frac.org/wp-content/uploads/2011/01/sbscorecard2010.pdf.

Smolak, L., Harris, B., Levine, M., & Shisslak, C. (2001). Teachers: The forgotten influence on the success of prevention programs. *Eating Disorders: The Journal of Treatment and Prevention, 9,* 261–5.

Smolak, L., Murnen, S.K., & Ruble, A.E. (2000). Female athletes and eating problems: A meta-analysis. *International Journal of Eating Disorders, 27,* 371–80. doi:10.1002/(SICI)1098-108X(200005)27:4<371::AID-EAT1>3.0.CO;2-Y.

Stice, E. (2002). Sociocultural influences on body image and eating disturbance. In C. G. Fairburn & K. D. Brownell (eds), *Eating disorders and obesity: A comprehensive handbook* (pp. 103–7). New York, NY: The Guilford Press.

Stice, E., & Whitenton, K. (2002). Risk factors for body dissatisfaction in adolescent girls. A longitudinal investigation. *Developmental Psychology, 28,* 669–78.

Strauss, R. S., & Pollack, H. A. (2001). Epidemic increase in childhood overweight. *Journal of the American Medical Association, 28,* 2845–8. doi:10.1001/jama.286.22.2845.

Striegel-Moore, R., Dohm, F., Pike, K., Wilfley, D., & Fairburn, C. (2002). Abuse, bullying, and discrimination as risk factors for binge eating disorder. *The American Journal of Psychiatry, 159,* 1902–7.

Taras, H., & Potts-Datema, W. (2005). Obesity and student performance at school. *Journal of School Health. 5,* 291–5. doi:10.1111/j.1746-1561.2005. tb07346.x.

The role of schools in preventing childhood obesity (2004). *The State Education Standard, 5,* 4–12. Http://www.cdc.gov/healthyyouth/physicalactivity/pdf/ roleofschools_obesity.pdf.

Thompson, J. K., & Spana, R.E. (1991). Visuospatial ability, accuracy of size estimation, and bulimic disturbance in a noneating-disordered college sample: A neuropsychological analysis. *Perceptual and Motor Skills, 73,* 335–8.

United States' Department of Agriculture (1994). *National school lunch program and school breakfast program nutrition objectives for school meals (Parts 210, 220).* Http://www.fns.usda.gov/cnd/Governance/regulations.htm.

—(2001). *Food sold in competition with USDA school meal programs: A report to congress.* Washington, DC. Http://www.cspinet.org/nutritionpolicy/Foods_ Sold_in_Competition_with_USDA_School_Meal_Programs.pdf.

United States Department of Health and Human Services National Women's Health Information Center (2005). *BodyWise Handbook Eating Disorders Information for Middle School Personnel.* Http://www.maine.g.ov/education/sh/ eatingdisorders/bodywise.pdf.

Vitousek, K., Watson, S., & Wilson, G. (1998). Enhancing motivation for change in treatment-resistant eating disorders. *Clinical Psychology Review, 18,* 391–420. doi:10.1016/S0272-7358(98)00012-9.

Vocks, S., Legenbauer, T., Ruddel, H., & Troje, N. (2007). Static and dynamic body image in Bulimia Nervosa: Mental representation of body dimensions and biological motion patterns. *International Journal of Eating Disorders, 40,* 59–66. doi:10.1002/eat.20336

Walsh, B. T., & Cameron, V. L. (2005). *If your adolescent has an eating disorder.* New York, NY: Oxford University Press.

Wertheim, E. H., Martin, G., Prior, M., Sanson, A., & Smart, D. (2002). Parent influences in the transmission of eating and weight related values and behaviors. *Eating Disorders, 10,* 321–34. doi:10.1080/10640260214507.

Woodside, B., Garfinkel, P., Lin, E., Goering, P., Kaplan, A., Goldbloom, D., & Kennedy, S. (2001). Comparisons of men with full or partial eating disorders, men without eating disorders, and women with eating disorders in the community. *American Journal of Psychiatry, 158,* 570–4.

Unoka, Z., Tölgyes, T., Czobor, P., & Simon, L. (2010). Eating disorder behavior and early maladaptive schemas in subgroups of eating disorders. *Journal of Nervous & Mental Disease, 198,* 425–31. doi:10.1097/NMD.0b013e3181e07d3d.

Yanovski, S. Z. (2002). Binge eating in obese persons. In, C. G. Fairburn & K. D. Brownell (eds), *Eating disorders and obesity* (pp. 403–7) (2nd ed.). New York: The Guilford Press.

CHAPTER NINE

Understanding and Managing Behaviors of Children Diagnosed with Mood Disorders

Lea A. Theodore and
Sandra B. Ward
The College of William and Mary

Melissa A. Bray and
Thomas J. Kehle
The University of Connecticut

Abstract

Childhood depression is a serious mental health disorder that affects up to 20% of school-age youth. Mood disorders in children, which include major depressive disorder, dysthymia, and bipolar disorder, are a growing public health concern with rising prevalence rates. It is well-established that mood disorders in children are common and recurrent, negatively impact academic performance, are accompanied by poor psychosocial outcomes, place children at greater risk for being diagnosed with at least one other psychological disorder, and greatly increase the risk for substance abuse and suicide attempts. The intent of this chapter is to provide classroom teachers with a knowledge-base of childhood depression so that they may identify and support children with depression to succeed academically and enhance their overall social and emotional functioning.

Overview

Childhood depression is a serious mental health disorder that affects up to 20% of school-age youth (Avenevoli, Knight, Kessler, & Merikangas, 2008). Even more alarming is that approximately 500,000 children and adolescents who are diagnosed with depression will attempt suicide (National Institute of Mental Health [NIMH], 2003). Mood disorders in children, which include major depressive disorder, dysthymia, and bipolar disorder, are a growing public health concern with rising prevalence rates (Horowitz & Garber, 2006; Rao, 2006). The extent to which mood disorders adversely affect the overall functioning of children and adolescents cannot be underestimated. It is well-established that mood disorders in children are common and recurrent, negatively impact academic performance, are accompanied by poor psychosocial outcomes, place children at greater risk for being diagnosed with at least one other psychological disorder, and greatly increase the risk for substance abuse and suicide attempts (Abela & Hankin, 2008; Rao, 2006). Given the negative consequences of childhood depression, prevention and intervention efforts in schools are warranted. This chapter provides an overview of mood disorders in children, including prevalence, associated characteristics, and classroom strategies, so that teachers may identify and support children with depression to enable them to succeed academically and socially in the classroom.

Psychoeducational Implications

Developmental Considerations

Depression can be experienced by all school-aged youth. However, the age and developmental level of a child influences how depression is expressed. Identifying childhood depression can be challenging because the level of cognitive development in young children affects how children express what they are feeling. That is, they do not have a solid understanding of depression in order to adequately explain their symptoms. Further complicating an accurate diagnosis of depression in children is that many of the symptoms occur in typically developing children and also overlap with other childhood disorders (Rudolph & Lambert, 2007). Despite the wide-range of symptoms that children and adolescents may display, the primary symptoms of depression include sadness, loss of interest, and irritability (DSM-IV-TR, American Psychiatric Association [APA], 2000; Rudolph & Lambert, 2007; Wilmhurst, 2005).

Characteristics of depression in preschool children include developmental delays, separation anxiety, irritability, sad affect, disinterest in play, and nightmares (Luby et al., 2003). School-age children demonstrate many of the same symptoms as preschool children. However, they also exhibit increased irritability, a lack of interest or pleasure in activities they used to enjoy, angry outbursts, depressed appearance, temper tantrums, low frustration tolerance, negative self-statements, and obstinance. They often present with physical symptoms such as headaches and stomach aches. They also experience academic problems and poor social relationships, including social rejection and not being accepted by their peers (DSM-IV-TR, APA, 2000; Hamen & Rudolph, 2003; Wilmhurst, 2005). Adolescents with depression may experience sleeping and eating disturbances; demonstrate low self-esteem; exhibit feelings of hopelessness, worthlessness, or guilt; a lack of energy; loneliness; declines in their academic performance; and increased thoughts about suicide (Huberty, 2008; Wilmhurst, 2005). They are also more likely to have eating and substance use disorders (Hammen & Rudolph, 2003). Regardless of the age of the child, the symptoms must be persistent over time, represent a change in functioning, and result in significant impairment in functioning (DSM-IV-TR, APA, 2000).

Major Depressive Disorder

Major depressive disorder (MDD) is considered to be the most severe form of depression and may be characterized by chronic feelings of sadness and loss of interest or pleasure. These behaviors significantly affect a child's daily functioning and impair their quality of life. While most children and adolescents experience mood swings, bad days, or feelings of sadness at some point in their lives, children with MDD are not able to recover from these feelings and resume their normal routine and activities (Merrell, 2008). Common characteristics of MDD include changes in sleep patterns; weight disturbances, including failing to make expected weight gains; decreased energy levels; feelings of worthlessness or guilt; and problems with concentration or decision-making. In addition, children may appear to be restless; demonstrate slowed thinking, speech, and/or body movements; and lack motivation. Children and adolescents are also more likely to exhibit irritability rather than sadness, manifest physical complaints (e.g.

headaches or stomach aches), demonstrate behavior problems in school such as being oppositional or exhibiting deficits in attention, and truancy (Huberty, 2008; Merrell, 2008).

Interpersonally, children and adolescents with MDD evidence a wide range of problem behaviors, from antisocial conduct such as aggression, impulsivity or inattention, to isolation and withdrawal (Hammen & Rudolph, 2003). Specifically, depressed children often have deficits with respect to prosocial behavior which often results in social difficulties and poor quality friendships. Since many of these children tend to isolate themselves, withdraw from others, or engage in disruptive behaviors, they are often socially rejected and less accepted by their peers (Hammen & Rudolph, 2003; Huberty, 2008). Academically, children with MDD have difficulty concentrating in school which makes it difficult for them to complete assignments or attend in the classroom. Further, their decreased motivation and energy levels negatively influence their ability to begin and complete assignments (Huberty, 2008). This often results in poor academic achievement, higher rates of absenteeism, and school failure (Hammen & Rudolph, 2003; Hubety, 2010). The combination of academic, interpersonal and academic difficulties experienced by children with MDD may result in risk-taking behaviors such as self-mutilation and experimentation with alcohol and drugs in an attempt to minimize their pain. Of particular concern is that they are also more likely to have recurrent thoughts of death (Merrell, 2008). Unfortunately, it is many of these associated problem behaviors that parents and teachers notice rather than the depression itself, which is the underlying cause (Huberty, 2010).

With respect to prevalence, estimates of MDD indicate that approximately 2% to 8% of school-aged children experience depression (Costello, Erkanli, & Angold, 2006), which suggests that in a classroom of 30 students, at least one child will have depression (Merrell, 2008). Adolescent prevalence rates indicate that as many as 20% of teens experience depression (Avenevoli et al., 2008). Significantly, 1 in 5 boys and 1 in 3 girls will have experienced an episode of major depression by the time they are 18 years of age (Merrell, 2008). Although MDD occurs equally in boys and girls during childhood, the prevalence rates increase dramatically during adolescence, with females being twice as likely to suffer from depression than males (Merrell, 2008; Zahn-Waxler, Race, & Duggal, 2005).

Childhood-onset of MDD occurs at approximately 13 to 15 years of age with an average duration of an MDD episode of 7 to 9 months (Kane & Garber, 2002). Although the first depressive episode will eventually remit, children often continue to exhibit milder symptoms of depression as well as psychosocial problems (Lewinsohn & Essau, 2002). This is particularly significant as these issues place children and adolescents at greater risk for recurrence of depressive episodes (Daley, Hammen, & Rao, 2000).

A number of other psychological disorders commonly co-occur with

MDD. Significantly, 40% to 70% of children and adolescents will have a co-existing disorder, with up to 50% having two or more co-occurring diagnoses (Rao, 2006). The most frequent co-occurring diagnoses include dysthymic disorder, anxiety disorders, disruptive behavior disorders including attention deficit hyperactivity disorder (AD/HD), oppositional defiant disorder and conduct disorder, and substance use disorders. Girls evidence higher rates of co-occurring internalizing disorders, such as anxiety, whereas boys tend to have a greater likelihood of co-existing externalizing disorders, particularly disruptive behavior disorders and substance use disorders (Hammen & Rudolph, 2003). The presence of co-occurring disorders is associated with negative outcomes and contributes significantly to the risk for recurrent depression, length of the depressive episode, and suicide attempts (Birmaher, Ryan, Williamson, Brent, & Kaufman, 1996; Kovacs, Akiskal, Gatsonis, & Parrone, 1994). If not addressed and treated, these problems will persist into adulthood with serious long-term consequences, including increased risk recurrence, educational failure, interpersonal and occupational problems, suicide attempts, criminal activity and legal problems, and suicide attempts (Klein, Torpey, Bufferd, & Dyson, 2008).

Dysthymic Disorder

Dysthymic disorder is less severe than a major depressive disorder, but is considered to be more chronic. Characteristic signs of dysthymic disorder, which must include depressed mood or irritability for at least one year, include a change in appetite, either eating too much or too little; a change in sleeping patterns; a decrease in energy or feelings of lethargy; low self-esteem; diminished ability to concentrate; and feelings of hopelessness. Additional symptoms include tearfulness, feelings of hopelessness and/or guilt, restlessness, irritability, and fatigue (DSM-IV-TR; APA, 2000).

Prevalence rates for dysthymic disorder are lower than those for MDD, and are seen in approximately 1 to 5% of school-age children (Birmaher et al., 1996). Whereas symptom duration for MDD is less than one year, the course of dysthymia is considered to be prolonged in that an episode may last from 2 to 5 years. Children and adolescents with dysthymia are also at an increased risk for developing other psychological disorders, including MDD, attention-deficit hyperactivity disorder, and anxiety disorders (Masi et al., 2003). Significantly, approximately 70% of children eventually develop a MDD within five years (Renouf & Kovacs, 1995). Dysthymic disorder often precedes the onset of a MDD, emerging approximately two to three years prior to the development of MDD (Kovacs, Obrosky, Gatsonis, & Richards, 1997; Rao & Chen, 2009). Diagnosis of both MDD and dysthymic disorder, known as double depression, is associated with a poorer prognosis and greater overall impairment.

Academically, children with dysthymia struggle in school because the depressive symptoms that they exhibit, including difficulty concentrating, loss of interest and slowed thinking, impact their ability to perform at their maximum potential. Therefore, grades are lower, they perform poorly on standardized tests, may refuse to come to school or there may be excessive absences, and homework assignments may be late and/or missing (Cole, 1990). Socially and emotionally, children with mood disorders experience substantial disruptions in their relationships. They tend to have fewer friends and close relationships, withdraw socially from others (Rudolph, Flynn, & Abaied, 2008), feel alone, have a great deal of conflict with parents and siblings (Hammen & Rudolph, 2003), and lose interest in activities that they once found pleasurable. Children with dysthymia also demonstrate negative self-esteem and deficits or distortions in their thinking. Specifically, they hold negative and critical beliefs about themselves and the world around them which results in ineffective styles of coping in many situations (Lakdawalla, Hankin, & Mermelstein, 2007). Consequently, children with dysthymia tend to make poor choices and may turn to alcohol or drugs to make them feel better.

Bipolar Disorder

Bipolar disorder (BD) in children has received increased attention in the last two decades among researchers and practitioners (Danner et al., 2009). It is well accepted that the presentation of symptoms in adult-onset BD differs from childhood/adolescent onset BD. Consequently, early onset bipolar spectrum disorder (EOBSD) is a term that has been used to refer to BD in youth under 18 years of age (Lofthouse & Fristad, 2006). EOBSD is a chronic condition that severely impairs functioning. In fact, periods of full recovery are rarely observed (Birmaher et al., 2006).

The Diagnostic and Statistical Manual of Mental Disorders-Fourth Edition-Text Revision (DSM-IV-TR) (APA, 2000) includes four subtypes of BD. However, there is no differentiation of BD in adults from that in children. Bipolar I disorder (BD I) is characterized by one or more manic episodes or mixed episodes that last for one week (APA, 2000). Many of these individuals also have had one or more major depressive episode as well. A manic episode is a specific period of elevated, expansive, or irritable mood that lasts for at least one week and represents a significant change from the individual's normal functioning (APA, 2000). Furthermore, at least three additional symptoms (four, if mood is irritable) must be present for a manic episode. These symptoms include inflated self-esteem/grandiosity; decreased need for sleep; pressured speech; flight of ideas; distractibility; increased goal-directed behavior/psychomotor agitation, and excessive involvement in pleasurable activities (APA, 2000). A mixed episode consists of a one-week period in which criteria are met for manic episode and major depressive with respect to BD I (APA, 2000).

The primary features of Bipolar II disorder (BD II) include one or more major depressive episodes with at least one hypomanic episode. Hypomania is defined by the same symptoms as a manic episode, but the duration is only four days (APA, 2000). The third subtype of BD, Cyclothymic disorder, is characterized by fluctuating moods with periods of hypomanic and depressive symptoms. However, the symptoms do not meet the criteria for manic or major depressive episodes (APA, 2000). Bipolar Not Otherwise Specified (BD NOS) features rapid alternating manic and depressive symptoms that do not meet criteria for manic or major depressive episodes (APA, 2000).

The diagnosis of EOBSD is complicated by the lack of consensus on the episodic nature of the disorder, the minimum duration of episodes to warrant a diagnosis, and the hallmark symptoms of mania in children and adolescents. While adults typically show discrete cycles of depression and mania, children often demonstrate rapid cycling of episodes without a distinct beginning and end (Miller & Barnett, 2008). Birmaher et al. (2006) found that children with EOBSD experienced frequent fluctuations of symptoms from subsyndromal to meeting full DSM-IV-TR criteria. Some children can show multiple episodes per day (Lofthouse, Mackinaw-Koons, & Fristad, 2004). This means that children can show depressive and manic symptoms within the same day. Due to these rapid alternating symptoms of depression and mania, children with EOBSD often do not satisfy the duration requirements for mania or hypomania in DSM-IV-TR (APA, 2000). In many circumstances, these children will receive a diagnosis of BD NOS (Baroni, Lunsford, Luckenbaugh, Towbin, & Leibenluft, 2009).

The prevalence of EOBSD is difficult to determine due to the debate over the diagnostic criteria for the disorder in children. Estimates of the occurrence of EOBSD range up to 5% of children (Youngstrom, Findling, Youngstrom, & Calabrese, 2005). The age of onset is also unclear, and several researchers have suggested that psychiatric symptoms evolve into BD (Grier & Wilkins, 2005).

EOBSD is a heritable disorder with a biological basis. Children with one or more parents who have BD have a greater risk for mood disorders (Birmaher et al., 2009). It is estimated that children who have a parent or sibling with EOBSD have a 4 to 6 times greater chance of having the disorder (Nurnberger & Foroud, 2000). The specific biological causes remain unknown and poorly understood (Grier, Wilkins, & Stirling Pender, 2007; Goldstein, 2010; Jerrell & Prewette, 2008; Luby & Navsaria, 2010; van der Schot et al., 2009), and it appears that environmental stressors can activate and exacerbate the expression of symptoms (Youngstrom et al., 2005). Researchers who have used structural MRI's have found that children with EOBSD tend to have differences in the activation in regions of the brain that are involved in emotional regulation (Frazier et al., 2005).

EOBSD in the School Setting

The symptoms and course of EOBSD are severe and limit a child's functioning (Goldstein, 2010). Additionally, the presenting symptoms may vary depending on the type of BD with which the child has been diagnosed. For example, children and adolescents with a diagnosis of BD II were more likely to have a co-morbid anxiety disorder, whereas, children and adolescents diagnosed with BD I were more likely to have a co-morbid diagnosis of attention deficit hyperactivity disorder (AD/HD) and/or oppositional defiant disorder (ODD) (Masi et al., 2007).

In general, children with EOBSD will demonstrate multiple intense mood swings each day (Kowatch et al., 2005; Lofthouse et al., 2004). The symptoms of a depressive episode in EOBSD are similar to those discussed in the previous section of this chapter. The three primary symptoms of a manic episode are persistent euphoria or irritability (APA, 2000). These will present as spontaneous changes in mood. Children and adolescents with euphoria/expansive mood are likely to be *extremely* happy, silly, and/or giddy, but their emotions do not match the context and are markedly different from their normal reactions to pleasant events (Kowatch et al., 2005). Irritability is manifested in extreme outbursts and temper tantrums (Kowatch et al., 2005). These children are often referred to as "out of control." Critical characteristics of these symptoms as they relate to EOBSD are their intensity, episodic nature, and lack of contextual relevance.

The additional symptoms for a manic and mixed episode (at least three symptoms required; four symptoms required if mood is irritable) (APA, 2000) and their expression in children/adolescents are as follows:

- Grandiosity: A characteristic of a grandiose mood is when the child cannot distinguish reality from fantasy (Kowatch et al., 2005). For example, a child may actually think that they can fly and jump out a window to prove it. These individuals may relate peculiar stories and often need to be the center of attention (Grier et al., 2007). Adolescents may overcommit to activities (McIntosh & Trotter, 2006).

- Decreased need for sleep: Children and adolescents with EOBSD tend to be full of energy while needing little sleep at night (4 to 5 hours). They may re-arrange room furniture, work on the computer, talk with others, and experience little fatigue during these activities (Grier et al., 2007; Kowatch et al., 2005). Due to their sleeping patterns, these children are often difficult to wake and may fall asleep during the day in school (McIntosh & Trotter, 2006).

- Pressured speech: In addition to talking more than usual, children and adolescents with EOBSD tend to talk rapidly and loudly. They are often perceived as intrusive because they do not let others contribute to the conversation (Grier et al., 2007; Kowatch et al., 2005).

- Flight of ideas/racing thoughts: Children and adolescents with EOBSD often change topics of discussion quickly, and others who listen to them are frequently confused (Kowatch et al., 2005). Additionally, they often have difficulty staying on task because their thoughts disrupt them (Grier et al., 2007).

- Distractibility: This symptom is common to several disorders and developmental stages, so it is important that distractibility occur with a mood shift from baseline to be considered a manic symptom (Kowatch et al., 2005). Distractibility in children and adolescents with EOBSD is often exhibited through an inability to focus, remember, or organize (Grier et al., 2007).

- Increase in goal-directed activity/psychomotor agitation: Since psychomotor agitation is a more common symptom of other disorders, goal directed activity is more functional in diagnosing EOBSD (Kowatch et al., 2005). This symptom is often presented as spending inordinate amounts of time on a task/activity, impulsive behavior, and feeling pressured (Grier et al., 2007).

- Excessive involvement in pleasurable activities that have high risk: Children and adolescents with EOBSD may show hypersexual behaviors, inappropriate displays of affection, or risk-taking behaviors (Grier et al., 2007; Kowatch et al., 2005).

Conceptual Foundations

Although the cause of childhood depression is largely unknown, genetic and environmental factors have been implicated in its development. Research from family and twin studies have suggested that depression runs in families, with heritability estimates ranging from 40 to 50% (Fava & Kendler, 2000). That is, children who have a parent that is diagnosed with MDD are fourteen times more likely to also experience depression themselves (Weissman et al., 2005). Significantly, children of parents with depression tend to have an onset before puberty. This is particularly noteworthy because when depression runs in families, there is a greater likelihood of recurrent depressive episodes, with depression persisting into adulthood (Wickramaratne, Greenwald, & Weissman, 2000). Studies investigating genetic influences on childhood depression have suggested that children may inherit vulnerability towards depression, and that environmental stressors may trigger a depressive episode (Rice, Harold, & Thapar, 2003).

Environmental causes for mood disorders in children and adolescents may include stressful, daily, and family life events. Depression may be triggered by a painful loss or significant event such as divorce, death of a family member or pet, a breakup, changing schools, moving to a new area, or accidents and illnesses within the family (Gilman, Kawachi, Fitzmaurice, & Buka, 2003). Daily life events may also serve as a trigger to depression. They include situations such as earning a bad grade on an exam, fighting with parents, siblings, or a significant other, having a chronic illness, and receiving criticism from parents and teachers (Wilmhurst, 2005). Finally, the family environment may also contribute to mood disorders in children, particularly under circumstances such as abuse, neglect, poor parenting, low socioeconomic status, single-parent families, and unemployment (Reinemann, Stark, Molnar, & Simpson, 2006). In addition to the genetic and environmental factors described above, a child's temperament, coping skills, and thoughts serve to moderate responses to life events that precede a depressive episode (Rao & Chen, 2009).

Three Tier Prevention/Intervention Strategy for Classroom Management for MDD and Dysthymia

The reauthorization of the Individuals with Disabilities Education Improvement Act in 2004 allowed local educational agencies (LEA's) to use evidence-based interventions in a Response to Intervention (RtI) model to identify specific learning disabilities in children. In order to help all children who are experiencing difficulty in school, the RtI model employed for academic problems has been expanded for social and emotional problems for children in schools, including depression (Huberty, 2008). As the trend in education is towards inclusion of students with various academic and social and emotional issues in the classroom, it is important for teachers to be knowledgeable regarding how to identify and help students with depression succeed in the classroom.

Tier I

At the school-wide level, universal prevention for depression may be provided by classroom teachers using social and emotional learning (SEL), whereby students are taught skills associated with self-management, developing positive relationships, and responsible decision-making (Merrell & Gueldner, 2010). The intent of SEL is to enhance social and emotional functioning, thereby improving mental health and academic success. By teaching students problem-solving skills and providing them with coping strategies, it is the premise of SEL that students will learn how to manage stress and set goals, thereby increasing their self-esteem (Merrell & Gueldner, 2010). Social and emotional learning may be employed using structured curricula addressing topics such as bullying and social skills. One such program is Strong Kids: A Social and Emotional Learning Curriculum, which may be used for all school-aged children, from kindergarten through 12th grade, in both regular and special education classrooms (Merrell, Carrizales, Feuerborn, Gueldner, & Tran, 2007). An attractive feature of such structured curricular programs is that teachers may incorporate these lessons into their daily academic curriculum (e.g. language arts). By incorporating SEL into educational lessons, it provides students with a place where they can safely express their feelings and concerns regarding a variety of issues (Merrell & Gueldner, 2010). In order for SEL programs to be maximally effective, they should be implemented on a regular basis throughout a child's schooling (Merrell & Gueldner, 2010).

Students in this tier may also be screened in order to identify children who are either at-risk or already have a depressive disorder. Two approaches have been identified as best practice in systematically and comprehensively screening children for depression (Huberty, 2008). First, for each child in the classroom, teachers may complete checklists or behavior rating scales, such as the Child Behavior Checklist (CBCL; Achenbach, 2001) or the Behavior Assessment System for Children—Second Edition (BASC–2; Reynolds & Kamphaus, 2004) (Huberty, 2008). Screening students using this methodology will identify not only depressive symptoms, but other emotional and behavioral issues that may be of concern as well. Despite the thoroughness of this type of screening, a drawback is that it takes a great deal of time for the teacher to complete the rating scales (Huberty, 2008). Second, teachers may identify students with the highest number of depressive symptoms in the class and subsequently rank order 5–10 children in terms of severity of behaviors exhibited. This type of screening process is considered efficient with respect to teacher time and in identification specific depressive behaviors. However, it also necessitates that teachers be knowledgeable of depressive symptoms in children (Huberty, 2008).

Students identified at Tier I with mild problems may benefit from strategies that the teacher can provide. For instance, these students may need minor accommodations in the classroom such as adjusting the workload or providing more time to complete assignments, modifying the class routine classroom, and fostering and enhancing social interactions (Huberty, 2008). This may be accomplished by providing the student with leadership experiences, or pairing students with peers who have similar interests (Huberty, 2010).

Tier II

Essentially, the SEL programs that are used for universal prevention in Tier I are also used as a secondary prevention strategy for students who are identified as at-risk or demonstrate some signs of depression. However, the curriculum is adjusted in order to meet the specialized needs of these students. For instance, teachers may spend more time covering various SEL issues by spending two lessons rather than one on certain topics, providing more opportunities for practice of newly developed skills, assigning homework or additional exercises that address the practicing of skills outside of the classroom setting, and regularly reviewing the skills so that students do not forget them (Merrell & Gueldner, 2010).

For children who are identified in the Tier I screening process as being at-risk for depression, there are several strategies that the classroom teacher can do to help the student succeed in school. Specifically, the teacher may provide academic accommodations such as breaking assignments into smaller and more manageable tasks, offering the student more time to complete tasks, and helping them develop good study habits. If the classroom teacher adjusts class-work or homework, it is important that expectations are not lowered for that child (Huberty, 2008). It is also important to incorporate positive experiences so that the student may experience success. This may be accomplished by giving the student special responsibilities in the classroom, providing them with leadership privileges, and peer mentoring which increase opportunities for reinforcement (Clark, DeBar, & Lewinsohn, 2003; Huberty, 2008). Since many children with depression withdraw socially from others, they tend to have few if any friends and often experience feelings of isolation. In order to foster positive interpersonal relationships, the teacher may match or team students with other confident and supportive peers as well as identifying peers with similar interests so that they may engage in social activities and make new friends (Clark et al., 2003; Huberty, 2008). Teachers should not hesitate to talk to the depressed child about their feelings and how they are doing. Often, children need someone to share their feelings and stresses with but do not know how to initiate this type of dialogue. When working with depressed or at-risk children, it is important to be maintain a positive attitude. This is because negative thoughts and behavior will only serve to reinforce the child's feelings of low self-esteem and incompetence (Huberty, 2010). Finally, teachers may employ relaxation strategies in her classroom which would not only help children with depression, but all students in the classroom (Huberty, 2008).

Tier III

Students who experience severe or chronic depression that negatively impacts their academic functioning require more intensive supports and services from specialized personnel outside of the classroom. However, teachers may continue to use the strategies of reducing stress and goal setting that were employed for prevention in Tiers I and II (Merrell & Gueldner, 2010). In addition, the classroom teacher can support these students by scheduling positive and pleasurable activities each day for the student, having students self-monitor their mood and behavior, and helping students develop and use problem-solving techniques (Huberty, 2008).

Children with serious depression will likely also receive treatment from specialized personnel, such as the school psychologist or school counselor. The most effective treatments for treating depression include behavioral and cognitive-behavioral techniques (CBT) (Huberty, 2008). Cognitive-behavioral approaches are designed to address a child's thoughts and feelings and their influence on behavior. There are several well-established CBT programs that are used to treat child and adolescent depression. They include the C.A.T. Project (Kendall, Choudhury, Hudson, & Webb, 2002), the ACTION program (Stark & Kendall, 1996), and the Adolescent Coping with Depression Program (CWD-A) (Clarke, Lewinsohn, & Hops, 1990). Since these programs may be implemented in the school environment, classroom teachers should be aware of them so that they may support students in identifying and changing negative thoughts that influence their behavior.

Three Tier Prevention/Intervention Strategies for Classroom Management for EOBSD

Considering the severity of EOBSD symptoms, their chronic occurrence, and the severe impairment they present, pharmacotherapy is often the first line of treatment for these children and adolescents. It is important to note that medication efficacy has not been validated, since few studies have been conducted with children and/or adolescents (McIntosh & Trotter, 2006). Medications typically include mood stabilizers, antipsychotics, and anti-hypertensives initially (Jerrell & Prewette, 2008; Lofthouse et al., 2004). Once the individual's mood is stabilized, anti-depressants may be prescribed in low doses. Even with these medications, patients are slow to recover and exhibit poor outcomes (Jerrell & Prewette, 2008). In another study, recovery was observed in 2 out of 3 children and adolescent participants with EOBSD, however, one-half of them had at least one full syndromal recurrence (Birmaher et al., 2006).

It is probable that children and adolescents with EOBSD will exhibit problem behaviors in the school setting, even with prescribed medications. With knowledge of the symptoms and course of the disorder, teachers and school personnel can take proactive measures to decrease the likelihood of disruptive episodes. Additionally, careful planning can help teachers respond more effectively to such episodes when they do occur. Although empirical studies are needed to provide evidence to support school-based interventions for EOBSD, teachers can apply strategies that can help children with EOBSD succeed in the classroom.

Tier I

Children with EOBSD will benefit from an organized classroom with a consistent schedule (Bardick & Bernes, 2005; Lofthouse et al., 2004; McIntosh & Trotter, 2006). A predictable routine may decrease the likelihood of negative reactions to transitions and unexpected events. At the secondary level, the adolescent's emotional and educational needs should be carefully considered in developing an individualized schedule (McIntosh & Trotter, 2006). A home-school log can facilitate consistency in practice and expectations between home and school (Bardick & Bernes, 2005). Within this structure it will be necessary for teachers, school personnel, and parents to be flexible in accommodating the child's episodic display of symptoms as well as medication side effects. For example, assignments and deadlines can be modified in response to the child's erratic attention, energy, and mood (Lofthouse et al., 2004). This may include shorter assignments, less homework, and breaking down larger assignments into smaller units (McIntosh & Trotter, 2006). Additionally, students with EOBSD may benefit from preferred seating and frequent breaks (Grier, Wilkins, & Szadek, 2005). The side effects of medications prescribed for EOBSD include increased thirst and need for urination as well as drowsiness. Students with EOBSD require free access to fluids and frequent restroom breaks (Lofthouse et al., 2004). They also may benefit from a shortened school day or a later start time to increase the probability of greater alertness at school (Grier et al., 2005).

Students with EOBSD, like most learners, respond better to a positive discipline approach (Grier et al., 2005). Consistent with their need for structure, a defined behavior management program for the classroom is recommended (Grier et al., 2005). In the context of a positive behavior plan, teachers and school personnel need to recognize the symptoms of an impending manic episode and take action to re-direct the student (McIntosh & Trotter, 2006). Such actions may include giving the student a choice to work alone, providing a quite place to calm down, and gently confronting the student on their behavior (Bardick & Bernes, 2005; McIntosh & Trotter, 2006). Additionally, the student and teacher can develop a private signal for the student to use to communicate potential difficulties and needs before behavior escalates (Bardick & Bernes, 2005).

Tier II

Children with EOBSD who demonstrate symptoms of a manic episode in school may benefit from a designated safe place to calm down (Bardick & Bernes, 2005; Lofthouse et al., 2004). This should be a private space agreed on by student, teacher, and school personnel. Although such a space should be away from other students, adult supervision is necessary. Additionally, a routine can be established so that the removal of the student with EOBSD does not disrupt the class.

In order to help the teacher anticipate and respond more effectively to the student's intense emotional episodes, school personnel can conduct a functional behavioral assessment (FBA) (Grier et al., 2005; Lofthouse et al., 2004). The results of an FBA can be used to identify the setting events and immediate triggers that lead to the student's emotional episodes as well as the consequences that contribute to the inappropriate behaviors. With this information, the teacher and the school team can develop a suitable behavior intervention plan that addresses the student's individual needs.

Children with EOBSD who are experiencing manic or depressive symptoms frequently experience social difficulties (Bardick & Bernes, 2005). They often don't respond appropriately to social cues. Additionally, they may be irritable, bossy, and intrusive; or they can be withdrawn. Consequently, these children may profit from social skills training. Depending on the needs of the student, this training can be in a group or individual format (Bardick & Bernes, 2005; Lofthouse et al., 2004). Cognitive-behavioral strategies are recognized as effective with students with EOBSD (Kowatch et al., 2005; McIntosh & Trotter, 2006).

Tier III

Students with EOBSD who experience chronic manic or depressive symptoms need more intensive services as their behaviors can be impairing and potentially harmful to themselves and others. In circumstances where the student exhibits suicidal ideation, it may be necessary to conduct a suicide threat assessment and take action based on the results (Bardick & Bernes, 2005). A crisis management plan may be necessary if the child exhibits manic behaviors to a degree that she/he may harm others. If serious symptoms persist, it may be necessary to consider more intense super-vision as well as alternative placements to a general education classroom (McIntosh & Trotter, 2006). These alternative placements can range from a self-contained classroom to a residential treatment center (Lofthouse et al., 2004). Students with EOBSD who have been hospitalized will need help transitioning back to school (Lofthouse et al., 2004). Such a transition should be planned carefully with the medical team.

Progress Monitoring of Interventions

There are numerous methods to assess depression including interviews, rating scales, record review, sociometrics and behavioral observations. School-based monitoring for major depressive and dysthymic disorder is an advantageous assessment to track student progress over time but it can be difficult to accomplish for two reasons: (1) Directly observing depression based on operational definitions of visible symptoms is difficult to define and code. Direct observations over time are only reliable if the symptoms are observable and thus measurable; and, (2) using interviews and rating scales in close proximity can also be unreliable.

Depressive characteristics can be viewed as being in four areas including emotional and affective (e.g. crying), cognitive (e.g. feelings of hopelessness), motivational (e.g. suicidal ideation), and physical (e.g. appetite changes, fatigue) (Rice & McLaughlin, 2001). Mood disorders have several unobservable characteristics such as cognitive distortions, lowered energy level, and lack of interest in school activities. However, there are some symptoms that are clearly apparent such as lack of eye contact, smiling, slow speech, and crying. Such observable behaviors have been suggested for direct observation.

School-based progress monitoring over time effectively employs direct observational methods since it is reliable when used across frequent, and relatively close in time, intervals (e.g. every week). Since schools are implementing the multi-tiered model of student support for assessment and intervention, a progress monitoring tool is needed within the three levels targeting social and emotional behaviors.

Progress monitoring specifically requires the direct and frequent collection of data across a representative sample of target behaviors, and employment of the data as a guide to facilitate the design of effective interventions (Hosp, Hosp, & Howell, 2006). Several problems exist with attempting to implement progress monitoring probes over time with internalizing problems. The assessments we do have are too long, not reliable over time, and include a broad array of behaviors rather than those that are the focus of the treatment being monitored. In order to address these issues, Levitt and Merrell (2009) recommended using small clusters of items from self-reports or rating scales. This allows for a unique assessment for the individual student being monitored. However, this procedure has limitations in that there exists the probability of invalidating the psychometric properties of self-reports or rating scales.

Volpe, Briesch, and Chafouleas (2010) have proposed an adaptive model of behavioral assessment to help with screening and progress monitoring of social and emotional behavior disorders. This work bridges a much needed gap as there are no viable methods linking screening to progress monitoring of treatment to date. Their model incorporates multiple gating procedures including teacher rankings, broad band measures, direct behavior ratings, and abbreviated behavior rating scales. The Systematic Screening for Behavior Disorders authored by Walker and Severson (1992) provides another appropriate option. It is also a multi-gated procedure for identifying internalizing behavior disorders. The final gate of this system employs a direct observational method of data collection.

Discussion and Final Recommendations

In sum, childhood depression is a serious disorder that negatively impacts academic performance, cognitive functioning, interpersonal relationships, and social and emotional functioning. Given the complexities associated with this disorder, school-based prevention and early identification efforts are essential. School psychologists and classroom teachers working within an RtI framework are ideally suited to support children with depression by providing them with effective interventions and classroom accommodations. In this manner, schools may help children and adolescents succeed academically and enhance their overall psychosocial functioning.

References

Abela, J. R. Z., & Hankin, B. J. (2008). *Handbook of depression in children and adolescents*. New York, NY: The Guilford Press.

Achenbach, T. M. (2001). *Child Behavior Checklist*. Burlington, VT: University Associates in Psychiatry.

American Psychiatric Association (2000). *Diagnostic and statistical manual of mental disorders* (4th ed., text rev). Washington, DC: Author.

Avenevoli, S., Knight, E., Kessler, R. C., & Merikangas, K. R. (2008). Epidemiology of depression in children and adolescents. In J. R. Z. Abela & B. L. Hankin (eds), *Handbook of depression in children and adolescents* (pp. 6–32). New York, NY: The Guilford Press.

Bardick, A. D. & Bernes, K. B. (2005). A closer examination of bipolar disorder in school-age children. *Professional School Counseling, 9*, 72–7. Accessed from http://schoolcounselor.metapress.com/content/k2153125rh611517/

Baroni, A., Lunsford, J. R., Luckenbaugh, D. A., Towbin, K. E., & Leibenluft, E. (2009). Practitioner review: The assessment of bipolar disorder in children and adolescents. *Journal of Child Psychology and Psychiatry, 50*, 203–15. doi:10.1111/j.1469-7610.2008.01953.x

Birmaher, B., Axelson, D., Monk, K., Kalas, C., Goldstein, B., Hickey, M. B. ... Brent, D. (2009). Lifetime psychiatric disorders in school-aged offspring of parent with bipolar disorder. *Archives of General Psychiatry, 66*, 287–96. doi:10.1001/archgenpsychiatry.2008.546

Birmaher, B., Axelson, D., Strober, M., Gill, M. K., Valeri, S., Chiappetta, L. ... Keller. M. (2006). Clinical course of children and adolescents with bipolar spectrum disorders. *Archives of General Psychiatry, 63*, 175–83. doi:10.1001/archpsyc.63.2.175

Birmaher, B., Ryan, N., Williamson, D., Brent, D., & Kaufman, J. (1996). Childhood and adolescent depression: A review of the past 10 years. Part II. *Journal of the American Academy of Child and Adolescent Psychiatry, 35*, 1575–83. doi:10.1097/00004583-199612000-00008

Birmaher, B., Ryan, N., Williamson, D., Brent, D., Kaufman, J., Dahl, R. E., ... Nelson, B. (1996). Childhood and adolescent depression: A review of the past 10 years. Part I. *Journal of the American Academy of Child and Adolescent Psychiatry, 35*, 1427–39. doi:10.1097/00004583-199611000-00011

Clark, G. N., DeBar, L. L., & Lewinsohn, P. M. (2003). Cognitive-behavioral group treatment for adolescent depression. In A. E. Kazdin & J. R. Weisz (eds), *Evidence-based psychotherapies for children and adolescents* (pp. 120–34). New York, NY: The Guilford Press.

Clarke, G., Lewinsohn, P., & Hops, H. (1990). *Adolescent coping with depression course*. Portland, OR: Kaiser Permanente Center for Health Research.

Cole, D. A. (1990). The relation of social and academic competence to depressive symptoms in childhood. *Journal of Abnormal Psychology, 99*, 422–9. doi:10.1037/0021-843X.99.4.422

Costello, E. J., Erkanli, A., & Angold, A. (2006). Is there an epidemic of child or adolescent depression? *Journal of Child Psychology and Psychiatry, 47*, 1263–71. doi:10.1111/j.1469-7610.2006.01682.x

Daley, S. E., Hammen, C., & Rao, U. (2000). Predictors of first onset and recurrence of major depression in young women during the 5 years following high school graduation. *Journal of Abnormal Psychology, 109*, 525–33. doi:10.1037/0021-843X.109.3.525

Danner, S., Fristad, M. A., Arnold, L. E. (2009). Early-onset bipolar spectrum disorders: Diagnostic Issues. *Clinical Child and Family Psychology Review, 12*, 271–93. doi:10.1007/s10567-009-0055-2

Fava, M., & Kendler, K. S. (2000). Major depressive disorder. *Neuron, 34*, 335–41. doi:10.1016/S0896-6273(00)00112-4

Frazier, J. A., Ahn, M. S., DeJong, S. Bent, E. K., Breeze, J. L., & Giuliano, A. J. (2005). Magnetic resonance imaging studies in early-onset bipolar disorder: A critical review. *Harvard Review of Psychiatry, 13*, 125–40. doi:10.1080/10673220591003597

Gilman, S. E., Kawachi, I., Fitzmaurice, G. M., & Buka, S. (2003). Family disruption in childhood and risk of adult depression. *American Journal of Psychiatry, 160*, 939–46. doi:10.1176/appi.ajp.160.5.939

Goldstein, B. J. (2010). Pediatric bipolar disorder: More than a temper problem. *Pediatrics, 125*, 1283–5. doi:10.1542/peds.2010-0494

Grier, J. E. C., & Wilkins, M. L. (2005). Bipolar disorder in children: Identification and diagnosis. Part I. *Communique, 34.* Accessed from http:// www.nasponline.org/publications/cq/mocq342bipolar.aspx

Grier, J. E. C., Wilkins, M. L., & Stirling Pender, C. A. (2007). Bipolar disorder: Educational implications for secondary students. *Student services.* (April 2007 ed.). Accessed from http://www.naspcenter.org/principals

Grier, J. E. C., Wilkins, M. L., & Szadek, L. (2005). Bipolar disorder in children: Treatment and intervention, part II. *Communique, 34.* Accessed from http:// www.nasponline.org/publications/cq/mocq342bipolar.aspx

Hammen, C., & Rudolph, K. D. (2003). Childhood mood disorders. In E. J. Mash & R. A. Barkley (eds), *Child psychopathology* (2nd ed., pp. 233–78). New York, NY: The Guilford Press.

Horowitz, J. L., & Garber, J. (2006). The prevention of depressive symptoms in children and adolescents: A meta-analytic review. *Journal of Consulting and Clinical Psychology, 74,* 401–15. doi:10.1037/0022-006X.74.3.401

Hosp, M. K. Hosp, J. L., & Howell, K. (2006). *The ABCs of CBM: A practical guide to curriculum-based measurement.* New York, NY: The Guilford Press.

Huberty, T. J. (2008). Best practices in school-based interventions for anxiety and depression. In A. Thomas & J. Grimes (eds), *Best practices in school psychology V* (Vol. 4, pp. 1473–86). Silver Springs, MD: National Association of School Psychologists.

—(2010). Depression: Supporting students at school. In A. Canter, S. Carroll, L. Paige, & I. Romero (eds), *Helping children at home and school III: Handouts from your school psychologist* (pp. S5H11-1-S5H11-3). Silver Springs, MD: National Association of School Psychologists.

Individuals with Disabilities Education Act, 20 US C. 1400 (2004).

Jerrell, J. M. & Prewette, E. D. (2008). Outcomes for youths with early- and very-early-onset bipolar I disorder. *The Journal of Behavioral Health Services and Research, 35,* 52–9. doi:10.1007/s11414-007-9081-3

Kane, P., & Garber, J. (2002). The relations among depression in fathers, children's psychopathology, and father-child conflict: A meta-analysis. *Clinical Psychology Review, 24,* 339–60. doi:10.1016/j.cpr.2004.03.004

Kendall, P. C., Choudhury, M., Hudson, J., & Webb, A. (2002). *The C. A. T. Project workbook for the cognitive-behavioral treatment of anxious adolescents.* Ardmore, PA: Workbook Publishing.

Klein, D. N., Torpey, D. C., Bufferd, S. J., & Dyson, M. W. (2008). Depressive disorders. In T. P. Beauchaine & S. P. Hinshaw (eds), *Child and adolescent psychopathology* (pp. 477–509). Hoboken, NJ: Wiley.

Kovacs, M., Akiskal, H., Gatsonis, C., & Parrone, P. (1994). Childhood-onset dysthymic disorder: Clinical features and prospective naturalistic outcome. *Archives of General Psychiatry, 51,* 365–74.

Kovacs, M., Obrosky, D. S., Gatsonis, C., & Richards, C. (1997). First-episode major depressive and dysthymic disorder in childhood: Clinical and sociodemographic factors in recovery. *Journal of the American Academy of Child & Adolescent Psychiatry, 36,* 777–84. doi:10.1097/00004583-199706000-00014

Kowatch, R. A., Fristad, M., Birmaher, B., Wagner, K. D., Findling, R. L., Hellander, M., & The Child Psychiatric Workgroup on Bipolar Disorder

(2005). Treatment guidelines for children and adolescents with bipolar disorder. *Journal of the American Academy of Child and Adolescent Psychiatry, 44,* 213–35. doi:10.1097/00004583-200503000-00006

Lakdawalla, Z., Hankin, B. L., & Mermelstein, R. (2007). Cognitive theories of depression in children and adolescents: A conceptual and quantitative review. *Clinical Child and Family Psychology Review, 10,* 1–24. doi:10.1007/s10567-006-0013-1

Levitt, V. H., & Merrell, K. W. (2009). Linking assessment to intervention for internalizing problems of children and adolescents. *School Psychology Forum, 3,* 13–26.

Lewinsohn, P. M., & Essau, C. A. (2002). Depression in adolescents. In I. H. Gotlib & C. L. Hammen (eds), *Handbook of depression* (pp. 541–59). New York, NY: The Guilford Press.

Lofthouse, N. & Fristad, M. A. (2006). Bipolar disorders. In G. G. Bear & K. Minke (eds), *Children's needs III* (pp. 211–24). Bethesda, MD: National Association of School Psychologists.

Lofthouse, N., Mackinaw-Koons, B., & Fristad, M. A. (2004). Bipolar spectrum disorders: Early onset. In A. Canter, L. Z. Paige, M. D. Roth, I. Romero, & S. A. Carroll (eds), *Helping children at home and school II: Handouts for families and educators* (pp. S5 13–16). Bethesda, MD: National Association of School Psychologists.

Luby, J. L., Heffelfinger, A., Mrakotsky, C., Brown, K., Hessler, M., Wallis, J., & Spitznagel, E. (2003). The clinical picture of depression in preschool children. *Journal of the American Academy of Child and Adolescent Psychiatry, 42,* 340–48. doi:10.1097/00004583-200303000-00015

Luby, J. L. & Navsaria, N. (2010). Pediatric bipolar disorder: Evidence for prodromal states and early markers. *Journal of Child Psychology and Psychiatry, 51,* 459–71. doi:10.1111/j.1469-7610.2010.02210.x

Masi, G., Millepiedi, S., Mucci, M., Pascale, R. R., Perugi, G., & Akiskal, H. S. (2003). Phenomenology and comorbidity of dysthymic disorder in 100 consecutively referred children and adolescents: Beyond DMS-IV. *Canadian Journal of Psychiatry, 48,* 99–105. Accessed from http://ww1.cpa-apc.org/Publications/Archives/CJP/2003/march/masi.pdf

Masi, G., Perugi, G., Millepiedi, S. (2007). Clinical implications of DSM-IV subtyping of bipolar disorders in children and adolescents. *Journal of the American Academy of Child and Adolescent Psychiatry, 46,* 1299–1306. doi:10.1097/chi.0b013e3180f62eba

McIntosh, D. E., & Trotter, J. S. (2006). Early onset bipolar spectrum disorder: Psychopharmacological, psychological, and educational management. *Psychology in the Schools, 43,* 451–60. doi:10.1002/pits.20159

Merrell, K. W. (2008). *Helping students overcome depression and anxiety: A practical guide* (2nd ed). New York, NY: The Guilford Press.

Merrell, K. W., Carrizales, D., Feuerborn, L., Gueldner, B. A., & Tran, O.K. (2007). *Strong kids: A social and emotional learning curriculum.* Baltimore, MD: Brookes.

Merrell, K. W., & Gueldner, B. A. (2010). Preventative interventions for students with internalizing disorders: Effective strategies for promoting mental health in schools. In M. R. Shinn and H. M. Walker (eds), *Interventions for achievement*

and behavior in a three-tier model including RTI (3rd ed., pp. 729–823).
Bethesda, MD: National Association of School Psychologists.

Miller, L., & Barnett, S. (2008). Mood lability and bipolar disorder in
children and adolescents. *International Review of Psychiatry*, 20, 171–6.
doi:10.1080/09540260801889088

National Institute of Mental Health (NIMH) (2003). *Breaking ground, breaking
through: The strategic plan for mood disorders research of the National
Institute of Mental Health*. Washington, DC: US Department of Health and
Human Services.

Nurnberger, J. I., & Foroud, T. (2000). Genetics of bipolar affective disorder.
Current Psychiatry Reports, 2, 147–57. doi:10.1007/s11920-000-0060-0

Rao, U. (2006). Development and natural history of pediatric depression:
Treatment implications. *Child Psychiatry*, 3, 194–204. Accessed from http://
www.clinicalneuropsychiatry.org/pdf/03_rao.pdf

Rao, U., & Chen, L. (2009). Characteristics, correlates, and outcomes
of childhood and adolescent depressive disorders. *Dialogues Clinical
Neuroscience*, 11, 45–62.

Reinemann, D. H. S., Stark, K. D., Molnar, J., & Simpson, J. (2006). Depressive
disorders. In G. G. Bear & K. Minke (eds), *Children's needs III* (pp. 199–210).
Bethesda, MD: National Association of School Psychologists.

Renouf, A. G., & Kovacs, M. (1995). Dysthymic disorder during childhood and
adolescence. In J. H. Kocsis & D. N. Klein (eds), *Diagnosis and treatment of
chronic depression* (pp. 20–40). New York, NY: The Guilford Press.

Reynolds, C. R., & Kamphaus, R. W. (2004). *Behavior Assessment System
for Children—Second Edition (BASC-2)*. Minneapolis, MN: Pearson
Assessments.

Rice, F., Harold, G., & Thapar, A. (2003). Negative life events as an account
of age-related differences in the genetic etiology of depression in childhood
and adolescence. *Journal of Child Psychology and Psychiatry*, 44, 977–87.
doi:10.1111/1469-7610.00182

Rice, K., & McLaughlin, T. F. (2001). Childhood and adolescent depression: A
review with suggestions for special educators. *International Journal of Special
Education*, 16, 85–96.

Rudolph, K. D., Flynn, M., & Abaied, J. L. (2008). A developmental perspective
on interpersonal theories of youth depression. In J. R. Z. Abela & B. L.
Hanking (eds), *Handbook of depression in children and adolescents* (pp.
79–102). New York, NY: The Guilford Press.

Rudolph, K. D., & Lambert, S. F. (2007). Child and adolescent depression. In
E. J. Mash & R. A. Barkley (eds), *Assessment of childhood disorders* (4th ed.,
pp. 213–52). New York, NY: The Guilford Press.

Stark, K., & Kendall, P. C. (1996). *Treating depressed children: Therapist manual
for Taking ACTION*. Ardmore, PA: Workbook Publishing.

van der Schot, A., Vonk, R., Brans, R., et al., (2009). Influence of genes and
environment on brain volumes in twin pairs of concordant and discordant for
bipolar disorder. *Archives of General Psychiatry*, 66, 142–51. doi:10.1001/
archgenpsychiatry.2008.541

Vople, R. Briesch, A. & Chafouleas, S. M. (2010). Linking screening for emotional
and behavioral problems to problem solving efforts: An adaptive model of

behavioral assessment. *Assessment for Effective Intervention, 35,* 240–4. doi:10.1177/1534508410377194

Walker, H. M., & Severson, H. (1992). *Systematic screening for behavior disorders* (2ⁿᵈ ed.). Longmont, CO: Sopris West.

Weissman, M. M., Wickramaratne, P., Nomura, Y., et al., (2005). Families at high and low risk for depression: A 3-generation study. *Archives of General Psychiatry, 62,* 29–36. doi:10.1001/archpsyc.62.1.29

Wickramaratne, P. J., Greenwald, S., & Weissman, M. M. (2000). Psychiatric disorders in the relatives of probands with prepubertal-onset or adolescent-onset major depression. *Journal of the American Academy of Child & Adolescent Psychiatry, 39,* 1396–405. doi:10.1097/00004583-200011000-00014

Wilmshurst, L. (2005). *Essentials of child psychopathology.* Hoboken, NJ: John Wiley & Sons Inc.

Youngstrom, E. A., Findling, R. L., Youngstrom, J. K., & Calabrese, J. R. (2005). Toward an evidence-based assessment of pediatric bipolar disorder. *Journal of Clinical Child and Adolescent Psychology, 34,* 433–48.

Zahn-Waxler, C., Race, E., & Duggal, S. (2005). Mood disorders and symptoms in girls. In D. J. Bell, S. L. Foster, & E. J. Mash (eds), *Handbook of behavioral and emotional problems in girls* (pp. 25–77). New York, NY: Kluwer/Plenum.

CHAPTER TEN

Understanding and Managing Behaviors of Children Diagnosed with Oppositional Defiant and Conduct Disorders (ODD/CD)

Tammy L. Hughes
Duquesne University

Michael E. Tansy
Private Practice Phoenix, Arizona

Kara G. Wisniewski
Brewer School Department, Brewer, Maine

Abstract

O how they cling and wrangle, some who claim
For preacher and monk the honored name!
For, quarreling, each to his view they cling.
Such folk see only one side of a thing.

Jainism and Buddhism. Udana 68–9:
Parable of the Blind Men and the Elephant

Like the blind men and the elephant, helping professionals, school personnel, parents, and children struggle to understand, and often disagree about the needs of individuals with oppositional defiant disorder (ODD) or conduct disorder (CD). Indeed, parents, teachers and other school personnel often staunchly and stubbornly hold fast to a narrow view of the cause and, in turn, remedy for the disruptive behaviors of ODD and CD. Stakeholders harboring narrow and rigid understanding of childhood conduct problems fail to appreciate the nature of their complexity, the challenge implicit in their treatment, and the importance of multiple interventions administered simultaneously, cooperatively, (Miller, Tansy, & Hughes, 1998) and with fidelity by qualified care providers (Rinsley, 1994). This chapter not only addresses the practical issues of understanding ODD and CD, but also prepares school professionals to understand effective treatments as well as the barriers to effective treatments.

Introduction

The diagnosis of Oppositional Defiant Disorder (ODD) or Conduct Disorder (CD) is a relatively straightforward process for the trained eye. That is, there is a list of behavioral characteristics that, when confirmed by a qualified professional (typically the school psychologist in a school district), come together to reach the threshold of a diagnosis. Compared to other psychological diagnoses that require assessment of thoughts and feelings, diagnosing ODD and CD is more straightforward and easier, as it relies on verification of observable behaviors.

ODD, often described as a milder form of CD, is characterized by negative and defiant behaviors such as: persistent stubbornness, resistance to directives, and unwillingness to compromise or negotiate with adults or peers. ODD has overlapping characteristics with CD, including disobedience and opposition to authority figures. In order to meet the criteria of ODD, at least four symptoms must be present for at least six months. In contrast to CD, ODD does not generally include aggression toward people or animals, destruction of property, or a pattern of theft or deceit. Indeed, individuals with ODD do not show a persistent pattern of the more serious behavior problems. Also, unlike CD, there tends to be an equal number of males and females who meet the criteria for ODD (Office of Child and Family Policy, 2008).

The essential features of CD are a repetitive and persistent pattern of behaviors that violate the basic rights of others or major age-appropriate societal norms or rules. Problem behaviors fall into four categories: a) causing or threatening physical harm to others, b) causing property loss or damage, c) deceitfulness or theft, and d) serious violations of rules. In order to diagnose CD, three or more characteristic behaviors must be present in the past 12 months, with at least one of them occurring in the previous 6 months. Moreover, the disturbance in behavior must cause significant impairment in the individual's (social, academic, or occupational) functioning. The onset of symptoms can occur when the individual is a child (age 10 or younger) or as an adolescent (age 11 or older).

Individuals with Childhood-Onset CD are: a) usually male, b) frequently display physical aggression toward others, c) likely to have disturbed peer relationships, d) may have had ODD behavior during early childhood, and e) usually have symptoms that meet full criteria for CD prior to adolescence. Many in this group have co-occurring AD/HD. Childhood-Onset CD is associated with persistent CD symptoms across the lifespan and into adulthood (American Psychological Association [APA], 2004) and many will also go on to develop Antisocial Personality Disorder (ASPD).

Adolescent-Onset CD is defined by the absence of CD symptoms prior to 10 years of age. Compared to Childhood-Onset CD, individuals with Adolescent-Onset CD are less likely to demonstrate aggressive behaviors and are more likely to have established relationships with peers. If, however, peers are engaged in antisocial acts (e.g. vandalism or truancy), this group can demonstrate antisocial behaviors alongside of peers. These adolescents are also less likely to have persistent CD or to develop adult antisocial patterns. Furthermore, like ODD, there is a more equal ratio of males to females in the Adolescent-Onset CD group.

Severity of CD is determined by the extent of harm to others. Behaviors described as Mild include: lying, truancy, and staying out after dark without permission. Behaviors described as Moderate include: vandalism and stealing that does not involve contact with the victim. Finally, behaviors described as Severe include: forced sex, physical cruelty, use of a weapon, and breaking and entering (APA, 2004).

When an individual's pattern of behavior meets the criteria for both ODD and CD, the diagnosis of CD takes precedence and only one diagnosis is given. Although rare, the onset of CD may occur after the age of 16. Typically, individuals diagnosed with CD are 18 years old or younger; however, adults may be diagnosed with CD if they do not meet the criteria for the more severe disorder of ASPD. If the onset of CD symptoms is unknown, then the diagnosis of CD—Unspecified Onset is used (APA, 2004).

The Developmental Course of ODD and CD

ODD, when present, commonly occurs prior to the onset of CD and ASPD (Loeber, Burke, Lahey, Winters, & Zera, 2000). The developmental course of ODD can begin as early as eight months; symptoms tend to be exhibited in the home with parents and then progress to other settings and interactions (APA, 2004). CD may begin as early as preschool, where early onset is reported between the ages of 4.5 and 5 years of age (Nock, Kazdin, Hiripi, & Kessler, 2006), although the first significant symptoms are usually evident during middle childhood to middle adolescence. Overall, the median age of onset for CD is 11.7 years (Nock et al., 2006). For those who meet the diagnostic criteria for ODD and CD early, there is a relatively stable pattern of behavioral problems and the child's difficulties are not simply transient (Keenan et al., 2010). Indeed, Early-Onset CD predicts more severe symptoms and a worse prognosis overall (e.g. increased risk for APSD, and Mood, Anxiety, Somatoform Disorders, and Substance-Related Disorders; APA, 2004; Stahl & Clarizio, 1999). In contrast, Adolescent-Onset CD and those with milder symptoms do not tend to continue on an antisocial path; rather, they show adequate adjustment in adulthood (Connor, 2002).

Loeber and colleagues (1993) have shown that there is a developmental pathway to delinquency in males that explains how childhood onset and adolescence onset symptoms unfold over the course of development. The three pathways are referred to as: authority conflict, overt aggression, and covert aggression. Others have replicated Loeber's model (e.g. Loeber, Keenan, & Zhang, 1997; Tolan & Gorman-Smith, 1998), supporting its value to parents and teachers when thinking about and monitoring children that may have demonstrate antisocial behavior.

In the Loeber et al. (1993) three-pathway model, individuals demonstrating *authority conflict*, the earliest entry point, present with ODD-like behaviors, including conflict with, and avoidance of, authority figures. There are three stages in this pathway, starting with stubborn behavior, then defiance (refusal, disobedience), and then authority avoidance (truancy). This pathway is only entered (starting at the stubborn behavior stage) prior to the age of 12 years. Typically, behaviors then increase in severity. After the age of 12 years, youth tend to exhibit behavior consistent with the highest stage of this pathway, authority avoidance. The second pathway of delinquency is *overt aggression*. The three stages comprising this pathway are minor aggression (annoying, bullying), physical fighting (gang fights), and violence (rape, assault). This path is marked by first ODD, then CD behaviors that result in aggression and inadequate positive problem-solving

(Loeber et al., 1993). The third pathway to delinquency is the pattern of *covert aggression*. This path is characterized by lying, vandalism, and theft and is only entered prior to the age of 15 years. Initial covert aggression starts with minor covert behavior (lying, shoplifting), then property damage (vandalism, fire setting), and finally serious property damage (burglary, theft). Those boys who enter a pathway early (e.g. authority conflict before the age of 12) were more likely to persist in their CD symptoms. Entry into the authority conflict pathway was noted as a forerunner to later escalation in covert or overt actions.

Associated Features and Differential Diagnosis

Although the diagnosis of ODD and CD is relatively straightforward, sometimes, behavior can be difficult to interpret. The stubbornness and argumentativeness of ODD can look similar to the irritability of depression or the disruptive behavior of hyperactivity. The impulsive behavior of AD/HD can be confused with the disobedience and opposition to authority figures in both ODD and CD. Importantly, no single behavior is considered alone. Rather, the associated symptoms and behaviors of each of the disorders are also taken into account when a diagnosis is made. Furthermore, ODD and CD often co-occur with other disorders (e.g. AD/HD, Depression, Anxiety and Learning Disabilities); therefore, it is essential that a comprehensive evaluation is completed when the diagnosis is made (Hughes, Crothers, & Jimerson, 2008). When criteria are met for CD and other co-occurring disorders, both diagnoses are given (e.g. CD and AD/HD and Depression, etc.).

Parents and teachers are especially important in the diagnostic process as they observe and describe patterns in a child's behavior (Loeber et al., 1993) in the child's natural context. Noting whether the behavior was an act of retribution for a perceived wrong, planned, or impulsive, an astute caregiver can identify early warning signs and as such, is able to implement interventions early.

Red flags and early warnings

There are few behaviors alone that require immediate diagnosis and treatment. That is, in general, ODD and CD symptoms tend to accumulate and progress as children age. One notable exception is the symptom of cruelty to animals (associated with CD). Retrospective reports from parents show that the median age of onset for hurting animals is 6.5 years—earlier than bullying, cruelty to people, vandalism, or fire setting (Frick et al., 1993). Further, cruelty to animals has been shown to be predictive of subsequent violent acts and ongoing antisocial behaviors. When parents, teachers or other school personnel become aware of an incident of cruelty to animals, a professional trained in identifying ODD, CD and other behavioral concerns should be notified so that appropriate intervention can be initiated. The best treatment outcomes occur when children are early in the development of CD and before the age of 8 years (Frick, 1998a; Kazdin 1996; McMahon & Wells, 1998; Shaw, Dishion, Supplee, Gardner, & Arnds, 2006).

Intervention

If forced to provide a simple summary, antisocial behavior appears to be the product of the interaction between genetic and cultural factors (Maes, Silberg, Neal, & Eaves, 2007; Justicia et al., 2006), particularly parenting styles (e.g., ineffective child raising style, insufficient supervision, low cognitive stimulation), individual factors (e.g., poor conflict management skills, low social skills, attention problems, learning problems), contextual family factors (e.g., poverty, parental delinquency, parental substance abuse, stress factors, family conflict), school and peer group factors (e.g., ineffective teacher responses, aggressive conduct in class, peer rejection, and association with deviant peers) that occur in combination (Webster-Stratton, 2001). Although the process of how to conduct a psychological assessment that determines the contributions of any or all of these factors for a given youth is beyond the scope of this chapter, it is important for teachers and parents to understand how central a role they play in helping to sort this information. Thus, in schools it is important to collect information from everyone who has contact with the child.

Response to Intervention

Although it is important to have an accurate diagnosis in order to plan for the best intervention strategy, schools are able to act quickly and apply strategies as soon as concerns are evident. Indeed, the Response to Intervention (RtI) model, now used in schools across the country, encourages educators to start interventions early and then provide more intensive services if the interventions fail to work or more information becomes available regarding the certainty of a diagnosis.

Students with ODD or CD demonstrate a variety of behavioral symptoms (as described above) that directly affect their academic functioning. That is, defiance for following rules of social conduct will also be evident when students are asked to complete academic assignments. As such, behavioral and academic issues should be addressed simultaneously.

Tiered interventions

In the RTI model, academic and behavioral interventions fall into one of three levels, described as Tier I, Tier II, or Tier III. Tier I interventions are proactive in nature and they have been shown (e.g. research evidence to support) their usefulness with all students—in the case of ODD and CD, Tier I interventions are beneficial for all youth with behavioral difficulties. It is expected, however, even with a proactive approach, that about 15% of students will require additional support (e.g. Tier II; Crone, Hawken, & Horner, 2010; Gresham, 2004). Furthermore, even when provided adequate Tier I and Tier II interventions, about 5% of students require the support provided only through individualized Tier III interventions (Colvin, 2007; Crone et al., 2010). Movement from Tier I to Tier II and then to Tier III matches the intensity of problems with a correspondingly intensive intervention. The decision to move between levels is based on the student's failure to benefit (e.g. failure to respond) and is referred to as the student's Response to Intervention (RTI). Interventions within this model are sometimes referred to as primary (Tier I), secondary (Tier II), and tertiary (Tier III).

Although the early research on RTI tended to focus on either academics (e.g. Fuchs & Fuchs, 2007) or behaviors (e.g. Sugai & Horner, 2009), more recently, schools have integrated these areas to improve their ability to provide comprehensive services (Hawken, Vincent, & Schumann, 2008; McKinney, Bartholomew & Gray, 2010; McIntosh, Bohanon, & Goodman, 2010; McIntosh, Horner, Chard, Dickey, & Braun, 2008; Stewart, Benner, Martella, & Marchand-Martella, 2007). The best outcomes for students occur when educators integrate academic and behavioral support (Stewart, Benner, Martella, & Marchand-Martella, 2007). Integrated models remind parents and professionals that there is a transactional relationship between academics and behavior that results in overall school performance (Lane & Wehby, 2002; Walker, Ramsey, & Gresham, 2005).

Tier I

As mentioned above, Tier I (primary interventions) are proactive, universal and provided for all students. Such interventions target system-wide concerns and involve all members of the school system, including school personnel, students, and families in order to build a healthy school environment through a focus on positive support. Effective instruction, monitoring a student's progress, and providing positive feedback and encouragement are quality practices in Tier I.

A high quality, scientifically-based general education experience is assumed to be the cornerstone of academic success for all students. Section

9101(37) of the *Elementary and Secondary Education Act* as amended as *No Child Left Behind (NCLB)*, defines scientifically-based research as "research that involves the application of rigorous, systematic, and objective procedures to obtain reliable and valid knowledge relevant to education activities and programs" (p. 540). Schools are required to show that: 1) the curriculums they deliver are research-based, that is students' learning can be measured, 2) that their teachers are delivering high quality instruction (e.g. the techniques used to teach the content) matches the needs of the students (see Tier II and Tier III) and 3) that changes to their teaching (either content or technique) are interventions supported by research evidence. There are many ways to meet these standards, including differentiating classroom instruction based on the child's skill, ensuring that there are sufficient opportunities to learn, and early screening followed by monitoring student progress (Hughes, Kaufman, & Hoover, 2010).

For youth showing behavioral concerns, teachers can provide academic support by identifying the essential learning content (e.g. the task is subtraction two-digit by two-digit numbers without borrowing). Teachers identify the content from the research-based curriculum used for the class. Next, teachers need to provide a structure (step-wise sequence) to move students toward that learning (Coyne, Kame'enui, & Camine, 2007). This structure is comprised of the techniques used to deliver the content. Often, hands-on, multisensory techniques have a strong research support (depending on the content you are trying to deliver). Then, students need to follow (by way of graphing or points) and be rewarded for their progress (e.g. provide positive feedback, encouragement, etc.). Teachers need to determine what may or may not be rewarding for any given student—for example, some children like private praise, while others enjoy acknowledgement in the large class settings.

For youth with behavioral concerns, teachers can provide behavioral support by clearly defining behavioral expectations (e.g. sit in your chair, face forward and keep your hands to yourself), setting clear and reachable goals (e.g. students may draw, read or pick a silent task when they have completed their assignment) and rewarding specified outcomes (e.g. may select to work on the computer, etc.). There are two well-developed primary intervention programs that support social development in youth that schools may adopt for their whole system. Both proactive classroom management (PCM) and positive behavior supports (PBS) have a research-base for their curriculum, methods, and delivery.

Proactive Classroom Management (PCM) is a recommended school-wide primary intervention that promotes high levels of academic engagement, and focuses on increasing students' on-task behavior and decreasing their disruptive behaviors (Gettinger, 1988; Rathvon, 2008; Wehby & Lane, 2009). PCM is designed to prevent opportunities for disruptive behavior, and include teaching strategies such as explicit instruction, guided practice, and ongoing feedback about class rules and routines. Classroom routines are established early in the year, and once established, teachers have been able to maintain an on-task rate of 80% or above for the classroom which has been described as ideal for optimal learning (Mitchem, Young, West, & Benyo, 2001).

Critical PCM tasks associated with prosocial behavior and optimal learning include organizing a productive classroom environment, providing instruction within close proximity of disruptive students and teacher movement within the classroom, establishing classroom rules and procedures, and managing transitions. There is a focus on small-group instruction and independent seatwork, communicating competently with students, and high levels of teacher-student interaction (e.g., behavior-specific praise, feedback, cueing, physical proximity, eye contact). Frequent reinforcement of prosocial behaviors and building positive relationships in the classroom are also important (Gunter, Kenton-Denny, & Venn; 2000; Hulac, Terrell, Vining, & Bernstein, 2011; Little, Akin-Little & Cook, 2009; Rathvon, 2008; Sutherland, Wehby, & Copeland, 2000; Wehby & Lane, 2009).

Many PCM interventions utilize the *Say, Show, Check* skill training strategy (Wolfgang & Wolfgang, 1995). This socialization technique provides direct instruction regarding how to behave during class, including rules and routines, using a three-step lesson format: the teacher demonstrates the rule, the teacher checks to verify students' understanding of the rule by role-playing breaking the rule, and then the teacher models the correct behavior again. Here, the students see both an example of the rule as well as a counter-example; both points allow the student to better understand what is expected of him or her in class.

Positive Behavior Support (PBS) is another recommended school-wide primary intervention. PBS focuses on the social culture of the school and behavioral supports needed for social and academic success by instituting the measurement of specific behaviors, using data-based decisions making to determine what is working and what is not, insuring that all interventions have an evidence-base and by using overt cues to implement setting-based change (Hulac et al., 2011; Sugai & Horner, 2006; Sugai et al., 2010). In order to be effective, PBS requires support from stakeholders (Turnbull et al., 2002) to develop the environments that facilitate universal, group, and individual student success. This includes time to effectively teach the entire school system the rules and procedures for implementation and to ensure that there are consistent consequences for behavior (Scott & Martinek, 2006). A strength of PBS is that schools can establish their own goals based on their own culture. However, the challenge then is to ensure multilevel support required to implement PBS. There are several steps that are identified as increasing the likelihood of effective implementation of PBS including: meeting with the school's key stakeholders, defining the team's vision, identifying the setting's strengths, weaknesses, opportunities, and threats, then developing an action plan, including both short-term and long-term actions (Ern, 2007). Similarly, Colvin (2007) provides a useful seven step plan to develop and maintain a proactive school wide discipline plan, including:

- developing a purpose statement;
- establishing school wide behavior expectations;
- teaching the behavior expectations;
- maintaining the behavior expectations;
- correcting problem behavior;
- using data gathered throughout before and since implementation; and
- sustaining the plan for the long haul.

Correspondingly, there are several specific pitfalls to avoid when planning a PBS intervention, including targeting only a few difficult students, seeking quick fixes, trying to find one powerful trick, revering outside experts, believing more is better, and ineffective communication of available resources (George & Kincaid, 2008; Horner, Sugai, & Horner, 2000).

In these integrated systems, interventions are designed to work in tandem to enhance students' social competence (Colvin, 2007; Crone, Hawken, & Horner, 2010; Gresham, 2004; McIntosh, Goodman, & Bohanon, 2010) and provide an effective delivery of core instruction (Fuchs & Fuchs, 2007). Regardless of the support shown in the research, teachers should monitor the outcomes of their efforts in their classroom, that is, how well their students are actually responding, academically and behaviorally. Student progress monitoring should occur in planned cycles (e.g. weekly, monthly) and interventions should be changed as needed (Sugai, 2009).

Tier II

Tier II, secondary interventions, are used with children who are less responsive to Tier I primary/universal interventions, are at risk for developing more significant academic delays and/or severely disruptive behavior, and need additional support for success. Secondary interventions may be provided to the whole class or to the smaller group. In these interventions, skills training tends to be more explicit, teacher monitoring is more frequent, self-monitoring is more emphasized and parent-teacher collaboration is more detailed. Generally, the 15% of students requiring Tier II interventions demonstrate persistent problems in general education settings (e.g. classroom, transitions, playground, cafeteria, etc.); yet, they are not students with serious, chronic academic and/or behavior problems requiring individualized attention. Some schools use Tier II interventions with all students as they can "improve the overall efficiency of the school wide procedures, while reducing the number of individualized interventions that are needed" (Crone et al., 2010, p. 1), which ultimately benefits all students and school personnel.

There are several published Tier II secondary intervention resources cited in the literature to support social, emotional, and behavioral difficulties, including such examples as the *Behavior Education Program* (BEP: Crone et al., 2010), *Resolving Conflict Creatively Program* (Brown, Roderick, Lantieri, & Aber, 2004), *Second Step* (Grossman et al., 1997; Duffell, Beland, & Frey, 2006), and *Social Emotional Learning* (Cohen, 1999; Elias, 2004; Elias & Arnold, 2006; Novick, Kress, & Elias, 2002; Zins et al., 2004). The task of identifying which, if any, of these programs may be best for your particular setting can be daunting. Crone et al. (2010) identified six key features of effective and comprehensive Tier II interventions that can be used when selecting a program:

- Can you implement the intervention across multiple students (e.g., students with similar Tier II risks)?

- Do you have quick and continuous access to the intervention?

- Are all school staff trained on the intervention?

- Is the intervention consistent with established school wide expectations?

- Is the intervention flexible enough to make modifications, if needed?

- Is the intervention meeting the specific needs of the children?

- Is there a data collection procedure that allows continuous monitoring of student progress as the intervention unfolds?

This list suggests that teachers should work collaboratively with other personnel (e.g., other teachers on the team, school principals, parents, etc.) to monitor success. Additionally, it is important to add that Tier II programs should not only be effective for participating students, but also acceptable to school personnel and not overly burdensome on school resources.

Maintaining a focus on academic success becomes increasingly critical for students requiring Tier II interventions. As mentioned, both academic and behavior support should have occurred together in Tier I. Moving to Tier II provides "supplemental" support to the "core" academic and behavioral instruction in Tier 1; Tier II additions are not a replacement for Tier 1 instruction (Burns & Gibbons, 2008). Additionally, there is strong evidence of a direct relationship between academic achievement and delinquency (e.g., Denno, 1990; Farrington, 1989; Hawkins et al., 1998; Loeber, Burke, Lahey, Winters, & Zera, 1998). As academic performance increases, delinquency rates decrease. Similarly, when delinquency is high, academic performance is found to be low. While a causal relationship between academic failure and delinquency has not been uncovered (Trout, Nordness, Pierce, & Epstein, 2003), academic underachievement is related to the onset, frequency, and persistence of delinquency in children and adolescents (McEvoy & Welker, 2000). Examining the developmental course of academic underachieving and delinquency reveals that the vast number of boys who go on to be delinquent were first failing in school (Wisniewski, 2006). Experience and research informs us that parents and teachers become distracted by behavior problems (Rivera, Al-Otaiba, & Koorland, 2006) and that teachers spend much time managing behaviors at the expense of instructional time, interfering with teachers' ability to address developing academic lags.

Tier III

Tier III, tertiary services, are those interventions developed for and delivered to students who demonstrate disruptive behavior and academic underachievement in spite of universal or group interventions. In contrast to primary and secondary interventions, tertiary services are more intensive and highly individualized. Children needing these services represent 3 to 5% of students. They may receive these services based on psychoeducational evaluation, often necessitating placement in special education and requiring coordinated community-based services. Interventions for children with behavioral problems that reach this level of severity are provided across a continuum of treatment settings (e.g., schools, clinics, residential facilities) targeting multiple systems (e.g., child, family, school, community) and engaging a comprehensive group of stakeholders (e.g., parents, educators, clinicians). This makes for a complex multi-systemic matrix that requires sustained and active coordination. In order to realize a lasting benefit, change must occur not only within the child but also within the family, the school, and community so that the adults are prepared to act in support of a child who has complex needs.

Conduct Problems: What Do We Need To Understand?

Effective Tier III services begin with an individualized assessment of the child. Although there is no "gold standard" for assessing children

(McConaughy, 2005), it is clear that the process requires a mindful study of the child using multiple methods, including interviews, observation, student record reviews, rating scales, and other forms of assessment (Steiner & American Academy of Child and Adolescent Psychiatry [AACAP], 1997; Connor, 2002). Ultimately, by examining this data the examiner needs to determine the cause or causes of the student's disruptive behavior in order to develop a plan that is effective, realistic, and individualized to decrease conduct problems and build resilience (Connor, 2002; Hughes et al., 2008). Incorporating traditional assessment data (from tests) along with observations, records, and functional behavioral assessment (FBA) improves our ability to select appropriate treatment strategies (Walker et al., 2005). In the case of ODD and CD, where social competence deficits are primary, it is considered a best practice (McNamara, 2002).

In recent years several authors have summarized Tier-III interventions developed to address conduct problems at school (Akin-Little, Little, Bray, & Kehle, 2009; McMahon, Wells & Kotler, 2006; Rathvon, 2008; Vannest, Reynolds, & Kamphaus, 2008). Many of the interventions outlined in these texts reveal a structuralist, rather than a functional, conceptualization of childhood psychopathology and treatment. A structuralist approach to treatment involves selecting interventions based on their demonstrated effectiveness with a percentage of individuals with the same problem. Essentially, interventions are selected because they work for the "average" person with the same problem. Functionalists, on the other hand, select interventions based on their demonstrated effectiveness in correcting the identified cause(s) of the behavior; for example, recommending family therapy if the source of disruptive behavior is family dysfunction (Miller et al., 1998). That is, regardless of how many other people also have a similar cause to their problem, the treatment selection for a specific person is based on their individual path to the problem (Shirk & Russell, 1996). A team that incorporates both approaches is more likely to be effective. Essentially, it is useful to start with what works for most people and then tailor interventions based on the needs of the specific person (Hughes & Theodore, 2009).

However, for youth with severe behavioral disturbances, like ODD and CD, even more effort is needed for success. Indeed, many researchers have observed that school-based interventions alone (those that do not attempt to intervene with families, communities and the other systems in the child's life that contribute to or maintain childhood conduct problems) are without significant and lasting effect (Henggeler & Lee, 2003; Henggeler & Schaeffer, 2010; Henggeler, Schoenwald, Borduin, Rowland, & Cunningham, 2009; Tarolla, Wagner, Rabinowitz, & Tubman, 2002; Vannest et al., 2008). Because of this concern, mutisystemic interventions for childhood conduct problems are required.

Interventions for Affective Regulation

Often children who demonstrate disruptive behaviors display impairment in affective (emotion) regulation (Cicchetti & Toth, 1995; Mullin & Hinshaw, 2007). Essentially, these youth have difficulty monitoring and evaluating their own emotional states (Campbell-Sills & Barlow, 2007) and can also have difficulty engaging in behavioral and cognitive sequences to maintain or change the intensity or duration of an affective state (Larsen & Prizmic, 2004), resulting in internalized and externalized behavior problems (Mullin & Hinshaw, 2007). In particular, children with high levels of negative affectivity employ faulty interpretations of social cues, and use reactive aggression in response to the perceived threat, resulting in high levels of peer, teacher, and parent rejection, and, ultimately, achieving a self-fulfilling prophecy that their faulty a priori beliefs that others reject them are correct and valid. Impairment of affective regulation may be directly observed in the form of strong emotional reactions to routine events or may be gleaned from interviewing the child, parents, or teachers. Note, this group of children will often qualify for special education under the category of ED regardless of or in addition to ODD or CD diagnosis.

Student-focused social competence, problem-solving and moral reasoning training programs are based on the assumption that children engage in conduct problems because they have not developed skills because it is not within their repertoire (skill acquisition deficit) or there is not sufficient motivation (reinforcement or discouragement) to maintain the prosocial skill. Based on the assumption that the skill is not sufficiently developed, interventions involve instructional time, discussion, modeling, role playing, coaching, practice, feedback, and positive reinforcement within a broader instructional and motivational context (e.g. why should you want to control yourself). These exercises often target feeling awareness, assertive communication, problem-solving, cooperation, self-control, and empathy training (Begun, 1995; Elliott & Gresham, 1991; Johnson & Johnson, 1995).

Reasoning and Social Judgment

Recognizing that conduct problems may be partially the result of errors in reasoning and judgment associated with poor emotional regulation, these programs provide direct training in social judgment, moral reasoning and development (Etscheidt, 1991; Hollin, 1990; Kazdin, 2003; Kendall, 1985, 1993; Lochman, Nelson, & Sims, 1981). Such programming stems from the recognition that when children with conduct problems are faced with frustrating situations, their reactions are determined by their perceptions of the situation, which may be erroneous, yet malleable. Focused on modifying these erroneous perceptions, teachers and other school personnel provide lessons (direct instruction, role-play, and feedback) and discussions of specific social skills, problem-solving skills and moral dilemmas.

Interventions for Communication Problems

Communication can be defined as the transmission of information and the exchange of ideas (Bedell & Lennox, 1997). It involves self-awareness of feelings and thoughts, an intent to make these feelings and thoughts known, the ability to initiate conversation, to maintain social interactions, to express your thoughts and feelings to another, and to comprehend what the other person is attempting to convey to you. It is an essential link in the interaction between thinking, feeling, and behavior.

Children with ODD and CD demonstrate impairment in their forms of communication. The origin of these communication difficulties are complex and include physiological/brain anatomy problems, temperament, reinforcement history, modeling, and family problems. Often, these youth display maladaptive forms of communication. For example, inappropriate classroom behavior may be behavioral manifestations communicating a need for attention, a need for control, an effort to extract revenge when needs aren't met, or complete frustration communicated by "shutting down" (Dinkmeyer, 1980).

Assertive Communication

A core component of any classroom designed to assist children with antisocial behavior must address prosocial communication. The goal of this component of the instructional environment is to teach assertive communication—a confident declaration or statement that affirms the person's point of view without threatening the rights of others or allowing others to ignore one's rights or point of view (Alberti & Emmons, 2008). Assertiveness is a communication style distinguished from both aggression and passivity. The goals of assertiveness training include: increased awareness of personal rights, differentiation between non-assertiveness and assertiveness, differentiation between passive–aggressiveness and aggressiveness, and learning both verbal and non-verbal assertiveness skills (Craighead & Nemeroff, 2001; Patterson, 2000). Typically, instruction in assertiveness training is conducted in small groups, making a classroom a natural setting for this experience. Often, the instructor guides the learner through specific assertive techniques, including "the broken record" (repeating your request of refusal of another's request like a broken record), "escalating assertion" (using stronger and firmer assertions as the situation warrants), "I-statements" and others (Jakubowski & Lange, 1978; Smith, 1975).

Interventions for Cognitive Distortion

Faulty cognitive processes are a primary factor contributing to the demonstration of ODD and CD behavior (Crick & Dodge, 1994, Kazdin, 1995). This group is more likely to misinterpret the verbal and nonverbal behaviors of others, behave in response to their own misinterpretations, and elicit hostile and controlling behaviors from others, thus generating a self-fulfilling prophecy of their initial misinterpretation. This sequence (trigger → misinterpretation → aggressive behavior → reactions from others outcome that is consistent with the misinterpretation → reinforcement and maintenance of a priori faulty belief system) is unconscious, unquestioned, automatized, habitual, and extremely resistant to change without intervention (Beck, 1999; Ellis & Bernard, 2006; Greenwald, 1980).

Cognitive Behavior Therapy

Fortunately, school-based interventions for children who engage in disruptive behavior as a result of impaired cognitive processes have good empirical support (Digiuseppe, 2010). These interventions are referred to as cognitive behavior therapy (CBT). CBT targets problematic thoughts. Some of the major advantages of CBT is that it is portable regardless of context and its usefulness is sustainable through self-feedback.

Social Problem Solving

Social problem solving interventions (Kendall & Braswell, 1993; Meichenbaum, 2002; Spivack, Platt, & Shure, 1976) assumes that children engage in problem behaviors because they suffer from habitually-employed deficits in the way they interpret, understand, and solve social problems, and that these maladaptive problem solving patterns may be changed through a planned set of activities that includes direct instruction, modeling, coaching, and reinforcement. The intervention focuses on choice. We begin by explaining to students that we actually choose how we think about problems and their solutions. We choose how we behave and that we can choose to behave differently, although it will require increased self-control and mindfulness as our current pattern of behavior may be habitual and operating outside of our awareness. The student is taught to define problems and to generate alternative problem-solving strategies. From this list of possible alternate ways to think about the situation and how to behave in relation to the social problem, the student is encouraged to stop, think and weigh the relative benefits of engaging in specific responses to the social problem. Through discussion and feedback on performance, the child develops more adaptive social problem solving skills that may be used in future social situations.

Rational Emotive Behavior Therapy

Rational Emotive Behavior Therapy (REBT) is based on the assumption that there is an objective reality with a layer of subjective interpretation we impose on it and that our construction of beliefs may be the root of our emotional problems (Dryden & Ellis, 2001; Ellis, 1994; McMullin, 2000). If our interpretation of the event is positive, we experience happiness and behave accordingly. If our belief about the event is negative, we have a negative emotion, such as sadness or anger, and act accordingly, as well. REBT interventions ask that we teach the student to dispute (engage in alternative countering, positive interpretations of the event) that are effective, or rational, rather than irrational and upsetting. As with CBT mentioned previously, REBT begins by explaining the concept, then guiding the student through direct instruction, modeling, exercises, homework, discussion, coaching, and reinforcement.

Cognitive Therapy

Cognitive therapy (Beck, 1976; DeRubeis, Tang, & Beck, 2001) is based on the understanding that people organize information and experiences in their mind according to a schemata (e.g. underlying mental structure). Faulty schemata form the basis for distorted thinking, emotional upset, and behavioral problems. Faulty thoughts or cognitive errors, include "all-or-nothing thinking", "discounting the positives," "jumping to conclusions,' "fortunetelling," and "making 'should' statements." Interventions using cognitive therapy are consistent with REBT, including explaining the error, then guiding the student through direct instruction, modeling, exercises, homework, discussion, coaching, and reinforcement. Additionally, the student is asked to monitor faulty schemata daily to offer the teacher insight into specific errors. When discussing the cognitive errors, the teacher is encouraged to ask the student three questions, "What's the evidence for and against the belief?" "What are the alternative interpretations of the event" and, "What's the real implication, if the belief were to be true?" (DeRubeis et al., 2001, pp. 360-1). Through these questions, countering thoughts may be developed that will lead to different schemata, feelings, and behavior. Countering thoughts may include a variety of techniques, depending on the nature of the faulty schemata, including: alternative interpretations, anti-catastrophic reappraisals, label shifting, perceptual shifting, and objective (rational) countering.

Interventions for Reinforcement Problems

Behavior modification strategies assume that an underlying cause of the child's behavior is his or her learning history and the number of rewards for disruptive behavior (Cooper, Heron, & Heward, 2007; Little et al., 2009; Vannest et al., 2008). Interventions based on this assumption include manipulating antecedents that trigger or anticipate the behavior, teaching new behaviors or strengthening the reward schedule for existing prosocial behavior, and facilitating the transfer of learning across settings. Contingency management may involve the teacher rewarding each individual student for demonstrating specific behaviors, independent of the other students' behavior (student-focused contingency management strategies), or by managing individual student's, groups' of students within a classroom, or entire classrooms' student behavior by rewarding the behavior of smalls groups within the classroom or the classroom as a whole (interdependent group-focused contingency management strategies).

A common student-focused contingency management strategy is token economies where teachers provide tangible (tokens, points, stickers, etc.) or non-tangible (praise, access to desirable activities, etc.) rewards to the student for demonstrating predetermined important prosocial behavior. Often, these tangible rewards are withheld or removed (response cost) when the student engages in predetermined targeted antisocial behavior. Accrued rewards can later be exchanged for larger rewards based on a preset menu.

Before beginning a contingency management intervention, it is essential that inappropriate behaviors (e.g. physical aggression, noncompliance) and the corresponding prosocial behavior (e.g. periods of non-aggressive behavior, promptly complying with teacher requests) are described in concrete and unambiguous terms. Once it is clear what is meant by positive and negative behaviors, an educator other than the teacher observes the student on multiple occasions to establish a pre-intervention record of the problem behavior. The problem behavior is described in terms of its frequency, level of intensity, duration, as well as what triggers and rewards the actions. This initial measurement will later be used to assess the effectiveness of the intervention, and modify the intervention, if needed. It is critical to develop a description of how rewards can be collected and a schedule that specifies how many tokens, points, or stickers must be spent to obtain items from a reinforcement menu.

Items on the reinforcement menu may include access to high interest activities, such as games, computer time, lunch-time with a high status individual, or other activities. Items on the menu can be inferred by observing activities the student naturally gravitates to or by asking the child what activities she or he may be willing to work for. To be most effective, rewards should occur instantaneously (praise), at set times throughout the day (e.g. points at the end of instructional blocks and transitions), at the end of the day (e.g. notes home to parents, formalized classroom recognition activities) and at the end of the week (e.g. classroom stores, recognition through campus-wide announcements). Having completed a comprehensive plan, the teacher must be alert to observe the student displaying the target positive behavior or negative behaviors. There should be a special effort to attend to and reward prosocial behaviors as they are less noticeable than antisocial behavior and more likely to be overlooked—thereby defeating the purpose of the intervention.

Two popular and well-researched examples of group-focused contingency management programs include the *Good Behavior Game* (GBG; Barrish, Saunders, & Wolf, 1969) and the *Good Behavior Game Plus Merit* (Darveaux,1984). When playing the GBG, students are divided into teams and compete to earn rewards based on their ability to maintain low levels of rule infractions. If all the teams remain below the threshold, all the teams are rewarded. Important elements of the GBG are positive peer pressure, establishing specific performance criteria for success, immediate feedback on behavior, and group-based reinforcement. The GBG program has been successful with a variety of age groups, in a variety of educational settings, and to have lasting benefit in the maintenance of desirable behaviors.

In the GBG Plus Merit, teams earn bonus points to offset lost points by demonstrating specific prosocial or academic behaviors. This variation of the GBG is particularly valuable as teachers appreciate that it rewards prosocial behaviors (unlike the GBG, which focuses on not engaging in disruptive behavior) and it allows students to self-correct, redeeming an otherwise failed day that holds no motivation to continue to behave. A variation of interdependent group-focused contingency management is the randomized group contingencies programs where the reward is unannounced or is a mystery until behavioral criteria is met. These programs are effective (Rhode, Jenson, & Reavis, 1996; Theodore, Bray, & Kehle, 2004) and popular with students and teachers (Madaus, Kehle, Madaus, & Bray, 2003; Moore, Waguespack, Wickstrom, Witt, 1994; Rhode, Jenson, & Reavis, 1996).

Interventions for Modeling

Several studies have examined and confirmed the important role of parent modeling in the development of childhood antisocial behavior (Baldwin & Skinner, 1989; Verlaan & Schwartzman, 2002; Vieno, Nation, Pastore, & Santinello, 2009). Others have targeted the role of deviant peer models in the development of adolescent antisocial behavior (Kimonis, Frick, &

Barry, 2004; Lee, 2011; Snyder, Dishion, & Patterson, 1986). Additionally, the media and video games have been identified as sources of deviance modeling contributing to antisocial behavior (APA, 1993, Buckley & Anderson, 2006; Centerwall, 1992; Derksen & Strasburger, 1996; Gentile & Anderson, 2006). Indeed, there are many models engaged in antisocial behavior that predispose children to oppositional, defiant, and conduct-disordered behaviors.

Providing alternative prosocial models for children with difficult behaviors is a challenge because the best outcomes are associated with modeling when the actor (i.e. model) is similar to the child (Hurd, Zimmerman, & Reischl, 2010), but enjoys a higher status. Finding higher-status exemplars matched on the unique characteristics of children and who have forged a path marked by successes in school and behavioral control often proves to be very difficult. Consider the target child faced with a portfolio that may include being male, born addicted to a single mother, his father incarcerated for a history of violence, and having a male cousin who glorifies weapons and the power and dominance associated with weapon possession. Such a child may have a strong desire to play in the NBA or NFL but does not dress for gym nor will he practice, has a learning disability that makes the experience of school burdensome and lives in a neighborhood where street violence rules and survival is predicated on assimilation into that system. Now consider how many youth just like him have survived as role models useful for interventions. Though daunting, it is imperative to educators and families to expose these at-risk children to these accepted models of prosocial behavior.

Interventions for Family Issues

Noncompliance, a keystone behavior in the development and maintenance of ODD and CD, may occur in a variety of forms, including passive noncompliance, simple refusal, direct defiance, and negotiation (Walker & Walker, 1991). Long before the child enters school, noncompliance becomes an established pattern. Specifically, feeling in control over child-parent social interactions rewards the child and avoiding interaction with the difficult and noncompliant child also rewards the parent. This dynamic is particularly evident within families where parents rely on harsh, coercive, and punitive methods to discipline. Children of these parents more frequently develop defiance, passive noncompliance, and oppositional behavior to resist parental demands (Dishion & Patterson, 1996; Dishion & Kavanagh, 2002, 2005; Dishion & Stormshak, 2006; Patterson, 1975, 1976, 2002). Once the pattern is developed within the home, children transfer that learning to the school and elsewhere. When patterns are reinforced, they are strengthened and made more resistant to change (see behavior management systems above).

Parent-Training

The underlying assumption of parent training is that parenting skills deficits have been partially responsible for the development and/or maintenance of the conduct-disordered behaviors. The primary focus of parent-training is altering the parents' behavior to change the child's behavior, teach the parent more effective behavior management skills, encourage the parent to model prosocial behavior to the child, and decrease stress levels for the student, the parents and the family. Parent training may occur at school or in community-based settings.

The key processes in parent training include direct teaching of behavioral techniques, social-problem solving and the influence of modeling to improve the child's prosocial behaviors. As each are described above, recall that these objectives are achieved through direct instruction, modeling, role-playing effective parent practices, rehearsal, coaching, feedback, bibliotherapy (e.g. reading relevant books), on-going homework assignments, between-session monitoring and support, and establishing parent support networks.

Interventions for Physiological and Constitutional Problems

Several sources have asserted that there are psychophysiological (Moffitt & Lynam, 1994; Tranel, 2000), physiological (Blair, 2003, 2006; Bradley, 2000; Minzenberg & Siever, 2006; Raine & Yang, 2006; Rogers, 2006) and temperamental (Keogh, 2003) indicators of oppositional, defiant, and conduct disordered precursors. Based on standardized measures of intelligence, it appears that children with less language skills (i.e. less lateralized language functions, less efficient left-hemispheric information processing) are at increased risk to develop antisocial behavior; perhaps because these deficits result in inefficient use of the internal language necessary to comprehend the complexities of social exchanges, to develop their lexicon of emotional language, appreciate reciprocal role-taking (empathy) and may contribute to risk for increased academic failure—all factors predisposing the child to the development of conduct problems (Connor, 2002). Physiological findings utilizing PET, SPECT, MRS, and fMRI imaging suggest impairment of the prefrontal cortex, temporal cortex, amygdala, hippocampus, and corpus callosum anomalies among subgroups of children with CD (Aggleton & Young, 2000; Bradley, 2000; Dolan & Morris, 2000; Emery & Amaral, 2000; Raine & Yang, 2006; Reiman, Lane, Ahern, Schwartz, & Davidson, 2000). Furthermore, others have identified metabolic impairment of neurotransmitters (serotonin, dopamine, norepinephrine), testosterone, and cortisol among subpopulations of adults demonstrating antisocial behavior, suggesting a significant physiologic involvement in these behaviors (Bradley, 2000; Minzenberg & Siever, 2006).

Medications

At this time, a review of the literature does not reveal any known medication targeted to treat childhood antisocial behavior. However, as noted previously, a disproportionate number of children with ODD and CD demonstrate co-occurring psychiatric conditions, including mood disorders (anxiety, depression, dysthymic disorder, bipolar disorder, and cyclothymia), attention deficit/hyperactivity disorder, obsessive compulsive disorder, adjustment disorders, somatoform disorders, and other conditions (APA, 2004). Though not directly addressing the child's oppositional, defiant, and conduct problems, medications addressing these co-occurring conditions is often warranted and has also been shown to also improve the success of interventions directly targeting the antisocial behavior.

Although medications may benefit the student suffering from any of these conditions, a federal law was introduced, HR 1170, which states as a condition of receiving federal funds, each state shall develop policies and procedures to prohibit school personnel to obtain a prescription for substances covered by section 202(c) of the Controlled Substances Act (21 USC. 812(c)) as a condition of attending school or receiving services (Fight for Kids, 2012). However there is no "prohibition against teachers and other school personnel consulting or sharing classroom-based observations with parents or guardians regarding a student's academic and functional performance, or behavior in the classroom or school, or regarding the need for evaluation for special education or related services" (20 USC. 1412(a) (25)).

Temperament

Temperament refers to those aspects of an individual's personality that are innate rather than learned (Chess & Thomas, 1968; McCrae & Costa, 1990). There are nine traits in children that appear to be innate and resistant to change over the course of a lifetime. These traits are activity level, rhythmicity, approach or withdrawal (initial reaction), adaptability, threshold of responsiveness, intensity of reaction, quality of mood, distractibility, attention span and persistence (Chess & Thomas, 1996). Most children could be categorized into one of three groups: easy, difficult, and slow-to-warm-up (Chess & Thomas, 1996). Simply put, "temperament plays an important role in shaping the course of school functioning" (Chess & Thomas, 1996, p. 117). Keogh (2003) identified three primary temperamental dimensions within school settings: Task Orientation (persistence, distractibility, and activity), Personal Social Flexibility (approach/ withdrawal, positive mood, and adaptability), and Reactivity (negative mood, sensory threshold, and intensity). Keogh found that teachers rated students with Task Orientation as more teachable. Furthermore, when teachers estimated student ability, their perception was influenced by the student's temperament, that is, teachers believed that children with difficult temperaments were thought to have lower academic potential. Given the robust evidence of self-fulfilling prophecies, caution and re-examination of teachers perceptions of students is warranted and should be considered routinely. In the case of student with ODD and CD, these difficult behaviors can have a negative influence on classroom experiences.

Intervention for Curriculum and Instruction

The literature emphasizes a close functional relationship between academic variables and behavioral problems (Filter & Horner, 2009; McIntosh, Horner, Chard, Boland & Good, 2006). Unfortunately, most interventions for children with behavioral disorders focus exclusively on managing behavioral difficulties and ignore any academic deficits (Rivera, Al-Otaiba, & Koorland, 2006). Additionally, there are very few studies at the secondary level (Lane, 2004) where we often find students requiring Tier III behavioral supports, but now also require very intensive academic support due to limited progress.

Function-Based Academic Interventions

The role of academic failure needs to be carefully considered for students with disruptive behavior. Academic problems sometimes precede problem behaviors (Umbreit, Ferro, Liaupsin & Lane, 2007). For example, a mismatch between student's skill level and task demand is frequently identified as a condition that results in the student seeking to escape the task, with some acting negatively to do so. When presented with a task that is below skill level, students may become bored, disengaged or insulted. In contrast, presentation of an academic task that is above skill level may also lead to avoidance, frustration, or aggression. Additionally, a student's interest-level in the subject task can also result in escape problem behavior (Hoff, Ervin, & Friman, 2005).

The nature of the teacher-student relationship and how that is related to academic interactions can precede and often predict a student's problem behaviors. The teacher-student relationship can be very strained and characterized by poor interaction patterns for youth with ODD and CD. Once these patterns are established, they are difficult to change.

There is no doubt that teaching students who present with the significant challenges associated with ODD and CD is a formidable task. This group of children can be described as fearing failure, being slow to develop trust in their teachers, difficult to keep engaged, and emotionally variable (Coleman & Vaughn, 2000). They tend to receive more negative attention from teachers following inappropriate behavior and little teacher attention for appropriate behavior (Lago-Dellalo, 1998). Unfortunately, as aggressive behavior increases so too does the likelihood that students will develop negative relationships with their teachers (Gunter & Coutinho, 1997; Ladd & Burgess, 1999). In fact, a cycle of negative reinforcement often characterizes the teacher-student relationship in classrooms for students with behavioral problems (Shores, Gunter, & Jack, 1993). More clearly, disruptive behaviors are (negatively) reinforced by the removal of academic task demands, while teachers are (negatively) reinforced by the removal of the disruptive behaviors when students do not have to complete the task. Note the similarity in relationships styles reviewed in the parenting section.

The classroom experience is also important to consider (Connell, 1990). Learning contexts that satisfy a student's need to belong or feel socially connected play a role in determining their motivation to engage. Students who feel emotionally secure with their teachers are more likely to be active participants in class and be more motivated in their work (Connell & Wellborn, 1991). On the contrary, students who have conflict with their teachers are more likely to feel alienated, and as a result, disengage from the learning process (Connell, 1990).

Without a functional focus on the curricular contribution to the probability of negative behavior for youth with ODD and CD, an otherwise strong intervention may result in poor outcomes. Furthermore, it is critical for teachers to carefully consider their role in the student-teacher relationship and seek to only contribute that which will support positive outcomes for their students. Engaging teachers (and parents for that matter) in how their stress and humiliation can add to an already difficult task is difficult; however, when done within the context of the need for the child and the support of a school system that recognizes the challenges—modification in this area can be successful (Rinsley, 1994).

Direct Instruction

Because students with behavioral problems evidence a range of problem behaviors which undermine their learning (Kauffman & Landrum, 2009), Benner, Nelson, Ralston, and Mooney (2010) stress that academic interventions "should include embedded instructional management procedures and motivators to help students regulate their attention and behavior as well as actively engage during instruction" (p. 99). In addition to the behavior management strategies provided earlier in this chapter, direct instruction is often identified as a necessary and appropriate intervention for students with ODD or CD who present with more significant academic underachievement. Key features of direct instruction, including the structure, sequencing, pacing of instruction, as well as opportunities for frequent feedback and practice of newly learned skills, are noted to be beneficial to students with behavioral difficulties (Landrum, Tankersley, & Kauffman, 2003). What follows are a few additional strategies used to support direct instruction. These strategies can be used with direct instruction in any subject or they may be used alone. The goal is the same: increase academic performance.

Student choice

Maximizing student interest is particularly important for youth with ODD and CD. Increasing interest is accomplished by relating new topics to those previously learned, relating topics to the student's life, explaining why a topic is of particular importance, and explaining why the student is being asked to learn the topic (Bloomquist & Schnell, 2002). Providing students with opportunities to make choices (e.g. where they will work, the order of task completion) is effective in increasing task completion and accuracy as well as decreasing disruption (Ramsey, 2010). Teachers report that giving students choices is manageable and the activity tends to be well-liked by the students.

Peer tutoring

One-to-one peer tutoring improves time-on-task and increased positive peer-to-peer comments for youth with disruptive behaviors (Locke & Fuchs, 1995). It is effective for students with the same or differing ability levels (Kunsch, Jitendra, & Sood, 2007). Most interestingly, a meta-analysis, comparing the results from 38 studies, found that the most effective tutoring occurred when students regularly reversed the roles of tutor and tutee (Spencer, 2006).

Tracking Intervention Impact: Progress Monitoring

Determining the usefulness of any of these interventions is accomplished by tracking the child's progress. Once each area of concern is identified (e.g. child has difficulty managing frustration, models inappropriate language from home and is failing math), the intervention selected (e.g. emotion regulation, exposure to appropriate role models, and direct instruction based on the child's math skills) and progress is defined (e.g. keeps hands and feet to himself 80% of the time during classroom instruction, responds appropriately to feeling provoked 90% of the time, uses appropriate language 95% of the time, completes homework for 6 out of 10 assignments), then the interval for review should be designated. Behaviors that require smaller changes (e.g. improving homework completion from 80% to 100%) can be reviewed less often; behaviors that have been intractable or are very far from acceptable (e.g. time on-task during math is 20% at baseline) need to be tracked often so that modifications can be made in a timely fashion (Miller et al., 1998).

Tracking a child's progress is accomplished easily by using a graph. First, a baseline needs to be established (in a day or week how often is the student exhibiting the problem behavior). That is, how often is the student expressing his or her frustration inappropriately, is noncompliant, is out of seat, is cussing, is failing to complete math work, etc. On the graph it is useful to put time, such as number of minutes or days, (on the X-axis) and percent of activity (on the Y-axis), allowing the teacher, team and child to review daily or weekly progress. It is recommended that the child review (if old enough he or she can make his or her own graphs) of positive behaviors so there is a focus on positive actions (review Positive Behavior Support section above). When it is clear that there is no (further) improvement in a given area, then the intervention should be reviewed, modified or changed completely.

The following case study illustrates how conduct problems look in young children and how the patterns of behavior look as the child ages. Parents and teachers note behavioral difficulties. However, as the case shows only a comprehensive plan where home and school efforts are coordinated is likely to result in behavioral change.

Case Study

Alex is the oldest of three children born to parents Mary and Jake. By parent report, Alex's prenatal period was unremarkable; however, his birth was complicated due to a low heart rate. His infancy was marked with jaundice and colic. At 9 months, Alex sustained a head injury which required medical intervention. Developmental milestones were reportedly attained as expected, with the exception of walking which was described as "late." At 18 months of age, Alex demonstrated signs of severe AD/HD and ODD. As a toddler, Alex reportedly tried to suffocate his younger sister with a pillow and was noted to have a fascination with guns and fire. At the age of five, Alex was hospitalized and medicated for these disorders.

In late elementary school, teachers described Alex as noncompliant; he had difficulty controlling his behaviors (e.g. did not keep his hands and feet to himself) and had few friends. If you were to observe Alex you would note that he did not stay in his seat during assignments—rather he would sit with his leg underneath him, bounce, and stand in 30-second cycles. Alex liked to roam the halls and whenever possible would ask (or leave) to go to the bathroom, library, nurse, or office. If he went to the bathroom he would be gone for long periods, returning only when staff retrieved him. He would be very talkative and would announce out loud his plans for an activity; for example, he may say, "I will only play freeze tag if there are no girls" and then he would discourage girls from play often by making fun of them. The few friends he did have were younger and often served as gofers to his requests. Parents of younger children registered their concerns regarding Alex's access to their children on the bus and his demands for them to bring him their Pokémon cards.

In middle school, Alex described himself as a loner and reported he was involved in witchcraft and fascinated by horror movies. He continued to start fires at the home and in vacant lots. At school he would make verbal threats to students, teachers and the assistant principal. He showed extreme difficulty learning new concepts, failed math, reading and science courses. His homework completion was less than 20% in any class. His teachers began to describe Alex as moody, hostile, and unresponsive to academic support.

In high school, Alex became aggressive to people and property. He destroyed bathrooms, parked cars and was suspended for hitting students he believed were taunting him. He also hit a teacher with whom he had the best rapport—the attack was unexpected and during a time when only Alex and the teacher were present in the classroom. He showed a lack of empathy and was adept at justifying all of his actions; except for the attack on his teacher, where he simply stated he "did not know why" he had hit her. In seeking help for dealing with his behavior, Alex's mother reported to the school that he was involved in inappropriate touching of family members.

A review of Alex's records indicate that Alex's father moved out and ceased all contact with Mary and the three children when Alex was four years old. The family history was remarkable for the presence of sexual and substance abuse, as well as mental illness. Alex was prescribed and compliant with medications for AD/HD.

Alex's case illustrates early problems that progressed and intensified as he aged. His case also highlights opportunities for early intervention and the need to coordinate home and school services across the developmental period. Alex's teachers were able to control some behaviors in their specific classrooms with sticker charts and rewards for good behaviors—but without comprehensive services his pervasive and persistent pattern conduct problems were unchanged.

Summary

Oppositional Defiant Disorder and Conduct Disorder are behavioral difficulties that demand an enormous amount of energy from teachers, parents, and community service agencies to address and resolve in children and adolescents. Early symptoms should be taken seriously, as they tend to persist throughout the developmental period and into adulthood. The best treatments are comprehensive in nature, occur in a coordinated effort and are in place before the child is age eight. There are different drivers of child behavior and an intervention that may work for one student may not work for another. As such, although the process of establishing a diagnosis is relatively straightforward, the process of understanding and treating the complexities of ODD and CD is far more difficult and typically results in modest gains. Adults who engage with children who are ODD and CD are often very frustrated and their frustrations can compound the difficulties these children demonstrate. It is easy to feel overwhelmed, give up and/or blame the child for his or her difficulties.

Schools are required to provide an education to all students regardless of their disruptive behaviors. Services for children with ODD and CD may occur in general (e.g. alternative) or special education. The purpose of separating these youth is based on their treatment needs and not on the diagnosis of ODD or CD alone. Students who have an emotional disability lag behind in skill development (how and why varies from child to child) and require skill development. Parents and teachers are strongly encouraged to seek support from an experienced multidisciplinary team when planning interventions. Adults also require support in their efforts to intervene with this group. There is no simple, single solution for an intervention team. Rather, sustained, good faith efforts that are monitored and adjusted have the best chance of success—and even then gains are often incremental and irregular. Early academic successes are associated with lower levels of delinquent acts—as such schools should focus every effort on reaching young learners as soon as they show signs of academic difficulty.

References

Aggleton, J. P., & Young, A. W. (2000). The enigma of the amygdala: Concerning its contribution to human emotion. In R. D. Lane & L. Nadel (eds), *Cognitive neuroscience of emotion* (pp. 106–28). New York, NY: Oxford University Press.

Akin-Little, A., Little, S. G., Bray, M. A., & Kehle, T. J. (eds). (2009). *Behavioral interventions in schools: Evidence-based positive strategies.* Washington, DC: American Psychological Association.

Alberti, R. E., & Emmons, M. L. (2008). *Your perfect right: Assertiveness and equality in your life and relationships* (9th ed.). Atascadero, CA: Impact.

American Psychological Association (1993). *Violence and youth: Psychology's response: Vol. 1: Summary report of the American Psychological Association Commission on Violence and Youth.* Washington, DC: Author.

—(2004). *Diagnostic and statistical manual of mental disorders-Text Revision* (4th ed.). Washington, DC: Author.

Baldwin, D. V., & Skinner, M. L. (1989). Structural model for antisocial behavior: Generalization to single-mother families. *Developmental Psychology, 25,* 45–50. doi:10.1037/0012-1649.25.1.45

Barrish, H. H., Saunders, M., & Wolf, M. M. (1969). Good behavior game: Effects of individual contingencies for group consequences on disruptive behavior in a classroom. *Journal of Applied Behavior Analysis, 2,* 119–24. doi:10.1901/jaba.1969.2-119.

Beck, A. T. (1976). *Cognitive therapy and the emotional disorders.* New York, NY: New American Library.

—(1999). *Prisoners of hate: The cognitive basis of anger, hostility, and violence.* New York, NY: Harper Collins.

Bedell, J. R., & Lennox, S. S. (1997). *Handbook for communication and problem-solving skills training*: A cognitive-behavioral approach. New York, NY: Wiley.

Begun, R. W. (ed.). (1995). *Ready-to-use social skills lessons & activities for grades 1–3.* West Nyack, NY: Center for Applied Research in Education.

Benner, G. J., Nelson, R. J., Ralston, N. C., & Mooney, P. (2010). A meta-analysis of the effects of reading instruction on the reading skills of students with or at risk of behavioral disorders. *Behavioral Disorders, 35,* 86–102. Accessed from http://www.ccbd.net/sites/default/files/bed-35-02-86.pdf

Blair, R. J. R. (2003). Neurological basis of psychopathy. *British Journal of Psychiatry, 182,* 5–7.

—(2006). The amygdala and ventromedial prefrontal cortex in morality and psychopathy. *Trends in Cognitive Sciences, 11,* 387–92. doi:10.1192/bjp.182.1.5.

Bloomquist, M. L., & Schnell, S. V. (2002). *Helping children with aggression and conduct problems: Best practices for intervention.* New York, NY: The Guilford Press.

Bradley, S. J. (2000). *Affective regulation and the development of psychopathology.* New York, NY: The Guilford Press.

Brown, J. L., Roderick, T., Lantieri, L., & Aber, J. L. (2004). The Resolving Conflict Creatively Program: A school-based social and emotional learning program. In J. E. Zins, R. P. Weissberg, M. C. Wang, & H. J. Walberg (eds), *Building academic success on social and emotional learning: What does the research say?* (pp. 151–69). New York, NY: Teachers College.

Buckley, K. E., & Anderson, C. A. (2006). A theoretical model of the effects and consequences of playing video games. In P. Vorderer & J. Bryant (eds), *Playing video games—Motives, responses, and consequences* (pp. 363–78). *Mahwah, NJ: LEA.*

Burns, M. K., & Gibbons, K. A. (2008). *Implementing response-to-intervention in elementary and secondary schools: Procedures to assure scientific-based practices.* New York, NY: Routledge.

Campbell-Sills, L., & Barlow, D. H. (2007). Incorporating emotion regulation into conceptualizations and treatments of anxiety and mood disorders. In J. J. Gross (ed.), Handbook of emotion regulation (pp. 542–60). New York, NY: The Guilford Press.

Centerwall, B. S. (1992). Television and violence: The scale of the problem and where to go from here. *Journal of the American Medical Association, 267,* 3059–63. doi:10.1001/jama.1992.03480220077031

Chess, S., & Thomas, A. (1968). *Temperament and behavior disorders in children.* New York, NY: New York University.

—(1996). *Temperament: Theory and practice.* New York, NY: Brunner/Mazel.

Cicchetti, D., & Toth, S. (1995). Developmental psychopathology and disorders of affect. In D. Cicchetti, D. J. Cohen (eds), *Developmental psychopathology, Vol 2: Risk, disorder and adaptation.* (pp. 369–420). Oxford: John Wiley & Sons.

Cohen, J. (ed.). (1999). *Educating minds and hearts: Social emotional learning and the passage into adolescence.* New York, NY: Teachers College Press.

Coleman, M., & Vaughn, S. (2000). Reading interventions for students with emotional/behavioral disorders. *Behavioral Disorders, 25,* 93–104.

Colvin, G. (2007). *7 steps for developing a proactive schoolwide discipline plan: A guide for principals and leadership teams.* Thousand Oaks, CA: Sage.

Connell, J. P. (1990). Context, self, and action: A motivational analysis of self-system processes across the life span. In D. Ciccheti & M. Beeghly (eds), *The self in transition: Infancy to childhood* (pp. 61–98). Chicago, IL: The University of Chicago Press.

Connell, J. P., & Wellborn, J. G. (1991). Competence, autonomy, and relatedness: A motivational analysis of self-system processes. In M. R. Gunnar & L. A. Sroufe (eds), *Self process and development: The Minnesota symposia on child development* (Vol. 23, pp. 43–77). Hillsdale, NJ: Erlbaum.

Connor, D. F. (2002). *Aggression and antisocial behavior in children and adolescents: Research and treatment.* New York, NY: The Guilford Press.

Cooper, J. O., Heron, T. E., & Heward, W. L. (2007). *Applied behavior analysis.* Columbus, OH: Merrill.

Coyne, M. D., Kame'enui, E. J., & Carnine, D. W. (2007). *Effective teaching strategies that accommodate diverse learners* (3rd ed.). Columbus, OH: Merrill Publishing Company.

Craighead, E., & Nemeroff, C. B. (eds). (2001). *The Corsini encyclopedia of psychology and behavioral science* (3rd ed., Vol. 4). New York, NY: John Wiley & Sons.

Crick, N. R., & Dodge, K. A. (1994). A review and reformation of social information-processing mechanisms in children's social adjustment. *Psychological Bulletin, 115,* 74–104. doi:10.1037/0033-2909.115.1.74.

Crone, D. A., Hawken, L. S., & Horner, R. H. (2010). *Responding to problem behavior in schools: The behavior education program* (2nd ed.). New York, NY: The Guilford Press.

Darveaux, D. X. (1984). The good behavior game plus merit: Controlling disruptive behavior and improving student motivation. *School Psychology Review, 13,* 510–14.

Denno, D. W. (1990). *Biology and violence: From birth to adult*hood. Cambridge, UK: Cambridge Press.

Derksen, D. J., & Strasburger, V. C. (1996). Media and television violence: Effects on violence, aggression, and antisocial behaviors in children. In A. M. Hoffman (ed.), *Schools, violence, and society* (pp. 62–77). Westport, CT: Praeger.

DeRubeis, R. J., Tang, T. Z., & Beck, A. T. (2001). Cognitive therapy. In K. S. Dobson (ed.), *Handbook of cognitive-behavioral therapies* (2nd ed., pp. 349–92). New York, NY: The Guilford Press.

Digiuseppe, R. A. (2010). Rational-emotive behavior therapy. In N. Kazantzis, M. A. Reinecke, & A. Freeman (eds), *Cognitive and behavioral theories in clinical practice* (pp. 115–47). New York, NY: The Guilford Press.

Dinkmeyer, D. (1980). *Systematic training for effective teaching*. Circle Pines, MN: American Guidance Service.

Dishion, T. J., & Kavanagh, K. (2002). The Adolescent Transitions Program: A family centered prevention strategy for schools. In J. B. Reid, G. R. Patterson, & J. Snyder (eds), *Antisocial behavior in children and adolescents: A developmental analysis and model for intervention* (pp. 257–72). Washington, DC.: American Psychological Association.

—(2005). *Intervening in adolescent problem behavior: A family-centered approach*. New York, NY: The Guilford Press.

Dishion, T. J., & Patterson, G. R. (1996). *Preventive parenting with love, encouragement and limits*. Eugene, OR: Castalia.

Dishion, T. J., & Stormshak, E. K. (2006). *Intervening in children's lives: An ecological, family-centered approach to mental health care*. Washington, DC: American Psychological Association.

Dolan, R. J., & Morris, J. S. (2000). The functional anatomy of innate and acquired fear: Perspectives from neuroimaging. In R. D. Lane & L. Nadel (eds), *Cognitive neuroscience of emotion.* (pp. 225–41). New York, NY: Oxford University Press.

Dryden, W., & Ellis, A. (2001). Rational emotive behavior therapy. In K. S. Dobson (ed.), *Handbook of cognitive-behavioral therapies* (2nd ed., pp. 295–348). New York, NY: The Guilford Press.

Duffell, J. C., Beland, K., & Frey, K. (2006). The Second-Step Program:

Social-emotional skills for violence prevention. In M. J. Elias & H. Arnold (eds), *The educator's guide to emotional intelligence and academic achievement: Social-emotional learning in the classroom* (pp. 161–74). Thousand Oaks, CA: Corwin.

Elias, M. J. (2004). Strategies to infuse social and emotional learning into academics. In J. E. Zins, R. P. Weissberg, M. C. Wang, & H. J. Walberg (eds), *Building academic success on social and emotional learning: What does the research say?* (pp. 113–34). New York, NY: Teachers College Press.

Elias, M. J., & Arnold, H. (eds). (2006). *The educator's guide to emotional intelligence and academic achievement: Social-emotional learning in the classroom.* Thousand Oaks, CA: Corwin.

Elliott, S. N., & Gresham, F. M. (1991). *Social skills intervention guide: Practical strategies for social skills training.* Circle Pines, MN: American Guidance Service.

Ellis, A. (1994). *Reason and emotion in psychotherapy: A comprehensive method of treating human disturbances: Revised and Updated.* New York, NY: Citadel.

Ellis, A., & Bernard, M. E. (2006). *Rational emotive behavioral approaches to childhood disorders: Theory, practice, and research.* New York, NY: Springer Science.

Emery, N. J., & Amaral, D. G. (2000). The role of the amygdala in primate social cognition. In R. D. Lane & L. Nadel (eds), *Cognitive neuroscience of emotion* (pp. 156–91). New York, NY: Oxford University Press.

Ern, G. (2007). Applying general systems thinking to positive behavioral support implementation: A framework for school psychologists. *Communiqué, 36*, 4–6.

Etscheidt, S. (1991). Reducing aggressive behavior and increasing self control. A cognitive-behavioral training program for behaviorally disordered adolescents. *Behavioral Disorders, 16*, 107–15.

Farrington, D. P. (1989). Early predictors of adolescent aggression and adult violence. *Violence and Victims, 4*, 79–100.

Fight for Kids. *Bills and resolutions: US Bills and resolutions introduced or passed against psychiatric labeling and drugging of children.* Retrieved from http://www.fightforkids.com/bills_and_resolutions.php.

Filter, K. J., & Horner, R. H. (2009). Function-based academic interventions for problem behavior. *Education and Treatment of Children, 32*, 1–19. doi:10.1353/etc.0.0043.

Frick, P. J. (1998a). Conduct disorder. In T. Ollendick & M. Hersen (eds), *Handbook of child psychopathology* (3rd ed., pp. 213–337). New York, NY: Plenum Press.

Frick, P. J., Lahey, B. B., Loeber, R., Tannebaum, L., Van Horn, T., Christ, M. A. G. ... Hanson, K., Loeber, R. (1993). Oppositional defiant disorder and conduct disorder: A meta-analytic review of factor analyses and cross-validation in a clinic sample. *Clinical Psychology Review, 13*, 319–40. doi:10.1016/0272-7358(93)90016-F.

Fuchs, L. S., & Fuchs, D. (2007). A model for implementing responsiveness to intervention. *Teaching Exceptional Children, 39*, 14–20.

Gentile, D. A., & Anderson, C. A. (2006). Violent video games: Effects on youth and public policy implications. In N. Dowd, D. G. Singer, & R. F. Wilson (eds),

Handbook of children, culture, and violence (pp. 225–46). Thousand Oaks, CA: Sage.

George, H. P., & Kincaid, D. K. (2008). Building district-level capacity for positive behavior support. *Journal of Positive Behavior Interventions, 10,* 20–32. doi:10.1177/1098300707311367

Gettinger, M. (1988). Methods of proactive classroom management. *School Psychology Review, 17,* 227–42.

Greenwald, A. G. (1980). The totalitarian ego: Fabrication and revision of personal history. *American Psychologist, 35,* 603–18. doi:10.1037/0003-066X.35.7.603

Gresham, F. M. (2004). Current status and future directions of school-based behavioral interventions. *School Psychology Review, 33,* 326–43.

Grossman, D. C., Neckerman, H. J. (1997). Effectiveness of a violence prevention curriculum among children in elementary school. *Journal of the American Medical Association, 277,* 1605–11. doi:10.1001/jama.1997.03540440039030.

Gunter, P. L., & Coutinho, M. J. (1997). Negative reinforcement in classrooms: What we're beginning to learn. *Teacher Education and Special Education: The Journal of the Teacher Education Division of the Council for Exceptional Children, 20,* 249–64. doi:10.1177/088840649702000306.

Gunter, P. L., Kenton-Denny, R., & Venn, M. L. (2000). Modification of instructional materials and procedures for curricular success of students with emotional and behavioral disorders. *Preventing School Failure, 44,* 116–21. doi:10.1080/10459880009599793.

Hawken, L. S., Vincent, C. G., & Schumann, J. (2008). Response to intervention for social behavior: Challenges and opportunities. *Journal of Emotional and Behavioral Disorders, 16,* 213–225. doi:10.1177/1063426608316018

Hawkins, J. D., Herrenkohl, T., Farrington, D. P., Brewer, D., Catalano, R. F., & Harachi, T. W. (1998). A review of predictors of youth violence. In R. Loeber & D. P. Farrington (eds), *Serious and violent juvenile offenders: Risk factors and successful interventions* (pp. 106–46). Thousand Oaks, CA: Sage.

Henggeler, S. W., & Lee, T. (2003). Multisystemic treatment of serious clinical problems. In A. E. Kazdin & J. R. Weisz (eds), *Evidence-based psychotherapies for children and adolescents* (2nd ed., pp. 301–22). New York, NY: The Guilford Press.

Henggeler, S. W., & Schaeffer, C. (2010) Treating serious antisocial behavior using multisystemic therapy. In J. R. Weisz & A. E. Kazdin (eds), *Evidence-based psychotherapies for children and adolescents* (3rd ed., pp. 259–76). New York, NY: The Guilford Press.

Henggeler, S. W., Schoenwald, S. K., Borduin, C. M., Rowland, M. D., & Cunningham, P. B. (2009). *Multisystemic therapy for antisocial behavior in children and adolescents* (2nd ed.). New York, NY: The Guilford Press.

Hoff, K. E., Ervin, R. A., & Friman, P. C. (2005). Refining functional behavioral assessment: Analyzing the separate and combined effects of hypothesized controlling variables during ongoing classroom routines. *School Psychology Review, 34,* 45–57. Accessed from http://www.nasponline.org/publications/spr/pdf/spr341hoff.pdf

Hollin, C. R. (1990). *Cognitive-behavioral interventions with young offenders.* Elmsford, NY: Pergamon Press.

Horner, R. H., Sugai, G., & Horner, H. F. (2000). A schoolwide approach to student discipline. *School Administrator, 57,* 20–3.

Hughes, T. L., Crothers, L. M., & Jimmerson, S. R. (2008). *Identifying, assessing, and treating conduct disorder at school.* New York: Springer.

Hughes, T. L., Kaufman, J., & Hoover, S. A. (2010). Creating congruent change in training and field based practice. In J. Kaufman, T. L. Hughes, & C. A. Ricco (Vol. Eds.), *Handbook of education, training and supervision of school psychologists in school and community Volume II: Bridging the training and practice gap: Building collaborative university/field practices* (pp. 309–19). New York, NY: Routledge.

Hughes, T. L., & Theodore, L. A. (2009). Conceptual frame for selecting individual psychotherapy in the schools. *Psychology in the Schools, 46,* 218–24. doi:10.1002/pits.20366

Hulac, D., Terrell, J., Vining, O., & Bernstein, J. (2011). *Behavior interventions in schools: A response-to-intervention guidebook.* New York, NY: Routledge.

Hurd, N. M., Zimmerman, M. A., & Reischl, T. M. (2010). Role model behavior and youth violence: A study of positive and negative effects. *Journal of Early Adolescence, 31,* 323–54. doi:10.1177/0272423161036163160

Individuals with Disabilities Education Act, 20, USC. & Sect. 1401, et. Seq. (I.D.E.A. 1997).

Individuals with Disabilities Education Improvement Act of 2004. 20 USC 1400.

Jakubowski, P., & Lange, A. J. (1978). *The assertive option: Your rights and responsibilities.* Champaign, IL: Research.

Johnson, D. W., & Johnson, R. T. (1995). *Teaching students to be peacemakers.* Edina, MN: Interaction.

Justicia, F., Benítez, J. L., Pichardo, M. C., Fernández, E., García, T., & Fernández, M. (2006). Towards a new explicative model of antisocial behaviour. *Electronic Journal of Research in Educational Psychology, 4,* 131–50.

Kauffman, J. M., & Landrum, T. J. (2009). Politics, civil rights, and disproportional identification of students with emotional and behavioral disorders. *Exceptionality, 17,* 177–88. doi:10.1080/09362830903231903

Kazdin, A. E. (1995). *Conduct disorders in childhood and adolescence* (2nd ed.). Thousand Oaks, CA: Sage.

—(1996). Combined and multimodal treatments in child and adolescent psychotherapy: Issues, challenges, and research directions. *Clinical Psychology: Science and Practice, 3,* 69–100. doi:10.1111/j.1468-2850.1996.tb00059.x

—(2003). Problem-solving skills training and parent management training for conduct disorder. In A. E. Kazdin & J. R. Weisz (eds), *Evidence-based psychotherapies for children and adolescents* (2nd ed., pp. 241–62). New York, NY: The Guilford Press.

Keenan, K., Boeldt, D., Chen, D., Coyne, C., Donald, R., Duax, J., … Humphries, M. (2010). Predictive validity of DSM-IV oppositional defiant and conduct disorders in clinically referred preschoolers. *Journal of Child Psychology and Psychiatry, 52,* 47–55. doi:10.1111/j.1469-7610.2010.02290.x

Kendall, P. C. (1985). Toward a cognitive-behavioral model of child psychopathology and a critique of related interventions. *Journal of Abnormal Psychology, 13,* 357–72. doi:10.1007/BF00912722

—(1993). Cognitive-behavioral therapies with youth: Guiding theory, current status, and emerging developments. *Journal of Consulting and Clinical Psychology, 61,* 235–47. doi:10.1037/0022-006X.61.2.235

Kendall, P. C., & Braswell, L. (1993). *Cognitive behavioral therapy for impulsive children* (2nd ed.). New York, NY: The Guilford Press.

Keogh, B. K. (2003). *Temperament in the classroom: Understanding individual differences.* Baltimore, MD: Paul H. Brookes Publishing.

Kimonis, E. R., Frick, P. J., & Barry, C. T. (2004). Callous-unemotional traits and delinquent peer affiliation. *Journal of Consulting and Clinical Psychology, 72,* 956–66. doi:10.1037/0022-006X.72.6.956

Kunsch, C. A., Jitendra, A. K., & Sood, S. (2007). The effects of peer-mediated instruction in mathematics for students with learning problems: A research synthesis. *Learning Disabilities Research & Practice, 22,* 1–12. doi:10.1111/j.1540-5826.2007.00226.x

Ladd, G. W., & Burgess, K. B. (1999). Charting the relationship trajectories of aggressive, withdrawn, and aggressive/withdrawn children during early grade school. *Child Development, 70,* 910–29. doi:10.1111/1467-8624.00066

Lago-DeLello, E. (1998). Classroom dynamics and the development of serious emotional disturbance. *Exceptional Children, 64,* 479–92.

Landrum, T. J., Tankersley, M., & Kauffman, J. M. (2003). What is special about special education for students with emotional or behavioral disorders. *Journal of Special Education, 37,* 148–56. doi:10.1177/00224669030370030401

Lane, K. L. (2004). Academic instruction and tutoring interventions for students with emotional/behavioral disorders: 1990 to present. In R. B. Rutherford, M. M. Quinn, & S. R. Mathur (eds), *Handbook of research in emotional and behavioral disorders* (pp. 426–86). New York, NY: The Guilford Press.

Lane, K. L., & Wehby, J. (2002). Addressing antisocial behavior in the schools: A call for action. *Academic Exchange Quarterly, 6,* 4–9.

Larsen, R. J., & Prizmic, Z. (2004). Affect regulation. In R. F. Baumeister & K. D. Vohs (eds), *Handbook of self-regulation: Research, theory, and applications* (pp. 40–61). New York, NY: The Guilford Press.

Lee, S. S. (2011). Deviant peer affiliation and antisocial behavior: Interaction with Monoamine Oxidase A (MAOA) genotype. *Journal of Abnormal Child Psychology, 39,* 321–32. doi:10.1007/s10802-010-9474-2

Little, S. G., Akin-Little, A., & Cook, C. R. (2009). Classroom application of reductive procedures: A positive approach. In A. Akin-Little, S. G. Little, M. A. Bray, & T. J. Kehle (eds), *Behavioral interventions in schools: Evidence-based positive strategies* (pp. 171–88). Washington, DC: American Psychological Association.

Lochman, J. E., Nelson, W. M., & Sims, J. P. (1981). A cognitive-behavioral program for use with aggressive children. *Journal of Clinical Child Psychology, 10,* 146–8. doi:10.1080/15374418109533036

Locke, W. R., & Fuchs, L. S. (1995). Effects of peer-mediated reading instruction of the on-task behavior and social interaction of children with behavior disorders. *Journal of Emotional and Behavioral Disorders, 3,* 92–9. doi:10.1177/106342669500300204

Loeber, R., Burke, J. D., Lahey, B. B., Winters, A., & Zera, M. (2000). Oppositional defiant and conduct disorder: A review of the past 10 years, Part

I. *Journal of the American Academy of Child and Adolescent Psychiatry, 39,* 1468–84. doi:10.1097/00004583-200012000-00007

Loeber, R., Farrington, D. P., Stouthamer-Loeber, M., & Van Kammen, W. B. (1998). *Antisocial behavior and mental health problems: Explanatory factors in childhood and adolescence.* Mahwah, NJ: Lawrence Erlbaum Associates.

Loeber, R., Keenan, K., & Zhang, Q. (1997). Boys' experimentation and persistence in developmental pathways toward serious delinquency. *Journal of Child and Family Studies, 6,* 321–57. doi:10.1023/A:1025004303603

Loeber, R., Wung, P., Keenan, K., Giroux, B., Stouthamer-Loeber, M., & Van Kammen, W. B. (1993). Developmental pathways in disruptive child behavior. *Developmental Psychopathology, 5,* 101–32. doi:10.1017/ S0954579400004296

Madaus, M. M. R., Kehle, T. J., Madaus, J., & Bray, M. A. (2003). Mystery motivator as an intervention to promote homework completion and accuracy. *School Psychology International, 24,* 369–77. doi:10.1177/01430343030244001

Maes, H. H, Silberg, J. L., Neal, M. C., & Eaves, L. J. (2007). Genetic and cultural transmission of antisocial behavior: An extended twin parent model. *Twin Research and Human Genetics, 10,* 136–50. doi:10.1375/twin.10.1.136

McConaughy, S. H. (2005). *Clinical interviews for children and adolescents: Assessment to intervention.* New York, NY: The Guilford Press.

McCrae, R. R., & Costa, P. T., Jr. (1990). *Personality in adulthood.* New York, NY: The Guilford Press.

McEvoy, A., & Welker, R. (2000). Antisocial behavior, academic failure, and school climate: A critical review. *Journal of Emotional and Behavioral Disorders, 8,* 130–40. doi:10.1177/106342660000800301

McIntosh, K., Bohanon, H., & Goodman, S. (2010). Toward true integration of academic and behavior response to intervention systems part three: Tier III supports. *Communiqué, 39,* 4.

McIntosh, K., Goodman, S., & Bohanon, H. (2010). Toward true integration of academic and behavior response to intervention systems part one: Tier I supports. *Communiqué, 39,* 2.

McIntosh, K., Horner, R. H., Chard, J. B., Boland, J. B., & Good, R. H. (2006). The use of reading and behavior screening measures to predict nonresponse to school-wide positive behavior support: A longitudinal analysis. *School Psychology Review, 35,* 275–91. Accessed from http://www.nasponline.org/ publications/spr/pdf/spr352mcintosh.pdf

McIntosh, K., Horner, R. H., Chard, D. J., Dickey, C. R., & Braun, D. H. (2008). Reading skills and function of problem behavior in typical school settings. *The Journal of Special Education, 42,* 131–47. doi:10.1177/0022466907313253

McKinney, E., Bartholomew, C., & Gray, L. (2010). RTI and SWPBIS: Confronting the problem of disproportionality. *Communiqué, 38,* 28–9.

McMahon, R. J. & Wells, K. C. (1998). Conduct problems. In E. J. Mash & R. A. Barkley (eds), *Treatment of childhood disorders* (2nd ed., pp. 111–207). New York, NY: The Guilford Press.

McMahon, R. J., Wells, K. C., & Kotler, J. S. (2006). Conduct problems. In E. J. Mash & R. A. Barkley (eds), *Treatment of childhood disorders* (3rd ed., pp. 137–268). New York, NY: The Guilford Press.

McMullin, R. E. (2000). *The new handbook of cognitive therapy techniques*. New York, NY: Norton.

McNamara, K. (2002). Best practices in promotion of social competence in schools. In A. Thomas & J. Grimes (eds), *Best practices in school psychology IV* (Vol. 2, pp. 911–27). Bethesda, MD: National Association of School Psychologists.

Meichenbaum, D. (2002). *Cognitive-behavior modification: An integrative approach*. New York, NY: Springer.

Miller, J. A., Tansy, M., & Hughes, T. L. (1998). Functional behavioral assessment: The link between problem behavior and effective intervention in schools. *Current Issues in Education, 1*, 1–18. Accessed from http://cie.ed.asu.edu/volume1/number5/

Minzenberg, M. J., & Siever, L. J. (2006). Neurochemistry and pharmacology of psychopathy and related disorders. In C. J. Patrick (ed.), *Handbook of psychopathy* (pp. 251–77). New York, NY: The Guilford Press.

Mitchem, K. J., Young, K. R., West, R. P., & Benyo, J. (2001). CWPASM: A classwide peer-assisted self-management program for general education classrooms. *Education and Treatment of Children, 24*, 110–40.

Moffitt, T. E., & Lynam, D. (1994). Neuropsychology of delinquent behavior: Implications for understanding the psychopath. In D. Fowles, P. Sutker, & S. Goodman (eds), *Psychopathy and antisocial personality: A developmental perspective* (pp. 233–62). New York, NY: Springer.

Moore, L. A., Waguespack, A. M., Wickstrom, K. F., & Witt, J. C. (1994). Mystery motivator: An effective and time efficient intervention. *School Psychology Review, 23*, 106–18.

Mullin, B. C., & Hinshaw, S. P. (2007). Emotion regulation and externalizing disorders in children and adolescents. In J. J. Gross (ed.), *Handbook of emotion regulation* (pp. 523–41). New York, NY: The Guilford Press.

No Child Left Behind Act of 2001, 9 USC. § 9101 *et seq.*

Nock, M. K., Kazdin, A. E., Hiripi, E., & Kessler, R. C. (2006). Prevalence, subtypes, and correlates of DSM-IV conduct disorder in the National Comorbidity Survey Replication. *Psychological Medicine, 36*, 699–710. doi:10.1017/S0033291706007082

Novick, B., Kress, J., & Elias, M. J. (2002). *Building learning communities with character: How to integrate academic, social, and emotional learning*. Alexandria, VA: ASCD.

Office of Child and Family Policy (2008). A clinical information guide: Conduct disorder and oppositional defiant disorder. Accessed September 10, 2008, from DCFS Web Resource Web site: resources/conductdisorder_guide.php

Patterson, G. R. (1975). *Families: Applications of social learning to family life* (rev. ed.). Champaign, IL: Research Press.

—(1976). *Living with children: New methods for parents and teacher* (rev. ed.). Champaign, IL: Research Press.

—(2002). The early development of coercive family process. In J. B. Reid, G. R. Patterson, & Snyder, J. (eds), *Antisocial behavior in children and adolescents: A developmental analysis and model for intervention* (pp. 25–44). Washington, DC: American Psychological Association.

Patterson, R. J. (2000). *The assertiveness workbook: How to express your ideas and stand up for yourself at work and in relationships.* Oakland, CA: New Harbinger.

Raine, A., & Yang, Y. (2006). The neuroanatomical bases of psychopathy: A review of brain and imaging findings. In C. J. Patrick (ed.), *Handbook of psychopathy* (pp. 278–95). New York, NY: The Guilford Press.

Ramsey, M. L. (2010). *Using function-based choice-making interventions to increase task completion and accuracy and to reduce problem behaviors for students with E/BD* (Doctoral dissertation). Accessed from http://digitalarchive.g.su.edu/epse_diss/69/

Rathvon, N. (2008). *Effective school interventions: Evidence-based strategies for improving student outcomes* (2nd ed.). New York, NY: The Guilford Press.

Reiman, E. M., Lane, R. D., Ahern, G. L., Schwartz, G. E., & Davidson, R. J. (2000). Positron emission tomography, emotion, and consciousness. In S. R. Hameroff, A.W. Kaszniak, & A. C. Scott (eds), *Toward a science of consciousness: The first Tucson discussions and debates* (pp. 311–20). Boston, MA: MIT Press.

Rhode, G., Jenson, W. R., & Reavis, H. K. (1996). *The tough kid book: Practical classroom management strategies.* Longmont, CO: Sopris West.

Rinsley, D. B. (1994). *Treatment of the severely disturbed adolescent.* Northvale, NJ: Jason Aronson.

Rivera, M. O., Al-Otaiba, S., & Koorland, M. A. (2006). Reading instruction for students with emotional and behavioral disorders and at risk of antisocial behaviors in primary grades: Review of literature. *Behavioral Disorders, 31,* 323–37.

Rogers, R. D. (2006). The functional architecture of the frontal lobes: Implications for research with psychopathic offenders. In C. J. Patrick (ed.), *Handbook of psychopathy* (pp. 313–3). New York, NY: The Guilford Press.

Scott, T. M., & Martinek, G. (2006). Coaching positive behavior support in school settings: Tactics and data-based decision-making. *Journal of Positive Behavior Interventions, 8,* 165–73. doi:10.1177/10983007060080030501

Shaw, D. S., Dishion, T. J., Supplee, L, Gardner, F., & Arnds, K. (2006). Randomized trial of a family-centered approach to the prevention of early conduct problems: 2-Year effects of the family check-up in early childhood. *Journal of Consulting and Clinical Psychology, 74,* 1–9. doi:10.1037/0022-006X.74.1.1

Shirk, S. R., & Russell R. L. (1996). *Change processes in child psychotherapy.* New York, NY: The Guilford Press.

Shores, R. E., Gunter, P. L., & Jack, S.L. (1993). Classroom management strategies: Are they setting events for coercion? *Behavioral Disorders, 18,* 92–102.

Smith, M. J. (1975). *When I say no, I feel guilty.* New York, NY: Bantam.

Snyder, J., Dishion, T. J., & Patterson, G. R. (1986). Determinants and consequences of associating with deviant peers during preadolescence and adolescence. *The Journal of Early Adolescence, 6,* 29–43. doi:10.1177/0272431686061003

Spencer, V. G. (2006). Peer tutoring and students with emotional and behavior disorders: A review of the literature. *Behavior Disorders, 31,* 204–22.

Spivack, G., Platt, J. J., & Shure, M. B. (1976). *The problems-solving approach to adjustment.* San Francisco, CA: Jossey-Bass.

Stahl, N. D., & Clarizio, H. F. (1999). Conduct disorder and comorbidity. *Psychology in the Schools, 36,* 41–50. doi:10.1002/(SICI)1520-6807(199901) 36:1<41::AID-PITS5>3.0.CO;2-9

Steiner, H., & American Academy of Child and Adolescent Psychiatry (AACAP) (1997). Practice parameters for the assessment and treatment of children and adolescents with conduct disorder. *Journal of the American Academy of Child and Adolescent Psychiatry, 36,* 122S–39S.

Stewart, R. M., Benner, G. B., Martella, R. C., & Marchand-Martella, N. E. (2007). Three-tier models of reading and behavior: A research review. *Journal of Positive Behavior Interventions, 9,* 239–53. doi:10.1177/109830070700900 40601

Sugai, G. (2009). *School-wide positive behavior support and response to intervention.* Accessed January 31, 2011 from http://www.rtinetwork.org/learn/ behavior/schoolwidebehavior

Sugai, G., & Horner, R. H. (2006). A promising approach for expanding and sustaining the school-wide positive behavior support. *School Psychology Review, 35,* 245–59.

—(2009). Defining and describing schoolwide positive behavior support. In W. Sailor, G. Dunlap, G. Sugai, & R. Horner (eds), *Handbook of positive behavior support* (pp. 307–26). New York, NY: Springer.

Sugai, G., Horner, R. H., Algozzine, R., Barrett, S., Lewis, T., Anderson, C., … Simonsen, B. (2010). *School-wide positive behavior support: Implementers' blueprint and self-assessment.* Eugene, OR: University of Oregon.

Sutherland, K. S., Wehby, J. H., & Copeland, S. R. (2000). Effect of varying rates of behavior-specific praise on the on-task behavior of students with EBD. *Journal of Emotional and Behavioral Disorders, 8,* 2–8. doi:10.1177/106342660000800101

Tarolla, S. M., Wagner, E. F., Rabinowitz, J., & Tubman, J. G. (2002). Understanding and treating juvenile offenders: A review of current knowledge and future directions. *Aggression and Violent Behavior, 7,* 125–43. doi:10.1016/S1359-1789(00)00041-0

Theodore, L. A., Bray, M. A., & Kehle, T. J. (2004). A comparative study of group contingencies and randomized reinforcers to reduce disruptive classroom behavior. *School Psychology Quarterly, 19,* 253–71. doi:10.1521/ scpg.19.3.253.40280

Tolan, P.H., & Gorman-Smith, D. (1998). Development of serious and violent offending careers. In R. Loeber & D. P. Farrington (eds), *Serious and violent juvenile offenders: Risk factors and successful interventions* (pp. 68–85). Thousand Oaks, CA: Sage.

Tranel, D. (2000). Electrodermal activity in cognitive neuroscience: Neuroanatomical and neuropsychological correlates. In R. D. Lane & L. Nadel (eds), *Cognitive neuroscience of emotion* (pp. 192–224). New York, NY: Oxford University.

Trout, A. L., Nordness, P. D., Pierce, C. D., & Epstein, M. H. (2003). Research on the academic status of children with emotional and behavioral disorders. *Journal of Emotional and Behavioral Disorders, 11,* 198–210. doi:10.1177/106 34266030110040201

Turnbull, A., Edmonson, H., Griggs, P., Wickham, D., Sailor, W., Freeman, R.,

... Warren, J. (2002). A blueprint for schoolwide positive behavior support: Implementation of three components. *Exceptional Children, 68*, 377–402.

Umbreit, J., Ferro, J., Liaupsin, C. J., & Lane, K. L. (2007). *Functional behavioral assessment and function-based intervention: An effective, practical approach.* Upper Saddle River, NJ: Prentice-Hall.

Vannest, K. J., Reynolds, C. R., & Kamphaus, R. W. (2008). *BASC–2 intervention guide.* Minneapolis, MN: NCS Pearson.

Verlaan, P., & Schwartzman, A. E. (2002). Mother's and father's parental adjustment: Links to externalizing behavior problems in sons and daughters. *International Journal of Behavioral Development, 26*, 214–24. doi:10.1080/01650250042000717

Vieno, A., Nation, M., Pastore, M., & Santinello, M. (2009). Parenting and antisocial behavior: A model of the relationship between adolescent self-disclosure, parental closeness, parental control, and adolescent antisocial behavior. *Developmental Psychology, 45*, 1509–19. doi:10.1037/a0016929

Walker, H. M., Ramsey, E., & Gresham, R. M. (2005). *Antisocial behavior in school: Evidence-based practices* (2nd ed.). Belmont, CA: Wadsworth/Thomson Learning.

Walker, H. M., & Walker, J. E. (1991). *Coping with noncompliance in the classroom: A positive approach for teachers.* Austin, TX: Pro-Ed.

Webster-Stratton, C. (2001). *Parents and children training series.* (rev. ed.). Seattle, WA: Incredible Years.

Wehby, J. H., & Lane, K. L. (2009). Classroom management. In A. Akin-Little, S. Little, M. Bray, & T. Kehle (eds), *Handbook of behavioral interventions in schools* (pp. 141–56). Washington, DC: American Psychological Association.

Wisniewski, K. G. (2006). *Delinquency, academic underachievement, and attention deficit hyperactivity disorder: A longitudinal investigation of developmental sequencing and interrelated risk factors* (Unpublished doctoral dissertation). Duquesne University, Pittsburgh, PA.

Wolfgang, C. H., & Wolfgang, M. E. (1995). *The three faces of discipline for early childhood: Empowering teachers and students.* Boston, MA: Allyn & Bacon.

Zins, J. E., Weissberg, R. P., Wang, M. C., & Walberg, H. J. (eds). (2004). *Building academic success on social and emotional learning: What does the research say?* New York, NY: Teachers College.

CHAPTER ELEVEN

Understanding and Managing Behaviors of Children Diagnosed with Post Traumatic Stress Disorder (PTSD)

Kathleen M. Chard
Cincinnati VA Medical Center and University of Cincinnati

Rich Gilman
Cincinnati Children's Hospital and University of Cincinnati

Lauren Holleb and Angelique Teeters
Cincinnati Children's Hospital

Abstract

Posttraumatic stress disorder (PTSD) is a mental health disorder that can develop in individuals who have been exposed to a traumatic event and have not been able to naturally recover from the experience. Children and adolescents risk developing PTSD due to events such as child abuse, bullying, car accidents, domestic violence, and natural disasters to name a few. The high potential for experiencing trauma as a child, combined with the significant likelihood of developing PTSD, makes it imperative that educators are prepared to respond to the emotional and behavioral needs of children and adolescents with PTSD symptoms in their classrooms. This chapter will review the diagnostic criteria for PTSD, describe the extant literature on school based PTSD interventions, and offer suggestions for teachers and school personnel interacting with children who they believe to have a trauma history.

Overview

Posttraumatic stress disorder (PTSD) is a mental health disorder that occurs in individuals who have been exposed to a traumatic event and have not been able to recover from the experience. Lifetime prevalence for PTSD is approximately 8%, and the prevalence of the disorder is estimated at 3.5% for the past year (Kessler, Chiu, Demler, Merikangas, & Walters, 2005). The likelihood of developing PTSD after a traumatic event is determined by a number of factors, such as proximity to the event itself, the closeness of the relationship to the victim or perpetrator, demographic background (e.g. gender) and internal resources (e.g. genetic expression, positive coping styles) and external supports (family and/or interpersonal relationships; Adams & Boscarino, 2006; Galea et al., 2007; Johnson, Maxwell, & Galea, 2009; Yehuda et al., 2009).

Until rather recently, the question of whether children or adolescents could develop PTSD was controversial (Sheeringa, 2008). This question is no longer debated. Recent data suggests that child protection service agencies in the United States receive approximately three million referrals each year, regarding approximately 5.5 million children (US Department of Health and Human Services, 2006, 2008). Those figures may only represent a portion of the child maltreatment cases that occur; researchers estimate that two-thirds of maltreatment cases are unreported. Of those cases referred, about 30% are substantiated and occur with the following frequencies: 65% neglect, 18% physical abuse, 10% sexual abuse, and 7% psychological abuse. In addition, anywhere from 3 to 10 million children are thought to be exposed to domestic violence each year, 40 to

60% of which cases also involve child physical abuse (Jouriles, McDonald, Norwood, & Ezell, 2001). A percentage of these children/adolescents will be diagnosed with PTSD.

Although no population-based study has examined the prevalence of PTSD in children and adolescents, children and adolescents who are kidnapped, witness the death of a parent, or are exposed to domestic violence have shown rates of PTSD as high as 95%, while children exposed to a sniper attack at school have evidenced PTSD rates around 40%. In addition, rates of PTSD in children subjected to sexual abuse are typically in the 60s and rates for exposure to physical abuse are in the 40s. In one of the more comprehensive studies to date, Kilpatrick et al. (2003) estimated a six-month prevalence of PTSD as 3.5% among adolescent males and 6.3% for adolescent females. Similar rates have been reported for younger children (e.g. Meiser-Stedman, Smith, Glucksman, Yule, & Dagleish, 2008). Factors that explain, in part, the likelihood of developing PTSD are similar to what has been reported in the adult literature (see Nickerson, Reeves, Brock, & Jimerson, 2009).

The high potential for experiencing trauma as a child, combined with the significant likelihood of developing PTSD, makes it imperative that educators are prepared to effectively support and manage the emotional and behavioral needs of children and adolescents with PTSD symptoms in their classrooms. This chapter will a) review the diagnostic criteria for PTSD, b) present information on PTSD symptoms commonly seen in schools, c) describe the extant literature on school based PTSD interventions, and d) offer suggestions for teachers and school personnel interacting with children who they believe to have a trauma history.

Conceptual Foundations

Studies have shown that individuals who experience a traumatic event may develop acute or chronic PTSD (Kessler, Sonnega, Bromet, Hughes, & Nelson, 1995) or, for a relatively smaller number of individuals, they may be diagnosed with a different mental health disorder altogether (e.g. acute stress disorder, specific phobia or depression; Kassam-Adams & Winston, 2004). Genetic, pretrauma, event-based and post-trauma factors have all been shown to predict who does/does not develop PTSD. Having parent(s) who experienced PTSD or having other family members who have experienced psychological problems can be indicative of potential diagnostic vulnerability within children (True et al., 1993). Age is also a factor, with very young or very old individuals being statistically more likely to develop PTSD. Pre-trauma variables, such as having experienced another traumatic event in the past, having premorbid psychological difficulties, and being raised in a blaming, shaming or guilt inducing environment are all predictive of developing PTSD (Koenen, Moffitt, Poulton, Martin, & Caspi, 2007). Possible traumatic, event-based variables that may increase the likelihood of developing PTSD include the extent with which there was a threat to life during the traumatic event, the ongoing chronicity of the traumatic experience, the person's emotional response (e.g. fear, helplessness, horror, guilt, and/or shame) at the time of the traumatic event, and dissociation at the time of the traumatic event (i.e. peri-traumatic dissociation; Johnson, Pike, & Chard, 2001). Finally, post-trauma variables can also impact the development of PTSD, including the amount of positive support the individual perceived receiving after the event (protective) versus the amount of negative, blaming social support they felt after the event (Schnurr, Lunney, & Sengupta, 2004).

Although no studies have been conducted that can determine which variables are more predictive of PTSD, social support and peri-traumatic dissociation appear to have some of the most support in research studies to date (Schnurr et al., 2004). Peri-traumatic dissociation can lead the individual feeling separated or cut-off from themselves and/or their surroundings. When in a "dissociative state," the individual may feel numb, lose track of time, feel as though they are floating outside of his or her body, or have no memories about a certain period of time. Dissociation at the time of a traumatic event suggests that a person was not connected with what was happening during the traumatic event. This may limit the extent with which a person can fully process his or her thoughts and emotions about a traumatic event, and thus, his or her ability to cope with the event (Birmes et al., 2003).

Although significant research has helped to identify variables that contribute to development or resistance to the disorder, there is still much that is unknown regarding who develops PTSD, suggesting that therapists, counselors, and teachers should be vigilant with all children known to have or suspected of having experienced a traumatic event.

Definition of PTSD

PTSD first came into existence in the 1980 third edition of the *Diagnostic and Statistical Manual of Mental Disorders* (DSM: American Psychological Association, [APA] 1980). Only in the revised 1987 version were traumatized children added. The diagnosis of PTSD consists of six integral criteria. In Criterion A, the clinician establishes if the child has experienced, witnessed, or learned about an event involving real or assumed physical harm or threat to physical integrity (A1). In response to the event, the child experiences fear, helplessness or horror (or confusion or agitation in young children) (A2). The characteristic symptoms that appear after experiencing the traumatic event are broken into three categories: re-experiencing, avoidance, and arousal. In the re-experiencing category (Criterion B), the child must endorse at least one of the following symptoms: intrusive memories of the traumatic event, recurrent, distressing dreams about the traumatic event, acting or feeling as if the traumatic event is reoccurring, or mental and/or physical discomfort when reminded of the traumatic event. To meet the Avoidance category (Criterion C), the child must have at least three of the following symptoms: avoiding thoughts, feelings, people, or situations associated with the traumatic event, not being able to recall an important aspect of the traumatic event, reduced interest or participation in significant activities, feeling disconnected from others, showing a limited range of emotion, and having a sense of a shortened future (e.g. not expecting to have a normal life span). For the Arousal category (Criterion D), the child must report at least two of the following symptoms: difficulty concentrating, exaggerated watchfulness and wariness, irritability or outbursts of anger, difficulty falling or staying asleep or being easily startled. All symptoms must be present for more than 1 month (Criterion E), and the disturbance must cause clinically significant distress or impairment in social, educational, or other important areas of functioning (Criterion F; American Psychological Association, 1994).

Symptomatology Most Likely Seen in Schools

Although it is generally accepted that children and adolescents with PTSD display or report many of the symptoms commonly found in adults, unique developmental factors as well as potential methodological/diagnostic issues contribute to how symptoms are reported in the literature. For example, factors, such as the individual's age and cognitive level, other demographic characteristics such as gender and socioeconomic status, the nature of the traumatic experience itself, and more distal factors (e.g., cultural background) appear to influence how PTSD symptoms are expressed (Schnurr et al., 2004). In addition, few measures are developmentally sensitive enough to capture the full array of symptoms as they may manifest in young (preschool) children. For example, Stover, Hahn, Im, and Berkowitz (2010) reported that while determination of PTSD in children is partially based on parent report, agreement between parent and child reports of traumatic experiences was not significant for avoidance and hyperarousal (i.e. Criteria C and D of the APA diagnostic taxonomy). Further, few self-report measures for young children possess adequate reliability and validity data (Stover & Berkowitz, 2005). Moreover, criteria listed in the current DSM taxonomy are universally applied regardless of age, making the wording of some of the PTSD criteria difficult to translate to very young children (Scheeringa, 2003). Thus, the differential symptomatic expression may partially be explained as a methodological/diagnostic artifact.

With the above stated, various studies have reported developmental variations of PTSD (see Nickerson et al., 2009 for a review). Given that preschool children do not have the cognitive capacity to understand or verbalize their experiences, reactions to traumatic events tend to be expressed non-verbally (e.g. through repetitive play that focuses on themes or aspects of the trauma). Further, reactions by the child may not necessarily be seen as directly related to the event itself. Sudden temper tantrums, disorganized, or agitated behaviors without apparent reason may be expressed. Finally, emerging skills just being mastered by the preschool child (e.g. toileting, speech complexity, sleep/eating habits) may regress to pre-mastery levels due to heightened anxiety and the child's overall difficulty coping with the traumatic experiences. For school-age children, reactions may continue to be displayed non-verbally, but as the child's cognitive level matures, reaction to the traumatic event may be verbally described in a straightforward manner. Such statements may be based on a specific aspect of the experience, rather than in its entirety. Cognitive complexity at this age level also entails that play behaviors may focus on the traumatic experience but the themes within the play behavior are more complex and elaborate than among preschool children. Behavioral reactions may be more directly connected to the traumatic experience and specific fears as the child continues to process through the event(s). Finally, although more verbally advanced than preschool children, school-aged children may find it difficult to verbalize their emotions to adults, and thus their feelings may be expressed through physical symptoms (frequent headaches or stomachaches) or behavioral cues, such as avoidance of activities/environments that may trigger a reminder of the event(s), problems paying attention to the teacher/parent, social withdrawal, or aggression.

Adolescents with PTSD often express emotions and display behaviors that are similar to adults who have been diagnosed with PTSD. Behaviors that can be expressed at this age level include oppositional/aggressive behaviors, (which can be due to their attempting to regain a sense of self-control or in response to their perceived foreshortened future), social withdrawal, participation in risk behaviors (e.g. substance abuse, sexual activity), and self-injurious behaviors (including suicide attempts). Adolescents can and often verbalize their experiences, with the verbalizations tied to the larger experience than one specific aspect. Behaviors consistent with a sudden disruption of normal life routines are common, including attention and learning problems, and sudden emotional outbursts.

Three-Tier Prevention/Intervention Strategies Used to Help Children with PTSD

Given the nature of the disorder, children and adolescents diagnosed with PTSD are often placed in situations where heretofore coping strategies may no longer be effective in coping with the aftermath of the traumatic event(s). Before describing specific strategies within each tier, it is important to emphasize that the primary role of teachers is to create a structured, supportive environment that is stable and psychologically safe for the child. The role of the teacher is not to diagnose or even treat PTSD, but rather to create a safe environment to promote the student's self-initiative and re-establish their focus to learning tasks. As noted in Nickerson et al. (2009; see also Brock, 2007; Foa, Keane, & Friedman, 2009), teachers are most often the key personnel to address and implement Tier I strategies, such as providing consistent and predictable daily routines, establishing more frequent breaks between learning tasks, and allowing extra-time for the child to follow through with requests (rather than to expect immediate compliance). Further, given that the disorder is often associated with memory and attention difficulties (Daud & Rydelius, 2009), teacher-delivered Tier I strategies can and should focus on strengthening the child's working memory and attention span. Specific strategies may include, a) reducing the number of requests made at the same time, b) providing visual aides, c) providing set routines with written guidelines, and d) modeling meta-cognitive strategies to help the child stop and anticipate the consequences of their choices (and prompting the student of these strategies if they fail to initiate them). Other Tier I strategies are designed to embed the needs of the student within the larger classroom context. Such strategies would include establishing clear guidelines for acceptable behaviors, anticipating when the child's behavior may be problematic to him/herself or to others, and identifying antecedent behaviors that may trigger an emotional response and altering the environment accordingly.

Teachers may be involved in a number of Tier II strategies to alleviate moderate classroom disruptions. With the aid of the school's mental health professional, such strategies would include serving as a trusted adult to teach, monitor, and reward stress management strategies, to serve as a soundboard whereby the child's reactions are addressed and normalized, and to help correct inaccurate attributions that the child may have made about the traumatic experience. In addition, depending on the age of the child, relationship with the child's family, and/or the nature of the traumatic experience, the teacher may help clarify the facts of the experience for the child, or to understand the child's perspective of the event, which can then be forwarded to the mental health professional and incorporated into future treatment strategies.

Given the nature of PTSD and its associated symptoms, Tier III strategies are often embedded within a larger systems intervention framework, which includes school- and community-based services. The teacher's role is often as a liaison between the components in this larger framework (e.g. sharing treatment efficacy data with the behavioral specialist, passing along information to the child's mental health specialist). Nevertheless, this is not to imply that teachers are excluded from delivering Tier III strategies. For example, in a recent randomized pilot study that implemented a ten-lesson curriculum designed to reduce PTSD symptoms among middle school youth exposed to traumatic events, Jacox and colleagues (2009) used teachers to deliver the entire curriculum. Components of the curriculum included providing: a) psychoeducation, b) relaxation training, c) cognitive coping strategies, d) strategies to process traumatic memories, e) gradual in vivo mastery of traumatic reminders, and f) social problem-solving strategies. None of the teachers had any previous clinical training. Results showed improvement in both self-reported and teacher-reported PTSD and depressive symptoms. Although additional studies are necessary, the findings are promising and indicate that teachers could be in a position to independently provide Tier III strategies in the future, at a level previously not assumed.

School-Based Research Findings

In addition to Jaycox et al. (2009), numerous other authors have explored the possibility of implementing PTSD interventions in the school setting (rather than a clinic setting). The impetus for this area of research is based on the knowledge that interventions delivered within an environment that is both familiar and accessible can increase treatment adherence and monitoring, and can utilize multiple levels of care within a single setting. In the case of PTSD, providing treatment in the school may contribute to minimize potential barriers towards receiving treatment (e.g. family financial resources, transportation, or possible stigmatization).

Although few in number, results of these studies collectively support the efficacy of school-based interventions. For example, a recent meta-analysis evaluating nineteen school-based studies (conducted between 1997 and 2010) found effect sizes ranged from medium to large (depending on sample and outcome measure; Rolfsnes & Idsoe, 2011). The majority (16) of these treatments employed cognitive-behavioral treatment (CBT) interventions, with eleven resulting in medium to large treatment effect sizes (Rolfsnes & Idsoe, 2011). Other interventions based on different treatment approaches (e.g. meditative exercises, art therapy, and play exercises) also showed promise. Other studies not incorporated in the meta-analysis have yielded similar findings (Morsette et al., 2009; Wolmer, Hamiel, & Laor, 2011), supporting further research in this area.

The International Society for Traumatic Stress Studies (ISTSS) has published practice guidelines for PTSD (Foa et al., 2009), including assessment and treatment suggestions. The guidelines also review the methodological considerations that should be taken into account when conducting a clinical trial. Foa and Meadows (1997) outlined the seven "gold standards" that can be used to evaluate the methodological rigor of PTSD treatment studies. The standards include: 1) clearly identified target symptoms; 2) reliable and valid measures; 3) use of blind evaluators; 4) assessor training; 5) manualized, replicable, specific treatment protocols; 6) unbiased assignment to condition; and 7) treatment adherence. More recently, Harvey, Bryant, and Tarrier (2003) expanded on these standards suggesting: 1) the use of independent evaluators; 2) blind assessors guess at the condition of each participant; 3) the investigator be blind to random assignment; and 4) evidence be provided that indicates the treatment was administered in its pure form, without the influence of other treatments, was received by the client and applied outside of the session.

Given these parameters, there are a number of limitations to the existing school-based studies. First, school-based treatments constitute a newly developing field and few rigorous evaluations have been made (Foa et al., 2009). Designs that incorporate random placement, compare the intervention to a controlled condition, and are based on longitudinal data are needed. Second, a large number of studies (Jordans et al., 2010; Rolfsnes & Idsoe, 2011; Wolmer et al., 2011) used school-based service providers to deliver the intervention. Securing trained professionals and its associated costs can potentially be prohibitive for a number of school districts who are resource-poor. Third, although expected in an emerging field, the age range of participants across studies was quite broad (typically between 8 and 16 years). Studies to examine the efficacy of interventions among preschool children are clearly needed. Fourth, the sample size in many of the published studies is variable, with the results of some studies based on four individuals while other studies (using a different intervention) yield results based 2500 participants. Fifth, the manner with which school-based treatments are delivered widely varies. While the majority of published studies appear to be based on a manualized treatment, some are not. Finally, treatment modality also varied across studies. In Rolfsnes and Idsoe's (2011) meta-analyses, the majority of studies targeted the classroom, although some interventions targeted both the individual and the group. While these particular findings suggested that group treatment (alone) effectively attenuated PTSD symptoms, treatments that combined group and individual modalities also yielded positive effect sizes (although not to the level of group treatment alone). Nevertheless, given the limited number of studies in general, it is difficult to comment on their generalizability. Overall, the provision of group or classroom treatment may serve an important therapeutic function for children with symptoms of PTSD in that they are able to garner support from their peers while also normalizing many of the symptoms they are experiencing.

Specific School-Based Interventions

Over the past several years, a number of studies have examined the effectiveness of treating traumatized children in the school environment. The majority of these studies have followed children who have witnessed terror attacks, war, or natural disasters.

Most recently, Wolmer and colleagues (2011) investigated the effectiveness of an intervention with fourth and fifth grade students who had been exposed to continuous rocket attacks during Operation Cast Lead near the Gaza Strip (Wolmer et al., 2011). Half of eligible students (N= 748) underwent a stress inoculation intervention while the other half of the students served as a control group. Students participated in fourteen, 45-minute weekly group sessions facilitated by school counselors. Session one consisted of psychoeducation about PTSD, while sessions 2 through 5 involved identifying emotions and working through positive and negative experiences and identifying and balancing bodily tension. Session 6 and 7 focused on coping with and managing fears, session 8 included identifying and challenging negative thoughts, session 9 focused on the power of positive experiences, session 10 taught the effect of humor as coping and ways to control attention, session 11 focused on imagery to enhance the ability to make decisions, the feeling of internal balance, and integrative rehearsal of coping skills, session 12 focused on emotional processing and regulation of strong emotions, and sessions 13 and 14 focused on the power of the group and creating a vision for the future. Results found that in comparison to the control group, children placed in the intervention group displayed significantly lower symptoms of posttraumatic stress and stress/mood than the control group. The effects of the intervention were moderated by gender, with boys reporting lower levels of PTSD post-intervention.

Jaycox (2004) developed the Cognitive Behavioral Intervention for Trauma in Schools (CBITS), which is a 10-week curriculum designed to be implemented for children between the ages of 11 to 15. The curriculum is sequenced to provide education and processing of the trauma, and each component within the curriculum incorporates key aspects of cognitive behavior therapy. The skills are learned, practiced, and monitored both in the group, as well as in individual sessions. Parent and teacher education sessions are also included. The curriculum has effectively reduced PTSD symptoms in a number of independent studies (e.g. Morsette et al., 2009; Ngo, Langley, Kataoka, Nadeeem, Escudero, & Stein, 2008), although few studies have conformed with ISTSS guidelines to this point.

Berger and Manasra (2005) established the ERASE-Stress to help children exposed to a large number of terrorist attacks. The curriculum consists of twelve classroom sessions, each lasting 90 minutes, to help reduce and prevent posttraumatic reaction in secondary students. Specific sessions include understanding internal feelings, controlling emotions, coping with grief and loss, and boosting self-esteem. Using a quasi-randomized controlled trial among 114 7th and 8th-grade students in Isreal, Gelkopf and Berger (2009) reported that students in the experimental group reported significant reductions on measures of PTSD symptoms, depression, somatic symptoms, and functional problems at 3-month post-intervention.

Berger, Pat-Horenczyk, and Gelkopf (2007) evaluated the effectiveness of a classroom-based program designed to help younger children cope with the threat and exposure to terrorism called Overshadowing the Threat of Terrorism (OTT). The curriculum, designed for children 7 to 11 years old, consists of psychoeducational materials and skills training with meditative practices, bio-energy exercises, art therapy, and narrative techniques for reprocessing traumatic experiences, delivered in eight, ninety-minute sessions. Specific sessions include an overview of the stress continuum during session 1, enhancing and developing coping skills during session 2, understanding somatic cues and strategies to control the body during stressful situations during session 3, developing emotional awareness during session 4, stopping emotional flooding and dealing with fears during session 5, building a social shield and enhancing the support system during session 6, reframing negative experiences during session 7, and looking for a better future and building a plan for the future during session 8. In the pilot study, seventy 2nd through 6th grade children participated in the intervention, and seventy-two children served as waitlist controls. At two month post-intervention, children in the intervention group reported significant improvement in PTSD symptoms (somatic complaints, generalized and separation anxiety). Boys in the treatment condition tended to improve more than girls.

Layne and colleagues (2008) investigated the effectiveness of a school-based psychotherapy program with adolescents exposed to war. The intervention was conducted with sixty-six high school students and sixty-one comparison children from Central Bosnia. The first tier of the intervention consisted of classroom-based psychoeducation and skills intervention while the second tier of the intervention was a manual-based seventeen-session trauma and grief focused group treatment called Trauma and Grief Component Therapy for Adolescents (TGCT). The intervention is assessment-driven and designed specifically for adolescents exposed to trauma, traumatic loss, and severe adversity that place them at high risk for PTSD. Results indicated that 73% of participating students reported direct life threat arising from close proximity to exploding shells or rifle fire, 36% reported witnessing violent death or serious injury, 12% reported witnessing torture, and 46% reported serious injury of a person to whom they were close. Among participating students, 55% reported abandoning their homes, 54% reported changing schools, 14% reported violent death in their nuclear family, and 73% reported death of at least one person with whom they were close. Both tier 1 and tier 2 interventions resulted in significant posttreatment PTSD and depressive symptom reductions and significant reduction in maladaptive grief reactions in the treatment condition. Significant symptom improvement between posttreatment and 4 month follow-up was observed in both conditions. In the treatment condition, 58% showed reductions in PTSD symptoms at posttreatment, and 81% at 4 month follow-up (Layne et al., 2008).

The School Reactivation Program was designed for children exposed to an earthquake in Turkey. The intervention consisted of eight two-hour meetings led by teachers over four weeks that combined psychoeducational modules and cognitive-behavioral techniques (Wolmer, Laor, Dedoglu, Siev, & Yazgan, 2005). Sixty-seven children participated in the School Reactivation Program and there was a control group of children as well. Results indicated that children who participated in the intervention showed significant symptomatic decrease in posttraumatic stress symptoms, grief, and dissociation. A large proportion of the children in both the intervention and control group still reported moderate to severe posttraumatic stress symptoms. Teachers blind to group assignment rated participating children higher than control children in terms of adaptive functioning.

Discussion and Recommendations

Trauma in children and adolescent is a significant societal issue that can have a profound detrimental effect on individuals who are not able to recover from the experience. Without intervention, research has shown that PTSD can have a monumental impact on brain development, psychological health, physical health, well-being, scholastic functioning, occupational functioning and proclivity toward risk taking, substance use, and crime (Nemeroff, 2004; Schnurr, Green, & Kaltman, 2008), thus creating a social and fiscal burden on society. While there are protective variables that can be implemented to try and prevent the development of PTSD, e.g., positive social support, for the majority of children and adolescents who develop PTSD, a structured trauma-focused intervention will need to be utilized to facilitate the individual's return to optimal functioning.

The existing research suggests that school-based interventions may be just as effective as clinic-based interventions for the treatment of PTSD. In addition, school-based treatments can often be easier to administer, as they allow for greater access to the children and adolescents on a daily/weekly basis as the need for transportation and parent/guardian time off work are not necessary to implement the therapy. Thus, these treatments can allow for greater treatment fidelity and adherence on the part of the children, thus increasing the amount of treatment they receive in a controlled period of time. Future research needs to be done to formally compare effective school based interventions with clinic based interventions in addition to comparing levels of family involvement in both of these settings. In addition, future studies should focus on improving the design rigor of the existing school based studies as indicated by the treatment guidelines for PTSD studies outlined above. Finally, studies should strive to expand the sample populations to include younger children and children and adolescents with diverse or multiple traumatic experiences to make the studies more applicable to the population as a whole. Any attempts to improve the care of traumatized youth will only further reduce the dramatic personal and societal impact of PTSD.

References

Adams, R. E., & Boscarino, J. A. (2006). Predictors of PTSD and delayed PTSD after disaster: The impact of exposure and psychosocial resources. *Journal of Nervous and Mental Disease, 194,* 485–93. doi:10.1097/01. nmd.0000228503.95503.e9

American Psychiatric Association (1980). *Diagnostic and statistical manual of mental disorders* (3rd ed.). New York, NY: American Psychiatric Press.

—(1994). *Diagnostic and statistical manual of mental disorders* (Rev. 4th ed.). New York, NY: American Psychiatric Press.

Berger, R., & Manasra, N. (2005). *Enhancing resiliency among students experiencing stress (ERASE-STRESS CHERISH): A manual for teachers.* Tel Aviv, Israel: Natal Trauma Center for Victims of Terror and War.

Berger, R., Pat-Horenczyk, R., & Gelkopf, M. (2007). School-based intervention for prevention and treatment of elementary students' terror-related distress in Israel: A quasi-randomized controlled trial. *Journal of Traumatic Stress, 20,* 541–51. doi:10.1002/jts.20225

Birmes P., Brunet A., Carreras D., Ducassé, J. L., Charlet, J-P. Lauque, D., .. Schmitt, L. (2003). The predictive power of peritraumatic dissociation and acute stress symptoms for posttraumatic stress symptoms: A three-month prospective study. *American Journal of Psychiatry, 160,* 1337–9. doi:10.1176/appi.ajp.160.7.1337

Brock, S. E. (2007, August). *Post-traumatic stress disorder: Effective school mental health response.* Workshop presented to the Chicago Public School District, Chicago, IL.

Daud, A., & Rydelius, P-A. (2009). Comorbidity/overlapping between AD/HD and PTSD in relation to IQ among children of traumatized/non-traumatized parents. *Journal of Attention Disorders, 13,* 188–96. doi:10.1177/1087054708326271

Foa, E. B., Keane, T. M., & Friedman, M. J. (eds). (2009). *Effective treatments for PTSD: Practice guidelines from the international society for traumatic studies* (2nd ed.). New York, NY: The Guilford Press.

Foa, E. B. & Meadows, E. A. (1997). Psychosocial treatments for posttraumatic stress disorder: A critical review. *Annual Review of Psychology, 48*, 449–80. doi:10.1146/annurev.psych.48.1.449

Galea, S., Ahern, J., Resnick, H., Kilpatrick, D., Bucuvalas, M., Gold, J., & Valahov, D. (2007). Psychological sequelae of the September 11 terrorist attacks in New York City. In Y. Neria, S. Galea, & F. Norris (eds). *Mental health and disasters.* London, England: Cambridge.

Gelkopf, M., & Berger, R. (2009). A school-based, teacher-mediated prevention program (ERASE-Stress) for reducing terror-related traumatic reactions in Israeli youth: A quasi-randomized controlled trial. *Journal of Child Psychology and Psychiatry, 50*, 962–71. doi:10.1111/j.1469-7610.2008.02021.x

Harvey, A. G., Bryant, R. A., & Tarrier, N. (2003). Cognitive behavior therapy for posttraumatic stress disorder. *Clinical Psychology Review, 23*, 501–22. doi:10.1016/S0272-7358(03)00035-7

Jaycox, L. H. (2004). *Cognitive Behavioral Intervention for Trauma in Schools (CBITS).* Longmont, CO: SoprisWest.

Jaycox, L. H., Langley, A. K., Stein, B. D., Wong, M., Sharma, P., Scott, M., & Schonlau, M. (2009). Support for students exposed to trauma: A pilot study. *School Mental Health, 1*, 49–60. doi:10.1007/s12310-009-9007-8

Johnson, D., Pike, J., & Chard, K. M. (2001). Factors predicting PTSD, depression, and dissociative severity in female treatment-seeking childhood sexual abuse survivors. *Child Abuse & Neglect, 25*, 179–98. doi:10.1016/S0145-2134(00)00225-8

Johnson, J., Maxwell, A., & Galea, S. (2009). The epidemiology of posttraumatic stress disorder. *Psychiatric Annals, 39*, 326–34. doi:10.3928/00485713-20090514-01

Jordans, M. J. D., Komproe, I. H., Tol, W. A., Kohrt, B. A., Luitel, N. P., Macy, R. D., & De Jong, J. (2010). Evaluation of a classroom-based psychosocial intervention in conflict-affected Nepal: A cluster randomized controlled trial. *Journal of Child Psychology and Psychiatry, 51*, 818–26. doi:10.1111/j.1469-7610.2010.02209.x

Jouriles, E., McDonald, R., Norwood, W., & Ezell, E. (2001). Issues and controversies indocumenting the prevalence of children's exposure to domestic violence. In S.A. Graham-Bermann & J.L. Edelson (eds), *Domestic violence in the lives of children: The future of research, intervention, and social policy* (pp. 13–34). Washington, D.C.: American Psychological Association.

Kassam-Adams, N. & Winston, F. K. (2004). Predicting child PTSD: The relationship between acute stress disorder and PTSD in injured children. *Journal of the American Academy of Child and Adolescent Psychiatry, 43*, 403–11. doi:10.1097/00004583-200404000-00006

Kessler, R. C., Chiu, W. T., Demler, O., & Walters, E. E. (2005). Prevalence, severity, and comorbidity of 12-month DSM-IV disorders in the National Comorbidity Survey Replication. *Archives of General Psychiatry, 62*, 617–27. doi:10.1001/archpsyc.62.6.617

Kessler, R. C., Sonnega A., Bromet E., Hughes, M., & Nelson, C. B. (1995).

Posttraumatic stress disorder in the National Comorbidity Survey. *Archives of General Psychiatry, 52,* 1048–60.

Kilpatrick, D. G., Ruggiero, K. J., Acierno, R., Saunders, B. E., Resnick, H. S., & Best, C. L. (2003). Violence and risk of PTSD, major depression, substance abuse/dependence, and comorbidity: Results from the National Survey of Adolescents. *Journal of Consulting and Clinical Psychology, 71,* 692–700. doi:10.1037/0022-006X.71.4.692

Koenen, K. C., Moffitt, T. E., Poulton, R., Martin, J., & Caspi, A. (2007). Early childhood factors associated with the development of post-traumatic stress disorder: Results from a longitudinal birth cohort. *Psychological Medicine, 37,* 181–92. doi:10.1017/S0033291706009019

Layne, C. M., Saltzman W. R., Poppleton, L. (2008). Effectiveness of a school-based group psychotherapy program for war-exposed adolescents: A randomized controlled trial. *Journal of the American Academy of Child and Adolescent Psychiatry, 47,* 1048–62. doi:10.1097/CHI.0b013e31817eecae

Meiser-Stedman, R., Smith, P., Glucksman, E., Yule, W., & Dagleish, T. (2008). The posttraumatic stress disorder diagnosis in preschool- and elementary school-age children exposed to motor vehicle accidents. *American Journal of Psychiatry, 165,* 1326–37. doi:10.1176/appi.ajp.2008.07081282

Morsette, A., Swaney, G., Stolle, D., Schuldberg, D., van den Pol, R., & Young, M. (2009). Cognitive behavioral intervention for trauma in schools (CBITS): School-based treatment on a rural American Indian reservation. *Journal of Behavior Therapy & Experimental Psychiatry, 40,* 169–78. doi:10.1016/j.jbtep.2008.07.006

Nemeroff, C. B. (2004). Neurobiological consequences of childhood trauma. *Journal of Clinical Psychiatry, 65(Suppl 1),* 18–28.

Ngo, V., Langley, A., Kataoka, S. H., Nadeeem, E., Escudero, P., & Stein, B. D. (2008). Providing evidence-based practice to ethnically diverse youths: Examples from the Cognitive Behavioral Intervention for Trauma in Schools (CBITS) program. Journal of the American Academy of Child & Adolescent Psychiatry, *47,* 858–62. doi:10.1097/CHI.0b013e3181799f19

Nickerson, A. B., Reeves, M. A., Brock, S. E., & Jimerson, S. R. (2009). *Identifying, assessing, and treating PTSD at school.* New York, NY: Springer.

Rolfsnes, E. S., & Idsoe, T. (2011). School-based intervention programs for PTSD symptoms: A review and meta-analysis. *Journal of Traumatic Stress, 24,* 155–65. doi:10.1002/jts.20622

Scheeringa, M. (2003). Research diagnostic criteria for infants and preschool children: The process and empirical support. *Journal of the American Academy of Child and Adolescent Psychiatry, 42,* 1504–12. doi:10.1097/00004583-200312000-00018

Scheeringa, M. S. (2008). Developmental considerations for diagnosing PTSD and Acute Stress Disorder in preschool and school-age children. *American Journal of Psychiatry, 165,* 1237–39.

Schnurr, P. P., Green, B. L., & Kaltman, S. (2008). Trauma exposure and physical health. In M. Friedman, T. Keane, & P. Resick (eds). *Handbook of PTSD.* New York, NY: The Guilford Press.

Schnurr, P. P., Lunney, C. A., & Sengupta, A. (2004). Risk factors for the development versus maintenance of posttraumatic stress disorder. *Journal of Traumatic Stress, 17*, 85–95. doi:10.1023/B:JOTS.0000022614.21794.f4

Stover, C. S., & Berkowitz, S. (2005). Assessing violence exposure and trauma symptoms in young children: A critical review of measures. *Journal of Traumatic Stress, 18*, 707–17. doi:10.1002/jts.20079

Stover, C. S., Hahn, H., Im, J. J. Y., & Berkowitz, S. (2010). Agreement of parent and child reports of trauma exposure and symptoms in the early aftermath of a traumatic event. *Psychological Trauma: Theory, Research, Practice, and Policy, 2*, 159–68. doi:10.1037/a0019156

True, W. R., Rice J., Eisen, S. A., Heath, A. C., Goldberg, J., Lyons, M. J., & Nowak, J. (1993). A twin study of genetic and environmental contributions to liability for posttraumatic stress symptoms. *Archives of General Psychiatry, 50*, 257–64.

US Department of Health and Human Services, Administration on Children, Youth and Families. *Child Maltreatment 2006* (Washington, DC: US Government Printing Office, 2008). United States Department of Health and Human Services, Administration on Children, Youth and Families, 2006.

Wolmer, L., Hamiel, D., & Laor, N. (2011). Preventing children's posttraumatic stress after disaster with teacher-based intervention: A controlled study. *Journal of the American Academy of Child and Adolescent Psychiatry, 50*, 340–8. doi:10.1016/j.jaac.2011.01.002

Wolmer, L., Laor, N., Dedoglu, C., Siev, J., & Yazgan, Y. (2005). Teacher-mediated intervention after disaster: A controlled three-year follow-up of children's functioning. *Journal of Child Psychology and Psychiatry, 46*, 1161–8. doi: 10.1111/j.1469-7610.2005.00416.x

Yehuda, R., Cai, G., Golier, J. A., Sarapas, C., Galea, S., Ising, M., … Buxbaum, J. D. (2009). Gene expression patterns associated with posttraumatic stress disorder following exposure to the World Trade Center attacks. *Biological Psychiatry, 66*, 708–11. doi:10.1016/j.biopsych.2009.02.034

CHAPTER TWELVE

Understanding and Managing Behaviors of Children During the Preschool Years

Jinhee Kim and Sierra Brown
Duquesne University

Abstract

Children with behavioral and emotional disorders often demonstrate delays in the typical developmental trajectory and exhibit challenging behaviors that often cause teachers to feel very frustrated. The disorders can impact children's daily functioning, development, behavioral adjustment, and academic ability. Teachers in early childhood education programs have a critical responsibility to enhance and support those children's development and learning. This chapter provides ways for teachers to understand and manage the behaviors of children with psychological disorders in early childhood education settings. This chapter begins by introducing a defining term, "disorder," noting the symptoms frequently observed in preschool settings, and discussing the specifics of intervention strategies available to teachers in the classroom. Finally, implications and recommendations for teachers are presented.

Overview

During preschool, important changes and learning occur in all areas of children's development. For example, preschool children engage in many gross motor skills, such as jumping, skipping, and hopping, and also slowly develop their fine motor skills. They are able to practice and improve information-processing skills such as paying attention (Bredekamp & Copple, 2009; Landry, Smith, Swank, & Miller-Loncar, 2000). Typically, preschoolers also show affection for their playmates and start cooperating with other children during play. Every child does not always follow the exact developmental trajectory. There are variations of children's developmental stages because of various reasons such as individual child, family backgrounds, or cultural backgrounds. Children experience different rates and amounts of growth based on who they are and where they come from (Bredekamp & Copple, 2009). In particular, children with behavioral and emotional disorders often demonstrate delays in the typical developmental trajectory. Moreover, young children can be affected by disorders that impact their daily functioning, development, behavioral adjustment, and academic ability.

Children exhibiting challenging behaviors, such as not following teachers' directions, often cause teachers to feel very frustrated. In illustration of this, preschoolers exhibiting challenging behaviors are three times more likely than older children to be expelled from programs (Gilliam, 2005). Teachers in early childhood education programs have a critical responsibility to enhance and support those children's development and learning. The responsibility for supporting children with special needs is not only that of special education specialists and school psychologists. Compared to older grade classroom teachers, early childhood teachers tend to have less training for children with special needs (Klein, Cook, & Richardson-Gibbs, 2001). To this end, this chapter provides ways to understand and manage the behaviors of children with psychological disorders for teachers in early childhood education settings. This chapter begins by introducing a defining term, "disorder," noting the symptoms frequently observed in preschool settings, and discussing the specifics of intervention strategies available to teachers in the classroom. Finally, implications and recommendations for teachers are presented.

Conceptual Foundations

Over the past ten years, the number of preschool children receiving special education services in the United States has steadily increased. About 5% of preschool children in the United States have special needs, including behavioral and emotional needs. The number of the age group from 3 to 5 years with disabilities receiving services under the Individuals with Disabilities Education Act (IDEA) was reported at 455,425 in 1992–93 to 620,182 in 2001–2, respectively. In addition, 51% of preschoolers with special needs received special education and related services in their early childhood education settings in 2003 (US Department of Education, 2003).

The Individuals with Disabilities Education Act (IDEA) legislates that all children with disabilities from birth to 21 years of age receive necessary services and a quality education. Along with No Child Left Behind (NCLB), IDEA clearly delivers the message that all children are expected to have access to special education and other relevant services. In particular, IDEA ensures that states provide a free and appropriate public education (FAPE) to preschool children with disabilities. Under Part B of IDEA, states must implement policies and procedures of the Preschool Grants Programs to enable eligible preschool children to benefit from special education and related services. Part C of IDEA requires that families enrolled in early intervention programs be provided with a service coordinator and an individualized family service plan (IFSP), which includes a treatment plan and identifies the outcome goals of the services provided. In states that choose not to apply for Part C funds, only children starting at the age of three who meet eligibility for a disability can receive special education services. States that have applied for Part C funds, (e.g. Arizona and Wisconsin), can provide interventions to young children who exhibit developmental delays, as well as physical or psychological disabilities.

Under IDEA, a child is eligible for special education services if the child has "mental retardation, hearing impairment, speech or language impairment, a visual impairment, a serious emotional disturbance, an orthopedic impairment, autism, traumatic brain injury, another health impairment, a specific learning disability deaf-blindness, or multiple disabilities" (IDEIA, 2004, Sec. 300.8). As noted earlier, there are difficulties in identifying young children's disorders. In this context, for young children under six (particularly for three to five), "developmental delay" has been also recommended as a more flexible term for covering all developmental problems (Allen & Cowdery, 2005). Children with a developmental delay have a deficit in at least two of the following functioning areas: cognitive, social and emotional, adaptive, physical, or language (Merrell, Ervin, & Gimpel, 2006; Shevell, Majnemer, Platt, Webster, & Birnbaum, 2005). States that adopt a delay model, such as Arizona, have specific definitions for preschool delay when a preschool child shows low performance on a norm-referenced test (e.g. below the mean for children of the same chronological age in one or more of the functional areas—cognitive, social and emotional, adaptive, physical, or language). Yet, most other states typically specify preschool delays in standard deviations to be 1.5 SD or 2 SD below the mean. These include moderate delay, preschool severe delay, and preschool speech/language delay.

Researchers have claimed that the systems approach allows educators to understand children's disabilities or delays and to lead appropriate interventions. The ecological system perspective, drawn from Bronfenbrenner's (1992) theory, is a provocative framework for understanding children with special needs and providing them with developmentally appropriate interventions. In the ecological system perspective (Bronfenbrenner, 1992), children's development can be understood within a series of nested systems, including the biosystem (the child), microsystem (e.g. families, classroom teachers, classroom practices), mesosystem (e.g. professional collaborations) exosystem (e.g. public policy, regulations), and macrosystem (e.g. beliefs, values). Each system level also influences others and is influenced by them. This perspective helps teachers to identify children's special needs and support them through closely examining the links among different system levels and collaborating with key persons at each system level (Sontag, 1996). In other words, children with special needs can be understood and approached through examining the interplay of the influential factors in both children and their environments. The child development-in-context model proposed by Bronfenbrenner (1992) identifies ways in which educators can support children with special needs through examining the nature of the different systems (e.g. family, school, and community) and finding the gaps in the linkages among them.

Similarly, Dunst (1985, 2000) suggested that direct and indirect social support for children, family, and community functioning should be considered when implementing intervention. From the perspective of the social support model suggested by Dunst, early intervention is defined as "the provision of support and resources to families of young children from members of informal and formal social support networks that both directly and indirectly influence child, parent, and family functioning" (Dunst, 2000, p. 99). In this sense, the social support model opens many possibilities for integrated strategies of intervention for young children through considering children's learning opportunities, parenting support, and family/community supports in multiple ways. Understanding that parents know the most about children's needs is crucial for planning and providing appropriate interventions. Collaboration between parents and service personnel is also critical for empowering children's strengths and for supporting children's needs (Beganto, 2006; Coleman, Roth, & West, 2009). In particular, this perspective allows educators to implement early interventions with family-centered strategies as family characteristics (e.g. parenting styles, parenting resources) are the most influential factors for young children's cognitive, social, and/or emotional development (Bailey et al., 1986; Bayat, Mindes, & Covitt, 2010; Ramey & Ramey, 1998). In particular, strong relationships have been reported between family characteristics and children's social behaviors (e.g. Jenkins, Simpson, Dunn, Rasbash, & O'Connor, 2005; Parcel & Menaghan, 1993). Collectively, within these frameworks, children with special needs can receive developmentally appropriate interventions based on their specific needs, reflecting the proximal (e.g. home, classroom, school) and distal environments (e.g. relevant community resources for special services, local state regulations) surrounding children.

Defining Disorders

As mentioned earlier, defining disorders of young children such as preschoolers is quite challenging because of the nature of young children's development. Every child does not always follow the exact developmental trajectory as there are variations of children's developmental stages due to variables such as individual child, family backgrounds, or cultural backgrounds.

All children may display some behaviors of inattention, hyperactivity, or impulsivity, such as inability to sit still during a game, or running around a lot. However, as with all disorders, the distinction between normal and abnormal behavior is chronicity, severity, and whether the behavior causes impairment in functioning. If the child is only running around at home and being disobedient to his or her mother and does not exhibit these behaviors during school, this may be an indication that the environment is having an effect on the child's behavior, and a disorder is not necessarily present.

Specifically, preschool children with behavioral and emotional disorders often do not come to school prepared to succeed, and their behaviors are a barrier to their learning and are one of the greatest challenges that teachers face. The National Mental Health and Special Education Coalition (Forness & Knitzer, 1992) defines a behavioral or emotional disorder as a disability characterized by behavioral or emotional responses in school that differ from typical age, cultural, or ethnic norms and which adversely affect educational performance. Educational performance includes academic, social, vocational, and personal skills. In particular, psychological disorders are mental disorders that produce behavioral or emotional symptoms that impact a person's life in maladaptive ways. Emotional or behavioral disorders can be associated with other developmental problems, such as academic failure. For example, researchers have found that children with behavioral or emotional disorders tend to exhibit low reading achievement (e.g. Mastropieri, Jenkins, & Scruggs, 1985) and that low reading skills in older children can be linked to other disorders (e.g. Hinshaw, 1992). In addition, when a child is diagnosed with a psychological disorder, "the symptoms occur often and last a long time, are present in more than one setting, and cause significant distress or impairment in functioning or both" (Bilmes & Welker, 2006, p. 21).

Raver and Knitze (2002) noted that approximately 10% of preschool children exhibit noticeable challenging behaviors, while about 4 to 6% of this population exhibits serious behavior problems. The challenging behaviors of this population include behavioral or emotional disorders such as externalizing behaviors (e.g. AD/HD), internalizing behaviors (e.g. anxiety disorder), and low incidence disorders (e.g. Schizophrenia). Due to the rarity of low incidence disorders in preschoolers, they are not discussed in this chapter.

Although studies vary in their assessments of the prevalence of preschool children's behavioral or emotional disorders (e.g. August, Braswell, & Thuras, 1998; Costello, Mustillo, Erkanli, Keeler, & Angold, 2003), they agree that one of the most common disruptive behavior disorders affecting preschool-aged children is Attention-Deficit/Hyperactivity Disorder (AD/HD). Barkley (1998) indicated that preschool age is the mean age for reports of any type of AD/HD. Similarly, in their study of 4 year-olds, Lavigne, LeBailly, Hopkins, Gouze, and Binns (2009) reported that AD/HD (12. 8%) was the most common disorder, followed by ODD (Oppositional Defiant Disorder, 13.4%). AD/HD is marked by developmentally inappropriate degrees of inattention, hyperactivity, and/or impulsivity (Campbell, 2002; Gadow, Sprafkin, & Nolan, 2001; Webster-Stratton, 1997). Boys are five times more likely to be identified as having behavior disorders than girls (Patterson, Capaldi, & Bank, 1991). The frequency of AD/HD is significantly higher for preschool boys than preschool girls (e.g. Lavigne et al., 2009). Researchers have noted that impaired brain functioning and environments that adversely influence brain development may cause AD/HD (Weyandt, 2005). In order to be diagnosed with AD/HD, the child should exhibit at least six symptoms explained by the guidelines of the Diagnostic and Statistical Manual of Mental Disorders—Fourth Edition—Text Revision (DSM-IV-TR). The behaviors of the child have to occur across different settings, must cause clear impairment within each setting, must be long lasting and persistent, and must have been present prior to the age of seven (American Psychiatric Association, 2000).

Oppositional Defiant Disorder (ODD) is another common disruptive behavior disorder that affects preschool-aged children. Weis (2008) reported that about 3% of preschoolers have ODD, compared to less than 1% of adolescents. Lavigne et al. (2009) indicated that ODD is the most common disorder among preschoolers. This disorder is marked by a persistent and frequent pattern of negative behaviors (e.g. loss of temper, becoming very angry or argumentative often, breaking rules, being noncompliant, being aggressive) over at least six months (Bilmes & Welker, 2006). Children with ODD often exhibit other disorders such as AD/HD, learning disabilities, and anxiety disorders (Lavigne et al., 1998). Diagnosing a child with ODD requires an informed school team with experience comparing developmental delays and disordered behavior under the guidelines of DSM-IV-TR (Hughes, Crothers, & Jimerson, 2007). Moreover, diagnosing AD/HD and ODD, as with many psychological disorders, relies on interviews with parents, teachers, or caregivers of the child, rating scales completed by adults familiar with the child, or observations typically conducted in a home, school, or clinic setting (Luby, 2006).

It is normal for young children to experience some anxiety. However, if children exhibit persistent fears, tension, or worry in more than one setting for a long time with significant distress and impairment in functioning, they may be diagnosed with an anxiety disorder. One of the most common is Generalized Anxiety Disorder (GAD), in which children exhibit frequent and intensive worries about many different things, including particular events, activities, and relationships. Researchers have reported that preschool children tend to have more fears related to animals and imaginary creatures than fears of natural disasters and physical danger (e.g. Bauer, 1976; Maurer, 1965).

Another anxiety pattern that preschool children experience is Separation Anxiety Disorder (SAD), which is marked by higher than normal anxiety levels when the child is separated from his or her primary caregivers (APA, 2000). Due to the nature of preschool children, prevalence data and the gender effects of SAD are not clear (Lyman & Hembree-Kigin, 1994). The prevalence range of SAD in preschoolers varies across studies from 0.3% (Lavigne et al., 1998) up to 5% (Kessler, Chiu, Demler, & Walters, 2005) (see Egger & Angold, 2007). Children often experience SAD when they experience significant changes in their lives, such as attending a new school, moving to a new area, or having new siblings. Separation anxiety usually diminishes around the age of two. However, in the diagnostic criteria of the DSM-IV-TR, if children demonstrate excessive fear or nightmares of being separated causing impairment over at least four weeks, it is time to consider a diagnosis of SAD. These behaviors can be observed within the classroom, especially in the morning when parents and caregivers are dropping the children off at preschool.

Autism spectrum disorders (ASD) are neurodevelopmental disorders that are diagnosed primarily in early childhood, and include Autism, Asperger's syndrome, Pervasive Developmental Disorder–Not Otherwise Specified (PDD- NOS), Rett syndrome, and Childhood Disintegrative Disorder (CDD; Luby, 2006; Volkmar, Lord, Bailey, Schultz, & Klin, 2004). Compared to school-aged children, preschool children have higher rates of SAD. For example, one study reported that in 2002, ASD prevalence among 4-year-olds in 2006 was 8.0 per 1000, compared to school-aged children (7.0; Nicholas, Carpenter, King, Jenner, & Charles, 2009). Children with ASD demonstrate impaired social interactions, communications, and restricted and repetitive behavior ranging from very mild to severe.

Symptoms Frequently Seen in Preschools

Children's challenging behaviors can easily be considered typical behaviors because such demonstrations in young children are still on the developmental continuum. Researchers have noted that it is more challenging to identify disorders in young children such as preschoolers because of the nature of young children's development. Many characteristics of behavioral and emotional disorders are also typical characteristics of preschool children (Bilmes & Welker, 2006; Lavigne et al., 2009; Steele, 2004). Furthermore, there has been much debate about identifying disorders at a young age (Barnett & Carey, 1992; Webster-Stratton, 1997). Even when symptoms of disorders are observed in young children, the symptoms often do not fit as cleanly into specific categories of disorders as those of older children.

Another reason for the difficulty in the early identification of young children's disorders is the lack of developmentally appropriate assessment tools and procedures for the young age group. For example, the Diagnostic and Statistical Manual of Mental Disorders, Fourth Edition, Text Revision (DSM-IV-TR) can be inappropriate for young children due to their limited language ability, as the framework heavily relies on the children's ability to express their feelings and experiences (Bilmes & Welker, 2006). With regard to the classification systems such as the DSM-IV-TR, children's anxiety may not represent clear subtypes of anxiety disorders because their anxiety may present in a more diffuse manner (Spence, Rapee, McDonald, & Ingram, 2001).

In this context, in order to understand and manage the behaviors of children with behavioral or emotional disorders, it is critical for teachers to be able to identify those symptoms. Symptoms frequently observed in preschool settings follow.

Children with Attention Deficit Hyperactivity Disorder (AD/HD)

Within the classroom, children with AD/HD often exhibit disruptive classroom behaviors. AD/HD is one of the most common disorders challenging teachers in the classroom, largely due to the symptoms becoming externalized as behavior problems viewed as "annoying" behaviors (Campbell, 2002; Gadow et al., 2001). Children with the inattentive form of AD/HD show inattentiveness, have difficulty finishing tasks or following multi-step directions, are easily distracted, or have difficulty concentrating on classroom activities. Alessandri (1992) indicated that preschoolers with AD/HD often change their activities during free play and tend to spend more time in sensorimotor play. Teachers also might observe that children with the hyperactive-impulsive type of AD/HD have a developmentally inappropriate inability to wait their turn in the classroom, talk excessively, get out of their seats often, or have difficulty playing quietly. In addition, children with AD/HD often exhibit deficits in social skills development (DuPaul, McGoey, Eckert, & VanBrakle, 2001; Egger & Angold, 2007). During the preschool years, children are able to be involved in more complex sociodramatic play with peers and start to value their friendships (Bodrava & Leong, 2007). However, children with AD/HD often fail to respect other children's boundaries, showing interruptive behaviors when they play with peers or are required to wait their turn. This can lead to rejection from their peers.

Children with Oppositional Defiant Disorder (ODD)

Oppositional Defiant Disorder is a common disorder in classroom and often co-occurs with AD/HD (Rey, 1993). ODD seriously interferes with children's daily routines, as children with ODD easily lose their temper and are annoyed, argue with adults, or refuse adults' directions or requests (Bilmes & Welker, 2006). Some of the behaviors of ODD can be seen as typical behaviors of a preschooler, such as temper tantrums and noncompliance; however, ODD is marked by severe behaviors and noncompliance for the child's age and development with the key indicator of impairment caused by the behaviors (e.g., noncompliance with parent or teacher requests and annoying others without regard to feedback from primary authority figures). Like children with AD/HD, children with ODD have fewer social skills and are less popular than their peers (Coy, Speltz, DeKlyen, & Jones, 2001; Webster-Stratton, 1993).

Children with Anxiety Disorders (AD)

Anxiety disorders are also common in preschool children. Children with anxiety disorders are more likely to be impaired and also diagnosed with ODD (Egger & Angold, 2007). Children with anxiety disorder have difficulty maintaining emotional stability and in transitioning between activities. Specifically, children with Separation Anxiety Disorder (SAD) struggle with separation when their primary caregivers leave. They cannot be soothed after separation from their caregivers. They are hesitant or refuse to go to school without their primary caregivers. Children experiencing SAD will often become upset, cry, and may be inconsolable for an extended period of time. Children with Generalized Anxiety Disorder (GAD) worry all the time, show reckless and defiant behavior, and are unable to sit still at rest time (Bilmes & Welker, 2006; Egger & Angold, 2007).

Children with Autism Spectrum Disorders (ASD)

Children diagnosed with autistic spectrum disorders exhibit atypical and repetitive behaviors (e.g. hand flapping, walking in circles, excessive finger tapping), a lack of reciprocal language, and restricted interests (Luby, 2006). They seem to obsess over a particular interest and are unable to switch easily from one activity to another when they are focused on their restricted interest. For instance, a child with autism may move a toy car back and forth over and over again without actually playing with the toy. Children with autism also show social skill deficits, as they are unable to engage in reciprocal play, have difficulty using their imagination, and do not have a developed theory of mind, a capability of understanding another's perspective (Siegler, DeLoache, & Eigenberg, 2003; Luby, 2006; Volkmar et al., 2004). During social interaction, children with autism do not engage in eye-to-eye gazing, a key component of social competence. Instead, children may focus more on another's mouth, limbs, or objects in the area (Klin, Jones, Schultz, Volkmar, & Cohen, 2002).

Similarly, a child diagnosed with Asperger's syndrome, a high functioning type of autism, may present similar behaviors to those of autistic children, such as stereotyped interests, repetitive behaviors, and social impairments. However, whereas children with autism have significant language and cognitive delays, children diagnosed with Asperger's typically have normal language and cognitive functioning (APA, 2000; Luby, 2006). Children with Asperger's syndrome may seem typical in their cognitive development, but they do not understand how to interact with their peers, making it difficult for them to make friends. Children diagnosed with PDD-NOS may also exhibit significant impairment to functioning, social and language impairments, and stereotyped interests. However, a diagnosis of PDD-NOS is intended for children who do not meet the full diagnostic criteria for autism, Asperger's, Rett syndrome (a neurological disorder affecting girls), Childhood Degenerative Disorder (CDD), or a disorder characterized by a developmental regression around toddlerhood (APA, 2000).

Response to Intervention (RtI)

Response to Intervention, or RtI, is a multi-tiered problem-solving model that utilizes a data-driven approach to prevention of and intervention with both academic and behavioral problems. Implementing RtI within the preschool classroom involves several benefits for all children, both with and without delays or disabilities. Through RtI, teachers can take appropriate actions when they notice a child may not be learning in an expected manner, instead of waiting for children to be diagnosed and receive special education services. For typically developing children or at-risk children,

RtI provides interventions and services supporting social, emotional, and academic needs to prevent future problems and possible unnecessary diagnosis of a disability. RtI also benefits children with disabilities by providing the necessary support and potentially effecting a better academic or behavioral outcome (Coleman, Buysse, & Neitzel, 2006; Greenwood, Bradfield, Kaminski, Linas, Carta, & Nylander, 2011).

Recently, RtI models for early childhood program settings adapted from RtI for school-aged children have been discussed. For example, the Pyramid model[1] (e.g. Fox, Dunlap, Hemmeter, Joseph, & Strain, 2003) is a three-tiered intervention practice for children who have social-emotional delays or behavioral challenges in early childhood education settings. The model includes "universal promotion for all children; secondary preventions to address the intervention needs of children at risk of social-emotional delays; and tertiary interventions needed for children with persistent challenges" (p. 6). Similarly, a Recognition and Response model targeting young children such as preschoolers in a variety of early childhood education settings is being developed, and includes key components of RtI (e.g. screening, assessment and progress monitoring) and multiple-tiered implementation (Coleman et al., 2006).

Tier I

Tier I is designed as a global intervention that can include either a classroom-based or a school-wide intervention. Interventions that target specific behaviors or academic problems can also be used as classroom or school-wide Tier I interventions. Preschool teachers at this tier should consider high quality curriculums to meet the needs of the classroom. Teachers can support children with challenging behaviors by consulting with specialists and implementing effective classroom management techniques which provide children with positive reinforcement and structure, including a classroom schedule, a rule chart, and transition activities (e.g. Allen & Cowdery, 2005; Barnett, VanDerHeyden, & Witt, 2007; Bayat et al., 2010).

A common intervention that can be implemented in a preschool classroom to manage children's anger or aggressive behaviors is called the "Turtle Technique," which was created by Schneider and Robin (1978) and was adapted into the Promoting Alternative Thinking Strategies (PATHS) curriculum (Domitrovich et al., 2008). This manualized curriculum, which includes a corresponding story, shows children how to control their behavior by calming down when getting angry or frustrated. To "Do the Turtle" the child hugs him- or herself and practices breathing to promote better impulse control and emotion regulation (Domitrovich et al., 2008).

Teachers can also integrate relevant storybooks into existing curriculums for all children and provide positive attention and praise, including descriptive praise (e.g. "You are sharing the blocks with your friend!") whenever positive behaviors are observed (Allen & Cowdery, 2005; Bayat et al., 2010). Providing and reviewing classroom rules and consequences of behaviors daily will give all children clear expectations for their behaviors. Teachers can also develop transition strategies when moving from one activity to another by warning children several minutes before transition and repeating the warning until the next activity occurs (Allen & Cowdery, 2005; Barnett et al., 2007; Bayat et al., 2010). This advance notice can help children to understand which activity will be next and move at their own pace. Using multiple modes of communication, such as pictures and songs, may help children respond to the teacher's directions more effectively (Allen & Cowdery, 2005; Johnson, Christie, & Wardle, 2005).

Similarly, Fox and Lentini (2006) identified useful strategies for teaching social skills and appropriate behaviors, including modeling the teacher's own social skills, modeling with puppets, doing finger plays, or playing games to introduce or discuss social skills. Fox and Lentini also introduced the idea that children can learn social skills through three stages of learning (skill acquisition, skill fluency, and skill maintenance and generalization). For example, teachers can support children in solving sharing problems with concrete examples of what the sharing skill is and how to use it through modeling or through embedded classroom activities. Children should have many opportunities to practice these skills and be encouraged to use the skill.

In addition, in paralleling National Association for the Education of Young Children (NAEYC) guidelines (Bredekamp & Copple, 2009) for early childhood education, teachers need to design physical environments that promote all children's appropriate behaviors. The classroom space and materials should be arranged in such a way that children can access them independently and feel actively involved with their environment (Allen & Cowdery, 2005; Fox et al., 2003; Klein et al., 2001).

When children do not improve either academically or behaviorally at Tier I, they will move on to Tier II, which provides additional support. Data should be collected and analyzed through validated progress monitoring methods such as anecdotal observations or behavior rating scales to identify which children should transition to Tier II (Bayat et al., 2010; Fox et al., 2003; Hawken, Vincent, & Schumann, 2008).

Tier II

Children who do not show progress from the universal intervention will transition to the second tier under the RtI model, which is implemented in a small group. The specific intervention in Tier II should be chosen based on the needs of the children. Teachers can adjust the existing curriculum for small groups and receive additional support from professionals to provide intervention and/or progress monitoring.

Children exhibiting disruptive behaviors tend to lack social and emotional skills. Katz and McClellan (1997) argue that children struggling with social and emotional skills need to have immediate and continual intervention. Fox and her colleagues (e.g. Fox et al., 2003; Fox & Lentini, 2006) suggest that teachers explain social skills, demonstrate them for the children, and provide opportunities for children to practice them. To do this, teachers need to make opportunities to coach the target children while standing nearby the children's activities (Bilmes & Welker, 2006). For example, a child with AD/HD symptoms often has difficulty waiting his or her turn, which often results in a distracted classroom atmosphere and high rates of peer rejection, as noted earlier. If the child has difficulty sharing toys with peers during free-play time, a teacher can help him or her by identifying (e.g. "Ask to take your turn") or demonstrating the sharing skills (e.g. "See how Kevin asks Emily to play with the blocks? Why don't you ask Kevin to play with the blocks together? Let me see if I can help you."). Teachers can form social skills groups for children who do not exhibit appropriate social skills, so that they can receive assistance from their peers (Bayat et al., 2010; Fox & Lentini, 2006).

Tier II interventions for academic problems, or specifically school readiness for preschoolers, could utilize tutors or classroom teachers to give further academic support to children who may be at risk of falling behind their peers. For example, through embedded small group activities, a teacher could work with a small group of preschoolers who do not yet have letter or color naming skills.

As with the first tier, progress monitoring should also be implemented to track children's progress, with the expectation that children who do not respond to the second tier of RtI should move to the third tier and children showing marked progress could also transition back to the first tier.

Tier III

Tier III consists of highly individualized plans based on the needs of the child, and includes increased progress monitoring. Children who do not respond to the first two tiers are included in Tier III, and require interventions that are tailored directly to their needs. Children who show academic delays and are in need of special education services may have an individualized family service plan (IFSP) or individualized education plan (IEP). An IFSP is used for infants and toddlers who receive support under Part C of IDEA (Jung, 2007). The IFSP is highly individualized to the child, addressing the child's needs and establishing a plan for how the family will address those needs and achieve the desired outcomes. Jung (2007) identifies several important aspects of the IFSP, which include the integration of outcomes and evidence-based interventions into daily activities, clear expectations for outcomes, comprehensibility to those who will use the IFSP, incorporation of all services utilized by the child, being nonjudgmental, and implementation by the caregivers. For example, if a child is experiencing language delays, the IFSP would address specific interventions and identify possible routines in which the child can practice his or her language skills, such as encouraging the child to verbalize his or her choice of toy during play time.

For children exhibiting behavioral issues, the preschool teacher and parents can integrate social stories, daily schedules, or a functional behavioral analysis (FBA) to create a behavior intervention plan for the child (Barnett et al., 2006; Bayat et al., 2010). An FBA incorporates multiple measures of the child's behavior, including observation, interviews, and behavior rating scales, to provide an assessment of the behavior (Merrell et al., 2006). The FBA identifies the function of the child's behavior (i.e. to escape a non-preferred activity or to gain a preferred activity) and provides appropriate interventions and consequences for the behavior, thus minimizing undesirable behaviors. It is important for the specific intervention that is used to be appropriate for the child in Tier III. This requires analysis of data, whether it is behavioral observations or permanent academic products, and continued progress monitoring.

Monitoring the Progress of Interventions

Ongoing assessment and progress monitoring are critical components of early intervention for young children, as they enable teachers to make informed decisions for the target children in a timely manner while collaborating with other intervention team members (e.g. parents, specialists, and school psychologists). Careful monitoring of progress toward specific outcomes can provide important information about the effectiveness of an intervention. One of the basic methods that teachers in early childhood programs can use to monitor children's progress is observation. Systematic observation of children's patterns can be very helpful for progress monitoring of interventions, as well as early identification of disorders (Steele, 2004). On a regular basis, teachers can observe targeted outcomes or objectives using various types of recording formats (e.g. anecdotal records, checklists, rating scales) for observation (Barnett & Carey, 1992; Bredekamp & Copple, 2009).

Specific documentation and procedures should be used to monitor the progress of children with special needs. For example, IFSP and IEP require that specific goals, outcomes, and strategies for the target child should be documented. Specific data recording to monitor progress is particularly necessary when a child's progress is very slow, because informal observation alone cannot objectively evaluate the child's progress. Teachers can also utilize the Work Sampling System (WSS), an authentic and performance-based tool. WSS is designed for children from 2 to 12 years old and can be used in regular classroom settings. Through careful observation and documentation (e.g. developmental checklists, portfolio collections, and summary reports) three times per year, teachers can gain knowledge about whether progress is being made and whether intervention strategies should be changed or added (Meisels, Liaw, Dorfman, & Nelson, 1995). Parents' reports and interview data are also used to implement comprehensive interventions with children's challenging behaviors (e.g. Barnett et al., 1999; Bayat et al., 2010; Fox, Carta, Strain, Dunlap, & Hemmeter, 2009).

Suppose a teacher consistently observes that a child has difficulty in interacting with peers, exhibiting aggressive behaviors. The teacher would examine how frequently a child's aggressive behaviors occur each day for several days. Once the teacher establishes the baseline of a child's disruptive behaviors, intervention will begin while the teacher continues to monitor the frequency of the behaviors. At Tier I of RtI, the teacher would collect data through formal/informal tools, such as a behavioral checklist and/or anecdotal records, to measure the frequency of the child's aggressive behaviors during the entire day (e.g. free play, transition, outdoor play) with the collaborative team. Progress monitoring varies according to frequency, duration and intensity. The teacher can monitor children's challenging behaviors (e.g. hitting or biting) by counting the frequency of those behaviors over a specific time period. In each tier of RtI, interventions that may increase or decrease in intensity should be evaluated and a data-based decision should be made (e.g. Brown, Odom, & Buysee, 2002; Kratochwill & Shernoff, 2003; Tilly, Reschly, & Grimes, 1999). The teacher can also involve parents in monitoring the child's progress in order to determine whether any intervention strategies (e.g. responding consistently to the child's biting, providing anticipatory and multimodal cues to predict the next activity) work for the child at home. At Tier II, the teacher would follow similar progress monitoring to Tier I. Progress monitoring in each tier would continue in the child's classroom as well as at home (e.g. Bayat et al., 2010). Through this process, the teacher can confirm how interventions are working based on data collected and make informed decisions about further intervention. This process also provides teachers with information about the functional or causal relationships between an intervention and children's behavioral or/and academic outcomes (Barnett & Carey, 1992; Horner, Car, Gail, Odom, & Wolery, 2005). If the child fails to respond to intervention at Tier III, the child would be referred for diagnostic testing and evaluation.

In RtI, assessments are used to identify which children do not meet academic or behavioral progress at expected rates, to determine what specific tasks children can and cannot do, and to monitor their progress regarding intervention effectiveness (National Association of State Directors of Special Education [NASDSE], 2005). In particular, in Tier I, all children should be screened comprehensively within three months of beginning the program. If 80% of children do not meet academic objectives and behavioral benchmarks, classroom-wide intervention should be followed. In Tier II, teachers can expect that 15% of children have received additional instruction. Small percentages of children may not show sufficient progress even with the use of intensive individualized instruction (NASDSE, 2005).

Discussion and Final Recommendations

In preschool students, many challenging behaviors are typical for this age level. However, when children exhibit repetitive challenging or disruptive behaviors in the classroom that are rooted in behavioral and emotional disorders, teachers in early childhood education programs can effectively manage them if they have detailed information about children's symptoms of different disorders. Teachers can utilize specific strategies and recourses available to reduce problematic behavior, generally by providing consistent, predictable, and clear directions (e.g. clear transition cues) and arranging classroom environments to reduce challenging behaviors. By dividing new or difficult tasks into small steps, teachers can encourage children to complete their work.

Working closely with primary caregivers and/or family members has been an essential factor for the successful schooling of young children (Wardle, 2003) and has been strongly recommended for successful intervention of children with disorders (e.g. Dunst, 2000). In particular, considering that preschool children have a limited ability to present their feelings or experiences compared to older children, primary caregivers play an important role in determining whether special education services are warranted. By communicating with parents about a child's behavior, teachers can help the child receive appropriate professional evaluations, accommodations, and modifications suited for a child's unique needs. The reports of parents, including interviews with parents about a child's behavior, can be a very basic component for making a decision about intervention.

Parental involvement is also important in deciding how deeply parents should be involved in the process of intervention. At Tier III within RtI, parents may be more involved in the process of intervention, because individual targeting practices for the child may be required across both home and school. Researchers have reported that individualized parent and family intervention programs for children are very effective (e.g. Powell,

Dunlap, & Fox, 2006). Therefore, collaboration should occur between and among school personnel, including school staff teachers, to produce positive intervention outcomes with empirically derived contents at all process of interventions (Lentz, Allen, & Ehrhardt, 1996).

Today, the number of minority children from culturally and linguistically different backgrounds is increasing in early childhood education programs, necessitating carefully planned interventions reflecting children's social and cultural contexts. When examining the rates of referral and placement in special education, the literature shows that minority students are overrepresented in special education, meaning the proportion of minority students in special education is greater than that of the general student population (Zhang & Katsiyannis, 2002).

Overrepresentation, or even inappropriate placement, in special education poses many problems, such as the stigma of the label "special education" and a possible failure to benefit from the educational programming provided in special education. Early identification and intervention can have a significant impact on daily functioning and academic performance, thus preventing more negative outcomes later in a child's education. Though special education can provide educational benefits to a child, it also has the potential to prevent academic growth. Students receiving special education in restrictive environments often do not receive the benefits that a general education can provide, such as challenging academics and social opportunities (Patton, 1998).

For example, studies have shown that African American students have a higher referral rate for assessment and intervention and also experience a greater likelihood of a more restrictive learning environment, (De Valenzuela, Copeland, Huaquing Qi, & Park, 2006; Hosp & Reschly, 2003). Furthermore, African American students are labeled with mental retardation and emotional disturbance at higher rates than other ethnic and racial groups (Hosp & Reschly, 2003). Immigrant children from different backgrounds may be easily perceived as having behavior disorders such as AD/HD by school personnel and be referred to special education services due to different cultural expectations and beliefs about children's behaviors (e.g. McDermott & Varenne, 1996; Kim, 2011; Medina, Lozano, & Goudena, 2001). For example, Kim (2011) found that a Korean immigrant child was recommended for a diagnosis of AD/HD because he often moved around the classroom, was easily distracted, and did not seem to listen carefully to the teacher's direction. His behavior was actually found to be typical, but it was treated as problematic and was exacerbated by the language barrier. In the same vein, psychometric bias can also contribute to the disproportionate number of minority children in special education. Item biases on psychometric tests and language differences of diagnosis for disorders may also contribute to a child obtaining lower test scores on such tests. Children taking the test may not fully understand the directions or may be unfamiliar with the items from a cultural standpoint, which may contribute to lower test scores (Skiba et al., 2008). Thus, teachers need to be aware of culturally sensitive intervention strategies regarding each child's different social and cultural context.

Teachers in early childhood education programs are significant caregivers who strongly influence children throughout their childhood and even into adulthood in many ways. Therefore, teachers should assess appropriate educational opportunities, including interventions, and work collaboratively with other educational support personnel to prevent children from being inappropriately placed in special education services. This can be accomplished by using data-based decision-making and evidence-based practices based on knowledge of children's disorders and interventions. Sometimes, despite following such procedures and utilizing evidence-based practices, teachers may not able to see meaningful outcomes or progress. Behavior change is slow, and rarely absolute. Nevertheless, attention to the ongoing data analysis and objective information about children is important for teachers to be able to understand and support those children rather than simply labeling them as children with disorders or disabilities.

Note

1   For more Pyramid model resources, see the Center on the Social Emotional Foundations for Early Learning (www. vanderbilt.edu/csefel) and the Technical Assistance Center on Social Emotional Interventions for Young Children (www. challengingbehavior.org)

References

Alessandri, S. M. (1992). Attention, play, and social behavior in AD/HD preschoolers. *Journal of Abnormal Child Psychology, 20,* 289–302. doi:10.1007/BF00916693

Allen, K. E., & Cowdery, G. E. (2005). *The exceptional child: Inclusion in early childhood education*. Albany, NY: Thomson Delmar Learning.

American Psychiatric Association (2000). *Diagnostic and statistical manual of mental disorders* (4th ed., Text Revision). Washington, DC: Author.

August G. J., Braswell, L., & Thuras, P. (1998). Diagnostic stability of AD/HD in a community sample of school-aged children screened for disruptive behavior (attention deficit hyperactivity disorder). *Journal of Abnormal Child Psychology, 26,* 345–60. doi:10.1023/A:1021999722211

Bailey, D. B., Simeonsson, R. J., Winton, P. J., Huntington, G.S., Comfort, M., Isbell, P., ... Helm, J. M. (1986). Family-focused intervention: A functional model for planning, implementing, and evaluating individualized family services in early intervention. *Journal of the Division for Early Childhood, 10,* 156–71. doi:10.1177/105381518601000207

Barkley, R. A. (1998). Attention-deficit by hyperactivity disorder. *Scientific American,* 44–49.

Barnett, D. W., Bell, S. H., Gilkey, C. M. (1999). The promise of meaningful eligibility determination: Functional intervention-based multifactored preschool evaluation. *The Journal of Special Education, 33,* 112–24. doi:10.1177/002246699903300205

Barnett, D. W., & Carey, K. (1992). *Designing interventions for preschool learning and behavior problems.* San Francisco, CA: Jossey-Bass Publisher.

Barnett, D. W., Elliott, N., Wolsing, L., Bunger, C. E., Kaski, H., McKissick, C., & Vander Meer, C. D. (2006). Response to intervention for young children with extremely challenging behaviors: What it might look like. *School Psychology Review, 35,* 568–82.

Barnett, D. W., VanDerHeyden, A. M., & Witt, J. C. (2007). Achieving science-based practice through response to intervention: What it might look like in preschools. *Journal of Educational and Psychological Consultation, 17,* 31–54. doi:10.1080/10474410709336589

Bauer, D. H. (1976). An exploratory study of developmental changes in children's fears. *Journal of Child Psychology and Psychiatry, 17,* 69–74. doi:10.1111/j.1469-7610.1976.tb00375.x

Bayat, M., Mindes, G., & Covitt, S. (2010). What does RTI (Response to intervention) look like in preschool? *Early Childhood Education Journal, 37,* 493–500. doi:10.1007/s10643-010-0372-6

Beganto, S. J. (2006). Of helping and measuring for early childhood intervention: Reflections on issues and school psychology role. *School Psychology Review, 35,* 615–20.

Bilmes, J., & Welker, T. (2006). *Common psychological disorders in young children.* St. Paul, MN: Redleaf Press.

Bodrava, E., & Leong, D. (2007). *Tools of the mind: The Vygotskian approach to early childhood education* (2nd ed.). Upper Saddle River, NJ: Pearson/Merrill Prentice Hall.

Bredekamp, S. & Copple, C. (2009). *Developmentally appropriate practices in early childhood programs* (Rev. ed.). Washington, DC: National Association for the Education of Young Children.

Bronfrenbrenner, U. (1992). Ecological systems theory. In R. Vasta (ed.). *Six theories of child development: Revised formulations and current issues* (pp. 187–249). London: Jessica Kingsley Publishers.

Brown, W. H., Odom, S. L., & Buysse, V. (2002). Assessment of preschool children's peer related social competence. *Assessment for Effective Intervention, 27,* 61–71. doi:10.1177/073724770202700407

Campbell, S. B. (2002). *Behavior problems in preschool children: Clinical and developmental issues* (2nd ed.). New York, NY: The Guilford Press.

Clay, D. L. (2004). *Helping schoolchildren with chronic health conditions: A practical guide.* New York, NY: The Guildford Press.

Coleman, M. R., Buysse, V., & Neitzel, J. (2006). *Recognition and response: An early intervening system for young children at-risk for learning disabilities.*

Chapel Hill: The University of North Carolina at Chapel Hill, FPG Child Development Institute.

Coleman, M. R., Roth, F. P., & West, T. (2009). *Roadmap to Pre-K RTI: Applying response to intervention in preschool settings.* National Center for Learning Disabilities, Inc. Accessed July 7, from http://www.rtinetwork.org/images/stories/learn/roadmaptoprekrti.pdf.

Costello, E. J., Mustillo, S., Erkanli, A., Keeler, G., & Angold, A. (2003). Prevalence and development of psychiatric disorders in childhood and adolescence. *Archives of General Psychiatry, 60,* 837–44. doi:10.1001/archpsyc.60.8.837

Coy, K., Speltz, M., DeKlyen, M., & Jones, K. (2001). Social-cognitive processes in preschool boys with and without oppositional defiant disorder. *Journal of Abnormal Child Psychology, 29,* 107–19. doi:10.1023/A:1005279828676

De Valenzuela, J. S., Copeland, S. R., Huaqing, Qi, C., & Park, M. (2006). Examining the educational equity: Revisiting the disproportionate representation of minority students in special education. *Exceptional Children, 72,* 425–41.

Domitrovich, C. E., Gest, S. D., Gill, S., Bierman, K. L., Welsh, J. A., & Jones, D. (2008). Fostering high-quality teaching with an enriched curriculum and professional development support: The Head Start REDI program. *American Educational Research Journal, 46,* 567–97. doi:10.3102/0002831208328089

Dunst, C. J. (1985). Rethinking early intervention. *Analysis and Intervention in Developmental Disabilities, 5,* 165–201. doi:10.1016/S0270-4684(85)80012-4

—(2000). Revisiting "rethinking early intervention". *Topics in Early Childhood Special Education, 20,* 95–104. doi:10.1177/027112140002000205

DuPaul, G. J., McGoey, K. E., Eckert, T. L., & VanBrakle, J. (2001). Preschool children with Attention-Deficit/Hyperactivity Disorder. *Journal of the American Academy Child and Adolescent Psychiatry, 40,* 508–15. doi:10.1097/00004583-200105000-00009

Egger, H., & Angold, A. (2007). Common emotional and behavioral disorders in preschool children: Presentation, nosology, and epidemiology. *Journal of Child Psychology and Psychiatry, 47,* 313–37. doi:10.1111/j.1469-7610.2006.01618.x

Forness, S. R., & Knitzer, J. (1992). A new proposed definition and terminology to replace 'serious emotional disturbance' in Individuals with Disabilities Education Act. *School Psychology Review, 21,* 12–21.

Fox, L., Carta, J., Strain, P., Dunlap, G., & Hemmeter, M.L. (2010). Response to intervention and the Pyramid model. *Infants & Young Children, 23,* 3–13. doi:10.1097/IYC.0b013e3181c816e2

Fox, L., Dunlap, G., Hemmeter, M. L., Joseph, G., & Strain, P. (2003). The Teaching Pyramid: A model for supporting social competence and preventing challenging behavior in young children. *Young Children, 58,* 48–53. Accessed from http://sesa.org/2010/05/the-teaching-pyramid/

Fox, L., & Lentini, R. H. (2006). "You got it!" Teaching social and emotional skills. *Young Children, 61,* 36–42.

Gadow, K. D., Sprafkin, J., & Nolan, E. E. (2001). DSM-IV symptoms in community and clinic preschool children. *Journal of the American*

Academy of Child and Adolescent Psychiatry, 40, 1383–92. doi:10.1097/00004583-200112000-00008

Gilliam, W. S. (2005). *Prekindergarteners left behind: Expulsion rates in state prekindergarten systems.* (Unpublished doctoral dissertation, Yale University). Accessed from http://www.challengingbehavior.org/explore/policy_docs/prek_expulsion.pdf.

Greenwood, C. R., Bradfield, T., Kaminski, R., Linas, M., Carta, J. J., & Nylander, D. (2011). The response to intervention (RtI) approach in early childhood. *Focus on Exceptional Children, 43*, 1–24. Accessed from http://www.crtiec.org/aboutcrtiec/documents/FOEC-V43-9-May-v5.pdf

Hawken, L. S., Vincent, C. G., & Schumann, J. (2008). Response to intervention for social behavior. *Journal of Emotional and Behavioral Disorders, 16*, 213–25. doi:10.1177/1063426608316018

Hinshaw, S. P. (1992). Academic underachievement, attention deficits, and aggression: Comorbidity and implications for intervention. *Journal of Consulting and Clinical Psychology, 60*, 893–903. doi:10.1037/0022-006X.60.6.893

Horner, R. Car, E., Gail, M., Odom, J., & Wolery, M. (2005). The use of single-subject research to identify evidence-based practice in special education. *Exceptional Children, 71*, 165–79.

Hosp, J. L., & Reschly, D. J. (2003). Referral rates for intervention or assessment: A meta-analysis of racial differences. *The Journal of Special Education, 37*, 67–80. doi:10.1177/00224669030370020201

Hughes, T. L., Crothers, L. M., & Jimerson, S. R. (2007). *Assessing, identifying, and treating conduct disorder at school.* New York, NY: Springer.

Individuals with Disabilities Education Improvement Act of 2004, P.L. 108–446, 20 USC. § *1400 et seq.*

Jenkins, J., Simpson, A., Dunn, J., Rasbash, J., & O'Connor, T. (2005). Mutual influence of marital conflict and children's behavior problems: Shared and nonshared family risks. *Child Development, 76*, 24–39. doi:10.1111/j.1467-8624.2005.00827.x

Johnson, E. J., Christie, J. F., & Wardle, F. (2005). *Play, development, and early education.* Boston, MA: Pearson.

Jung, L. A. (2007). Writing individualized family service plan: Strategies that fit into the routine. *Young Exceptional Children, 10*, 2–9. doi:10.1177/109625060701000301

Katz, L., & McClellan, D. (2005). *Fostering social competence: The teacher's role.* Washington, DC: National Association for the Education of Young Children.

Kessler, R. C., Chiu, W. T., Demler, O., & Walters, E. E. (2005). Prevalence, severity, and comorbidity of 12-month DSM-IV disorders in the national comorbidity survey replication. *Archives of General Psychiatry, 62*, 617–27. Accessed from http://psychopathology.fiu.edu/Articles/Kessler%20et%20al_2005.pdf

Kim, J. (2011). Korean immigrant mothers' perspectives: The meanings of a Korean heritage language school for their children's American early schooling experiences. *Early Childhood Education Journal. 39*, 133–41. doi:10.1007/s10643-011-0453-1

Klein, D., Cook, R., & Richardson-Gibbs, A. (2001). *Strategies for including children with special needs in early childhood settings.* Albany, NY: Delmar.

Klin, A., Jones, W., Schultz, R., Volkmar, F., & Cohen, D. (2002). Visual fixation patterns during viewing of naturalistic social situations as predictors of social competence in individuals with Autism. *Archives of General Psychiatry, 59,* 809–16. doi:10.1001/archpsyc.59.9.809

Kratochwill, T. R., & Shernoff, E. S. (2003). Evidence based practice: Promoting evidence-based interventions in school psychology. *School Psychology Quarterly, 18,* 389–408. doi:10.1521/scpq.18.4.389.27000

Landry, S. H., Smith, K. E., Swank, P. R., & Miller-Loncar, C. L. (2000). Early maternal and child influences on children's late independent cognitive and social functioning. *Child Development, 71,* 358–75. doi:10.1111/1467-8624.00150

Lavigne, J. V., Arend, R., Rosenbaum, D., et al., (1998). Psychiatric disorders with onset in the preschool years: I. Stability of diagnosis. *Journal of the American Academy of Child and Adolescent Psychiatry, 37,* 1246–54. doi:10.1097/00004583-199812000-00007

Lavigne, J. V., LeBailly, S. A., Hopkins, J., Gouze, K. R., & Binns, H. J. (2009). The prevalence of AD/HD, ODD, depression and anxiety in a community sample of 4-year-olds. *Journal of Clinical Child and Adolescent Psychology, 38,* 315–28. doi:10.1080/15374410902851382

Lentz, F. R., Allen, S. J., & Ehrhardt, K. E. (1996). The conceptual elements of strong interventions in school settings. *School Psychology Quarterly, 11,* 118–36. doi:10.1037/h0088924

Luby, J. L. (2006). *Handbook of preschool mental health: Development, disorders, and treatment.* New York, NY: The Guilford Press.

Lyman, R., & Hembree-Kigin, T. (1994). *Mental health interventions with preschool children.* New York, NY: Plenum.

Mastropieri, M., Jenkins, V., & Scruggs, T. (1985). Academic and intellectual characteristics of behavior disordered children and youth. In R. B. Rutherford, Jr. (ed.), *Severe behavior disorders of children and youth* (pp. 86–104). Reston, VA: Council for Children with Behavior Disorders.

Maurer, A. (1965). What children fear. *Journal of Genetic Psychology, 106,* 265–77.

McDermott, R., & Varenne, H. (1996). Culture, development, disability. In R. Jessor, A. Colby, & R. A. Shweder (eds), *Ethnography and human development: Context and meaning in social inquiry* (pp. 101–26). Chicago, IL: The University of Chicago Press.

Medina, J. S., Lozano, V. M., & Goudena, P. P. (2001). Conflict management in pre-schoolers: A cross-cultural perspective. *International Journal of Early Years Education, 9,* 153–60. doi:10.1080/09669760125528

Meisels, S. J., Liaw, F., Dorfman, A., & Nelson, R. F. (1995). The work sampling system: Reliability and validity of performance assessment for young children. *Early Childhood Research Quarterly, 10,* 277–96. doi:10.1016/0885-2006(95)90008-XMerrell, K. W., Ervin, R. A., & Gimpel, G. A. (2006). School psychology for the 21st century. New York, NY: The Guilford Press.

National Association of State Directors of Special Education (2005). *Response* to intervention: Policy considerations and implementations. Alexandria, VA: Author.

Nicholas, J. S., Carpenter, L. A., King, L. B., Jenner, W., & Charles, J. M. (2009). Autism spectrum disorders in preschool-aged children: Prevalence and comparison to a school-aged population. *Annals of Epidemiology, 19*, 808–14. doi:10.1016/j.annepidem.2009.04.005

Parcel, T. L., & Menaghan, E. G. (1993). Family social capital and children's behavior problems. *Social Psychology Quarterly, 56*, 120–35. Accessed from http://www.jstor.org/stable/2787001

Patterson, G. R., Capaldi, D., & Bank, L. (1991). An early starter model for predicting delinquency. In D. J. Pepler & K. H. Rubin (eds), *The development and treatment of childhood aggression* (pp. 139–68). Hillsdale, NJ: Erlbaum.

Patton, J. M. (1998). The disproportionate representation of African Americans in special education. *The Journal of Special Education, 32*, 25–31. doi:10.1177/002246699803200104

Perrez, M., & Reicherts, M. (1992). *Stress, coping, and health*. Seattle, WA: Hogrefe & Huber.

Powell, D., Dunlap, G., & Fox, L. (2006). Prevention and intervention for the challenging behaviors of toddlers and preschoolers. *Infants and Young Children, 19*, 25–35. doi:10.1097/00001163-200601000-00004

Ramey, C. T., & Ramey, S. L. (1998). Early intervention and early experience. *American Psychologist, 53*, 109–20. doi:10.1037/0003-066X.53.2.109

Raver, C. C., & Knitze, J. (2002). *Promoting the emotional well-being of children and families: Ready to enter: What research tells policymakers about strategies to promote social and emotional school readiness among three- and four-year-old children*. Policy Paper #3. Columbia University, New York: National Center for Children in Poverty.

Rey, J. M. (1993). Oppositional defiant disorder. *American Journal of Psychiatry, 150*, 1769–78.

Schneider, M., & Robin, A. L. (1978). *Manual for the turtle technique*. Unpublished manual, Department of Psychology, State University of New York at Stony Brook.

Shevell, M., Majnemer, A., Platt, R. W., Webster, R., & Birnbaum, R. (2005). Developmental and functional outcomes at school age of preschool children with global developmental delay. *Journal of Child Neurology, 20*, 648–54. doi:10.1177/08830738050200080301

Siegler, R. S., DeLoache, J. S., & Eisenberg, N. (2003). *How children develop*. New York, NY: Worth Publishers.

Skiba, R. J., Simmons, A. B., Ritter, S., Gibb, A. C., Rausch, M. K., Cuadrado, J., & Chung, C. (2008). Achieving equity in special education: History, status, and current challenges. *Exceptional Children, 74*, 264–88. Accessed from http://www.tdsb.on.ca/wwwdocuments/programs/Equity_in_Education/docs/Achieving%20Equity%20in%20Special%20Education%20History,%20Status,%20and%20Current%20Challanges.pdf

Sontag, J. C. (1996). Toward a comprehensive theoretical framework for disability research: Bronfenbrenner revisited. *The Journal of Special Education, 30*, 319–44. doi:10.1177/002246699603000306

Spence, S. H., Rapee, R., McDonald, C., & Ingram, M. (2001). The structure of anxiety symptoms among preschoolers. *Behaviour Research and Therapy, 39,* 1293–316. doi:10.1016/S0005-7967(00)00098-X

Steele, M. (2004). Making the case for early identification and intervention for young children at risk for learning disabilities. *Early Childhood Education Journal, 32,* 75–9. doi:10.1007/s10643-004-1072-x

Tilly, W. D. III, Reschly, D. J., & Grimes, J. (1999). Disability determination in problem solving systems: Conceptual foundations and critical components. In D. J. Reschly, W. D. Tilly, & J. P. Grimes (eds), *Special education in transition: Functional assessment and noncategorical programming* (pp. 221–51). Longman, CO: Sopris West.

US Department of Education (2003). Executive summary -- Twenty-fifth annual report to congress on the implementation of the individuals with disabilities education act. Accessed from http://www2.ed.gov/about/reports/annual/osep/2003/index.html

Volkmar, F. R., Lord, C., Bailey, A., Schultz, R. T., & Klin, A. (2004). Autism and pervasive developmental disorders. *Journal of Child Psychology and Psychiatry, 45,* 135–70. doi:10.1046/j.0021-9630.2003.00317.x

Wardle, F. (2003). *Introduction to early childhood education: A multi-dimensional approach to child-centered care and learning.* Boston, MA: Allyn and Bacon.

Webster-Stratton, C. (1993). Strategies for helping families with young oppositional defiant or conduct-disordered children: The importance of home and school collaboration. *School Psychology Review, 22,* 437–57.

—(1997). Early intervention for families of preschool children with conduct problems. In M. J. Gurlanick (ed.), The effectiveness of early intervention (pp. 429–53). Baltimore, MD: Boorks.

Weis, R. (2008). *Introduction to abnormal child and adolescent psychology.* Thousand Oaks, CA: Sage.

Weyandt, L. L. (2005). Executive function in children, adolescents, and adults with attention deficit hyperactivity disorder: Introduction to the special issue. *Developmental Neuropsychology, 27,* 1–10. doi:10.1207/s15326942dn2701_1

Zhang, D. & Katsiyannis, A. (2002). Minority representation in special education: A persistent challenge. *Remedial and Special Education, 23,* 180–7. doi:10.1177/07419325020230030601

CHAPTER THIRTEEN

Understanding and Managing Behaviors of Children Involved with Relational and Social Aggression (RA/SA)

Julaine E. Field

University of Colorado at Colorado Springs

Abstract

This chapter examines relational and social aggression among school-age students. The definition of relational aggression is discussed, including how this unique form of bullying differs from physical or overt acts of bullying behavior. Relationally-aggressive behaviors appear in children as young as preschool; however, as students' cognitive, language, and social skills become more sophisticated, so too do the covert relationally-aggressive strategies to exercise power and influence over members of one's peer group. A developmental overview of relational aggression is provided as well as a focused discussion on social informational processing, which is often skewed by children or adolescents who use relational aggression. Finally, specific educator intervention strategies are discussed and align with the Response to Intervention (RtI) model (i.e. universal, prevention, and remediation approaches).

Introduction

Bullying is a destructive force in any school environment. In a US national study comprised of over 15,000 students in grades 6 to 10, 8.4% of students reported that they were bullied at least once a week or more while at school (Nansel et al., 2001). Other estimates of school-based bullying range from 30% to 80% of students reporting that they have personally experienced bullying at school and 10% to 15% indicating being chronic victims of peer abuse (Card & Hodges, 2008). Research (e.g. Gendron, Williams, & Guerra, 2011) over the last two decades has clearly demonstrated that all forms of bullying interfere with student learning and compromise the physical, psychological, and/or emotional safety of K-12 students. Yet, not all bullying behavior is physical, overt, or typically aggressive.

Relational aggression is a form of bullying that involves specific behaviors that harm peer relationships, social status, or a student's sense of belonging or connection to a group of peers or peers in general. It is an interpersonal problem that exists within the context of relationships and involves a misuse of personal and/or social power to dominate others (Pepler et al., 2006). Relational aggression involves the use of rumors, gossip, "the silent treatment," or other interpersonal practices that lead to social isolation. Rather than physical dominance or the threat of physical force, students who use relationally-aggressive strategies exercise relational and social dominance to damage a peer's social status or reputation.

Being liked, valued, and connected with peers is a major contributor to psychological stability for many K–12 students and takes on increasing importance as students move toward middle and high school. When friendships or one's social status is in jeopardy, students are often distracted and lack academic focus until the social rupture is repaired or at least stabilized. This is particularly true for school-age girls, who report more emotional intimacy with friends as well as more psychological distress when involved in incidents involving relational aggression.

Students who are repeatedly subjected to relational aggression by their peers may begin to experience somatic symptoms, an increased chance of illness (Fekkes, Pijpers, Fredriks, Vogels, & Verloove-Vanhorick, 2006), avoid school, retaliate through physical means, experience increasing levels of anxiety and depression, and may even become suicidal (Kumpulainen et al., 1998). Unfortunately, the covert, social nature of this particular type of bullying causes many teachers to identify it as a "student-owned" problem versus a "teacher-owned" (Walker, 2010) problem that requires intervention on the part of the teacher. Teachers often do not witness relational aggression due to the "invisibility" of the behaviors and may minimize them even if they are observed because of their relationship to friendship or social dynamics. At the same time, the school environment is where these behaviors are likely to occur and create disruption. Walker (2010) writes, "School settings provide one of the very best settings available for addressing this phenomenon that is causing increasing concern, and even alarm, among parents, school staff, legislators, policy makers, and mental health professionals" (p. 594).

Defining Relational Aggression

Indirect aggression (similar to relational and social aggression) was first mentioned in the bullying literature by Feshbach in 1969 to identify and name covert aggressive behaviors that are used by students to manipulate their peers. Lagerspetz, Björkqvist, and Peltonen (1988) found that indirect aggression allowed the perpetrators to be anonymous due to the covert nature of the behaviors (e.g. it is highly unlikely that a teacher will observe a student initiating a rumor). Indirect aggression is now commonly called relational or social aggression and many researchers use the term "relational aggression" to capture all behaviors, whether over or covert, that involve the social manipulation of peers to damage a person's social standing or reputation.

Researchers such as Crick and Grotpeter (1995), Crick (1996), Crick and Grotpeter (1996), Crick et al. (1999), and Coyne, Archer, and Eslea (2006) have explored the various behavioral subsets associated with covert aggression in hopes of arriving at a well-established research construct (or constructs) for the purposes of describing, measuring, and educating important stakeholders regarding this form of bullying. Researchers continue to hold different views in defining relational aggression and in determining whether it encompasses a different set of behaviors than social aggression and indirect aggression.

For example, the term, social aggression (Underwood, Galen, & Paquette, 2001) is often used to describe ganging up behaviors in which a group of students use psychological and emotional abuse (e.g. name-calling, shunning, spreading rumors), and sometimes physical or overt behaviors (e.g. tripping someone, shoving someone into a locker) to target an individual victim. Typically, there is a peer leader who initiates the attacks and other students will follow and participate in the aggression. Wiseman's (2002) "Queen Bee" metaphor exemplifies this practice.

Archer and Coyne (2005) attempted to clarify if relational and social aggression is the same phenomenon, or if the two terms actually describe separate sets of behaviors. Currently, many researchers use the term, relational aggression, to describe all indirect bullying behaviors (e.g. Leff et al., 2010; Mathieson & Crick, 2010). Because this book is designed to assist classroom teachers in managing disruptive behaviors and behaviors that are symptomatic of childhood disorders, relational and social aggression will be briefly discussed separately, as both sets of behaviors are clearly visible in any school setting, the intent of the aggression may differ, and intentional use of specific intervention strategies to target these types of bullying is recommended.

Relational aggression and social aggression may involve covert or overt (usually verbal) behaviors which cause peer victimization. These behaviors are often described as part of the "normal socialization process" of school-age students, adults are often unaware that both forms of bullying are occurring, and both relational and social aggression capitalize on students' emotional vulnerability related to peer acceptance and approval. Whether relational or social aggression, the associated behaviors are not easily detected by adults because they are not traditional bullying behaviors (i.e. physical bullying) and both target social connections, friendships, or students' need for peer approval, acceptance, and belonging.

Relational aggression can be differentiated from social aggression because the intent is to harm a specific student's friendships or feelings of belonging in a particular peer group (Crick & Grotpeter, 1995). Additionally, relational aggression typically occurs between students who previously identified as friends, experience a conflict, and then use specific social isolation strategies (e.g. gossip, "the silent treatment") to demonstrate their anger or seek revenge for a perceived friendship slight or conflict. Relational aggression may include ignoring, socially isolating, spreading rumors, pretending to like a friend and then engaging in backstabbing discussion with others, and lying to the target/victim about one's true feelings. Much of these behaviors are easily linked with passive-aggressive approaches to demonstrating anger or frustration toward a friend.

Social aggression, which is often associated or used concurrently with relational aggression, is defined as behaviors that seek to compromise a student's social standing or popularity through attacking the student's social status among a group of peers. Social aggression typically involves at least one perpetrator, who often has a network of peers to help spread negative rumors, engage in social shunning or isolation, and participate in negative "group think" and behaviors toward the identified target/victim. Social aggression is considered to be successful when the victim becomes disconnected from peers or is socially alone and when others attribute various negative characteristics to the target/victim.

Cyberbullying is aggression that is perpetrated through cellphones, text messages, social networking sites, blogs, and online videos (e.g. *You Tube*). Cyberbullying may be used in relational or social aggression to insult, mock, or spread rumors about a target or victim. Unfortunately, cyberbullying allows the audience of the bullying incidents to be extremely large, which serves to humiliate and further intimidate a victim. In conclusion, the author recognizes that relational and social aggression and cyberbullying often overlap or are used simultaneously. For simplicity and to maintain continuity with current research studies, the author will refer to relational aggression throughout this chapter, as this is the most researched and stable construct to describe this form of aggression (see Crick & Grotpeter, 1995; Crick, 1996; Crick & Grotpeter, 1996; Crick et al., 1999; Crick et al., 2006; Mathieson & Crick, 2010).

Impact of Relational Aggression on Students and Schools

Many school administrators, teachers, and parents are beginning to appreciate the impact of relational aggression on the school culture as well as the short and long term consequences for both victims and perpetrators. Maintaining a safe, positive school climate is essential for students to maximize their learning potential; yet, many schools may promulgate a culture of bullying if administrators or teachers turn a blind eye to students who use relational and social aggression to wield power over their peers or are simply unaware of what to look for or how to intervene when they witness the behaviors. Additionally, administrators and teachers who engage in relational aggression themselves further contribute to a contentious school culture. Goldstein, Young, and Boyd (2008) conducted a study with 1,335 African American and European American students (52% female and 49% African American) in grades 7–12. They found that students who were exposed to numerous incidents of relational aggression reported feeling less safe at school and less satisfaction overall with the school environment. Boxer, Edward-Leeper, Goldstein, Musher-Eizenman, and Dubow (2003) noted that when relational aggression was included in school climate/school safety assessments, the presence of widespread relational aggression was specifically linked to a negative psychological and social environment at school.

Students who are victims of relational aggression at school have been found to have a reduction in class participation (Buhs, Ladd, & Herald, 2006), a decline in academic focus or concentration, decrease in school affiliation, and a poor sense of belonging at school (Hill & Werner, 2006). Moreover, such students often will engage in school avoidance to eliminate the possibility of being victimized at school (Buhs et al., 2006). After an incident of relational aggression, victims often immediately feel anxiety, frustration and/or anger, alienation, confusion, and disconnected from others. Students who respond with anxiety may also use a great deal of energy to investigate what has occurred with their peers and attempt to make amends. Additionally, students who were victimized may then engage in reactive relation aggression due to feeling wronged by what has occurred (Mathieson & Crick, 2010). Some males who are the targets of relational aggression may escalate their response and physically fight to get revenge. Of course, both males and females may choose to use relational aggression or physical aggression in the form of bullying in response to being targeted.

In the last ten years, numerous studies have discovered the long-term consequences for both victims and perpetrators of relational aggression. Victims of relational aggression often experience long term peer rejection, peer avoidance, loneliness and isolation, a decrease in self-esteem, increased distress (Craig, 1998; Crick & Grotpeter, 1996), increased conflict with peers, depression and anxiety (Prinstein, Boergers, & Vernberg, 2001). Perpetrators of relational aggression are also vulnerable to long term consequences. This includes social isolation (Crick & Grotpeter, 1995), rejection from peers, increased conflict at school, decreased self-reported life satisfaction, fewer close relationships, maladaptive problem solving and conflict resolution skills, difficulty regulating emotion (e.g. abuse substances, see: Sullivan, Farrell, & Kliewer, 2006), difficulty managing competition among peers, and depression (Loukas, Paulos, & Robinson, 2005).

Interestingly, there are mixed findings when examining the social skills and social status of perpetrators of relational aggression. Some studies report limited social skills of perpetrators while others discuss sophisticated social skills that assist with peer manipulation and remaining undetected by adults while bullying others (e.g. Puckett, Aikins, & Cillessen, 2008; Shoulberg, Sijtsema, & Murray-Close, 2011). Still other studies show decreased popularity among peers for aggressors (Olweus, 1993), while several investigations suggest that relationally-aggressive youth may be quite popular with their peers due to an elevated social status and the capacity for "ruling peers" through fear of victimization (Pellegrini, Bartini, & Brooks, 1999); however, these social strategies contribute to greater maladjustment after high school (e.g. Sandstrom & Cillessen, 2010).

Development of Relational Aggression

Studies over the last twenty years have examined relational aggression among pre-school to college students in order to analyze the nature of these behaviors at particular stages of development. Björkqvist, Osterman, and Kaukiainen (1992) proposed a developmental theory, which states that as children develop cognitive, language, and social skills, their aggressive behaviors can become increasingly more covert and psychological versus overt and physical.

Relationally-aggressive behaviors can be used and detected during preschool. Crick et al. (2006) studied the development of relationally-aggressive behaviors among ninety-one pre-school age children over the course of eighteen months. This study found that due to sexually segregated play, female preschool students as young as 2 1/2 years of age were more relationally aggressive with their female peers, while male preschool children were more physically aggressive with their male peers. Relational aggression among preschool children often includes overt verbal exclamations (e.g. *I don't like you. I won't play with you anymore*), as children this young are egocentric and have not mastered social subtleties or clandestine strategies to manage their social circumstances. Crick et al. (2006) also found that "relationally aggressive behavior patterns may begin to crystallize at relatively young ages for girls" (p. 264) and those relationally-aggressive actions were more likely to be repeated by female preschool children than males over the eighteen month period.

Several researchers have studied relational aggression among elementary age children. During this time, students will increase the sophistication of their social skills, which also equates to a greater possibility of covert, manipulative behaviors to manage peer conflict, peer competition, and to increase the social power that is demonstrated with peers. Mandates for stereotypical behaviors by gender require that girls identify social strategies to deal with disagreements or quarrels in ways that are within the confines of being a "good girl." Male students may also resort to relational aggression while in conflict with a female student (i.e. physical aggression demonstrated toward a girl is taboo) or while in a social setting that maintains severe consequences for physical fighting.

Numerous studies have assessed various aspects of relational aggression among elementary age children. Underwood (2003) found that relational aggression is a normative or typical form of aggression by middle childhood. The enhanced cognitive and language skills and social intelligence of this developmental period allow students to engage in more covert forms of aggression and social manipulation.

Relational aggression is so common among this age group that Mathieson and Crick (2010) propose two different forms of relational aggression to understand how these behaviors are used and why they are demonstrated. Proactive (also referred to as *instrumental*; see Walker, 2010) relational aggression refers to behaviors that are meant to instigate aggression, manipulate relationships, and damage another student's social standing (Mathieson & Crick, 2010). Students demonstrating proactive relational aggression may initiate a period of social unrest among peers by targeting an individual student. In the case of social aggression (as discussed earlier in this chapter), several students may become involved as fellow perpetrators, active participants who serve as "go-betweens" between the victim and perpetrator, etc.

Reactive relational aggression involves a response to proactive relational aggression that may include becoming socially manipulative to "right a wrong" or retaliate (Mathieson & Crick, 2010). Depending upon the social standing of the student who perpetrates reactive relational aggression, their attempts to aggress may or may not be effective in stopping the perpetrator or securing the support of their peers. Finally, Mathieson and Crick (2010) found that students who demonstrate reactive relational aggression tend to be students who internalize social problems and conflict, while students who engage in proactive relational aggression tend to be externalizing, more socially callous and unemotional toward victims. Interestingly, the authors also note that students who use proactive relational aggression are more likely to exhibit antisocial traits, are socially skilled, and are able to use these skills to bring about their social goals. Therefore, because they are socially savvy, such children can demonstrate proactive relational aggression and prosocial skills simultaneously.

Sex differences and the use of relational aggression is a popular research topic with many researchers (e.g. Crick & Grotpeter, 1995; Kistener et al., 2010). Several researchers (e.g. Crick & Grotpeter, 1995; Hayward & Fletcher, 2003; Owens, Shute, & Slee, 2000) have found that girls are more likely to be relationally aggressive than boys; girls rate the use of relational aggression more favorably than boys (Crick & Werner, 1998), and yet girls are more likely to view relational aggression and verbal aggression as more harmful to themselves than boys (Coyne, Archer, & Eslea, 2006).

Subsequent studies, however, have not found a significant difference between males' and females' use of relational aggression (see Archer, 2004). Kistner et al. (2010) studied developmental differences between boys and girls and their use of physical and relational aggression. These researchers found that between 3rd and 5th grade, girls increased their use of physical and relational aggression and boys did not. Kistener et al. (2010) also found that relational aggression increased in 4th and 5th grade girls and lessened among 4th and 5th grade boys. However, it is important that school personnel avoid applying gender based stereotypes when monitoring for bullying or relational aggression among students to avoid attribution bias or the failure to identify aggressive acts because of the gender of the child exhibiting them.

Although relational aggression is most frequently associated with middle school age children, high school and college students may also demonstrate relational aggression. Crothers, Field, and Kolbert (2005) conducted a qualitative study with fifty-two 9th and 10th grade students to explore their use of relational aggression. The participants were diverse (69.2% White, 13.5% Multiracial, 11.5% African American, 3.8%, Latina and 1.9% Native American) and each responded to semi-structured prompts related to relational aggression. The study found that the participants "identified four primary motivations for the relational aggression described in the scenario: jealousy/envy, fun/entertainment, social status, and deflection" (p. 352). The results of this study help to shed light on why high school students may be motivated to continue these social strategies despite the assumed increase in psychological maturity.

Belonging to a particular peer group may also influence why high school students engage in relational aggression. Pokhrel, Sussman, Black, and Sun (2010) found that high school students who identify with high risk peer groups tend to use more relational aggression, while students who identify with elite or popular groups tend to use more relational aggression over time than other students. Finally, many high school students are involved in dating or romantic relationships. As a result, jealousy, desires to control one's romantic partner, and emotional volatility are often characteristics associated with learning how to negotiate romantic boundaries and the intense feelings associated with adolescents' emerging sexuality. Relational aggression may be present among adolescents who are competing with others to secure particular romantic partners. For example, questioning an adolescent male or female's sexuality through rumors and gossip is one way of attempting to attack a peer's social standing or status—thus reducing the likelihood that this peer will be a romantic competitor. Field, Kolbert, Crothers, and Hughes (2009) write that for female adolescents, "Appearing kind and amiable while strategically cutting off or shunning a woman from a group allows a female to maneuver socially among the possible mates and among her competition" (p. 15).

Across age groups, social information processing is also associated with a student's use of relational aggression (e.g. Crick & Grotpeter, 1995). SIP refers to cognitive skills related to "reading" a social situation accurately or interpreting social cues in ways that most children or adolescents would interpret them. Students who use relational aggression tend to assign hostile intent to peers in indistinct relational situations. Rather than remaining open to learning about what is happening in a particular social situation, quick judgments or interpretations may be made and students may act on this negative interpretation by becoming relationally aggressive with their peers. Further, students who have deficits in SIP are more likely to believe that aggressive solutions are favorable (Crick & Werner, 1998). When guiding students through the specific cognitive steps of SIP, a teacher may help students with: a) encoding environmental cues, b) interpreting those cues, c) selecting social goals based on interpretation, d) generating alternative responses and the consequences associated with those responses and, e) making decisions to enact a behavioral response.

Relational Aggression in the Classroom and Response to Intervention

While many teachers in the US will report that their main professional objective is to facilitate student learning and academic achievement, educational professionals also recognize that the social dynamics within the classroom either contribute to or distract from a positive learning environment. Academic instruction and a student's capacity to focus, concentrate, and retain information can be derailed when that same student is actively under attack by perpetrators before, during, or after class (Greenberg et al., 2003).

Allen (2010) writes, "The relationships of students to one another and the teacher within classrooms are reciprocal and interconnected. In other words, the actions of all members of the classroom affect the behaviors of everyone in that environment, creating a dynamic context and culture" (p. 2). Thus, in order to foster an educational environment that is conducive to learning, teachers must be aware of relational aggression among students, understand who the participants are in such conflicts, and know sound practices for intervention to benefit the victims, the perpetrators, and the classroom environment, overall.

The Response to Intervention model (RtI) is a preventative science framework for the early prevention and identification of learning and behavioral problems for students having difficulty in school. Using RtI, students are exposed to increasing levels of evidence-based practices to avoid placement in special education or unnecessary consequences in school (e.g. expulsion; National Research Council and the Institute of Medicine, 2009). Students who do not make adequate progress from such evidence-based practices are often thought to have an intrinsic disorder which prevents them from benefitting from the strategic implementation of these practices.

Tier I

According to the RtI model, tier one or universal responses to relational aggression include preventative programming. Effective classroom management is the single most important variable in whether or not relational aggression or other bullying behaviors are present in any given class. Roland and Galloway (2002) found a significant relationship between classroom management, the social structure of a class, and bullying behavior. Teachers with effective classroom management strategies positively influenced the social structure of a class and reduced the likelihood of relationally aggressive behaviors. Interestingly, this research also accounted for family background and family dynamics, which did not have a direct or indirect impact on whether or not a student exhibited bullying behavior.

Fonagy et al. (2009) found that teacher implemented anti-bullying programming, which includes curricular opportunities to develop perspective taking abilities among students, was effective in reducing the number of bullying incidents and the number of students identified as bullies in the participating schools. These findings may be partially explained by students' daily involvement with classroom teachers as well as the influence of classroom teachers in creating a more positive school climate. Gendron, Williams, and Guerra (2011) found that students with high self-esteem, but immersed in a negative school climate, were more likely to perpetrate bullying (including relational aggression), while students with a high self-esteem, immersed in a positive school climate, were less likely to engage in bullying behaviors.

Effective classroom management and the creation of a positive classroom climate require that teachers closely monitor the social dynamics of their students. This includes understanding relational aggression and the associated behaviors. Novick and Isaacs (2010) recommend that teachers have specific training about the different types of bullying (e.g. relational aggression). When teachers recognize all forms of bullying, they are more likely to intervene. Allen (2010) states "that it seems very possible for teachers who appear to have perfectly behaved classes to provide havens for bullies that shelter them against detection. This speaks to the savvy ability of some bullies to manipulate the classroom environments of well meaning, yet unsuspecting teachers and to hide behind facades of innocence" (p. 6). Teachers must acknowledge that relational aggression can be invisible to a teacher, that the students are aware that it is occurring, and that these covert behaviors undermine the emotional and psychological safety of students and distract from their ability to concentrate and learn.

Specific Tier I strategies may include teachers talking about classroom rules and clear expectations for behavior with peers, discussing the school's anti-bullying policy with students and reinforcing cooperation, empathy, and perspective taking among students. Structured pair work and group work are academic strategies which may enhance cooperation among students and reduce strict social hierarchies (i.e. social dominance associated with increased levels of relational aggression) among students. The teacher may emphasize what empathy and perspective taking are and how each is demonstrated when these topics emerge in English, social studies, and health related classes. Teachers intervening at the primary level of RtI may also want to invite a professional school counselor, school psychologist, or school social worker to conduct classroom guidance lessons to reinforce effective social skills, problem solving, and conflict management for all students. Also, teachers who model these social behaviors or interpersonal skills themselves increase the likelihood that students will follow their example.

Mishna, Wiener, and Pepler (2008) found that most of their research participants did not tell their teachers when they were being bullied by a friend (i.e. relational aggression). Participants in Fekkes et al. (2005) reported that they infrequently report bullying incidents to their teachers and are more likely to inform their parents when bullying has taken place at school. Therefore, teachers may need to directly inquire about relational aggression when they notice changes in students that may be a result of peer victimization. For example, if teachers notice a change in a student's mood, body language, social engagement, or participation in class, teachers should inquire with the students about these changes in a compassionate, yet subtle, private manner.

Additionally, if the teacher overhears students being particularly negative about another student, the teacher should intervene, and ask questions in order to understand the social climate of their respective classroom. Demonstrating care and an interest in understanding the target/victim may permit the student to disclose relational aggression. Students who take the risk of disclosing relationally-aggressive incidents to their teacher may or may not invite teacher intervention. Many students desire intervention from school staff to assist with bullying (Frisén & Holmqvist, 2010); however, teachers must cautiously proceed to avoid re-victimizing the student or managing the social dynamics of the classroom without exacerbating the problem.

Tier II

Tier II interventions at the system or classroom level involve specific interventions to curb relational aggression and other bullying behaviors. When relational aggression occurs in the classroom or when teachers suspect that it has occurred, he or she can choose to indirectly or directly address the class as a whole prior to or after intervening with the individual perpetrator. Indirect approaches include reminding students of the rules for the classroom and expectations for social behavior, discussing how relational aggression impacts the classroom environment and school environment, self-disclosing how relational aggression impacted the teacher at some point in his or her academic career, and describing the specific consequences of bullying at school.

Direct approaches include naming the relationally-aggressive behaviors that were witnessed or reported and the students involved and asking the class to discuss how these incidents impact the class and class climate. This approach can certainly be deemed risky as students may be embarrassed by such a direct discussion of the social dynamics; however, this strategy also may help reduce the shame of the victim who may have suffered in silence and decrease the power of the perpetrator who believes that he or she has been engaging in undetected, albeit socially-powerful behaviors. The teacher may also directly ask the class how to decrease the use of relational aggression and how to support the students who are routinely victimized. Teachers who use direct approaches must be prepared to facilitate the class discussion, manage strong emotions, and help the class achieve closure to move forward with class material. Teachers may want to solicit the support of a school counselor, school psychologist, or school social worker to facilitate class discussions.

Tier II responses for specific students may include social skills training and the implementation of specific anti-bullying curriculum (including intervention strategies for student bystanders to bullying) for the entire class. For example, the Early Childhood Friendship Project (Ostrov et al., 2009) is a classroom level intervention for young children. Preliminary evidence suggests that this program is effective in reducing relational aggression among students. Students involved in perpetrating relational aggression may also benefit from small group counseling with a psychoeducational focus, such as social problem solving, emotional regulation and/or anger management, and healthy conflict resolution. The Good Will Girls (Field et al., 2009) is a small group curriculum designed specifically for adolescents who are struggling with relational and social aggression. Although originally designed for females, the activities are also appropriate for male students. Topics addressed in the Good Will Girls small group curriculum include: the meaning of friendship, conflict in friendships, relational and social aggression, approaches to conflict, practicing alternative approaches to conflict, the power of assertiveness, the power of words, and effective friendship skills.

When addressing the perpetrators of bullying, it is beneficial to understand the perpetrator and his or her behaviors. For example, some students may be "trying on" particular bullying behaviors (e.g. such as relational aggression), in attempt to establish more power with peers or to gain more social standing. In other words, some students may be caught early in their development of relationally-aggressive behaviors and may be able to learn alternative strategies to win peer approval through group counseling or individual counseling. Teachers who support these interventions (and the efforts of the school counselor) may in fact eliminate the probability that these types of behaviors continue to occur in their respective classrooms.

Other students may demonstrate relational aggression as part of a consistent pattern of interpersonal behaviors, which includes dominating or attempting to control others. Operating from a consistent position of power may allow students to firmly establish their place in the social dominance hierarchy among their classmates. Interestingly, teachers may be surprised by some students who fit this description or are described this way by their peers, as these same students may be quite savvy at pleasing teachers, appear to be rule-abiding students, and maintain a strong peer following. Students who occupy "top" positions in the social dominance hierarchy may increase the amount of relationally-aggressive behaviors they engage in if their social position appears threatened (e.g. a new, attractive student enrolls at school, another student receives school-wide recognition, particularly if he or she is of the same gender, etc.).

Students who are particularly vicious in their relationally-aggressive behaviors, even after being confronted by school personnel or developing an awareness of how they are impacting the victim, may meet the criteria for a behavioral disorder. Oppositional Defiant Disorder (ODD) is an example of a behavioral disorder that may be associated with extreme, frequent relational aggression. ODD is diagnosed in students who demonstrate hostile and defiant behavior that lasts at least six months and includes four of the following behaviors: student loses temper, argues with adults, defies adults' requests or rules, deliberately annoys people, blames others for his or her mistakes, is touchy or easily annoyed by others, is angry and resentful, and who is often spiteful and vindictive. Due to the aforementioned behaviors, such students experience a significant impairment in their social and academic functioning. In the case of a student with ODD, teachers will most likely not be surprised by reports of bullying. Students diagnosed with ODD will most likely be referred for counseling services outside of school, and teachers often will engage in ongoing consultation with school counselors, school psychologists, and school social workers to troubleshoot and develop behavior modification plans for these students (Tier III interventions).

Allen (2010) proposes a novel approach to working with individual perpetrators of relational aggression and other forms of bullying. This approach fits a Tier II intervention, as the focus is on intervening in the relationally-aggressive cycles of behaviors exhibited by identified students. Whether used by the classroom teacher or a school counselor after a teacher referral, the focus of this approach is brainstorming specific behaviors that may assist with solving the problem rather than focusing on punishment or disciplinary consequences. Therefore, this intervention is highly relevant for classroom teachers.

There are six specific steps are included in this process, including: 1) Meet with the individual student who is perpetrating the relational aggression and express concern about Student X and the problem (i.e. relational aggression) that is causing Student X unhappiness at school, 2) Ask the student what he or she knows about the problem, which may provide for a greater understanding of the problem, 3) Share specific information with the student that may help him or her better understand the problem from the teacher's perspective, 4) Ask the student what he or she believes could happen to solve the problem and increase Student X's happiness at school,

5) Thank the student for his or her assistance and suggestions for solving the problem, and 6) Meet with the victim of relational aggression one to two days later to assess the progress that has been made.

Allen's approach may be especially helpful if the identified student commits to specific behaviors that he/she is willing to contribute to step four or the problem solving phase of the interview. Additionally, this approach may also be most beneficial for students who do not regularly engage in bullying and may benefit from identifying steps to be prosocial or engage in behaviors that may lead to positive peer power and influence. Finally, this approach may be useful as an initial bullying intervention to be followed by a more punitive intervention if necessary.

For students who are known to frequently engage in relationally aggressive behaviors, a more direct, punitive approach may be necessary to emphasize clear expectations for a student's social behaviors. If the teacher observes the relational aggression or receives repeated, reliable reports from peers, it is important for the teacher to react immediately by indicating that he or she saw or has been told about what happened, has identified the behaviors as relational aggression, and will not permit that type of behavior to continue within the classroom. This action is necessary to send a clear message to the perpetrator, the victim, and the active or passive bystanders within the class. After this initial acknowledgement by the classroom teacher, the teacher must decide if he or she is going to take time during the class to engage in a systemic intervention to address the classroom climate, rules regarding classroom behavior and expectations for how students should relate to one another.

Addressing the individual bully, particularly when the teacher has witnessed the relationally-aggressive behavior, is incredibly important. Although time consuming, when the teacher intervenes one-on-one, such interventions may be the best approach to eliminating relational aggression and reinforcing a positive learning environment. When meeting with the individual perpetrator, the teacher should: 1) Specifically state the behavior that was observed and why the behavior is consistent with relational aggression, 2) Ask the aggressor to describe how this behavior impacts the targeted student and the class overall, 3) Remind the student of related classroom and school rules that relate to the student's behavior, 4) State the specific behaviors that the teacher would like to have the student demonstrate (e.g. how might the student manage aggravation with a fellow student, how might the student treat a student who is not popular and is frequently bullied or teased, etc.), 5) Discuss specific consequences for the behavior (e.g. writing a letter of apology, cleaning a classroom, detention, staying after school with the teacher, sitting in isolation in the classroom during the next day's class, a phone call to parents, etc.), 6) Discuss the next set of consequences that will occur if the behavior continues (e.g. report to administration, parental conference, suspension from school, etc.), 7) Remind the student that the teacher will more closely monitor the student's behavior as a result of this incident, 8) Talk about strategies to use social power/popularity in positive ways while at school and, 9) Summarize the content of the meeting with the student.

Two additional considerations for the above intervention are a discussion of mentalization and the completion of a behavioral contract. Mentalization is described as the opportunity to examine one's own (i.e. bully) and someone else's (i.e. target/victim) mental states as they relate to relationally-aggressive behavior. Fonagy et al., (2009) describes mentalization as thinking prompts that encourage students to consider their own beliefs, wishes, and feelings when engaging in bullying and to consider the beliefs, wishes, and feelings of the victim or target. This process fosters mindfulness about one's own internal states and also prompts a student toward empathy for the victim (if the student is capable of empathy). Using mentalization as an intervention strategy may involve questions like the following:

1 When you think about Student X, what do you believe about him/ her?

2 When you are being relationally aggressive toward Student X, what do you wish will happen? What do you hope will happen?

3 How do you feel when you are being relationally aggressive toward Student X? How do you feel when the bullying episode is over?

4 When you think about Student X, what do you think he/she believes about the way that he/she is treated?

5 What do you think that Student X wishes for at school? With his/ her peers?

6 How do you think that Student X feels when you _____?

Whether mentalization is used with elementary age or high school students, the teacher must remember to be patient when waiting for a perpetrator's responses. He or she may not be asked to think in a reflective manner on a regular basis and may need support in learning how to do so. Additionally, it is also important for teachers, when using this intervention, to not give in to annoying or disrespectful behaviors (e.g. eye rolling while hearing the prompts) demonstrated by adolescent perpetrators, as these behaviors are also a tactic to avoid this form of thinking and the subsequent feelings this thinking may produce.

Another strategy that a teacher can use to reinforce a particular relational aggression intervention is to create a behavioral contract with the perpetrator. A behavioral contract may include a specific listing of behaviors that will be extinguished, new behaviors that will be used, and an acknowledgement of the consequences that will occur if the student violates or breaks the contract. The perpetrator should participate in the creation and writing of the behavioral contract and should receive a copy when the meeting/intervention is complete. The teacher(s) should retain a copy of the behavioral contract with the understanding that it will be referred to in the future if the student is identified as a perpetrator again and may be shared with parents and/or school administrators if further intervention is needed.

Each of the individual interventions previously discussed assumes that the teacher has observed the bullying behavior directly or has enough information to strongly suspect that such behavior has happened and thus should take action to intervene. Unfortunately, some students may make an accusation of bullying when the behavior is reciprocal (i.e. the bully and the victim are not easily identified) or other mediating variables do not contribute to a clear understanding of what has happened (e.g. lack of witnesses, bystanders claim that the victim is not being honest, etc.).

Behavioral Contract for:_____

Date Completed: _____

I, _____, understand that this behavioral contract has been created because I have been engaging in the following bullying behaviors:
Spreading negative rumors about Student X
Laughing at Student X when she participates in class
Rolling my eyes when Student X walks by my desk
Texting threatening messages to Student X
Whispering to my friends about Student X and provoking them to treat her poorly

Instead of engaging in the above behaviors, I will:
Ignore Student X when I am irritated by her
Remain silent and respectful when Student X participates in class
Use my cell phone for positive interactions with my peers
Tell my friends that I am not going to bully Student X anymore
I understand that I have one day of detention due to the bullying behaviors listed above.

I understand that_____ (my teacher) will notify my parents, the school principal if I continue to bully Student X. Additionally, my teacher will recommend that I be suspended from school if I continue to bully Student X.

_____   _____
Signature of Student   Date

_____   _____
Signature of Teacher   Date

Figure 13.1 An example of a behavioral contract

In these cases, it is important for the teacher to report the issue to school administrators or support personnel (e.g. school counselors or school social workers) so that they can investigate the claim of bullying. Schools may benefit from using a Bullying Reporting Form so that information is gathered in an organized, systematic manner and so that students who are named in multiple reports or are frequently named can receive disciplinary consequences that are consistent with the number of infractions. A sample Bullying Reporting Form can be found in Appendix A of this chapter.

Tier III

Although teachers are not typically involved in organizing or implementing Tier III remediation efforts, supporting these efforts when possible may play a significant role in student "buy-in" and send a consistent message to students and parents about behavioral expectations at school. Tier III interventions at the systems level require that school administrators, teachers, and staff address the overall bullying culture at a school. This may include the implementation of a school-wide curriculum. For example, Walk Away, Ignore, Talk, Seek Help (WITS) is a comprehensive curriculum designed to reduce victimization among students, improve social skills and increase social responsibility for elementary age children. More research is needed to document the efficacy of this program; however, initial research is promising and this curriculum represents a school-wide initiative intended to alter school climate (Leadbeater, Hoglund, & Woods, 2003).

Additionally, ongoing staff trainings and teacher and staff meetings to address bullying are necessary so that the adults feel that they have the necessary tools to intervene effectively at the class and individual levels. Whole-school assemblies designed to focus specifically on bullying, and grade level meetings with the school administrators to review anti-bullying policies and specific consequences for students who are caught bullying, are also useful. Comprehensive remediation efforts may also include parent trainings and involve students directly in altering a school culture that permits bullying (e.g. peer educator or peer helping programs).

Tertiary intervention for individual perpetrators of relational aggression may include group counseling, which focuses on remediating students' use of relational aggression and promotes alternative social skills which will foster student success at school. Individual counseling interventions may also be structured to hold students accountable for altering their relationally-aggressive behaviors. Parent meetings and follow up will assist with emphasizing the required changes that will assist students with avoiding long-term consequences associated with relationally-aggressive behavior (e.g. suspension from school).

Conclusion

This chapter has focused on relational aggression; a unique, covert set of behaviors that wreak havoc among peer relationships in school-age students. Research related to relational aggression is discussed as well as developmental implications. Specific prevention, intervention, and remediation strategies are reviewed, with emphasis being placed on Tiers I and II interventions that may be directly enacted by classroom teachers. Classroom or system interventions are outlined, as well as different models for intervening with individual perpetrators of relational aggression. In conclusion, teachers are powerful agents in reducing the presence of relational aggression at school because of their consistent contact with students and their potential to be significant, positive social influences for their individual classes as well as the entire school culture.

References

Allen, K. (2010). A bullying intervention system: Reducing risk and creating support for aggressive students. *Preventing School Failure, 54*, 199–209. doi:10.1080/10459880903496289

—(2010). Classroom management, bullying and teacher practices. *The Professional Educator, 34*, 1–16. Accessed from http://theprofessionaleducator. org/articles/Allen_final.pdf

Archer, J. (2004). Sex differences in aggression in real-world settings: A meta-analytic review. *Review of General Psychology, 4*, 291–322. doi:10.1037/1089-2680.8.4.291

Archer, J., & Coyne, S.M. (2005). An integrated review of indirect, relational, and social aggression. *Personality and Social Psychology Review, 9*, 212–30. doi:10.1207/s15327957pspr0903_2

Björkqvist, K, Osterman, K., & Kaukiainen, A. (1992). The development of direct and indirect aggressive strategies in males and females. In K. Björkqvist & P. Niemela (eds), *Of mice and women: Aspects of female aggression* (pp. 51–64). San Diego, CA: Academic Press.

Boxer, P., Edwards-Leeper, L., Goldstein, S. E., Musher-Eizenman, D., & Dubow, E. F. (2003). Exposure to "low-level" aggression in school: Associations with aggressive behavior, future expectations, and perceived safety. *Violence and Victims, 18*, 691–704.

Buhs, E. S., Ladd, G. W., & Herald, S. L. (2006). Peer exclusion and victimization: Processes that mediate the relation between peer group rejection and children's classroom engagement and achievement. *Journal of Educational Psychology, 98*, 1–13. doi:10.1037/0022-0663.98.1.1

Card, N., & Hodges, E. V. (2008). Peer victimization among schoolchildren: Correlates, causes, consequences and considerations in assessment and intervention. *School Psychology Quarterly, 23*, 451–61. doi:10.1037/a0012769

Coyne, S. M., Archer, J., & Eslea, M. (2006). We're not friends anymore!

Unless ... : The frequency and harmfulness of indirect, relational, and social aggression. *Aggressive Behavior, 32,* 294–307. doi:10.1002/ab.20126

Craig, W. M. (1998). The relationship among bullying, victimization, depression, anxiety, and aggression in elementary school children. *Personality and Individual Differences, 24,* 123–30. doi:10.1016/S0191-8869(97)00145-1

Crick, N. R. (1996). The role of overt aggression, relational aggression, and prosocial behavior in the prediction of children's future social adjustment. *Child Development, 67,* 2317–27. doi:10.1111/j.1467-8624.1996.tb01859.x

Crick, N. R., & Grotpeter, J. (1995). Relational aggression, gender, and social-psychological adjustment. *Child Development, 66,* 710–22. doi:10.1111/j.1467-8624.1995.tb00900.x

—(1996). Children's treatment by peers: Victims of relational and overt aggression. *Development and Psychopathology, 8,* 367–80. doi:10.1017/S0954579400007148

Crick, N. R., Ostrov, J. M., Burr, J. E., Cullerton-Sen, C. Jansen-Yeh, E., & Ralston, P. (2006). A longitudinal study of relational and physical aggression in preschool. *Applied Developmental Psychology, 27,* 254–68. doi:10.1016/j.appdev.2006.02.006

Crick, N. R., & Werner, N. E. (1998). Response decision processes in relational and overt aggression. *Child Development, 69,* 1630–9. doi:10.1111/j.1467-8624.1998.tb06181.x

Crick, N. R., Werner, N., Casas, J., O'Brien, K., Nelson, D., Grotpeter, J., & Markon, K. (1999). Childhood aggression and gender: A new look at an old problem. In D. Bernstein (ed.). *Gender and Motivation: Nebraska Symposium on Motivation* (Vol. 45, pp. 75–142). Lincoln, NE: University of Nebraska Press.

Crothers, L. M., Field, J. E., & Kolbert, J. B. (2005). Navigating power, control, and being nice: Aggression in adolescent girls' friendships. *Journal of Counseling and Development, 83,* 349–54.

Fekkes, M., Pijpers, F.I., Fredriks, A. M., Vogels, T., & Verloove-Vanhorick, S.P. (2006). Do bullied children get ill, or do ill children get bullied? A prospective cohort study on the relationship between bullying and health-related symptoms. *Pediatrics, 117,* 1568–74. doi:10.1542/peds.2005-0187

Feshbach, N. (1969). Sex differences in children's modes of aggressive responses toward outsiders. *Merrill-Palmer Quarterly, 15,* 249–58.

Field, J., Kolbert, J., Crothers, L., & Hughes, T. (2009). *Understanding girl bullying and what to do about it: Strategies to heal the divide.* Thousand Oaks, CA: Corwin.

Fonagy, P., Twemlow, S. W., Vernberg, E. M., Nelson, J. M., Dill, E. J., Little, T. D., & Sargent, J. A. (2009). A cluster randomized controlled trial of child-focused psychiatric consultation and a school systems-focused intervention to reduce aggression. *The Journal of Child Psychology and Psychiatry, 50,* 607–16. doi:10.1111/j.1469-7610.2008.02025.x

Frisén, A., & Holmqvist, K. (2010). Adolescents' own suggestions for bullying interventions at age 13 and 16. *Scandinavian Journal of Psychology, 51,* 123–31. doi:10.1111/j.1467-9450.2009.00733.x

Gendron, B. P., Williams, K. R., & Guerra, N. G. (2011). An analysis of bullying among students within schools: Estimating the effects of individual normative beliefs, self-esteem and school climate. *Journal of School Violence, 10*, 150–64. doi:10.1080/15388220.2010.539166

Goldstein, S. E., Young, A., & Boyd, C. (2008). Relational aggression at school: Associations with school safety and social climate. *Journal of Youth & Adolescence, 37*, 641–54. doi:10.1007/s10964-007-9192-4

Greenberg, M., Weissberg, R., O'Brien, M., Zins, J., Fredewricks, L., Resnik, H., & Elias, M. (2003). Enhancing school-based prevention and youth development through coordinated social, emotional and academic learning. *American Psychologist, 58*, 466–74. doi:10.1037/0003-066X.58.6-7.466

Hayward, S. M., & Fletcher, J. (2003). Relational aggression in an Australian sample: Gender and age differences. *Australian Journal of Psychology, 55*, 129–34. doi:10.1080/00049530542000298572

Hill, L. G., & Werner, N. E. (2006). Affiliative motivation, school attachment, and aggression in school. *Psychology in the Schools, 43*, 231–46. doi:10.1002/pits.20140

Kistener, J., Counts-Allen, C., Dunkel, S., Drew, C. H., David-Ferdon, C., & Lopez, C. (2010). Sex differences in relational and overt aggression in the late elementary school years. *Aggressive Behavior, 36*, 282–91. doi:10.1002/ab.20350

Kumpulainen, K., Rasanen, E., Henttonen, I., Almqvist, F., Kresanov, K., Linna, S., …Tamminen, T. (1998). Bullying and psychiatric symptoms among elementary school-age children. *Child Abuse and Neglect, 22*, 705–17. doi:10.1016/S0145-2134(98)00049-0

Lagerspetz, K. M., Björkqvist, K., & Peltonen, T. (1988). Is indirect aggression typical of females? Gender differences in aggressiveness in 11-to-12-year-old children. *Aggressive Behavior, 14*, 403–14. doi:10.1002/1098-2337(1988)14:6<403::AID-AB2480140602>3.0.CO;2-D

Leadbeater, B., Hoglund, W., & Woods, T. (2003). Changing contexts? The effects of a primary prevention program on classroom levels of peer relational and physical victimization. *Journal of Community Psychology, 31*, 397–418. doi:10.1002/jcop.10057

Leff, S. S., Wassdorp, T. E., Paskewich, B., Gullan, R. L., Jawad, A. F., MacEvoy, J. P., … Power, T. J. (2010). The preventing relational aggression in schools everyday program: A preliminary evaluation of acceptability and impact. *School Psychology Review, 39*, 569–87. Accessed from http://www.nasponline. org/publications/spr/39-4/spr394leffwaasdroppaskewich.pdf

Loukas, A., Paulos, S. K., & Robinson, S. (2005). Early adolescent social and overt aggression: Examining the roles of social anxiety and maternal psychological control. *Journal of Youth and Adolescence, 35*, 335–45. doi:10.1007/s10964-005-5757-2

Mathieson, L. C., & Crick, N. R. (2010). Reactive and proactive subtypes of relational and physical aggression in middle childhood: Links to concurrent and longitudinal adjustment. *School Psychology Review, 39*, 601–11. Accessed from http://www.nasponline.org/publications/spr/39-4/spr394mathieson.pdf

Mishna, F., Wiener, J., & Pepler, D. (2008). Some of my best friends—Experiences of bullying within friendships. *School Psychology International, 28*, 549–73. doi:10.1177/0143034308099201

Nansel, T. R., Overpeck, M., Pilla, R. S., Ruan, W. J., Simons-Morton, B., & Scheidt, P. (2001). Bullying behaviors among US youth: Prevalence and association with psychosocial adjustment. *Journal of the American Medical Association, 285*, 2094–100. doi:10.1001/jama.285.16.2094

National Research Council and the Institute of Medicine (2009). *Preventing mental, emotional, and behavioral disorders among young people: Progress and possibilities.* Washington, DC: National Academies Press.

Novick, R. M., & Isaacs, J. (2010). Telling is compelling: The impact of student reports of bullying on teacher intervention. *Educational Psychology, 30*, 283–96. doi:10.1080/01443410903573123

Olweus, D. (1993) *Bullying at school: What we know and what we can do.* Cambridge, MA: Blackwell.

Ostrov, J. M., Massetti, G. M., Stauffacher, K., Godleski, et al., (2009). An intervention for relational and physical aggression in early childhood: A preliminary study. *Early Childhood Research Quarterly, 24*, 15–28. doi:10.1016/j.ecresq.2008.08.002

Owens, L., Shute, R., & Slee, P. (2000). Guess what I just heard! Indirect aggression among teenage girls in Australia. *Aggressive Behavior, 26*, 67–83. doi:10.1002/(SICI)1098-2337(2000)26:1<67::AID-AB6>3.0.CO;2-C

Pellegrini, A. D, Bartini, M., & Brooks, F. (1999). School bullies, victims, and aggressive victims: Factors relating to group affiliation and victimization in early adolescence. *Journal of Educational Psychology, 91*, 216–24. doi:10.1037/0022-0663.91.2.216

Pepler, D. J., Craig, W. M., Connolly, J. A., Yuile, A., McMaster, L., & Jiang, D. (2006). A developmental perspective on bullying. *Aggressive Behavior, 32*, 376–85. doi:10.1002/ab.20136

Pokhrel, P., Sussman, S., Black, D., & Sun, P. (2010). Peer group self-identification as a predictor of relational and physical aggression among high school students. *Journal of School Health, 80*, 249–58. doi:10.1111/j.1746-1561.2010.00498.x

Prinstein, M. J., Boergers, J., & Vernberg, E. M. (2001). Overt and relational aggression in adolescents: Social-psychological adjustment of aggressors and victims. *Journal of Clinical Child Psychology, 30*, 479–91. doi:10.1207/S15374424JCCP3004_05

Puckett, M. B., Aikins, J. W., & Cillessen, A. H. N. (2008). Moderators of the association between aggression and perceived popularity. *Aggressive Behavior, 34*, 563–76. doi:10.1002/ab.20280

Roland, E., & Galloway, D. (2002). Classroom influences on bullying. *Educational Research, 44*, 299–312. doi:10.1080/0013188022000031597

Sandstrom, M. J., & Cillessen, A. H. N. (2010). Life after high school: Adjustment of popular teens in emerging adulthood. *Merrill-Palmer Quarterly, 56*, 474–99. doi:10.1353/mpq.2010.0000

Shoulberg, E., Sijtsema, J. J., & Murray-Close, D. (2011). The association between valuing popularity and relational aggression: The moderating effects of actual popularity and physiological reactivity to exclusion. *Journal of Experimental Child Psychology, 110*, 20–37. doi:10.1016/j.jecp.2011.03.008

Sullivan, T. N., Farrell, A. D., & Kliewer, W. (2006). Peer victimization in early adolescence: Associations between physical and relational victimization and drug use, aggression, and delinquent behaviors among urban middle school students. *Development and Psychopathology, 18,* 119–37. doi:10.1017/S095457940606007X

Underwood, M. K. (2003). *Social aggression among girls.* New York, NY: The Guilford Press.

Underwood, M.K., Galen, B.R., & Paquette, J.A. (2001). Top ten challenges for understanding gender and aggression in children: Why can't we all just get along? *Social Development, 10,* 268–71. doi:10.1111/1467-9507.00162

Walker, H. M. (2010). Relational aggression in schools: Implications for future research on screening intervention and prevention. *School Psychology Review, 39,* 594–600. Accessed from http://www.nasponline.org/publications/spr/39-4/spr394walker.pdf

Wiseman, R. (2002). *Queenbees and wannabes: Helping your daughter survive cliques, gossip, boyfriends, and other realities of adolescence.* New York, NY: Three Rivers Press.

Appendix A

Bullying Reporting Form
_____ School

Name of the Person Completing the Report: _____

Date of Report: _____ **Date of Bullying Incident**: _____

Where the Incident Happened:

_____

Who Was Involved:

_____

_____

_____

_____

What Happened:

_____

_____

_____

_____

My Role in this Situation:

____I was the Bully

____I was the Target/Victim

____I was the Victim/I have been the Bully before

____ I was a Bystander (*I saw it happen but did not intervene*)

____I was an Advocate (*I saw it happen and I tried to help*)

____I am the Teacher who heard about this incident

Type of Bullying:

____Relational Aggression

____Physical Aggression

____Cyber Bullying

What I Would Like to See Happen (What I Would Like the Administrators to Do):

Printed Name (First and Last Name)   Signature

Understanding and Managing Behaviors of Children Diagnosed with Substance Abuse Disorders (SAD)

Amanda Clinton

University of Puerto Rico

Abstract

This chapter addresses individual and classroom behavior management related to issues of substance use and abuse for children and adolescents. Substance abuse is an issue of concern among our nation's youth. Although the types of drugs consumed by youth may vary, recent numbers indicate a rise in usage and a decreasing age of initiation. The formal definition of substance abuse refers to a predominantly clinical issue, rather than a school-based diagnosis. However, as addressed within a three-tiered model, a number of evidence-based and relatively easy-to-use prevention and intervention curricula are available to classroom teachers. These types of programs may help reduce initiation of substance use and aid teachers in managing related behaviors before they reach clinically significant levels, at which point displinary action and external consultation are common. Conclusions highlight the importance of behavior management by the classroom teacher at the early stages of substance use development.

Introduction

From the Beatles' 1967 hit song, *Lucy in the Sky with Diamonds* to the Eagles', *Hotel California*, 10 years later and, more recently, Sean Paul's, *We Be Burnin'*, or Weezer's, *We're All on Drugs*, the theme of substance use occupies a position at the forefront of popular culture in the United States and abroad. Since adolescents are both the major consumers of the latest fashions and fads, particularly in regards to music (Nielsenwire, 2011), and are at a developmental stage marked by the emergence of independent interests (Aries, 2001), it comes as no surprise that song lyrics reflect youth's curiosity in substances. Adolescent drug use appears to be on the rise, as per the National Institute on Drug Abuse's (NIDA) 2011 publication, "High School and Youth Trends." In fact, the most recent survey data available in the US suggests that the age of initiation (first use) is decreasing for adolescents, while the overall use of drugs seems to be reversing its downward trend to be on the rise for the first time in about a decade (NIDA, 2011).

In 2008, adolescent substance use and abuse reached its lowest levels since NIDA began applying its biennial Monitoring the Future survey on drug, alcohol, and cigarette use and related attitudes in 1975 (NIDA, 2011). However, NIDA's most recent data "raises concerns about increases in drug use among our Nation's teens, particularly the youngest" (p. 1). The numbers reflect worrisome trends in the patterns of use and abuse in America's school-aged population.

In general, the 2011 report indicates that previous declines in substance use have stalled as compared to prior years. Of the drugs measured in the NIDA survey, only alcohol and Vicodin use fell across all grades measured (8th, 10th, and 12th). Marijuana use increased notably for students; beginning in 8th grade and continuing through the high school years, as did the non-medical use of prescription and over-the-counter medications, including drugs such as Adderall, Oxycontin and cough medicine (NIDA, 2011). Previously at 2.4%, the lifetime use of Ecstasy rose to 3.3% for 8th graders; a similar pattern was observed for 10th graders (NIDA, 2011). In addition to consumption increases, students across grade levels reported a frightening perceptual change: in general, adolescents describe drugs such as marijuana and MDMA as "relatively low-risk" (NIDA, 2011). Alcohol use, while decreasing slightly, remains high at a level of approximately 42% for youth from the 8th through the 12th grades (NIDA, 2011).

The cost to the US economy of addressing drug abuse reached nearly $193 billion in 2007 (Cratty, 2011; Join Together, 2011). These numbers put the financial burden related to drug abuse at the level of treating a number of chronic health problems in the country, such as diabetes, even minus the inclusion of alcohol, inhalants, and prescription drug abuse. Obviously, the issue is a serious one for the US and, in turn, it's youth population.

The appropriate and responsible consumption of controlled drugs, such as cigarettes, alcohol, and prescription medication, is defined as "substance use." The term "substance (or drug) abuse," however, indicates "a maladaptive pattern of use leading to significant impairment" (American Psychological Association [APA], 2000). Significant impairments are broadly categorized as problems in daily functioning, taking unnecessary risks, legal problems related to drug use, and social-familial conflicts. "Substance dependence," like substance abuse, leads to significant impairment or distress but differs from substance abuse in that it involves an ever-increasing and uncontrollable need for one's drug of choice. This insatiation persists, in spite of a desire to the contrary; the addict continues to desperately need his drug of choice in order to avoid the consequences resulting from a lack of use.

Substance abuse can have severe negative effects on various aspects of a student's life functioning. In terms of academic performance, grades often fall as a result of poor study habits and frequent absenteeism (Breslau, Miller, Chung, & Schweitzer, 2010). Furthermore, social and emotional consequences may be grave, including the loss of friendships. Since drug abuse is not widely accepted, one may be largely rejected by peers other than those who are also utilizing illicit drugs or abusing controlled substances. Consequences extend far beyond the school setting, however, in that familial conflicts typically arise or become exacerbated when a young person is addicted (Maggs, Patrick, & Feinstein, 2008) and legal problems frequently arise (Doherty, Green, Ensminger, 2008; Maggs et al., 2007). In general, the long-term outcomes for adolescents who abuse drugs tend to be poor and may include school failure, legal problems, unhealthy relationships, and difficulties obtaining and sustaining employment.

Issues that affect youth necessarily impact the school system and professionals who work with children and adolescents as educators and support staff. For this reason, school-based professionals should possess knowledge that may contribute to the identification, prevention, and support of students at-risk for substance use or substance abuse. While the educational system cannot provide treatment for addicted students, educators should be able to offer school-based support to students with addiction issues. The current chapter highlights recent research in the area of adolescent substance abuse with specific attention to behavioral and classroom management.

The chapter is organized in the following manner: subsequent to this introduction, a specific definition of the disorder is provided along with symptoms that educators may observe. Next, the conceptual foundations important to understanding substance abuse issues and potential behavior management concerns within the classroom are addressed. A prevention/intervention strategy using a three-tier model is discussed next, and, finally, progress monitoring of strategies that have been presented in earlier parts of the chapter. The chapter concludes with a discussion and recommendations related to classroom behavior management of the substance-abusing adolescent.

Definition of the Disorder

The Diagnostic and Statistical Manual, Fourth Edition-Text Revision (DSM-IV-TR) published by the APA (2000) and the International Classification of Diseases, 10th Edition (ICD–10) published by the World Health Organiztion (WHO, 1990) contains clinical diagnostic criterion for Substance Abuse and Substance Dependence. These diagnoses are not considered qualifying conditions for special education services under federal law, for which reason diagnostic criterion are not typically distributed and discussed in educational settings. However, students with special education classification under the emotional-behavioral disorders (EBD) category may be at particularly high risk for drug abuse. This is because of the frequent co-morbidity between conditions such as depression and substance abuse (Swendsen et al., 2010).

As per the DSM-IV-TR (APA, 2000), substance abuse and substance dependence are mutually exclusive diagnostic options. A diagnosis of substance abuse mandates a maladaptive pattern of use over a year-long period. Observation of one or more of the following behaviors during this time may be indicative of the disorder:

- Recurrent substance use resulting in a failure to fulfill major role obligations at work, school, or home;

- Recurrent substance use in situations in which it is physically hazardous (such as driving an automobile);

- Recurrent substance-related legal problems;

- Continued substance use despite having persistent or recurrent social or interpersonal problems caused or exacerbated by the effects of the substance.

A diagnosis of substance dependence differs from substance abuse in that it is characterized by a maladaptive pattern of behavior marked by increasing tolerance for drugs and/or withdrawal symptoms over the course of a year. Specifically, substance abuse refers to:

- Tolerance, as defined by either of the following: (a) A need for markedly increased amounts of the substance to achieve intoxication or the desired effect or (b) Markedly diminished effect with continued use of the same amount of the substance;

- Withdrawal, as manifested by either of the following: (a) The characteristic withdrawal syndrome for the substance or (b) The same (or closely related) substance is taken to relieve or avoid withdrawal symptoms;

- The substance is taken in larger amounts or for a longer period than intended;

- There is a persistent desire or unsuccessful efforts to cut down or control substance use;

- A great deal of time is spent in activities necessary to obtain the substance, use the substance, or recover from its effects;

- Important social, occupational, or recreational activities are given up or reduced because of substance use;

- The substance use is continued despite knowledge of having a persistent physical or psychological problem that is likely to have been caused or exacerbated by the substance.

Symptomatology Commonly Observed in School Settings

A substantial body of research indicates that children may demonstrate behaviors as early as preschool that are predictive of very high risk for later drug abuse. That is, children who have difficulties controlling impulses, managing emotions, coping with frustration, and establishing friendships are at particular risk for illicit substance usage in the future (Fothergill et al., 2008). These include difficulties resolving conflicts and frequent aggressive behavior (Swan, 1995), poor school performance (Maggs et al., 2008; Williams et al., 2007), co-morbid disorders, such as depression or attention-deficit hyperactivity disorder (Hayatbakhsh et al., 2008), and social withdrawal or a lack of healthy friendships (Grella, Hser, Joshi, & Rounds-Bryant, 2001; Mason, 2010). As such, children who may be inclined toward drug abuse in their adolescence can potentially be identified early in their school careers and directed toward participation in universal prevention programs, such as those discussed below.

When an adolescent is actively engaged in substance use or is abusing or dependent on drugs, inappropriate behaviors tend to become pronounced and may be extreme. For example, his or her grades may decline significantly (Williams et al., 2007), delinquency, such as violence, and stealing may be observed (Botvin, Griffin, & Nichols, 2006), he or she may be caught in a number of lies (Botvin et al., 2006), may engage in a shift in peer group, and conflicts with family or friends typically arise. Behaviors specific to the influence of the substance being ingested, such as confusion, slurred or accelerated speech, drowsiness, or unexplained euphoria may further be observed. In the school setting, peers may be aware of their friend's unusual behaviors and report them to adults, or classroom teachers may notice a shift in academic performance, attitude, and attendance.

Conceptual Foundations

The subject of substance abuse in youth represents a rapidly evolving sub-specialization in addiction research and practice. Within the past 20 years, significant organizational, treatment, and research advances specific to working with adolescents with drug use problems have been made (see Liddle & Rowe, 2006). This is important, since drug use and abuse tends to peak during the teen years (NIDA, 2010). The broader approach to substance abuse prevention, diagnosis, and treatment that has developed for work with teenagers is based on biopsychosocial models and emphasizes a series of interrelated factors. Currently, an increasing emphasis is being placed on the biological aspects of substance abuse disorders, as well (NIDA, 2010). In general, the biopsychosocial model of substance abuse conceptualizes addiction as the result of a biological predisposition toward addiction, or a particular inclination to "enjoy" and, later "crave" more drugs as a result of the way in which the individual's brain perceives pleasure in relation to drugs.

The biological factors are, then, exacerbated by a psychological profile marked by depression, anxiety, or explosive anger from which drugs may offer relief. Additional contributions to the cycle result when the social milieu encourages drug use. This may occur through accessibility or role models, for example. If it is socially acceptable to use drugs, initiation and continued consumption may be indicated where a different environment might *not* provide another youth the opportunity to acquire illicit or controlled substances despite having a similar profile.

Protective Factors and Risk Factors

Addiction research and practice organizes fundamental concepts according to a model of protective and risk factors (Brook, Brook, & Pahl, 2006; Mason, 2010; NIDA, 2010). This organization of protective and risk factors elucidates interrelationships between positive influences, or protective factors, such as attachment, healthy peer influences, and temperament, that may act as buffers when a child is confronted with drugs and potential negative influences, or risks (Mason, 2010). Risk factors may include a genetic predisposition (Saba et al., 2011; Tsuang, Bar, Harley, & Lyons, 2001), poor parenting (Williams, 2007), a difficult temperament (Giancola & Mezzich, 2003), poverty (Mason, 2010), and inadequate community norms (Carpiano, Kelly, Easterbrook, & Parsons, 2011; HeavyRunner-Rioux & Hollist, 2010), to name a few.

The model of protective and risk factors describes interrelated individual, familial, and community tendencies, contexts, and experiences. For this reason, intervention by school-based educational and mental health personnel may be complex. Teachers can help address related behaviors in the classroom, ensure student health safety, and participate in progress monitoring, for example. He or she may need to contribute a significant amount of information to the case management process. This is because, while abuse treatment is typically beyond the scope of the educational setting, the teacher's observations and input will be critical to a successful intervention effort. Key components of the protective/risk factor model are discussed in more detail in subsequent paragraphs and summarized in Table 14.1.

Table 14.1 Examples of Risk and Protective Factors

Risk Factors	Domain	Protective Factors
Early Aggressive Behavior	Individual	Self-Control
Poor Social Skills	Individual	Positive Relationships
Lack of Parental Supervision	Family	Parental Monitoring and Support
Substance Abuse	Peer	Academic Competence
Drug Availability	School	Anti-Drug Use Policies
Poverty	Community	Strong Neighborhood Attachment

Source: National Institute on Drug Abuse, 2010

Biological Factors

Addiction is influenced by numerous factors. However, addiction is increasingly recognized as a fundamentally biologically-based disorder (Quenqua, 2011). Genetic research indicates that certain individuals are more likely to become addicts than others due to biological predispositions that result in higher consumption and a stronger sense of reward and reinforcement after consuming (Saba et al., 2011; Wheeler & Carelli, 2009). Studies of twins estimate that genetic factors may account for as much as 74% of the variance in the addiction to marijuana, for example (Kendler, Jacobson, Prescott, & Neale, 2003). In general, a "modestly high [genetic] heritability is irrefutable, but that heritability is likely due to many variants of very small effect" (Brion, personal communication, September 7, 2011). Though a disorder might be genetic, that does not mean it cannot be resolved. As explained by Dr Nora Volkow, NIDA Director, "Addiction is a brain disease that can be treated" (NIDA, 2010). A key factor in this process may be pharmacological, in addition to behavioral interventions (Quenqua, 2011).

Peer/School Context

Adolescents are at a developmental stage marked by separation from parents and an increasing emphasis on the establishment of key relationships with peers (Mason, 2010). As a result, friends tend to have a very strong influence on an individual's behavior during adolescence. A large body of evidence supports the idea that socializing with drug-using peers represents a risk factor that increases the probability of adolescent drug use (Davis & Spillman, 2011). Moreover, adolescents not only tend to perceive drug use as an exciting opportunity to test limits but also as a means of fostering bonding with peers (Berger, 2009).

Certain teens are at greater risk of drug use and abuse during adolescence than others. The child who is doing poorly in school and tends to vacillate between timidity and aggression—behavior that results in compromised social relationships—is particularly vulnerable to the suggestion by peers that she try drugs (Gorman, Zhu, & Horel, 2005; Maggs et al., 2008).

While genetic factors and the familial environment also contribute to the probability that an adolescent abuses drugs, deviant socialization represents another key predictor. Youth who demonstrate a preference for peers who violate social norms and express non-traditional attitudes toward rules and laws are more likely to engage in substance use (Tarter et al., 2011). In fact, this very behavior, in combination with other risk factors, has been shown to increase the incidence of cannabis use disorder in youth (Tarter et al., 2011).

Indeed, peer relationships seem to be more important than issues of culture, according to a recent publication (Miller, 2011). Although it has long been thought that a positive correlation exists between level of acculturation and drug use, this recent work brings this belief into question. That is, a body of research previously suggested that immigrant or ethnic minority students who identify more strongly with American culture and less-so with their familial roots appeared to consume higher amounts of illicit substances (e.g. Akins, Mosher, Smith, & Gauthier, 2008; Gilbert, 1987; Yin, Zapata, & Katims, 1995). However, when acculturation level was compared with other factors, it was not related to either low or high levels of drug use. Instead, social factors such as gang membership and peer influence weighed heavily as predictors. As explained by Miller, "the social context in which acculturation occurs may have a greater impact than the [acculturation] process itself" (2011, p. 102).

Research indicates that peers can, conversely, influence anti-drug decisions. A study by Davis and Spillman (2011) specifically evaluated the relationship between more positive and less positive peer relationships and substance use. The researchers asked participants questions such as, "I felt comfortable talking to my friends about problems I was having." They reported differences between young adults who had utilized illicit substances and those who had not, the latter indicating significantly higher levels of positive peer relationships.

Family Context

Healthy attachments to adults in the home are extremely important in the development of positive life outcomes (Roche, Ensminger, & Cherlin, 2007). Children of caring parents who are involved in their lives and establish and enforce clear expectations fare better than those of disengaged or punitive parents independent of cultural group (Pittman & Chase-Lansdale, 2001; Samaniego & Gonzales, 1999). Parents and family members further serve as models for children and adolescents; youngsters who observe the abuse of alcohol and drugs at home are more likely to experience addiction problems of their own (Collins, Grella, & Hser, 2003; NIDA, 2010).

In addition to being role models for their children, parents specifically establish relationships with their children and, furthermore, socialize them through home-based tasks requiring cooperation. These include helping with household chores and jobs. Data suggest that the quality of parent-child relationships and collaboration in the home are related to substance use disorders, in that deviant attitudes and inappropriate peer relation ships appear to result from negative home environments and relations (Tarter et al., 2011).

Community Context

Societal and cultural norms play a role in the consumption of drugs and alcohol (Spoth, Greenberg, & Turrisi, 2008). These communal influences may be particularly worrisome in the context of impoverishment (Gorman et al., 2005). However, the degree to which communities either explicitly or implicitly approve of substance use can vary in degree even in high risk environments (Roche, Ensminger, Cherlin, 2007). Frequently, poverty is accompanied by high levels of violence, mental health issues (Grella et al., 2001), familial disintegration (Pittman & Chase-Lansdale, 2001) and violence (Gorman et al., 2005). These factors all correlate with substance abuse.

In conclusion, the conceptualization of drug abuse during adolescence must be conducted utilizing a multi-faceted approach. Otherwise, understanding the multiple causes that contribute to addiction may not be sufficiently understood in order to allow for development of meaningful and effective prevention and intervention strategies. Best practices in the case of a pre-teen or adolescent who is using or abusing drugs considers genetic, individual and school, family, and community factors. While teachers most typically address school-based behaviors—usually within their particular classrooms—they must also be aware of the broader biopsychosocial nature of the disorder to ensure appropriate advocacy.

Prevention/Intervention Strategies

Substance abuse is a highly complicated problem that results from multiple influences. The notion of protective and risk factors helps explain the way in which different variables can counterbalance one another and potentially lead to either a drug-free life or result in a pattern of substance abuse. These influences may be biological, individual, familial, school, and/or community related. Addressing each of these areas is beyond the scope of this chapter. However, the following paragraphs aim to help teachers address issues related to substance abuse within the educational setting. This is done in a tier-based framework that begins with universal prevention programs at Tier I, continues with directed intervention at Tier II, and finishes with individualized treatment considerations within the school environment at Tier III. In effect, a tier-oriented approach mirrors what may also be considered primary, secondary, and tertiary prevention. The difference with a tier-based framework is the emphasis it places on progress monitoring and data-based decision-making.

Before describing a three-tiered strategy for addressing substance abuse related behaviors in the school setting, it is important to understand the management of drug and alcohol use on the school campus. As previously mentioned, Substance Abuse Disorder and Substance Abuse Dependence are *not* qualifying conditions for special education services. If a student is suspected of being under the influence of any substance while on school grounds, school administration typically addresses the physical consequences of their condition immediately (i.e. contacting parents and requesting the student be transported to their doctor or hospital). Subsequent to ensuring the student's safety, the issue is most commonly referred for disciplinary evaluation. Suspension from school attendance is frequently incurred even at the initial offense and proof of outside treatment is required in order to return to classes. School officials may further refer the case to the relevant legal authorities depending on its nature. Most schools will provide Student Study Team (SST) support throughout this process in order to ensure that the student receives appropriate follow-up and guidance, even though it is not relevant for special education referral (unless EBD is suspected).

Tier I

Tier I strategies related to behaviors exhibited in the case of substance abuse actually address early prevention. That is, Tier I interventions are based on preventing drug initiation through classroom-based programs designed for all students, commonly called universal prevention programs.

A number of studies indicate that very young children, such as preschool and early elementary school-aged boys and girls, may demonstrate personality characteristics and behaviors indicative of future problems (Doherty et al., 2008; Swan, 1995). Risk factors that have been identified as childhood markers of potential substance abuse problems in adolescence include aggression, poor adherence to rules and norms, rebelliousness and low acceptance of responsibility (Brook, Whiteman, Cohen, & Tanaka, 1991). Further longitudinal data indicate a relationship between aggression or aggression combined with shyness and later substance abuse, with the latter condition being the most serious of the two (Ensminger, 1990; Fothergill et al., 2008; Green, Doherty, Stuart, & Ensminger, 2010; Green & Ensminger, 2006).

As previously mentioned, individuals may present behaviors and personality characteristics as early as preschool that suggest they are at high risk for substance abuse disorders. Recent government reports further indicate that the age at which children first try illicit substances, or the age of initiation, seems to be decreasing (NIDA, 2011; Sharp, McLaughlin, & McClanahan, 1999). According to NIDA (2011), for example, 8th grade students demonstrate greater substance use in their most recent study than in prior years. The combination of early predictors and younger ages of initiation suggests that Tier I programs may be of both increasing utility and importance.

Since children with characteristics indicative of future substance abuse problems show these behaviors from a young age and since the age of initiation is decreasing, Tier I strategies may be implemented as soon as the children enter the school setting and should be supported with continued reinforcement throughout the school years. In fact, the types of social-emotional and problem-solving skills emphasized in universal prevention programs largely require frequent re-teaching, or booster sessions, throughout one's academic career in order to increase effectiveness (Botvin, Renick, & Baker, 1983).

Specific examples of Tier I strategies may be broadly categorized as psychosocially-oriented life skills programs. Such programs typically include a series of lessons that highlight a combination of techniques ranging from social, emotional, behavioral, and cognitive components while including drug-specific scenarios to aid in development of refusal skills. Drug prevention curricula are frequently provided to teachers for use within the classroom setting. These materials are directed at the whole-class rather than any particular student. Certainly, the idea is to help those youngsters who have not developed emotion management, pro-social, and problem-solving techniques to do so with the hope that they might avoid the negative consequences that accompany aggression, withdrawal, and poor coping as they continue their academic careers.

Programs selected for the depth of research litereature supporting their effectiveness are described in the following paragraphs.

Drug Abuse Resistance Education (D.A.R.E.)

Created in 1983, the D.A.R.E. program is promoted by a non-profit organization with the same name. The curriculum is implemented in approximately 80% of US school districts (Hanson, 2007). The most recent incarnation of the D.A.R.E.[1] curriculum focuses on teaching children from kindergarten through 12th grade how to focus on positive strengths and largely avoid harmful influences such as drugs (www.dare.com). Although sessions are presented in the school setting, D.A.R.E. recruits law enforcement officials to implement the program, rather than requesting that the classroom teacher or another school employee present the lessons.

Research findings on D.A.R.E. in the US have not been encouraging. Comparison between students who received D.A.R.E. lessons versus those who participated in a standard drug education program demonstrated few differences between groups and no significant advantage for D.A.R.E., although the program continues to be highly popular (Ennett, Tobler, Ringwalt, & Flewelling, 1994). Other studies have indicated that although D.A.R.E. resulted in changes in attitudes and knowledge regarding drug use, actual consumption of substances was not impacted (Rosenbaum, Gordon, & Hanson, 1998).

Some prevention professionals posit that the limited long-term effects of D.A.R.E. may result from the need for "booster" sessions, or annual review and renewed emphasis on drug refusal skills. Others have argued that these results are misleading since the majority of drug resistance program evaluations do not adequately assess key factors in their curricula. The D.A.R.E. program is based on relationships between students and law enforcement professionals, particularly police, and improvements in this area are not measured (Birkeland, Murphy-Graham, & Weiss, 2005). Furthermore, Birkeland and her colleagues (2005) note that school administrators do not expect overwhelming results in terms of all participants meeting the behavior change goals indicated in the curriculum. Instead, they anticipate slow progress in a small number of individuals. For this reason, they do not tend to be concerned by limited improvements. Educators tend to consider the program a success despite the lack of support from large-scale studies. In sum, D.A.R.E. remains highly popular and widely used in the US and across the world.

Life Skills Training

Another recognized universal primary prevention program utilized in high schools is Botvin's *Life Skills Training Program* (LST; 2000). LST learning objectives are directed toward personal self-management skills (i.e. problem-solving and emotional coping), social skills (i.e. establishing friendships, confidence development, communication), and drug resistance (i.e. methods of defending against pressures related specifically to drugs and alcohol). LST is designed to be presented by classroom teachers to their students in 30–45 minute sessions over the course of several weeks.

A significant body of research suggests the LST curriculum is highly effective at reducing drug and alcohol use as well as violent behaviors (e.g. Botvin et al., 2006; Griffin, Botvin, & Nichols, 2004; Spoth, Clair, Shin, & Redmond, 2006), although it is important to highlight the fact that much of this literature is published by the program's developer and colleagues. Criticism regarding LST suggests that the encouraging data about the program's effectiveness has more to do with the (misleading) presentation of statistics and does not support the degree of impact reported (Gorman, Conde, & Huber Jr., 2007).

Seattle Social Development Project

The Seattle Social Development Project (SSDP)[2] is directed toward children beginning in first grade and continuing through the sixth grade. This school-based universal curriculum was established in 1981, and aims to reduce the risk of long-term drug abuse by enhancing protective factors such as a child's sense of school affiliation, positive behavior in the school setting and academic achievement. This multi-component program achieves its stated prevention goals in part by offering workshops for parents and teachers. In this way, the adults in children's lives learn to engage their youngsters in learning, to facilitate the development of positive relation-ships, and to encourage pro-social behaviors.

Research demonstrates more positive outcomes for students receiving the SSDP curriculum than those who do not. Specifically, SSDP participants demonstrate less drug use and reduced delinquency as compared to control subjects (Hawkins & Catalano, 2005). Long-term results of the program further support the importance of the SSDP emphasis on positive social, family, and academic behaviors (Oesterele, Hill, Hawkins, & Abbott, 2008). In fact, Oesterele and her colleagues (2008) provide longitudinal data showing that high adaptive functioning from an early age has an impact on outcomes in adulthood.

Criticism of the SSDP focuses on the quasi-experimental nature of data collection. Specifically, Gorman (2002) argues that the SSDP claims are overstated, since some of its participants were initially recruited as 1st graders for a project funded by the Department of Justice (DOJ). When the DOJ program lost its monies, the children—then in the 4th grade—were recruited to the SSDP. However, the SSDP principal investigators made certain to identify distinct experimental groups: those who participated in the DOJ program initially and then joined the SSDP, those who received only the SSDP intervention, and controls (Hawkins & Catalano, 2005).

Adolescent Transitions Program (ATP)

Although best described as a Three-Tiered Program, ATP[3] is discussed in each of the three-tiered sections. ATP (Dishion & Kavanaugh, 2003) provides educational and therapeutic support at Tier I, Tier II, and Tier III levels, depending upon the needs of the adolescent and his or her family. At the Tier I level, which the authors title the "Universal Level," ATP is designed for use in school settings, although its focus is largely on parenting pre-adolescents and adolescents in order to reduce risky behaviors, such as drug use. Parents attend a series of classes that help them learn to focus on their child's positive qualities, establish norms, and implement fair and consistent consequences, solve problems, and improve communication.

Tier II

At the Tier II level, interventions are directed toward students who are at particularly high risk due to significant risk factors and/or prior experience with illicit substances. Within the school setting, Tier II interventions may take the form of establishing positive peer supports, matching students with mentors, further drug and alcohol educational classes, and group-based therapeutic approaches (Sharp et al., 1999). Some specialists have argued that this level of service is important in school-based prevention and early intervention efforts, since an estimated 9 out of every 10 adolescents with a substance problem do not receive treatment (Clark, Horton, Dennis, & Babor, 2002). The reason for lack of treatment is directed at the "traditional service model," which requires that the adolescent and his family seek clinical treatment, which rarely occurs (Wagner & Macgowen, 2006).

The best researched and potentially the most effective—both in terms of abuse issues and application in the school context—are cognitive-behavioral group interventions (Plant & Panzarella, 2009; Sloboda, 2009; Winters, Botzet, Fahnhorst, Stinchfield, & Koskey, 2009), or skills-based therapies (Wagner & Macgowen, 2006). The skills-oriented therapy recommended by Wagner and Macgowen (2006), however, proposes inviting independent experts in substance abuse into the school to conduct the intervention and, as such, is not addressed in detail in the present chapter, since it is a systems issue.

Cognitive-behavioral substance abuse interventions within the school setting may be implemented in a time-limited fashion by a mental health professional, such as the school psychologist, in conjunction with other support personnel. A cognitive-behavioral intervention typically targets the thoughts and actions of adolescents. In behavioral terms, specific goals are developed that can reduce the influence of environmental factors—such as social situations that provoke a desire to use—on drug use. As described by Winters and his colleagues (2009), participants develop plans for avoiding situations that provoke consumption, such as parties, hang-outs, and drug-using peers. In cognitive terms, participants rehearse conversations related to refusal, and "rewrite" their inner dialogue to develop a more adaptive future direction and thinking patterns. Furthermore, contingency management systems may also be utilized for students who remain abstinent since they have been demonstrated to be effective (Roll & Watson, 2006). Since these programs often involve "testing clean," the school nurse should also be an active member of the team in order to conduct drug tests.

Adolescent Transitions Program (ATP)

As previously mentioned in the Tier I section, ATP is a combined program/method organized within a Three-Tiered Program (Dishion & Kavanaugh, 2003). At the Tier II level, which the authors title the "Selective Intervention Level," ATP implements a "Family Check-Up," which consists of a complete assessment and provides the professional support to address issues that are of increasing severity.

Tier III

In the case of students exhibiting behaviors indicative of a serious problem with alcohol or drugs, Tier III interventions are typically so intensive and requiring of specialized services that they would be provided in settings external to the school. The teacher's role in a Tier III intervention would be largely geared toward providing information regarding behavioral, social, and academic observations prior to and during the adolescent's treatment.

Furthermore, the teacher would typically be asked to complete rating scales regarding progress in each of these areas prior to, during, and subsequent to the student's treatment. The school psychologist could request this information, as well as clinicians working in the treatment intervention setting.

Due to the frequent co-morbidity of psychiatric conditions such as depression, anxiety, and behavior disorders with substance abuse, it is possible that the teacher would refer the student for a thorough social-emotional-behavioral evaluation and actively participate in this process. This assessment will help the SST determine if the substance abuse is a result of another disorder, particularly one which qualifies for special education support.

Although treatment is not typically a responsibility of the classroom teacher, it would be useful for the educators, administrators, and support staff in the school to learn more about the myriad factors contributing to serious substance issues. This is important because an effective treatment program will involve coordination with medical professionals, family members, and other mental health workers as well as the adolescent himself or herself. In an effort to assist the intervention, the school psychologist can also conduct weekly and, later, bi-weekly to monthly behavioral observations and request the completion of behavioral questionnaires from teachers, parents, and the student. In this way, adaptive behaviors can be monitored and maladaptive behaviors rapidly identified in order to seek appropriate services immediately.

Adolescent Transitions Program (ATP)

As previously mentioned in the Tier I and Tier II sections, ATP is a combined program/method organized within a Three-Tiered Program (Dishion & Kavanaugh, 2003). At the Tier III level, which the ATP authors call the "Indicated Level," direct professional help is provided to the family in order to address abuse issues.

Progress Monitoring of Interventions

In the context of substance abuse during adolescence, progress monitoring of interventions will be an important component of the process. However, the degree of involvement from school personnel will likely be significantly reduced if Tier II and, particularly, Tier III interventions are required, since substance abuse treatment is not a qualifying condition for special education supports under federal law.

Tier I Progress Monitoring.

Tier I interventions related to substance issues are administered in the school setting as universal prevention programs. Often, prevention programs are presented to students long before substance use disorders may be observed. That is, universal prevention programs that focus on making good decisions, addressing peer conflicts, and understanding emotions are developed for children as young as preschool age. Progress monitoring for these types of programs would most commonly occur on an annual basis at a pre-test and post-test level.

Before beginning the lessons in the universal prevention curriculum, the teacher could complete behavioral rating scales for each student and/or request that parents do the same. Another option would be to administer basic knowledge and skills tests to those students who are old enough to read and respond to these types of tasks. In this way, behavior and/or knowledge change can be evaluated. Children who present with at-risk levels of behaviors (i.e. rejection, aggression, etc.) predictive of later substance abuse problems should continue to be monitored throughout their school careers.

Tier II Progress Monitoring

At the Tier II level, progress monitoring data will not likely be the direct responsibility of the classroom teacher due to the nature of substance abuse and treatment. However, if a student is participating in a small-group intervention either on-campus or in a clinical setting external to school grounds, the teacher will likely be requested to provide individual information about a particular student's behaviors, academic progress, and social activities in their classroom. This type of data is commonly obtained from teachers using behavior rating scales and subjective reports. Additionally, attendance records and grades or homework completion rates may be useful. While this information does not directly address the frequency and degree of substance abuse, it does provide useful data regarding behaviors related to substance abuse. This can be valuable to treatment planning, whether the focus is cognitive-behavioral or behavioral and advises clinicians about compliance with age-appropriate expectations (such as attending classes).

Tier III Progress Monitoring

Similar to the Tier II level, the clinical nature of substance abuse means that classroom teachers will not be directly involved in monitoring physical indicators of addiction, such as blood alcohol level, for example. This kind of data is collected by professionals working in either clinical or legal settings or, potentially, both. However, as with tier II, teacher report is invaluable to clinicians working with addicted adolescents.

Conclusion

Substance use and abuse are critically important topics for parents of adolescents and, importantly, the educators who work with such students. Data from NIDA (2011) suggest that the age of initiation appears to be decreasing. Furthermore, the use of controlled prescription drugs is on the rise while consumption of illicit substances continues to be of concern.

Teachers can make a significant impact in positive long-term outcomes for their students if they advocate for Tier I strategies from the earliest grades. Primary prevention in the form of universally-oriented programs may be one of the most successful means of combating drug use of any kind as children move into upper elementary, junior high, and high school. Providing children with direct instruction in problem-solving, emotion management, and social skills from as young as the pre-school years can help them to develop positive behaviors in the years prior to those that typically bring peer pressure for drug consumption. Furthermore, if universal prevention programs are implemented at the classroom level on a yearly basis, children receive "booster" sessions annually and can refine these abilities which are critical to rejecting drugs later in life.

In addition to advocating for universal prevention programs and implementing them with fidelity at the classroom level, teacher input regarding student behavior—either erratic if drug abuse is suspected but not yet confirmed or in response to Tier II and Tier II treatments external to the school setting—is very important. Providing responses to rating scales and/ or consulting with mental health professionals working in or outside of the school provides key information to the treatment team. In summary, the classroom teacher can make a significant contribution to every student, particularly those at high-risk for controlled or illicit substance use or abuse and even from a very young age.

Notes

1 Interested readers are encouraged to consult http://www.dare.com/home/about_ dare.asp for more information about the D.A.R.E. program as well as annual reports that the group publishes

2 Interested readers are encouraged to consult http://www.ssdp-tip.org/ssdp/ index.html for more information about the program.

3 Interested readers are encouraged to consult http://www.strengtheningfamilies. org/ for more information about the program.

References

Akins, S., Mosher, C., Smith, C. L., & Gauthier, J. F. (2008). Effect of acculturation on patterns of Hispanic substance use in Washington state. *Journal of Drug Issues, 38,* 103–18.

American Psychiatric Association (2000). *Diagnostic and statistical manual of mental disorders: DSM-IV* (text revision). Washington, DC: American Psychiatric Association.

Aries, E. (2001). *Adolescent behavior: Readings & interpretations.* Highstown, NJ: McGraw-Hill/Dushkin.

Berger, K. (2009). *The developing person: Through childhood and adolescence.* New York, NY: Worth Publishers.

Birkeland, S., Murphy-Graham, E., & Weiss, C. (2005). Good reasons for ignoring good evaluation: The case of the drug abuse resistance education (D.A.R.E.) program. *Evaluation and Program Planning, 28,* 247–56. doi:10.1016/j.evalprogplan.2005.04.001

Botvin, G. J. (2000). *Life skills training.* Princeton, NJ: Princeton Health Press.

Botvin, G. J., Griffin, K. W., & Nichols, T. D. (2006). Preventing youth violence and delinquency through a universal school-based prevention approach. *Prevention Science, 7,* 403–8. doi:10.1007/s11121-006-0057-y

Botvin, G., Renick, N. L., & Baker, E. (1983). The effects of scheduling format and booster sessions on a broad-spectrum psychosocial approach to smoking prevention. *Journal of Behavioral Medicine, 6,* 359–79. doi:10.1007/BF00846324

Breslau, J., Miller, E., Chung, W. J., & Schweitzer, J. B. (2010). Childhood and adolescent onset psychiatric disorders, substance use, and failure to graduate high school on time. *Journal of Psychiatric Research, 45,* 295–301. doi:10.1016/j.jpsychires.2010.06.014

Brook, J. S., Brook, D. W., & Pahl, K. (2006). The developmental context for adolescent substance abuse intervention. In H. A. Liddle & C. L. Rowe (eds), *Adolescent substance abuse: Research and clinical advances* (pp. 25–51). New York, NY: Cambridge University Press.

Brook, J. S., Whiteman, M., Cohen, P., & Tanaka, J. S. (1991). Childhood precursors of adolescent drug use: A longitudinal analysis. *Genetic, Social, and General Psychology Monographs, 118,* 195–213.

Carpiano, R. M., Kelly, B. C., Easterbrook, A., & Parsons, J. T. (2011). Community and drug use among gay men: The role of neighborhoods and networks. *Journal of Health and Social Behavior, 52,* 74–90. doi:10.1177/0022146510395026

Clark, H. W., Horton, A. M., Dennis, M., & Babor, T. F. (2002). Moving from research to practice just in time: The treatment of cannabis use disorders comes of age. *Addiction, 97,* 1–3. doi:10.1046/j.1360-0443.97.s01.11.x

Collins, C. C., Grella, C. E., & Hser, Y-I. (2003). Effects of gender and level of parental involvement among parents in drug treatment. *The American Journal of Drug and Alcohol Abuse, 29,* 237–61. doi:10.1081/ADA-120020510

Cratty, C. (2011, May 26). Drug abuse costs rival those of chronic diseases, report says. *CNN*. Accessed from http://edition.cnn.com/2011/HEALTH/05/26/drug.abuse.costs/index.html

Davis, S. J., & Spillman, S. (2011). Reasons for drug abstention: A study of drug use and resilience. *Journal of Psychoactive Drugs, 43,* 14–19. doi:10.1080/02791072.2011.566492

Dishion, T. J., & Kavanaugh, K. (2003). *Adolescent behavior: A family-centered approach*. New York, NY: The Guilford Press.

Doherty, E. E., Green, K. M., & Ensminger, M. E. (2008). Investigating the long-term influence of adolescent delinquency on drug use initiation. *Drug and Alcohol Dependence, 93,* 72–84. doi:10.1016/j.drugalcdep.2007.08.018

Drug Abuse Resistance Education (n.d.). *About D.A.R.E.* Accessed from http://www.dare.com/home/about_dare.asp

Ennett, S. T., Tobler, N. S., Ringwalt, C. L., & Flewelling, R. L. (1994). Resistance education? A meta-analysis of Project D.A.R.E. outcome evaluations. *American Journal of Public Health, 84,* 1394–401. doi:10.2105/AJPH.84.9.1394

Ensminger, M. E. (1990). Sexual activity and problema behaviors among black, urban adolescents. *Child Development, 61,* 2032–46. doi:10.1111/j.1467-8624.1990.tb03585.x

Fothergill, K. E., Ensminger, M. E., Green, K. M., Crum, R. M., Robertson, J., & Juon, H. (2008). The impact of early school behavior and educational achievement on adult drug use disorder: A prospective study. *Drug and Alcohol Dependence, 92,* 191–9. doi:10.1016/j.drugalcdep.2007.08.001

Giancola, P. R., & Mezzich, A. C. (2003). Executive functioning, temperament, and drug use involvement in adolescent females with a substance use disorder. *Journal of Child Psychology and Psychiatry, 44,* 857–66. doi:10.1111/1469-7610.00170

Gilbert, M. J. (1987). Alcohol consumption patters in immigrant and later generation Mexican American women. *Hispanic Journal of Behavioral Sciences, 9,* 299–313. doi:10.1177/07399863870093006

Gorman, D. M. (2002). Overstating the behavioral effects of the Seattle Social Development Project. *Archives of Pediatrics & Adolescent Medicine, 156,* 1155–6.

Gorman, D. M., Conde, E., & Huber, J. C., Jr. (2007). The creation of evidence in 'evidence-based' drug prevention: A critique of the Strengthening Families Program Plus Life Skills Training evaluation. *Drug and Alcohol Review, 26,* 585–93. doi:10.1080/09595230701613544

Gorman, D. M., Zhu, L., & Horel, S. (2005). Drug 'hot-spots', alcohol availability and violence. *Drug and Alcohol Review, 24,* 507–13. doi:10.1080/09595230500292946

Green, K. M., Doherty, E. E., Stuart, E. A., & Ensminger, M. E. (2010). Does heavy adolescent marijuana use lead to criminal involvement in adulthood? Evidence from a multiwave longitudinal study of urban African Americans. *Drug and Alcohol Dependence, 112,* 117–25. doi:10.1016/j.drugalcdep.2010.05.018

Green, K. M., & Ensminger, M. E. (2006). Adult social behavioral effects of heavy adolescent marijuana use among African Americans. *Developmental Psychology, 42,* 1168–78. doi:10.1037/0012-1649.42.6.1168

Grella, C., Hser, Y., Joshi, V., & Rounds-Bryant, J. (2001). Drug treatment outcomes for adolescents with comorbid mental and substance use disorders. *Journal of Nervous and Mental Diseases, 189*, 384–92. doi:10.1097/00005053-200106000-00006

Griffin, K. W., Botvin, G. J., & Nichols, T. R. (2004). Long-term follow-up effects of a school-based drug abuse prevention program on adolescent risky driving. *Prevention Science, 5*, 207–12. doi:10.1023/B:PREV.0000037643.78420.74

Hanson, D. (2007). Drug abuse resistance education: The effectiveness of DARE. *Alcohol Abuse Prevention: Some serious problems.* Accessed from http://www.alcoholfacts.org/DARE.html

Hawkins, J. D., & Catalano, R. F. (2005). Doing prevention science: A response to Dennis M. Gorman and a brief history of the quasi-experimental study nested within the Seattle Social Development Project. *Journal of Experimental Criminology, 1*, 79–86. doi:10.1007/s11292-004-6463-x

Hayatbakhsh, M. R., Najman, J. M., Jamrozik, K., Mamun, A. B., Bor, W., & Alati, R. (2008). Adolescent problem behaviors predicting DSM-IV diagnoses of multiple substance use disorder: Findings of a prospective birth cohort study. *Social Psychiatry & Psychiatric Empidemiology, 43*, 356–63. doi:10.1007/s00127-008-0325-1

HeavyRunner-Rioux, A. R., & Hollist, D. R. (2010). Community, family, and peer influences on alcohol, marijuana, and illicit drug use among a sample of Native American youth: An analysis of predictive factors. *Journal of Ethnicity in Substance Abuse, 9*, 260–83. doi:10.1080/15332640.2010.522893

Join Together (2011, May 26). New report estimates illicit drug use costs US economy more than $193 billion annually. Accessed from http://www.drugfree.org/join-together/drugs/new-report-estimatesillicit-drug-use-costs-u-s-economy-more-than-193-billion-annually

Kendler, K. S., Jacobson, K. C., Prescott, C. A., & Neale, M. C. (2003). Specificity of genetic and environmental risk factors for use and abuse/dependence of cannabis, cocaine, hallucinogens, sedatives, stimulants, and opiates in maletwins. *American Journal of Psychiatry, 160*, 687–95. doi:10.1176/appi.ajp.160.4.687

Liddle, H. A., & Rowe, C. L. (eds). (2006). *Adolescent substance abuse: Research and clinical advances.* New York, NY: Cambridge University Press.

Maggs, J. L., Patrick, M. E., & Feinstein, L. (2008). Child and adolescent predictors of alcohol use and problems in adolescence and adulthood in the National Child Development Study. *Addiction, 103*, 7–22. doi:10.1111/j.1360-0443.2008.02173.x

Mason, M. (2010). Mental health, school problems and social networks: Modeling urban adolescent substance use. *Journal of Primary Prevention, 31*, 321–31. doi:10.1007/s10935-010-0227-3

Miller, H. V. (2011). Acculturation, social context, and drug use: Findings from a simple of Hispanic adolescents. *The American Journal of Criminal Justice, 36*, 93–105. doi:10.1007/s12103-010-9086-y

National Institute on Drug Abuse (2011). *NIDA InfoFacts: High school and youth trends.* Accessed from http://www.drugabuse.g.ov/infofacts/HSYouthtrends.html

—(2010). *The science of addiction: Drugs, brains, and behavior.* Washington, DC: National Institutes of Health.

Nielsenwire (2011, June 8). Kids today: How the class of 2011 engages with media. Accessed from http://blog.nielsen.com/nielsenwire/consumer/kidstoday-how-the-class-of-2011-engages-with-media

Oesterle, S., Hill, K. G., Hawkins, J. D., & Abbott, R. D. (2008). Positive functioning and alcohol-use disorders from adolescence to young adulthood. *Journal of Studies on Alcohol and Drugs, 69,* 100–11.

Plant, R. W., & Panzarella, P. (2009). Residential treatment of adolescents with substance use disorders. In C. G. Leukefeld, T. P. Gullotta, & M. Staton-Tindall (eds), *Adolescent substance base: Evidence-based approaches to prevention and treatment* (pp. 135–54). New York, NY: Springer.

Pittman, L. D., & Chase-Lansdale, P. L. (2001). African American adolescent girls in impoverished communites: Parenting style and adolescent outcomes. *Journal of Research on Adolescence, 11,* 199–24. doi:10.1111/1532-7795.00010

Quenqua, D. (2011, July 10). Rethinking addiction's roots, and its treatment. *The New York Times.* Accessed from http://www.nytimes.com/2011/07/11/health/11addictions.html?_r=1&emc=eta1

Roche, K. M., Ensminger, M. E., & Cherlin, A. J. (2007). Variations in parenting and adolescent outcomes among African American and Latino families living in low-income, urban areas. *Journal of Family Issues, 28,* 882–909. doi:10.1177/0192513X07299617

Rosenbaum, D. P., Gordon, S., & Hanson, S. (1998). Assessing the effects of school based drug education: A six-year multilevel analysis of project D.A.R.E. *Journal of Research in Crime and Delinquency, 35,* 381–412. doi:10.1177/0022427898035004002

Roll, J. M., & Watson, D. (2006). Behavioral management approaches for adolescent substance abuse. In H. A. Liddle & C. L. Rowe (eds), *Adolescent substance abuse: Research and clinical advances* (pp. 375–95). Cambridge: Cambridge University Press.

Saba, L. M., Bennett, B., Hoffman, P. L., Barcomb, K., Ishii, T., Kechris, K., & Tabakoff, B. (2011). A systems genetic analysis of alcohol drinking by mice, rats, and men: Influence of brain GABAergic transmission. *Neuropharmacology, 60,* 1269–80. doi:10.1016/j.neuropharm.2010.12.019

Samaniego, R. Y., & Gonzales, N. A. (1999). Multiple mediators of the effects of acculturation status on delinquency for Mexican American adolescents. *American Journal of Community Psychology, 27,* 189–210. doi:10.1023/A:1022883601126

Sharp, R. N., McLaughlin, R. J., & McClanahan, K. K. (1999). Psychology in school based prevention, early intervention, treatment and abstinence maintenance. *School Psychology International, 20,* 87–103. doi:10.1177/0143034399201007

Sloboda, Z. (2009). School prevention. In C. G. Leukefeld, T. P. Gulotta, & M. Stanton-Tindall (eds), *Adolescent substance abuse: Evidence-based approaches to prevention and treatment* (pp. 191–212). New York, NY: Springer.

Spoth, R. L., Clair, S., Shin, C., & Redmond, C. (2006). Long-term effects of universal preventive interventions on methamphetamine use among adolescents.

Archives of Pediatric & Adolescent Medicine, 160, 876–82. doi:10.1001/archpedi.160.9.876

Spoth, R. L., Greenberg, M., & Turrisi, R. (2008). Preventive interventions addressing underage drinking: State of the evidence and steps toward public health impact. *Pediatrics, 121*, S311-S5336. doi:10.1542/peds.2007-2243E

Swan, N. (1995). Early childhood behavior and temperament predict later substance use. *NIDA Notes, 10*. Accessed from http://archives.drugabuse.g.ov/NIDA_Notes/NNVol10N1/Earlychild.html

Swendsen, J., Conway, K. P., Degenhardt, L., et al., (2010). Mental disorders as risk factors for substance use, abuse and dependence: Results from the 10-year follow-up of the National Comorbidity Survey. *Addiction, 105*, 1117–28. doi:10.1111/j.1360-0443.2010.02902.x

Tarter, R. E., Fishbein, D., Kirisci, L., Mezzich, A., Ridenour, T., & Vanyukov, M. (2011). Deviant socialization mediates transmissible and contextual risk on cannabis use disorder development: A prospective study. *Addiction, 106*, 1301–8. doi:10.1111/j.1360-0443.2011.03401.x

Tsuang, M. T., Bar, J. L., Harley, R. M., & Lyons, M. J. (2001). The Harvard twin study of substance abuse: What we have learned. *Harvard Review of Psychiatry, 9*, 267–79. doi:10.1093/hrp/9.6.267

Wagner, E. F., & Macgowan, M. J. (2006). School-based group treatment for adolescent substance abuse. In H. Liddle and C. L. Rowe (eds), *Adolescent substance abuse: Clinical research and advances* (pp. 333–56). Cambridge: Cambridge University Press.

Wheeler, R. A., & Carelli, R. M. (2009). Dissecting motivational circuitry to understand substance abuse. *Neuropharmacology, 56*, 149–59. doi:10.1016/j.neuropharm.2008.06.028

Williams, J. H., Davis, L. E., Johnson, S. D., Williams, T. R., Saunders, J. A., & Nebbitt, V. E. (2007). Substance use and academic performance among African American high school students. *Social Work Research, 31*, 151–61.

Winters, K. C., Botzet, A. M., Fahnhorst, T., Stinchfield, R., & Koskey, R. (2009). Adolescent substance abuse treatment: A review of evidence-based research. In C. G. Leukefeld, T. P. Gullotta, & M. Staton-Tindall (eds), *Adolescent substance base: Evidence-based approaches to prevention and treatment* (pp. 73–96). New York, NY: Springer.

World Health Organization (2004). *International Classification of Diseases* (10th ed.). Geneva, Switzerland: Author.

Yin, Z., Zapata, J. T., & Katims, D. S. (1995). Risk factors for substance use among Mexican American school-age youth. *Hispanic Journal of Behavioral Sciences, 17*, 61–76. doi:10.1177/07399863950171004

CHAPTER FIFTEEN

Understanding and Managing Behaviors of Children Diagnosed with Traumatic Brain Injury (TBI)

Lindsay McGuirk and Jeffrey A. Miller
Duquesne University

Stacie Leffard
The Children's Institute

Abstract

This chapter provides an introduction to the types, severity and causes of traumatic brain injury (TBI). Within the introduction, the authors provide a context for school personnel to notice, respond to, and advocate for youth who have sustained a TBI. This is critical because early and consistent support and intervention can reduce the learning and behavior problems that can manifest as a result of TBI. Details are provided about how assessment and intervention are linked for youth with TBI. Finally, the chapter includes an extended discussion of ways that teachers and other school personnel can help youth with TBI recover faster and maintain appropriate behavior in the school setting as they recover.

Overview

Children and adolescents who have sustained a traumatic brain injury (TBI) are at-risk for developing cognitive, emotional, and behavioral impairments, which may persist or worsen over time. In severe cases, children with TBI can have dramatic changes in personality, decreased impulse control, and sometimes aggression (Kim, 2002). The child with TBI may require interventions that address cognitive, academic, emotional and behavioral issues and his or her family may need assistance in helping the child with issues in these areas. Such intervention is necessary particularly during the school years when cognitive and social-emotional abilities are maturing quickly.

Children and adolescents who have sustained a TBI often return to the classroom setting in need of school-based educational and social support services. Because the recovery process of a TBI is dependent on several factors, including the cause, the severity of the injury, and the brain structures and systems affected, interventions implemented in the school setting must account for the individual characteristics of the injury and the student. Schools that provide education about TBI to teachers and staff, make students aware of TBI, and work to prevent TBI in school-related activities, will likely see a lower incidence of TBI because these are protective factors. In those same schools, in part due to early intervention, those who have sustained a TBI will have an increased probability of maximum recovery compared to schools that do not provide these services.

Types of TBI

Brain injury is an umbrella term, which encompasses a variety of traumas that affect the brain. A brain injury acquired after the birth process can be designated as either a non-traumatic brain injury or traumatic brain injury. A non-traumatic brain injury involves an internal brain process, and includes meningitis, brain cancer, or a vascular problem, such as a stroke. The other type of brain injury, traumatic brain injury, and the type we will focus on in this chapter, is due to an external process, usually physical force, which causes trauma.

Traumatic brain injuries are divided into three types of injuries: penetrating, open, or closed. If the force is strong enough to penetrate the skull and directly injure the head, as in a gunshot wound, then it is diagnosed as a penetrating head injury. When an injury such as this occurs, damage to the brain is restricted to the path of the object, although additional damage may be caused by factors such as bleeding of the brain, swelling, and/or infection (Farmer & Peterson, 1995). If the skull is fractured and broken open, this results in an open injury. An open head injury often damages the brain tissue or the surrounding membranes. In contrast, if there is no evidence of the injury penetrating the skull, then it is diagnosed as a closed head injury. Injury to the brain in closed head cases occurs due to the compression or rotation of the brain inside the skull (Canto, Chesire, & Buckley, 2011). Even though the skull is not penetrated or broken open, closed head injuries can cause even more damage than open injuries because there is no room for the brain to compensate for swelling or pressure. There are several different types of closed head TBIs, including concussions, brain contusions, diffuse axonal injuries, and hematomas. The causes of TBIs can result in either an open or closed injury. For example, in one case a car accident could cause an open head injury, whereas in another case it may result in a closed head injury; for instance, a concussion.

Severity of TBI

Determination of the severity of a TBI is dependent upon the type of injury, the location of injury, and the amount of damage to the brain of the injured. TBIs are classified by severity, and interventions and prognosis vary according to the severity of the TBI. The Glasgow Coma Scale (Arffa, 2006), a common assessment scale used to classify a TBI, categorizes TBI into mild, moderate, and severe cases. This assessment measures such factors as eye opening, verbal response, and motor response.

Mild TBI occurs most often, and accounts for 80 to 90% of all TBI cases (Kirkwood et al., 2008). The most common and well-known mild TBI is a concussion. A concussion is a bump, blow, or jerk to the head that changes the way the brain works; more specifically, the brain cells, but does not appear to change brain anatomy (Kirkwood et al., 2008). Even though concussions are usually not life threatening, those who sustain one still may experience serious effects that last for extended periods of time, which is referred to as "post-concussion" syndrome. Immediately after a concussion occurs, a child may experience disorientation and confusion. The child may also experience headaches, dizziness, poor concentration and memory, irritability, and sleep disturbance up to 6 months after the injury.

Moderate to severe TBIs can have much more serious and lasting effects. There is usually a loss of consciousness and memory loss (known as post-traumatic amnesia). The difference between a moderate TBI and a severe TBI is how long the loss of consciousness and memory loss lasts. When someone sustains a moderate or severe TBI, the axons in the brain that transport electrical impulses throughout the body may be damaged from the forceful impact of the brain. This is known as a diffuse axonal injury. Density differences of the white and gray matter in the brain cause the nerve cells to pull apart from the axons, known as shearing. The amount of shearing that takes place is directly related to the severity of the TBI injury. Therefore, the more damage to the brain structure that occurs, the longer post-morbid symptoms will continue.

TBI is the leading cause of acquired disability in children in the United States. Schools are faced with the challenge of assisting students returning from a TBI who are still demonstrating negative effects from the injury (Chapman et al., 2010). Since the presentation and course of recovery of a TBI varies for each child, educators need to understand the degrees and distinctions of TBIs. If these nuances are ignored, the long-term consequences of TBI often may be misinterpreted (Savage, Depompei, Tyler, & Lash, 2005).

Prevalence

TBI was historically considered to be a relatively low-incidence disability (Canto et al., 2011). However, present prevalence data indicate that this is no longer the case. Indeed, the Center for Disease Control has characterized it as a serious public health problem at local, national, and international levels, especially for children and adolescents. In fact, children aged 0 to 4 years and adolescents aged 15 to 19 years represent the two groups most likely to suffer a TBI, besides adults aged 65 years and older (Faul, Xu, Wald, & Coronado, 2010; Gopinath & Narayan, 1992). An average of approximately 180 per 100,000 children ages 1 to 15 years of age are hospitalized for a head injury each year (Kraus, 1995). Other prevalence findings indicate that brain injury is the leading cause of death and disability for children and adolescents ages 0 to 19, and affects 635,000 in America (Langolis, Rutland-Brown, & Thomas, 2004). More specifically, of children between the ages of birth and 14 years, 435,000 trips to the emergency room are made because of a TBI, with nearly 37,000 hospitalizations and 2,700 deaths (National Dissemination Center for Children and Adolescents, 2011).

Bearing in mind that TBI is more common than originally considered, it is unsettling that, when surveyed, a vast majority of educators reported that they had very limited or no experience evaluating or consulting with students who have had a TBI (Canto, Chesire, & Buckley, 2010). In fact, when educators were asked about their experience with students with a TBI, 92% admitted having no training in the academic implications that arise from the injury (Glang, Dise-Lewis, & Tyler, 2006).

Figure 15.1 breaks down the leading causes of TBI, which include falls, motor vehicle-traffic accidents, struck by/against events, and assault. Faul and colleagues (2010) attribute half (50%) of TBIs among children aged 0 to 14 years to falls, making it the leading cause of TBI for children. "Struck by/against events" are defined as colliding with a moving or stationary object, and is identified as the second leading cause of TBI among children aged 0 to 14 years, comprising 25% of TBIs. Motor vehicle and traffic accidents are also identified as a leading cause of TBI, and more notably, represent the largest percentage of TBI-related deaths of all age groups.

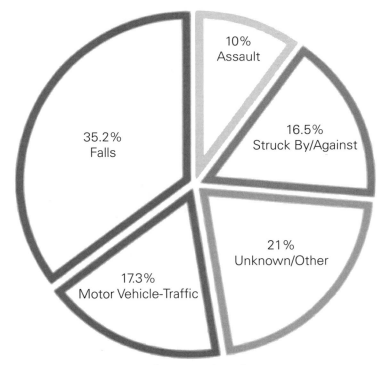

Figure 15.1 Leading causes of TBI (Faul et al., 2010)

Theoretical Framework

Transitioning children and adolescents who have endured a traumatic brain injury (TBI) back into the school environment can pose some challenging obstacles for students, their families, and school personnel. However, there are two models of assessment and intervention available that can make this transition more manageable: the Multistage Neuropsychological Assessment-Intervention Model (Teeter & Semrud-Clikeman, 1997) and the Developmental Neuropsychological Remediation/Rehabilitation Model (Rourke, Bakker, Fisk, & Strang, 1983). The Multistage Model divides TBIs into eight stages, ranging from the least severe at Stages 1 and 2, to the most severe at Stages 7 and 8. These are paired stages with the odd number stage indicating level of assessment and the even numbered state indicating level of intervention (see Table 15.1). Rourke's Remediation/Rehabilitation Model provides a bottom-up approach in providing support at each level of severity by examining factors that interact with recovery and rehabilitation, such as academic functioning, the demands of the environment, available protective resources, and ongoing assessment and intervention data. Therefore, the Multistage Neuropsychological Model and Rourke's Model of Remediation/Rehabilitation are integrated in the treatment of students with TBIs.

The Multistage Neuropsychological model, developed by Teeter and Semrud-Clikeman (1997), connects assessment with intervention at the stage most appropriate to the injury and proposes that an efficient identification and evaluation of the problems guide effective intervention strategies. Stage 1 of the model outlines the least severe of impairments, which are usually identified through pre-referral interventions. For example, a minor concussion may be identified at Stages 1 and 2 through teacher interview or student observation. This stage focuses on problem identification, which leads to the second stage of behavioral-based intervention planning. Once the problem is identified, school personnel can develop and implement an intervention based on initial observational or teacher interview data. During this stage, specific classroom interventions that address the problems identified are implemented. These interventions can include specific study skills and curriculum modifications, such as peer tutoring.

If an impairment is more severe, and a response to intervention yields unsuccessful results, it may be necessary to progress to higher stages. At this stage, a psycho-educational evaluation, or a cognitive child study is often required. More specifically, measures of intellectual, academic, and psychosocial functioning are utilized to better assess the presenting problem(s) (Teeter & Semrud-Clikeman, 1997). Therefore, a formal referral to complete an evaluation is required and may result in special education placement. Further, this would result in Stage 4 cognitive-based interventions being developed and employed. These interventions are based on the child's cognitive strengths and weaknesses determined through the psycho-educational evaluation. Teeter and Semrud-Clikeman (1997) assert that the interventions at Stage 4 can include those that target organizational and study skills, strategic instruction, and self-esteem and social relations. For children who do not respond to interventions in Stages 1 and 2 and 3 and 4, a neuropsychological evaluation may be justified. In addition to conducting a comprehensive neurological evaluation in Stage 3, psychological and academic functioning should also be assessed. If a school psychologist is not competent to administer a neuropsychological evaluation, a formal referral outside of school support should be utilized. Often, children with TBIs require neuropsychological testing (Semrud-Clikeman, 2010). Even if a child with a minor concussion responds to interventions at Stage 2, a neuropsychological evaluation may be completed to assess baseline functioning and progress monitoring to measure short-term and long-term effects of the concussion.

Stages 5 and 6 of the Multistage model utilize an integrated neuropsychological plan and incorporates treatment interventions from earlier

Table 15.1 Overview of the Multistage Neuropsychological Assessment-Intervention Model (Teeter & Semrud-Clikeman, 1997)

	Assessment	Intervention
Least Severe	*Stage 1*: Pre-referral through student observation and/or teacher interview	*Stage 2*: Curriculum modifications (e.g. peer tutoring)
	Stage 3: Psycho-educational or cognitive child study	*Stage 4*: Specific interventions that target cognitive weaknesses identified through evaluations (e.g. strategic instruction, one-on-one support, etc.)
	Stage 5: Neuropsychological evaluation	*Stage 6*: Interventions that utilize child's strengths and long-term management of symptoms and impairments
Most Severe	*Stage 7*: Intensive medical and neurological evaluation	*Stage 8*: Medical and neurological rehabilitation in hospital and/or rehabilitation setting

stages. Focus in this stage is on compensation for the child's weaknesses by using his or her strengths and long-term management of symptoms and impairments (Teeter & Semrud-Clikeman, 1997). Stages 7 and 8 of the model address those children with the most severe impairments, who may need intensive medical and neurological evaluation and remediation. Therefore, this stage is typically out of the realm of school supports in that the most severe impairments require medical and neurological rehabilitation that is provided in a hospital and/or rehabilitation setting. For example, a child with a TBI with the maximum severity of impairment requires MRI, PET, and/or CT imaging from a neurologist, and rehabilitation at a residential treatment center. Frequently, interventions are not focused on academic or psycho-social factors, but medical treatments, such as neurosurgery. Table 15.1 provides a more organized depiction of the Multistage Neuropsychological Assessment-Intervention Model.

At each stage of the Multistage Neuropsychological Model, Rourke's Developmental Neuropsychological Remediation/Rehabilitation Model (1994) suggests examining factors, which are categorized into seven steps. At the first step, interactions of assets/deficits across academic, social, and adaptive functioning should be assessed. Generally, an evaluation of the child's functional consistent with the severity of the injury and other factors related to the injury is conducted (Rourke et al., 1983). By triangulating data from the evaluation, a clearer picture of the child's TBI and how it relates to his/her functioning can be measured. Assessing the demands of the child's environment is the second step of Rourke's model. Immediate demands (e.g. school setting), as well as long-term demands (e.g. workplace environment) should be considered. While immediate demands for the child are concerned with learning and long-range demands are more concerned with after school goals, such as work, both require social interactions. When working with a child with a TBI, questions such as "what kinds of challenges is the child faced with currently, and what challenges will the child be faced with in the future?", must be asked.

By understanding the functionality of the child within specific frameworks, more appropriate intervention plans can be developed (Teeter & Semrud-Clikeman, 1997). Moreover, by gauging the child's functional status, short-term and long-term predictions can be established, which is the third step of Rourke's model. To form these predictions, families and school personnel must consider what is normal for child development, theories of information processing and cognition, and current research on the relationship between brain functioning and behavior in children (Rourke et al., 1983; Stein & Raudenbush, 2010). Once short- and long-term predictions are established, more appropriate treatment strategies and progress monitoring plans can be developed and modified according to the child's functioning.

The fourth step of Rourke's remediation/rehabilitative model is drawn from the results of the evaluation and the child's individual circumstances obtained in Steps 1 through 3, and aims to expand the short- and long-term predictions to "ideal" short- and long-term remedial plans (Teeter & Semrud-Clikeman, 1997). When developing the remedial plans, it is imperative to take into account the available resources of the individual child that will be utilized. If resources are not considered, or are over- or underestimated, the remedial plans will be unsuccessful. The resources include the family, therapists, teachers, and the setting of the context, whether it be a school or rehabilitative facility. Teeter and Semrud-Clikeman (1997) suggest specificity during this step concerning treatment goals, intervention strategies, and prognosis. Once the remedial resources are taken into consideration, a more "realistic" remedial plan can be formulated and Step 6 of Rourke's model can be undertaken. Generally, the "realistic" remedial plan begins to come together when short- and long-term remedial plans (Step 4) are developed with consideration of the available resources (Step 5; Teeter & Semrud-Clikeman, 1997).

Progress monitoring with any treatment plan is essential, especially for children with TBIs because of the individualized rates of improvement and varied skills and capacities that are affected by the lesion. Progress monitoring is Rourke's 7th and final step of his model, which entails ongoing assessment and intervention. Because of individual rates of improvement, interventions may need to be modified often and sometimes drastically, hence assessments must also be administered frequently to gauge what treatment goals are being reached and what aspect(s) of the interventions is working and what is not.

Due to changes in healthcare reimbursements and technological improvements, inpatient rehabilitation stays are getting shorter. This may result in students with more severe impairment returning to schools sooner than has been the case. Schools may have less time to prepare for students returning after an injury depending on injury severity and duration of required treatment (e.g. a student with mild TBI may return to school quickly with accommodations, whereas a student with a severe TBI may have an extended inpatient rehabilitation stay allowing the school more time to plan).

Traumatic Brain Injury and the Individuals with Disabilities Education Act

The Individuals with Disabilities Education Act, also known as IDEA, is a law developed within the United States that ensures services to children with disabilities. IDEA reaches out to more than 6.5 million infants, toddlers, children, and youth with disabilities. This is done through early intervention, special education, and related services by state and public agencies. It should be emphasized that a TBI is a category of eligibility entitled to all special education rights. Therefore, under the IDEA directive of Child Find, Local Education Agencies (LEAs) are required to identify children thought to be eligible for special education, including children with a TBI (IDEA, 2004).

According to IDEA, a TBI is:

> An acquired injury to the brain caused by an external physical force, resulting in total or partial functional disability or psycho-social impairment, or both, that adversely affects a child's educational performance. TBI applies to open or closed head injuries resulting in impairments in one or more areas, such as cognition; language; memory; attention; reasoning; abstract thinking; judgment; problem-solving; sensory, perceptual, and motor abilities; psychosocial behavior; physical functions; information processing; and speech. TBI does not apply to brain injuries that are congenital or degenerative, or to brain injuries induced by birth trauma. (IDEA, 2004)

Many children who suffer from a TBI will have difficulty learning and/ or may exhibit disruptive behaviors. IDEA emphasizes that teachers must recognize that a child's learning style and classroom behavior may have changed because of a TBI.

Children who have experienced a mild TBI, and are expected to fully recover, may be protected under Section 504 of the Rehabilitation Act of 1973, depending on the length of their functional impairments. Section 504 is a federal law protecting the rights of individuals with disabilities and requires public educational agencies to establish fair and equal opportunities for these students in school. Because of this protection, the school must provide the students with disabilities the maximum and appropriate assistance and opportunities (Pennsylvania Code, Chapter 15).

Children who have suffered a severe or chronic TBI may require an Individualized Education Program (IEP) from their school. This can address the child's new and specific educational needs following a TBI. The IEP will cover how the disability affects the child's functioning in the general curriculum; annual goals; related services and aids the child may receive; progress made; and overall participation in educational activities with children without disabilities (Pennsylvania Code, Chapter 14). It may also be beneficial for a child who suffered from a TBI to work one-on-one with a speech language pathologist (SLP), occupational therapist (OT), and/or physical therapist (PT). A SLP can work on cognitive-communication skills with the child, while an OT can evaluate self-help and fine motor skills, and a PT can assess the child's mobility, as a whole. This individualized hands-on work with the child is highly encouraged by IDEA, in hopes to bring any child with a TBI back to an acceptable level of functioning in the classroom and everyday life.

Three Tier Prevention/Intervention Strategy

When a child acquires a brain injury during their school years, he/she is faced with a variety of challenges, especially because it is a time of increased cognitive development and growth. Many children who have experienced a TBI will exhibit characteristics of learning and/or behavioral diffi-culties. In addition, if a child experiences a TBI, the injury can exacerbate pre-existing learning, behavioral, or psychological problems (Glang, Todis, Sublette, Brown, & Vaccaro, 2010). Therefore, additional supports and accommodations, and IEP and Section 504 teams are critically important to successful academic, social, and emotional outcomes (Todis & Glang, 2008). Furthermore, due to more awareness and knowledge of TBIs and more technology and therapeutic techniques, there has been dramatic progress in brain injury recovery rates over the past 20 years (Faul et al., 2010). This translates to an increasing number of young, otherwise healthy individuals with chronic, neurological disabilities returning to the schools. However, we are still struggling nationwide with TBI programming even though it was added as a special education eligibility category in 1990 through IDEA (Glang et al., 2010).

With any intervention, school personnel use a three tier prevention/inter-vention strategy for teachers to use in classroom management. This is often thought of as the three-tiered pyramid, with Tier I being addressed through prevention and awareness interventions, Tier II utilizing classroom interventions to assist in moderate disruptions or classroom dysfunction, and Tier III yielding special education placement or a Section 504 plan to address severe disruptions or classroom dysfunction. While the Tier III model may be more straightforward and comprehensible for other diagnoses, such as learning disabilities or AD/HD, moving from Tier I to Tier III TBI interventions are not as clear cut. Many students with a TBI do not function sufficiently in the classroom environment, and steps must be taken to rehabilitate those students to their optimal levels of functioning within the classroom environment just as with students with other diagnoses.

Tier I: Prevention and Awareness

In the Response to Intervention (RtI) model, Tier I encompasses all students; therefore, screening and intervention at this level are universal and aims to monitor student progress by identifying students who are not making expected gains or meeting specific milestones. The first line of intervention to consider for TBI should be prevention. One way to prevent TBI is by raising awareness of activities that pose a higher risk of head injury, and by teaching students and their families precautions that can limit those risks, such as appropriate fit and proper use of helmets during activities, such as bicycle riding and tackle football.

In addition to raising awareness in an attempt to prevent TBI, universal screening procedures that establish baseline levels of functioning and flag indicators of possible head trauma can be helpful in recognizing students that are already afflicted. Similar to the yearly physical exam that school children are required to have from a physician, a simple screening procedure, such as a question on the annual health contact sheet for the school, for current or past head trauma would help identify students who might be suffering from side effects of a TBI.

An example of a more sophisticated screening instrument being implemented in youth sports is the Heads Up program, which uses BASELINE ImPACT (Immediate Post-concussion Assessment and Cognitive Testing), a computer-based assessment tool, to establish pre-morbid or baseline functioning levels in young athletes (www. impacttest.com). Following a suspected TBI, the athlete's current levels of functioning can be compared to previously established baseline levels to determine if there are any deficits as a result of the injury and when it is safe for the athlete to return to play. The program is also a tool for educating coaches, players, and parents about concussions (www. pittsburghpenguinsfoundation.org).

Another simple screening measure is the HELPS Brain Injury Screening Tool (Picard, Scarisbrick, & Paluck, 1991) which identifies the possible presence of a current or past brain injury by answering the following questions:

H Have you ever Hit your Head or been Hit on the Head?
E Were you ever seen in an Emergency room, hospital or doctor's office because of an injury to your head?
L Did you ever Lose consciousness or experience a period of being dazed and confused because of an injury to your head?
P Do you experience any of these Problems in your daily life since you hit your head? (Includes a list of 11 problems commonly associated with TBI)
S Any significant Sicknesses?

Depending on the age of the child, this screening can be completed by the parent or student in just a few minutes and establish whether there is need for further evaluation to confirm TBI and its side effects (Picard et al., 1991).

A final way to address TBI universally is by raising awareness and educating teachers to recognize the symptoms and potential side effects that a child may experience as a result of a brain injury. When a child suffers head trauma, the impact on typical school activities may be difficult for a teacher to discern or accommodate because training is minimal for general education teachers. Therefore, professional development programs can be implemented to better educate teachers and provide them with strategies to recognize and serve children who have suffered from TBI.

One professional development model for training teachers to better deal with TBI when encountered in the educational setting is the TBI Consulting Team model (Glang et al., 2010), which utilizes a group of trained consultants who provide consultation services to schools in the form of in-service trainings and ongoing support for educators of children with TBI. One version of this model is Pennsylvania's BrainSTEPS (Strategies Teaching Educators, Parents, & Students). In this program, extensively trained consulting teams are available to families and schools throughout the state of Pennsylvania to aid in the development of educational programs and academic interventions, implementation of strategies, and progress monitoring of students receiving services. BrainSTEPS consultants do not provide direct services to students; rather, they teach educators and families in how to provide the necessary services (www.brainsteps.net).

Another evidence-based professional development program for TBI awareness is BrainSTARS, which is a manualized approach that highlights the link between observed behaviors and the underlying neurological trauma. The manual provides a stepwise, progressive technique for providing services and accommodations to students with brain injuries and "includes background information about brain injury, child and adolescent development, ways to create positive change, a comprehensive list of problems associated with brain injury, recommended interventions, and worksheets" (www.childrenscolorado.org/conditions/rehab/camps/brainstars.aspx). The manual may be implemented on its own or with ongoing support from expert consultants.

Tier II: Moderate disruptions of classroom dysfunction

Due to the fact that children with a TBI have increased behavioral problems and a stronger need for educational assistance in the classroom, it is imperative for the parents and teachers to intervene appropriately and affectively, based on the symptom severity of the TBI (Yeates & Taylor, 2006). When using a Tier II intervention, it is first important for the child who suffered from a TBI to understand what has happened, and also what to expect in the future regarding his or her abilities (Kirkwood et al., 2008). If a Tier II intervention is being implemented, this means the child has experienced a mild traumatic brain injury, whereas precautions must be taken in the school environment to a moderate extent.

For a child who has suffered a mild TBI, taking too much time away from school post-injury could actually cause recovery to digress into a negative state. A slow return to school has the potential to cause stress, loneliness from being away from friends and the familiar school environment, and even fear of falling behind academically (Kirkwood et al., 2008). An initial period of rest and recovery should be implemented for anyone with a TBI; however, the best medicine could potentially be returning to the pre-injury daily routine, and for children this is school.

Once a child with a mild TBI has returned to school effectively, teachers must intervene so that any emotional, behavioral, and academic concerns are recognized and addressed. Just as it is important to recognize the child's TBI, it is just as necessary to validate the injury. A child may feel as if his or her injury is not being taken seriously, due to the notion that it was a mild TBI. Psychotherapy can be beneficial intervention for children who have suffered from a mild TBI. This provides a place for the child to discuss his or her injury, coping strategies, as well as physical, emotional, and behavioral symptoms that he or she experiences (Kirkwood et al., 2008). Family-based therapy may also be recommended if the family system has changed or been altered because of the child's TBI. Training family members in rehabilitation has been shown to improve physical and cognitive recovery in children over and above clinician based interventions (Braga, Da Paz Júnior, & Ylvisaker, 2005).

Tier III: Severe Disruptions or Classroom Dysfunction

In the Response to Intervention (RtI) model, Tier III refers to the lowest percentage of students who require intensive planning and intervention services along with frequent progress monitoring in order for a student to benefit from his or her academic environment. Tier III generally refers to students who require either an Individual Education Program (IEP) or a 504 plan. Children who suffer moderate and severe TBIs often need specific care, services, and academic modifications upon their return to school, which can therefore, qualify them for an IEP or 504 plan.

The recovery of children who have suffered a TBI involves many inter-relating factors, including cognitive, behavioral, educational, social, and family issues, in conjunction with the type and severity of the TBI. Because of the interaction of these various factors, TBIs can cause a multitude of physical, cognitive, social, emotional, and behavioral effects, and long-term outcomes that can range anywhere from total recovery, long-lasting disabilities, or death (Dykeman, 2003; Ylvisaker et al., 2005).

Common long-term symptoms resulting from moderate to severe TBI are changes in appropriate social behavior, deficits in social judgment, and cognitive changes, especially problems with sustained attention, processing speed, and executive functioning (Kim, 2002; McDonald, Flanagan, Rollins, & Kinch, 2003; Stone, Baron-Cohen, & Knight, 1998). Although many of these symptoms can be gradually improved with appropriate rehabilitation, all of these symptoms have long-term consequences for the daily lives of people with moderate to severe TBI, especially school-aged children (Dahlberg et al., 2007; Milders, Fuchs, & Crawford, 2003; Ponsford, Draper, & Schonberger, 2008).

The transition from hospital or home to school reentry is a critical piece of the recovery process. When a child is transitioned back into the school environment after suffering a TBI, school personnel must consider the impact of learning on the recovery of the child. Moreover, it is important to note that a TBI not only affects the child's learning, but also may cause physical changes, speech and language impairments, social skills impairments, emotional changes, and behavioral changes. However, often a person with a TBI is not aware of these impairments, particularly ones that are unseen to the person, such as cognitive problems (Glang et al., 2010). Therefore, a person with a TBI may not recognize the need for help and can over-estimate his or her abilities. Because a TBI can alter the learning process, students who have experienced one must be told that they now learn differently than they had previously. It is estimated that 70% of school aged children with severe TBIs and 40% with moderate TBIs will require the onset of special education services and intensive treatments upon their return to school (Kinsella et al., 1997). Students may transition back to school through multiple steps. The student may originally be placed in a residential treatment center, followed by homebound instruction, followed by half a day in a special education classroom. This transition requires the successful partnership of the student's teachers, school psychologists, neuropsychologists, and school administrators. School staff may be unfamiliar with the language of medical reports and how they translate practically to educational planning. Ideally, a neuropsychologist and school psychologist should meet with the student's teachers and staff to discuss what the child's current level of functioning is and what should be expected of him or her upon his or her return to the classroom. Neuropsychologists and school psychologists can help to develop IEP or 504 plan and give realistic expectations of performance. They should also elaborate on any medications the child is taking and what the side effects of that medication may look like in a school environment. Finally, the line of communication should not be closed following the meeting. A plan to reconvene with both educational and psychological staff should be made in advance (Wade, Carey, & Wolfe, 2006).

Numerous studies have found that young children often experience poorer outcomes than do adolescents with equivalent injuries. Although general functioning typically seems to improve annually, the cognitive problems associated with impaired executive control and behavioral abilities often worsen over the child's developmental stages (Galvin & Mandalis, 2009). In a classroom, this may look like a child who is progressing normally during vocabulary instruction, but during math class the student may become overwhelmed and cannot understand simple concepts such as addition. Also, a child may function normally in terms of everyday living skills, but may not socialize appropriately.

Possible explanations for these continuing difficulties in younger children include the notion that because younger children have not yet learned or "overlearned" tasks such as reading, writing, problem solving, social skills, etc., it is harder for them to recover or relearn those skills than it is for an older child who has more years of experience with those skills prior to injury. The more natural a skill is, the easier it may be to retain or relearn.

An ideal course of recovery includes a decrease in symptom amount, as well as a reduction of the symptom severity. This means that a child may re-enter the school environment with several areas of severe impairment. The goal of recovery is not simply to decrease the number of impairments, but also to lessen the severity of the impairment. Trying to achieve this ideal course of recovery generally is not continuous improvement; rather, there are periods of improvement and decline. A study conducted on children who experienced TBIs indicated that although a significant amount of progress occurred during the first year post injury, only a very minor rate of change during the subsequent two years occurred in most areas. In addition, there were continuous neurobehavioral deficits present throughout all three years for moderately and severely injured children. The most significant slowing of recovery was evident in novel problem solving (Taylor et al., 2003). All three of these findings highlight the need for frequent and periodic observations of functional behavior both in school and in the home, with adjustments made to the medical and educational intervention to address the ever-changing symptomology of the child (Dykeman, 2009).

For individuals substantially affected by a TBI, Ben-Yishay and Prigatano (Prigatano, 1999) propose strategies that can be used as support on the road to recovery and "normality". It is important to consider what it really means to return to normality. In most cases, normality after the injury will not match the student's normality before the injury. Therefore, normality for a person with a TBI is that they are comfortable in his or her own skin, feel healthy and safe in his or her environment, and have insight and acceptance into his or her injury and future. The model also considers the deficits that can be experienced by a person with a TBI in all facets of his or her life. These deficits include feelings and impressions of their injury demonstrated through cognitive, interpersonal, social, and intrapsychic spheres. When working with a student who has suffered a TBI, it is critical that mental health is assessed, denial is confronted, and other feelings, such as anger, are discussed. Through these strategies of the model, the student is supported through his or her coping with the loss of his/her functioning, and as he or she gradually hits critical landmarks in his or her recovery.

Critical landmarks of a TBI do not necessarily include regaining of functioning because typically, especially with severe TBIs, this is improbable. However, critical landmarks outlined in the Ben-Yishay model still improve functioning in that individuals come to awareness and understanding of their challenges, which helps them become more malleable to treatments. Moreover, with this heightened awareness, individuals learn to compensate for their deficits by utilizing those skills they have mastered. Their newfound realism allows them to set practical limits, and they are able to cognitively overcome barriers by utilizing those skills that are proficient. In short, the idea of achieving normality for a person who has suffered a TBI is coming to a point in which he or she has achieved acceptance of not only his or her injury, but the deficits caused by that injury. To aid in this realization, school personnel can help the students observe their own behavior to become self-aware of their level of functioning and capabilities. This should be done at an acute period of the injury and should focus on ensuring that the child has a sufficient and realistic understanding of the events surrounding the injury and what can be expected in the future (Kirkwood et al., 2008). A child who does not have a realistic view of his/her abilities will be less likely to take to an intervention and use it properly in the classroom. Therefore, self-awareness is crucial before intervention implementation.

Tier II and Tier III Interventions

The line between a moderate and severe TBI is debatable, and therefore, so are the interventions used to address the deficits caused by each. Similar interventions are employed for moderate and severe TBIs because similar skills and functions are affected. The difference lies within how intrusive the interventions need to be and how often they are implemented based on how severely the skills and functions of the student are affected. Because TBIs depend on the various factors surrounding the injury, itself, and the student, the interventions we discuss do, as well. Therefore, it is up to the educator to determine which interventions can help to compensate for the student's deficits in the classroom environment, as well as which interventions match with the student's individual characteristics.

Therefore, similar to any diagnosis, TBIs do not have a "one-size-fits-all" intervention or treatment. As mentioned, many factors are dependent on a person's recovery, including the severity of the injury, the location of the injury, support system, personality characteristics, and age at which the injury occurred. Interventions and remedial treatments of a TBI must be custom made around these factors, and the presenting problems of the injury. In contrast to other diagnoses seen in the school setting, TBIs follow a functional model of rehabilitation, rather than a diagnostic model, in that students are rehabilitated to a point where they can engage or participate in the tasks and activities of everyday life (Galvin & Mandalis, 2009). In other words, many strategies and interventions intend to support the child in the classroom environment, but do not necessarily improve underlying skills or the injury, itself. Along the same lines, children with TBIs must learn to compensate for their injury. This is done by using their strengths that are intact after the injury to compensate for weaknesses that are a result of the injury.

Specific interventions for TBI can be broken into domains, including cognitive and academic training, study and organization skills, and social skills. With any intervention, it is important to teach through successive approximations or chaining strategies, meaning the student should learn and practice components of the intervention until mastery before moving onto more complex aspects.

Classroom Environment

Cognitive exertion and the added stimulation of the school environment can significantly increase symptoms of the injury, even when the student has begun to recover. As a result, there are a number of classroom and academic modifications that can be put in place to ease the recovery of students with TBIs. Adjusting the seating proximity of the student by seating him/her closer to the teacher can increase structure and instructional prompting that the student receives. Furthermore, depending on which specific interventions are being implemented, the teacher can keep a closer eye on the student to be sure he/she is properly using the intervention and that it is producing beneficial outcomes for the student. By being in the front of the class, other students who may be a source of distraction for the student with the TBI will not be in the foresight and therefore, less of a distraction.

Decreasing the size of the class also decreases the extra stimulation. However, due to a lack of school resources and school personnel, this may be unrealistic. If so, classroom teachers can modify the classroom atmosphere to decrease excess stimulation for the student by setting up individual work stations or centers where one, two, or three students can work at a time. Distractions outside of the classroom may also pose a problem. More specifically, a child with a TBI may be distracted if there is a lot of activity occurring in the hallway or outside of a window. In short, distractions should be kept to a minimum. Simply pulling down window blinds so the child is not distracted by activity outside or closing the door to reduce noise from the hallway can reduce the extra stimulation and help the child focus more readily. It may also be beneficial to keep the child in the same classroom throughout the school day. Moving between three or four classrooms creates added stimulation and can be another source of distraction.

Instructional Modifications

Adjusting the classroom environment can most definitely be beneficial for a student with a TBI, but the teacher may also have to adjust or increase certain teaching strategies in order for the student to truly be included in the learning environment. The teacher may have to repeat instructions and/ or minimize directions by providing one or two at a time instead of listing them. When repeating instructions, paraphrasing can often be ineffective. This means that teachers should not use phrases as, "well, let me explain it another way.." This will just further confuse the student. Because students with TBIs have slower processing speed, repeating exactly as before provides more time to absorb the information (Glang et al., 2010). Scaffolding by providing guided questions and providing clues to keep the student on topic can also be advantageous while providing the student with some independence, as well (Galvin & Mandalis, 2009). This strategy can also be utilized when the student is struggling to provide an answer. Often, the student does know the answer, but cannot form the actual wording due to deficits in executive functioning caused by the TBI.

Assignments

In terms of school assignments, a student with a TBI may become overwhelmed more quickly than his/her peers. By clearly defining class requirements, such as assignments and deadlines, the student will have a better chance of completing assignments on time. For example, a teacher can assist the student in chunking assignments or have another student create a timeline for long-term or large assignments. Because students with TBIs have difficulty remembering and are slower to complete tasks, teachers can provide notes, outlines, or presentation slides to the student prior to class to give him/her a head start on the class lessons for the day to organize his or her thoughts. Moreover, more time can be allotted to the student with the TBI to complete tasks.

As stated, children with a TBI often become cognitively exerted more quickly than the average student. By taking a break from academically-heavy tasks and simply focusing on non-academic activities, such as coloring or reading a magazine, the child will have a chance to cognitively rejuvenate. It may even be necessary for a teacher to lessen the workload for the student as to avoid cognitive fatigue. A consideration of modifications mentioned by teachers and parents as provisions for behavioral problems include preferential seating, small group instruction, one-on-one teaching, alternative testing procedures, decreased homework load, and alternative grading systems (Yeates & Taylor, 2006).

Social Skills

There has been limited support for behavioral interventions being utilized with a TBI diagnosis, largely because research has been conducted with small sample sizes or single case designs, thus restricting the capability to generalize (Noggle & Pierson, 2010; Wade et al., 2006; Ylvisaker et al., 2007). Furthermore, little research has been completed investigating the intervention outcomes solely of children and adolescents, let alone those outcomes in the classroom (Semrud-Clikeman, 2010). Often, children who experience a TBI can behave in socially inappropriate ways. They may have problems with social judgment, have trouble following along in a conversation, or may disclose information that is unsuitable in certain contexts. More specific symptoms consist of withdrawal from people, disinhibition, aggression, and confrontational behaviors (Dykeman, 2003). It is important to remember that these social behaviors are a result of the cognitive problems caused by the injury, which in turn, affect the emotional temperament of the child.

A behavioral plan and positive behavior supports that reinforce positive social behavior can minimize inappropriate conduct in the classroom (Ylvisaker et al., 2007). Modeling and prompting can be utilized for appropriate social behavior, while planned ignoring of the inappropriate behavior and redirection to another topic or task should be used until the student is able to use behavioral control (Dykeman, 2003). However, the student must be made aware of the inappropriate behaviors they exhibit after the fact and receive clear feedback concerning those behaviors, as they may be oblivious to the negative effects those behaviors could have on their social interactions. Self-monitoring can increase the student's awareness by redirecting his/her attention to those behaviors by using problem solving techniques to formulate goals, develop alternative solutions, identify consequences of those solutions, and finally, choose which solution is the best fit for the situation. Self-monitoring also develops the student's ability to engage in reflective listening to identify conversation content, affect, and the context of the conversation (Dykeman, 2003).

There has been some empirical evidence in support of the use of cognitive-behavioral therapy to treat emotional and cognitive skills (Williams, Evans, Needham, & Wilson, 2002). Decreased frequency of challenging behaviors, decreased intensity of challenging behaviors, and improvement of relationships with peers and educational staff have been documented results of CBT for the treatment of TBIs (Feeney & Ylvisaker, 2003). Further research that examined the efficacy of a cognitive-behavioral intervention on TBI diagnoses determined that CBT is helpful in improving child self-management and compliance (Wade, Carey, & Wolfe, 2006). Counselors and/or teachers can use prepared scripts in individual counseling sessions or within the classroom to help students confront complicated or confusing social situations (Dykeman, 2003). Moreover, emotional difficulties, such as anxiety, can be remediated by teaching the student to employ relaxation techniques.

Treatment Integrity

Treatment integrity (also known as fidelity) is the degree of compliance to an explicitly described intervention. This is important because the probability of replicating the research outcomes of evidence-based treatments declines if the procedures are deviated from significantly. However, local constraints often force deviations from the prescribed methods carried out in a laboratory or other tightly controlled setting and it is possible that an intervention will still work to some degree with minor modifications; thus, it is better to attempt a reasonably modified version of the intervention than to bypass it completely because the optimal resources or setting are not available. Members of a problem-solving team should complete frequent integrity checks to ensure that they are implementing an intervention as intended (or as closely as possible), especially if they feel that an intervention is not producing the desired outcome (Hulac, Terrell, Vining, & Bernstein, 2011).

Progress Monitoring

TBIs can cause disturbances in all spheres of a child's life, including cognitive, interpersonal, social, and intrapsychic. Progress monitoring is essential for students with TBIs to assess improvement, lasting effects, and decreases in performance and functioning. The ongoing assessment of students with TBIs can assess baselines and continued functioning of those students. Specific assessments and measures that can be utilized for progress monitoring of TBIs include: cognitive tests, memory and language tests, measures of visuospatial functioning, tests of motor abilities, tests that assess attention and concentration, personality assessments, and adaptive functioning measures. However, traditional tests of intelligence are not always a good measure of cognitive recovery after a brain injury since they measure acquisition of prior knowledge. Considering that memory and the learning of new information is generally affected to a greater extent than other cognitive skills in a TBI, neuropsychological tests are more efficient at detecting how a person learns. Functional Behavioral Assessment (FBA) and cognitive assessment should also be conducted to examine, measure, and treat many deficits associated with TBI, particularly behavioral changes related to increased impulsiveness, inappropriate emotional outbursts, aggression, and inattention. A TBI can produce immediate, short-term, and/or long-term effects on the functioning of any of these domains. Therefore, it is imperative to gauge a baseline of functioning to assess the varying effects that are often produced by TBIs.

Case Example

Ashley is a 17-year-old female in her junior year of high school. She is on her school's basketball team and has been playing competitively for six years. About two weeks ago, Ashley was playing in a basketball game and was dribbling down the court when she lost control of her balance, proceeded to move past the basketball hoop, and hit the front of her head on the wall behind the basket. Once Ashley hit the front of her head on the wall, she fell backward, hitting the back of her head against the court floor.

Ashley suffered from an immediate, brief loss of consciousness. Once she regained consciousness, Ashley was taken to the hospital to have some tests conducted in order to better assess her situation. It was found that Ashley suffered from a mild TBI from a concussion. Persisting post-concussive symptoms included sensitivity to light and noise, frequent headaches, and irritability. Her irritability translated into difficult interpersonal clashes with teachers, mood swings, and intolerance for inconsistency. Ashley's cognitive presentation included impaired sustained attention, slowed processing speed, and impaired verbal fluency. It was recommended that Ashley return to school one week after her injury.

Once Ashley returned to school, the school team considered several potential intervention recommendations. She was provided with a modified school schedule with initial half-days, then with a gradual increase to full days of school. Rest breaks in the nurses' office as needed throughout the school day were also recommended, particularly when her low frustration tolerance secondary to irritability was prominent. She was offered extended time for assignment completion, a reduced work load for graded assignments, and postponement of significant exams until her symptoms subsided. Finally, she was provided with previous notes she missed while out of school due to her injury and new notes and assignments. Ashley was also excused from PE class, physical recreation, or any other physical activity that has the potential to exacerbate her symptoms.

Since Ashley is a competitive basketball player, a decision was made as to when she was allowed to return to practicing and playing with her high school's team. Since Ashley's brain had not fully healed immediately following her concussion, re-injury is a major concern that her physicians and coaches must consider. If Ashley were to hit her head again soon after this injury, very serious damage could occur. There is no specific time limit for how long Ashley should sit out from basketball, and the final decision for her to practice and play was made by her physician and neurologist. A slow, gradual reintroduction to playing with the team again is recommended as the ideal route for Ashley.

Ashley's case illustrates what is an unfortunately common scenario of a mild TBI caused by a sports-related injury. Since Ashley's TBI is mild, her transition back to the school environment is rather quick. However, once she is back at school, gradual modifications need to be made so she is not simply thrown back into daily life pre-injury state. Ashley's post-concussive symptoms and cognitive and behavioral presentation was closely monitored by her parents, teachers, and physicians. It was also prudent for Ashley's physicians to make appropriate decisions in her return to her high school's basketball team, as to avoid another injury. Ashley's case shows a range of approaches to supporting a student's return to school following mild TBI with the goal of preventing further injury, providing support to behavioral problems secondary to the injury, and to the extent possible minimizing the amount of school she would miss that could lead to further frustration.

Conclusion

TBI is an increasingly identified problem that affects students' learning and functional performance in schools. Indeed, school-aged children are at the highest risk of experiencing a TBI. As has been shown, the severity and range of affected systems can vary from child to child based on preexisting skills, the nature of the injury, and the amount of support that is available. Simply, each child with a TBI needs to be treated individually with specialized assessment and intervention. Further, it has been shown that teachers and other school personnel can play a critical role in the prevention, recovery, and rehabilitation of students who experience a TBI. The most important role that school personnel can play is to identify the need for assessment and intervention for a child suspected of experiencing a TBI and work as a team with other health care personnel to support a maximal return to premorbid functioning.

References

Arffa, S. (2006). Traumatic brain injury. In C. E. Coffey, R. A. Brumback, D. R. Rosenberg, & K. Voeller (eds), *Textbook of Essential Pediatric Neuropsychiatry* (pp. 507–48). Philadelphia: Lippincott Williams & Wilkins.

Braga, L. W., Da Paz Júnior, A. C., & Ylvisaker, M. (2005). Direct clinician-delivered versus indirect family-supported rehabilitation of children with traumatic brain injury: A randomized controlled trial. *Brain Injury, 19,* 819–31. doi:10.1080/02699050500110165

BrainSTEPS (2011). www.brainsteps.net

Canto, A. J., Chesire, D. J., & Buckley, V. A. (2010, April). *Serving students with traumatic brain injury (TBI): Preliminary findings.* Presented at the annual Florida State University First Year Assistant Professor Grant Program Research Colloquium.

Canto, A. I., Chesire, D. J., & Buckley, V. A. (2011). On impact: Students with head injuries. *Communiqué, 40,* 1–5.

Chapman, L. A., Wade, S. L., Walz, N. C., Taylor, H. G., Stancin, T., & Yeates, K. O. (2010). Clinically significant behavior problems during the initial 18 months following early childhood traumatic brain injury. *Rehabilitation Psychology, 55,* 48–57. doi:10.1037/a0018418

Children's Hospital Colorado (2011). www.childrenscolorado.org/conditions/rehab/camps/brainstars.aspx

Dahlberg, C. A., Cusick, C. P., Hawley, L. A., Newman, J. K., Morey, C. E., Harrison-Felix, C. L., & Whiteneck, G. G. (2007). Treatment efficacy of social communication skills training after traumatic brain injury: A randomized treatment and deferred treatment controlled trial. *Archives of Physical Medicine and Rehabilitation, 88,* 1561–73. doi:10.1016/j.apmr.2007.07.033

Dykeman, B. F. (2003). School-based interventions for treating social adjustment difficulties in children with traumatic brain injury. *Journal of Instructional Psychology, 30,* 225–30.

—(2009). Response to intervention: The functional assessment of children returning to school with traumatic brain injury. *Education, 130,* 295–300.

Farmer, J. E., & Peterson, L. (1995). Pediatric traumatic brain injury: Promoting successful school reentry. *School Psychology Review, 24,* 230–43.

Faul, M., Xu, L., Wald, M. M., & Coronado, V. G. (2010). *Traumatic brain injury in the United States: Emergency department visits, hospitalizations, and deaths.* Atlanta, GA: Centers for Disease Control and Prevention, National Center for Injury Prevention and Control.

Feeney, T. J., & Ylvisaker, M. (2003). Context-sensitive behavioral supports for young children with TBI: Short term effects and long term outcomes. *Journal of Head Trauma and Rehabilitation, 18,* 33–51. doi:10.1097/00001199-200301000-00006

Galvin, J., & Mandalis, A. (2009). Executive skills and their functional implications: Approaches to rehabilitation after childhood TBI. *Developmental Neurorehabilitation, 12,* 352–60. doi:10.3109/17518420903087293

Glang, A., Dise-Lewis, J., & Tyler, J. (2006). Identification and appropriate service delivery for children who have TBI in schools. *Journal of Head Trauma Rehabilitation, 21,* 411–12. doi:10.1097/00001199-200609000-00013

Glang, A., Todis, B., Sublette, P., Brown, B. E., & Vaccaro, M. (2010).

Professional development in TBI for educators: The importance of context. *Journal of Head Trauma Rehabilitation, 25,* 426–32. doi:10.1097/HTR.0b013e3181fb8f45

Gopinath, S. P., & Narayan, R. K. (1992). *Clinical treatment: Head injury.* New York, NY: Oxford University.

Hulac, D., Terrell, J., Vining, O., & Bernstein, J. (2011). *Behavioral intervention in schools.* New York, NY: Routledge.

ImPACT Applications Inc. (2011). http://impacttest.com/Individuals with Disabilities Education Act, 20 USC. § 1400 (2004).

Kim, E. (2002). Agitation, aggression, and disinhibition syndromes after traumatic brain injury. *NeuroRehabilitation, 17,* 297–310.

Kinsella, G. J., Prior, M., Sawyer, M., et al., (1997). Predictors and indicators of academic outcome in children 2 years following traumatic brain injury. *Journal of the International Neuropsychological Society, 3,* 608–16.

Kirkwood, M. W., Yeates, O. W., Taylor, H. G., Randolph, C., McCrea, M., & Anderson, V. A. (2008). Management of pediatric mild traumatic brain injury: A neuropsychological review from injury through recovery. *Child Neuropsychology, 22,* 769–800. doi:10.1080/13854040701543700

Kraus, J. F. (1995). Epidemiological features of brain injury in children: Occurrence, children at risk, causes, and manner of injury, severity, and outcomes. In S. H. Broman & M. E. Michael (eds), *Traumatic head injury in children* (pp. 22–39). New York, NY: Oxford University Press.

Langolis, J. A., Rutland-Brown, W., & Thomas, K. E. (2004). *Traumatic brain injury in the United States: Emergency department visits, hospitalizations, and deaths.* Atlanta, GA: Center for Disease Control and Prevention, National Center for Injury Prevention and Control.

McDonald, S., Flanagan, S., Rollins, J., & Kinch, J. (2003). TASIT: A new clinical tool for assessing social perception after traumatic brain injury. *Journal of Head Trauma Rehabilitation, 18,* 219–23. doi:10.1097/00001199-200305000-00001

Milders, M., Fuchs, S., & Crawford, J. R. (2003). Neuropsychological impairments and changes in emotional and social behavior following severe traumatic brain injury. *Journal of Clinical and Experimental Neuropsychology, 25,* 157–72. doi:10.1076/jcen.25.2.157.13642

National Dissemination Center for Children and Adolescents (2011). Traumatic brain injury. *NICHCY Disability Fact Sheet, 18.* Washington, DC: Author.

Noggle, C. A., & Pierson, E. E. (2010). Psychosocial and behavioral functioning following pediatric TBI: Presentation, assessment, and intervention. *Applied Neuropsychology, 17,* 110–15. doi:10.1080/09084281003708977

Picard, M., Scarisbrick, D., & Paluck, R. (1991). *HELPS—A brief screening device for traumatic brain injury.* New York, NY: Comprehensive Regional Traumatic Brain Injury Rehabilitation Center.

Pittsburgh Penguins Foundation (2011). http://pittsburghpenguinsfoundation.org/programs/headsup.html

Ponsford, J., Draper, K., & Schonberger, M. (2008). Functional outcome 10 years after traumatic brain injury: It's relationship with demographic, injury severity, and cognitive and emotional status. *Journal of International Neuropsychological Society, 14*, 233–42. doi:10.1017/S1355617708080272

Prigatano, G. P. (1999). *Principles of neuropsychological rehabilitation*. New York, NY: Oxford University Press.

Rourke, B. P. (1994). Neuropsychological assessment of children with learning disabilities: Measurement issues. In C. R. Lyon (ed.), *Frames of reference for the assessment of learning disabilities: New views on measurement issues* (pp. 475–514). Baltimore, MD: Paul H. Brookes.

Rourke, B. P., Bakker, D. J., Fisk, J. L., & Strang, J. D. (1983). *Child neuropsychology: An introduction to theory, research, and clinical practice*. New York, NY: The Guilford Press.

Savage, R. C., Depompei, R., Tyler, J., & Lash, M. (2005). Pediatric traumatic brain injury: A review of pertinent issues. *Pediatric Rehabilitation, 8*, 92–103. doi:10.1080/13638490400022394

Semrud-Clikeman, M. (2010). Pediatric traumatic brain injury: Rehabilitation and transition to home and school. *Applied Neuropsychology, 17*, 116–22. doi:10.1080/09084281003708985

Stein, N. L. & Raudenbush, S. (eds). (2010). *Developmental cognitive science goes to school*. New York, NY: Routledge.

Stone, V. E., Baron-Cohen, S., & Knight, R. T. (1998). Frontal lobe contributions to theory of mind. *Journal of Cognitive Neuroscience, 10*, 640–56. doi:10.1162/089892998562942

Taylor, H., Yeates, K. O., Wade, S. L., Drotar, D., Stancin, T., & Montpetite, M. (2003). Long term educational interventions after traumatic brain injury in children. *Rehabilitation Psychology, 48*, 227–36. doi:10.1037/0090-5550.48.4.227

Teeter, P. A. & Semrud-Clikeman, M. (1997). *Child neuropsychology: Assessment and interventions for neurodevelopmental disorders*. Needham Heights, MA: Allyn & Bacon.

Todis, B. & Glang, A. (2008). Redefining success: Results of a qualitative study of post-secondary transition outcomes for youth with traumatic brain injury. *Journal of Head Trauma Rehabilitation, 23*, 252–63. doi:10.1097/01. HTR.0000327257.84622.bc

Wade, S. L., Carey, J., & Wolfe, C. R. (2006). The efficacy of an online cognitive-behavioral family intervention in improving child behavior and social competence following pediatric brain injury. *Rehabilitation Psychology, 51*, 179–89. doi:10.1037/0090-5550.51.3.179

Williams, W. H., Evans, J. J., Needham, P., & Wilson, B. A. (2002). Neurological, cognitive, and attributional predictors of posttraumatic stress symptoms after traumatic brain injury. *Journal of Traumatic Stress, 15*, 397–400. doi:10.1023/A:1020185325026

Yeates, K. O., & Taylor, H. G. (2006). Behavior problems in schools and their educational correlates among children with traumatic brain injury. *Exceptionality, 14*, 141–54. doi:10.1207/s15327035ex1403_3

Ylvisaker, M., Adelson, D., Braga, L. W., Burnett, S. M., Glang, A., Feeney, T., ... Todis, B. (2005). Rehabilitation and ongoing support after pediatric TBI: Twenty years of progress. *Journal of Head Trauma Rehabilitation, 20*, 95–109.

Ylvisaker, M., Turkstra, L., Coehlo, C., Yorkston, K., Kennedy, M., Sohlberg, M. M., & Avery, J. (2007). Behavioral interventions for children and adults with behaviour disorders after TBI: A systematic review of the evidence. *Brain Injury, 21*, 769–805. doi:10.1080/02699050701482470

CHAPTER SIXTEEN

Conclusion: Promoting and Maintaining Intervention Success when Working with Children and Adolescents with Emotional and Behavioral Disorders

Laura M. Crothers and
Jered B. Kolbert
Duquesne University

Abstract

In this chapter, the authors will review some of the considerations that may be helpful to the reader when determining which intervention structure to follow in responding to children's problematic emotional or behavioral responses associated with various child and adolescent disorders.

Overview

Throughout the process of reading the valuable information presented in the chapters of this book, it is our hope that the reader has learned about the choices and structure of interventions for children with a variety of emotional and behavioral problems. In accordance with the Response to Intervention (RtI) model framework, such interventions can be differentiated for use in Tiers I, II, or III, and implemented accordingly depending upon the intensity and/or chronicity of the behavior or emotional symptomatology. In this chapter, the authors will review some of the considerations that may be helpful to the reader when determining which intervention structure to follow in responding to children's problematic emotional or behavioral responses associated with various disorders.

Perhaps the most important recommendation is that the social ecology of the child's functioning be acknowledged and included in the interventions developed. Second, it may be helpful to consider utilizing school-based consultation as a means of introducing and maintaining the use of the interventions recommended in the classroom and school system. Third, it is vitally important that educators choose interventions based upon the evidence base attesting to their effectiveness. Fourth, as necessary as it is to use evidence-based interventions, it is just as essential to monitor the child's progress in response to those interventions. Finally, as we know that behavior change is rarely absolute, it is crucial to be reasonable in our expectations for success.

Social Ecology of Emotional and Behavioral Problems

Although the research attesting to the importance of considering the social ecology of children when planning for behavioral intervention has existed for decades, this theoretical framework has been re-invigorated; for example, in considering the reasons for the limited success of whole-school anti-bullying intervention programs (Swearer, Espelage, Vaillancourt, & Hymel, 2010). In explanation, social ecology focuses upon the dynamic relations between people and their environment (Stokols, 2000). Social ecological analyses of emotional and behavioral problems highlight the symptoms associated with such difficulties in reference to the causal circumstances of their physical and social environments (Stokols, 2000). Thus, social ecology provides a conceptual framework that can be used to understand the etiology of emotional and behavior problems (Stokols, 2000). Perhaps of greater importance, however, such an approach allows the design of therapeutic interventions to be accomplished to respond to the realities of children's environmental contexts.

The preeminent theoretical approach referenced in the social ecological theoretical framework is Bronfenbrenner's (1979) ecological framework of the microsystem, the mesosystem, the exosystem, and the macrosystem, each of which describe the complexity of interactions of a variety of factors that exist within an individual and also his or her proximal and distal environments (Stacks, 2005). Using this theoretical approach, Stacks (2005) describes the factors related to the onset and persistence of externalizing behavior problems.

In the *microsystem*, which is the pattern of activities, roles, and interpersonal relations experienced by the person that allow or inhibit interaction with the immediate environment (Bronfenbrenner, 1993), factors such as the quality of preschool educational environment and parenting behavior have been found to contribute to the development of externalizing behavior (Stacks, 2005). The *mesosystem,* comprised of the relationships existing between two or more settings (Bronfenbrenner, 1993), consists of factors that account for some of the variability in externalizing behavioral problems, such as the strength of the relationship between home and school (Stacks, 2005). *Exosystemic* factors (linkages between two settings, in one of which the developing person has no part) may refer to such variables as stress at the parent's employment context that indirectly affect the development of the child's externalizing behavior problems by means of the parent's behavior (Stacks, 2005). Finally, in the *macrosystem,* which includes belief systems, resources, and patterns of social exchange in systems-level culture (Bronfrenbrenner, 1993), factors that may contribute to the development and maintenance of problem behavior include stressful life events and conditions, such as poverty (Stacks, 2005).

The consideration of these spheres of influence upon a child's behavior suggests that alterations in one environment are not wholly sufficient for behavioral change; instead, intervention must occur at or at least acknowledge the role of each environmental level in order for emotional or behavioral change to be long-lasting. This recognition is not meant to stymie intervention efforts when it seems impossible to address a problem behavior at every environmental level of a child's functioning. Such knowledge instead should guide our efforts to include as much information about the child and his or her environments into our intervention planning efforts as possible. At the least, attempting to include the child's family or caregivers in intervention planning and implementation is likely prudent in order to increase the success of such efforts.

Ecological analyses have implied that certain behaviors and environmental conditions for a child can wield a powerful impact upon his or her well-being, and thus can be termed "leverage points" for their high-impact influence (Stokols, 2000). Thus, although educators work with children at school, certain behaviors are best addressed through changes made outside the educational context, such as at home or in the child's neighborhood. Educators should be cognizant that sometimes, the most efficient means to impact a child's behavior at school might mean that a behavioral intervention does not actually occur *at* school.

Using School-Based Consultation to Deliver Evidence-Based Interventions

One of the challenges of implementing tiered interventions is that teachers are expected to assume greater responsibility in educating children who have been identified with emotional and behavioral disorders. In the Response to Intervention (RtI) model, teachers are expected to apply educational interventions to students who are just beginning to exhibit symptoms of behavioral and mental health disorders. Furthermore, new legislation such as the No Child Left Behind (NCLB) Act of 2001 (US Department of Education, 2001) and the Individuals with Disabilities Education Act (IDEA) 2004 has resulted in the increased inclusion of students with emotional and behavioral disorders in regular education classrooms. In previous decades, students with emotional and behavioral disorders were more likely to be educated or treated by special educational teachers and educational specialists, including school psychologists and school counselors than by regular education teachers. Now, the expectation in the RtI model is that regular education teachers will receive support from educational specialists either by way of the educational specialist working with the student in the general education setting, which is referred to as "push-in" services, or through receiving consultation from the educational specialist.

The new expectation is that regular education teachers will be able to identify and use differentiated instructional and classroom management strategies that have empirical support in working with children identified with emotional and behavioral disorders. The increasing complexity of the teacher's role demands the need for more effective and intense teacher preparation and the need for consultation from fellow teachers and from experts who have specialized knowledge and training. Consultation is generally defined as a non-hierarchical problem-solving relationship between a consultee and consultant, in which the goal of the consultative relationship is to improve the consultee's functioning with clients (e.g. students, schools, caregivers) and to improve the skills of the consultee (e.g. classroom teacher, principal) so that he or she will be able to independently provide services to the client in the future (Caplan, 1970; Zins & Erchul, 2002).

School-based consultation typically is characterized by a problem-solving process that is primarily guided by the consultant but continually adjusts according to the needs of the consultee/teacher (Crothers, Hughes, & Morine, 2008). Furthermore, it usually involves elements of both a collaborative relationship, in that the consultant assists the consultee/teacher in identifying his or her ideas and strengths regarding the issue, and a directive relationship in that the consultant may provide direct suggestions based on his or her technical expertise and prepare the consultee/teacher to utilize new or improved skills.

Using behavioral consultation in school settings

Behavioral consultation is probably the most common model of consultation used by educational support personnel in the schools, and includes the following steps: 1) establishment of a cooperative partnership, 2) problem identification and analysis, 3) intervention development and selection, and 4) intervention implementation, evaluation and follow-up (Crothers et al., 2008). In the problem identification stage, the consultant helps the consulting teacher in defining the problem, identifying the antecedent determinants of the identified problem, identifying the consequences that may maintain the behavior, assessing relevant variables within the environment, and identifying the available resources. During the problem definition step, the problem behavior is operationally defined so that the behavior is easier to measure. In addition, the frequency and duration of the problem as well as the intensity and severity of the behavior is assessed.

When identifying the antecedents of the target behavior, temporal and situational variables are considered. The consultant and consulting teacher then explore possible positive consequences that could improve the target behavior, as well as possible inappropriate consequences that may maintain the behavior. After such consequences are explored, other environmental variables are assessed, such as instruction, school routines, and the child's attitudes and behaviors. Finally, the student's strengths and potential resources, such as peer tutors, are identified to ensure the most success (Peterson, 1968).

Using systems consultation in school settings

Despite the numerous strengths of the behavioral consultative model, some educational support personnel may use a systemic approach to consultation, which also incorporates a problem-solving process, but diverges in some important ways from the behavioral model. The systemic approach focuses less on the specific behavioral interactions between the student and teacher, and more on the nature of the relationships between the child and their significant others, including parents, teachers, and peers, and the nature of the relationships between the child's significant others (White & Mullis, 1998). In the systemic approach, the problems and potential solutions are not seen as existing within the child, but rather the nature of the interactions between the student and teacher and between the teacher and parents is the focus of intervention. Indeed, Westwood (2002) found that some of the important components of successful inclusion plans for children with emotional and behavioral disorders included a positive teacher-child relationship, the child's counselor's support in the inclusion process, and parental involvement.

Additionally, Weintraub (1998) found that regular education teachers thought that some of the most effective interventions for students with troubling behavior were consulting with parents to address problems perceived to be related to the student's home life and developing a relationship with the child to decrease alienation. The systemic approach to consultation is also holistic in that it recognizes the children's emotions and cognitions are interconnected, and that the thoughts, feelings, and behaviors of their parents and teachers are also interconnected. As in behavioral consultation, the child's behavior is seen as functional, and exploration of the various contexts of the child's life is necessary to determine the potential purpose of the behavior. The school-based systemic consultant might first assist the teacher in examining the history of his or her relationship with the child, exploring the reciprocal nature of the interactions between the teacher and child.

The relationship between the teacher and child is explored, and the teacher may be asked to consider how his or her behaviors, thoughts, and feelings impacted the child, and reciprocally, how the child's behaviors, thoughts, and feelings influenced the teacher. Through such questions, the consultant attempts to assist the teacher in developing new perspectives of the child and his or her relationship with their child that results in the teacher generating new solutions. According to the systems perspective, a consultant is often necessary when there is tension between a student and teacher because the teacher's perspective of the child and the situation has become restricted by his or her emotional intensity. In such cases, the consultant uses his or her objectivity and ability to see the relationship patterns to guide the teacher and/or patterns to perceive the situation from a broader perspective.

In the systemic approach to school-based consultation, there is also considerable emphasis on facilitating collaboration between the home and school (White & Mullis, 1998). The primary goals of involving the parents are to better understand the family context that may be contributing to the child's difficulties, obtain the parents' perspective and ideas to address the problem, and to increase family-school collaboration in and of itself given the considerable empirical support demonstrating the relationship between academic achievement and family involvement (e.g. Epstein, 2005). Interested readers are encouraged to review Epstein's work on family-school collaboration, as a full explanation is beyond the scope of this text.

The consultant often acts a facilitator of family-school collaboration. Often, the relationship between the teacher and parents has been soured by their mutual frustrations in addressing the challenging behaviors of the child. Frequently, the teacher and parents focus on each other as a source of the problem. In such situations, the consultant seeks to rebuild the relationship between the teacher and the parents through hosting parent-teacher conferences. In these meetings, the consultant uses a structured format of a problem-solving model to reestablish a more functional hierarchy and increased trust among the adults, thus facilitating more constructive communication between the parents and teachers and blocking unproductive communication. However, sometimes teachers are most concerned about remedying the academic difficulties that children are experiencing related to their emotional or behavioral problem(s). In such cases, instructional consultation may be a valuable tool to help facilitate a change in a student's academic performance.

Using instructional consultation in school settings

Another form of consultation that may be particularly valuable in helping teachers to remedy the academic weaknesses associated with children's emotional or behavioral problems is instructional consultation. Rosenfield (1995), the pioneer of instructional consultation (IC), describes the process as a merging of instructional psychology in the discipline of school psychology with the process of collaborative consultation from the field of special education. Because educational professionals are often called upon to engage in consultation regarding students' educational progress and problems, IC is an excellent fit because of its focus upon evidence-based practices (EBP's). Although IC has a specific focus on academic concerns, with consideration of appropriate academic progress, it can also be used to address issues of classroom management (Rosenfield, 2003).

There is much evidence that instructional quality and time spent in learning both powerfully influence students' learning outcomes (Walberg, 1985). These factors appear to be particularly important in preschool and early elementary school, and also for children demonstrating low academic achievement. Unfortunately, teachers often fail to use high-quality instructional strategies, ensure that children are actively working on academic tasks, or encourage mastery learning through their teaching behaviors (Rosenfield, 1995). Furthermore, there is research documenting that teachers tend not be as current with the professional source literature as would be desirable, consequently failing to use the recent EBP described in scholarly journals and other such sources, preferring more practical approaches (Rosenfield, 1995). Thus, there appears to be a need to use IC in helping teachers to improve their pedagogical practices.

While "within-child" attributions have been historically made for students' academic difficulties, in which problems that children are experiencing in their educational achievement are believed to be due to characteristics of the child, there is increased emphasis in the discipline of education in examining more-easily-altered variables, such as quality of instruction. Within the field of special education, a strong movement toward pre-referral interventions in the form of high quality instruction and EBPs has occurred, with a view toward reducing the number of students being classified as disabled and found eligible for special education services. Such pre-referral interventions have also been designed in order to help diminish the disproportionate referral and placement of students of diverse backgrounds into special education (Gravois & Rosenfield, 2006; Rosenfield, 1995). Focus on the instructional system, including the task (what is to be learned), the learner (his or her readiness to undertake the learning task), and the treatment (the instructional and management strategies), instead of upon the concept of a malfunctioning learner, allows consultants to avoid making within-child attributions for learning diffi-culties (Rosenfield, 1984).

Children's difficulties in learning can be conceptualized as an instruc-tional mismatch, and consultation may be used by educational specialists or master teachers to work with teachers, analyze this mismatch, and facil-itate a synchronized interaction of the task, the learner, and the treatment (Rosenfield, 1995). Through the consultative process, the relationship between the teacher and the consultant is of utmost importance in encouraging the change process (Rosenfield, 1995). Thus, the underlying assumptions of IC are that: 1) All children can learn, 2) The appropriate place for intervention is the interaction between teachers and students in the classroom and, 3) It is productive for teachers to consult with each other and other educational support personnel in a collegial, problem-solving relationship (Rosenfield, 1992; Wizda, 2004).

Rosenfield (1995, 2002) describes IC as a problem-solving process that is similar in its underlying structure to other forms of consultation that have been detailed in the psychological literature. It may encompass all four levels of consultation described by Meyers, Parsons, and Martin (1979): 1)

Providing direct service to the client by assembling data about the student through assessment, interviewing, or observation; 2) Providing indirect service to the client through the consultee (the level most often used with IC in which the consultee is responsible for most of the data gathering and intervention implementation; 3) Providing service to the consultee when the primary goal is to change the consultee's behavior in order to encourage subsequent change to the student clients and; 4) Providing service to the system in order to effect change in the instructional system in the school, hopefully leading to improved organizational functioning (Rosenfield, 1995).

Knotek, Rosenfield, Gravois, and Babinski (2002) found that IC works as a socially constructivistic endeavor due to features associated with consultee-centered consultation (Caplan & Caplan, 1993; Caplan, Caplan, & Erchul, 1995), including effective alliance-building, orderly reflection, and the generation of alternative hypotheses. Moreover, IC has stages, much like other models of consultation, including entry, problem identification, intervention design, intervention implementation, and finally, intervention evaluation (Gravois, Rosenfield, & Gickling, 1999; Rosenfield, 2002). Interested readers are encouraged to consult Rosenfield's and Gravois' and colleagues' various writings on this topic for greater detail.

Outcomes of consultation

There is limited research examining the outcome of consultation (Crothers et al., 2008), but there is evidence supporting the importance of consultation and training for teachers working with children with emotional and behavioral disorders. Regular education teachers tend to have more negative attitudes towards teaching students with emotional and behavioral disorders in a mainstream setting than with students with intellectual and physical disabilities and learning disorders, but teachers who had specific training for working with such children have more positive attitudes than teachers who lack such training (Cagran & Schmidt, 2011). Teachers report wanting more training in behavior management when providing an education to a student with an emotional or behavior disorder than a student with a learning disability (Otto, 1999). Moreover, regular education teachers who receive training in the use of behavior management and instruction skills appear to positively impact the academic engagement of students with emotional and/or behavior disorders (McConnell, 1996). Scott et al. (2008) found that the degree to which teachers followed a behavioral management plan designed for students with emotional and behavioral disabilities who were being considered for a restrictive placement, and which was constructed through consultation with a school psychologist, predicted decreases in students' inappropriate behaviors.

Teachers may seek different educational specialists to access their respective areas of expertise and training. School psychologists, school counselors, school social workers and special education teachers are likely to have received training in behavioral modification, but school psychologists may be the most knowledgeable about creating a behavior intervention plan. Consistent with the orientation of their training programs, school psychologists and special education teachers are expected to have received the most intensive training in differentiating instructional practices to address the needs of students experiencing academic difficulties. Generally, school counselors' area of expertise includes the recognition of the socio-emotional and career development needs of students. School social workers tend to receive training regarding social systems, and thus may best understand the community resources for students and families with mental illness. School counselors, school psychologists, and school social workers all may be competent in helping teachers promote parent involvement. As the research literature expands to identify instructional and classroom management strategies that are differentiated according to students' emotional and behavioral disorders, teachers may find that the respective educational specialists are more likely to be aware of empirically-supported interventions related to their area of expertise.

Importance of Using Evidence-Based Interventions

Whiston, Tai, Rahardija, and Eder (2011) explain that in the disciplines of education, counseling, and psychology, there has been an increased emphasis upon the use of evidence-based practice. This call-to-arms has encouraged a surge of research exploring the effectiveness of the psychological and educational interventions used with children in school systems. Although there are countless promising interventions designed to prevent or address problem behavior, often, rigorous experimental evaluations of these strategies and programs do not exist (Buckley, 2009). Specifically, many interventions are lacking in sufficient information regarding their application, scalability, and sustainability for students with behavior problems (Buckley, 2009).

Horner, Sugai, and Anderson (2010) propose a set of core features that can be used to determine whether an intervention has an evidence base to support its effectiveness. First, the practice needs to be operationally defined, ensuring that the specific features of the intervention can be observed and counted. Second, the environments in which the intervention is expected to be effective are defined. Is the intervention uniquely suited to one context, such as a preschool, or are the features of the intervention designed to work in multiple settings? Third, the target population for the intervention is defined. For whom is the intervention likely to be effective? Is the intervention designed for a specific population of children or adolescents? Fourth, the qualifications for those who will implement the intervention are specified. While some interventions may be used by all educators, others require that they are used by those with specific training. If specific training is required, the qualifications of the implementers should be explicit, and tools or measures for assessing intervention efficacy should be available with the technical adequacy of these devices defined. Fifth, the outcomes expected from using the interventions should be specified. This is the designation of the measurable outcomes that are expected if the intervention is used with integrity. These outcomes may include effects measured by proximal assessments (concurrent criterion-referenced validity) and/or distal assessments (future criterion-referenced validity). Benchmarks, mastery criteria, corollary benefits, contraindications, and adverse side effects should also be described. Finally, the conceptual theory and basic mechanisms of the intervention are explained. This step allows the framework of an intervention from which to operate in investigating why a practice works. This step also allows for additional development, modification, and adaptation (Horner et al., 2010).

However, there are significant challenges involved in implementing evidence-based interventions in schools. Evans and Weist (2004) argue that providing empirically supported practice, particularly in the area of mental health services, requires staffing, training, and supervision practices that many schools are not able to provide.

Thus, the question may be posed: What factors are associated with implementing and maintaining the use of evidence-based practices? In a study examining the correlates of the sustainability of evidence-based practices in a delinquency and violence prevention initiative, researchers found that financial sustainability planning and aligning the intervention with the goals of the school predicted the sustainability of evidence-based interventions (Tibbits, Bumbarger, Kyler, & Perkins, 2010). The literature regarding systems change enumerates the challenges in moving an educational system to a new way of doing things. Regardless of such challenges, however, the historic underservice of children with emotional and behavioral disorders, particularly those of different ethnic or racial backgrounds, demands accountability to ensure that appropriate, supportive services are provided for children whose behavior is impeding their learning and overall school functioning (Harry, Hart, Klingner, & Cramer, 2009).

The Necessity of Progress Monitoring

As mentioned, determining the efficacy of school-based prevention and intervention strategies focusing upon healthy social, emotional, and behavioral skills is important for reasons such as preventing the underservice of children with emotional and behavioral disorders (EBD). Such poor service delivery is particularly concerning considering the historic and implacable overrepresentation of certain subgroups in this disability category in school systems. In their research, Harry et al. (2009) found that the referral process for classifying students with emotional and behavioral disorders "was arbitrary and subjective and the assessment itself fraught with cultural and social-class misconceptions" (p. 166).

Despite the inherent problems with the service of children with EBD in school systems, Evans and Owens (2010) describe remarkable progress within the past decade in developing and evaluating such behavioral school-based intervention strategies, particularly through evaluations characterized by pre-post and follow-up designs. However, Evans and Owens (2010) also indicate that the assessment points in such evaluations often are months apart; for practical reasons, educators may be in need of tools to measure a student's response to intervention in a shorter period of time, known as short-cycle assessments. Such assessments may be more feasible (requiring less effort, training requirements, or time) or relevant (with an emphasis upon the demonstration of the association between assessment and practice, including academic outcomes; Evans & Owens, 2010). In a special issue (2010) on using behavioral assessment within problem-solving models in the journal, *School Psychology Review,* edited by Evans and Owens, a number of low-effort assessments that may be used to screen and monitor responses to intervention over time were presented (interested readers are encouraged to consult this issue for additional information).

However, yet another important reason for progress-monitoring, perhaps, is to provide objective ratings of students' behavioral change for educators. Indeed, Evans and Owens (2010) make the case for the need for measures that are sensitive to small improvements. When mired in the problem of addressing a student's emotional or behavioral difficulties at school, educators may lose a sense of perspective and objectivity in measuring behavior change, since the emotional or behavioral difficulties requiring intervention may be disruptive, intrusive, or irritating. Another complication is that students' behavioral improvements are often modest and occur gradually over time. Therefore, quantitative evidence of students' behavioral change may actually be encouraging for educators who perceive that improvements are not occurring with any magnitude, or at all.

Keeping Reasonable Expectations

Finally, is critical to recognize that behavioral change is rarely absolute. In fact, unless the behavior is dangerous to the child or others, it may be argued that even a modest change can result in improved outcomes not only for the student, but also for those educators and family members who work with or spend time with the child. For example, one potential problem of using a behavioral intervention, such as operant conditioning, is the issue of extinction burst, which may occur when a behavioral extinction has just begun. An extinction burst refers to a rapid but temporary increase in the target behavior's frequency, which is followed by the eventual diminishment and then extinction of the behavior identified for elimination. However, in an examination of the prevalence of extinction burst in applied research, Lerman and Iwata (1995) found that the rate of such a problem was only 24%, and may be less likely when extinction is implemented with alternative procedures rather than as the sole intervention (i.e. bursting was evident in 12% of the former cases and 36% of the latter). Therefore, in order to decrease the risk for extinction burst, it is recommended that extinction procedures be combined with another technique, such as differential reinforcement of behavior.

Summary

Teachers are increasingly being called upon to provide differentiated instruction not only for students with learning difficulties, but also for students identified with behavioral or emotional disorders or students who are sub-threshold for these disorders. While the expectation that teachers should provide preventative assistance in the mainstream setting to students demonstrating symptoms of behavioral and emotional disorders has long existed, this expectation has often not been realized. The advent of the RtI framework and the increased emphasis and availability of evidence-based approaches provides teachers with the organizational structure and strategies necessary to address the needs of students with emotional and behavioral disorders in a systematic manner.

Implicit assumptions of the RtI model are that teachers are highly trained and motivated to learn about the unique characteristics of their students, and that teachers work closely and collaboratively with educational support personnel to identify students' symptoms, design interventions that are consistent with evidence-based approaches, and monitor the effectiveness of these interventions. In some respects, the role of the teacher in the RtI model is refined to include expertise in the empiricism of instruction and behavioral management as well as to develop a working understanding of mental illness. We hope and expect teachers to find this book to be a valuable resource in the pursuit of meeting such challenging expectations.

References

Bronfenbrenner, U. (1979). *The ecology of human development.* Cambridge, MA: Harvard University Press.

—(1993). The ecology of cognitive development: Research models and fugitive findings. In R. H. Wozniak & K. Fischer (eds), *Development in context: Acting and thinking in specific environments* (pp. 3–44). Hillsdale, NJ: Erlbaum.

Cagran, B., & Schmidt, M. (2011). Attitudes of Slovene teachers towards the inclusion of pupils with different types of special needs in primary school. *Educational Studies, 37,* 171. doi:10.1080/03055698.2010.506319

Caplan, G. (1970). *The theory and practice of mental health consultation.* New York: Basic Books.

Caplan, G., & Caplan, R. B., (1993). *Mental health consultation and collaboration.* San Francisco: Jossey-Bass.

Caplan, G., Caplan, R. B. & Erchul, W. P. (1994). Caplainian mental health consultation: Historical background and current status. *Consulting Psychology Journal: Practice and Research, 46,* 2–12. doi:10.1037/1061-4087.46.4.2

Crothers, L. M., Hughes, T. L., & Morine, K. A. (2008). *Theory and cases in school-based consultation: A resource for school psychologists, school counselors, special educators, and other mental health professionals.* New York: Routledge.

Epstein, J. L. (2005). Results of Partnership Schools-CSR model for student achievement over three years. *Elementary School Journal, 106,* 151–70. doi:10.1086/499196

Evans, S. W., & Owens, J. S. (2010). Behavioral assessment within problem-solving models: Finding relevance and expanding feasibility. *School Psychology Review, 39,* 427–30.

Evans, S. W., & Weist, M. D. (2004). Implementing empirically supported treatments in the schools: What are we asking? *Clinical Child and Family Psychology Review, 7,* 263–7. doi:10.1007/s10567-004-6090-0

Gravois, T. A., & Rosenfield, S. A. (2006). Impact of instructional consultation teams on the disproportionate referral and placement of minority students in special education. *Remedial and Special Education, 27,* 42–52. doi:10.1177/07419325060270010501

Gravois, T., Rosenfield, S., & Gickling, E. (1999). *Instructional consultation teams: Training manual.* College Park: University of Maryland, Instructional Consultation Lab.

Harry, B., Hart, J. E., Klingner, J., & Cramer, E. (2009). Response to Kauffman, Mock, & Simpson, (2007): Problems related to underservice of students with emotional or behavioral disorders. *Behavioral Disorders, 34,* 164–72.

Horner, R. H., Sugai, G., & Anderson, C. M. (2010). Examining the evidence base for school-wide behavior support. *Focus on Exceptional Children, 42,* 1–14.

Individuals with Disabilities Education Improvement Act (2004). Public Law 108–446 (20 U. S. C. 1400 et seq.).

Knotek, S. E., Rosenfield, S. A., Gravois, T. A., & Babinski, L. (2003). The process of fostering consultee development during instructional consultation.

Journal of Educational and Psychological Consultation, 14, 303–28. doi:10.1207/s1532768xjepc143&4_6

Lerman, D. C., & Iwata, B. A. (1995). Prevalence of the extinction burst and its attenuation during treatment. *Journal of Applied Behavior Analysis, 28,* 93–4. doi:10.1901/jaba.1995.28-93

McConnell, M. E. (1996). *Instructional and classroom management training for general education teachers working with students with emotional and/or behavior disorders, grades 6–12.* Dissertation Abstracts International: Section A. The Humanities and Social Sciences, 58(03), 819.

Meyers, J., Parsons, R. D., & Martin, R. (1979). *Mental health consultation in the schools: A comprehensive guide for psychologists, social workers, psychiatrists, counselors, educators and other human service professionals.* San Francisco: Jossey-Bass.

Otto, K. H. (2000). *Teacher identified staff development needs when including students with learning disabilities and emotional and behavioral disorders.* Dissertation Abstracts International: Section A: Humanities and Social Sciences, 60(09), 3323.

Peterson, D. W. (1968). *The clinical study of social behavior.* East Norwalk, CT: Appleton-Century-Crofts.

Rosenfield, S. A. (1984, August). *Instructional consultation.* Paper presented at the annual meeting of the American Psychological Association, Toronto, Canada.

—(1995). The practice of instructional consultation. *Journal of Educational and Psychological Consultation, 6,* 317–27. doi:10.1207/s1532768xjepc0604_2

—(2003). Consultation as dialogue: The right words at the right time. In N. M. Lambert, J. Sandoval, & I. Hylander (eds), *Consultee-centered consultation: Improving professional services in schools and community organizations* (pp. 339–47). Mahwah, NJ: Lawrence Erlbaum Associates, Inc.

Scott, A. S., Jackson, H. G., Jensen, M. J., Moscovitz, K. K., Bush, J. W., Violette, H. D., … Pious, C. (2008). A validity of the study of functionally-based behavioral consultation with students with emotional/ behavioral disabilities. *School Psychology Quarterly, 23,* 327–9. doi:10.1037/1045-3830.23.3.327

Sokols, D. (2000). Social ecology and behavioral medicine: Implications for training, practice, and policy. *Behavioral Medicine, 26,* 129–38. doi:10.1080/08964280009595760

Stacks, A. M. (2005). Using an ecological framework in understanding and treating externalizing behavior in early childhood. *Early Childhood Education Journal, 32,* 269–78. doi:10.1007/s10643-004-0754-8

Swearer, S., Espelage, D. L., Vaillancourt, T., & Hymel, S. (2010). What can be done about school bullying?: Linking research to educational practice. *Educational Researcher, 39,* 38–47. doi:10.3102/0013189X09357622

Tibbits, M. K., Bumbarger, B. K., Kyler, S. J., & Perkins, D. F. (2010). Sustaining evidence-based interventions under real-world conditions: Results from a large-scale diffusion project. *Prevention Science, 11,* 252–62. doi:10.1007/s11121-010-0170-9.

US Department of Education (2002). No Child Left Behind Act of 2001. Executive summary. Accessed from http://www.ed.gov/nclb/overview/intro/execsumm.doc

Walberg, H. J. (1985). Instructional theories and research evidence. In M. C. Wang & H. J. Walberg (eds), *Adapting instruction to individual differences* (pp. 3–23). Berkeley, CA: McCutchan Publishing Company.

Weintraub, A. L. (1998). *Tipping the balance: Perspectives of teachers in a regular elementary school on educating students with troubling behavior.* Dissertation Abstracts International: Section A. The Humanities and Social Sciences, 59(10), 3741.

Westwood, C. A. (2002). *The successful inclusion of children with emotional and behavioral disorders into general education settings.* Dissertation Abstracts International: Section A. The Humanities and Social Sciences, 64(02), 401.

Whiston, S. C., Tai, W. L., Rahardija, D., & Eder, K. (2011). School counseling outcome: A meta-analytic examination. *Journal of Counseling and Development, 89,* 37–55.

White, J., & Mullis, F. (1998). A systems approach to school counselor consultation. *Education, 119,* 242–52.

Wizda, L. (2004). An instructional consultant looks to the future. *Journal of Educational and Psychological Consultation, 15,* 277–94. doi:10.1080/104744 12.2004.9669518 http://dx.doi.org/10.1207/s1532768xjepc153&4_5

Zins, J. E., & Erchul, W. P. (2002). Best practices in school consultation. In A. Thomas & J. Grimes (eds), *Best practices in school psychology* (4th ed., Vol. 1, pp. 625–43). Bethesda, MD: National Association of School Psychologists.

INDEX